70 -

Consumer Law and Socioeconomic Development

Claudia Lima Marques • Dan Wei
Editors

Consumer Law and Socioeconomic Development

National and International Dimensions

Springer

Editors
Claudia Lima Marques
Faculty of Law
Federal University of Rio Grande do Sul
Porto Alegre, Brazil

Dan Wei
Faculty of Law
University of Macau
Macau, Macau

ISBN 978-3-319-55623-9 ISBN 978-3-319-55624-6 (eBook)
DOI 10.1007/978-3-319-55624-6

Library of Congress Control Number: 2017942776

Printed on acid-free paper

This Springer imprint is published by Springer Nature
The registered company is Springer International Publishing AG
The registered company address is: Gewerbestrasse 11, 6330 Cham, Switzerland

Foreword: Consumer Law in a Changing World

In a world where the fabric of reality is sewn in astounding speed, some will call current times "post-modernity," while others would rather name it "liquid modernity," not to mention those who say we live in a "risk society." In any of these scenarios, the only thing we can be sure about is that change is constant, transition is perennial, and ephemeral and virtual things triumph over durable, long-lasting, perpetual, or concrete things. For this reason, the decision of Springer Publishing to bring this volume into print could not have come at a better moment. This is a collection of creative and in-depth essays that address current relevant aspects of consumption relations in a time of global uncertainty.

As a matter of fact, one of the best things about being invited to introduce a new book, when one has been involved with a group of authors who have been writing on the subject for a rather long time, is the opportunity to remember, rethink, evaluate, and appreciate the evolution of a (in this case, legal) subject in a (constantly and increasingly) changing world, this time faced with new problems caused and influenced by new technological and physical circumstances . . . which call for new solutions of a legal nature.

This book is the result of the work of the ILA Committee on the International Protection of Consumers, in itself, a result of the 2008 73rd Conference of the International Law Association, hosted in Rio de Janeiro by the Brazilian Branch of the ILA, to discuss "Law for the Future." The Brazilian Branch sponsored the idea, advanced by Professor Claudia Lima Marques (then already a leading Brazilian authority on the subject), that a major factor, when considering the requirements of Law for the Future, would be how to regulate the effects of globalized consumption upon the weaker link of the chain: consumers.

Professor Lima Marques had already managed to attract to that Rio conference members and (until then) non-ILA members of both legal and political communities that shared this concern and were ready to engage in serious work and present their contribution. The Brazilian Branch, jointly with Claudia and Professor Diego Arroyo (the Committee´s first Rapporteur), convinced the ILA International Board of their seriousness in purpose and capacity to carry out the obligations undertaken. Thus, in

November of that year, the first ILA Committee on Consumer Law was created; it was headed by two representatives of the Global South but already assembled members from all continents, legal traditions, and professional backgrounds.

The Committee's work soon resulted in a first book (*The Global Financial Crisis and Consumer Regulation: New Developments on International Protection of Consumers*), launched during the ILA Conference in Sofia (2012). It is a pleasure to note that eight authors of that first book—Claudia Lima Marques, Dan Wei (now Committee Rapporteur), Thierry Bourgoignie, James Nehf, Louise Teitz, David Stewart, Gail Pearson, and Hector Valverde Santana—contribute texts to this second publication, which testifies to a continued research group work. They are now joined by 25 new names who preserve the diversity of geographic origins, professional backgrounds and legal traditions—which comes as no surprise to those who attended the Committee meetings during the 2008 (Rio de Janeiro), 2010 (The Hague), 2012 (Sofia), 2014 (Washington), and 2016 (Johannesburg) ILA Conferences.

It should also be noted that this book assembles texts of ILA Committee members, as well as writings of guests sponsored by the Brazilian NGO Brasilcon, academic institutions, international organizations linked to consumer protection, and the Chinese government. This rich diversity of authors resulted in a work that plurality of themes must also be highlighted. The articles now published undoubtedly manage to address in a global way the most up-to-date, fascinating, and relevant aspects in the issue of consumer protection, its multiple connections with international law, domestic law, economics, politics, and the environment. The quality of the work herein gathered, in addition to the seriousness and political ability of the Committee Officers, always backed by the Brazilian Branch and ILA Headquarters, making the best use of the ILA brand in the international legal arena, has given their work access to new fora that discuss consumer protection, such as the UNCTAD and The Hague Conferences.

For all these reasons, readers are herein presented with rewarding papers that enrich international bibliography on the issue, clearly distancing themselves from the "prêt à penser" juridical literature, and make the Brazilian Branch and ILA Headquarters very proud.

Belo Horizonte and João Pessoa, Brazil

Marcílio Toscano Franca Filho
Susana A.C. Vieira

Preface

Consumers become more important in pushing economic recovery in developed countries and as a growing source of domestic demand in developing countries. Consumer law faces numerous challenges today. Globalization made international transaction of goods and services easier than ever before, and a joint international effort to develop fair, equitable, and nondiscriminatory principles to protect effectively consumers is needed.

For a long time, regulation and enforcement of consumer law issues focused essentially on the national level. In recent years, the international dimension of consumer protection has also been acknowledged. The United Nations General Assembly approved the revised UN Guidelines for Consumer Protection in December 2015 by setting a goal to promote international cooperation among Member States. The UNGCP incorporates new important issues, public utilities, data protection and privacy, e-commerce, financial services, tourism, energy, and others. International and regional endeavors mainly produce soft laws in order to assist states to deal with consumer issues and achieve a certain degree of harmonization by drafting principles, which can be incorporated in their national laws. Following the same line, some of the most important efforts undertaken by leading institutions, including the newly formed Intergovernmental Group of Experts (IGE), focus, among other aspects, on undertaking studies and research on consumer protection related to the UNGCP and providing capacity building and technical assistance to developing countries and economies in transition.

This book is presented as a contribution to such broader effort, taking an opportunity for the discussion and understanding of important consumer law issues, at national, regional, and international levels. It contains contributions from prominent scholars in the area; some of them play important roles in leading global and national academic societies. A number of chapters were written by the members of the Committee on International Protection of Consumers of the International Law Association (London), which well reflects the current Committee's mandate. The Committee has been accepted to act in the role of an observer, not only at UNCTAD IGE but also at the Hague Conference on Private International Law.

Together with the work of the Committee, the book also collected other contributions from experts from Brazil and China, in a joint effort of Brasilcon (*Instituto Brasileiro de Política e Direito do Consumidor*, Brasília); the Federal University of Rio Grande do Sul, Porto Alegre (PPGdir./UFRGS); and the University of Macau, China. The chapters cover a considerable range of issues and take on different perspectives, from a look at the trends and challenges in the international protection of consumers to a reflection at experiences of some emerging economies' legal systems and to the issue of consumer protection in the context of financial crisis. We are confident that the works presented here will provide a meaningful contribution for the subject of consumer law by shedding light on complicated issues, highlighting the different dimensions of consumer law and bringing on a more updated view on them.

We would like to thank all the contributors and institutions, namely, the ILA and BRASILCON, for the support provided in different forms for the success of this work.

Porto Alegre, Brazil
Macau, Macau China

Claudia Lima Marques
Dan Wei

Contents

List of Contributors

Káren Rick Danilevicz Bertoncello Department of the Consumer Law at the Center of Studies of AJURIS, School of Magistracy of the State of Rio Grande do Sul, Porto Alegre, Brazil

Leonardo Roscoe Bessa Brasilcon Board, Brasília, Brazil

University Center of Brasília (UniCEUB), Brasília, Brazil

Brasilcon, Brasília, Brazil

Thierry Bourgoignie Research Group on International and Comparative Consumer Law, Université du Québec à Montreal, Montreal, QC, Canada

Rosangela Cavallazzi PROURB, Federal University of Rio de Janeiro, Rio de Janeiro, Brazil

Law Department, Pontifical Catholic University of Rio de Janeiro (PUCRJ), Rio de Janeiro, Brazil

Diogenes Faria de Carvalho Faculty of Law, Federal University of Rio Grande do Sul, Porto Alegre, Brazil

André de Carvalho Ramos Faculty of law, University of São Paulo, São Paulo, Brazil

Ana Cândida Muniz Cipriano Faculty of Law, University of Buenos Aires, Buenos Aires, Argentina

Clarissa Costa de Lima Department of the Consumer Law at the Center of Studies of AJURIS, School of Magistracy of the State of Rio Grande do Sul, Porto Alegre, Brazil

Walter José Faiad de Moura Brasilcon Board, Brasília, Brazil

University Center of Brasília (UniCEUB), Brasília, Brazil

Amanda Flávio de Oliveira Faculty of Law, Federal University of Minas Gerais, Belo Horizonte, Brazil

Vitor Hugo do Amaral Ferreira Faculdade Antonio Meneghetti, Centro Universitário Franciscano, Santa Maria, Rio Grande do Sul, Brazil

Alberto do Amaral Junior Faculty of Law, University of São Paulo, São Paulo, Brazil

Johannes Doll Faculty of Education, Federal University of Rio Grande do Sul, Porto Alegre, Brazil

Shan He Association of Consumer Law, China Law Society, Beijing, China

Antonia Espíndola Longoni Klee Faculty of Law, Federal University of Rio Grande do Sul, Porto Alegre, Brazil

Maria Goretti Sanches Lima International Forum of Travel and Tourism Advocates, São Paulo, Brazil

Claudia Lima Marques Faculty of Law, Federal University of Rio Grande do Sul, Porto Alegre, Brazil

Bruno Miragem Faculty of Law, Federal University of Rio Grande do Sul, Porto Alegre, Brazil

Ana Cândida Muniz Faculty of Law, University of Buenos Aires, Buenos Aires, Argentina

James P. Nehf Robert H. Mckinney School of Law, Indiana University, Indianapolis, IN, USA

Luke Nottage Faculty of Law, University of Sydney, Sydney, NSW, Australia

Adalberto Pasqualotto Faculty of Law, Pontifical Catholic University of Rio Grande do Sul, Porto Alegre, Brazil

Faculty of Law, Federal University of Rio Grande do Sul, Porto Alegre, Brazil

Gail Pearson Business School, University of Sydney, Sydney, NSW, Australia

Roberto Augusto Castellanos Pfeiffer Faculty of Law, University of São Paulo, São Paulo, Brazil

Fabiana D'Andrea Ramos Universidade Federal do Rio Grande do Sul, Porto Alegre, Brazil

Héctor Valverde Santana Faculty of Law, University Center of Brasília, Brasília, Brazil

David P. Stewart Faculty of Law, University of Georgetown, Washington, DC, USA

Louise Ellen Teitz Faculty of Law, Roger Williams University School of Law, Bristol, RI, USA

Luciane Klein Vieira Faculty of Law, University of São Paulo, São Paulo, Brazil

Dan Wei Faculty of Law, University of Macau, Macau, China

Ying Yu Wolfson College, University of Oxford, Oxford, UK

Yixian Zhao East China University of Political Science and Law, Institute of BRICS Legal Studies, Shanghai, China

About the Editors and Authors

Káren Rick Danilevicz Bertoncello, Judge in the State of Rio Grande do Sul, Brasilcon's Director Department, specialist in Civil Law by the Universidade Federal do Rio Grande do Sul, Master in Private Law by the Universidade Federal do Rio Grande do Sul, Member of the Research Group about overindebtedness coordinated by Professor Dr. Claudia Lima Marques, coordinator of the Department of the Consumer Law at the Center of Studies of AJURIS (School of Magistracy of the State of Rio Grande do Sul).

Leonardo Roscoe Bessa, Attorney General at the Brazilian Federal District, Master and PhD in Law, Director of Brasilcon.

Thierry Bourgoignie, Full Professor, Director, Groupe de recherche en droit international et comparé de la consommation (GREDICC), Université du Québec à Montréal, Montréal Québec, Canada.

Rosangela Cavallazzi, Retired Professor of Law School of the Federal University of Rio de Janeiro (Brasil), Professor of PROURB-UFRJ and PUC-Rio, Director of Brasilcon, Researcher 1B CNPq.

Diogenes Faria de Carvalho, Postdoctoral PhD in progress at the Federal University of Rio Grande do Sul (UFRGS); Doctor in Psychology from the Catholic University of Goiás (PUC-GOIÁS); Masters in Economic Law from the University of Franca (UNIFRAN); Effective Professor of the Federal University of Goiás (UFG), Pontifical Catholic University of Goias (PUCGO), and Salgado de Oliveira University (UNIVERSO); Coordinator of the graduate and postgraduate programs in Law at the University Salgado de Oliveira (UNIVERSE-Campus: Goiania); Practicing lawyer with Velasco, Vellasco & Simonini Law Firm; Member and Director of the Brazilian Institute of Policy and Consumer Law (Brasilcon). Main areas of interest: consumer rights, consumer indebtedness, consumption psychology, and intellectual property.

André de Carvalho Ramos, Associate Professor of International Law and Human Rights Law at the Faculty of Law of the University of São Paulo (USP), PhD in International Law at University of São Paulo, Visiting Fellow at the Lauterpacht Centre for International Law (Cambridge), Member of the American Society of Private International Law (ASADIP), Member of the Brazilian Society of International Law, Member of the Brazilian Branch of the International Law Association, Member of the National Executive Group of the International Legal Cooperation Department of the Federal Prosecution Office, Federal Prosecutor, Head of Regional Electoral Prosecutor Office in São Paulo State (2012–2016).

Clarissa Costa de Lima, Judge in the State of Rio Grande do Sul, Brasilcon's Review Director Assistant, Specialist in Consumer Law by the Universidade de Coimbra, Master in Private Law by the Universidade Federal do Rio Grande do Sul, Member of the Overindebtedness Research Group coordinated by Professor Dr. Claudia Lima Marques, Coordinator of the Department of the Consumer Law at the Center of Studies of AJURIS (School of Magistracy of the State of Rio Grande do Sul).

Walter José Faiad de Moura, Lawyer, Postgraduate and Master in Law, Director of Brasilcon.

Amanda Flávio de Oliveira, LL.M. and PhD, Federal University of Minas Gerais (UFMG), Belo Horizonte, Brazil; Professor of Economic Law at Federal University of Minas Gerais (UFMG), Belo Horizonte, Brazil; Vice President of Brasilcon (Brazilian Institute for Consumer Law and Policy), Brasília.

Vitor Hugo do Amaral Ferreira, Master in Latin American Integration from the Universidade Federal de Santa Maria; Professor of Law courses at the Centro Universitário Franciscano and Faculdade Antonio Meneghetti; Coordinator of the Group of Education, Research, Extension and Practice on Consumer Law and the Group of Politic Research and Consumer Society; Lawyer. Email: vitorhugodir@hotmail.com.

Alberto do Amaral Junior, Associate Professor of Faculty of Law of University of São Paulo, Brazil; PhD (University of São Paulo, 1987).

Fabiana D'Andrea Ramos, graduated in Law and Social Sciences from the Federal University of Rio Grande do Sul (1997), a Masters in Law from the University of Heidelberg (1998) and Doctorate in Law from the State University of Rio de Janeiro (2005), an Associate Professor at the Universidade Federal Fluminense in the disciplines of Civil and Private International Laws. Email: fabianadramos@gmail.com.

Johannes Doll, Pedagogue, gerontologist, Doctor of Philosophy; Professor at the School of Education, Undergraduate and Graduate Studies, of the Federal University of Rio Grande do Sul (Porto Alegre/Brasil).

He Shan, President of Chinese Law Research Society on the Protection of the Rights and Interests of Consumers, China Law Society.

Antonia Espíndola Longoni Klee, LL.M. and S.J.D from the UFRGS (Federal University of Rio Grande do Sul), Specialist in International Law from the UFRGS, Guest Professor in the Specialization Course Lato Sensu in Consumer's Law and Fundamental Rights (UFRGS), Member of the Special Monitoring Committee of the Bills of Updating of the CDC (Brazilian Institute of Consumer's Politics and Right (Brasilcon)), Director of Brasilcon, Member of the Lawyers Institute of Rio Grande do Sul (IARGS), Lawyer in Porto Alegre.

Maria Goretti Sanches Lima, Specialist at Travel and Tourism; Executive Vice President of IFTTA (International Forum of Travel and Tourism Advocates); Doctor jur. by University of Rostock, Germany; Master of Laws by PUC São Paulo, Brazil. Email: goretti@ifttabrasil.org.

Claudia Lima Marques, Professor at the Federal University of Rio Grande do Sul (Porto Alegre), Former President of Brasilcon and Chief Editor of the Consumers Law Journal/Thompson Reuters (Brasília), Chair of the Committee of International Protection of Consumers, International Law Association (London).

Bruno Miragem, Professor at the Federal University of Rio Grande do Sul (UFRGS), President of the Brazilian Institute of Policy and Consumer Law (Brasilcon), Lawyer.

Ana Cândida Muniz, Expert in Politics and International Relations, Fundação Escola de Sociologia e Política de São Paulo (FESPSP); PhD Candidate in Law at the University of Buenos Aires, Argentina; Lawyer.

James P. Nehf, Professor of Law, Indiana University; Professor of Law and Cleon H. Foust Fellow at the Indiana University Robert H. McKinney School of Law; serves on the Executive Board of the International Association of Consumer Law and has chaired the Consumer Law Working Group of the Cyberspace Committee in the American Bar Association (Business Law Section).

Luke Nottage, Professor of Comparative and Transnational Business Law, University of Sydney Law School.

Adalberto Pasqualotto, Professor of Consumer Law in undergraduate, master, and doctor degrees in the Law School of the Pontifical Catholic University of Rio Grande do Sul; Legum Doctor by the Federal University of Rio Grande do Sul.

Gail Pearson, Professor of Business Law at the University of Sydney, President of the International Association of Consumer Law (IACL).

Roberto Augusto Castellanos Pfeiffer, Professor of the Faculty of Law of the University of São Paulo (USP), Professor of the School of Economics of Fundação Getúlio Vargas (FGV), Doctor and Master in Law by USP, Attorney of the State of São Paulo, Former Executive Director of PROCON of São Paulo, Commissioner of the Administrative Council for Economic Defense (CADE), Legal Consultant of the Ministry of Justice, Brazilian Supreme Court Law Clerk.

Héctor Valverde Santana, PhD and LL.M. in Law at Pontifícia Universidade Católica de São Paulo (PUC-SP), Law Professor on Consumer Protection and Civil Responsibility at Centro Universitário de Brasília (UniCEUB), Judge in the Federal District Area, Brazil.

David P. Stewart, B.A., Princeton; M.A., J.D., Yale; LL.M., New York University; Codirector, Global Law Scholars Program; Codirector, Center on Transnational Business and the Law; Professor from Practice of Georgetown University Law Center.

Louise Ellen Teitz, Professor of Law at Roger Williams University School of Law, former First Secretary at The Hague Conference on Private International Law in The Hague, the Netherlands, from 2012 to 2015, with primary responsibility for family law areas, including the 1980 Child Abduction Convention, the 1996 Child Protection Convention, and related projects, including mediation in family law matters, the "Malta Process" involving Sharia-based legal systems, and relocation.

Luciane Klein Vieira, PhD in International Law from the University of Buenos Aires (2015), Master in Private International Law from the University of Buenos Aires (2012), Master in Law of Economic Integration from Universidad del Salvador and Université Paris I – Panthéon – Sorbonne (2010), Specialist in Management of Schools by the University Castelo Branco (2006), Bachelor's Degree in Law from the University of Vale do Rio dos Sinos (2004), Professor for Integration Law at the University of Buenos Aires, Public International Law and Professor of Private Law at FACAMP and PUCC, Former Fellow of CONICET (National Council of Scientific and Technical Research of Argentina), Researcher at the Institute of Investigaciones Sociales y Legales Dr. Ambrosio L. Gioja of the Buenos Aires University, Deputy Director of the Brazilian Institute of Politics and Consumer Law (Brasilcon), Member of the American Association of Private International Law (ASADIP).

Dan Wei, Ph.D. in Law of University of Coimbra, Full Professor and Associate Dean of Faculty of Law of the University of Macau, Rapporteur of the Committee of International Protection of Consumers of International Law Association.

Ying Yu, Dr., Research Fellow, Wolfson College, University of Oxford, UK; Former Chief Research Fellow of Centre for International Consumer Protection Policy & Law, Wuhan University, China. E-mail: ying.yu@csls.ox.ac.uk.

Yixian Zhao, Assistant Researcher and Chief of Office in Legal Research Institute of BRICS of East China University of Political Science and Law. Research fields: legal systems of Brazil, law and development of BRICS, comparative laws, etc. E-mail: evaaiw@outlook.com.

Part I
International Protection of Consumers: Trends and Challenges

Chapter 1
Consumer Protection in the Global Context: The Present Status and Some New Trends

Dan Wei

1.1 Transnationalization and the International Dimension of Consumer Law

Economic globalization, a state of flux, can be understood as transnational circulation of goods, services, essential factors of production and information. Economic activities are no longer confined to national borders but are underway in global sphere.[1] Nowadays, with the constant reduction of barriers for international trade in goods and services, digital economy, and mass tourism, a global citizen is also a global consumer.[2]

The benefits brought by trade liberalization and new technologies since 1990s are both numerous and stimulating. Consumers are able to use the abundant information on the Internet to make better-informed decisions. Transactions become cheaper, quicker, easier, and more convenient. There are more avenues for shopping, more options in terms of price and services, and more access to an endless collection of products.

In an era of transnationalization, consumers are also facing more challenges. Due to the diversity of selling methods and new technology, the changing way of business practices, and the phenomenon of mass tourism, consumers are being exposed to new risks and fraudulent, deceptive, and unfair practices. Products and services (financial products in particular) are becoming progressively sophisticated and are difficult to assess even for experts. Subprime lending to lower-income consumers is considered the root cause of recent global financial crisis. In many

[1]This study is a part of research project "Global Governance and International Protection of Consumers" (MYRG2015-00100-FLL) sponsered by the University of Macau. See Wei (2002), p. 64.

[2]Discussion Report of the Hague, International Law Association, available at http://www.ila-hq.org/en/committees/index.cfm/cid/1030.

D. Wei (✉)
Faculty of Law, University of Macau, Macau, China
e-mail: danwei@umac.mo

C. Lima Marques, D. Wei (eds.), *Consumer Law and Socioeconomic Development*,
DOI 10.1007/978-3-319-55624-6_1

occasions, consumers are provided with misleading information and advertisement. The disputes arising from cross-border consumption often turn out to be burdensome with low efficiency for consumers.

Originally, consumer protection has been envisaged at a national level. Today, economic globalization increases the need to have universal standards to protect consumers both nationally and internationally and consumer law requires incorporating the international dimension. As an autonomous discipline, consumer law is distinct from traditional legal branches like civil law and commercial law by giving priority to the consumer rather than the transaction itself. Just as Thierry Bourgoignie has put it, consumer law offers a subjective understanding (instead of an objective conception) of the phenomenon of consumption as consumption is not a neutral process of technical destruction and the consumer plays a vital role on the market.[3] The specificity of consumer law stands the recognition of the principle of vulnerability of the consumer in terms of information, choice, and negotiation capacity. In cross-border consumption relationships, the vulnerability of the consumer still remains and in most cases turns out to be much more obvious than the one reflected in internal transactions. Claudia Lima Marques pointed out some peculiar characteristics of international consumer transactions, namely, international consumer contracts are not long-lasting and repetitive, the cost for upholding rights are much higher, the consumer, in addition to language barriers, is not familiar with foreign laws and jurisdictions and has more difficulty in having access to justice.[4]

In the global context, consumer law has to develop to "a truly international discipline."[5] The international community needs to develop common principles as well as concrete instruments to implement the goals or objectives of "consumer protection" listed in international treaties or legal documents. Taking into account the internationalization of consumer transactions, the international dimension of consumer law has to contain a number of themes.

First, since the consumer and the trader are located in different jurisdictions, there is a need to elaborate rules of private international law, which are specifically targeted at cross-border consumption relationships. Currently, different approaches have been adopted by different jurisdictions, for example, the approach of "excluding party choice of law," the approach of "limiting party choice of law," and the approach of "curtailing party choice of law."[6] Private international lawyers have proposed "the most favorable law approach" in order to provide a better protection to the consumer.[7] However, there does not yet exist a consensus so far about essential philosophies of conflict of laws and conflict of jurisdiction rules applicable to transnational consumption relations.

---

[3]Bourgoignie (1992), p. 297.

[4]Lima Marques (2012); Pearson (2012), pp. 37–40.

[5]Micklitz and Twigg Flesner (2010), p. 206.

[6]Ruhl (2011), pp. 585–591.

[7]Lima Marques (2001), pp. 657–779.

Second, although economic integration sets sight on the creation of a single global market, the reality is that the world market is still legally fragmented. Consumer protection legal standards and substantive rules are different across different countries. Empirical studies show that differences in national consumer law have impacts on the development of cross-border consumption.[8] Producers, service providers, and traders adapt sales practices to suit each country's legal setting. On one hand, the international consumer law necessitates efforts and impetus toward increased harmonization and standardization[9]; on the other hand, problems related to cross-border transactions call for transnational responses and solutions.

Third, there is also a need to establish regional and international institutional frameworks or regulatory networks. International consumer protection will never turn out to be effective without coordinated enforcement and a well-functioning network among national regulators and agencies. Given the fact that the judicial redress as doctrinal solutions to consumer law issues is always troublesome and arduous for consumers, moreover, anticonsumer jurisprudence has emerged in some jurisdictions[10]; alternative mechanisms such as regulatory initiatives and administrative measures can facilitate the rights to access to justice of the consumer. Therefore, there is a need to assume *ex ante* approach to avoid individual and collective damages in consumer society, and perhaps some global agencies that centralize such functions may offer some innovative contributions.

1.2 Legal Scholarship and Reconceptualization of International Consumer Law

Generally speaking, legal scholarship focusing on international consumer law is falling behind the process of globalization of markets and internationalization of consumers. Compared with the blooming scholarship of international trade law and international commercial law, the research on international protection of consumers is largely marginalized and only represents concerns of minority of the jurists.

The International Association of Consumer Law (IACL)[11] and the Committee of International Protection of Consumers of International Law Association (ILA)[12] are two main global academic societies aimed at fostering the study and international understanding of consumer law and policy. IACL, initially composed by some

[8]Ramsay (2006), p. 35.

[9]Howells et al. (2011), p. 17.

[10]See for example, Helveston (2015), p. 1739.

[11]More information about the association can be found at http://www.iaclaw.org/association/association.html.

[12]More information about the committee can be found at http://www.ila-hq.org/en/committees/index.cfm/cid/1030.

leading scholars such as Iain Ramsay, Sothi Rachagan, Thierry Bourgoignie, Antonio Benjamin, and so forth, grew from a number of successful international conferences on consumer law and now gathers scholars from all parts of the world and regularly proposes different themes for international dialog on consumer law. The Committee of International Protection of Consumers of the ILA was created in 2008, and among several objectives its mandate is to "...look at how national legislation on the conflict of laws and jurisdiction, as well as international treaties, model laws and regional legislation on consumer issues deal with the issue of consumer protection in a transboundary context..."[13]

The Committee has proposed five guiding principles in the Sofia Declaration, which had been adopted by the ILA as Resolution No. 4/2012. The Sofia Declaration is the very first international resolution on consumer protection made by the ILA in more than a hundred years and was approved by unanimity. The Sofia Declaration states five principles: principle of vulnerability, principle of more favorable protection to consumer, principle of contractual justice, principle of responsible lending, and principle of participation of consumer groups and associations.[14]

Several important endeavors of research outputs are the *Handbook of Research on International Consumer Law* (edited by Geraint Howelles, Ian Ramsay, and Thomas Wilhelmsson, 2010, Edward Elgar) and *The Global Financial Crisis and the Need for Consumer Regulation: New Developments on International Protection of Consumers* (edited by Claudia Lima Marques, Diego Fernández Arroyo, Iain Ramsay, and Gail Pearson, 2012, Orquestra). A number of research papers also cut across the challenge of consumer law in the globalized world and analyze the transnational dimension and transnational instruments of consumer law. Hans-W. Micklitz in his essay "The Expulsion of the Concept of Protection from the Consumer Law and the Return of Social Elements in the Civil Law: A Bittersweet Polemic" argued a new theoretical paradigm in favor of separating general civil law from consumer law.[15] Christian Twigg-Flesner and Hans Micklitz drew a framework of international consumer law and identified succinctly potential fields of research.[16] Claudia Lima Marques recognized the paradox of international protection of consumers and analyzed relations between international law and consumer

[13]http://www.ila-hq.org/en/committees/index.cfm/cid/1030.

[14]The text of the ILA's Resolution reads as follows: "*Consumer protection should be guided by the following general principles: 1. Consumers are the weaker party in situations of mass contracts or standard form contracts, in particular concerning information and bargaining power. 2. It is desirable to develop standards and to apply rules of private international law that would entitle consumers to take advantage of the most favorable consumer protection. 3. Regulation of consumer contracts should be effective and fair and ensure transparency. 4. Responsible lending is incumbent on all those involved in consumer credit transactions, including credit providers, brokers and advisors. 5. Consumer groups should participate actively in the development and regulation of consumer protection.*"

[15]Micklitz (2012), p. 296.

[16]Micklitz and Twigg Flesner (2010), pp. 201–207.

law.[17] Recently, the research of international consumer law has gone further by deepening specific issues such as financial services, e-commerce, online dispute resolution, tourism, food safety, and collective enforcement, in addition to traditional standpoints of private international law.[18] As more and more global problems are increasing due to market distortions and failures of "efficient market hypotheses,"[19] international trade lawyers now become more aware of collective public goods and optimal intervention[20]; in this sense, competition laws and consumer protection laws offer alternative policy instruments and can be more efficient.[21]

In the globalized world, the foundation and the development of international consumer law need reconceptualization and new philosophical formulations. All trade and services should be eventually to the benefit of consumers, and consumer confidence leads to constant economic growth and sustainable development. Consumers have a great impact on the economy, both nationally and internationally. In accordance with the report released by the World Bank, household consumption alone represents 60% of GDP as a global average.[22]

The United Nations (UN) Summit in 2015 adopted the 2030 Agenda for Sustainable Development, which makes a list of five areas of critical importance for humanity and the planet, being people, planet, prosperity, peace, and partnership, and the Agenda sets out seventeen UN sustainable development goals.[23] In order to make globalization socially sustainable, consumers have a dynamic role to play in all mentioned five areas.[24] International legal instruments need an equitable balance between economic growth and social justice. In this context, international consumer law should develop toward a human-centered approach, a rights-centered approach, and social-value-centered approach.

The human-centered approach inspires a change of thinking pattern from a mercantilist one to a more humanitarian one and requires that consumers as individuals are enabled by "constitutional protection"[25] and consumers' fundamental rights (such as access to basic goods and services, health rights, dignity rights,

[17]Lima Marques (2012); Pearson (2012), pp. 37–40.

[18]Toniollo (1998), pp. 837–865.

[19]Mailkiel (2003); Wink (2015), pp. 369–390.

[20]See for example Corden (1974).

[21]Petersmann (2012), p. 375.

[22]World Bank, *2010–2014 Figures*, Household Final Consumption Expenditure (% of GDP), available at http://data.worldbank.org/indicator/NE.CON.PETC.ZS.

[23]United Nations (2015), pp. 14–28. The 17 goals are poverty eradication, food security and nutrition, health and well-being, education, gender equality and women's empowerment, water and sanitation, energy, inclusive and sustainable economic growth, employment and decent work, infrastructure and sustainable industrialization, reducing inequality, sustainable cities and settlements, sustainable consumption and production, peaceful and non-violent societies and capable institutions, implementation and global partnership.

[24]Consumers International (2015), available at http://www.consumersinternational.org.

[25]Petersmann (2012), pp. 173–175. The author commented that the paradigm of "negative liberty" was successfully challenged by constitutional paradigms of "positive liberty."

liberty rights, and equality rights)[26] should be taken into full consideration at par with the objectives of economic dimension. Erik Jayme believes that the protection of the consumer, as a person and as a weaker party, is one new trend in international law.[27] For nearly three decades, international trade and investment liberalization have facilitated multinational enterprises' commercial expansion worldwide. The mercantilist thought and liberal proposals have dominated the rulemaking of international economic law, according to which consumer law might be an obstacle to free trade. While consumer rights and the concerns of consumer protection have been reflected in international law, the current legal framework still lacks a holistic machinery that effectively integrates patchy gaps. The reason behind this fact is that participation of rent-seeking interest groups (business lobbies) other than consumers is predominant in lawmaking process. There is a great disparity between consumers who do not have sufficient bargaining power and the organized business groups, which concentrate huge capitals and economic forces.

The rights-centered approach requires a balance between economic efficiency and social justice and, perhaps more importantly, a holistic mode of operation aiming to incorporate consumer rights into other areas of law (such as trade law, investment law, competition law, intellectual property law, and many more). Consumer interests comprise three levels: fundamental interests, economic interests, and societal interests.[28] Fundamental interests refer to access to the market and rational and fair distribution of those goods that are vital for survival. Economic interests relate to classical consumer protection within the market. Societal interests are those that consumers have in wider social and ecological environment. All these need rights-oriented legal regulations to ensure that the interests need to be realized in practice. In international arena, neither substantive nor procedural rights of consumers in many areas decisive for economic development have been provided for. For example, the world trade impacts consumers extensively; however, there is still no reference to consumer rights in the WTO Agreements.[29] Prior to the most recent revision of the UN Guidelines for Consumer Protection (referred to as UNGCP, adopted in 1985, revised in 1999 and 2015), the Guidelines did not use the term "rights"; instead of that, the wording "legitimate needs" was adopted. After nearly 30 years since the Guidelines were agreed, policy makers have realized

[26]Consumer protection as a constitutional right has been incorporated in no less than 25 countries. See Rachagan (2010), p. 49.

[27]Jayme (2003), p. 186.

[28]Ecologic—Institute for International and European Environmental Policy, (2003), *Consumer Interests and Sustainable Development in International Trade Law*, Federation of German Consumer Organisations (vzbv), Policy Brief, available at www.vzbv.de.

[29]It should be noted that the General Agreement on Trade in Services (GATS) of the WTO defines the framework of cross-border services in Article 1, namely, cross-border supply, consumption abroad, overseas commercial presence and provision of services through presence of natural persons. The Agreement on the Application of Sanitary and Phytosanitary Measures (SPS) has played an important role in harmonization of sanitary and phytosanitary measures among the members-states.

that the rights-centered approach is reasonable in order to better facilitate implementation.

The social-value-centered approach requests the awareness of social rights, as well as the implementation of corporate social responsibility through ethic management system. Iain Ramsay defends that consumer rights are "part of new range social rights" in modern society.[30] Consumers' right to satisfaction of basic needs, to safety, to be informed, to choose, to be represented, to redress, to a healthy environment, etc. are also public interest. Jagielska and Jagielski comment that the new generation of human/fundamental rights combines the idea of "social state concept," which means that the function of the state is to direct the processes of social development and to guarantee fair and equitable distribution of benefits. To protect the interests of consumers is to serve the common good.[31] National consumer agencies should fight against fraudulent and deceptive cross-border commercial practices, and the protection of consumers at an international level aims to offer a global public good. Consumers' movement toward a better social well-being may act as agents of social change.

As far as its discipline contribution, international consumer law can help to bridge the gap between private law and public law and consequently to reach beyond the public–private divide. It might be seen as an example of a new form of global governance regimes.[32] Market incentives should be harnessed aiming to guarantee the legitimacy and accountability to stakeholders, including consumers. Many times, global problems have surpassed national sovereignty's capacity; they require nontraditional forms of deliberation with border-crossing regulatory reach. During the process of norm creation and lawmaking, international consumer law offers a new understanding about a methodological approach and the boundaries of law. For instance, private lawmaking employed in international commerce and Internet standards has become a robust component of commercial and consumer life. A number of soft law represented by G-20 High Level Principles on Financial Consumer Protection and World Bank 39 Generalized Good Practices for Consumer Financial Protection, etc. react to the financial crisis and proliferate and establish reformed regulatory structures for international financial consumer protection. In the evolving normative regimes of international consumer law, different legal cultures interact with each other, hard law and soft law coexist, official and unofficial rules are all encompassed, public, private, and hybrid norm-producing entities are all engaged in lawmaking. Perhaps the true theoretical and methodological values that international consumer law offer allow us to reconceptualize the future trends of consumer law in terms of development paths: if consumer law justifies a state-originated approach and how national states operate through soft law for transnational transactions.

[30] Ramsay (2012), pp. 27–29.

[31] Jagielska and Jagielski (2012), p. 343.

[32] Calliess and Zumbansen (2012), p. 23.

1.3 Mappings of International Efforts: The Present Status

In the absence of a universal instrument that contains specifically rules vis-à-vis international consumer protection, the UNGCP (adopted in 1985, revised in 1999 and 2015) is the most important reference. The UNGCP provide policy advice for member states and leave them enough flexibility when transposing principles into national laws. More than one hundred countries now have laws based on the Guidelines. The very recent revision of the UNGCP in 2015[33] aimed to achieve an effective protection for consumers at the national, regional, and international levels while maintaining the balance between a high level of consumer protection and the competitiveness of businesses.[34] Now, the Preamble of the UNGCP sets out expressively the Millennium Development Goals, and the areas covered by the UNGCP are much broader by adding new themes such as state-provided services, privacy, e-commerce,[35] financial services,[36] energy,[37] public utilities,[38] travel and tourism,[39] and so forth. Moreover, in implementing one of the objectives of the Guidelines, which is to further international cooperation in the field of consumer protection, the revision of the Guidelines in 2015 encourages national enforcement agencies to coordinate and cooperate in cross-border cases, to utilize existing international networks, to enter into bilateral and multilateral arrangements, and to improve international judicial and interagency cooperation. Finally, the Guidelines also guarantee the establishment of international institutional machinery (an Intergovernmental Group of Experts on Consumer Protection Law and Policy) to provide capacity building and technical assistance to developing countries and economies in transition in formulating and enforcing consumer protection laws and

[33]UNCTAD (2015), Draft Resolution on Consumer Protection for Consideration by the General Assembly, Paragraphs 82–90, available at http://unctad.org/Sections/ditc_ccpb/docs/UNGCP_DraftResolution2015_en.pdf.

[34]UNCTAD (2015), *Report on Modalities for the Revision of the United Nations Guidelines for Consumer Protection*, available at http://unctad.org/en/Pages/DITC/CompetitionLaw/UN-Guidelines-on-Consumer-Protection.aspx.

[35]UNCTAD (2015), Draft Resolution on Consumer Protection for Consideration by the General Assembly, Paragraphs 63–65, available at http://unctad.org/Sections/ditc_ccpb/docs/UNGCP_DraftResolution2015_en.pdf.

[36]UNCTAD (2015), Draft Resolution on Consumer Protection for Consideration by the General Assembly, Paragraphs 66–68, available at http://unctad.org/Sections/ditc_ccpb/docs/UNGCP_DraftResolution2015_en.pdf.

[37]UNCTAD (2015), Draft Resolution on Consumer Protection for Consideration by the General Assembly, Paragraph 76, available at http://unctad.org/Sections/ditc_ccpb/docs/UNGCP_DraftResolution2015_en.pdf.

[38]UNCTAD (2015), Draft Resolution on Consumer Protection for Consideration by the General Assembly, Paragraph 77, available at http://unctad.org/Sections/ditc_ccpb/docs/UNGCP_DraftResolution2015_en.pdf.

[39]UNCTAD (2015), Draft Resolution on Consumer Protection for Consideration by the General Assembly, Paragraph 78, available at http://unctad.org/Sections/ditc_ccpb/docs/UNGCP_DraftResolution2015_en.pdf.

policies, among other mandates.[40] In sum, compared with the previous version in 1999, the new UN Guidelines revised in 2015 has improved in building capacity through forming an expert group with the participation of consumer authorities, in building international cooperation with more interactions at the governmental level and in building an environment favorable for digital economy and many services.

Some United Nations' agencies are also engaged in consumer protection at international level. The Agriculture and Consumer Protection Department of the Food and Agriculture Organizations (FAO) has established "Food Chain Crisis Management" (FCC) and "Emergency Prevention System for Food Safety" (EMPRES Food Safety), which assist FAO members in early warning, emergency prevention, and rapid response.[41]

Codex Alimentarius Commission (CAC), jointly created by FAO and the World Health Organization (WHO) as the world's most relevant food standard body covering 99% of the earth's population, has established more than 200 food standards and more than 100 guidelines and codes for food production and processing. The Food Code, or Codex Alimentarius,[42] is now a global reference for both food industries and consumers. Top priority has been given to the protection and interest of consumers. It serves as an important basis for national food legislation and has far-reaching implications for resolving trade disputes among the WTO members.

The World Health Organization has launched numerous programs and initiatives related to consumer protection.[43] For instance, in 2003, the WHO Framework Convention on Tobacco Control, as the first international treaty negotiated under the support of the WHO, was adopted and eight implementation guidelines covering nine articles of the Convention have been approved.[44] Since 2004, the International Food Safety Authorities Network (INFOSAN) has facilitated information and data sharing regarding food safety issues.

The International Organization for Standardization (ISO) through the Committee on Consumer Policy (COPOLCO) develops standards together with the active participation of consumer organizations, a network called Priorities from a Consumer's Point of View.[45] According to the project overview dated January 2016, COPOLCO has advanced in total 29 key areas for consumers.[46] In recent years,

---

[40]UNCTAD (2015), Draft Resolution on Consumer Protection for Consideration by the General Assembly, Paragraph 96, available at http://unctad.org/Sections/ditc_ccpb/docs/UNGCP_DraftResolution2015_en.pdf.

[41]More information can be found at http://www.fao.org/food/food-safety-quality/empres-food-safety/en/.

[42]World Health Organization and Food and Agriculture Organization of the United Nations (2006), p. 25.

[43]More information can be found at http://www.who.int/entity/en/.

[44]FCTC (2015), *The WHO Framework Convention on Tobacco Control: an Overview*, http://www.who.int/fctc/WHO_FCTC_summary_January2015_EN.pdf?ua=1.

[45]http://www.iso.org/sites/ConsumersStandards/4_interests.html.

[46]ISO/COPOLCO, (2016), COPOLCO WG2, N 099, available at http://www.iso.org/iso/key_areas_programme_copolco.pdf.

much progress has been achieved in the areas of customer satisfaction (the right to be informed and the right to redress of consumer), product safety (recall procedure, food safety, consumer safety guidance, child-resistant packaging, and cross-border trade),[47] more vulnerable consumers (children, older people, persons with disabilities, etc.),[48] services (energy and finances),[49] and so forth.

The World Intellectual Property Organization (WIPO) adopted the WIPO Development Agenda in 2007, which contains 45 recommendations and aims to care for especially the rights of intellectual property users in developing countries, through a demand-driven approach.[50]

The International Telecommunication Union (ITU) adopted in 2014 GSR14 Best Practice Guidelines on Consumer Protection in a Digital World, which highlights the need to redefine legitimate consumer rights and to establish effective mechanisms for cooperation with relevant bodies at the national, regional, and international levels; service providers; and consumer authorities.[51] The Guidelines encourages effective systems to safeguard consumer privacy and data, consumer right to information, multiple channels for redress, as well as the particularly vulnerable consumers.

The UN World Tourism Organization created a working group on the protection of tourists/consumer and travel organizers in 2010.[52] The mentioned working group proposed in 2013 a Draft Convention on the Protection of Tourist and Tourism Service Providers,[53] which has a special focus on force majeure and emergencies such as disasters and bankruptcies of travel agencies. The UNWTO proposal purports to standardize national laws and to protect mainly *ex post* tourism services

[47]For example, ISO 10001, Customer Satisfaction—Guidelines for Codes for Organizations, ISO 10002, Customer Satisfaction—Guidelines for Complaints Handling, ISO 10003, Customer Satisfaction—Guidelines for Dispute Resolution External to Organizations, ISO 10008, Customer Satisfaction—Guidelines for Business to Consumer Electronic Transactions, ISO 10377, Consumer Product Safety—Guidelines for Suppliers, ISO10393, Consumer Product Recall—Guidelines, ISO 14452, Network Services Billing—Requirements, ISO/TSA 20245:2014, Cross-border trade of second-hand goods, ISO 22000:2005, Food Safety Management Systems—Requirements for Any Organization in the Food Chain, etc.

[48]For example, ISO/IEC Guide 71:2014, Guide for Addressing Accessibility in Standards.

[49]For example, ISO/IEC Guide 76:2008, Development of Services Standards—Recommendations for Addressing Consumer Issues, ISO/TC 224, Services activities relating to Drinking Water Supply Systems and Wastewater Systems—Quality Criteria of the Services and Performance Indicators.

[50]http://www.wipo.int/ip-development/en/agenda/recommendations.html.

[51]http://www.itu.int/en/ITU-D/Conferences/GSR/Documents/GSR14_BPG_final_en.pdf.

[52]UNWTO (2011), *Activities towards a legal instrument on tourist/consumer protection general debate*, CE/90/7 and UNWTO, (2012), *Report of the Secretary-General, Part I (e) Protection of tourist/consumer and travel organizers*, CE/94/3(I)(e).

[53]UNWTO (2013), *Draft Convention on the Protection of Tourists and Tourism Service Providers*, WCTE/12/5.

providers. In the absence of indicated responsible authorities, the effectiveness of tourist/consumer protection remains to be improved.

Other international organizations have also raised awareness on consumer rights and promoted consumer empowerment. In the area of financial services, after the world financial crisis, the Organization for Economic Cooperation and Development (OECD) assisted G20 countries and other economies in adopting G20 High-level Principles on Financial Consumer Protection in 2011.[54] The Financial Stability Board (FSB) delivered Consumer Finance Protection with particular focus on credit in 2011.[55] The World Bank issued Good Practices for Financial Consumer Protection in 2012.[56] In the area of electronic commerce, OECD approved in 1999 OECD Guidelines for Consumer Protection in the Context of Electronic Commerce.[57] The United Nations Commission on International Trade Law's (UNCITRAL's) Working Group III has drafted preliminary procedural rules for online dispute resolution (ODR) cross-border electronic commerce transactions (including business-to-consumer transactions)[58] and an outcome document regarding the elements and principles.[59] In 2013, the International Financial Consumer Protection Organization (FinCoNet) was created with a purpose of institutionalizing cooperation among financial supervisory authorities.[60] The FinCoNet issued a Report on Responsible Lending—A Review of Supervisory Tools for Consumer Lending Practices, which summarized the responses to financial crisis from 20 jurisdictions worldwide and reported that a great majority of jurisdictions were in the process of developing or implementing measures of responsible lending.[61] In the area of tourism services, as early as 1970, the International Institute for the Unification of Private Law (UNIDROIT) adopted an International Convention on Travel Contracts (CCV), aiming at safeguarding the rights and interests of travelers.[62] However, little progress has been achieved in terms of ratifications by member states of the UNIDROIT. The Hague Conference on Private International Law (HCCH) decided to include a proposal submitted by the Brazilian government on "Draft Convention on Cooperation and Access to Justice Concerning International Tourists" into its working agenda, and the Permanent Bureau of the HCCH

[54]http://www.oecd.org/daf/fin/financial-markets/48892010.pdf.

[55]http://www.fsb.org/wp-content/uploads/r_111026a.pdf.

[56]The document can be found at http://www.worldbank.org.

[57]http://www.oecd.org/sti/consumers/34023811.pdf.

[58]UNCITRAL (2015), *Online dispute resolution for cross-border electronic commerce transactions: draft procedural rules*, A/CN.9/WG.III/WP.133.

[59]UNCITRAL (2016), *Draft outcome document reflecting elements and principles of an ODR process*, A/CN.9/WG.III/WP.140.

[60]http://www.finconet.org.

[61]FinCoNet (2014), *FinCoNet report on responsible lending: Review of supervisory tools for suitable consumer lending practices*, p. 118, full text available at http://www.finconet.org/FinCoNet-Responsible-Lending-2014.pdf.

[62]http://www.unidroit.org/instruments/transport/ccv.

will conduct a study on the desirability and feasibility of the topic.[63] From the perspective of international protection of consumer/tourist, the HCCH proposal advances a great step compared with the UNWTO proposal because the draft convention aims to protect *ex ante* tourists as consumers in any market niche with direct consumption relations through international cooperation among administrative authorities and judicial cooperation, including small claims courts.[64]

The International Consumer Protection and Enforcement Network (ICPEN) has gathered together 55 countries as member organizations and three countries as partner organizations since 1992 to cooperate in information sharing and enforcements for cross-border commercial activities affecting consumers. Instead of handling individual consumer complaints, ICPEN promotes collective actions to be taken by consumer agencies of its participants in order to facilitate cross-border remedies and effective international consumer protection. A few initiatives of this kind are international Internet sweeps; filing of complaints in up to eight languages related to cross-border transactions such as online shopping, ecommerce services, traveling, phone services, financial services, etc. through alternative dispute resolution (ADR) with the supervision of national consumer authorities[65]; and education campaigns such as fraud prevention project.

The International Consumer Product Safety Caucus (ICPSC) is an international organization with a view to sharing information and enhancing cooperation among consumer product safety regulatory and market surveillance authorities. The ICPSC develops knowledge-based projects and individual topics such as international cooperation, products recalls, recall effectiveness, and product safety initiatives.[66]

The International Consumer Product Health and Safety Organizations (ICPHSO), as another international forum, is composed of governmental agencies, consumers, business, legal firms, trade associations, and all stakeholders, to study non-food consumer product safety issues.[67]

Consumers International (CI) is the worldwide federation of consumer groups (nongovernmental organizations—NGO) with over 240 member organizations in 120 countries and represents the global voice defending consumer rights in other important international organizations. The unique contributions and achievements of CI refer to empowerment of consumers and participation in national and international consumer protection legislation.[68]

---

[63]Hague Conference on Private International Law (2015), Conclusions & Recommendations Adopted by the Council, Council on General Affairs and Policy of the Conference, 24–26 March 2015.

[64]Hague Conference on Private International Law (2015), *Proposal by the Government of Brazil on a Draft Convention on Cooperation and Access to Justice for International Tourists*, Prel.Doc. No. 2, at Annex III, prepared by Claudia Lima Marques and Nadia de Araújo.

[65]More information on this project "Econsumer.gov" can be found at http://www.icpen.org.

[66]See membership information at http://www.icpsc.org.

[67]http://www.icphso.org/about-icphso.

[68]See for example, Consumers International (2010), *Consumer International, 50 Years of the Global Consumer Movement*, available at http://www.consumersinternational.org/media/33263/ci50ebook-english.pdf.

Consumer protection policy is involved in regional integration processes. Different regional blocs set up different priorities. The European Union (EU) has become a global reference in breaking down trade barriers without prejudice to the high level of protection for the consumers. The European Consumer Agenda adopted by the European Commission purports to maximize consumer participation and trust in the single market. The European treaties and the Charter of Fundamental Rights of the European Union[69] establish the general principles of promoting balanced and sustainable development while ensuring free movement of persons, services, goods, and capital. A number of directives at EU level[70] effectively facilitated legislative harmonization among EU member states. In the area of enforcement, EU regulation No. 2006/2004 lays down a structure for enforcement cooperation among national authorities of the EU member states. Where consumers' collective interests in the internal market are at stake, a court or an administrative entity can grant injunctions, in accordance with Injunctions Directive 2009/22/EC. Regarding the disputes, the EU consumers may benefit from the European Consumer Centers (ECC-Net),[71] as well as alternative dispute resolution[72] and online dispute resolution.[73]

The Southern Common Market (Mercosur) has made some progress in consolidating a Mercosur system of consumer defense,[74] which is structured based on a common information system, a regional action of capacity building, a norm applicable for international consumer contracts.[75] The Mercosur legislation sets an aim of harmonizing basic concepts (such as consumer and provider) regarding consumer protection adopted by members. It is technical committee 7 with the participation of national consumer protection agencies in the discussion of policies and actions in order to improve and develop the protection and defense of consumers within Mercosur.[76]

Compared with the EU and Mercosur, the North American Free Trade Agreement (NAFTA) holds a more mercantilist position since there is no common consumer policy or primary objective to harmonize consumer protection laws.[77]

[69]Charter of Fundamental Rights of the European Union, 2010/C 83/02.

[70]For instance, the Directive on Consumer Rights, the Directive on certain aspects of the sable of consumer goods and associated guarantees, the Directive on unfair terms in consumer contracts, the new package travel directive, the Directive on the protection of consumers in respect of certain aspects of timeshare, the Unfair Commercial Practices Directive, the Price Indication Directive, the Directive on Misleading and Comparative Advertising and so forth.

[71]In 2014 alone, the ECC-Net dealt with more than 37,000 complaints. See European Commission, (2015), *The European Consumer Centres Network: 10 Years serving Europe's consumers, Anniversary Report 2005–2015*, available at http://ec.europa.eu/consumers.

[72]Directive 2013/11/EU on ADR for consumer disputes.

[73]EU Regulation No. 524/2013 and Commission Implementing Regulation (EU) 2015/1051.

[74]Junior Antônio (2014).

[75]Estatuto da Cidadania do Mercosul Plano de Ação, Mercosul/CMC/DEC. N° 64/10.

[76]More projects can be found in National Secretariat of Consumer of the Ministry of Justice of Brazil (2015), *Manual de Defesa do Consumidor Mercosur e Peru*, 1st Edition, pp. 23–26.

[77]Nehf (2008).

NAFTA gives each member state the freedom to impose restrictions due to public policy purposes.

In other parts of the world, consumer protection plans and people-orientated development models have become a concern in the regional integration context. In Asia, a cross-border consumer redress mechanism to handle consumer complaints has been created within the ASEAN through the ASEAN Committee on Consumer Protection (ACCP).[78] In Asia-Pacific Economic Cooperation (APEC), the blueprint in 1998 declared to develop and implement consumer protection.[79] The Electronic Commerce Steering Group (ECSG) is in charge of the cross-border privacy rules (CBPR) system from which consumers may benefit.[80] It should be noted that APEC only operates in nonbinding commitments and consensus among its member states and therefore the ongoing projects are only of advisory nature. In Africa, the Southern African Development Community (SADC) adopted a draft declaration on regional cooperation in competition and consumer policies[81] and the Communications Regulators' Association of Southern Africa (CRASA) formulated Information and Communications Technology Consumer Rights and Protection Regulatory Guidelines[82] for its member states.

In the megaregional trade agreement negotiations, one can find two different approaches. In the recently concluded Trans-Pacific Partnership Agreement (TPP), the achievement on consumer protection is quite modest since TPP members "agree to adopt and maintain consumer protection laws related to fraudulent and deceptive commercial activities online and to ensure that privacy and other consumer protections can be enforced in TPP markets."[83] While in the ongoing Transatlantic Trade and Investment Partnership (TTIP) negotiations, the approach seems more ambitious because the TTIP's goal is to harmonize consumer protection standards, according to the announcement of political leaders. As the negotiations continue, more time will be needed to verify if the potential closer economic partnership may imply deregulation of consumer protection in the EU or instead intensify harmonization between the EU and the US.

---

[78] http://www.aseanconsumer.org/accp.

[79] http://www.apec.org/Meeting-Papers/Leaders-Declarations/1998/1998_aelm/apec_blueprint_for.aspx.

[80] Barrad and Raul (2014), pp. 19–30.

[81] http://www.sadc.int/files/4813/5292/8377/SADC_Declaration_on_Competition_and_Consumer_Policies.pdf.

[82] http://www.crasa.org/common_up/crasa-setup/10-03-2015_SADC%20ICT%20CONSUMER%20RIGHTS%20AND%20PROTECTION%20%20REGULATORY%20GUIDELINES%20%202011.pdf.

[83] The Summary of the TPP can be found at the website of Office of the United States Trade Representative at http://ustr.gov.

Finally, the global business sector has also been engaged in self-regulation harmonization to ensure consumer confidence and establish industry standards.[84] In the global economy, self-regulation, many times elaborated through a multistakeholder's approach, has become an important tool complementing state regulation. Even though self-regulation initiated by industries as a useful component in the complete regulatory system has benefits and merits, there are still legal limitations,[85] especially where market incentives and the goals of self-regulation do not coincide. One empirical study about privacy disclosures of the websites pointed out that a full self-regulatory regime had not been able to emerge despite the existence of such regulation.[86] Some concerns of skepticism can be illustrated by an antitrust action brought by the US Department of Justice against the National Association of Realtors for certain rules related to Internet brokers.[87]

1.4 Some New Trends

Based on the above snapshot of the current efforts of consumer protection in the international community, one can find some new trends of the development path of international consumer law.

1.4.1 Components of Legal Regime and Protagonists in Lawmaking

In the medium and long term, the legal regime of international consumer protection will continue to resemble the characteristics of pluralism and fragmentation. The norm production landscape is highly diversified and fragmented. Unlike in the domestic context where state intervention exists through coercive rules and judicial review, in cross-border transactions, however, states' roles are reduced since national borders are also legal borders, especially in the implementation. To take an example of cyber law, the dilemma we face is that without a supportive legal framework for consumer protection, cross-border transaction is forced into the national legal system, which is not adequate anymore.[88] Furthermore, the application of national law, including conflict of laws, is always costly and tricky. This feature of "lawlessness" or "inefficiency of national legal systems" gives rise to the

[84]For example, International Chamber of Commerce (ICC) elaborated Advertising and Marketing Communication Practice Consolidated ICC Code.

[85]Reich (2008), pp. 859–868.

[86]Culnan (2000), pp. 20–26.

[87]Castro (2011), p. 8.

[88]Reich (2008), p. 860.

proliferation of norm producing originated by other bodies such as international organizations, industries, traders, and even hybrid entities composing the public, the private sector, and the civil society. In consumer electronic commerce transactions, the new reality is characterized by the overwhelming privatization of lawmaking (such as codes of conduct, best practices, etc.) and the abundance of autonomous self-regulation, which is independent from national legal order.[89]

The phenomenon of the rise of private lawmaking in the sphere of consumer protection law requires plenty of attention. Although norms such as codes of conduct and best practices originating from industries can increase regulatory efficiency, facilitate consumer redress, and help businesses to assume ethical manners, and a violation of certain norms might even generate social and economic sanctions, it is necessary to scrutinize legitimacy, transparency, and fairness from a consumer point of view. In many cases, consumer involvement is absent in the elaboration of such self-regulation and effective public supervision is not sufficient. Considering the nature of consumption relationship (the vulnerability of consumer, limited freedom of choice of consumer, and information asymmetry), it is justified that states and public policy decision makers should be protagonists in formulating the legal order and national consumer authorities must take quicker actions. The privatization of lawmaking will continue to exist; however, it should be merely complementary in enhancing the level of consumer protection and should be always subject to judicial control and monitoring system.

To juxtapose "private soft law" originated from businesses, there is also "public soft law" originated from governments and international organizations. The main technique used by international organizations in pursuit of consumer protection is soft law. Similar to the situation in international environmental law, soft law is also predominant in international consumer law and embodies a method of global governance. The picture exactly illustrates the development paths of these fields where the international society has an anxiety to transform political assertions into lawful rights. Soft law exemplifies a starting point that reproduces the consensus on guiding principles, basic issues, and development priorities. On one hand, soft law encounters less barriers than hard law: it is easier to consolidate because the texts and the instruments are not binding and therefore do not need ratification, which is always time consuming and complicated; it leaves flexibility in targeting problems, thus creating room for maneuver for national authorities. On the other hand, soft law is the precursor and the base of potential binding treaties. One can see the example of the implementation of the United Nations Guidelines on Consumer Protection; as soft law, the Guidelines have remained relevant and valid after three decades since 1985. Some intergovernmental organizations (like ICPEN and the OECD) have embraced the objectives of the guidelines.[90] All countries now have a consumer law, and the Guidelines have provided useful inspirations for a good

---

[89] Calliess and Zumbansen (2012), pp. 153–180.

[90] UNCTAD (2013), *Implementation report on the United Nations Guidelines on Consumer Protection (1985–2013)*, TD/B/C.I/CLP/23, p. 3.

number of national consumer laws.[91] In some countries, consumer rights have already been enshrined constitutionally and recognized as human rights. The future path of consumer protection is that soft law will not be an alternative to hard law but a forerunner of hard law. The experimenting trails of soft law will always stimulate states to foster confidence and crystallize toward mandatory rules of hard law. The proposal submitted by the Brazilian government on "Draft Convention on Cooperation and Access to Justice Concerning International Tourists," which aims to guarantee the rights of tourist consumers and to safeguard access to justice and administrative intervention, is an indication of such a trend.

1.4.2 Harmonization of Consumer Protection Norms

Harmonization of standards, codes of conduct, and good practices has already taken place through international organizations and global businesses. However, in relation to harmonization of consumer laws among different countries, there have been skeptical views regarding such feasibility, taking into account varying levels of institutional development. Thomas Bernauer explains "variation of consumer protection standards across countries may be a source of trade disputes."[92] Since the past decade, harmonization of consumer law has been achieved or at least advocated at regional levels. Harmonization easily starts within a region since regional integration creates opportunities for approximation of legal infrastructures. The EU is a very successful case in harmonizing consumer laws further guaranteed by a strong judicial system. In Latin America and in Asia, harmonization projects are ongoing and similar initiatives have also been supported.

As the megaregional trade agreements negotiations continue, harmonization of consumer protection rules will no longer be a fiction.

1.4.3 Shift of Paradigm of Ex Post Redress to Ex Ante Protection

A court of law can be always the last resort for consumers to claim their interests in cross-border transactions. Nevertheless, international litigations are time consuming, costly, and inefficient. In order to ensure consumers' access to low-cost, simple, and efficient ways of resolving disputes, ADR has been offered to solve problems both online and offline. ODR is also widely used in online transactions and cross-border trade. However, ADR and ODR are not yet developed

[91]UNCTAD (2013), *Implementation report on the United Nations Guidelines on Consumer Protection (1985–2013)*, TD/B/C.I/CLP/23, p. 1.
[92]Bernauer and Meins (2002).

sophisticatedly and have only limited functions because many times proposed solutions are not binding and not many consumers know how to file complaints with ADR entities. In addition, sometimes it is difficult for consumers to know who on earth (content provider or Internet intermediary) is responsible.

A new trend in international consumer protection is to change the ex post model into an ex ante one aiming to avoid consumer litigations. The Draft Convention on Cooperation and Access to Justice Concerning International Tourists at the Hague Conference has been designed for this purpose. Through international legal cooperation, competent administrative authorities of members states shall guarantee in a nondiscriminatory manner international tourists-consumers' right to access to justice, i.e., to facilitate their utilization of consumer protection system, including the use of courts of small claims in the country visited. To achieve the shift of paradigm, national agencies should cooperate with each other and promote cooperation among all concerned domestic entities.

On the way of building global cooperation platforms among competent authorities, in the future, there will be new initiatives that are more institutional based and focus on special sectors. Similar to the newly established International Financial Consumer Protection Organization (FinCoNet), which replaced the previous informal network among the national financial supervisory agencies, probably other global agencies will also appear in the future, for instance, a global food safety agency,[93] a global digital agency, and so on. Considering that the WTO is not an ideal forum to fulfill the objectives of consumer protection, perhaps there is a possibility to create a global agency that has jurisdiction for setting mandatory standards for public interests. Nevertheless, such option will be too difficult to realize.

1.4.4 Empowerment of Consumers

Although it is not possible to draw an exhaustive list on the new trends of international consumer protection, one that is certain to appear is the increasing empowerment of consumers.

The increasingly important role of consumers has been recognized and included in the UN Agenda 2030 (Goal 12 of the sustainable development goals), and UNCTAD will have a new mandate through the Intergovernmental Group of Experts in Consumer Protection Law and Policy to help consumers organize better and coordinate their concerns and interests globally. Consumers are the largest group in the world economy and can be powerful agents for transformation by obliging multinationals to protect consumers' rights and raise standards[94] as major

[93] Snuder (2013), pp. 162–209.

[94] For example, the recent Volkswagen emission scandal has triggered millions of consumer complaints and the consumer watchdog in the U.S., the Federal Trade Commission filed a lawsuit against the multinational for its deceptive and unfair practices.

economies have shifted their development strategy in the direction of new sources of domestic demand. Media and technology have empowered multinational companies' outreach, on one hand, and will multiply consumers' impact in the future. Consumers need empowerment and innovative organization to exert more influence and economic pressure on businesses.

Consumers should not be only passive recipients in global markets; consumers should also be active participants as well as contributors of a fair global governance. As stated in the Sofia Declaration adopted by the ILA, "consumer groups should participate actively in the development and regulation of consumer protection." Consumers' involvement in regulation can ensure accountability, transparency, and due process.

1.5 Concluding Remarks

Consumers become more important in pushing economy recovery in developed countries and as a growing source of domestic demand in developing countries. International consumer law is not antitrade law. The European Union's successful experiences demonstrate that better consumer protection is not antithetical to progressive economic integration. Effective consumer protection can enhance and facilitate trade. Trade expansion needs to be regulated in order to achieve better quality and equilibrium between economic growth and social justice. The core value established by international consumer law is that world trade should transform from being producer oriented to being more people centered, and consumers, as the weaker party, can enjoy fairness and lawful rights. International trade is borderless, but consumers' interest does not stop over at national borders. The new environment of digital economy in the global context has reshaped marketplaces and brought disruptive changes for consumer behaviors and traditional notion of consumers (in the case of consumer to consumer, C2C). International consumer law, as a newly emerged discipline, needs to keep up to date with global developments and functions like an engine to drive legislative and regulatory process.

The Chinese great philosopher Mencius once said: "Without the compass and the ruler, a carpenter cannot form squares and circles." Mencius taught us that nothing could be accomplished without norms or standards. Without effective consumer protection, international trade cannot achieve a healthy sustainability. Consumer protection, as an international public good, requires mandatory rules and standards, including information, nondiscrimination, good faith, fairness in preformulated contract terms, access to justice, and conflict laws.[95]

Originally, there is no path in the world, but after many people have walked upon it, there became a way. It illustrates the case of international consumer law. The

[95] Reich (2008), pp. 860–861.

discipline creates opportunities for the development of global governance. International consumer lawyers have begun with the first step in a long journey.

References

Barrad CV, Raul AC (2014) APEC overview. In: Raul AC (ed) The privacy, data protection and cybersecurity law review. Law Business Research

Bernauer T, Meins E (2002) Consumer protection in a global market. Available at https://www.researchgate.net/publication/241075756

Bourgoignie T (1992) Characteristics of consumer law. J Consum Policy 14:293–315

Calliess G-P, Zumbansen P (2012) Rough consensus and running code: a theory of transnational private law. Hart Publishing, Oxford and Portland, Oregon

Castro D (2011) Benefits and limitations of industry self-regulation for online behavioral advertising. The Information Technology & Innovation Foundation

Consumers International (2015) The role of consumer protection in meeting the UN sustainable development goals. Available at http://www.consumersinternational.org

Corden WM (1974) Trade policy and economic welfare. Oxford University Press, Oxford

Culnan MJ (2000) Protecting privacy online: is self-regulation working? J Public Policy Market: Spring 2000 19:1

European Commission (2015) The European Consumer Centres Network: 10 years serving Europe's consumers, Anniversary Report 2005–2015. Available at http://ec.europa.eu/consumers

Helveston MN (2015) Judicial deregulation of consumer markets. Cardozo Law Rev 36:1739–1783

Howells G, Ramsay I, Wilhelmsson T (2011) Consumer law in its international dimension. In: Howells G, Ramsay I, Wilhelmsson C (eds) Handbook of research on international consumer law. Edward Elgar, Northampton

Jagielska M, Jagielski M (2012) Are consumers rights human rights? In: Devenney J, Kenny M (eds) European consumer protection: theory and practice. Cambridge University Press, Cambridge

Jayme E (2003) Gesammelte Schriften, Band 3. C.F. Müller, Heidelberg

Junior Antônio PG (2014) O Consumidor e sua Proteção na União Europeia e Mercosul: Pesquisa Conjuntural como Contribuição à Política Desenvolvimentista de Proteção Consumerista nos Blocos. Juruá Editora

Lima Marques C (2001) A Proteção do Consumidor: Aspetos de Direito Privado Regional e Geral, XXVII Curso de Derecho Internacional – OEA/CIJ. Ed. Secretária General – Subsecretária de Asuntos Jurídicos, Washington

Lima Marques C (2012) Relations between international law and consumer law in the globalized world: challenges and prospects. In: Lima Marques C, Arroyo DPF, Ramsay I (eds) The global financial crisis and the need for consumer regulation: new developments on international protection of consumers

Mailkiel BG (2003) The efficient market hypothesis and its critics. CEPS Working Paper No. 91. Princeton University, https://www.princeton.edu/ceps/workingpapers/91malkiel.pdf

Micklitz H-W (2012) The expulsion of the concept of protection from the consumer law and the return of social elements in the civil law: a bittersweet polemic. J Consum Policy 35:283–296

Micklitz H, Twigg Flesner C (2010) Think global—towards international consumer law. J Consum Policy 33:201–207

Nehf JP (2008) Principles of consumer protection in the North American Free Trade Agreement. Available at http://dx.doi.org/10.2139/ssrn.1208822

Pearson G (2012) Porto Alegre, Asunción

Petersmann E-U (2012) International economic law in the 21st century: constitutional pluralism and multilevel governance of interdependent public goods. Hart Publishing, Oxford and Portland, Oregon

Rachagan S (2010) Development and consumer law. In: Howells G, Ramsay I, Wilhelmsson (eds) Handbook of research on international consumer law. Edward Elgar, Cheltenham and Northampton

Ramsay I (2006) Consumer law, regulatory capitalism and the 'New Learning' in regulation. Sydney Law Rev 28(9):10–35

Ramsay I (2012) Consumer law and policy: text and materials on regulating consumer markets, 3rd edn. Hart Publishing, Oxford

Reich N (2008) Transnational consumer law-reality or fiction? Penn State Int Law Rev, Vol. 27 (3/4): 859

Ruhl G (2011) Consumer protection in choice of law. Cornell Int Law J 44:569–601

Snuder F (2013) We need a global food safety agency: reflections on the hidden jurisprudence of the WTO. PKU Transnatl Law Rev 1(2):162

Toniollo JA (1998) International protection of the consumer. ILSA J Int Comp Law 4:837

United Nations (2015) Transforming Our World: The 2030 Agenda for Sustainable Development, A/RES/70/1

Wei D (2002) Globalization and China's pathway in quest for a new identity. J Int Trade Law Policy 6(2)

Wink SP (2015) The bankruptcy of the securities market paradigm. Virginia Law Bus Rev 9 (3):369

World Health Organization and Food and Agriculture Organization of the United Nations (2006) Understanding the Codex Alimentarius, 3rd edn. Rome

Chapter 2
The UN Guidelines for Consumer Protection: Review and Next Steps

Ana Cândida Muniz Cipriano and Héctor Valverde Santana

2.1 Introduction

When consumer rights first began to be internationally considered, following North American President John Kennedy's speech to the United States Congress on March 15, 1962,[1] it was unlikely to predict that such theme would become an international concern.

The advent of the United Nations Guidelines on Consumer Protection, first adopted on April 9, 1985, was a clear recognition of the importance of the basic rights outlined by John Kennedy in 1962: the right to safety, the right to be informed, the right to choose, and the right to be heard. It was certainly a direct effect from historic facts that followed 1962: the first UN Conference on Trade and Development in 1964, the collapse of the Soviet Union and the end of the Cold War, and the independence of many countries and the fall of dictatorship in others, followed by the considerable increase of UN membership from 159 countries (1989) to 192 (1997).[2]

The independent countries, as well as the new members, required a special strategy in what concerns development. Hence, the attention to the theme of consumption and therefore consumer protection became inevitable.

Today, about 30 years later, the United Nations General Assembly has recently approved the second review of the UN Guidelines on Consumer Protection. But

[1] http://www.jfklibrary.org/Asset-Viewer/Archives/JFKPOF-037-028.aspx (accessed on March 25th, 2016).

[2] Hanhimaki (2008), pp. 20–25.

A.C. Muniz Cipriano (✉)
Faculty of Law, University of Buenos Aires, Buenos Aires, Argentina
e-mail: munizymuniz@hotmail.com

H.V. Santana
Faculty of Law, University Center of Brasília, Brasília, Brazil

C. Lima Marques, D. Wei (eds.), *Consumer Law and Socioeconomic Development*,
DOI 10.1007/978-3-319-55624-6_2

what does this review mean? What is expected from the UN members to do, and what can consumers expect from the adoption of the revised Guidelines?

2.2 The Advent of the United Nations Guidelines for Consumer Protection Adopted in 1985

Following the discussion settled by President Kennedy in 1962, the United Nations members launched a discussion on consumer protection matters, first, within the Economic and Social Council (ECOSOC), which requested the Secretary General a survey on the institutions and legislation among the country members (1970). Following such survey, a first report was to be considered by Member States, in which within the ambit of the ECOSOC it was agreed the need for a general and international "guidance" setting specific objectives, considering, as well, the needs of developing countries.

It was only in the early 1980s that the Economic and Social Council formally requested the Secretary General to continue consultations and a first guidelines draft was presented.

On April 9, 1985, the General Assembly approved, under Resolution 39/248, adopted by consensus, the Guidelines for Consumer Protection, providing an international framework for the development and evaluation of consumer policy.

There is no doubt that the Guidelines became an international reference regarding minimum consumer protection standards. Many country members' legislation, including the Brazilian one, is mostly based and inspired by the UNGCP.

Following such approval, the Economic and Social Council adopted resolution 1990/85,[3] specifically on consumer protection, which referred to the necessary implementation of the Guidelines for Consumer Protection, rendering special attention to developing countries.

The United Nations Guidelines on Consumer protection constitute a policy framework also urging governments to promote consumer protection, at first, in eight areas: *basic needs*, *safety*, *information*, *choice*, *representation*, *redress*, *consumer education*, and *healthy environment*. The Guidelines are particularly designed for governments of developing and newly independent countries to use in structuring and strengthening consumer protection policies and legislation.[4] The Guidelines were adopted "recognizing that consumers often face imbalances in economic terms, education levels and bargaining power." That is the reason why the UNGCP is a reference officially recognising that consumer protection is a tool for social justice and economic development.

It is important to mention, it was as well predicted the settlement of an international program regarding the implementation of the Guidelines. Such program

[3]Resolution A/C.2/54/L.24 9TH.

[4]http://www.un.org/documents/ga/res/39/a39r248.htm.

would be under the Secretary General's leadership and would be based on the cooperation of the members, regional commissions, and other relevant bodies and agencies. The program was to be implemented subject to the availability of extrabudgetary resources and to be reviewed in 1995, on the occasion of the tenth anniversary of the adoption of the Guidelines.

Despite the aforementioned difficulty, the UNGCP managed to address and include very important and basic interests and needs of consumers worldwide, considering *the imbalance that consumers face in economic terms, educational levels and bargaining power* and the importance of promoting just, *equitable and sustainable economic and social development.*

According to the first United Nations reports on the activities of the UNGCP and the impact of its worldwide implementation, there were taken two surveys carried out by members' governments regarding the UNGCP's implementation (1992 and 1995).

Such reports recognized that the UNGCP were still very much important and relevant for social development, especially in developing countries. Even in developed countries, where there are already considerably strong consumer laws, the UNGCP constitute a reference, even in order to achieve objectives and goals.

As for the objectives of the United Nations Guidelines on Consumer Protection, at that time the Member States considered that among the interests and needs of consumers, "particularly those in developing countries," the ones that deserved attention were the ones related to economic terms, education and access to nonhazardous products, promoting just, equitable, and sustainable economic and social development. Therefore, the UNGCP of 1985 had the aim not only to appoint the main consumers' rights but also to assist country members in order to achieve adequate and proper protection in this very specific area.

That is the reason why the UNGCP became such an important international document; it became an international reference establishing minimum standards in the field of consumer protection, including the need to "facilitate the production and distribution patterns responsive to the needs and desires of consumers," "assist countries in curbing abusive business practices by enterprises at the national and international levels which adversely affect consumers," "facilitate the development of independent consumer groups," "further international co-operation," and "encourage the development of market conditions which provide consumers with greater choice at lower prices."

The UNGCP settled a new standard concerning governments' responsibility in developing proper policies on consumer protection, settling priorities according to the country's economic status and needs. So it is recommended that governments should provide or maintain adequate infrastructure to develop, implement and monitor consumer protection policies, taking special attention to certain sectors of the population such as the rural population.

Thus, it became crucial for Member States to create proper organisms or agencies to implement, follow and enforce the basic consumer protection standards settled in the UNGCP in all foreseen areas: (a) physical safety, (b) promotion and protection of consumers' economic interests, (c) standards for the safety and quality of consumer goods and services, (d) distribution facilities for essential consumer goods and services, (e) measures enabling consumers to obtain redress, (f) education and information programs, (g) measures relating to specific areas (food, water, pharmaceuticals, including pesticides and chemicals) and international cooperation.

2.3 The Review of the UNGCP in 1999

The review of the United Nations Guidelines on Consumer Protection, in 1999, was mainly focused on environmental matters. Following all summits and conferences in order to call attention to our planet's preservation, the review of the UNGCP took no different path.

In the 1972 Conference on Human Environment, the International Organization of Consumers Unions settled the basis for environmental discussions within the ambit of consumer matters. It was recognized that environmental matters were basically "ordinary people's matters" and the well-being and survival of all individuals the main concern.

Considering that the environment was (and still is) being damaged, mainly due to all sorts of consumption (energy, water, food, electronics, etc.), the need to call people's attention to this matter became inevitable.

The UNGCP, in order not only to consider the theme of environmental matters in its new version but also to be successfully calling attention to the need for sustainable consumption, also called for new consumer protection and awareness policies, as well as international cooperation.

An Inter-Regional Expert Group Meeting on Consumer Protection and Sustainable Consumption took place in São Paulo, in January 1998, in order to think of and provide a proper framework on the matter of sustainable consumption regarding consumer rights. The results of such meeting were presented and discussed at the Ad Hoc Inter-Sessional Working Group of the Commission on Sustainable Development (CSD) in February 1998, the sixth session of the CSD in April 1998, and the Substantive Session of the Economic and Social Council (ECOSOC) in July 1998.

The important results of such discussions are based on the recognition for the need for expanding the Guidelines, including the theme of sustainable consumption. The Member States were urged to continue efforts to implement the Guidelines, including the theme of sustainable consumption: (a) to assist countries in achieving or maintaining adequate protection for their population as consumers, (b) to facilitate production and distribution patterns responsive to the needs and desires of consumers, (c) to encourage high levels of ethical conduct for those engaged in the production and distribution of goods and services to consumers, (d) to assist countries in curbing abusive business practices by all enterprises at the national and international levels that adversely affect consumers, (e) to facilitate the development of independent consumer groups, (f) to further international cooperation in the field of consumer protection, (g) to encourage the development of market conditions that provide consumers with greater choice at lower prices, (h) to promote sustainable consumption.

The review of the UNGCP that was finalized in 1999 did not suppress or change any of the first settled objectives but highlighted previous ones and established new ones according to the need for considering environmental limitations and global warming. Themes like the protection of consumers from hazards to their health and safety; the promotion and protection of the economic interests of consumers; access of consumers to adequate information to enable them to make informed choices according to individual wishes and needs; and consumer education were maintained, having included themes like education on the environmental, social, and economic impacts of consumer choice; consumer redress; and the promotion of sustainable consumption patterns.

The United Nations considered that the industrialized countries' unsustainable patterns of production and consumption were the major cause of the continued deterioration of the global environment, the lead of such countries being therefore crucial in achieving sustainable consumption patterns. As for developing countries, their needs and economic status are to be taken under consideration, together with the goals of development, health care and eradicating poverty.

Apart from the governments, the Guidelines also establish the participation of providers (enterprises) in the processes of guaranteeing consumer protection, stating that they *should obey the relevant laws and regulations of the countries in which they do business*, complying with international appropriate standards.

The participation of universities and public and private enterprises, as well as the civil society is also officially considered in the process of developing consumer protection policies. Within such ambit, the participation of the civil society is very much important, highlighting the example of Consumers International (CI), which participated both in the process of creating the UNGCP itself and in the discussions for expanding the Guidelines, including the theme of sustainable consumption.

2.4 The First Meeting of the Ad Hoc Expert Group on Consumer Protection

It is important to take into account that in almost over 30 years of the UNGCP, there was no official group of experts or a specific committee regarding consumer protection matters within the ambit of the United Nations. The only existing group for over 18 years on competition and policy within UNCTAD was the one to organize ad hoc meetings on consumer protection. Although both themes are related, considering the existence of an official international document on consumer protection for over 30 years, the lack of a proper and specific group to discuss consumer matters within the ambit of the United Nations was for a while the object of great criticism. The Sixth United Nations Conference to Review All Aspects of the Set of Multilaterally Agreed Equitable Principles and Rules for the Control of

Restrictive Business Practices (Geneva, November 8–12, 2010) invited UNCTAD to convene two expert meetings on consumer policy between the Review Conferences.

The *First Ad Hoc Expert Meeting*[5] actually undertaken by UNCTAD had as its main focus the revision of the United Nations Guidelines on Consumer Protection. It followed the results of the *Sixth United Nations Conference to Review All Aspects of the Set of Multilaterally Agreed Equitable Principles and Rules for the Control of Restrictive Business Practices*, which recommended UNCTAD to convene two expert meetings on consumer policy between the Review Conferences, separate from the Intergovernmental Group of Experts on Competition Law and Policy.

The *First Ad Hoc Expert Group Meeting on Consumer Protection* took place in July 2012 and had as its first aim to prepare an Implementation Report on the UNGCP: considering that the Guidelines were issued in 1985, and following its review in 1999, it was necessary the investigation on its implementation and the possible need for a new review. The first investigations were coordinated by UNCTAD with the participation of several countries, which contributed handling information on whether the Guidelines were still valid and useful. The result was that the UNGCP remained not only valid and useful, but some other themes and areas new in commerce should be studied and included as well, such as e-commerce, financial services, data protection, tourism, energy, and cross-border trade.

Country members considered the necessary attention to the "new products, services," and tools offered by the continuous development of technology and that special attention should be given to developing countries and countries with economies in transition.

The *Second Ad Hoc Expert Group Meeting on Consumer Protection*[6] took place in July 2013, and country members took the chance to discuss not only the need for a UNGCP review but also the need for establishing a proper official group of experts on consumer protection. In order to promote further investigation and studies, there were created four working groups focusing on the main theme object of concern: E-commerce (chaired by France), Financial Services (chaired by Malaysia), Other Issues (chaired by Brazil and Germany), and Implementation of UNGCP (chaired by Gabon).

The process counted again on the participation of Consumers International,[7] which expertise provided investigation, campaigns, and reports that contributed to the attention to many specific themes such as public services, energy, e-commerce, and financial services and updates related to water, pharmaceutical products, and food.

[5]http://unctad.org/en/pages/MeetingDetails.aspx?meetingid=65.

[6]http://unctad.org/en/pages/MeetingDetails.aspx?meetingid=350.

[7]http://unctad.org/Sections/ditc_ccpb/docs/UNGCPCont_CI_en.pdf.

For each working group, there were prepared questionnaires so that opinion among Member States and other related stakeholders would be collected on a number of themes and their relevance.

2.5 The Review Process of UNGCP 2012–2015

Following a process coordinated by UNCTAD, which consulted country members regarding the most important and urgent matters on consumer protection, it was recommend that "UNCTAD should undertake discussions regarding the possibility of updating the United Nations Guidelines for Consumer Protection" and "undertake to collaborate on the content of potential revisions."[8]

The conclusion that followed the discussions was that, despite the UNGCP remained a valid international reference for many countries and national consumer protection laws, after a very important review in 1999, it was urgent the attention to new themes, which are a result of new times. At the time of the last revision (1999), for instance, mobile phones were not so popular and common, and the functions of mobile phones were not so diverse and essential as nowadays. Today, just one product—mobile phone—can be a tool for several other products and services. Therefore, e-commerce, financial issues, data protection, privacy, and tourism were among the very discussed themes and object of considerable concern.

The document compiled by UNCTAD, "Implementation Report," was the object of discussions at the 13th Intergovernmental Group of Experts (IGE), Second Ad Hoc Expert Group Meeting on Consumer Protection, held in Geneva in July 2013. More than 120 participants from over 55 Member States and intergovernmental and nongovernmental organizations attended the meeting. The Implementation Report identified a number of areas for the improvement of the UNGCP, to ensure that they address new and contemporary issues that are at the forefront of consumer protection policy. An additional Ad Hoc Expert Meeting on Consumer Protection, which was planned under the regular work of the Secretariat and arising from the Doha Mandate in January 2015, discussed the Modalities Report and its conclusions.

The chairs for the working groups (E-Commerce, Financial Services, Other Issues, and Implementation) presented their respective reports and results concluding that there are new challenges such as e-commerce and financial services, as well as other issues such as data protection, false advertisement, and cross-border consumer protection matters, that merit further discussion.[9]

In March 2015, an Informal Expert Meeting was held again in Geneva, which was attended by more than 60 participants from over 40 Member States and intergovernmental and non-governmental organizations. Experts exchanged views on the content of the Draft Resolution for consideration by the General Assembly

[8]http://unctad.org/meetings/en/SessionalDocuments/ADHOC2013_CCPB_FullReport_en.pdf.
[9]http://unctad.org/meetings/en/SessionalDocuments/ADHOC2013_CCPB_FullReport_en.pdf.

(Draft Resolution) to revise the United Nations Guidelines for Consumer Protection (UNGCP), in preparation for the Seventh United Nations Review Conference of July 2015. Although it was officially an informal meeting, this was perhaps one of the most important moments in the discussions related to the UNGCP review. At this point, most country members had confirmed their support on the new UNGCP version and strongly affirmed the need for establishing an intergovernmental group on consumer protection.

UNCTAD representatives explained the implications regarding the creation of an intergovernmental group within the ambit of the United Nations, (the soonest budgetary moment to include any new projects would be 2017–2018). But Member States, especially developing countries ones, considered crucial the preview of such group in the present UNGCP review. The Member States considered that the social and political impact of officially creating an intergovernmental group of experts within the ambit of the UN was too important, yet even without a proper budget: "Most experts called for the establishment of an IGE on consumer protection as soon as possible, so as to ensure consumer protection finds a proper forum for policy discussion within the United Nations."[10]

In June 2015, UNCTAD organized a last meeting before the Seventh United Nations Conference for the Review of the Set of Multilaterally Agreed Equitable Principles and Rules for the Control of Restrictive Business Practices: *Informal Consultations on the Revision of the United Nations Guidelines for Consumer Protection (UNGCP)*, which was attended by 27 delegates from Member States' permanent missions in Geneva, including the Brazilian one.

The Draft Resolution for the Revision of the UNGCP was then submitted and discussed and adopted in the *Seventh United Nations Conferences to Review All Aspects of the United Nations Set of Multilaterally Agreed Equitable Principles and Rules for the Control of Restrictive Business Practices* (UN Review Conference).

Considering the financial implications of creating an intergovernmental group of experts, the Draft Resolution of the Reviewed UNGCP should be submitted to two different Committees: Second Committee (Economic and Financial Committee) and Fifth Committee (Administrative and Budgetary Committee). Thanks to the close work and support of the Member States, particularly by their respective consumer protection agencies, the aim to create an intergovernmental group on consumer protection was achieved: the General Assembly decided to establish such a group referring its decision to the Trade and Development Board, to be included in the 2017–2018 biannual budget of UNCTAD: "As a provisional measure, annual Expert Group Meetings on Consumer Protection could be convened (with existing resources) pending the eventual implementation of the Intergovernmental Group of Experts on Consumer Protection Law and Policy (IGE)."[11]

[10]http://unctad.org/meetings/en/SessionalDocuments/DITC_CCPB2015_Informal%20Expert%20Meeting%2027.03.15_FullReport.pdf.

[11]http://unctad.org/meetings/en/SessionalDocuments/DITC_CCPB2015_UNGCP_InformCons_04.06.2015_Report.pdf.

The agreed Draft Resolution was presented and approved at the Seventh United Nations Conference to Review the Set, in July 2015, and then submitted to the United Nations General Assembly for final approval.

On the December 22, 2015,[12] at the 81st plenary meeting of the United Nations General Assembly, the revised UNGCP and its new draft was officially approved. The UNGCP now was further expanded, including specific topics for e-commerce (letter I.), financial services (letter J.), public utilities (item 77), tourism (item 78), data protection and privacy (5, k; 11, e; 14, h), and the creation of an intergovernmental group of experts, under item N. 95 of the UNGCP.

The intergovernmental group of experts on consumer protection law and policy shall operate within the framework of an existing commission of the Trade and Development Board of the United Nations Conference on Trade and Development having the mandate to provide forums and modalities for multilateral consultations, discussions, and exchanges of views between Member States; undertake studies and research periodically on consumer protection; conduct voluntary peer reviews of national consumer protection policies of Member States, as implemented by consumer protection authorities; collect and disseminate information; provide capacity building and technical assistance to developing countries and economies in transition in formulating and enforcing consumer protection laws and policies; consider relevant studies, documentation, and reports from relevant organizations of the United Nations system and other international organizations and networks; make appropriate reports and recommendations on the consumer protection policies of Member States, including the application and implementation of these guidelines; and conduct a periodic review of the guidelines, when mandated by the United Nations Conference to Review All Aspects of the Set of Multilaterally Agreed Equitable Principles and Rules for the Control of Restrictive Business Practices.

Under item 3, General Principles, number 5, there are listed the main needs that the Guidelines are intended to meet: (a) access by consumers to essential goods and services; (b) the protection of vulnerable and disadvantaged consumers; (c) the protection of consumers from hazards to their health and safety; (d) the promotion and protection of the economic interests of consumers; (e) access by consumers to adequate information to enable them to make informed choices according to individual wishes and needs; (f) consumer education, including education on the environmental, social, and economic consequences of consumer choice; (g) availability of effective consumer dispute resolution and redress; (h) the freedom to form consumer and other relevant groups or organizations and the opportunity of such organizations to present their views in decision-making processes affecting them; (i) the promotion of sustainable consumption patterns; (j) a level of protection for consumers using electronic commerce that is not less than that afforded in other forms of commerce; and (k) the protection of consumer privacy and the global free flow of information.

[12] http://unctad.org/meetings/en/SessionalDocuments/ares70d186_en.pdf.

It is known that some of the included themes, such as data protection, privacy and tourism, have already been developed and even included in national consumer protection policies such as in Germany (data protection) and Brazil (tourism), which also explains the partnership of both countries in defending the inclusion of those themes even leading the discussions in the Working Group "Other Issues."

It is at the same time known that there is a considerable imbalance of policies and attention to consumer protection matters among UN country members. The remaining question is therefore related to the implementation of the new themes (or at least the attention to those themes) and the commitment of governments implementing the UNGCP in their respective countries.

2.6 Recognition of the Importance of Protecting the Consumers as Tourists: Discussions Within the United Nations and the Private International Law Hague Conference

As already mentioned, among the various themes discussed within the "Other Issues" Group, coordinated by Brazil and Germany, there was the theme of tourism. Tourism has become one of the most important (and lucrative) sectors worldwide, specially thanks to the participation of the BRICS members (Brazil, Russia, India, China, and South Africa).

Following a South American experience by the members of the Southern Common Market (MERCOSUR) regarding consumer protection focused on the attention to conflict resolution regarding tourist among the country members (which at first even counted with the participation of Venezuela), the Brazilian government, with the collaboration of Professor Claudia Lima Marques,[13] drafted a proposal for an international convention in order to protect international consumers.[14]

Such proposal was first presented at The Hague Conference level on 2012, and on the following year, with the support of members such as Portugal and China (and most of South American countries), the theme was included in the Conference Agenda.[15] The importance of such inclusion lies on the fact that for the first time in The Hague Conference on Private International Law, a theme, proposed by a developing country, was considered to be officially discussed and therefore included in the Conference Agenda.

The parallel discussions at the United Nations concerning the inclusion of the same theme in the review of the UNGCP also rendered the proper importance to the

[13]Rodriguez José and Marques (Coord.) (2014), pp. 829–834.

[14]https://assets.hcch.net/docs/5de9c911-2516-45ca-a995-23f3d3dea2d8.pdf.

[15]https://assets.hcch.net/upload/wop/genaff2015pd02.pdf.

theme. Perhaps the parallel discussion itself rendered the proper support of the theme in both forums. But how can the UNGCP related to consumer protection and tourism be implemented? How are Member States working this topic?

As above mentioned, Latin American countries have already some experience related to the theme of consumer protection in tourism. Within the ambit of MERCOSUR, country members have been working on a project, which has been led by Brazil and has proven to be efficient, according to the work done during the 2014 Football World Cup. The network of consumer protection agencies and governmental officials of tourism, health, sport, and security affairs have proven to be very efficient. During the World Cup, for instance, other stakeholders also joined the task force; even providers were invited to be part of it. The ideals of having a network of consumer protection agencies providing assistance to international consumers also became one of the main topics under the Governmental Forum of Ibero-American Consumer Protection Agencies (FIAGC).

Considering that the theme has been maintained in The Hague Conference Agenda and considering that the theme is already officially one of the UNCGP's official objectives, country members are now urged to debate and include the topic in their own political/social agendas. May the work developed by South American countries be an example of new paths to follow regarding international consumer protection?

In this very specific topic, not only has Brazil been an example for launching the debate at The Hague or defending the theme at the United Nations, but Brazil also officially included the theme in a political agenda: Presidential Decree 7.963 of 2013[16] included the theme of tourism as one of the main topics to develop consumer protection.

Although Brazil has been developing a significant work in this area,[17] there is much work to be done: when it comes to international tourism, the role of several countries (and most importantly UN country members) is more than crucial to the development and success of the theme.

As already mentioned before, there are some issues that are inevitable to be dealt with, and tourism is one of them. Technology, development, costs, and needs have even "created" new categories of tourists and travelers, who also need and deserve the proper protection. According to the World Tourism Organization (UNWTO), the number of tourists is increasing—worldwide. The inclusion of the theme "tourism" in the UNGCP not only confirms such tendency but also urges governments of country members to take necessary and efficient measures related to this specific area.

[16]http://www.planalto.gov.br/ccivil_03/_ato2011-2014/2013/decreto/d7963.htm.

[17]Cipriano Ana Cândida Muniz et al. (2014), pp. 39–45.

2.7 The Need for Internalization of the UNGCP by the UN Member Countries

It is undeniable that the United Nations Guidelines on Consumer Protection constitute an international reference for consumer protection and policy standards. The UNGCP certainly goes beyond that, being an international recognition of consumers' vulnerabilities and a necessary tool for development and even human rights.

In the year that marked the UNGCP's 30th anniversary, country members made a special effort to the inclusion and creation of an intergovernmental group on consumer protection within the United Nations. As stated in the previous versions of the UNGCP, country members were urged to take appropriate measures to implement the Guidelines. Whether regionally or nationally, the governments of Member States are demanded to take the necessary measures to respect the standards established in the UNGCP, as well as to take actions in order to achieve such standards: "4. Member States should develop, strengthen or maintain a strong consumer protection policy, taking into account the guidelines set out below and relevant international agreements. In so doing, each Member State must set its own priorities for the protection of consumers in accordance with the economic, social and environmental circumstances of the country and the needs of its population, and bearing in mind the costs and benefits of proposed measures."[18] Such demand also leads to a question of how all the "new" UNGCP topics will be implemented. How will Member States develop consumer protection policies to attend the UNGCP? Will the Intergovernmental Group on Consumer Protection take part in such implementation (considering that there will only be a specific budget in 2017/2018)? Brazil was one of the leading countries in this area since it has already developed a specific policy for consumer protection matters, but unfortunately the political and economic crises endured by the country seem to have as well compromised such development.

2.8 Conclusion

It is undeniable that the United Nations Guidelines on Consumer Protection constitute an international reference for consumer protection and policy standards. The UNGCP certainly goes beyond that, being a recognition of consumers' vulnerabilities and a necessary tool for development and even human rights.

The two updates suffered by the UNGCP may be considered a little too shy for some critics and experts, but they certainly attended significant themes that are the result of new times and technologies. The attention to the theme of sustainable

[18]http://unctad.org/meetings/en/SessionalDocuments/ares70d186_en.pdf.

consumption was so much important and actual in 1999 as it is nowadays. As in the United Nations Secretary General's own words, for the occasion of the Paris Treaty signature on April 22, 2016, "The era of consumption without consequences is over."[19] The connection between consumer protection, development, and environment is therefore inevitable. It is more than time to not think but take actions concerning these topics. Following the reviewed version of the United Nations Guidelines on Consumer Protection, it is urgent for Member States' governments to create, deliver, and develop policies regarding consumer protection in accordance with the international standard established by the UNGCP.

The constant evolution of the means of communication and related technologies are providing all of us new products and services, shrinking barriers and distances. The inclusion of "new themes" such as data protection and privacy, e-commerce, financial services, and tourism is the proper example of all this process. At the same time, it is necessary to recognize that the constant change in our societies will demand other reviews in the future. Governments, civil society, as well as other stakeholders must therefore consider all those changes and all of today's recognized rights, bearing in mind that consumer protection has an impact on development, access to information, access to justice, and thus impact people's lives.

References

Cipriano ACM et al. (2014) A proteção internacional do consumidor turista e visitante: Ministério da Justiça - Ministério do Turismo, Brasilia

Hanhimaki JM (2008) The United Nations: a very short introduction. Oxford University Press, Oxford

Rodriguez José AM, Marques CL (Coord.) (2014) Los servicios en el Derecho Internacional Privado. RJR, Porto Alegre

[19]http://www.un.org/sg/statements/index.asp?nid=9641.

Chapter 3
The UNGCP Guidelines: Some Comments

Gail Pearson

Now that the General Assembly has passed the revised Consumer Protection Guidelines in December 2015, we have two tasks. The first is to critique the Guidelines themselves and ask whether they are sufficiently protective for the lived conditions of the world's natural persons who have a personal family or household purpose.[1] The second is to ask whether the proposed international infrastructure can effectively add to safeguarding all of us, all of the world's natural persons.

The original Guidelines spoke primarily of consumers. We were an undifferentiated lot with mention of the low income, rural, and illiterate partly buried in wordy principles,[2] but we did have extensive economic interests to be promoted and protected.[3] This Revision has added the protection of vulnerable and disadvantaged consumers to the General Principles.[4] This speaks to a long-articulated concern, most recently prominent in the discussions of developed world consumer credit. A further theme beyond protection is "access" or "inclusion." Not only should consumers be protected in their transactions, but they should also have the opportunity to make those transactions. This is expressed in a new General Principle as access by consumers to essential goods and services.[5] Taking the world's population of natural persons as a whole, even modifying this by the 'circumstances of the country,' this is sadly aspirational.

[1]UNGCP para 4.

[2]1985paras 27, 34, 36.

[3]1985 B paras 13–23.

[4]UNGCP 111 para 5 (b).

[5]UNGCP 111 para 5 (a).

G. Pearson (✉)
Business School, University of Sydney, Sydney, NSW, Australia
e-mail: gail.pearson@sydney.edu.au

C. Lima Marques, D. Wei (eds.), *Consumer Law and Socioeconomic Development*,
DOI 10.1007/978-3-319-55624-6_3

The chief innovations in this Revision are the addition of four new General Principles; new sections for Business Practices, National Policies, Electronic Commerce and Financial Services, and International Institutional Machinery; as well as significant additions to Dispute Resolution; Specific Areas, namely, Energy, Public Utilities, and Tourism; and International Cooperation. There are new roles envisaged for national consumer protection agencies cooperating across borders, businesses providing initial dispute resolution, and a newly established Intergovernmental Group of Experts on Consumer Protection Law and Policy. Taken together, this should revitalize and energize global attention to fundamental questions of consumer protection, and particularly for cross-border activities. The world of digital transactions across countries is the modern challenge to consumer protection, but it is not the challenge to the entirety of the world's population of consumers.

3.1 Choice and the Market

What is the underlying philosophy of the Guidelines? They promote a "choice" model of consumer protection tempered by information and education, along with certain protection. These choices are to be tempered by environmental, social, and economic concerns.[6] Choice is a multiedged sword. It speaks to absence of choice in nonmarket economies and subsistence economies. It evokes manipulation of choice by sophisticated advertising and the microeconomic modeling of economists. The Guidelines take little note of the psychology-infused insights of the behavioral economists who have told us (or at least those of us of certain parts of the globe) that we are overburdened with information; that even if we wished, we could not read all the information provided to us for us to make mundane or important consumer decisions; that if we did, we would not have the expertise to make decisions in our own best interests. They do encourage disclosure and responsible conduct by third parties and agents.[7]

A key aspect of this Revision is the emphasis on knowledge. Information and knowledge complement a choice model, for without information and the ability to use that information there can be no informed choice, optimum or otherwise. In addition to promoting global flows of knowledge, there is an interesting change to the preposition in the General Principles concerning adequate information for informed choices.[8] Instead of access "of" consumers, this now reads access "by" consumers. "By" connotes a more positive involvement of consumers with information.

---

[6]UNGCP para 5 (e) (f).

[7]UNGCP V J (e) (f).

[8]UNGCP 111 para 5(e).

This choice model was present in the Consumer Protection Guidelines in earlier iterations. The previous Guidelines grew from the articulation of consumer rights and the addition of concern for sustainability. They were linked to the evolution of post-WWII globalization that contrasted rapacious transnational enterprises of the then developed world with the needs and portrayal of innocence in the then developing world. According to Consumers International, the UNGCP Guidelines were developed at the same time as those to "contain the excesses" of transnationals and were the repository for measures to regulate business lost from the Transnational Corporation Guidelines.[9] A choice model for consumer protection is intimately connected to economic theories that pose an efficient market based on optimal choices, which will reach equilibrium and distribute resources not only efficiently, that is, to those who will use them for the general good, but also equitably.

The original 1985 Consumer Protection Guidelines encouraged "the development of market conditions" and concern that consumer protection measures would not be inconsistent with international trade obligations and prove a barrier to international trade.[10] This was the pre-GATT and pre-rise of China as "manufacturer to the world" era. Although *developing* market conditions are still present,[11] on one reading the new Guidelines assume the market and the centrality of business.[12] They recognize that not all goods and services are delivered by private enterprise, and the Guidelines specifically include State-owned enterprises in the scope of application clause.[13]

The clause that procedures and regulations should not become barriers to international trade is still there, as is the application of the Guidelines to both "home-produced and imported goods and services."[14] So too is a focus on international standards for both safety and quality purposes.[15] There is an important addition to the General Principles that as well as protection of consumer privacy, consumers should have access to knowledge through the "global free flow of information."[16]

There is a revitalized focus on international cooperation particularly for cross-border transactions and enforcement.[17] This is welcomed, but does it go far enough? The great conundrum for the digital revolution and the ubiquity of cross-

[9]Updating the United Nations Guidelines for Consumer Protection For the Digital Age 2013 Kuala Lumpur 2013 pp. 6–8.

[10]Guidelines for Consumer Protection UN General Assembly a/RES/39/248 16 April 1985 111 Guidelines para 8.

[11]UNGCP 1 para 1 (g).

[12]UNGCP 1V para 11.

[13]UNGCP 11 para 2.

[14]UNGCP V paras 12, 13.

[15]UNGCP para 16, para 33, para 34.

[16]UNGCP 1 para 1 (k).

[17]UNGCP V1 paras 82–90; V11 paras 95–97.

border consumer purchases of goods and services is how to create effective consumer dispute resolution.

It almost goes without saying that a global market is a competitive market. In some situations, consumer protection has been relegated as a subsidiary of competition policy. The importance of competition is highlighted by the Implementation Report on the UNGCP 1985–2013 being produced by the Intergovernmental Group of Experts on Competition Law and Policy[18] and reference to the UNCTAD mandate to help all countries with the implementation of competition and consumer protection policies.[19] In the original Guidelines, governments were to control restrictive business practices and encouraged to promote competition as an aid to a range of consumer choice at the lowest price.[20] In the Revision, States should encourage fair and effective competition for choice and also ensure that consumer protection policies do not protect domestic businesses from competition.[21] The new Intergovernmental Group of Experts on Consumer Protection Law and Policy is to report to the United Nations Conferences to Review All Aspects of the United Nations Set of Multilaterally Agreed Equitable Principles and Rules for the Control of Restrictive Business Practices.[22] Effective consumer protection measure is a goal in itself and a key to preserving competition and guarding against monopolies.

3.2 Spotlight on Business

The tenor of the Guidelines has shifted from the earlier focus on the "legitimate needs" of consumers (perhaps diplomatic speak for rights) to setting out benchmarks for good practice for business in interacting with consumers. This is an important development. In many countries, a hollow invocation of rights does little to change business culture and/or less than effective protection via limited dispute resolution. A strong emphasis on business behavior may lead to changes in business practices and reduction in the need for dispute resolution for domestic and cross-border transactions. Ethical conduct by businesses that takes account of the objectives of the Guidelines in dealings with consumers should benefit both business and consumers.

The Good Business Practices Principles are for both online and offline activities.[23] This accords with the new General Principles that the protection for

[18]UNCTAD Implementation Report United Nations Guidelines for Consumer Protection (1985–2013) July 2013, TD/B/C.1/CLP.

[19]UNCTA Draft Resolution on Consumer Protection for consideration by the General Assembly 25 June 2015.

[20]Guidelines for Consumer Protection UN General Assembly a/RES/39/248 16 April 1985 111 Guidelines para 15, 17.

[21]UNGCP V C para 24.

[22]UNGCP V11 para 97 (h).

[23]UNGCP 1V para 11.

consumers using electronic commerce should not be less than those afforded to other forms of commerce.[24] Technology neutrality is also embedded.[25] Put briefly, businesses should treat consumers fairly and equitably, behave legally and ethically, practice transparency and easy access to information, assist consumers to develop knowledge and skills through education and awareness programs, protect the privacy of consumers, and have complaints handling and internal dispute resolution mechanisms in place.[26]

While many businesses in many countries already abide by these principles through either conviction or law, others do not. Since the task of ensuring good business practice has been cast as essential to consumer protection, that is, central to the lived conditions of the natural persons of the globe, it is worth elaborating.

Fair and equitable treatment requires that "at all stages of their relationship" businesses should deal fairly and honestly with consumers and avoid practices that harm consumers. Fairness and honesty should be integral to business culture. This suggests that in anticipation of a contract or otherwise, and certainly pre- and post-contract, businesses should act in good faith and with good conscience and not exploit consumer vulnerabilities and cognitive biases. The current "culture" debate in global banking institutions suggests that if in parts of an organization there is a culture of profit at any cost, there are inherent difficulties in shifting cultural attitudes and behavior. The Principle that condemns illegal, unethical, discriminatory, or deceptive commercial behavior explicitly includes abusive marketing, debt collection, and other practices that pose unnecessary risk or harm to consumers. This commercial behavior Principle exhorts both businesses and their agents to take responsibility for upholding consumer protection objectives. This Principle may be useful, for instance, in those jurisdictions where there have been disturbing reports of debt collection practices.

The Principle of access to information "by" consumers is reinforced by the Good Business Principles, which include the measures that business should take to enable consumers to make informed decisions. It is the role of business to ensure easy access to information that is complete, accurate, not misleading, that includes terms, conditions, fees, and final costs.[27] Business also has a part to play in ensuring, through education, that consumers have the knowledge and skills to do three things: understand risks, take informed decisions, and access advice (preferably independent third-party advice). These have a clear applicability to financial decision making, but this is not the only area where appreciation of the risks and final costs of a product are important, particularly given the prevalence of drip pricing in some industries and interminable automatic renewal clauses in others. The intermediary or independent third-party adviser has been put forward as the solution to information overload and cognitive bias. Third-party advisers can put a

[24]UNGCP 111 para 5 (j).

[25]UNGCP 1V 11 (c).

[26]UNGCP 1V para 11 (a)–(f).

[27]UNGCP 1V (11) (c).

brake on otherwise potentially harmful transactions but may not be without their own biases. Nevertheless, in jurisdictions that do not mandate independent third parties for some situations, this will be a powerful Principle to invoke.

The Business Principles concern the protection of privacy through a combination of methods—control, security, transparency, and consent.[28]

If business can resolve disputes with consumers, this should be faster, more flexible, and less costly than complex ombudsman, tribunal, or court procedures. There may be a question of trust, but the consumer complaints and dispute Principle refer to well-established international standards.[29] An additional benefit for businesses that are dealing fairly with consumers is that complaints and dispute data can assist them to improve their treatment, behavior, and culture.

The Business Principles are complemented by a section entitled "National Policies for Consumer Protection." The Principles for business are not directive. The Guidelines are not legally binding. The UN General Assembly resolution recommends that Member States implement the Guidelines while reiterating that despite the diversity of rules and legal cultures, there is consensus on the need for common principles. The national policy principles state that "Member States should establish consumer protection policies that encourage: - -."[30] The matters to be encouraged are good business practices; information to allow consumers to contact business and enable regulatory authorities to identify and locate them; information about the goods and services and their terms and conditions; intelligible contract terms that are not unfair; a transparent process for, among others, return and refunds; secure payment mechanisms; dispute resolution and redress; privacy and data security; and consumer and business education. In addition, another Guideline says States should work toward the necessary human and financial resources for consumer protection agencies to ensure both compliance and redress.[31] A Guideline that calls for regulatory resources to promote effective business compliance may have great utility in jurisdictions where the focus has been on elaborate mechanisms for redress and less attention given to regulatory intervention.

3.3 Electronic Commerce

The digital world is the greatest revolution of our time. It has been accorded only three Guidelines compared with sustainability, the cause for the 1990 Revision, which required fourteen Guidelines.[32] The latter looks to measures to preserve the

---

[28]UNGCP 1V 11 (e).

[29]UNGCP 1V 11 (f).

[30]UNGCP V A para 14.

[31]UNGCP V A para 15.

[32]UNGCP V H para 49–62.

future, while the "digital marketplace" is the current reality for much of the world, including the rural, vulnerable, and disadvantaged. States are asked to promote consumer confidence, provide the same level of protection as with other forms of commerce, accommodate the "special features" of electronic commerce, and make consumers and businesses aware of their digital rights and obligations.[33] It is suggested that States may wish to consider relevant international standards and guidelines, adapt these to their own circumstances, and collaborate to implement them across borders.

The OECD Guidelines for Consumer Protection in the Context of Electronic Commerce are specifically mentioned.[34] These were formulated in 1999 and address a range of matters, including transparent protection, fair advertising and marketing, online disclosure, confirmation, payment, dispute resolution, privacy, education, and global cooperation.[35] There is tension between the digital marketplace, which is global, and law and jurisdiction, which is national. This is a problem that will not be solved by the appeal to the better nature of business or better resources for national enforcement. Cooperation and joint initiatives as recommended in the OECD Guidelines, and the new UNGCP Guidelines discussed below, are important and may lead to some useful results, but they do not solve the problem of consumer redress for defective cross-border transactions. In addition to global cooperation, there is scope to intensify regional cooperation.

In electronic transactions, there are deficits in the easy accessibility of pricing, contractual terms, and ease of termination. Individuals do not click through or, if forced to do so, deal with information in a perfunctory manner. Further payment options for add-ons may be embedded within digital products. It is not enough for national regulators to refer to reputational ratings as a way of preserving fair dealing with digital services or services advertised digitally. Concern for individual privacy does not address issues of algorithmic production of marketing for particular products. Third-party liability has been mentioned below, and attention needs to be given to platform liability issues and consumer protection.

While there are issues about the digital marketplace, there are also great opportunities to use data analytics to produce information and products that are suitable for particular individuals and for their benefit. This also articulates with a new addition discussed below that financial services be suitable for the needs and means of consumers.

This part of the Guidelines should be slated for further revision in the not too distant future.

[33]UNGCP V I para 63, 64.

[34]UNGCP V I para 65.

[35]OECD Guidelines for Consumer Protection in the Context of Electronic Commerce, 1999.

3.4 Financial Services

As the Implementation Report noted, there has been both an exponential growth in global access to financial services and detailed rules to protect consumers.[36] Member States are exhorted to "establish or encourage." As appropriate, they should create and set up regulatory and enforcement policies; oversight bodies; mechanisms to protect consumer assets, including deposits; improved financial education strategies for financial literacy; fair treatment and disclosure so that institutions and their agents are responsible and accountable; written policies for financial institutions on conflict of interests and disclosure of conflicts between providers and third parties; responsible conduct by providers and lenders, including by responsible lending and the sale of products that are suitable to the consumer's needs and means; controls to protect consumer data from fraud and abuse; a regulatory framework for cost-efficiency and transparency in remittances; measures to reinforce financial inclusion, education, and protection of consumers in the access and use of financial services. In addition States should consider relevant international Guidelines including the OECD High-Level Principles on Financial Consumer Protection, the G20s Principles for Financial Inclusion and the World Bank's Good Practices for Financial Consumer Inclusion.

The goals of financial inclusion and financial literacy are widely addressed and, even if they would score "could do better," are implanted in national as well as global agendas. Remittances sustain many economies and are a crucial issue for the growing populations of temporary workers and displaced persons. Many States have deposit insurance and other mechanisms to protect depositors. There are ongoing issues with conflicts of interest, responsible behavior, and product suitability. Every day brings fresh stories from different parts of the globe. These Guidelines can be more than an aspiration and should help set some parameters to debate domestic regulatory developments. Together, with the encouragement of oversight bodies and regulatory and enforcement policies for consumer protection for financial services, a future implementation report for these Guidelines should be able to point to the moral force and practical impacts of this new inclusion in the Guidelines.

3.5 Specific Areas

The General Principles of access to essential services has been made concrete in the provisions on Energy and Public Utilities. States should promote universal access to clean energy and have policies for supplying affordable energy.[37] This Guideline

[36] UNCTAD Implementation Report United Nations Guidelines for Consumer Protection (1985–2013) July 2013, TD/B/C.1/CLP p 17.

[37] UNGCP V I para 76.

stresses community participation and awareness raising programs. The Public Utilities Guideline is similar, promoting access and policies to improve rules. The rules are to do with service provision, information, security deposits, advance payment, late fees, termination and restoration of service payment plans, and dispute resolution. These should take into account the situation of the disadvantaged and vulnerable.[38]

Forms of energy to cook and heat vary throughout the globe and are essential to sustain human life. In many parts of the developed world, some forms of energy have been public utilities and are now privatized. Other services once regarded as public utilities such as telephone services have also been privatized. In some places, even water is privately delivered. It is difficult to know what Member States may or may not regard as a public utility.

3.6 Dispute Resolution and Redress

The original Guidelines on redress have evolved to include alternative and other dispute resolutions and specifically to include cross-border disputes. They also include exhortations for inexpensive, expeditious access to remedies, including collective resolution procedures (for overindebtedness and bankruptcy also) and ensuring that these are not an undue burden on society and businesses.[39] Other additions are cooperation of States with business and consumer groups to further the understanding on avoiding disputes, the availability of mechanisms for redress, and where consumers can file complaints.[40] States are asked to encourage businesses to do their part by resolving disputes fairly and expeditiously and informally and to have voluntary mechanisms and informal complaint procedures to help consumers.[41] Can business be the champion of cross-border dispute resolution? Who will monitor business in its cross-border guise?

The final new addition is tourism. Instead of "should promote" or "should develop," this Guideline says States "should ensure." This is about adequate policies regarding marketing and goods and services related to travel, traveler accommodation and timeshares, as well as other tourism. The cross-border challenges should be addressed and include cooperation with other States for enforcement and information sharing and cooperation with other relevant stakeholders.[42] International tourism is a very important sector in the global economy and, for many, services are delivered digitally. The protection of tourists as consumers has e-commerce and platform liability challenges.

[38]UNGCP V I para 77.
[39]UNGCP V F para 37, 40.
[40]UNGCP V F para 41.
[41]UNGCP V F para 38.
[42]UNGCP V K para 78.

3.7 International Cooperation

This is potentially the most important development for substantive protection in cross-border transactions. Nine new Guidelines have been added to this part. International cooperation among consumer protection enforcement agencies may be the consumer's best at this point in time with no international tribunal, court, or ADR forum to resolve cross-border disputes for consumers who face problems of jurisdiction, applicable law, and access to an appropriate forum. In some jurisdictions such cooperation already assists individual consumers, but there is a major ease of access problem. The new Guidelines should strengthen the movement toward greater cooperation between enforcement agencies.

Cooperation is not mandatory, and States are asked to improve their ability to cooperate to combat cross-border commercial practices that are fraudulent and deceptive. It is, of course, discretionary for agencies to respond when asked to cooperate.[43] A number of Guidelines set out the parameters for cooperation among consumer protection enforcement agencies. They should coordinate and avoid interference with activities taking place in other jurisdictions; they should try to resolve any disagreements; they should make use of existing international networks and enter into bilateral and multilateral arrangements to implement the Guidelines.[44] To facilitate this, States are asked to give the authority to enforcement agencies to investigate, pursue, obtain, and share relevant information and evidence relevant to cross-border fraudulent and deceptive practices, as well as the authority to cooperate with foreign consumer protection and other agencies.

The Guidelines envisage a framework to combat fraudulent and deceptive practices and ask that consumer protection policy agencies should take a lead role in developing this.[45] There should be a designated consumer protection policy or enforcement agency to facilitate cooperation under the UNGCP, and this should be notified to the Secretary General.[46] States are asked to consider international standards in considering the legal authority to provide to their consumer protection agencies and in particular the OECD Guidelines for Protecting Consumers from Fraudulent and Deceptive Commercial Practices Across Border adopted in 2003. For some States, this should require domestic legislation. Other States may need to review existing mutual assistance legislation.

It is relevant to ask, what is the width of "fraudulent and deceptive?" Will all goods and services that fail to meet quality, purpose, safety, or description standards be the result of fraudulent and deceptive commercial practices? Are there some practices that are short of being "fraudulent and deceptive," such as "misleading" or sharp dealing, that do not fall within these Guidelines? The OECD Guidelines set out an understanding of commercial and deceptive practices such as

---

[43]UNGCP V1 para 82.
[44]UNGCP V1 para 83–85.
[45]UNGCP V1 para 86.
[46]UNGCP V1 para 87.

those that harm or pose an imminent threat of harm, including misrepresentations of material fact that cause detriment to the economic interests of consumers, failure to deliver products after a consumer has been charged, and charging or debiting without authorization.[47] The cause of international cooperation among enforcement agencies should not rest on limited or legalistic distinctions, and it is hoped that Member States will take a broad approach.

It is of little use to consumers requiring redress if they cannot obtain it, and there are real problems with amounts that may seem trivial to business but are important to individuals. The Guidelines state that States should consider bilateral and multilateral arrangements to improve cooperation to enforce decisions across borders and recover foreign assets.[48] These objectives pose difficulties for business and could be exponentially difficult for consumers. When considering international cooperation, should consideration be given to an international compensation fund to which States would contribute, funded by businesses that conduct cross-border consumer transactions?

There is an existing forum for enforcement cooperation—the International Consumer Protection and Enforcement Network (ICPEN). Thirty-six consumer protection agencies participate in its econsumer.gov portal for complaint reporting. Given the functions of the newly set up Intergovernmental Group of Experts discussed below, consideration should be given to assessing the effectiveness of these and other transnational portals in resolving complaints for individuals, as well as providing data for systemic issues of international consumer protection.

3.8 International Institutional Machinery

The Guidelines will not exist in a vacuum. Member States are asked to take steps at national and regional levels to implement the Guidelines.[49] There is now a firm institutional base for Member States to exchange views and experiences in developing policy and consumer protection implementation. An Intergovernmental Group of Experts on Consumer Protection Law and Policy within the existing framework of UNCTAD will provide the institutional machinery.[50] This has been established and will meet for the first time at Geneva in October 2016. It shall have a number of functions. These are as follows:

- conduct an annual forum for Member States to discuss the Guidelines and particularly their implementation;

[47] OECD Guidelines for Protecting Consumers from Fraudulent and Deceptive Commercial Practices Across Borders para 1 Scope and definitions, B.

[48] UNGCP V1 para 89.

[49] UNGCP V11 para 96.

[50] UNGCP V11 para 95.

- undertake studies and research on consumer protection issues related to the Guidelines (based on a consensus and the interests of Member States) and disseminate these to increase the exchange of experience and effectiveness of the Guidelines;
- conduct voluntary peer reviews of national consumer protection policies as implemented;
- collect and disseminate information about the steps that Member States have taken nationally and regionally to implement the objectives and principles of the Guidelines;
- provide capacity building and technical assistance to developing countries and economies in transition in formulating and enforcing consumer protection laws and policies;
- consider studies, documents, reports from UN organizations, other international organizations, and networks in order to exchange information on work programs, topics for consultation, identification of work-sharing projects, and cooperation to provide technical assistance;
- make appropriate reports and recommendations on Member States' consumer protection policies, including the implementation of the Guidelines;
- operate between and report to the UN conferences to review all aspects of the Agreed Principles and Rules to Control Restrictive Business Practices;
- review the Guidelines when the UN Conferences to Review All Aspects of the UN Set of Multilaterally Agreed Equitable Principles and Rules for the Control of Restrictive Business Practices mandate this;
- establish procedures and methods of work for the IGECP to carry out its mandate, including for confidentiality.[51]

There is an important safeguard for Member States and business. In the performance of its functions, neither the IGE nor its subsidiary organs should pass judgment on the activities or conduct of individual Member States or individual enterprises in connection with a specific business transaction and should avoid becoming involved in business transaction disputes.[52]

There is tremendous potential for this body, located within UNCTAD to wield both moral and practical authority in developing consumer protection that serves the interests of the lived conditions of individuals in the very diverse parts of our globe. As well as providing a forum for States, it also provides the opportunity for others to contribute through research and work initiatives. Without business, there is no competitive marketplace to provide for consumer needs, and the emphasis on good business practices within the Guidelines should continue to be reflected in the work of the IGECP. The economic interests of consumers should be well served by this and further iterations of these Guidelines. They will not solve all problems of imbalances in power and information between those requiring goods and services and those providing them.

---

[51]UNGCP V11 para 97, 99.

[52]UNGCP V11 para 98.

Chapter 4
Common Law and International Consumer Protection in the Global Orbit of Consumption

Fabiana D'Andrea Ramos and Vitor Hugo do Amaral Ferreira

4.1 Introduction

> We must put human dignity at the heart of every perspective and every gesture. Other interests, though legitimate, are secondary.—Pope Francis

In an ever-growing consumerist society, being capable of averting trends is a condition of individual freedom, freedom of being different, and freedom of having an identity. The same man that once imprisoned others in the past is today enslaved by products and false consumption needs. These are times of "having" prevailing over "being."

The effort of protecting those involved in more vulnerable consumer relations resulted in consumer vulnerability to be legally recognized. In Brazil, the Federal Constitution of 1988 introduced this field by determining that it was the duty of the State to promote consumer protection, thus listing it among the fundamental rights and guarantees.

In 1990, Brazil took a new step toward consumer protection with the enactment of Law 8.078/90 (Consumer Protection Code—CDC), and over the years the CDC became well known for numerous achievements in consumer relations, especially in favor of consumers. However, although its applicability and effectiveness have been proven countless times, there are still many challenges to be faced.

In its 25 years of existence, the CDC sought to defend basic rights, product and service quality, consumer health and safety, fulfillment of offers; questioned the

F. D'Andrea Ramos, Ph.D/UERJ (✉)
Universidade Federal do Rio Grande do Sul, Porto Alegre, Brazil
e-mail: fabianadramos@gmail.com

V.H. do Amaral Ferreira, Ph.D. Candidate/UFRGS
Faculdade Antonio Meneghetti, Centro Universitário Franciscano, Santa Maria, Rio Grande do Sul, Brazil
e-mail: vitorhugodir@hotmail.com

C. Lima Marques, D. Wei (eds.), *Consumer Law and Socioeconomic Development*,
DOI 10.1007/978-3-319-55624-6_4

appeals of advertising; alerted consumers about abusive practices and liabilities; and created mechanisms and instruments that qualify and facilitate consumer protection.

On grounds of the above, it is possible to affirm that although the first 25 years were meritorious, even more attention should be paid in the next 25 years. Achieving more levels of success in the next 25 years will require even greater care regarding easy credit and the consequent indebtedness, the organization of policies for waste from consumption, and understanding of the psychological vulnerability of the consumer and consumer behavior. Days of greater effectiveness of the CDC, clarification and operationalization of rights, and, the theme of this study, international consumer protection—these are the challenges of the coming years.

4.2 Mundialization and Globalized Consumption

The twentieth century is known for outlining new rights, which gave birth to many branches of law, including environmental law, biolaw, and consumer law. The multiplicity of paradigms that explain the construction of the world leads to the understanding that human thought and science, allied with technology, have made man a thinking and domineering animal par excellence. Their discoveries, combined with knowledge and the need to feel increasingly effective, lead to exaggeration.

The phenomena of today are dominated by mundialization and globalization, the consequences and causes of multiple changes that are directly related to the development of society. Mundialization is a concept that translates all kinds of changes: innovation, creation, destruction, acculturation, and discoveries. As mundialization increases, the integration of different parts of the world expands under the effect of the acceleration of trading and development, thus fostering the taste for knowledge and the desire to intervene in the construction of the future.

In this manner, civilization and its relations continuously develop, and society consequently becomes more and more complex. It is understood, therefore, that there is law wherever there is society.

This same law also becomes more complex with human and social evolution, given that men naturally gather in order to form communities. Certainly, congregating interests, which arise from this approach, consequently results in tensions that require the legal system to have solutions for social harmony to always be guaranteed as a principle of peaceful coexistence.

The international panorama cannot be put apart from all the issues that affect life of society and individuals in posmodern times. The world, which was once something distant, wide, is today something global, close.

From the fall of the Berlin Wall to the fall of the Twin Towers, 10 years have passed. The same September 11th that marks one of the greatest tragedies in the world marks the celebration of the 25th anniversary of the enactment of the Consumer Protection Code.

From the speech of peace times and just societies, which have been so often announced, a dangerous world was declared, a world that is more difficult to decipher and immersed in the desire to be guided in a place that has lost its sources of reference.[1]

Notably, it is essential to mention that trade issues, which are the base of interest for countries to come together in blocks, guide other issues that turn into the object of observation. In this sense, the construction of globalization or mundialization is a structure that has already begun to take shape.

In posmodern times, people are closer and more connected, and facts and events have matured into the global level. Tracing the progress of global society requires efforts that go beyond market rumors and national policies. The aspirations for a better civilization must gain strength from within, projecting, from the outset, a profile of peace, justice, and respect for the differences found in all domains.[2]

Globalization is on the agenda. It is "a buzz word that quickly turns into a motto, a magical incantation, a password able to open the doors of all present and future mysteries" are the words of Zygmunt Bauman[3] in his work on the human consequences aroused by globalization.

The author goes even further by contrasting that being local in the face of a world of globalization is a sign of deprivation and social degradation. The discomforts of localized existence seeks salvation in globalization.

Accepting globalization today is not a choice, but a basic requirement to avoid stagnation. The process is consolidated, an upgrade that cannot be undone; it is irreversible. Humanity is characterized by movement, in which is addressed by the author, when moving, be it unwillingly or by default, humanity moves. Movement spawns not only new inventions and theories but also effects that are sometimes uneven or uncertain.

On one hand, there are those who adhere to these new inventions and, on the other, those who work outside of this context. These are known as "globals" and "locals" at which, at the same proportionality, can be called the included and the excluded.

Alain Rouquié[4] contributes to the theme by saying that the communication society defies borders and customs. Governments almost have no means to control or limit flows. It is true that after these technological and economic phenomena, such as the *Internet*, the State took new shape. It tends to transform itself, thus losing its substance in the two ends: both at the regional and the supranational scale. The latter constitutes a new dimension of international relations. A new law arises beyond borders: justice, which is a royal title par excellence, is no longer a national monopoly.

[1]Rouquié (2004).
[2]Ventura Deisy (2003).
[3]Bauman (1999), p. 07.
[4]Rouquié (2004).

Studies, in posmodern times, are in charge of checking opportunities that may facilitate the (re)organization of the process of globalization, or even the resulting consequences.

A greater understanding of the process of globalization is relevant and ranges from the concept that more effective and productive actions for the development and strengthening of global society are necessary.

Changes are rapidly occurring on a scale never before seen. The concept of globalization indicates a process of economic restructuring in which the relations among its agents gain a global reach, producing significant changes in the production system, both commercial and political interactions, and therefore going beyond national borders.

This process, however, encompasses much more profound and challenging changes, consequently creating dilemmas and opening new horizons in regard to ways of life, currents of thought, and social relations.

The consumer society, which is the result of this process and consequence of the globalized era, carries with it a potential contradiction: it values the human factor in the creation process but simultaneously disqualifies those who do not participate in the inclusion/consumption process.

Consumer relations, as seen in the technological and geographical aspect, over time, have proven to be increasingly more comprehensive. In this scenario, the unquestioned misguidance of man cannot be reason to condemn technological and productive progress, thus refusing the acceptance of new scenarios. There is no different way of accepting the cell phone, interactivity, the *Internet,* new products, and the diversity of the offered services. For this purpose, the consumer must be provided with the proper knowledge that enables the implementation of his rights, wherever he may be.

By breaking borders, the consumer is not limited to his space, which enables him to create a new space: the world. Although the consumer becomes a citizen of the world, he still lacks a world that protects him. The eternal desire for conquest that motivates human beings has also turned them into pathfinders, driven by the expansion of land and the need for trade. Today, silks and spices no longer tempt humans as in the past. Humans are still subject to colonization, and consumers are placed to expect, for example, the launch of a new mobile phone—still colonized by major brands, the inventions of modern man.

The colonizing masters of another era are, nowadays, still the first ones to create spaces; they have lands to conquer and people to colonize. They do not cross oceans as they once did; they are everywhere. The era of the crusades and industrial revolution paralleled the time of expansion, mass production, and globalized consumption (consumerism).

Luciane Klein[5] makes it clear that from the assumptions that guide the agenda, it is possible to identify that the consumer, given his vulnerability, needs protection when consuming within the inner scope of his country. Furthermore, it is also

[5]Vieira (2015), p. 159.

within his right to be granted with minimum protection when consuming beyond the borders of his country.

The remarkable technological and scientific progress of the last century has brought significant changes to the contemporary world. Thus, if contemporaneity reaps benefits of a promising moment of thought and human evolution, it stands the abuses and (in)consequences of mass production.

The Industrial Revolution is known for massively increasing the capacity of production in the late seventeenth and early eighteenth centuries. According to Claudia Lima Marques,[6] the Industrial Revolution possessed three important moments. The revolution was initially fueled by coal and steel, which resulted in the massification of the form of production, reaching an unspecified number of consumers and creating new forms of distributing consumer goods. The second phase is characterized by Taylorism and Fordism. This phase secured a differential in production and mass distribution, resulting in different consumer habits, since the workers, which became consumers, started buying the goods they produced. The third phase is based on information technologies and the globalization of the economy organized in big chain stores, brands, and *shopping centers*, which now offer a variety of products and services. These products and services are allied to technology and tend to create consumer relationships in a single *click*, i.e. virtual consumer relations, but with real consequences.

Furthermore, a new scenario was redesigned after the Industrial Revolution, in which the change in economy and society considerably increased the vulnerability of consumers and started to challenge the legal doctrine to promote the protection of consumers; this is consumer law. In times of the internationalization of spaces, subjects, and institutions, it has become more than necessary; it has become urgent to deal with the international protection of the consumer among the perspectives and challenges that await him.

4.3 For a Common Basis of Consumer Rights

The consumer society, by itself, is not part of an enclosed and isolated system. Education plays an important role that involves a number of factors inherent to the human condition. By admitting the need for recognizing human cultural diversity, one must seek to understand it before anything else.

Knowing man is situating him in the universe and contemplating the idea that all knowledge should contextualize its object. Thus, "Who are we?" is inseparable from "Where are we?" and "Where did we come from?" and "Where are we going?"[7]

[6] Lima Marques et al. (2008).

[7] Morin (2002), p. 47.

In this way, it is safe to say that in any analysis of consumer society, it, the society, is an entity associated with the world, with reality. Consequently, the question that should be asked must not be fragmented. Therefore: *What is consumer society? Where is consumer society? Where is consumer society heading?*

Paulo Freire[8] addresses this issue stating that "an aware person is able to relate facts and problems, they are able to understand." In the same way, they have a different understanding of history and their role in it. Similarly, an aware person also has a different understanding of history and their role in it. "Refuse becoming accommodated, mobilize and organize to change the world."

This positioning is in accordance with Edgar Morin,[9] in which there is a need to proportionally recompose the whole in order to recognize the parts. Thus, analyzing the consumer society requires an understanding of the environment in which it is inserted in, whereas "contextualization is an essential condition of effectiveness."

By agreeing to this assumption, a way is found to (ac)knowledge(ment) of multidimensional and complex issues, which involves not only the problem of consumer society but also the world, which is the reorganization of thought.

In this sense, the primary foundation to build a common law is found, on the outline proposed here, a common law for the consumer, as a premise of international consumer law.

The idealization of a proposal that embraces such an expectation cannot contemplate a different feeling of the ideal of change. It must take on questions different from the hopelessness and alienation of modern man immersed in a world that he cannot fully understand.

The Illuminist universalism present in the Universal Declaration of 1789 and later the Universal Declaration of Human Rights of 1948 urged the gullible that the process of universality, or mundialization, was slow but impossible to be fought against.[10]

The possibility of making a common law, in the mundialization of law, is defined as real and at the very least necessary, to the extent that society, which is also global, is faced with problems, situations of universal nature, which lack common, global, universal referrals.

In consumer law, Héctor Valverde Santana[11] claims that the process of globalization imposes a specific analysis for the balance of consumer relations at the international level, while consumer vulnerability may be highlighted in the face of the complexity of the transborder transactions. In this context, the author writes about international principles of consumer protection.

---

[8]Freire (2003), p. 236.

[9]Morin (2002), p. 37.

[10]Delmas-Marty (2003).

[11]Santana (2015), p. 135.

Regarding the future protection of vulnerable consumers in private law, Claudia Lima Marques and Bruno Miragem[12] highlight the need for new fraternity in which identities and cultures are coordinated by human rights in a private law liability, which is able to build a common origin and dialogue of differences.

These authors also reinforce the need to revisit the expression fraternity.

In spite of this, globalization has brought forth a new time with reflections in various sectors and, of course, consumer society, and consequently on consumer law. Thinking of the consumer in a globalized sense is associating his *status* to the internationalization of law.

Private law recognizes its role in balancing its own legal relations. This is because the consumer today is a citizen of the world; growing and broad is his work in spaces beyond the borders of his country. Thus, the balance of consumer relations cannot be restricted to a specific geographical limit. It should rather recognize regional and global spaces and promote private international law in the field of consumer law that is capable of protecting against vulnerability beyond its borders, or rather in the absence of them.

Professor Claudia Lima Marques[13] emphasizes that consumer law is a private law of material freedom and equality. For this reason, consumer law is at the intersection of public and private laws. Systematically, consumer law is founded on constitutional values, promoting the protection of the weakest consumers (vulnerable consumers) in the dogmatic philosophical conception against the mass consumer society, taking into account the socioeconomic aspect of consumer law. The brazilian code today works as a system, the main set of rules and principles, insofar as it is a duty of the State; on the other hand, it is an essential guarantee for the consumer.

The private law of the future will safeguard the vulnerable with more fraternal instruments, equivalent to private law liability, essentially common in origin, making itself more human, just as in brotherhood in which brothers recognize each other as equals. The visionary contribution of Antonio Herman Benjamin[14] stands out in stating that at the beginning of the 1990s, the protection of the vulnerable becomes both a supraindividual and an internationalized issue as well as a supranational problem, consubstantiated with common issues, among which protection of the vulnerable is a universal requirement.

For an "international consumer law," Eduardo Antonio Klausner[15] structures, in short, the idea that contemporaneity is made by a globalized society, structured at international trade and consumption. Thus, the principle of consumer vulnerability turns to the principle of protection in international law.

[12]Lima Marques and Mirage (2014).

[13]Lima Marques et al. (2008), p. 47.

[14]Benjamin (1993), p. 200.

[15]Klausner (2012), p. 172.

The author asserts, considering the insufficiency of the current legal instruments, the methodology used, and the inefficacy of the existing theories, that to think, as suggested by an International Consumer Law, is opportune for adapting the protection of consumers to the globalized environment, that is, the international consumer protection.

4.4 The (Mis)Directions and the Hope for an International Consumer Law

When it comes to a common ground for protecting consumer rights in the international arena, it is preliminary knowledge that we are faced with a dialogue in search for equality. Sponsoring such a desire is to believe in the hope of recognizing individuals who require protection because of their inequality.

At this rate, it is up to the twentieth century to identify the new subjects of rights, and since the beginning of the twenty-first century, the role of these subjects has become even broader. These subjects draw the attention of the legal order by the context in which they are inserted in—as consumers, who are obviously vulnerable—but, given the global consumer context, require tutelage to go beyond the jurisdictional limits of their country.

Being a consumer is a fact of vulnerability. A consumer in a worldwide consumer society has the opportunity of acquiring goods and services in a different country from that of his origin; even if the consumer does not move from his physical-territorial space (such as in e-commerce), one must consider that vulnerability (ever present) takes other forms and proportions and is put into question in new spaces.

The present meaning may yield the hope of an international consumer law capable of recognizing the vulnerability (essential condition) of consumers in an international space. The meaning that conveys this ideal is the one of maximum guarantee of equality. "If equality can be said as natural to the 'human being', the truth is that, in the historical experience, society (and its rights) has always destroyed this equality," as highlights Claudia Lima Marques.[16]

International consumption, as asserted by Eduardo Antônio Klausner,[17] has peculiarities and demands even more special care of the law in the face of a lack of continuity in international consumption, difficulty in reexecuting a service in tourist contracts, language barrier that hinders access to information, differences between the laws of the country of origin and the country of the consumer relation.

[16]Lima Marques and Mirage (2014).

[17]Klausner (2008), pp. 59–76.

The European Commission, when elaborating the Guide for the European Consumer in the Single Market, reported that the consumer, when litigating abroad, is faced with a variety of setbacks: (1) determining the appropriate jurisdiction at the international level and the real possibility of the consumer litigating in the court that has jurisdiction; (2) the diversity of national rules on consumer rights and the existence of different legal systems; (3) the cost of sustaining a dispute in which all procedural steps or part of them will develop abroad, compared to the small value of the consumer contract; (4) compliance of acts abroad; (5) the recognition and enforcement of foreign judgments.[18] Notably, the protection of consumers lacks an agenda that includes an integrated international system for defending their rights. The free trade agreements have contributed significantly to more effectively thinking of a protectionist approach.

Among the consequences of the globalized world for the consumer market are questioning who the international consumer is, what the main issues of cross-border consumer relations are, and what the global actions (regional and global) of consumer protection are. This is essential for establishing perspectives, hopes for a new look at consumer protection, and a globalized view capable of understanding the international space.

From international trade to international consumption, it is possible to observe a postmodern world wrapped in the plurality of standards, methods, and subjects. This scenario presents a variety of multiconnected consumer relations, and private international law is still limited in face of this diagnosis.

Currently, the international consumer does not have a conceptual uniformity, thus limiting himself to the ideal of active and passive consumer, the discussions of the consumer in the virtual space, and the tourist consumer, as well as discussions that support related issues such as financial services, advertising, data protection, and entity rights. Therefore, the essence of consumer protection is recognized as the recognition of consumer vulnerability.

The protection of the vulnerable by law stems from the many new subjects worthy of protection that dwell within inequality, as ensure Claudia Lima Marques and Bruno Miragem.[19] "In the case of the Consumer Protection Code, rights are ensured for consumers in order for the unequal to achieve material equality, thus guaranteeing the right to choose, right to information and right to transparency in order to protect their shattered freedom or autonomy."

An interesting discussion that allows the expansion of the agenda is potential vulnerability, considering that the international consumer is in a situation of greater informational, technical, legal, or simply phatic dependence. There is a multiplicity of suppliers, depersonalized/impersonal services, and fragility in the foreign language, in addition to the lack of continuity in the contracted service. Of course, the (international) context that the consumer is inserted in exacerbates his status as a vulnerable consumer.

[18]European Commission (1996), pp. 17–19.

[19]Lima Marques and Mirage (2014), p. 127.

Claudia Lima Marques[20] clarifies that the analysis of the balance of consumer relations at international level is inherent in the process of globalization. The complexity of cross-border transactions enhances consumer vulnerability through the difficulties in acquiring information about safety and quality of products and services, resulting in major obstacles for compensation of unfair damage suffered by the consumer.

The process of globalization has a direct impact on national and international consumer relations. In this sense, "from this observation many efforts are made to establish measures that minimize the negative effects of globalization on consumer rights," as describes Hector Valverde Santana.[21]

The author also states that consumer protection is essential for strengthening market economy, considering that the consumer holds the largest share of money in circulation. This alone is reason enough to substantiate their protection, but even more appropriate is the condition to manage and reaffirm the fundamental rights and full exercise of their citizenship.

In short, the hope of establishing a protective agenda for the international consumer must not stray far from the recognition of the principle of basic vulnerability, which is fundamental in consumer protection. At the same time, this protective agenda should ensure more favorable consumer protection based on contractual justice, in responsible credit transaction and with the effective participation of groups and consumer associations.

Similarly, UN Resolution No. 39/248 aimed to establish guidelines that assist countries in achieving or maintaining adequate protection for their consumer population by offering consumption and distribution patterns that meet the needs and desires of consumers, encouraging high levels of ethical conduct for those engaged in the production and distribution of goods and services for consumers. This document also aimed to assist countries by reducing unfair trade practices that harm consumers using all means, both nationally and internationally; assisting in the development of independent consumer groups; promoting international cooperation in the consumer protection area; and encouraging the development of market conditions that provide consumers greater choice at lower prices.

This is the challenge between the (mis)direction and hope of consolidating international consumer protection in face of globalization/mundialization. It is essential to (re)structure basic consumer rights in the national space in order for such rights to be then extended to the international scenario. Member States of the international community must commit in order to allow consumers to be on level and have their economic interests protected, with safety standards and quality of services and goods, with concrete measures of compensation, with information and educational program, with access to information related to specific areas.

---

[20] Lima Marques (2013), p. 39.

[21] Santana (2015), p. 579.

4.5 Conclusion

The international panorama is inseparable from all the issues affecting life in society and individuals in posmodern times. It is essential to mention that trade issues, a basis of interest for countries to be grouped together, are directed at other issues that are now the object of study of dogmatics and legal practice.

The possibility of making common law through the globalization of law is embodied as real, at the very least necessary, to the extent that society, which is also global, is faced with problems of universal nature of situations, which in turn needs common, global, universal referrals.

Private law recognizes its role in balancing its own legal relation. The consumer is also a citizen of the world, ever growing and broad is his performance in areas beyond the borders of his country. Thus, the balance of consumer relations cannot be restricted to specific geographical borders and locations. It should rather be recognized as regional and global spaces and promote private international law in the field of consumer law, which is able to protect vulnerability beyond its borders, or rather in the absence of them.

However, consumer protection lacks an agenda that includes an integrated international system for the protection of consumer rights.

As stated, consumer society contains within itself a potential contradiction: it values the human factor in the creative process but simultaneously disqualifies those who do not participate in the inclusion/consumption process.

After 25 years of enactment of the Consumer Protection Code, there have been many achievements, but even more challenges are still to come. In times of internationalization of space, subjects, and institutions, perhaps even more than necessary, it is urgent to discuss international consumer protection among the prospects and challenges that await.

The characteristics of the post Industrial Revolution era brought a new scenario that greatly increased the vulnerability of consumers and went on to challenge the legal doctrine by promoting the protection of consumers; this is consumer law. Twenty-five years later, society is not the same, the spaces are different, and it would be incoherent to limit consumer protection to national legislation in a moment in which consuming has become a globalized act (beyond borders), lacking the proper norms that meet the contemporary environment characterized by a world citizen consumer.

References

Bauman Z, Penchel M (1999) Globalização: as consequências humanas. Zahar, Rio de Janeiro

Benjamin AHV (1993) A proteção do consumidor nos países menos desenvolvidos: a experiência da América Latina. Revista Direito do Consumidor 8:200. Ed RT, São Paulo

Delmas-Marty M, Choukr FH (2003) Três desafios para um Direito Mundial. Lumen Júris, Rio de Janeiro

European Commission (1996) Guide del consumidor europeo en el mercado unico, 2nd edn. European Commission, Brussels

Freire P, Freire AMA (2003) Cartas a Cristina: reflexões sobre minha vida e minha práxis. UNESP, São Paulo

Klausner EA (2008) Perspectivas para a proteção do consumidor brasileiro nas relações internacionais de consumo. Revista CEJ XII(42, jul./set): 59–76

Klausner EA (2012) Direito Internacional do Consumidor: a proteção do consumidor no livre-comércio internacional. Juruá, Curitiba

Lima Marques C (2013) Esforços para incluir o tema da proteção do turista na agenda de trabalho da Conferência de Haia e a proposta brasileira de "Convenção de Cooperação em Matéria de Proteção dos Visitantes e Turistas Estrangeiros". Revista Direito do Consumidor 90:39. Ed RT, São Paulo

Lima Marques C, Mirage B (2014) O novo direito privado e a proteção dos vulneráveis, 2nd edn. Editora Revista dos Tribunals, São Paulo

Lima Marques C, Bessa LR, Benjamin AHV (2008) Manual do Direito do Consumidor. Ed RT, São Paulo

Morin E (2002) Os Sete saberes necessários à educação do futuro, 6th edn. Cortez; UNESCO, São Paulo

Rouquié A (2004) Prefácio. In: Seintenfus R (ed) International relations. Manole, Barueri

Santana HV (2015) Globalização econômica e a proteção do consumidor: o mundo entre crises e transformações. Revista Direito do Consumidor 98:135. Ed RT, São Paulo

de Ventura Deisy FL (2003) As assimetrias entre o Mercosul e a União Europeia: os desafios de uma associação inter-regional. Manole, Barueri

Vieira LK (2015) El proyecto de acuerdo del Mercosur sobre derecho aplicable em materia de constratos internacionales de consumo. Revista Direito do Consumidor 99:159. Ed RT, São Paulo

Chapter 5
International Consumer Protection and Private International Law

Louise Ellen Teitz and David P. Stewart

5.1 The Current Architecture of International Consumer Protection

As other contributions to this volume demonstrate in greater detail, the international community lacks a coherent institutional structure for effective consumer protection on a global basis. No single organization or agency plays the central standard setting role in identifying the issues or articulating the rules to deal with difficulties encountered by individual consumers in an increasing globalized economy.

Rather, the international approach at this stage is characterized by at best poorly coordinated efforts in various forums, which to date have generated only a few largely nonbinding rules, principles, and precepts. Despite the absence of any centralized coordination, much less mechanisms for enforcement, the international approach has nonetheless generated increasing participation by national authorities and at least a measure of respect and implementation at the domestic level.

Among the more important global points of reference are the UN Guidelines for Consumer Protection adopted by the General Assembly in 1985.[1] These Guidelines are based on the proposition (among others) that there is a need to protect consumers from hazards to their health and safety, to promote and protect the economic interests of consumers, to guarantee consumer access to adequate information to enable them to make informed choices according to individual wishes and needs and to provide "effective consumer redress."[2] The Guidelines were expanded in

[1]See UNGA Res. 95/248 Annex (adopted by consensus on April 16, 1985).

[2]Id. at para. 3.

L.E. Teitz
Faculty of Law, Roger Williams University School of Law, Bristol, RI, USA

D.P. Stewart (✉)
Faculty of Law, Georgetown University Law Center, Washington, DC, USA
e-mail: stewartd@law.georgetown.edu

C. Lima Marques, D. Wei (eds.), *Consumer Law and Socioeconomic Development*,
DOI 10.1007/978-3-319-55624-6_5

1999, on the recommendation of the UN Commission on Sustainable Development, to address sustainable consumption.[3]

This articulation of basic consumer rights has been widely endorsed and accepted. On the basis of the UN Guidelines, some observers have identified the essential elements of consumer protection to consist of the rights to the satisfaction of basic needs, to safety, to be informed, to choose, to be heard, to redress, to consumer education, and to a healthy and sustainable environment.[4]

Although this articulation of the basic rights of consumers appears to have gained broad endorsement, it remains largely inspirational, a statement of goals to be achieved. The international system still lacks an institutional focus for efforts to protect and promote the interests of consumers. Instead, the issues are dealt with by a diversity of international entities.[5] For example, within the United Nations family of organizations, various aspects of consumer protection are dealt with by UNCTAD as well as the UN Commission on Sustainable Development, by the World Health Organization and the Food and Agricultural Organization, and by the World Bank and the International Monetary Fund, to name but a few.

Other international bodies also play a significant role. For example, the Organization for Economic Cooperation and Development (OECD) works to help countries develop effective consumer policies in order to promote efficient, transparent, and fair global markets for consumers. A major portion of its work in this regard is undertaken by its Committee on Consumer Policy, which prepared Guidelines for Consumer Protection in the Context of Electronic Commerce, approved in 1999 by the OECD Council. These Guidelines are specifically designed to protect consumers when they purchase goods "online" over the Internet, much as they are protected in buying from a local store or by mail order from a catalogue. In October 2011, the G-20 Finance Ministers and Central Bank Governors approved a set of "high-level principles on financial consumer protection," which had been developed within the OECD.[6]

Various initiatives are also underway within the Organization for American States (discussed below) and within the European Union, where a new "European Consumer Agenda" emphasizes reinforcing consumer safety, enhancing knowledge, stepping up enforcement and improving enforcement, and securing redress. Among the specific initiatives under consideration are proposals for online dispute resolution mechanisms and small claim procedures.[7]

Some other efforts at intergovernmental coordination have been undertaken. Most significantly, the International Consumer Protection and Enforcement

---

[3]See UNGA Decision 54/449 (Dec. 22, 1999), available at http://www.un.org/esa/sustdev/sdissues/consumption/cpp14.htm. See also the Report of the Secretary General, "Consumer Protection: Guidelines for Sustainable Consumption," UN Doc. E/CN.17/1998/5 (19 February 1998).

[4]See, e.g., http://www.consumersinternational.org/who-we-are/un-guidelines-on-consumer-protection.

[5]Howells and Weatherill (2005), Hueting (2011).

[6]The G-20 High Level Principles can be found at http://www.oecd.org/dataoecd/58/26/48892010.pdf.

[7]See http://ec.europa.eu/consumers/strategy/index_en.htm#agenda.

Network (ICPEN) is an organization established in 1992 and composed of consumer protection authorities from over 40 countries, whose goals are to protect consumers' economic interests around the world, to share information about cross-border commercial activities that may affect consumer welfare, and to encourage global cooperation among law enforcement agencies.[8]

Nongovernmental bodies of experts are making significant contributions to the field as well. Here, the work of the International Law Association, and in particular its Committee on the International Protection of Consumers, deserves special mention because it draws together a group of experts from a variety of national contexts, approaching the issues on a global and independent basis.

It is evident from this short overview that the field of international consumer protection remains decentralized and fragmented, still at an early stage of evolution and development, with an essentially protean international architecture. It lacks a foundation in any particular international organization or even a firm international charter. It represents at best the beginnings of a weak regulatory system, at this stage little more than a network that produces nonbinding instruments in the form of guidelines or norms.

In some respects, this situation is analogous to the emergent global financial system described in Professor Chris Brummer's new book entitled *Soft Law and the Global Financial System*.[9] Brummer describes in detail the institutional shortcomings in the international architecture of global finance and how they contributed to the 2008 financial crisis. He also reviews the challenges faced by those who now seek to reform that system. In his view, the global financial system continues to be characterized by "considerable heterogeneity" and varying levels of governance. In the absence of a central international regulatory authority, various actors (both international and domestic) serve as "standard setters" producing nonbinding instruments such as informal codes, standards, reports, and best practices. It falls to national authorities (with widely different formal mandates) to interpret and apply those instruments at the domestic level. As a consequence, the international system functions mostly by consensus.

Brummer views with "considerable skepticism" the calls that some make for the creation of a new supranational financial regulation organization—for example, perhaps a World Financial Organization built on the model of the World Trade Organization. Such an entity is unlikely to succeed, in his view. He concludes that for the foreseeable future, "national regulatory authorities will continue to play important roles in a constantly evolving regulatory architecture, just as the accumulating body of international codes and institutions will set (and reset) the rules of engagement for cross-border market supervision."[10]

In much the same way, one must view the international architecture of consumer protection as a weak, largely horizontal system lacking firm international

---

[8]See https://icpen.org.

[9]Brummer (2012).

[10]Id. at 266–267.

foundations whose main participants include interconnected, cooperative "standard setters" producing principles, norms, and recommendations rather than legally binding texts. And as Brummer notes, "[i]n a world of soft law, leading by example is critical."[11]

5.2 Domestic Enforcement Agencies in the United States

The "teeth" of the consumer protection movement continue to be found mostly at the domestic level and in national laws. Virtually, every country now boasts some form of domestic consumer protection legislation and some kind of governmental organization or agency to enforce the relevant rules. Domestic implementation models vary widely, however, and the extent of their regulatory and enforcement authority varies from country to country. It appears that most countries do accept and strive to implement the standards that have been adopted at the international level.

In the United States, consumer protection and regulation is decentralized.[12] Most of the 50 states and other subordinate jurisdictions have their own consumer protections laws and enforcement agencies, including many of the larger cities. At the federal level, Congress has approached the subject incrementally by adopting "separate laws targeting specific business practices, industries, and consumer products."[13] Despite its fragmented nature, this system as a whole provides strong and effective protection for most consumer issues.

For example, the Federal Trade Commission (an independent agency) has primary responsibility for promoting competition and protecting consumers from unfair or deceptive trade practices in advertising, marketing, or sale of goods and services.[14] The FTC's Office of International Affairs not only cooperates closely with foreign law enforcement agencies on investigations and cases that affect U.S. consumers but also works actively with consumer protection agencies around the world to promote cooperation and convergence toward best practices.

In addition, the Food and Drug Administration implements and enforces the various federal statutes regulating food and food additives, drugs and cosmetics, vaccines, tobacco, and medical devices.[15] A separate Consumer Product Safety Commission, established in 1972, works to protect the public from unreasonable

[11]Id. at 279.

[12]Generally, see Flayton and Letchiner (2011). An excellent overview can be found in Crane et al. (2011), p. 305. They observe "consumer protection law in the United States is not so much a cohesive body of law as it is a jumble of discrete (yet often interrelated and overlapping) federal and state laws."

[13]Crane et al. (2011), p. 305.

[14]Generally, see http://ftc.gov/bcp/about.shtm.

[15]See http://www.fda.gov.

risks of injury or death from thousands of types of consumer products, for example, those posing a risk of fire or electrical, chemical, or mechanical hazards.[16]

Issues related to the financial aspects of consumer transactions have generally been addressed in separate federal legislation, for example, in laws regulating discrimination in consumer credit markets, mandatory credit card disclosures, credit reporting and debt collection, financial date privacy, and similar issues.[17] More recently, the U.S. Congress established a new regulatory agency, the Consumer Financial Protection Bureau.[18] This body was created in response to the domestic financial crisis in which many Americans lost their savings, homes, and jobs because of failures in the banking system to protect against irresponsible lending. The CFPB consolidates most of the federal government's authority concerning consumer financial protection in one place. Its stated mission is to make domestic markets safer for consumer financial products and services, thus promoting the interests of consumers, whether they are applying for a mortgage, choosing among credit cards, or using any number of other consumer financial products.[19]

The CFPB began operations on July 21, 2012, and its new director has said that his focus will be on vigorous enforcement particularly in respect of the so-called nonbank financial companies—money transfer agencies, credit bureaus, and private mortgage lenders, for example—that previously have fallen outside the authority of most bank regulators and consumer protection agencies.

The legislation also had many other purposes relevant to consumer interests, including promoting equitable access to credit for consumers and to banking services among low-income and medium-income individuals, as well as the regulation of capital investment by banks and insurance companies and of hedge funds and private equity funds.

5.3 Recent Efforts at the Regional Level

Regional efforts promote the protection of health and safety of consumers by creating a hemisphere-wide Web that allows the compilation and publication, on a permanent basis, of major regional and global alerts on products. Likewise, such efforts are designed to offer a space for the collection of technical regulations and standards, best practices on market surveillance for the safety of products, directory

[16]For information about the CPSC, see http://www.cspc.gov.

[17]For example, the Consumer Credit Protection Act, 15 U.S.C. § 1601 et seq., and the Truth in Lending Act, id., and the Equal Credit Opportunity Act, 5 U.S.C. § 1691 et seq.

[18]Generally, see http://www.consumerfinance.gov.

[19]The CFPA was created by the so-called Dodd-Frank Wall Street Reform and Consumer Protection Act of 2010, Pub.L. 111–203.For background, see Chaffee (2011), 60 Amer. U. L. Rev. 1431.

of officials and experts, online training module, among others, as well as to serve as a tool for the secure exchange of information among authorities. For example, the European Union makes consumer protection a priority, using its treaty-based authority to promote consumers' rights to information and education, to impose safety requirements on various products, and to regulate unfair business practices, misleading and comparative advertising, and price indicators and labeling.[20]

Within the Organization of American States, attention has recently focused on issues related to the growth of Internet usage, and in particular on e-commerce as an increasingly important engine of economic development. One significant initiative is the Consumer Safety and Health Network (CSHN), described as the first inter-American effort to contribute to the development and consolidation of national and regional systems designed to ensure product safety. Conceived as a tool to allow consumers and regional authorities to exchange information and experiences, and to stimulate education on product safety, the CSHN aims to "provide easy access to relevant information on products deemed unsafe by markets from different parts of the world that count with advanced warning systems."[21] The overall purpose is to contribute to the development and consolidation of national and regional systems working on strengthening consumer product safety and thus protect consumer health through the early detection and coordinated action that may prevent the entry of unsafe nonfood consumer products to American markets.

A somewhat different approach has been attempted within the context of the Inter-American Specialized Conferences on Private International Law (known by their Spanish acronym CIDIP). By way of background, in 1994, the CIDIP produced (and the OAS subsequently adopted and opened for signature) the text of an Inter-American Convention on the Law Applicable to International Contracts (colloquially known as the "Mexico City Convention").[22] Essentially a choice-of-law instrument, the Convention honors party autonomy as its basic rule (Art. 7) but provides that in the event the contracting parties do not select the applicable law or if their selection should prove ineffective, then "the contract shall be governed by the law of the State with which it has the closest ties" (Art. 9). The Convention was not intended to be "consumer-specific" but applies to most consumer (B2C) contracts. To date, however, only Mexico and Venezuela have ratified this Convention.

More recently, in the context of CIDIP VII (first convened in 2003), attention turned more specifically to issues of consumer protection and the resolution of B2C disputes, including the question of applicable law as well as jurisdiction and monetary restitution (conventions and model laws). The process began with the submission of various proposals, including for a specific Convention on Consumer Protection and Choice of Law as well as a draft Model Law on Jurisdiction and Choice of Law, and proposals for a draft Model Law on Consumer Redress

[20]For additional information, see http://europa.eu/pol/cons/index_en.htm.

[21]See http://www.oas.org/en/sla/cshn/about_cshn.asp.

[22]The text is available at http://www.oas.org/juridico/english/treaties/b-56.html.

Mechanisms.[23] Despite genuine efforts to resolve differences in approach, these efforts have yet to find a successful conclusion.[24]

Two other important (and related) efforts within the OAS relate indirectly to consumer protection. One has resulted in the adoption in June 2011 of a Model Inter-American Law on Access to Public Information.[25] This Model Law aims to provide the necessary legal framework necessary for ensuring citizen participation in a democratic system, strengthening accountability of and trust in government institutions, and guaranteeing the fundamental human right to seek, receive, and impart information and ideas of all kinds, as articulated in Article 13 of the American Convention on Human Rights, Article 19 of the International Covenant on Civil and Political Rights, and the 2001 Declaration of Principles on Freedom of Expression of the Inter-American Commission on Human Rights.

The other pertains to privacy and the protection of personal data. At the request of the OAS General Assembly, and on the basis of responses by Member States to a questionnaire, the Department of International Law of the Secretariat for Legal Affairs prepared a comparative study of various data protection systems, including international instruments and national legislation.[26] In addition, the Inter-American Juridical Committee adopted several resolutions on this matter, all in an effort to address the regulation of data protection through potential international instruments, as well as at the level of the legislation of some OAS Member States, and of the processing of personal data by the private sector. In March 2012, the Committee adopted a proposed Statement of Principles on Privacy and Protection of Personal Data in the Americas.[27] This Statement articulated 12 basic principles to be adopted and followed in national law and practice in order to prevent harm to individuals from the wrongful or unnecessary collection or use of personal data and information. The Committee also recommended that each national system should adopt a clear and effective policy of openness and transparency about all developments, practices, and policies with respect to personal data and information.[28]

[23]Generally, see http://www.oas.org/dil/CIDIP-VII_consumer_protection.htm. For additional background, see Paula Serra Freire (2010).

[24]For one analysis, see Diego Fernandez (2009), p. 411.

[25]AG/RES. 2661 (XLI-O/11), adopted at the fourth plenary session, held on June 7, 2011). See http://www.oas.org/dil/AG-RES_2661_XLI-O-11_eng.pdf. For a detailed commentary and implementation guide, see http://www.oas.org/dil/CP-CAJP-2841-10_eng.pdf.

[26]OAS doc. OEA/Ser. G CP/CAJP-3063/12, Comparative Study: Data Protection in the Americas (3 April 2012).

[27]CJI/RES. 186 (LXXX-O/12). The text is available at http://www.oas.org/cji/eng/CP-INF_6418-12_eng.pdf.

[28]At its 2012 annual session, the OAS General Assembly took note of these Principles and referred them to the Committee on Political and Juridical Affairs.

5.4 Conclusion

In a decentralized, fragmented environment where international efforts continue to be focused largely on issues related to governmental regulation at the national or societal level, there is ample opportunity for the approaches and methodologies of private international law to make significant contributions to the development of effective and efficient solutions to the problems of consumer protection. The adoption of protective rules and regulations, and their enforcement by governmental agencies, is important, to be sure, but one cannot look to the government for all solutions.

Private international law can contribute to the avoidance as well as the resolution of disputes at the level of the individual consumer. Educating consumers and providing them with the information and means to avoid exploitation in the first instance reduces the need for governmental enforcement. Establishing effective measures for the prompt resolution of B2C disputes can frequently be a more effective solution than after-the-fact governmental enforcement. Development of private international rules and measures is also clearly linked to the promotion of the rule of law more generally. In this respect, one may hope that the recent experiences in CIDIP VII are not predictive of the future.

References

Brummer C (2012) Soft law and the global financial system. Cambridge University Press, Cambridge

Crane EM, Eichernseer NJ, Glazer ES (2011) U.S. consumer protection law: a federalist patchwork. Def. Couns J 78:305

Diego Fernandez A (2009) Current approaches to harmonization of consumer private international law in the Americas. IntComp L Q 58:411

Flayton D, Letchiner J (2011) United States. In: Campbell D (ed) International consumer protection, 2nd edn. Juris

Freire PS (2010) Regulation of international consumer contracts in the Americas. Bus Law Int 11:65

Howells G, Weatherill S (2005) Consumer protection law, 2nd edn. Ashgate, Farnham

Hueting D (2011) International regulatory regimes. In: Campbell (ed) International consumer protection, 2nd edn. Juris

Chapter 6
The Supranational Organizations' Initiatives Aimed at Protection of Tourists. Why International Conventions Are Needed

Maria Goretti Sanches Lima

6.1 Introduction

So far, the 1970 International Convention on Travel Contracts (CCV) and the OECD Council Recommendation on Package Holidays by Air dealt at the international level with the subject of travel.[1] Both notions of "traveller" and "travel contract" were introduced by the CCV. However, few countries have signed and ratified the CCV. From Europe, only Italy keeps its position to date.

Currently, the need to protect the *weaker party to the contract* is premised upon the threat of no transnational liability and lack of justice. The barriers between markets are being gradually eliminated due to the development of business relations, which have grown up in the last century. The markets that before were closed to exchanges started to open a revolution in international trade.

The convention's words provide the frame for ongoing efforts to fathom what the international understanding should be to boosting market growth. But cultural legal frame may trigger known problems in relation to cultural meanings. Whether or not there is a gap in the national legislation, the harmonization of international rules through a convention always overpasses the notion of need. Although the "need" is stronger than possibility, it is not always perceived or easily understood by the authorities. Due to the current need to protect tourists, two supranational organizations—the UNWTO, United Nations World Tourism Organization, and the HCCH, Hague Conference on Private International Law—have captured the core of the problem initiating an exhaustive work toward an international agreement to protect tourists.

[1]Without mention the Montreal Convention regarding liability of air carriers that carries a particular content.

M.G. Sanches Lima (✉)
International Forum of Travel and Tourism Advocates, São Paulo, Brazil
e-mail: goretti@ifttabrasil.org

C. Lima Marques, D. Wei (eds.), *Consumer Law and Socioeconomic Development*,
DOI 10.1007/978-3-319-55624-6_6

The article firstly tackles the discussion on the "legal status" of the natural person, as tourists, travellers, and consumers providing arguments to justify the need of protection due to vulnerability. Secondly, it describes the achievements of the initiatives adopted by supranational organizations. Finally, it demonstrates that both conventions are simultaneously needed because the "travel and tourism" sector works beyond national boundaries where the international tourist is vulnerable for several reasons. Therefore, the different scopes of the "draft conventions" complement each other better than what might have been expected.

6.2 Tourists, Travellers, Consumers

Fundamentally, tourists[2] are travellers. There is no unanimity among countries on the classification of such "legal status." To the Europeans, a "traveller" is a natural person who travels, including business travelers, as self-employed or members of liberal professional.[3] Although in the former Package Travel Directive the definition of traveller did not exist in European law, there are studies pointing that some Member States included the term traveller in their codes, such as Germany in the Bürgerliches Gesetzbuch (or BGB), the Netherlands in the Burgerlijk Wetboek (or BW), at the time of implementing the PTD. The term traveller was also adopted by Austria, Estonia, and Sweden. But France, Luxembourg, and Slovakia preferred the term "purchaser." Other countries such as Denmark, Czech Republic, and Poland used "customer," while Latvia and Portugal took "'client' and Lithuania, "tourist." Only a few Member States used the term consumer, such as Ireland, Cyprus, Greece, Malta, Spain, and the United Kingdom.[4]

In South America, the emphasis falls on the consumer. The concept of consumer in Brazil,[5] Peru,[6] and Paraguay[7] is similar. They classify as consumer not only those who acquire goods and services but also those who use them. All victims of the event, the so-called bystander, and any person exposed to commercial practices are equated with consumers. In those cases, there is no need of a contractual relationship. Conversely, in Argentina,[8] to characterize a consumer the contract must be always chargeable for goods and services.

It is feasible to say that the tourists usually purchase goods and/or services that fall into the scope of consumer law. All tourists are consumers due to the need to

[2]See 'UNWTO Global Code Ethics Tourism'. Available on: http://ethics.unwto.org/en/content/globalcode-ethics-tourism. Access on: 01 Set. 2013.

[3]Directive (EU) 2015/2302 on package travel and linked travel arrangements, Recital (7).

[4]Nölke-Schulte et al. (2008).

[5]Act 8.078/90, Consumer Defence Code (CDC).

[6]Decree (DL) 716/91—Ley de Protección al Consumidor.

[7]Act 1.334/98—Ley de Defensa del Consumidor y Del Usurário.

[8]Act 24.240/93—Ley de Defensa del Consumidor.

acquire goods and services. However, not all consumers are tourists as not everyone travels. In "strict sense," "travel and tourism" belongs to the field of consumer law.

One important point underlying the difference between the popular and scientific use of the words "tourist" and "traveller" is that "tourist" is an economic concept while "traveller" is easily attached with the fundamental right of "freedom to travel"[9] or "free movement of persons."[10] While "traveller" is clearly asserted as a subjective right, "tourist" is being used by policies targeting the tourism industry.

6.3 The Need for Protection

Beyond the discussion on the "legal status," it is unavoidable recognizing that the tourist needs protection. If the consumer is always in a weaker bargaining position than the supplier, there is more reason to pay attention to the tourist who usually is out of his domicile and jurisdiction. The tourist, mainly the international one, faces cross-border barriers such as different language, cultural differences, and foreign currency. So often she or he is a victim of xenophobia, racism or any other bias. The most experienced tourist always faces several difficulties abroad. It means that in such conditions, the tourist is under vulnerable situations.[11] One example is the closure of EU airspace in 2010 due to the volcanic ash cloud Eyjafallajökull. That captured the attention of authorities about the need to assist tens of thousands of tourists for days on end.

Other vulnerable situation is the problem of jurisdiction. The jurisdiction regards to competence, as to define which court of justice is competent to hear and decide a case or make a certain order, and also to legislation, *i.e.*, the law applicable to a particular case. It is difficult for the tourist to pursue an action against a tourism service provider located abroad (re to EU as a nonmember State) in case of non- or

---

[9]"Freedom to travel" is set forth by Art 77 (2) (c) of the TEU and TFEU, 2010/C 83/01. Consolidated versions of the Treaty on European Union and the Treaty on the Function of the European Union.

[10]The Brazilian Federal Constitution: "Art 5, item XV—it is free in time of peace the movement (of persons) within the national territory, and any person may, under the terms of the law, enter it, remain therein or leave it with her/his assets".

[11]See: European Commission, "Consumer vulnerability across key markets in the European Union" (January 2016) available online at: http://ec.europa.eu/consumers/consumer_evidence/market_studies/docs/vulnerable_consumers_exec_sum_27_01_2016_en.pdf. In the literature, there exists no single, commonly adopted definition of consumer vulnerability and most often vulnerability refers to an ex ante assessment of the likelihood of a potential negative outcome in terms of consumer well-being. It is an assessment of risk rather than a reflection of a negative outcome that has or is certain to materialize. Two broad vulnerability categories emerge from the literature, namely, vulnerability, which relates to personal characteristics of the consumer, and a broader concept, which takes into account the transactional situations in which consumers find themselves.

improper performance of the contract. In a modern high-technology society, the tourist has the feasibility to contact directly the hotel, the car rental, the restaurant, the travel agency established in another country concluding the contract through electronic means. There is no party autonomy as the contract is offered in terms of "take it or leave it" basis.[12] If things go wrong, usually the tourist can file a claim. Nevertheless, the question is how to enforce a foreign judgment. Cross-border tourist relationship is not compatible with the framework of the National Consumer Protection.

To deal with the negative externalities, created by the current consumer environment, legal change is needed. The recognition that the tourist is in vulnerable situation would ensure that the markets continue to develop properly. The change has to focus in an acceptable level of minimum harmonization particularly in terms of access to justice and regulation on emergency situations. The protection of tourist reverts in benefit of the tourism service providers as trust and confidence increase the transactions in the market.

6.4 The Differences Between the Conventions Drafted by UNWTO and the HCCH

6.4.1 Scope

Regardless of nomenclature, it is evident that the Conventions drafted by the UNWTO and HCCH are different in content and scope. While the UNWTO's Convention is fundamentally based on protect tourists in emergency situations, in line with rights and obligations of tourism service providers, the HCCH's Convention deals with cooperation and access to justice for international tourists.

One Convention focuses to assist tourists in emergency situations, including packages and accommodation issues, while the other focuses on access to justice that is a door to settle jurisdiction problems regarding competence. In addition, the level of coverage is different as the UNWTO's Convention underlies provisions in depth, while the HCCH deals mainly with principles and forms of cooperation among States. Although both are targeted to protect the tourist, they are different in content, scope, and essence.

Another aspect is the "niche of the market." The UNWTO's Convention focuses on the relation between the consumer and particular niches of the market directly involved in tourism, excluding stand-alone transport services such as air, rail, road, and maritime services.[13] Conversely, the HCCH's Convention covers any

[12]The expression is primarily found into Courts decisions from U.S.A. such as: Carlson v General Motors Corp. 883 F 2d 287 (4th Cir. 1989), Campbell Soup v Wentz, 172 F2d 80 (3rd Cir. 1948).
[13]Art 1 (3) of the 7th UNWTO's draft convention.

consumer relationship performed by the tourist as a consumer in any niche of the market, even stand-alone services. As the latter refers to access to justice without tackling the national legislation, there is no risk of conflict between the Conventions.

Although the draft conventions are independent, they complement each other as both are targeted to the development of the tourism sector. This is to say, while the UNWTO's Convention protects tourist *ex post* in an event of "emergency situation" regulating the interests of tourism services providers, the HCCH's Convention protects the tourist as a consumer *ex ante*, granting access to a foreign justice in order to mitigate economic losses.

6.4.2 *Developments*

6.4.2.1 The UNWTO's Draft Convention

The Convention was first inspired by the volcanic ash cloud that happened in 2010. The draft, however, goes beyond emergency situations (Annex I), including additionally two areas—package travel (Annex II) and, to a lesser extent, accommodation (Annex III). The project started in 2011 with a short pause in light of pending decisions on the revision of the European Union Directive on Package Travel. It was reactivated in 2014 at the occasion of the sixth Working Group by the new UNWTO Executive Director for Programme and Coordination.

Besides the delegates from the Member States and affiliated members, the work received contributions from international organizations and associations such as the International Forum of Travel and Tourism Advocates—IFTTA.

In 2014, IFTTA presented a document called "IFTTA Submission to the UNWTO Draft Convention on the Protection of Tourists and Tourism Service Providers." That document was the result of a half-day session held by the occasion of the 24th IFTTA Conference in Prague. The rapporteurs of the workshops presented conclusions to a plenary meeting. The conclusions were edited by Professor Klaus Tonner and circulated to IFTTA members. It was edited again and adopted by IFTTA Board. Afterwards, the IFTTA Law Journal published the outcome.[14]

Additionally, IFTTA presented two documents, which focused strictly on questions/points raised by the UNWTO concerning comments addressed in the sixth and seventh meeting of the WG. These documents reflected suggestions and dissenting opinions from IFTTA's members on many topics of the Convention.

[14]IFTTA L Rev, in RRa 2–2014 pp. 14–16, and IFTTA L Rev, in RRa 3–2014 pp. 18–22. IFTTA Law Review is published three times a year (April, August, December) as a supplement to the journal RRa—ReiseRecht aktuell.

Among definitions or phrases in the wording of the Convention, everything worth arguing had been presented to assist the UNWTO Secretariat. The UNWTO has now reached the eighth edition of the Working Group.

6.4.2.2 The HCCH's Draft Convention

The **HCCH's Convention** was idealized in 2010 by a committee of experts from the American Association on Private International Law (ASADIP). In 2012, ASADIP launched the "Declaration of Rio de Janeiro" containing the "Agenda of the Americas in Private International Law, on topics of interest to the States of the region."

Firstly, the draft approaches to protect tourists and visitors internationally. The first draft was called "Convention on the protection of tourists and visitors abroad." In 2013, the Government of Brazil endorsed those efforts submitting the draft to the Hague Conference.

A bulk of documents and letters supporting the initiative were delivered to the HCCH by the Brazilian Government's representatives. The Draft Convention was analyzed by the HCCH's Bureau, and in 2015 a significant change in the title occurred. It is now named "Draft Convention on cooperation and access to justice for international tourists."

Fundamentally it contains 10 articles, followed by one Annex. The Annex includes a model of a "Complaint Form," which intends to be multilingual.

6.4.3 Content

6.4.3.1 The UNWTO's Draft Convention

Significant results emerged from the eighth WG, but its main achievement in the last meeting was the change in the title, which was crucial to avoid misunderstandings related to B2B contracts and the adoption of the term "emergency situations" instead of "force majeure." Basically, "force majeure" drives the idea of exclusion of liability, which would be a contradiction if the intention is to encourage States Parties to assist the tourists and facilitate the satisfaction of their primary and basic needs in emergency situation.

Over the years, the title received amendments proposed by the WGs. Prior to the third WG, the Draft Convention was called Draft Convention on the Protection of Tourists/Consumers and Travel Organizers. Later it was changed to UNWTO Convention on the Protection of Tourists and Tourism Service Providers.

However, to avoid the idea of protection on B2B contracts, the title is now "UNWTO Convention on the protection of tourists and rights and obligations of tourism service providers."

Although it is slightly better, the emphasis on "rights and obligations of tourism service providers" still carries legal consequences inasmuch as the Draft Convention did not develop so far specific provisions on that. It is to say, the wording of the title logically still drives a separate idea on the "legal status." It was, however, emphasized by the UNWTO that there is not a logical, international, or national definition for tourist. The UNWTO emphasizes that tourist has an economical definition.

Bearing these considerations in mind, the question arises as to whether the Draft Convention in the form of double "legal status" should be envisaged to better fit into an interdisciplinary approach between law and economics. It seems much more likely that the issue has to be further deeply investigated.

Due to the density of ideas contained within the Draft Convention, the UNWTO's efforts are remarkable; the document comprises a preamble, followed by 16 articles and three Annexes. As mentioned, the Annexes enter in detail into areas that are relevant for the protection of tourists: emergency situations, package travel, and accommodation, where the members of the Working Group have made their most challenging contribution.

6.4.3.2 The HCCH's Draft Convention

The HCCH also changed the title of the Convention. It is now called "Draft Convention on cooperation and access to justice for international tourists."

Although there were changes in the title, the main motive power of the first draft remains the same. It is the idea of formation of a global network to protect foreign tourists as consumers allowing them to be benefited by the national consumer protection framework on the grounds of legal services. The new title just makes such idea more prominent, given its emphasis for access to justice and for *ex ante* cooperation, as the foreign tourist could use the alternative dispute resolution mechanisms already in force in the visited country. This would make feasible for the tourist to complain in the visited country by filling out a form written in her or his native language and being assisted by an authority.

As often happens in administrative grounds, the authorities own a list of businesses that provide tourism services. If the problem cannot be solved, there will start a cooperation of authorities between the home country of the tourist and the visited country.

At least the tourist would obtain an official document without the need of translation in order to activate other legal means to enforce a judgment. The idea is to set up an international instrument toward a multilateral global cooperation to facilitate access to justice without interference from national or Union legislation.

The core of the draft is the use of the already existing legal systems upon international consumer cases avoiding the costly and inefficient international litigations that usually fall into personal frustration.

6.5 Why International Conventions Are Needed

Apart from the obvious difficulties in international law,[15] the tourist needs protection because she/he is vulnerable mainly in cross-border transactions. From the current socioeconomic context have emerged important risk factors from consumer vulnerability as a result of market dispute and economic, social, and technological developments that create new sets of challenges. In terms of travel and tourism, those risk factors are oversized.

The tourist can conclude the contract in her/his own language but can also conclude it in a different language and different currency mainly through the Internet. There is an intercultural interaction between the tourist and the "tourism service provider" where often the commercial practices in the visited country is strongly different from the commercial practices of the market in the domicile of the tourist. Two ingredients of the interaction are language and culture. Even the literate tourist, who is fluent in a second language, will face many cultural obstacles to overpass cultural difficulties. The tourist has not enough length of time to assimilate a foreign culture and often will fall in misunderstandings.

That is why the tourist, as a consumer, is also a weaker party to the contract and especially vulnerable under several conditions. Sometimes globalization masks the tourist's vulnerability. Today the necessaries for life abroad are often minimal. The tourist can find shopping centers, restaurants, bus, and taxi everywhere. But a subtler set of challenges are always there, often related to things that may seem trivial at first.

Actually, the term vulnerability carries different contexts. It has different meanings in different legal systems, and explanations vary according to the approach in question. It is common to think of vulnerability as a kind of consumer characteristics or demographics such as age, disability, gender, race/ethnicity, low or limited literacy and level of education. These are useful indicators for governments, institutions, and businesses to operationalize programs and policies; however, there is no empirical proof that biophysical characteristics of individuals should be the sole basis to define vulnerability. In fact, any individual might experience vulnerability at a point in time.[16]

The sophistication of the concept of vulnerability goes beyond the essentials of the principle set forth by some legal systems.[17] Vulnerability applies to everyone who consumes—the rich, poor, educated, noneducated, credulous, or wise.[18]

---

[15]For instance: "dualism"; a position in which two systems of law (national and international) co-exist but function separately. "Monism", where international law is declared to be an integral part of national law. Such different legal frame drives problems as in "dualist" countries (*i.e.* England) it is common that a provision or executive act related to foreign affairs is lawful in national law, but a breach of international law, as in England, see: Bradley and Erwing (2003), p. 310.

[16]Stearn (2012).

[17]In Brazil, for instance, vulnerability is a principle set forth by Art 4 (I) of the Consumer Defence Code.

[18]Benjamin et al. (2010), p. 259.

Although everyone is vulnerable in the current environment of the market, there are consumers who are more vulnerable than others. It is unlikely that everyone who falls into one of these categories of individuals will face the same level of risk. They are the children, the elderly, and the disabled who also travel.

Thus, private market works well when there are many suppliers and consumers. But unfortunately, free markets by themselves are not able to ensure the efficiency of the economy.[19] Governments need to provide fairness or even efficiency to the travel and tourism sector, a sector that works beyond national boundaries, where the tourist is vulnerable for several reasons.

The international cooperation on the "draft conventions" would benefit both the "tourist" and the "tourism service providers," consequently the market as a whole. In this context, further technical adjustments on both "draft conventions" are still expected and very welcome.

References

Benjamin AH, Marques CL, Bessa LR (2010) Manual de Direito do Consumidor, 3a. ed. Rev. dos Tribunais, São Paulo

Bradley AW, Erwing KD (2003) Constitutional and administrative law, 3rd edn. Person Longman, London

Nölke-Schulte H, Christian F-T, Martin E (2008) EC consumer law compendium. Sellier European Law Publisher, Munich

Sachs J (2011) The price of civilization. Vitage, London

Stearn J (2012) Tackling consumer vulnerability. Consumer Focus, London

[19] Sachs (2011).

Chapter 7
Chinese Approaches to Reform Consumer Protection Law: Substantive Law and Conflict Law

Ying Yu

7.1 Introduction

The long-awaited first Act of China Private International Law, "Law of Application of Law for Foreign-Related Civil Relations of People's Republic of China" (LALFCR), was adopted on October 28, 2010, and came into force on April 1, 2011. Unprecedented, the legislation of China expresses its protective attitude of private international law to consumers evidenced by Article 42 of the LALFCR. There is one special article for consumer contract's applicable rule among all the 52 articles, which is the first protective choice of law rule in China's legislative history:

> Article 42: *Consumer contract shall be governed by the law of the country of the consumers' habitual residence. The law of the country where the products/commodities and services be supplied should govern the contract, provided that it was chosen by the consumer or there is no related business activities of supplier/professional in the country of the consumer's habitual residence.*

China is an impressive consumer market; not only its internal market has opened to foreign products, but also international tourism is flourishing and the Chinese products are available to consumers in all national markets. Anyway, it is remarkable that the first Act of China Private International Law, the "Law of Application of Law for Foreign-Related Civil Relations of People's Republic of China" (LALFCR), has a special article for consumer contract (Art. 42).

Part of this article was written in 2010, the rest was written in 2013. The article was originally published at Revista de Direito do Consumidor Vol. 103, pp. 143–154.

Y. Yu (✉)
Faculty of Law and Wolfson College, University of Oxford, Oxford, UK
e-mail: ying.yu@wolfson.ox.ac.uk

C. Lima Marques, D. Wei (eds.), *Consumer Law and Socioeconomic Development*,
DOI 10.1007/978-3-319-55624-6_7

7.2 Background and History of Article 42 of China's "Law of Application of Law for Foreign-Related Civil Relations of People's Republic of China"

7.2.1 Legal Background

On October 1, 1949, when the People's Republic of China was established, all the laws promulgated by the former government were abolished, including a code of private international law named "Regulation on Application of Law, 1918."[1] The following three decades, the development of private international law was stagnated by the prevalence of legal nihilism, coupled with the isolated situation of China.[2] From the opening and reforming policy adopted by China in 1978, legislative activity is getting into a prosperous phase during which foreign-related legal relations make itself a more and more significant attraction. Many codes were blooming with few conflict rules in its respect sphere, such as Succession Law 1985 (Art. 36), Adopting Law 1991 (Art. 20), Maritime Code 1992 (Chap. 14), and so forth. The most important achievement concerning the choice of law rules of the revival period is "General Principles of the Civil Law of the People's Republic of China" (GPCL) in 1986, in which chapter 8 embodies particular choice of law provisions for foreign-related civil matters.[3] Two years later, the Supreme People's Court issued the "Opinions of the Supreme People's Court on Several Issues concerning the Implementation of the General Principles of the Civil Law of the People's Republic of China" (for Trial Implementation) (Opinions of GPCL, 1988), which is a judicial interpretation to explain and expend the GPCL. Concerning contracts, the "Law of the People's Republic of China on Economic Contracts involving Foreign Interest" (ECFI 1985)[4] made its contribution to foreign-related contract, cooperating with its judicial interpretation of 1987[5] until the end of the twentieth century. In 1999, Contract Law of the People's Republic of China (Contract Law 1999) entered on the stage, instead of ECFI 1985 and its judicial interpretation of 1987, to regulate contract relationship. Article 126 of Contract Law is a choice of law rule specially for foreign-related contracts.[6] Moreover, a

---

[1]Han D P (2006), p. 59.

[2]Huang J (2006), p. 120.

[3]GPCL Chapter VIII: Application of Laws to Civil Matters involving Foreign Elements.

[4]ECFI was abolished in 1999.

[5]"Explanation of Supreme People's Court's on Selected Questions of Application of Foreign Economic Contract Law" was abolished in 2000.

[6]Article 126: The parties to a foreign-related contract may choose those laws applicable to the settlement of contract disputes, unless stipulated otherwise by law. If the parties to a foreign-related contract fail to make such choice, the State laws most closely related to the contract shall apply.

For the contracts to be fulfilled in the territory of the People's Republic of China on Chinese-foreign equity joint ventures, on Chinese-foreign contractual joint ventures and on Chinese-foreign cooperation in exploring and exploiting natural resources, the laws of the People's Republic of China shall apply.

judicial interpretation of 2007 made its effort on foreign-related contracts by concentrating its entire 12 articles on choice of law rules of contracts, "Rules of the Supreme People's Court on the Relevant Issues concerning the Application of Law in Hearing Foreign-Related Contractual Dispute Cases in Civil and Commercial Matters (2007 Rules)."

The consumer contracts had no chance to distinguish itself from business contracts between traders (B2B), concerning the choice of law rules among afore mentioned codes and judicial interpretations. Technically, the applying approach of consumer contracts should be implemented on the grounds of "Party Autonomy" doctrine, "Most Significant Relationship" doctrine, and "Characteristic Performance" doctrine[7]; there is no difference from that of B2B contracts.

7.2.2 *The Efforts of Legal Doctrine*

Chinese scholars keep efforts to ameliorate the fragmentation problem on private international law rules. The LALFCR adopted in October 2010 is a fruit of academic theories and the legislator's consideration of the present social conditions of China. First mooted back in 2002, when the government of the PRC launched a codification action on drafting a Civil Code, Part IX of the draft Code now accommodates eight chapters, including 94 articles on conflict rules,[8] on the basis of the Model Law of Private International Law of the People's Republic of China (hereinafter "Model Law"). The Model Law was presented by the China Association of Private International Law[9] on 2000.

The association not only supplies the legislative reference of the government by its proposal but also supplies theoretical resources of private international law by its dynamic academic activities. In 1993, the association began its draft works on Model Law. After several amendments, the final text is now the sixth edition,[10] which embraces 166 articles separated in five chapters of General Principle, Jurisdiction, Application of Law, Judicial Assistance, and Supplementary Provisions. The Model Law has no legal effect, whose aim is to supply the references to

[7]Article 145 of GPCL, and Article 142 of Contract Law, Article 5 of 2007 Rules, etc.

[8]Draft Civil Code of PRC, Part IX Application of law of Foreign-related Civil Matter. There are 8 chapters including 94 articles embodied in the Part IX.

[9]China Association of Private International Law was found in Oct, 1987. From 1993, the association began its draft works on Model Law under the efforts of former President Prof. Depei Han. After several amendments, the final text is the sixth edition which embracing 166 Articles separated in five Chapter of General Principle, Jurisdiction, Application of Law, Judicial Assistance and Supplementary Provisions.

[10]Huang J (2006), p. 129.

government legislation and academic research.[11] One noteworthy phenomenon that appeared in this Model Law is that, for the first time, consumers are, as concerned by scholars, to be treated as a special party. There are two articles particular for consumers both in jurisdiction[12] and applicable law[13] rules. The domicile or habitual residence of the consumer is regarded as the closest connection place of consumer contracts; as a result, consumer contracts should be governed by the law of the place where the consumer's domicile or habitual residence is located. However, the rule can only be applied under the circumstance where there is no effective choice of party autonomy according to the Model Law.[14]

Although the 2002 Civil Code failed to be approved, the scholars never gave up their diligence in pushing the government to enact a code of private international law in China. In 2008, the Chinese government scheduled to draft the Law of Application of Law for Foreign-Related Civil Relations again. The final text of the Proposal of Law of Application of Law for Foreign-Related Civil Relations[15] was presented by the Association in March 2010 (Final Proposal, 2010). Article 56[16] of the Proposal, which is a provision on consumer contracts, corresponds to the modern philosophy of consumer protection prevailing in the world of private international law. The majority evolution of the article is threefold: first, the article adopts the consumer's habitual residence as the primary connecting factor of consumer contracts. Second, the notion of distinguishing "active consumer" and "passive consumer" was first established in the article. Third, the party autonomy was limited in consumer contracts. This article supplied fundamental ideas to the legislator. Even though the consequence, that is, Article 42 of the LALFCR, is not satisfying scholars, to some extent, at least it is a great step forward for the Chinese

[11]See Preamble of The Model Law of Private International Law of The People's Republic of China, presented by the China Association of Private International Law, Law Press, China, 2000.

[12]Model Law Article 31: The court of PRC shall have jurisdiction over an action arising from a dispute in respect of consumer rights and interests, if the domicile or the habitual residence of the consumer is suited within the territory of the PRC.

[13]Model Law Article 101: Failing choice of law, the contract is governed by the law of the place with which it has a closest connection. Generally, the law of the closest connection with the following contracts is decided in accordance with the following provisions:. . .(18) The consumer contract is governed by the law of the place of the consumer's domicile or habitual residence. . ..

[14]Model Law Article 100: Contracts are governed by the law the parties agreed on and explicitly chose except as otherwise stipulated by the PRC law and by the treaties concluded or acceded to by the PRC. . . .

[15]The proposal includes 78 articles presented by the team lead by Prof. Jin Huang who is the present president of China Association of Private International Law.

[16]The Final Proposal Article 56: Consumer contracts should be governed by the law of consumer's habitual residence or the place where the commodities or services be supplied. The law chosen by the parties which has relative connection with the consumer contract shall be applied; except the circumstance of the consumer consumed in the place of business located without invited by the business, the choice of law shall not be contrary to the mandatory rules of consumer's habitual residence, provided the consumer's habitual residence is the place where the business has ever deal with any relative operations via any medium, or sent any individual invitation to consumer, or received the order form the consumer.

legislator to be concerned about consumer protection through private international law.

7.3 Sources of Chinese Private International Law and the 2010 Act

The three most important sources of Chinese private international law are international treaties, national legislation, and international practices, which are implied by a provision of the 1986 GPCL.[17] Judicial interpretations and explanations issued by the Supreme People's Court, which exercises its authority vested by law, are regarded are sources of Chinese private international law as well. Thus, the sources of Chinese private international law can be conveniently divided into two categories: national sources, including domestic legislation and judicial interpretation of laws, and international sources, consisting of international conventions and customs.[18] The hierarchy of application stipulated by Article 142 of the GPCL can be understood as follows: international treaties of which China is a party are superior to domestic legislation and judicial interpretations; international customs can only be applied as a supplement in case the area is lacking in international treaties, domestic legislation, and judicial interpretations.

The main current sources of private international law concerning the province of international sale of goods contracts include (1) international conventions to which China is a party: the United Nations Convention on Contracts for International Sale of Goods (CISG 1980 of UNCITRAL), (2) international custom: Principles of International Commercial Contracts (PICC 2004 of UNIDROIT) and International Rules for the Interpretation of Trade Terms (INCOTERMS 2000 of ICC), (3) domestic legislation in effect: General Principles of the Civil Law of the People's Republic of China (GPCL 1986)[19] and Contract Law of the People's Republic of China (CL 1999),[20] (4) judicial interpretations: Opinions of the

[17]GPCL Article 142: The application of law in civil relations with foreigners shall be determined by the provisions in this chapter.

If any international treaty concluded or acceded to by the People's Republic of China contains provisions differing from those in the civil laws of the People's Republic of China, the provisions of the international treaty shall apply, unless the provisions are ones on which the People's Republic of China has announced reservations.

International practice may be applied on matters for which neither the law of the People's Republic of China nor any international treaty concluded or acceded to by the People's Republic of China has any provisions.

[18]Huang J, Guo M L (2007), pp. 381–382. This paper was first published in Yearbook of Private International Law (Vol. 1, 1999), pp. 135–156.

[19]Chapter VIII of GPCL is a particular chapter for application of law rules in Civil Relations with Foreigners from Article 142 until Article 150.

[20]Article 126 of CL is a special choice of law rule of foreign-related contracts.

Supreme People's Court on Several Issues concerning the Implementation of the General Principles of the Civil Law of the People's Republic of China (for Trial Implementation) (Opinions of GPCL, 1988) and Rules of the Supreme People's Court on the Relevant Issues concerning the Application of Law in Hearing Foreign-Related Contractual Dispute Cases in Civil and Commercial Matters (2007), etc.

7.3.1 Scope of Application of the LALFCR and Article 42

The scope of the LALFCR is limited in the situation of "Foreign-related civil relation," according to Article 2.[21] The new law avoids repeating the definition of "Foreign-related civil relation," which can be traced back to the former judicial interpretation.[22] "Foreign-related civil relation" means the civil relation involving one or more foreign elements. "Foreign element" can be present in the party or parties who is not Chinese, the objective which situated and the fact what taken place beyond the territory of China. A fact that cannot be ignored is that Hong Kong, Marco, and Taiwan are treated as foreign in respect of civil contracts and commercial transactions.[23]

The general choice of law rules of contracts, except consumer contracts and labor contracts,[24] should comply with Article 41 of the LALFCR,[25] which observes the traditional doctrines of "Party Autonomy," "Characteristic Performance," and "Most Significant Relationship." Article 42 makes a remarkable innovation to separate consumer contracts (B2C) from commercial contracts (B2B), whose parties are both traders. According to Article 42, consumer contract enjoys its particular choice of law rules. Nevertheless, Chinese legislation fails to appreciate the significance of stipulating the definition of "consumer contract." But the

---

[21]Art 2. The application of laws concerning foreign-related civil relations shall be determined in accordance with this Law.

[22]Supreme people's Court, Opinions to Several Questions concerning Implementing the General Principle of Civil Law of the People's Republic of China, (1988), Art 178: Where either party or both parties in a civil legal relationship is an alien, a stateless person or a foreign legal person, and the object of the civil legal relationship is within the territory of a foreign country, and the legal facts that produce, alter or annihilate the civil relations of rights and obligations occur in a foreign country, such relationship shall be called foreign-related civil relations.

[23]Huang J & Qian X F (1995), p. 293.

[24]The choice of law rule of labor contracts is stipulated by Article 43 of LALFCR. Art 43: The laws at the working locality of laborers shall apply to labor contracts; if it is difficult to determine the working locality of a laborer, the laws at the main business place of the employer shall apply. The laws at the dispatching place of labor services shall apply to labor dispatches.

[25]LALFCR Article 41: The law chosen by the parties should be applied to the contract. In the circumstance where the parties failed to choose, the habitual residence's law of one party should be applied, provided the obligation implemented by that party is the most characteristic performance; or other law which possesses the most significant relationship with the contract.

meaning of "consumer" can be deduced from one article of domestic substantive law, "Law of the People's Republic of China on Protection of Consumer Rights and Interests" (LPCRI, 1993).[26] A consumer is a natural person who purchases and uses commodities or receives services for daily consumption, according to Article 2 of the LPCRI. Thus, we can understand that the "consumer contract" in Chinese legal system is contract concluded by the consumer and trader for purchase commodities and services for the consumer's daily life.

7.3.1.1 Choice of Law Approach of Consumer Contract Reconstructed by the LALFCR

From 2011 April 1, the LALFCR came into force anything but not alone. The mentioned sources of private international law should be applied together with the LALFCR for the regulation of sales contracts possessing foreign elements. With respect to consumer contracts, the following are the rules on application:

(1) The law applying process should be commenced from the international treaties, both multilateral and bilateral treaties. There is absence of multilateral treaty on what can be applied to consumer contracts, owing to the fact that consumer contracts are excluded by the one convention that applies to the sale of goods contracts, the United Nations Convention on Contracts for International Sale of Goods (CISG 1980).[27] The application of a bilateral treaty depends on whether the concerned foreign country in the individual case concluded a bilateral treaty with China. Seldom is a bilateral treaty in which China is a party designed to apply particular rules for consumer contract, until now.
(2) Under such circumstances when international treaties fail to be applied to foreign-related legal relation, conflict rules come into play. Article 42 would be the most significant choice of law rules on consumer contracts when the LALFCR comes into operation. The article indicates three rules, namely:
    (a) In general, the law of the habitual residence of the consumer governs the consumer contracts.
    (b) The law of the country where the commodities and services were supplied by the supplier should be applied, if it was chosen by the consumer.
    (c) The law of the country where the commodities and services were supplied by the supplier should be applied under the circumstance that the supplier did not deal with related operations in the country of the consumer's habitual residence.

[26] LPCRI Article 2: The rights and interests of consumers in purchasing and using commodities or receiving services for daily consumption shall be under the protection of the present Law, or under the protection of other relevant laws and regulations in absence of stipulations in this Law.

[27] CISG Article 2: This Convention does not apply to sales: *(a)* of goods bought for personal, family or household use, unless the seller, at any time before or at the conclusion of the contract, neither knew nor ought to have known that the goods were bought for any such use;...

(3) The chosen law must be exclusively substantive law due to the renvoi character of Chinese legislation according to Article 9[28] of the LALFCR. The *lex causae* resulting from the selection of Article 42 would be either Chinese law or foreign law. Mandatory rules of China are always prevalent over foreign substantive law as a general principle in Article 4 of the LALFCR.[29]
(4) The main domestic laws that are possible to be applied concerning consumer contract include (a) General Principles of the Civil Law of the People's Republic of China (GPCL), 1986; (b) Contract Law of the People's Republic of China (CL), 1999; (c) Law of the People's Republic of China on the Protection of Consumer Rights and Interests (PCRI), 1993, etc.

7.4 The First Amendment of China Consumer Protection Law

On 25 October 2013, China passed the first amendment to its Consumer Protection Law, *Law of the People's Republic of China on the Protection of Consumer Rights and Interests 2013*, which was originally adopted in 1993. The new law entered into force on the World Consumer Day, March 15, 2014.

There are several significant modifications in the law, which could have the following effects:

1. Empower consumers by enhancing the CCA's legal position.

There is only one well-known consumer association in China, named the CCA (Chinese Consumer Association), which was set up by the government rather than as a private consumer association. It is a generic quasi-government organization who has no any individual consumer members. With a confusing name, CCA performs a public interest function, apart from acting on behalf of consumers. The amendment characterizes the CCA as a "Social Organization" rather than as an association.[30]

With this new legal status, the CCA is, for the first time, authorized by statute to be funded by the government[31] and to be an active participant in the legislative process.[32] Besides the dispute resolution functions stipulated by the former law, the

[28]LALFCR Article 9: Foreign laws applicable to foreign-related civil relations do not include the Law of the Application of Law of this foreign country.

[29]LALFCR Article 4: If there are mandatory provisions on foreign-related civil relations in the laws of the People's Republic of China, these mandatory provisions shall directly apply.

[30]Art. 36, *Law of the People's Republic of China on the Protection of Consumer Rights and Interests 2013*.

[31]Art. 37 (8), *Law of the People's Republic of China on the Protection of Consumer Rights and Interests 2013*.

[32]Art. 37 (2), *Law of the People's Republic of China on the Protection of Consumer Rights and Interests 2013*.

CCA and its provincial branches are conferred the power to bring class action litigation against certain behavior considered to be detrimental to the public as consumers.[33]

2. Protect distance consumers by the "Right of Withdrawal" rules.

The right of withdrawal rules are for the first time introduced into the Chinese legal system. Distance consumers (i.e., those who buy at a distance, such as through mail order or the Internet) are allowed a 7-day cooling-off period and a right to obtain reimbursement from the seller within 7 days after the returned commodity has been received. The freight cost of returning the products should be paid by the consumer.[34]

3. Transfer the burden of proof from consumers to traders.

According to the Civil Procedure Law of China, the burden of proof currently lies with the plaintiff. The amendment transfers the burden of proof from the consumers to the traders, particularly in durable commodities and house decoration areas.[35]

4. Increase punishment compensation.

The consumer is to be allowed compensation amounting to three times the payment made if she/he is defrauded by the trader and up to twice the amount of personal injury damages.[36]

So far, there is no official English version of the 2013 amendment. The 1993 version of *Law of the People's Republic of China on the Protection of Consumer Rights and Interests* could be found on some websites.[37]

References

Huang J (ed) (2006) Private international law, 2nd edn. Law Press, China

Han DP (ed) (2006) New private international law. Wuhan University Press, China

Huang J, Qian XF (1995) "One country, two systems", three law families, and four legal regions: the emerging inter-regional conflicts of law in China. Duke J Comp Int Law 5:289–328

Huang J, Guo ML (2007) New development of Chinese private international law. In: Huang J (ed) International law from a marco-perspective. Wuhan University Press, pp 381–382

[33] Art. 47, *Law of the People's Republic of China on the Protection of Consumer Rights and Interests 2013*.

[34] Art. 25, *Law of the People's Republic of China on the Protection of Consumer Rights and Interests 2013*.

[35] Art. 23, *Law of the People's Republic of China on the Protection of Consumer Rights and Interests 2013*.

[36] Art. 55, *Law of the People's Republic of China on the Protection of Consumer Rights and Interests 2013*.

[37] Available at http://en.internationalconsumer.org/Plus/m_default/Cms/docDetail.php?ID=19.

Chapter 8
International Consumer Protection in Mercosur

Alberto do Amaral Junior and Luciane Klein Vieira

8.1 Introduction

Historically, consumer protection originated in developed countries with the consolidation of the Fordist mass production model. However, in the American continent, consumer protection had a close relation to the import-substitution model, which took place in Brazil, in the second half of the twentieth century. In parallel, the imperative to ensure access to consumption of the vast segments of the Brazilian population was a fundamental necessity.

Other Mercosur countries did not have an industrialization process, having remained largely to be agricultural economies. In those countries, the industrial activity was confined to processing primary goods. Consumer protection contributed to improving the quality of products at domestic level and to leading a more balanced relations between consumers and producers. In an economic integrated space with a number of international economic transactions, it is of utmost importance the existing rules of consumer protection.

Our aim is to analyze some principles and achievements of the Technical Committee 7 (CT n° 7), in charge of creating norms, adopting policies, and taking measures designed to ameliorate and develop international consumer protection in the Mercosur countries.

A. do Amaral Junior (✉) • L.K. Vieira
Faculty of Law, University of São Paulo, São Paulo, Brazil
e-mail: aamaralj@uol.com.br

C. Lima Marques, D. Wei (eds.), *Consumer Law and Socioeconomic Development*,
DOI 10.1007/978-3-319-55624-6_8

8.2 Consumer Law in the Founding of Mercosur States

Before the creation of Mercosur, Brazil, in a pioneering way, had specific rules for consumer protection. The Code of Consumer Protection, Law n° 8.098, was passed in the Brazilian Congress on September 11, 1990, in virtue of Article 5° XXXII of the 1988 Federal Constitution and Article 48 of its Transitional Provisions. Prior to 1991, the remaining countries, Argentina, Uruguay, and Paraguay, did not contain, in a particular instrument, rules on that matter.

In Argentina, for example, Law 24.240 on consumer protection[1] came to light on September 22, 1993, and is in force up to date. Only after 1 year, the Argentine Constitution, amended in 1994, included Articles 42 and 43 in order to solidify the regulation in this respect.

The 1992 Paraguayan Constitution solely indirectly alluded to consumer protection, although Law 1.334, passed on October 27, 1998, protecting consumers and users,[2] received influence from Brazilian and Argentine laws and the Mercosur Protocols,[3] mentioned below.

Finely, the Uruguayan Constitution does not contain any constitutional norm guaranteeing consumer's rights since the theme did not figure in the 2004 constitutional reform.[4] Nevertheless, on September 20, 1999, Law 17.189[5] disciplined the consumption relation for the first time in the history of that country. Due to lack of formality, such a law came to be replaced by Law 17.250[6]—Law of Consumer Protection—on August 11, 2000, and is still in force. Its main source finds itself in the Mercosur Protocol on Consumer Protection.[7]

As one can easily observe, both Paraguayan legislation and Uruguayan[8] legislation in this field were strongly inspired by attempts of legislative harmonization within the economic bloc.

[1]The law No. 24.240 was amended by various laws, among them: Law n° 24.568/1995 (Published in *Boletín Oficial de la República Argentina*, n° 28.260, on 31/10/1995); Law n° 24.787/1997 (Published in *Boletín Oficial de la República Argentina,* n° 28.617, on 2/4/1997); Law n° 24.999/1998 (Published in *Boletín Oficial de la República Argentina*, n° 28.948, on 30/7/1998); Law n° 26.361/2008 (Published in *Boletín Oficial de la República Argentina,* n° 31.378, on 7/4/2008); Law n° 26.993/2014 (Published in *Boletín Oficial de la República Argentina,* n° 32.972, on 19/9/2014) and Law n° 26.994/2014 (Published in *Boletín Oficial de la República Argentina,* n° 32.985, on 8/10/2014).

[2]Regarding this law, see: Ruiz Díaz Labrano (2014), pp. 75–438.

[3]Fellous (2003), p. 170.

[4]Bourgoignie (2009), p. 51.

[5]Law published in *Diario Oficial (D.O),* n° 25.368, on 30/9/1999.

[6]Law published in *Diario Oficial (D.O.),* n° 25.583, on 17/8/2000.

[7]Ribeiro and Zordan (2006), p. 469.

[8]With respect to Venezuela and Bolivia, countries that subsequently joined MERCOSUR as full members, it is important to point out that, at present, Venezuela does not have a consumer protection law, due to the repeal of the DEPABIS Law (Law for the Defense of People in Access to Goods and Services), 2010. Thus, from 23/1/2014, when the Organic Law on Fair Prices (later

8.3 The Harmonization of Legislation on Consumer Rights in Mercosur

Mercosur[9] is an integration project created by the Treaty of Asuncion on March 26, 1991, which falls within what is known as "new regionalism."[10]

Initially, Mercosur was composed of Brazil, Argentina, Uruguay, and Paraguay; since August 12, 2012, Venezuela[11] has become a full member of Mercosur. Furthermore, on December 7, 2012, the protocol of accession of Bolivia to Mercosur was signed, which is currently being ratified, pending only the acceptance of the Paraguayan Congress. In spite of the effectiveness of that protocol, the 48th summit meeting of Mercosur, held in Brasilia on July 17, 2015, rendered official Bolivia's entry to the bloc.

If member states are really interested in deepening the integration with a view to achieving the so-called four freedoms, the best way to do this is to jointly define public policies, among which is international consumer protection. Therefore, consumer protection is a natural goal when states seek to make up of an economic bloc in a globalized world.[12]

With that objective in mind, on April, 23, 1994, the finance ministers of the original Mercosur states signed a Joint Declaration conveying the willingness to make closer their legislation on competition and consumer protection.[13] Concomitantly, they stated the common intention to raise national rules of consumer protection at least in accordance with international standards.[14] This Declaration

amended on November 8, 2015), which explicitly repealed the legislation indicated, the Venezuelan consumer does not have a specific protective law. In Bolivia, the situation is different. On 6/12/2013, Law 453, known as the General Law of the Rights of Users and Consumers, was approved. (Published in *Gaceta Oficial del Estado Plurinacional de Bolivia*, n° 591NEC, on 6/12/2013), which regulates consumer rights in the country for the first time.

[9]About the historical background of the bloc, see: Scotti (2013), pp. 62–64; Amaral Júnior (2015), pp. 453–461.

[10]The new regionalism, a form of multilateralism that emerged from the demands of globalization since the 1980s, has as its main features: (a) broad trade liberalization with automatic tariff reductions; (b) market integration; (c) the inclusion of different materials of trade; (d) the low institutionalization and the existence of dispute resolution systems. Czar De Zalduendo (2013), p. 23.

[11]Venezuela entered MERCOSUR after the suspension applied to Paraguay, which prevented it from participating in the decision-making bodies of the bloc when the democratic order had not been reestablished in the country, supposedly breached after the removal of former president Lugo. The treaty that incorporated the country to the bloc has been in force since 14/1/2014, when Paraguay finally deposited the instrument of ratification.

[12]Stiglitz (1995), p. 1371.

[13]Ata da Reunião de Ministros de Economia de 23/4/1994, item 2 "Coordenação de políticas macroeconômicas e intercâmbio comercial entre os países membros", paragraph 2°. Available at: http://gd.mercosur.int/SAM/GestDoc/PubWeb.nsf/ListadoReunRealizadas?OpenForm&lang=POR, Accessed on 17/1/2016.

[14]Bourgoignie. *Op. cit.*, p. 47.

is in line with the provisions of Article 1 of the Treaty of Asuncion establishing the commitment of States Parties to harmonize their legislation in relevant areas in view of strengthening the integration process.

In the course of 25 years,[15] Mercosur has been fully engaged in creating standards to diminish negative legislative discrepancies. In this connection, the CT 7 has played a prominent role, as we will point out in the next section.

8.4 The Competence of the Technical Committee 7

The institutional concern for consumer protection gained room within the Common Market Group from the creation of Working Subgroup 10, linked to the Coordination of Macroeconomic Policies.[16]

It gave birth to the Committee on Consumer Law Studies, which in 1994 was transformed into Technical Committee of the MERCOSUR Trade Commission, a body created in the bloc under the Ouro Preto Protocol. Similar agreement is complementary to the Asuncion Treaty. Taking into account that the Internal Regulation of the Mercosur Trade Committee provides for creating a specialized Technical Committee to regulate[17] and safeguard consumer protection, the powers previously assigned to the Consumer Law Studies Committee were transferred to the CT 7.[18]

Thus, since its inception on February 15, 1995,[19] the CT 7 has been the chief body in charge of establishing proposals for legislative harmonization in the bloc aiming to improve and develop consumer protection in Mercosur. This goal presupposes a broad participation and support of national consumer protection agencies of member states, working on the basis of exchange of information on specific matters between law enforcement authorities.

The CT 7 has discussed the following subjects: (a) proposals and projects for legislative harmonization, (b) practical actions toward consumer protection, (c) exchange of information and know-how on states' projects and policies,

[15]Regarding the stages in which Mercosur has passed during its existence, related to initiatives to protect the consumer, see: Marques (2009), pp. 368–379.

[16]With the establishment of the Study Committee in April 1993, work on legislative harmonization of consumer law in GMC Subgroup No. 10 began. This Subgroup should prepare a document called "Basic Guidelines for Consumer Protection in Mercosur" and a set of basic, non-exhaustive standards that set a common minimum standard in this area. Marques (1999), p. 22.

[17]Regarding the possibility of Mercosur to legislate on consumer law, it is interesting to note that the Treaty of Asunción and the Protocol of Ouro Preto did not expressly attribute this competence to the bloc. In practice, the implied power theory is adopted to support the work that has been done. Marques (1997), p. 89.

[18]Marques. "Direitos do consumidor no MERCOSUL: algumas sugestões frente ao impasse". *Op. cit.*, p. 20.

[19]The CT n° 7 was created by the Directive n° 1/1995 of CCM. Available at: http://www.mercosur.int/innovaportal/v/703/2/innova.front/directivas_1995, accessed on 7/1/2016.

(d) institution of regulatory framework, (e) consumer education and protection measures, (f) implementing policies to further integration and improve the rights and interests of the consumers of the region.[20]

This Technical Committee proposes resolutions that are submitted to public consultation before their adoption by the Common Market Group. The procedure accomplished is transparent to deal with criticisms and suggestions coming from the Mercosur members.[21]

8.5 CT 7's Main Contributions to International Consumer Protection

Since 1995, the CT 7 has arduously worked on the task of harmonizing regional legislation. As a result of this work, there are plenty resolutions adopted by the Common Market Group, which is evidence of this body's activity. Nonetheless, its work is not limited to that kind of innovation as we will intend to demonstrate.

8.5.1 1995–2010 Contributions

Thanks to a great variety of initiatives, describing in detail CT 7's actions is quite difficult. By way of illustration, we will underline the following.

8.5.1.1 The Common Regulation for Consumer Protection

On November 29, 1997, the Protocol for Consumer Protection in Mercosur, containing unified standards, came to the fore. It disciplined the consumers' rights without indicating procedural instruments to safeguard their implementation. Without addressing international consumer relation, the text in question regulates the consumers' material rights without pointing to any procedure to make those rights effective.[22]

Drawn on five resolutions[23] discussed in Fortaleza, that measure was the object of critique on the part of the Brazilian government insofar as the Protocol

[20]Ministry of Justice (2015), p. 23.

[21]See Ata n° 4, da LXXII Reunião Ordinária do CT n° 7, Anexo IV (Proposta de Curso MERCOSUL de Defesa do Consumidor). Brasília, 6 e 7/12/2012. Available at: http://www.mercosur.int/innovaportal/v/383/2/innova.front/busqueda_avanzada, accessed on 7/1/2016.

[22]Marques (1997), p. 102.

[23]The resolutions that form part of the Protocol Project are: (a) Resolution n° 123/1996, on qualification of consumer, supplier, consumption relationship, product and service; (b) Resolution n° 124/1996, on basic consumer rights; (c) Resolution n° 125/1996, on the quality level, risks, health and safety of products and services; (d) Resolution n° 126/1996 on misleading and abusive advertising; (e) Resolution n° 127/1996, on contractual guarantee.

guarantees consumer rights far lower than those enshrined in the Brazilian law. During the 15th meeting of the Mercosur Trade Commission, held in Montevideo on December 9 and 10, 1997, the said Protocol was then rejected.

Thereby, resolutions already indicated could not enter into force.

Since then, the CT 7 had to renew its work on the drafting of legal instruments that brought together minimum guidelines instead of extensive and detailed rules.[24]

8.5.1.2 The Santa Maria Protocol on International Jurisdiction on Consumer Relations

In conformity with Decision n° 10, the Mercosur Common Market adopted the Protocol on International Jurisdiction of Consumer Relations on November 22, 1996.

The Protocol regulated the international jurisdiction for contracts[25] with consumers, limiting its scope to contracts of credit sale, supply of tangible goods, provision of services, including loans and other credit operations. Article 1 excludes contracts of carriage. It is silent about consumer relations through public means.[26]

To be applied, both the supplier and the consumer must have their domicile in different member states of Mercosur, or if they have their domicile in the same country, the most characteristic performance of consumer relation is carried out in another state of Mercosur. Yet to define the international nature of consumer relation is required an advertising or a proposal in the consumer's domicile, as well as the making of a contract in his domicile (Article 2).[27]

As regards the jurisdiction, the Protocol sets forth as a general rule the possibility for a consumer to lodge a judicial action where he has a permanent domicile (Article 4), given the huge obstacles of a foreign lawsuit.[28]

Moreover, it provides concurrent alternative jurisdictions for the benefit of the consumers, for instance, the jurisdiction of the states' courts in which the contract was concluded, of the service provision, of delivery of goods, of the defendant's domicile, since they belong to countries with reasonable links with consumer relation.[29]

---

[24] About the topic, see: Vieira (2013), pp. 61–64.

[25] Criticisms of this material delimitation can be found in: Klausner (2005), pp. 122–123.

[26] All. "Mercosur". In: Fernández Arroyo DP (ed) 2010, p. 627.

[27] Dreyzin De Klor et al. (2003), pp. 198–199.

[28] Wehner (2001), p. 156.

[29] Tellechea Bergman (2002), p. 92.

Yet the Protocol foresees rules on the effectiveness of foreign sentences, in consonance with Article 11 and following, being that cooperation will be conducted by central authorities.[30]

However, despite its vanguard nature, the Santa Maria Protocol has never entered into force since Article 18 subordinates its validity to the effectiveness of the Common Regulation of Consumer Protection.

8.5.1.3 The Inter-institutional Agreement Between Bodies of Consumer Protection of Mercosur Member States on Behalf of Visitor Consumer

Such agreement was approved on June 3, 2004, in Buenos Aires, Argentina.[31]

Pursuant to Article 3, consumer tourists in the region will be advised and informed with regard to their rights. Fast and efficient administrative mechanisms will be in force to settle disputes stemming from the consumer's stay in a distinct state, taking account of rules of the host country.

At the meeting on August 16 and 17, 2012, the member states of Mercosur decided to start the phase of implementation of that agreement. The pilot project had the support of the Superintendence of Consumer Protection (PROCON's) of Rio de Janeiro and São Paulo.

On January 10, 2013, the PROCONs, together with the Consumer National Bureau (SENACON) officially launched the Form[32] for Complaints of Visitor Consumer in conjunction with Uruguay and Venezuela.

Once a claim is lodged, authorities of both countries shall remain in contact for information exchange and cooperation in pursuit of a mutually satisfactory agreement.

In subsequent meetings of the CT 7, from 2013 onwards, other tourist destinations adhered to the pilot project, namely, the Autonomous City of Buenos Aires, San Carlos de Bariloche, Curitiba, Porto Alegre, Natal, and Fortaleza.

8.5.2 *The Legacy from 2011 to 2015*

From 2011 on, there has been a great intensity of movement in the development of projects and policies by the CT # 7. Many of these projects were born out of the

[30]About the topic, see: Vieira. *Protección Internacional del Consumidor. Procesos de Escasa Cuantía en los Litigios Transfronterizos*. Op. cit., pp. 73–75.

[31]MERCOSUR/LV GMC/DI n° 12/2004. Available at: http://www.mercosur.int/msweb/SM/DefCons/es/Acu_Def_Cons_Vis_ES.pdf, Accessed on 19/1/2016. (Effective.)

[32]The form to be presented by the tourist consumer is available at: http://www.procon.sp.gov.br/noticia.asp?id=3365; http://www.indepabis.gob.ve/MERCOSUR; http://www.consumidor.gub.uy/informacion/index.php?SectionCode=MENU&IndexId=433, both accessed on 7/2/2014.

Statute of Citizenship of Mercosur, approved by Decision n° 64-2010 of the Mercosur Common Group. It established the need to create, before the conclusion of that Statute, which would culminate on March 26, 2021, a System of Mercosur Consumer Protection comprising (a) a Mercosur Information System and Consumer Protection; (b) a regional action of capacity building, represented by the creation of the Consumer Protection Mercosur School; and (c) the drafting of Mercosur standards for international consumer contracts. The following are instances.

8.5.2.1 The Draft Agreement on Applicable Law Relating to International Consumer Contracts

The Brazilian delegation presented a draft resolution to Mercosur Common Group on law applicable to international consumer contracts during the regular meeting of the CT 7 on August 18 and 19, 2010, in Rio de Janeiro.

Analyzed, revised, and extended in the following meetings of the CT 7, this draft had four different versions.[33] Approved as Decision Project n° 15/2012, the latest version contains the Mercosur Agreement on the Applicable Law to International Consumer Contracts.[34]

Its first articles are dedicated to qualifications and to contracts that were excluded.[35]

With respect to the applicable law, Article 4, which governs the contracts concluded by the consumer, the latter being in the state of domicile, employs alternative connection elements, such as the consumer's domicile, place of conclusion or execution of the contract, and headquarters of the supplier of goods or services, allowing the parties to choose the applicable law. In the absence of a valid election or lacking the exercise of this right, the rule provides for the application of the law of the consumer's domicile since it is presumed to be the most favorable rule to the vulnerable party of the contractual relation.

Regarding the applicable law, Claudia Lima Marques points out that the law chosen in the adhesion contracts ought to be compared to that of the consumer's domicile law, and in case of conflict, the judge should opt for the most favorable law to the latter. According to the author, we seek a pedagogical effect in the sense that suppliers choose barely the most favorable law in an adhesion contract, which

[33]Comments on the four different versions of the Project can be found at: Vieira (2015), pp. 159–179.

[34]See Ata n° 3 da LXXXIX Reunião Ordinária do GMC. Anexo III. Cuiabá, 18/10/2012. Available at: http://www.MERCOSUR.int/innovaportal/file/4945/1/gmc_2012_ata03_pt.pdf, accessed on 19/1/2016.

[35]According to art. 3 of the standard in comment, the commercial contracts between professional suppliers of goods and services, questions arising from the marital status of the persons and the capacity of the parties, the contractual obligations that had as main objective succession questions, testamentary matters, matrimonial property regime, among others, are excluded.

is presumably that of the consumer's domicile. A judge must apply only the most beneficial law or, if necessary, decide grounded on the law of the consumer's domicile.[36]

In turn, Article 5 is intended to regulate contracts concluded by the consumer, being this out of his state domicile. For contracts concluded by a tourist, the consumer is equally permitted to choose the applicable law, whether the parties opt for the law in force where the contract was made or executed or the law of the consumer's domicile. The choice is solely valid if the law is the most favorable to the vulnerable party. The law of the place of contract shall be applied in case of absence or invalidity of the law previously chosen.

Still, the project provides the need for electing the applicable law in writing, after the parties' consent and knowledge. Likewise, in adhesion contracts, the law that the supplier chooses should be clearly expressed through information given to the consumer, as well as in the contract itself, with the goal of securing transparency and legal certainty.

The law in force in the state of the consumer' domicile must be applied to travel and tourism contracts, concluded in tourist packages or combined services, provided that such contracts have the place of performance outside that state (Article 7).

Unfortunately, we observe that the course of the project is paralyzed due to divergences pointed by the Venezuela delegation, which has interest in revising the entire proposal.

8.5.2.2 Resolution n° 34/2011 on Basic Concepts in Consumer Law

The Extraordinary Meeting of the Common Market Group, held in Montevideo, approved Resolution n° 34 on basic concepts in consumer protection[37] on December 17, 2011. That Resolution adopts definitions and concepts applicable to consumer relations within member states, employing uniform qualifications for consumers, suppliers, consumer relations, products, services and binding offer, and the information duty, as a corollary of the intrinsic obligation of transparency.

Thus, in accordance with Article 1 (a), "Consumer is any natural or legal person who acquires or uses products or services in the gratuitous or onerous way as a final recipient, in a consumer relation or as result or because of it. Consumer is not considered who do not constitute final recipient that acquires, stores, uses, or consumes products or services in order to integrate them as input directly to other products or services in the production process, processing, marketing or provision to third parties."

[36]Marques (2013), p. 180.

[37]MERCOSUR/GMC/RES. n° 34/2011. Published in: *Boletín Oficial del MERCOSUR*. N° 48. Available at: http://www.mercosur.int/innovaportal/v/3186/2/innova.front/resoluciones_2011, Accessed on 3/8/2015.

As can be seen, it is quite broad the autonomous qualification that Mercosur adopts to the extent that it is based on the finalist theory by considering the consumer as a final recipient of products and services purchased, without excluding the bystander or an assimilated consumer.[38]

8.5.2.3 The Products and Services Alert Protocol Project Considered Potentially Harmful or Dangerous

The meeting of the CT 7, held in Brasilia, began to debate a minute of a Protocol on Recall of Products and Services[39] on May 21, 2015.

That project reveals the concern of the CT 7 with the need to call consumers and the withdrawal of products and services that have been put into the market, which may pose a risk to consumer health and safety when they can cause consumption accidents.

Thus, the protocol project provides in Article 3 the supplier's duty, after taking cognizance of the harmfulness or dangerousness of a product or service, to report it immediately in writing to the national protection agencies to the consumer of the states and the regulatory bodies involved, describing, among others, the defect and risks, as well as indicating the geographical distribution of the product or service and steps that have been and will be taken. The project also warns that the direct individual communication to the consumer, through websites, does not extinguish the supplier's obligation to collective communication about the harmfulness and dangerousness of the products that were put into the market (Article 6, Paragraph 3). Further, pursuant to the project, the supplier has the obligation to send reports to national regulatory agencies for consumer protection, with a maximum time frame of 60 days, communicating the amount of recalled or repaired services, their geographical distribution, and the number of affected consumers while mentioning additional measures relative to products that have not been collected or repaired (Article 8).

8.5.2.4 The School of Consumer Protection in Mercosur

As referred to at the inception, the Statute of Mercosur Citizenship determines that the creation of Mercosur System for Consumer Protection shall be composed of a regional action of capacity building, represented by the School for Consumer Protection in Mercosur.

---

[38]Notwithstanding the importance of the mentioned Resolution, it still lacks validity.

[39]The entire content of the Project can be consulted in: Ata n° 01/2015 da LXXVII Reunião Ordinária do CT n° 7, Anexo VI. Brasília, 21 e 22/5/2015. Available at: http://www.mercosur.int/innovaportal/v/383/2/innova.front/busqueda_avanzada, Access on 19/1/2016.

This school began to be generated from the ordinary meeting of the CT 7, which took place in the city of Buenos Aires on April 12 and 13, 2012.

Afterward, the meeting of the CT 7 approved the proposal of a course for consumer protection[40] on the basis of a handbook especially conceived to this end, on December 6 and 7, in Brasilia. That handbook[41] was officially lunched at the ordinary meeting of the Mercosur Group, in August, 2015, in Brasilia, On that occasion, member states decided to announce the Mercosur Online Courses for Consumer Protection.

Of note, the Mercosur School for Consumer Protection finds itself in an implementation phase being expected to have positive results in the short run, such as regional actions of capacity building and the consumers' awareness on their rights.

8.6 Conclusions and Perspectives

To deepen economic integration, it is indispensable to put into practice measures protecting the consumer who acquires or uses foreign products or services without leaving his home state.

In that vein, the CT 7 plays a fundamental role constituting a touching stone of the process aimed at harmonizing legislation. In search of safety, transparency, and predictability to consumers, the CT 7 approved many projects that did not become binding because of national governments' disinterests, unpreparedness, divergences, or negligence.

Surely, in this scenario of back and forth, an unprotected consumer consumes less. Hence, GDP diminishes. Regional integration is reduced and weakened. Then international trade experiences a negative impact as a consequence of the drop in economic exchanges. We expected that the projects indicated above would gain strength in a way that Mercosur would serve as a reference to other integration projects in terms of favoring cross-border consumer to decisively influence national laws.

[40]See Ata n° 4/2012 da LXXII Reunião Ordinária do CT N° 7. Anexo IV. Brasília, 6 e 7/12/2012. Available at: http://www.mercosur.int/innovaportal/v/383/2/innova.front/busqueda_avanzada, Accessed on 19/1/2016.

[41]See the bilingual version of the manual mentioned in: Ministry of Justice. National Consumer Secretariat. Senacon. Op. Cit., 414 pp.

References

All PM (2010) MERCOSUR. Consumer Protection in International Private Relationships – La Protection des Consommateurs dans les Relations Privées Internationales. CEDEP, Asunción

Amaral Júnior Ado (2015) Curso de Direito Internacional Público, 5ª ed. Atlas, São Paulo

Bourgoignie T (2009) Integración regional y la protección del consumidor en las Américas y en Europa. Intégration Économique Régionale et la Protection du Consommateur. Éditions Yvon Blais, Cowansville-Québec

Czar De Zalduendo S (2013) Integración: nociones generales. Integración económica e integración regional. In: Negro S (Dir.) Derecho de la Integración (Manual), 2ª ed. BdeF, Buenos Aires

Dreyzin De Klor A, Uriondo De Martinoli A, Noodt Taquela MB (2003) Dimensiones convencional e institucional de los sistemas de jurisdicción internacional de los Estados mercosureños. Derecho Internacional Privado de los Estados del MERCOSUR. Zavalia, Buenos Aires

Fellous BE (2003) Proteção do Consumidor no MERCOSUL e na União Europeia. Revista dos Tribunais, São Paulo

Klausner EA (2005) Jurisdição internacional em matéria de relações de consumo no MERCOSUL – sugestões para a reedição do Protocolo de Santa Maria. Revista de Direito do Consumidor. N° 54. Abr./Jun.

Marques CL (1997) Regulamento comum de defesa do consumidor do Mercosul – Primeiras observações sobre o Mercosul como legislador da proteção do consumidor. Revista de Direito do Consumidor. N° 23-24. Jul./Dez

Marques CL (1999) Direitos do consumidor no Mercosul: algumas sugestões frente ao impasse, Revista de Direito do Consumidor. N° 32. Out./dez.

Marques CL (2009) Consumer protection policy in Mercosur: an evolution. Regional Economic Integration and Consumer Protection. Ivon Blais, Québec

Marques CL (2013) Comércio eletrônico de consumo internacional: modelos de aplicação da lei mais favorável ao consumidor e do privilégio de foro. A Proteção do Consumidor no Brasil e no Quebec: diálogos de direito comparado. La Protection du Consommateur au Québec et au Brésil: échanges de droit compare. Editora da UFF, Niterói

Ministério da justiça (2015) Secretaria nacional do consumidor. Senacon. Manual de Defesa do Consumidor. MERCOSUL e Peru. MJ, Brasília

Ribeiro BM, Zordan FHZ (2006) A necessidade da harmonização legislativa no Mercosul para a proteção jurídica do consumidor. In: Menezes W (Coord.) Estudos de Direito Internacional – Anais do 4° Congresso Brasileiro de Direito Internacional – 2006, vol VI. Juruá, Curitiba

Ruiz Díaz Labrano R (2014) Derechos del Consumidor y del Usuario de Servicios. Ley n° 1334/98 de Defensa del Consumidor y del Usuario. La Ley, Asunción

Scotti LB (2013) El derecho de la integración en el MERCOSUR. In: Inegro S (Dir.) Derecho de la Integración (Manual), 2ª ed. BdeF, Buenos Aires

Stiglitz G (1995) El derecho del consumidor en Argentina y en el MERCOSUR. La Ley, Tomo

Tellechea Bergman E (2002) La Dimensión Judicial del Caso Privado Internacional en el Ámbito Regional. Fundación de Cultura Universitaria, Montevideo

Vieira LK (2013) Protección Internacional del Consumidor. Procesos de Escasa Cuantía en los Litigios Transfronterizos. BdeF, Montevideo-Buenos Aires

Vieira LK (2015) El Proyecto de Acuerdo del MERCOSUR sobre Derecho Aplicable en Materia de Contratos Internacionales de Consumo. Revista de Direito do Consumidor. N° 99. Mai./Jun.

Wehner U (2001) Contratos internacionais: proteção processual do consumidor, integração econômica e internet. Revista de Direito do Consumidor. N° 38. Abr./Jun.

Chapter 9
25 Years to Celebrate: Horizons Reached by the 1990 Brazilian Consumer Protection Code and Horizons to Come, Especially on the International Protection of Consumers

Claudia Lima Marques

9.1 Introduction

The horizon is where the sky meets the earth, when they form a single line of blue and green, as if it were possible to achieve the impossible, to have the best of Earth and Heaven in only one destiny. Horizon is where we want to reach; it is the dream, very remote, but it is also the desirable, the success, and the way to the future. In this article, we will use the figure of speech "horizons reached" (Part I) and "horizon to come" (Part II) to tell the beautiful story of consumer law's 25 years of prosperity and victory since the enactment of the Brazilian Consumer Protection Code in 1990 due to the inspiration arising from the Review of the UN Guidelines for Consumer Protection in 2015, and the Brazilian Consumer Protection Code revision, in order to ponder how the future of consumer law could be in Brazil.

In Brazil, it was the Federal Constitution of 1988 that determined the establishment of a Consumer Protection Code (Article 48 of the Acts and Constitutional Provisions); thus, Law no. 8.078 of September 11, 1990, unanimously passed by the Brazilian Parliament and also known as the *Consumer Protection Code* (hereinafter CDC), completed, in March 2016, 25 years of being force.[1]

There is, indeed, much to celebrate in these 25 years. Many were the victories and achievements conquered by the civil society organizations, scholars and the

Some parts of the text were parts from my previous study, Marques, Claudia Lima. 25 years of the consumer defense code and the suggestions outlined by the 2015 review of the UN Guidelines for consumer protection to update, published in *Revista de Direito do Consumidor*, vol. 103 (2016).

[1]See Benjamin et al. (2014), p. 34 et seq.

C.L. Marques (✉)
Faculty of Law, Federal University of Rio Grande do Sul, Porto Alegre, Brazil
e-mail: cmarques.ufrgs@gmail.com

C. Lima Marques, D. Wei (eds.), *Consumer Law and Socioeconomic Development*,
DOI 10.1007/978-3-319-55624-6_9

Drafting Committee,[2] the Public Attorney's Office, the Public Defender's Office, the consumer agencies (called in Brazil PROCONs), the lawyers, and the judges. However, above all, these were achievements made by Brazil toward economic development and to a more harmonic and healthier consumer society in order to recognize the duty of the State to protect vulnerable individuals in the market, i.e., the consumer (as established by Article 5, XXXII, of the Brazilian Constitution of 1988).[3] Indeed, a law may help the development of a country, especially if it is an "economic" law, establishing conduct on how one should proceed in the market (as prescribed by Article 170 and Article 218 of the Brazilian Constitution of 1988), such as the Brazilian Consumer Protection Code.[4] A law with a social function and of public policy can consolidate and guide public policy, a policy of consumers' relations; create a national consumer protection system; and guide State agencies that defend consumers, individually and collectively, as the CDC has done for the past 25 years.[5]

As I have written before,[6] this law of "public order and social interest" (CDC, Article 1) that renewed the foundations of Brazilian civil law was innovative when regulating advertisement and the regime of service contracts and in introducing "the dialog between sources"[7] in Brazil. It was decisive in regulating the quality of products, subscription contracts, and debt collection and also in consolidating the principle of good faith in relations between experts-suppliers and lay consumers; it

---

[2]See Ada et al. (2007), p. 9 et seq.

[3]See Marques et al. (2010).

[4]So teach Bruno Miragem: "the consumer law also has clear promotional character in economic perspective. Not only is justified under the ethical basis of protection of the human person in the society of consumption, but also under the discretion of the economy that drives the content of legislative intervention of the State in regulating the market. It means saying: by imposing legal obligations to suppliers, aims at establishing a *standard* of conduct that not only individual relations between consumers and suppliers, but as a standard of quality and efficiency of the market as a whole, generating a positive effect not only the interests of individual consumers, but also to the development of economic relations. Is that factor contributes with its own economic development." (Miragem 2012, p. 41 et seq).

[5]See Miragem (2003), pp. 120–164.

[6]The next three paragraphs were removed from the article, Marques, Claudia Lima. 25 anos de Código de Defesa do Consumidor e as sugestões traçadas pela Revisão de 2015 das Diretrizes da ONU de proteção dos consumidores para a atualização, published in *Revista de Direito do Consumidor*, vol. 103 (2016), p. 1 (in press).

[7]Dialogue of the sources is an expression created by the German author, Erik Jayme, to indicate the simultaneous and coherent application of more than one legal source in time, that no more 'exclude', on the contrary, 'dialogue' under the guidance of the Constitution. "Dialogue" of laws/fonts" (di + a = two or more; logos = thinking or logic), an expression created in its course of the Hague (Jayme 1995, p. 259), meaning the current simultaneous, coherent and coordinated application of legislative sources plúrimas, special laws (such as the CDC) and General (as the CC/2002), with converging fields of application, but not more equal, so that there is no 'conflict of laws' and Yes, apparent conflict that is resolved by dialogue between the constitutional values and present in these standards. See Marques Claudia Lima, O 'diálogo das fontes' como método da nova teoria geral do direito: um tributo a Erik Jayme, in Marques (2012a) p. 18 and sec.

was revolutionary in harmonizing the activities of credit scoring and negative credit data, privatized public servers, and the suppliers of products and services in general. Important horizons of development have been achieved in the country as the CDC protected everyone equally—the rich and the poor,[8] PhDs and the uneducated, children and adults, respecting their dignity and differences,[9] imposing the same quality and fairness in performance, considering all the final recipients of products and services as consumers (CDC, Article 2), equating all to vulnerable people (CDC, Article 2—sole paragraph—and Article 29), and extending the protection to all victims of accidents originated from services and products (CDC, Article 17).[10] This equality of the different,[11] of the lay, of the nonprofessionals, of the weak and the recognition of the vulnerability of consumers (CDC, Article 4, I), as stated by Antonio Herman Benjamin, is the touchstone,[12] the cornerstone, that helped build this 25-year success.

There is also a future and a certain future![13] In celebrating its 30th anniversary, the UN General Assembly approved on December 22, 2015, the revision of the Guidelines for Consumer Protection (UN Guidelines for Consumer Protection of 1985, revised in 1999 to include sustainable consumption and then in 2015),[14] bringing important suggestions to address the newest issues of the consumer society, such as online consumption through mobile and other electronic means; privacy; the

---

[8]In this sense, see Benjamin (1993a), p. 200: "consumers are not equal to each other, either in the same country or in different countries. There are rich and poor consumers; There are informed consumers and others to ignore completely the new technologies; There are clamouring for this much yearned consumers and other liabilities; for consumers with access to justice and others that even on take your complaints to the courts." And, in paragraph 6, would state: "the right of the consumer, especially in least developed countries, with extremely heterogeneous populations, have to take into consideration such differences, because, otherwise, will reflect only the needs of those consumers with power of representation and be heard, taking them, therefore, to be used by the legal system. We have, then, a consumer law of the "gifts", which therefore ignores the "absent", those who, for various reasons, has no place or voice in the legislative process and the judicial process. ... In Latin America, in recent years, poverty has exploded. On the one hand, we have the upper class with only a privileged few; on the other, the middle class, subject to a continuous process of impoverishment, shrinking day by day. Soon, formulate the consumer law in such terms, as an instrument of protection fundamentally these two classes, is put in a position by removing his elitist acts of everyday consumers, of all consumers, wealthy or poor, informed or uninformed."

[9]Erik Jayme, commenting on a case of abusive publicity in Brazil says: "the reaction of the Brazilian law put in the foreground the dignity of the poor (*Würde der Armen*). The design of consumer ('*Verbraucherleitbild*') in Brazil was so impregnated of the need of material sectors of society, which could not be forgotten." (Jayme 1999, pp. 24–40).

[10]See about the definitions of consumers at the CDC Marques (2014a), pp. 300–415.

[11]So we defend in Marques and Miragem (2014), p. 191.

[12]See Benjamin and Marques (2014), pp. 303–365.

[13]Here Inspire me the Article about the present, past and future of the French Consumption Code of Mazeaud, Denis (2013), pp. 1–4.

[14]See the original version, A/RES/39/248, 16 April 1985 and its importance in Brazil, in the work of Sodre (2009).

protection of hypervulnerable consumers[15]; financial and credit services; tourism and mass transportation; the power densification of administrative consumer protection agencies; and international consumption—all exactly the themes of the Federal Senate Project now under consideration by the House of Representatives under PLS no. 281 from 2012 and PLS no. 283 also from 2012, which aim to update the CDC[16]—a process that began in 2010, while celebrating 20 years of the Code, with the inclusion of the international protection of consumers.[17]

As I had the honor to serve as Rapporteur-General of the Draft of the Bill, under the engaged chairmanship of Hon. Antonio Herman Benjamin[18] at the Legal Committee of the Senate[19] that prepared the CDC Update Bills[20] (PLS nos.

[15]In accordance to the Law, the expression is "vulnerable and disadvantage consumers" (CDC, article 5, III), as the expression hiper-vulnerable is Antonio Herman Benjamin's, who initially used it in lectures and, later, in his rulings, i.e.: "the ethical-political category, and also legal, of vulnerable subjects includes a subgroup of subjects hiper-vulnerable, [...] When you protect the hiper-vulnerable, strictly speaking ends benefited is truly the society itself, as expected respect for the collective social inclusion pact imperative, which is expensive, not for his patrimonial facet, but precisely by embracing the intangible and humanist dimension of the principles of human dignity and solidarity. Ensure judicial inclusion (that is, recognize the legitimacy to Act) of these people hiper-vulnerable, including of the intermediaries who is up to represent them, not to leave any rough justice for lack of rights spokesman offended" (Superior Court of Justice, Suit: REsp no. 931,513/RS, Rapporteur: Hon. Herman Benjamin, Judged in: 11/25/2009, Laurence 9/27/2010). See also, Marques (2014a), pp. 287–331.

[16]See the approval in the Committee on Constitution and justice of the Senate in September 2015, http://www.12.senado.leg.br and in plenary and referral to the Board in November 2015, in http://www25.senado.leg.br/web/atividade/materias/-/materia/106768. The projects now take the numbers 3514 PL, 2015 (PLS 281.2012) and PL 3515, 2015 (PLS 283, 2012), but in this text we will keep the numbers by which were known, of the Senate.

[17]See Senado (2010), p. 11ff.

[18]The General report of the Commission informs that the Commission began its work on 15 December 2010 and held 37 meetings (12 regular meetings, public hearings and 17 8 technical meetings) with the sectors concerned, looking to hear all representative segments operating in law and consumer protection, in order to complete their work as technique, democratic and transparent as possible. *Atualização do Código de Defesa do Consumidor – Relatório*, Presidency of the Federal Senate, Brasilia, 2012, p. 20.

[19]The Committee of legal experts was chaired by the Honorable judge from the Superior Court of Justice, Mr. Antonio Herman Benjamin, and having as members myself, Claudia Marques Lima (UFRGS), as Rapporteur-General, and Ada Grinover Pellegrini professors (USP), Leonardo Roscoe Bessa (UniCeub), Roberto Pfeiffer (USP) and Kazuo Watanabe (USP). The three focal points of the work of the Commission of Jurists was the credit scheme and the fight against the overindeptedness of the consumer, improving the effectiveness of the procedural part of the CDC and the phenomenon of e-commerce. See Marques and Miragem (2012), p. 331.

[20]See http://www.senado.gov.br/senado/codconsumidor/default.asp. In particular, the Senate projects that are being discussed today, Bill No. 281, from 2012, presented by Senator José Sarney, intended to amend Law no. 8.078 of September 11, 1990 (the Brazilian Consumer Protection Code), to improve the General provisions of chapter I of title I of the bill, and provide for electronic commerce; and Senate Bill No. 283, from 2012, also presented by Senator Jose Sarney, in order to amend the CDC to improve the discipline of consumer credit and on the prevention of over-indebtedness.

281/2012, 282/2012, and 283/2012), and to participate, along with Professor. Dr. Wei Dan, as an observer on behalf of the "International Law Association" at the meetings held in the UN to revise the Guidelines for Consumer Protection,[21] it seems to me that the coincidence of these two "revisions" theme necessarily leads me to the conclusion that the time is appropriate to advance the rights of the consumers and confirms the urgent necessity to revise the national bill, at least in the areas drawn by the UN Guidelines.

The purpose of this article is to demonstrate some of the contributions of the Consumer Protection Code for the country's development in civil law—leaving for other scholars to contribute in other areas such as administrative law, civil procedure, and criminal law—and, in a second part, this article will analyze the international protection of consumers according to the CDC updating proposal and toward the directions outlined by the UN Guidelines revisions of 1999 and 2015. The UN Guidelines revision of 2015 has been the most important one in the past 30 years, pointing to some changes that are about to be implemented in Brazil and that must serve as an inspiration to national legislators,[22] especially regarding the international protection of consumers.

9.2 The Consumer Protection Code: Horizons to Celebrate in These 25 Years

If there is a lot to celebrate in these 25 years of the enactment of the Brazilian Consumer Protection Code—a law that has profoundly changed the market and Brazilian law—I would like to analyze the points of greatest success and their impact in practice (letter A, below) in order to make, subsequently, an assessment of these 25 years, dividing them into eras, periods, or consumer protection stages in Brazil, also indicating the points at which the CDC did not achieve a continued success or the limits that had been identified regarding its implementation or the adjustments to the rules initially planned (letter B, below).[23]

---

[21] See http://www.ila-hq.org/en/news/index.cfm/nid/2F35999B-ADFA-4719-9DB11D5CECBAD1A8.

[22] The Department of Trade and Industry ('DTI') of the Philippines has announced it will update its consumer protection law (the Consumer Act of the Philippines) with the new issues raised by the updated Guidelines, see Philippines/United Nations: DTI welcomes revised UN guidelines for consumer protection, in *Thai News Service*, December 30, 2015 (available at http://academic.lexisnexis.nl/, 03.01.2015).

[23] The following excerpts were extract of the article, published in the Marques (2016) in press.

9.2.1 *The Success of the Brazilian Consumer Code: Guiding Principles*

In an assessment of the 25 years of the CDC, it is possible to say that the first success was the constitutional mandate to establish a "code"—a systematic and organized set of articles on consumer protection. This systematization of standards in a microsystem (as expressed by Natalino Irti) facilitated the awareness of the new rules, giving strength and promoting the microcode. As I have written before, three decisions of the authors of the Draft were basic to the success of the CDC, or even were the success of this microcodex "themselves": (a) the plural concept of consumer, with four different definitions to this economic agent (Article 2 caput and its sole paragraph, Article 17, and Article 29 of the CDC); (b) the incorporation of the pragmatic theory of quality, from North America,[24] which relativizes the *summa divisio* between contractual and noncontractual liability to ensure in all consumer relations a quality adjustment (without vices) of goods and services and quality assurance (without defects) of goods and services; (c) a new contract theory,[25] guided by the objective good faith principle—annexing duty of conducts and (basic) good faith rights in the law for consumption relations—as well as by viewing obligation as a process in time, valuating the *pre* and *post* contractual phases, and imposing a new regime to contracts that require (services) and contracts that provide (products). These decisions were, in my view, the "strategic bases" to the success of this Code and may be resystematized in two principles.

9.2.1.1 Principle of Material Equality and the Equality of the Group of Consumers

In 1990, before the enactment of the CDC, the legal situation of consumers was one of a deep inequality when compared to the suppliers, experts, and professionals who supply products and render services in the market. If there were formal equality, the material inequality was huge, and this was prejudicial for the consumer market's development in Brazil. As Antônio Herman Benjamin teaches: "Before the CDC, the Brazilian consumer did not have any general law acting on their behalf, considering their special condition as vulnerable individuals of the consumer market. Their protection, under the civil law, was made with great difficulties,

[24]The quality theory was brought to Brazil by Antonio Herman Benjamin, after his master's studies at the University of Illinois, USA and adapted to Brazilian reality, also with the help of law purchased, in particular European policy of 1985 on the subject, see details in Benjamin, Antonio Herman. Arts. 12–27. In: Oliveira, Juarez (coord.). *Comentários ao Código de Proteção do Consumidor*. São Paulo: Saraiva, 1991 and by the same author, Chapter 5, the Manual already quoted from Marques/Benjamin/Bessa.

[25]See the use of the expression "new contractual theory" since the first edition in 1992, in Marques (2014a), p. 57ff.

using the obsolete rules of Civil Code. There was no law (or legal mechanism) that would properly address, for instance, publicity, the general conditions of contracts or the civil responsibility of the supplier. Thus, the consumer in Brazil was, in fact, totally unsupported to face the abuses in the consumer market. The Civil Code, promulgated in January 1st 1916, still governed almost all the consumer relations. Unnecessary to say that there was a disparity between the economic development stage of the country and the Civil Code content, created for an agrarian (with an incipient industrialization) and rural society (with a great part of the population living outside the cities), very different from the current society."[26]

The first decision that assured the CDC's success and created great practical impact was the one that observed the consumer in a plural form, as an individual, homogeneously, collectively, and with diffuse interests (CDC, Article 81—sole paragraph), assigning the four different definitions of consumer,[27] being the consumer who is the final recipient of products and services (*ex vi* CDC, Article 2 caput), i.e., not only the economical agent who contracts or acquires but also the one who is the final user (in Portuguese, *destinatário final)*[28]; being the consumer the collectivity, which intervenes in consumer relation (*ex vi* CDC, Article 2—sole paragraph), or a group of people, specific or not, exposed to commercial practices, to consumer subscription contracts, to contractual practices, to debt collection, inserted in negatives databases (CDC, Article 29),[29] or even the consumers of current and future generations, victims of accidents caused by products or services (*ex vi* CDC, Article 17).[30]

Compared to the Civil Code of 1916 and its rural and individualist perception of the human person, this view of an active actor or of a group of people in the same situation in the market or a of group or individual who is a subject of rights (see the consumers' basic rights in CDC, Article 6)[31] was a huge evolution that allowed the Brazilian market to escape from an individualistic (material) view to accompany the perception of collective and diffuse interests, which have already been foreseen in the civil procedure since the Public Civil Action Law of 1985. There is no doubt that this four consumer definitions are an elementary key in the practical success of

[26]Benjamin (1993b), pp. 269–270.

[27]Marques (2013), p. 25.

[28]See the work of Almedia (2003).

[29]See Miragem (2014), p. 147. See an example of a case law about negative database adjudged by the Brazilian Superior Court of Justice, in the Special Repetitive Motion no. 1.424.792/BA (Rapporteur: Hon. Luis Felipe Salomão, judged in 24/9/2014), that declared that: "*Considering the rules laid down in the Consumer Protection Code, even with the regular registration of the name of the debtor in the registration of credit protection agency, after full payment of the debt, it is for the lender to require the exclusion of discreditable record, within 5 (five) working days from the first working day after the full availability of the cash needed for the discharge of overdue debt*" (Superior Court of Justice, *AgRg in EDcl in REsp 1368258/MG*, Rapporteur Hon. Raul Araújo, fourth group, judged in 10/13/2015).

[30]See about the subject Bessa (2009), p. 55.

[31]See the leading cases, in Benjamin et al. (2013), p. 119ff.

the Code. This view of a more vulnerable agent or actor in the market was decisive for the evolution of the Brazilian consumer market, and also the consumer market development, which helped to stabilize the economy and to face economic crises.

The individual view of the problems was also prejudicial to the solution of collective problems. Even the public policies to the consumer society suffered because of this individualistic view that prescribed that a contract was just a concern to the parties, that the consumer accidents were "fatalities," and that only the proved guilt of the supplier could lead to liability and compensation. Damage prevention policies could only be born with the overcoming of this "individualistic" paradigm and when the notion of the consumer groups has triumphed.[32] The 2015 revision of the UN Guidelines for Consumer Protection has stressed the need of this collective paradigm on consumer protection.[33]

The notion of consumer in these 25 years has evolved. Before the Civil Code of 2002, a more maximalist view of the consumer (*maximalismo*) prevailed, being replaced by a finalistic view (*finalista*), which only considers as a consumer those that are vulnerable (it is assumed that every natural person is vulnerable) or that act after their area of expertise (if it is a legal entity). This finalistic view was even more humanized by the vulnerability test, as prescribed by the Superior Court of Justice to be "deep finalism" (*finalismo aprofundado*), which benefits embroiders, farmers, truck and taxi drivers, and small and microbusinesses, if outside of their professional activity or if they proved their technical, legal, informational, or factual vulnerability against those that render services or product supplier.[34]

The Brazilian legal definition of consumer is not a negative one (consumer would be the nonprofessional, for example). Instead, it is a positive definition (the last one to consume, who takes the product or service to the market, with no intention of reselling,[35] final, factual and economical user of the product and service).[36] Thus, we had overcome the initial criticisms for the inclusion of legal entities into the main definition of consumer, in CDC Article 2 caput.[37]

During the updating of the CDC, no definition was changed; on the contrary, the definitions were all preserved, proving the success of the preliminary draft. The

[32]See Marques (2013), p. 31.

[33]The new number 40 of the directive is a good example: "40. Member States should ensure that collective resolution procedures are expeditious, transparent, fair, inexpensive and accessible to both consumers and businesses, including those pertaining to over-indebtedness and bankruptcy cases."

[34]See the leading, in Garcia (2007), p. 9. Also, see Morato (2008).

[35]The jurisprudence teaches till today: "O Código de Defesa do Consumidor não se aplica ao caso em que o produto ou serviço é contratado para implementação de atividade econômica, já que não estaria configurado o destinatário final da relação de consumo." (STJ, EDcl no AREsp 122.199/SP, Rel. Ministro João Otávio de Noronha, Terceira Turma, julgado em 09/12/2014, DJe 12/12/2014).

[36]See Benjamin (1993), p. 269.

[37]See Miragem (2014), p. 143.

CDC's touchstone—vulnerability—was even extended and nuanced, be it through "deep finalism"[38] or through Antônio Herman Benjamin's hypervulnerability theory, or even by the decisions about the most vulnerable consumers (children, sick, illiterate,[39] elderly,[40] disabled people, etc.).[41] *Vulnus, vulnerare*—the origin of such expressions means injured.[42] Vulnerable is the one who can be or was injured.[43] Vulnerability has levels, and the law must recognize the necessity to effectively protect the weaker ones.[44] Currently, the hypervulnerability notion about some consumer groups is exactly the recognition that there are consumers that are more vulnerable (children, sick, elderly, disabled people, etc.) than others and that the market harasses them and tries to take advantage of their great vulnerability. The equality has to be "material," from opportunities to results—and not a mere formal equality. The CDC, in its 25 years of being in force, has helped the Brazilian market to understand this.

The CDC brought a new legal and political view on consumer protection: the one of prevention and integral reparation of damages. Not only that, but it also fights against the abuse of consumers, not just individually but also collectively (CDC, Article 4 and Article 6). This way, it finally consolidates the paradigm of equality of all group (collectivity) of consumers in a similar situation in Brazil, which was started by the Public Civil Action Law of 1985. Thus, this material autonomy of consumers having been set, it is necessary to ensure as well the autonomy of the weakest and most vulnerable ones.

9.2.1.2 Principle of Responsible Autonomy or "Framed" Autonomy Principle

True autonomy is always the freedom of others; the autonomy of the lay, the weaker, which are invited to negotiate; the consumer against the supplier. Nevertheless, private rights were all intended to protect the one who negotiates, who is a professional, who renders services or provides goods. In this sense, a substantial paradigm change was necessary in contracts and in noncontractual consumption relations. The

---

[38]This term was well accepted in the country, see the initial ideas in Marques, *Contratos*, p. 342 and following. Veja também, defendendo fortemente sua extensão aos micro e pequenos empresários, Oliveira, Júlio Moraes. *Consumidor-Empresário – A defesa do finalismo aprofundado*. Belo Horizonte: Arraes, 2012.

[39]See the Observatório do Crédito e Superendividamento MJ/UFRGS data, in Marques, Claudia Lima. A vulnerabilidade dos analfabetos e dos idosos na sociedade de consumo brasileira: primeiros estudos sobre a figura do assédio de consumo, in Marques and Gsell (2015), pp. 46–87.

[40]See about the elderly consumer subject the great book of Schmitt (2014).

[41]See about the subject, which supports that the hypervulnerables are mentioned in the Federal Constitution, Nishiama (2010), p. 229.

[42]This way teaches Fiechter-Boulvard (2000), p. 14.

[43]Lacour (2007), p. 28.

[44]Marques and Miragem (2014), p. 17.

CDC performed this substantive renovation of the consumption juridical relation, through the quality theory and a new contractual theory. Norbert Reich identified in European law what he called framed autonomy principle (*framed autonomy*).[45] The idea is inspiring because it recalls that the stronger autonomy is limited or is inserted in a legal "framework or frame"; in the definition of the legal transaction, such figurative speech is used to express the reserved space of the autonomy of will of the parties, the law being the framework or frame that upholds this private autonomy space. In this article, nevertheless, and in Portuguese law, I did not find a similar expression. I would like to nominate it as the "responsible autonomy principle," in order to recall its limits (contractual rights abuse) and its consequences, which is the suppliers' liability in case of autonomy abuse.

As I have already written, the CDC changed the contractual theory (from *pacta sunt servanda* to the good faith principle) and civil liability (from the "guilt" principle to the strict liability) paradigms in Brazil. These changes have helped a lot in the improvement of the quality of the Brazilian products and services, facilitating their exportation and acceptance—with security and adequacy—in the internal market.

Without doubt, the two biggest dogmatic changes in the Brazilian Civil Law originated from the Consumer Code: first, the theory of quality, which approximated the *summa* division between contract and tort laws with a pragmatic liability at the providers' chain for quality adequacy (faults of product or services—CDC, Article 18 and following) and for security quality (defects of product or services—CDC, Articles 12–17). That has strengthened the duty to inform, as well as the duty to prevent and reimburse the individual—homogeneous, collective, and diffuse—moral or material damages. Second is the new contractual theory, which approximated the contractual regimes for providing (product supply) and rendering (service supply), preparing Brazil for a new economy of services—a technological and informational one—valuing good faith throughout the entire period or for all the contractual *iter*, as well as the consumer's trust, and innovating when regulating publicity and its obligatory effects. The significant jurisprudence arising from this "material" section of the CDC (Articles 8–54) attests to the success of this renewing dogmatic view, which infuses, nowadays, the 2002 Civil Code itself.

Since I have approached both matters in previous occasions,[46] it seems unfit to repeat the idea here; hence, I will just highlight one conclusion: the CDC's practical success is directly linked to the realistic and pragmatic way it controlled the service regime, approximating the "production" and the "delivery." Services are better regulated in the CDC system than in the 2002 Civil Code, whose service supply view is still almost the same as the 1916 Civil Code, with merely two new articles on this section.[47] and lots of appendixes, such as the duty to inform, publicity, and

---

[45] Reich (2014), p. 48 and following.

[46] On the new contractual theory (p. 57 a 296) and the responsibility for the quality (p. 1285 a 1378), see Marques (2014a).

[47] See Miragem (2013), pp. 67–114.

the offer to an undetermined person to receive special attention, to the point that the CDC "objectifies" the noncompliance of the duty to inform in case of fault (CDC, Article 18) or defect (CDC, Article 12) of the information rendered as a contractual noncompliance (CDC, Article 35). Article 84 of the CDC, regulating the specific execution of the obligation, as well as Article 42, concerning debt collection, are examples of this pragmatic and very practically useful view, and so is Article 28, on disregarding the company's legal entity. The CDC is a postmodern law,[48] adapted to the increasingly virtual current consumer society, highly dependent on services and indebtedness. Below, there is a quick demonstration of the phases, ages, or stages that this Code went through in the past 25 years and its future prospects.

9.2.2 The "Ages" or "Stages" of the Consumer Code: CDC Assessment and Topics to Improve Consumer Protection in Brazil

As written by Ada Pelegrini Grinover and Antônio Herman Benjamin, each and "every consumer protective law has, therefore, the same ratio, in other words, to re-balance the consumer relation, by reinforcing, when it is possible, the consumer position, or by prohibiting and limiting certain practices on the market."[49] Consumer protection norms helped Brazil develop and increase its internal market and, with it, its economy. The second consumption stage, which arrived in Europe after the Second World War, arrives in Brazil after the Federal Constitution of 1988 and the restoration of democracy, with a mass consumption, a consumption of quality and generalization, no longer restricted to a privileged class. It is increasingly democratized in all social classes.[50]

In a realistic assessment, the CDC is one of the most breakthrough laws in the Brazilian legal system, especially in relation to private law, a dogma breakthrough that changed paradigms, hence its systematic valuation and the strong acceptance of the sources conversation theory by the Supreme Courts. But not all is good; lots of subjects have suffered a "step backwards" in these 25 years. Just as some stages had increased consumer protection, others saw its decrease and thus had less consumer protection.

[48] *See also:* Contratos bancários em tempos pós-modernos – Primeiras reflexões. *Revista de Direito do Consumidor* 25, p. 19 and following.

[49] Introdution by Benjamin Antônio Herman e Grinover, Ada Pellegrini, in Grinover et al. (2007).

[50] About Europe, see Lipovetzky (2006), p. 25: "La segunda fase del consumo, que nace alredor de 1950, señala el momento en el que la producción y el consumo de masas dejan de estar reservados para una clase privilegiada, en el que el individualismo se libera de las normas tradicionales y en el que aparece una sociedad cada vez más volcada hacia el presente y las novedades que trae, cada vez más regida por una lógica de seducción pensada bajo la forma de una hedonazación de la vida accesible a todas las capas sociales."

Just as observed in Mercosur,[51] the assured protection by the CDC for the consumer was not always the same. There have been stages when this protection was bigger and stages of less protection. In this article, we are going to call "CDC ages" this "age" or stages, in a retrospective of these 25 years.

9.2.2.1 Golden Age: The New Law Sparkle and the CDC Maximalist View (1988–2000)

The link between its protection in the 1988 Federal Constitution, in Articles 5, 170, V and 48 of ADCT, was decisive for the success of consumer law in Brazil.[52] The constitutional command was complied with only in September 1990 with the promulgation of the Consumer Defense Code (CDC). This Code's approval—which was made unanimously—was not an easy task. It is necessary to honor the authors of the Consumer Defense Code Preliminary Draft Bill.[53] They were pioneers in consumer protection, and under the wise coordination of Professor Ada Pellegrini Grinover (University of São Paulo) they achieved the creation of a renewing and effective law, whose success is due to an excellent adaptation effort of comparative law to the Brazilian reality. I had the honor to serve as Advisor of the Ministry of Justice at that time, and I could verify the solid ideas and theories used at the Consumer Code Bill. Many people helped to include the mention of consumer protection at the Federal Constitution of Brazil in 1988. Here I want to honor agricultural engineer Marilena Lazzarini, who then led the NGO IDEC, in São Paulo, and later became a member with outstanding performance of Consumers International, London.

The engaged work of the authors of the Preliminary Draft Bill was very important. After the approval of the Consumer Code, the authors of the Bill performed conferences in the whole of Brazil, in partnership with the Brazilian Bar Association (OAB), the Public Attorney Office, and the judiciary. It is worth mentioning the creation in 1991 of "Brasilcon," the Brazilian Institute of Politics and Consumer Law, in order to bring closer and empower the civil society and all the legal careers, highlighting the importance of this protective law, the Consumer Code. This was further enabled, by initiative of the visionary Antônio Herman Benjamin, who created the Journal of Consumer Law (*Revista de Direito do Consumidor*, edited by Thompson Reuters), in 1992, an important vehicle to

[51]See my opinion about the stages of the consumer protection in Mercosul, in the English chapter, Marques Claudia Lima. The Consumer Protection Policy in Mercosur. In: Marcílio Toscano Franca Filho, Lucas Lixinski, María Belén Olmos Giupponi. (Org.) (2010).

[52]This way also Nishiama (2010).

[53]The Committee that wrote the Draft Bill had the following members: Ada Pellegrini Grinover (Coordinator), Daniel Roberto Fink, José Geraldo Brito Filomeno, Kazuo Watanabe, Zelmo Denari, Antonio Herman V. Benjamin, Nelson Nery Junior, Marcelo Gomes Sodré and Mariângela Sarrubbo.

disseminate scientific and practical information and debates, to analyses case law and examples of the practice of the new consumer law.[54]

It is important to highlight that the Brazilian Consumer Code as a law has qualities (dogmatically and practical) infinitely greater than the 1916 Civil Code—which did not even include a good faith general clause.[55] It was also superior to the 1850 Commercial Code, very distant from the Brazilian reality in the '90s. The result of this success was the widespread application of the Consumer Code to approximately all contractual cases, also between businesses, which is called a "maximalist" or extensive interpretation of the notion of consumer, "maximizing" the scope of application of the Consumer Code also to these B2B contracts. The reaction—to this extensive use of the Consumer Code—comes in the form of a set of new special laws, for example, the Health Insurance Law in 1996. This golden age, with the acceptance and widespread application of the Consumer Code, lasted until 2000. In 2001, the Bank's Federation (hereinafter CONSIF, in the Portuguese acronym) has proposed a constitutional claim against the CDC (*Unconstitutionality Direct Action*—'ADIN' no. 2591), and in 2002 the new Civil Code was approved. The golden age came to an end.

9.2.2.2 The Silver Age: Doubts About the CDC's Application (2001–2006)

Doubts are like heavy clouds on the horizon, and the golden age of Consumer Protection Law ended exactly with the reaction of the most conservatives sections of economy, which launched a serious doubt regarding the CDC's application on some economic sectors. In the end of December in 2001, the Bank's Federation CONSIF filed an unconstitutionality claim against CDC Article 3, second paragraph, looking to achieve a privilege that the CDC would not be applicable to banks, insurers, credit cards, financial companies.

The ADIN of the banks was the greatest consumerist victory in those 25 years,[56] stopping the privilege of certain economic sectors (in this case banks, financial institutions, insurers, and credit card administrators) to be immune from the application of the Consumer Code. The CDC's rules of conduct would not apply to them because CONSIF claimed that, according to Article 192 of the Brazilian Constitution of 1988, only complementary laws could be applied to banks and financial service enterprises. This claim was dismissed by the expressive quorum of nine votes in favor of the entire CDC's constitutionality and 2 votes against it,

[54]Brasilcon was created by the Draft Law authors, as a scientific academic institute and it had as the first President, Antônio Herman Benjamin, who one year later was the founder of Revista de Direito do Consumidor, since the published and distributed by Ed. Revista dos Tribunais/Thompson Reuters, São Paulo. See details in Miragem et al. (2015), pp. 13–15.

[55]See more about the good faith general clause in the work of Martins (2002).

[56]See Marques (2007), pp. 40–75.

considering any interpretation of Article 3, paragraph 2, of the Consumer Code' constitutionally.[57]

The court stated in ADIN no. 2591 that "The protection to the consumer and the integrity of their rights represent mandatory commitments that the Brazilian State consciously assumed our legal system plan. (...) The National Constitutional assembly, in character absolutely groundbreaking, rose up the consumer protection to the main position of fundamental rights (Brazilian Constitution, art. 5, XXXII), assigning, yet, the principal structuring condition to our legal order (Brazilian Constitution, article 170, V)."[58]

Nevertheless, the victory of ADIN no. 2591 would only come in 2006, after even motions of clarifications under the decision's syllabus, considering if it would or not mention interest. The case solution took more than 6 years, a silver age, in which the initial force of the law was stopped. In 2002, the new Civil Code (Federal Law no. 10.406/2002) was approved, which repealed 1916's Civil Code and the first part of 1850's Commercial Code,[59] unifying the obligations regimen but preserving a special regimen to consumption relations, hence the importance of a dialogue between the sources.

Today there are still limit themes that escape from the CDC's application. In the definition of its scope of application, it is worth mentioning that the CDC is not yet applicable to residential rentals,[60] neither to the relations between the client and the

---

[57]See the final decision: "*Requests for clarification. Appellate legitimacy limited to the parties. Disregard of appeal submitted by amicus curiae. Requests for clarification opposed by the attorney general. Alleged contradiction. Changing the decision's summary. Restriction. Requests for clarification considered. (...) 5. Requests for clarification provided to reduce the summary of the judgment of the unconstitutionality direct action no. 2591, which shall have the following content, excluded statements for which there is no consensus: Article 3, § 2, of the CDC. Consumer Protection Code. Art. 5, XXXII, Constitution of 1988. Art. 170, V, Constitution of 1988. Financial Institutions. Subjecting them to the Consumer Protection Code. Unconstitutionality Direct Action Rejected. 1. Financial institutions are, all of them, reached by the rules conveyed by the Consumer Protection Code. 2. "Consumer" for the purposes of the Consumer Protection Code, is any person or entity that uses, as a final recipient, banking, financial and credit activity. 3. Direct Action Rejected.*" (Federal Supreme Court, ADI no. 2591 ED, Rappourteur: Hon. Eros Grau, Full Court, judged in: 12/14/2006).

[58]Extract of Hon. Celso de Mello vote, Federal Supreme Court ('STF'), in the ADIn n. 2.591, known as "ADIN of the banks", cited by Bessa, Leonardo Roscoe, Relações de consumo e Aplicação do Código de Defesa do Consumidor, 2. Ed., São Paulo: RT, 2009, p. 7.

[59]The text is: "Art. 2.045. Revokes Law No. 3.071, of January 1st 1916 - Civil Code; and Part One of the Commercial Code - Law No. 556 of June 25th 1850".

[60]See Garcia (2007), p. 9 and following. See also Superior Court of Justice decision as the summary: "*Non-applicability of the Consumer Protection Code to lease governed by Law n. 8.245/1991, because in addition to being part of different microsystems the regulatory framework of private law, the legal relationships regarding leases do not have the characteristic features of the consumption relations set forth in articles 2 and 3 of CDC (Law no. 8.078/1990. Previous judgments*" (Superior Court of Justice, AgRg in AREsp no. 101.712/RS, Rapporteur: Hon. Marco Buzzi, Fourth Group, Judged in: 11/03//2015).

lawyer,[61] and it has low effectiveness in matters of data banks of positive data.[62] In Europe, rental is currently considered a relation of consumption, especially to receive protection from the policy of abusive clauses, like recent decisions of the Court of Justice of the European Union clarify.[63] There are special laws about privacy and database sensitivity of consumption society, themes that the CDC could not include yet.

9.2.2.3 The Bronze Age: The Dialogue Between the CDC, the 2002 Civil Code, and Special Laws (2006–2010)

Every time a code as important as a Civil Code enters into force, like it happened in Brazil in 2003, the other laws of the legal system have to "adapt" and the case law/jurisprudence tend to use the newest laws and not the older. The 2002 Civil Code took almost 30 years to be approved, demonstrating certain limits as its up-to-datedness[64] and the projects that currently move to create a new Commercial Code.

Nevertheless, the dialogue between the CDC and the Civil Code was established by the previously mentioned ADIN no. 2.591 reported decision. In such decision, for the first time in Brazil, the "sources dialogues" theory, envisioned by German author Erik Jayme,[65] was accepted by a higher court. The Federal Supreme Court

---

[61]See Prux, Oscar Ivan. Responsabilidade civil do profissional liberal no Código de Defesa do Consumidor. Belo Horizonte: Del Rey, 1998; and the Superior Court of Justice decision as the summary follows: "*Special Appeal. Forum selection clause Validity. Contract to provide legal services. 1. The mere difference in the economic level between the parties - the lawyer and his former constituent defendant in action for recovery of attorneys' fees – does not features economic* "hiposuficiency" *to remove the selection forum clause. 2. In the absence of subscription contract nor contract governed by the Consumer Protection Code, there is no circumstance in fact from which one could infer the intellectual or economic* hiposuficiency *of the defendant, the election of jurisdiction established in the contract, under art. 111 of the Civil Procedural Code and in accordance to the Precedent no. 335 of the Federal Supreme Court STF ("Valid the choice of court clause for processes arising from the contract.") should be upheld. 3. Special Appeal provided.*" (Superior Court of Justice. REsp no. 1263387/PR, Rapporteur: Hon. Maria Isabel Gallotti, Fourth Group, Judged in: 06/04//2013).

[62]See "defendendo o diálogo entre as regras do CDC e a lei de cadastros positivos", Bessa (2009), p. 101.

[63]See Gsell (2014), pp. 375–387.

[64]The Civil Code of 2002 was approved more than 30 years after the draft bill. Its "Revision Commission and Elaborating Civil Code" started its Works in May 23, 1969, composed by the following lawyers: José Carlos Moreira Alves (Parte Geral); Agostinho Alvim (Direito das Obrigações), Silvio Marcondes (Direito da Empresa), Erbert Chamoun (Direito das Coisas), Clóvis do Couto e Silva (Direito de Família), Torquato Castro (Direito das Sucessões). Four bill essays were published (in 1972, 1973, 1974 and the final in 1975, which number is 634-D/1975). About lawyers who composed the Comission and their academic formation, see Lotuffo, Renan, Da oportunidade da codificação civil e a Constituição, in Sarlet, Ingo Wolfgang (Org.), *O novo Código Civil e a Constituição*, Porto Alegre, Livraria do Advogado Ed., 2003, p. 11ff.

[65]71 See about the theory: Marques Claudia Lima, O ´diálogo das fontes´ como método da nova teoria geral do direito: um tributo a Erik Jayme, in Marques (2012a), p. 18.

(STF in the Portuguese acronym), in the very memorable case of ADIN no. 2.591, ruled in favor of the constitutionality of the application of the CDC to all bank activities, recognizing the need of the dialogue between all sources of law. From the Honorable Joaquim Barbosa's vote, the following is extracted: "I understand the financial system regulation and the discipline of consumption and consumer defense may perfectly coexist. In many cases, the operator of rights will find facts that call upon standards application as much as from one area as another from the legal knowledge. That occurs because of the different aspects that one reality presents, making it surround the different normative scope of the law."

Related to what was claimed about complementary laws on the financial system structure and the CDC, Honorable Joaquim Barbosa, referring to the dialogue of sources technique, pointed out that "There isn't, *a priori*, a reason to talk about formal exclusions between those normative species, but about reciprocal influence, about joint implementation of both at the same time, being complementary or secondary or allowing the volunteer option of the parts about the preponderant source."[66]

As I have written, the expression created by Erik Jayme in his famous Hague General Course,[67] "the dialogue of sources," refers to "the simultaneous and consistent application of many laws or private sources of law, under the light (or with the values guide) of the 1988 Federal Constitution. [. . .] Erik Jayme, in his general course of 1995, taught that in light of the 'postmodern pluralism' of a law with many sources, the need to coordinate the laws originated from the same legal order resurges, as a requirement for an efficient and fair judicial system (*Identité culturelle et intégration: le droit internationale privé postmoderne, Recueil des Cours*, II, p. 60 e 251 and following). The use of Jayme's expression, *dialogue de sources*, is an attempt to express the need for a consistent application of all private laws that coexist in the system. It is the derivative or mended consistency (*cohérence dérivée ou restaurée*), that in a time of decodification and of micro recodification, searches for efficiency not only hierarchically but also functionally from the plural and complex system of our contemporary law, in order to avoid the *antinomie*, the incompatibility, or nonconsistency. "Dialogue" arises due to the fact that there is mutual influence; there is "dialogue" because there is joint application at the same time and in the same case, one being complementary or subsidiary to the other, allowing one to opt for the prevailing source or even allowing one to opt for one of the laws in an abstract conflict—a flexible and open solution, interpenetration, or even the most favorable solution for the weakest party in the relation (different treatment for different people). The dialogue of sources is a rhetorical expression (and semiotics = tells its own purpose to impose two logics, to apply simultaneous and coherently two laws)."[68]

---

[66]See details either in Almeida João Bastista de, Pfeiffer Roberto (coord.) (2006).

[67]See Jayme (1995).

[68]Marques (2015a), p. 128.

CDC's Article 7[69] has foreseen since 1990 that the sources should be applied together, in favor of the consumers, allowing consumer law to be in other laws other than the CDC. As the Superior Court of Justice clarifies: "article 7 of Law no. 8.078/90 fixes the so-called dialogue of sources, according to whom, every time a law guarantees any right to the consumer, it may be included into the CDC micro-system, as if it were incorporated under the special protection of the CDC and also having the same preference regarding its application in consumption relations."[70]

In the lecture for the Brazil-Germany Network in Consumer Law Research, held on November 13, 2005, at the Federal University of Rio Grande do Sul (UFRGS), the Honorable Antonio Herman Benjamin considered this theory as one of the most used in court with "hundreds" of quotes.[71] Effectively, the "sources dialogue theory" had a good reception in State Court's jurisprudence.[72] For instance, in the beginning of 2016, on the Superior Court of Justice website, 29 collegiate decisions about the theme and more than 1,200 monocratic decisions were found quoting such theory.[73]

In fact, the dialogue of sources is a sophisticated theory, but especially useful for hard cases, as I have written: "on those hard cases there are intimacy in law from different fields of application, fields sometimes convergent, and in general, different (regarding subjects), in the same legal system, there is a dialogue between special and general sources, applying to the equal concrete case, all lighted by the constitutional values system and the fundamental rights."[74] If the initial reaction to CDC Article 7 in jurisprudence was not as positive as the theory, its use would tend

---

[69]Article prescribes that: "Art. 7°:The rights under this code do not exclude others arising from international treaties or conventions to which Brazil is a signatory, the ordinary domestic law, the regulations issued by the competent administrative authorities, as well as those derived from general principles of law, analogy, customs and equity".

[70]Superior Court of Justice. REsp no. 1037759/RJ, Rapporteur: Hon. Nancy Andrighi, Third Group, Judged in 02/23//2010.

[71]See the summary of leading case judged in 12/19/2008 by the Superior Court of Justice, in the case 'REsp. no. 1.024.128/PR', Rapporteur Hon. Herman Benjamin: "The novel legislation is another step called 'reform of the Civil Procedural Code – CPC', set of measures that are modernizing the legal system to make the suit faster and more effective. Under this approach, the granting of a suspensive effect to the debtor's defense no longer automatically come to its simple filing. Under the principles of good faith and procedural loyalty, the effective willingness to cooperate for quick and fair settlement of the dispute and the proof that one's right is good are required. This is new concept applied to the general theory of the execution suit, which, in this *ratio*, reflects in the sparse procedural law governing the microsystems of execution suits, provided that the rules of the CPC can be alternatively used to fill gaps. Applied in the procedural context, the sources dialogue theory".

[72]Read about the good reception by Theory of the Dialogue of Sources in the case law, in Bessa Leonardo Roscoe. Diálogo das fontes no direito do consumidor. In: Marques (org.) (2012a), p. 183.

[73]See the expression. "dialogue of sources" on the official website of STJ: http://www.stj.jus.br/SCON/ (Acesso em 12.01.2015).

[74]Marques (2015a).

to increasingly establish itself in Brazil and face the legislative pluralism we live in (see the example of the "Elderly Act" from 2013).

9.2.2.4 The Age of Hope: The Process of Updating the CDC and Review of UN Guidelines (2010–2016)

In 2010, when celebrating 20 years of CDC, the Federal Senate began a review and updating process of CDC,[75] which brings a lot of hope to consumers, and culminate on our law projects in transition at Brazilian Parliament (PLS no. 281 from 2012 changing the initial part of the CDC, and including the Introduction Law to Brazilian Law standards, currently PL no. 3514 from 2015, at plenary, and PLS no. 283 from 2012 about credit to consumers, prevention and treatment of the major debt, currently PL no. 3515 from 2015, in exam by the special commission).

In 2012, the process to review the guidelines on consumer protection (UN Guidelines for Consumer Protection 1985, revised in 1999 to include sustainable consumption) began,[76] finalized with the approval of the revised version of the UN General Meeting on December 22, 2015. The UN Guidelines for Consumer Protection are the only real international instrument about consumer protection, and they celebrate their 30 years with deep updating. Indeed, the globalized society of information, credit, and technology of today is very distant from the consumption society of 1985. If the first theme of updating in 1999 after the ECO 1922, was the sustainable consumption,[77] currently the schedule is broad. Documents from UNCTAD inform "The DNUPC review covers all content of the existent DNUPC, as in some areas still not reached in the guidelines (electronic commerce, financial service, another points and implementation), the goal is to improve consumers protection in a world constantly changing and the need to update it in areas which are, increasingly, an essential part of daily consumption. The review's goal is to reach an effective protection in national, regional, and international levels, with respect to the balanced right between a high level of protection and business competitiveness."[78]

Accordingly, the 2015 Guidelines have the following new parts: II—Field of application and III—General Principals, which was expanded to include electronic commerce, financial services, database protection, privacy, access and renewable

[75]See Senado (2010), p. 11.

[76]See the original version, A/RES/39/248, de 16 de Abril de 1985 e sua importância no Brasil, na obra de Sodré, Marcelo Gomes. *A construção do direito do consumidor*. São Paulo: Atlas, 2009

[77]In 1999, was included on United Nation Guidelines for Consumer Protection a new chapter, letter G, about "The Promotion of sustainable consumption patterns", that states (nr. 42) "sustainable consumption includes meeting the needs of present and future generations for good and services in ways that are economically, socially and environmentally sustainable".

[78]UNCTAD, Report on the modalities for the review of the United Nations Guidelines for Consumer Protection, Preparatory Meeting for the Review Conference VII for Consumer Protection Geneva, January 2015.

energy, public service, and tourism and reinforce international cooperation in the theme. At IV. Principles for Good Business Practices, information and the transparency were reinforced, as well as the protection of privacy, mechanisms of dispute resolution (F. Dispute Resolution and Redress Mechanisms), prevention of disputes (G. Dispute Avoidance and Awareness of Resolution Mechanism), promotion of sustainable consumption (K. Promotion of Sustainable Consumption—included since 1999), electronic commerce (L. E-commerce), financial services (M. Financial Services), and measures about specific themes and new articles of energy, public service and general service, and tourism (N. Measures Relating to Specific Areas; 88. Energy. 89. Public Utilities, 90. Tourism, VI. International Co-operation), with reinforcement of international protection to consumers in case of fraud.

The greatest novelty was the creation of a permanent matter in the UN dedicated to consumers, that is, VII. International Institutional Machinery, which assures the creation not of a UN Commission but at least of an intergovernmental group of consumer law inside UNCTAD (Intergovernmental Group of Experts on Consumer Law and Policy operating within the framework of an existing Trade and Development Commission of UNCTAD). This review of the Guidelines brings a lot of hope for better days on consumer protection all over the world.

In Brazil, the updating of the CDC also brings a lot of hope. As I previously wrote, the CDC is a law with constitutional origin, send to elaborate from the legislator himself (Article 48 of the Acts and Constitutional Provisions). As affirmed by the Federal Supreme Court in the ADIN no. 2591, it is a value constitutionally fixed, as stony clause, guaranteed as fundamental right by Article 5, XXXII of 1988 Federal Constitution in which the State, being State-judge (the judiciary in all instances), being State-executive (administration, prosecutors and public defenders, public law, Procon state and municipal, regular agencies) and State legislator (Federal Senate, representative body and further legislative organs) must promote the consumer defeat.[79]

Accordingly, attention was brought upon the fact that the Supreme Court House has consolidated, since 2013, its jurisprudence at Pronouncement 381,[80] limiting the application of CDC ex officio to bank contracts—despite the ADIN victory.

The Supreme Court House itself is reviewing this emplacement, face to the entrance in force of the new Civil Procedure Code, in March 2016, in Brazil, and in special appeal nr. 1.465.832- RS (Rel. Ministro Paulo de Tarso Sanseverino), studies how to change the Pronouncement 381.[81] In fact, considering the automatic nullity provided at CDC Article 51, as 2002 Civil Code and 2015 Civil Procedure

---

[79]See in Marques (2002), pp. 9–398.

[80]The text is: Súmula 381/STJ—"In banking contracts is forbidden to judge know of craft, unconscionability clauses".

[81]"In the declaration of nullity of unfair terms provided for in art. 51 of the CDC, the contradictory and full defense should be respected and cannot be recognized ex-officio in the second sphere of jurisdiction", Superior Court of Justice, Document no. 51882822—Decision—website—DJe: 15/09/2015.

Code, the nullity of abusive clauses in any contract, must be declared ex officio by the all judges, because it's irremediable by the parts manifestation or unavailable to them.

The society of information and widespread credit was also a challenge to the CDC, which is now updated with a law project of the Federal Senate specifically designed to regulate the growing phenomenon of hiring in electronic commerce, PLS no. 281 from 2012, and a second project, PLS no. 238 from 2012, designed to regulate with more detail the granting of credit to consumers and prevent and treat the problem of overindebtedness.[82]

Two advances on the notion of consumer are already found in the CDC updating process. The first is the deepening of the notion of a [more] "vulnerable" consumer (vulnerable consumer or disadvantaged consumer)[83] or a consumer with aggravated vulnerability, the hypervulnerable. UN's Guidelines, in its 2015 updating, stresses the importance of States to recognize that there are consumers that are more vulnerable,[84] for example, illiterates who cannot read information, deaf mutes who cannot call to complain, a sick person who cannot move away from home, the blind who cannot read a contract that is not written in Braille, thus preparing its standards (and jurisprudence) to this group.[85] Even though the CDC already mentioned children (Article 37 on advertising) and level of knowledge and age (Article 39), PLS no. 281 and PLS no. 283, both from 2012, will now include, while prohibiting consumption harassment, the elderly, the sick ones, and the illiterate in a special manner. The norm of the PLS no. 281 from 2012 brings a basic right of protection against harassment, and PLS no. 283 from 2012 defines consumer harassment as an abusive commercial practice in credit, mentioning the hypervulnerable (Article 54-F).

---

[82]See Marques, Claudia Lima e Benjamin, Antonio Herman. Consumer over-indebtedness in Brazil and the need of a new consumer bankruptcy legislation. In: Niemi J, Ramsay I, Whitford W. C. (ed.) (2009), p. 55ff.

[83]Andreasen, A. R., The disadvantaged consumer, New York: The free Press, 1975 e é uma expressão muito usada por Iain Ramsay, para consumidores jovens ou idosos superendividados, Ramsay, Iain. The alternative consumer credit market and financial sector: regulatory issues and approaches, in The Canadian Business Law Journal, vol. 35, nr. 3, October 2001, p. 328 e seg. Também na Europa a expressão é bem conhecida, veja Domont-Naert, F. Consommateurs défavorisés: crédit et endettement – Contribution à l´étude de l´efficacité du droit de la consommation, Centre de Droit de la Consommation/Kluwer Story Sciencia: Bruxelles, 1992, p. 1 e seg.

[84]See the United Nations Guidelines reviewed in 2015 "11. The principles that establish benchmarks for good business practice for conducting online and off-line commercial activities with consumers are as follows: (a) Fair and equitable treatment- Businesses should deal fairly and honestly with consumers at all stages of their relationship, so that it is an integral part of the business culture. Businesses should avoid practices that harm consumers, particularly with respect to vulnerable and disadvantaged consumers."

[85]Beautiful example is the decision of the Superior Court of Justice in the civil action to impose the financial institution demanded the obligation to adopt the Braille method in the accession bank contracts with person with visual impairment. See: Superior Court of Justice. Case REsp no. 1315822/RJ, Rapporteur: Hon. Marco Aurélio Bellizze, Third Group, Judged in 23/07/2015.

In the definition of provider of products and services (CDC, Article 3) the State and, with the privatization, all the companies that provide these services (which used to be public services) are included. Furthermore, CDC Article 22 reaffirms the implementation of CDC to issues resulting from public services and services that used to be public. However, the dialogue between administrative law and the CDC has shown its limits. If we are to celebrate the implementation of the CDC to public services, we cannot ignore that it is a border topic, meaning the CDC cannot be implemented with all its strength. Thereby, despite all the efforts of jurisprudence regarding the regulation of prior debts,[86] indicators,[87] and the recovery of supply,[88] the protection of consumers of those services or of those who use the services of general interest has failed,[89] and since those are primarily private services and services that used to be public, offered in a remunerated way in the market, they consist of consumer relationships.[90] Therefore, CDC Article 22 is still the main article—alongside CDC Article 2—to establish that the consumer of public services *uti singuli* is a real consumer and must be protected by the CDC.[91]

The revision of the UN Guidelines for Consumer Protection[92] states that this issue must be a priority for developing countries, but in the projects to update the

---

[86]This leading case mentions the victory as the collection of past debts: "1. The Supreme Court's case law established the understanding that it is forbidden to suspend the supply of electricity and water services due to past tenses debts. The court assumes the regular account of default, for the month of consumption. (...) 4. special appeal not provided" (Superior Court of Justice, Case AgRg in AREsp no. 752030/RJ, Rapporteur: Hon. Benedito Goncalves, First Group, judged in 10/22/2015).

[87]It should be mentioned that "it is illegal to cut the supply of essential public service, if the debt is caused by alleged fraud in the meter device, which was determined unilaterally by the concessionaire. (Superior Court of Justice. Case AgRg in AREsp no. 412849/RJ, Rapporteur: Hon. Minister Humberto Martins, Second Group, judged in 12/10/2013). See also: Superior Court of Justice. Case AgRg in REsp no. 1398768/AM, Rapporteur: Hon. Herman Benjamin, Second Group, judged in 06/03/2014 and Superior Court of Justice. Case AgRg in AREsp no. 581826/RS, Rapporteur: Hon. Magalhães, Second Group, judged in 15/10/2015.

[88]See leading case: Superior Court of Justice. Case REsp no. 1529820/SE, Rapporteur: Hon. Herman Benjamin, Second Group, judged in 06/16/2015.

[89]In these 25 years, we went from more effective protection against cutting public services, a law that does not prohibit consumers cut defaulter (Superior Court of Justice. Case Resp no. 1062975/RS, Rapporteur: Hon. Eliana Calmon, Secong Group, judged in 09/23/2008) and prohibits the discontinuance of service in municipalities (Superior Court of Justice. Case REsp no 742640/MG, Rapporteur: Hon. Eliana Calmon, Second Group, judged in 09/06/2007), or in case of danger of death or serious violation of human dignity, sick, disabled, etc. (Superior Court of Justice. Case Resp 647853/RS, Rapporteur: Hon. Luiz Fux, judged in 09/28/2004).

[90]See details in Marques Contratos, op. cit., p. 623 and following.

[91]Thus seminal work Pasqualotto (1992), pp. 130–148.

[92]The new text is UNGCP: "K. Measures Relating to specific areas (...). 69. In advancing consumer interests, Particularly in Developing Countries, Member States should not, where appropriate, give priority to areas of essential concern for the health of the consumer, such as food, water, pharmaceuticals, energy, and public utilities, and Also address the specificities of tourism" (the bold part is the revised).

CDC, this issue was not dealt with.[93] The new Article 77 of the UN Guidelines includes a simple text about the duties of the States and establishes the fact that the user of public-paid services is a real consumer and must be protected by the States, especially if hypervulnerable.[94]

One of the main topics of the UN Guidelines in its reviewed version of 2015 is the right to access essential products and services (5, a), the protection of hypervulnerable consumers (5, b), and also ensuring that the level of protection of an e-consumer is not lesser than that of a regular consumer (5, i), as well as the protection of consumer's privacy and the flow of information (5, k).[95]

The beginning of 2016 comes with a lot of hope regarding the approval of the update of the CDC (PLS no. 281 from 2012 and PLS no. 283 from 2012), and as prescribed by PLS no. 281 from 2012, the international protection of consumer is an issue that also deserves our special attention, which will be discussed in the next section of the present article.

9.3 Horizons to Come After 25 Years of the CDC, Especially Regarding International Protection of Consumers

If the consumer protection stages in Brazil demonstrate a cyclical change in the issue, it is important to analyze the projects on updating the CDC under this angle, especially paying attention to a new theme: the international protection of consumers. The UN Guidelines clarified the theme, specifically mentioning the necessity of concern from States regarding the redress of damages and consumer dispute settlement in international trade, in international financial system, and especially in case of international aspects of tourism.

[93]See Martins and Ferreira (2012), p. 11 et seq.

[94]The new text UNGCP is: "77. *Public utilities*. Member States should not promote universal access to public utilities as well as formulate, maintain or strengthen national policies to Improve Articles and statutes dealing with provision of service, consumer information, security deposits and advance payment for service, late payment fees, termination and restoration of service, establishment of payment plans, and dispute resolution between Consumers and utility service providers, taking into account the needs of vulnerable and disadvantaged Consumers".

[95]The original texts are: "II - General principals. 5. The legitimate needs Which the Guidelines are intended to meet are the Following: (A) Access by Consumers to essential goods and services; (B) The protection of vulnerable and disadvantaged Consumers; (. . .) (I) the level of protection for Consumers using electronic commerce que is not less than that afforded in other forms of commerce; (K) The protection of consumer privacy and the global free flow of information."

9.3.1 International Consumer Protection According to the Sofia Declaration and Updating the CDC

In 2008, at the ILA Biennial Conference, in Rio de Janeiro, by suggestion of ILA Brazil directors, there was the establishment—for the first time in over 100 years—of an International Law Association Committee dedicated to protecting consumers: the Committee on International Protection of Consumers.[96] From this committee came the Sofia Declaration on the development of international principles on consumer protection.[97]

In 2012, the International Law Association, gathered in Sofia, made its first resolution on consumer protection (ILA Resolution 4/2012, London), which suggests five principles that must guide international consumer law development: consumers are the weaker party in situations of mass or standard form contracts, in particular concerning information and bargaining power (vulnerability principle); it is desirable to develop standards and to apply articles of private international law that would entitle consumers to take advantage of the most favorable consumer protection (most favorable protection principle); regulation of consumer contracts should be effective and fair and ensure transparency (fairness principle); responsible lending is incumbent on all those involved in consumer credit transactions, including credit providers, brokers, and advisors (responsible lending principle); and consumer groups should participate actively in the development and regulation of consumer protection (active participation on the regulation principle).[98]

These principles were used at the update of the Brazilian Consumer Code (CDC).[99] Now, let us observe how the CDC updating process (PLS 281, 2012, and PLS 283, 2012), current in the Chamber of Deputies (PL 3514, 2015 e 3515, 2015), is in accordance with the principle of vulnerability and the principle of the most favorable consumer protection.

---

[96]International Law Association, Report of the Seventy-Fourth Conference—The Hague (London, 2010), 259. (www.ila-hq.or/en/committees/index.cfm/cid/1030).

[97]Resolution ILA 4/2012 75° ILA Conference, Sofía, Bulgaria, from 26 to 30 August 2012.

[98]The Declaration of August 30, 2012, the first in consumer law of the ILA, in over 130 years, is as follows: "Sofia Statement on the development of international principles on consumer protection - Consumer protection should be guided by the following general principles: 1. Consumers are the weaker party in situations of mass or standard form contracts, in particular concerning information and bargaining power. 2. It is desirable to develop standards and to apply rules of private international law that entitle consumers to take advantage of the most favorable consumer protection. 3. Regulation of consumer contracts should be effective and fair and ensure transparency. 4. Responsible lending is incumbent on all those involved in consumer credit transactions, including credit providers, brokers and advisers. 5. Consumer groups should participate actively in the development and regulation of consumer protection." See Conference Resolution Sofia 2012. Available in: <http://www.ila-hq.org/en/committees/index.cfm/cid/1030>. Access: 02 Sept. 2012.

[99]Senado (2012), pp. 139 and 140.

9.3.1.1 The Principle of Vulnerability

The first principle recognized as "international" by ILA is the principle of consumer vulnerability, a principle that guides almost all national laws[100] and European Union laws for the protection of weaker party.[101] As we have seen in this text, the Brazilian Consumer Code updating and the 2015 UN Guidelines review build a sense of aggravated vulnerability, distinguishing between all the "weaker" consumers themselves and the group of consumers with aggravated vulnerability or hypervulnerability.[102]

The Consumer Code updating process in Brazil supports that basic principle, especially with respect to harassment of particularly vulnerable consumer groups, the elderly, the patients, the illiterate, for example. As I have written,[103] in the projects to update the Brazilian Consumer Code (PLS no. 281 and PLS no. 283, both from 2012), the special committee of jurists, headed by Hon. Antônio Herman Benjamin, introduced to the Brazilian law the idea of a fight against harassment of consumers, identifying harassing and overly aggressive marketing strategies focused on certain groups, such as the elderly and illiterate. The standard used was the Unfair Commercial Practices Directive, 2005/29/CE, which at its Article 8 uses as a general definition the idea of aggressive practice, in which are included harassment, coercion, physical force and undue influence.[104] The option of the Brazilian legislator was to consider consumer harassment as the gender of all aggressive commercial practices[105] that limit the freedom of consumer choice.

In this way, in PLS no. 281 from 2012, a new consumer right was created, prohibiting any kind of discrimination and consumer harassment, strengthening freedom of choice, as follows:

> Art. 6°...
> XII – the freedom of choice, especially due to new technologies and data networks, prohibited any kind of discrimination and consumer harassment;

Also in the PLS no. 283 from 2012, there are standard typifying the consumer harassment and unfair commercial practices, as follows:

> [Art. 54-C] It is prohibited, explicitly or implicitly, in consumer credit offering, advertising or not [...]

---

[100] See on the *principle of debilis*, Lorenzetti (2006), p. 455ss.

[101] See the '*principle of protection of the weaker party*', in Reich (2014), p. 37ff.

[102] See on the demand for real equality of unequal and most vulnerable among them, Marques and Miragem (2014), p. 85ss.

[103] This paragraph is based on the study, Marques and Gsell (2015), pp. 46–87.

[104] Micklitz (2014), p. 113, states que such a standard is likewise the general clause.

[105] Note that the aggressive commercial policy expression was not known in many European countries before the Directive 2005, as reported Howels, Geraint. Aggressive Commercial Practices. In: Howels Geraint, Micklitz Hans, Wilhelmsson Thomas (2006), p. 168.

IV – harass or pressure the consumer to hire the product supply, service or credit, including the distance, electronically or by telephone, especially in case of elderly consumers, illiterate, sick or high state of vulnerability or if the purchase involved prize...

In the Brazilian Consumer Code updating general report, we suggest that these standards are part of an increase in the ethical and inclusive dimension of the Consumer Code.[106] This social inclusion directive seeks to adapt the Consumer Code to the challenges of Brazil today, where democratization and generalization of consumer credit, especially payroll credit, finds its main target in the groups of the elderly,[107] the illiterate, or the functional illiterate.[108] Recognizing the special vulnerability of these consumer groups is an important step and, as we have seen, coincides with the UN Guidelines. It is expected that the update of the Brazilian Consumer Code will soon be approved.

The UN Guidelines still mention consumer vulnerability in financial services and in international relations, especially in e-commerce and in the case of tourists, strengthening the principle that consumer law in the virtual world or online must be at least the same as that of consumers in the offline world, equal rights being of paramount importance. Let us see the second principle of the Sofia Declaration.

9.3.1.2 The Principle of the Most Favorable Protection

This principle applies especially in cross-border cases where it is possible to apply more than one legal system, taking under consideration the articles of private international law of countries and transnational status of the private consumer relationship. To develop an international consumer protection, it is really necessary to think of applying that to ensure greater protection of their rights and not the one in a written contract of adhesion made, for example, by the creator of a digital service or a product purchased at a distance.

The European Union has consolidated this principle in Article 5 of the former Rome Convention, currently the Rome I Regulation, stating that it should apply the law chosen by the parties only if it were more favorable than the mandatory articles of the country's consumer protection of the residence of consumers. This rule of "favor" does not exist in Brazil yet, but the Commission responsible for updating the CDC accepted my suggestion to include this reference to the most favorable consumer protection. This concern for international consumer protection moved the Brazilian Parliament,[109] and in the substitutionary Bill of Senator Ricardo Ferraço,

[106] Benjamin and Marques (2012), pp. 23–24.

[107] See Marques (2015b).

[108] See Marques (2014b), pp. 99–146.

[109] As Nadia de Araújo teaches, "Opinión No. 243/2014" expressly mention the need to also update the Articles governing international trade, which were provided for in art. 9 of LINDB. According to Senator Ricardo Ferraço, there was no way to ignore, the substitute Bill proposed the PLS 281, the new international dimension of consumption, otherwise it will not prepare the Consumer Code and the Brazilian legislation for the coming years." Araujo (2015), pp. 451–471.

it was possible to suggest a new Article 9 in the Introductory Law, with special articles for consumer protection (Article 9, B, and Article 9, C). The suggestion applies only to consumers in the shape of individuals, as has been the trend around the world[110] and in Brazilian jurisprudence.[111] The rules for the international protection of consumers, in PL no. 3414 from 2015 (former PLS no. 281 from 2012) pending before the House of Representatives, are as follows:

> Art. 9. The obligations, except for specific cases provided by law, shall be governed by the law of the country where they were established [. . .].
>
> Art. 9 ° -B. The international consumption contract, understood as the one carried out between a natural consumer person and a supplier of goods and services whose establishment is located in a country other than that of the consumer's domicile shall be governed by the celebration of the place of law or, if executed in Brazil, by Brazilian law, since more favorable to consumer.
>
> § 1. If the contract is preceded by any negotiations or marketing by the supplier or its representatives, addressed to Brazil and it held, in particular sending advertising, correspondence, e-mails, commercial messages, invitations, prizes or offers, mandatory provisions of Brazilian law will be apply, since more favorable to consumers.
>
> § 2. Contracts for international travel packages or package tours involving tour groups or hotel and tourism services, fulfillment outside of Brazil, contracted with tour agencies and operators located in Brazil, will be governed by Brazilian law.
>
> Art. 9 ° -C. The law applicable to non-contractual obligations, if none of the parties has domicile or an establishment in the country where the accident occurs, damage, fact or tort, will be the law of the place where its effects are felt. [. . .]

The option of the Brazilian Parliament was to modify my initial suggestion that established a legal connection with the consumer's domicile (as presumably the most favorable law), choosing to remain with the law of the celebration as the main law for international contracts (Article 9), even consumption (Article 9, B) and compare it to Brazilian law (Article 9, B, *in fine*). Thus, it excludes the party autonomy or the choice of law in consumer contracts between those present. The article is conservative, but it is still a strong advance. The many references in this article designed to the most favorable law are positive and demonstrate the growing importance of this principle in the future of Brazilian law, such as the Brazilian suggestion of the Organization of American States International Private Law Interamerican Conference ('CIDIP' in the Portuguese acronym) n. VII- Part II,[112] and Mercosur Technical Committee ('CT' in the Portuguese acronym) n. 7.

For international contracts of e-commerce or distance contracting, a special article drafted by the Jurists Committee, allowing freedom of choice—because in such cases it is difficult to establish which is the law of celebration—is present in Article 101 of the CDC, to wit:

---

[110]See Marques (2006), p. 145ss.

[111]Thus concludes in Marques (2010), p. 47ff.

[112]See my suggestion for this CIDIP VII, accepted by the Brazilian government in Marques (2001), pp. 657–780.

Art. 101...

§ 2. To the conflicts arising from the supply international distance, applies to consumer's domicile law, or, if more favorable to this, the state standard chosen by the parties, provided, in any event, the consumer access to justice. (NR)

In comparative law, we have seen other models,[113] besides the mentioned model of the European Union, with provisions on immediate application or international imperative. The most interesting is the Chinese model.[114] The Chinese law of 2010 (the "Law of Application of Law for Foreign-related Civil Relations of the People's Republic of China"—LALFCR) entered into force in 2011, and, among its 52 articles, it sets Article 42 as a special article for consumer contracts. The provision of Article 42 of the Chinese law LALFC[115] ensures the applicability of the laws of the consumer's domicile, but the consumers—and only they—can choose the law of the place of performance of the contract, or this shall be applied when the supplier/provider has no significant operations in the country of residence of the consumer, like e-commerce. The rule translated by Prof. Dr. Wei Dan is as follows: "Article 42. The laws at the habitual residence of consumers shall apply to consumer contracts; if a consumer chooses the applicable laws at the locality of the provision of goods or services or an operator has no relevant business operations at the habitual residence of the consumer, the laws at the locality of the provision of goods or services shall apply."[116]

The interesting aspect about the Chinese model is considering the consumer's habitual residence as the main connection (certainly the most favorable) and permitting the autonomy of the will/freedom of choice only to the consumer, and limitedly to the local law of the celebration of the contract, like the Brazilian law, for instance.

The Chinese law also proves to be wise when excluding the applicability of the habitual residence law when the supplier has no business operations in the consumer's country of residence, similar to the case of tourists.[117] The Chinese model

[113] See Marques (2012a), p. 151ff.

[114] See, for all the text Dan (2016).

[115] Translation by Prof. Dr. Yu Ying: "Article 42: Consumer contract shall be governed by the law of the country of the consumers' habitual residence. The law of the country where the products/commodities and services be supplied should govern the contract, provided that it was chosen by the consumer or there is no related business activities of supplier/professional in the country of the consumer's habitual residence." See her article Ying (2016).

[116] Dan (2014), pp. 13–24.

[117] Affirms Dan (2014), pp. 13–24: ("It can be seen that under Chinese Law on Choice of Law for Foreign-related Civil Relationships, the parties of consumer contract are not allowed to choose the applicable law. Only the consumer is allowed to choose the applicable law and the applicable law to be chosen by the consumer must only be the laws at the locality of the provision of goods or services. To put into other words, for an inter-regional consumer dispute, the laws to be the applied are the laws at the locality of the provision of goods or services chosen by a tourist consumer. If the tourist does not choose any applicable law, the laws at the habitual residence of the tourist will be applied. However, if an operator has no relevant business operations at the habitual residence of the consumer, the laws at the locality of the provision of goods or services will apply.")

has influenced the works of the Jurist Commission of the Brazilian Federal Senate.[118]

In Latin America, the Argentine model is the most important and has also influenced the Brazilian Parliament in a positive manner, demonstrating the necessity of a special consumer protection provision. The article of the new Civil and Commercial Code of Argentina (Law n. 26.994 of October 7 2014) establishes the consumer's domestic law as a basis, but only for cases of passive consumer; otherwise, the law of the place of performance or the place of celebration applies. The article, deeply influenced by the Rome Convention (1980) in its first part, is as follows:

> Article 2655. – Applicable Law. The consumer contracts are determined by the Member State Law of the place of domicile of the consumer in the following cases: a. if the conclusion of the contract was preceded by an offer, publicity or activity fulfilled at the State of the consumer's dwelling place and if he/she complied all the necessary acts for the conclusion of the contract; b. if the supplier received/accepted the order at the State of the consumer's domicile; c. if the consumer was induced by the supplier to travel to a foreign State aiming to complete the order; d. if the travel contracts, with a global price, include combined installments of transportation and accommodation. To cases not included in this article, the consumer contracts are determined by the law of the country of place of performance. In case of it not being possible to determine the place of fulfillment, the contract rests determined by the law of the place of celebration.

Besides the Argentinian model, particularly similar to the European model, two new pieces of legislation have recently been elaborated. In the Dominican Republic, the new Law n. 544, known as *Ley de Derecho Internacional Privado* (International Private Law Legislation), dated October 15, 2014, brought a new consumer special protection standard, which allows the choice of the applicable law but restricts its effects to the chosen law, never excluding the standards foreseen on the habitual residence law for consumer protection. The considered enigmatic excerpt from Article 63, from Law n. 544 is as follows: "The contracts celebrated by consumers are Articled by the law of the country of habitual activity, in absence of election by the parties shall be applied the law of the consumer habitual residence." Sole Paragraph: "On consumer contracts celebrated by the aspects of this article, the applicable law election by the parties may lessen/diminish the consumer protection standards foreseen on the law of their habitual residence, on those cases which the contracting party has a business establishment in the mentioned country or at any rate had directed its commercial activities to this country."[119]

Panama published Law n. 7 of 2014, *Codigo de Derecho Internacional Privado* (International Law Code), considered a paramount general principle on consumer

[118]See Benjamin and Marques (2012), p. 65ff.

[119]See more on Luciane Klein Viera's docatorate thesis, at UBA, named "Bases para la Armonización Legislativa en Materia de Derecho Aplicable a los Contratos Internacionales con Consumidores en el MERCOSUR, orientadas hacia al reconocimiento de una nueva categoría de consumidor transfronterizo".

protection (Article 8: "The international community's fundamental principles are part of the judges' rules of application, like the supremacy of interests of the children and consumers which prevail over all other aspects;... the protection of the weak, the international obligation erga omnes and the rights derived from ius cogens, the environmental responsibility and other universal law principles applicable"). Article 95 provides: "The consumer contracts are ruled by the law of the place of transaction. The election by the consumers may be invoked on their domicile jurisdiction, the place of contract fulfillment or the one that is most favorable, in regard to the supremacy of consumer interest principle. The most favorable law stands for the most adequate law to repair and protect the interests of the consumer." This model is very interesting for it establishes the most favorable law as the most favorable and suitable approach to repair and protect the interests of the consumer—certainly a model to be followed on the Brazilian CDC's reform.

According to Nadia de Araújo, in the substitute Bill "was created an applicable legislation for active consumer relations in cases of touristic packages to foreign countries. In this case, the binding law shall be the Brazilian law, whenever the contracts for the services are settled there. Thus, it enables the national judge in charge to apply the CDC, even if the package service was executed in a foreign country. This legislation is in accordance to the rule of place of celebration connection and aims to offer a larger protection to the tourist-consumer while on the place of contract."[120] The CDC reform, on its first Bill by Senator Ferraço,[121] had also brought another special article on tourist-consumer protection. The article was withdrawn at the Federal Senate plenary due to the project proposal made by the Brazilian Government at the Hague Conference. The project it is still under negotiation.

9.3.2 *Protection of Tourist-Consumer: Advances Under the Hague Conference*

In fact, the tourist[122] protection is the horizon for the international consumer protection, considering that this consumer is distant from its country, culture, and

---

[120]Araujo (2015), pp. 451–471.

[121]See Marques and Lima (2013), pp. 265–294.

[122]According to World Tourism Organization (UNWTO), tourist is the visitor that stays more than 24 h in a different place from its habitual residence, and so, is a participating subject of a movement of people who seeks different locations other than their origin place. "2.9. A visitor is a traveler taking a trip to a main destination outside his/her usual environment, for less than a year, for any main purpose (business, leisure or other personal purpose) other than to be employed by a resident entity in the country or place visited. These trips taken by visitors qualify as tourism trips. Tourism refers to the activity of visitors (...). 2.13. A visitor (domestic, inbound or outbound) is classified as a tourist (or overnight visitor), if his/her trip includes an overnight stay, or as a same-day visitor (or excursionist) otherwise." Available at: [http://unstats.un.org/unsd/statcom/doc08/BG-TourismStats.pdf]. Access: 08.01.2013.

native language and does not know the local costumes or where to seek help in case of disrespect to his/her rights.[123] Thus, in the past, under the law of the place of celebration, the tourists as active consumers (who willingly crossed borders) always had less attention from the doctrine than the electronic commerce consumers or the passive consumers.[124] As I have written, the "actual tourist protection models on the international private law are essentially four: 1. *Establishment of special homogenous and material legislation for contracts* of sector interest, like the UNIDROIT International Convention on the Travel Contracts ('CVV') of 1970 or the ones concerning air transport; 2. *Production of legal articles for conflicts of special laws for the consumer protection*, applicable –sometimes- to tourists, like the European Union's Rome I Regulation...; 3. *Establishment of networks for administrative cooperation of rapid legal settlements*, like the 2005 Mercosur Agreement on Visiting Consumers, indication of judicial administrative bodies for the realization of rapid conciliations, for instance the Brazilian's Small Claims Court (available 24 hours at the airports); and 4. *Warranty of privileged access to the Court of domicile*, even when the consumer is a tourist and the demand's plaintiff, for cross-border litigations, on the return of travel; what is not certainty of success on demand, [...] for the difficulties of enforcement and liability of chain of suppliers, for the small value of the claim and the existence of *forum non conveniens* in some legislations."[125]

It is worth pointing out that international tourism accounts for more than one billion people per year on the move, and 45% of the tourist destinations are developing or emerging countries,[126] where consumer protection is not always strong. Furthermore, the consumer profile has changed, from the multilingual and universally "cultured" elite to the people from ascending countries such as China and Russia, the top two biggest on consumer spending; Brazil in ranked in the fifth place. The current distinction between the definitions of passive consumer (stays in his/her origin country and for that reason must be protected) and the active consumer (the tourist and for that reason must receive less protection) is no longer appropriate. The UN Guidelines, 2015 revision, provide the assurance of the same rights and protection for online consumers as for offline consumers, whether tourists or not, and determine the Member States to protect the tourists so that they can claim their rights regardless of their short period of stay in the country. Today, the tourist may be simultaneously an active and a passive consumer since it is possible to perform purchases by electronic means during the time of travel. According to Brazilian data, 64% of foreign tourists traveling to Brazil do not have

[123] See, for all, Dan (2014), pp. 13–24.

[124] See the details in Klausner (2015), pp. 78–82.

[125] Marques (2013), pp. 39–64.

[126] http://www.dadosefatos.turismo.gov.br/export/sites/default/dadosefatos/estatisticas_indicadores/downloads_estatisticas/Estatxstica_e_Indicadores_de_turismo_no_Mundo_-_2009_1__3_.pdf.

any travel agent and come by themselves.[127] These changes on international tourism claim for a better protection of the tourist.

The UN General Assembly's Resolution of December 21, 2001 (A/RES/56/212), approved the Global Code of Ethics for Tourism organized by the UNWTO, with headquarters in Madrid. The Code of Ethics' first article determines the duty of the authorities of the visiting countries to protect the tourist: "4. The public authorities have the mission to ensure the protection of the tourists and visitors and their respective goods. In this duty, they must have special attention to the security of foreign tourists, in view of their particular vulnerability. With this purpose, they will facilitate the enactment of means concerning information, prevention, protection, security and specific assistance corresponding to their needs."[128] Following Article 8, there is a thoughtfulness to inform the tourist-consumer of a warranted access to local administrative and judicial authorities and of equal rights: "2. To tourists and visitors is recognized (...). Will benefit of an easy and rapid access to administrative, judicial and sanitation local services (...). 3. Tourists and visitors will enjoy the same rights of the citizens of the visiting country in situations of confidentiality of personal data, in especial when the data are in accordance to the current diplomatic agreements (...)."

The UN Guidelines on consumer protection, in its 2015 revision, included a special section for the protection of the tourist, which essentially mentions the challenges of an international protection of tourist-consumers and the necessity to collaborate in this matter. The new guideline of the UNGPC is as follows:

> 78. Tourism. Member States should ensure that their consumer protection policies are adequate to address the marketing and the provision of goods and services related to tourism, including, but not limited to, travel, traveller accommodation and timeshares. Member States should, in particular, address the cross-border challenges raised by such activity, including enforcement cooperation and information sharing with other Member States, and should also cooperate with the relevant stakeholders in the tourism-travel sector.[129]

In the field of tourist protection as international consumers, a lot has been developed. On March 23, 2012, more than 100 members of ASADIP from 14 different countries showed their support to a 'proactive agenda' , and in the Declaration of Rio de Janeiro[130] they considered it to be possible to advance in terms of international tourist protections, proposing its study at the Hague Conference—set as the principal global forum to discuss cooperation and protection of the weaker on the international private law.

---

[127] http://www.dadosefatos.turismo.gov.br.

[128] Available at: [www.unwto.org/ethics/full_text/en/pdf/Codigo_Etico_Espl.pdf]. Access: 17.09.2013.

[129] See the original in Spanish in *Revista de Direito do consumidor*, vol. 104 (2015).

[130] Available at: [http://asadip.files.wordpress.com/2012/04/carta-de-rio-de-janeiro8asadip230312en-espac3b1ol-y-portviii.pdf]. Access: 21.01.2013.

At the Costa Rica ASADIP meeting, the Brazilian Government was present and, represented by the Consumer Defense States' Secretary, Dr. Juliana Pereira (SENACON/MJ), stood up in favor of the matter, considering it to be important that the consumer defense bodies engage together in the protection of the foreign tourist consumers, in the face of their linguistic, time, and information disadvantages. Today, only the transport and travel agency matters have special articles on international private law, a more *a posteriori* protection than *ex ante*.

At the Peru ASADIP Congress, the Brasilcon (Brazilian Institute for Consumer Law and Politics) organized, within the ASADIP, a side event to study tourist-consumer protection and putting it into practice, and so the Director of the Consumer Defense Department (DPDC) of the Ministry of Justice, Dr. Amaury Oliva, once again showed support to the ASADIP initiative. Encouraged by the Brazilian Government, as an *expert*, to present a proposition, I have chosen to take inspiration from the pragmatism of the *soft* cooperation model of Mercosur and the strong cooperation of the European Union and it's ECC-NET.[131]

The Brazilian Government accepted my academic suggestion and, based on that, presented its proposition on April 2013 at the Hague Council of General Affairs: the "Convention on Co-operation for Foreign Tourists and Visitors Protection." The subject of tourist-consumer protection was included on the Hague Academy subjects with the support of many countries, among them Argentina, Peru, Uruguay, China, the European Union, the United States, and South Africa and also the support of ASADIP. In 2014, after the successful FIFA World Cup experience, a second version of this Convention (*Draft Convention on Co-Operation and Access to Justice for International Tourists*)—similar to the Hague Convention on International Access to Justice of 1980—was organized by the SENACON and presented by the government.

In March 2015, with the assistance of China—holder of more than 100 bilateral tourism treaties[132]—the Hague Council decided to include the subject of tourist protection in the work agenda of the Permanent Bureau in order to analyze the viability of a global convention on cooperation on the subject. The UNWTO is working on a material convention to help tourists and stakeholders in cases of emergency and cataclysms; hence, this Hague Convention would play as a supplement to the UNWTO's. However the expert hired to carry studies on the feasibility and the convenience of the proposed convention has not yet finished his work.

---

[131] See Marques (2012b), pp. 425–455.

[132] See Dan (2012) 40, quoting Zhang Buhong, Lai Bao (2009), pp. 16–20.

9.4 Final Considerations

There has been 25 years of sheer success of the Brazilian Code of Consumer Defense and Protection, but there is still a lot to be done. The revision of the UN Guidelines, concluded in 2015, points toward these future vision subjects: international consumer protection, electronic commerce, access to essential goods and services, security on financial services, avoidance of overindebtedness, international cooperation, mass tourism, et cetera. The still-to-be accomplished horizons are important, but Brazil is demonstrating to be in the right path with the CDC reform, in particular the Federal Senate Bills: PLS no. 281 from 2012 on the general part of the CDC, *e-commerce*, and international consumer protection, and PLS no. 283 from 2012 on consumer credit, combat against abusive acts on consumers, prevention of overindebtedness, and treatment of natural people, now in discussion at the Chamber of Deputies. We hope that soon this dream of reforming the CDC, while celebrating 25 years of being in force, may come true.

In the field of international protection of consumers, the national projects are varied, such as PLS no. 281 from 2012, but one that deserves to be highlighted is the Brazilian project of Co-operation Convention to Protect Tourists, being advanced at the Hague Conference, joining efforts already existent in Europe (ECC-NET)[133] and Mercorsur (*Acuerdo interinstitucional de entendimiento entre los organismos de defensa del consumidor de los Estados Parte del Mercosur para la defensa del Consumidor visitante*)[134] with world powers like China and friend countries from Latin America. What we see ahead is a great prospect of a better cooperation and care with tourists.

Returning the initial argument, consumer protection serves as a development instrument for countries, promoting the quality of goods and services at the national market and increasing consumer reliance on the national market.

Sociologists well describe the importance of consumption nowadays, in this globalized and technological society. The consumer is the active agent of the market; to have access to the consumption of national and foreign goods is to have access to wealth and the positive effect of globalization. Hence, being excluded, not being a consumer, is to be in "poverty," being excluded from this new world.

As Bauman asserts: "In a consumerist society, the 'normal life' is the consumers' life, always worried in choosing among the great variety of opportunities, enjoyable

[133]Source: http://ec.europa.eu/consumers/ecc/index_en.htm.

[134]Source: www.mj.gov.br. See: http://blog.justica.gov.br/inicio/tag/acordo-institucional-para-protecao-do-consumidor-visitante/.

sensations and the rich experiences offered by the world. A 'happy life' (. . .)."[135] In opposition to the consumers included in a globalized consumerist society, "the poor of this consumerist society don't have access to a normal life; even less to a happy existence. . .abandoned consumers (. . .) exiled from the market (. . .). In a society of consumers, this inability is determinant to social degradation and 'internal exile'. This lack of appropriateness, this impossibility to obey the consumer duties, transforms into resentment: Who suffers it is excluded from the social feast shared amongst the others."[136]

In this sense, the horizons will only be reached by those consumers protected by the law and by the practice of this law, nationally and internationally. We hope this friendship between Brazil and China may help both countries find these new development horizons!

References

Ada PG et al (2007) Brazilian consumer defense code reviewed by the authors of the draft, 9th edn. Forense Universitária, Rio de Janeiro

Almeida JB (2003) Manual de direito do consumidor. Saraiva, São Paulo

Araujo Nde (2015) A proteção do consumidor nos contratos internacionais: necessidade de regulamentação específica se torna realidade no Brasil e demais países do Mercosul. Revista de Direito do Consumidor, vol 100, Jul–Ago

Benjamin AH (1993) A proteção do consumidor nos países menos desenvolvidos – A experiência da América Latina. Revista de Direito do Consumidor 8:200 et seq

Benjamin AHdeV (1993a) A proteção do consumidor nos países menos desenvolvidos – A experiência da América Latina. Revista de Direito do Consumidor, vol 8, Oct-10

Benjamin AH (1993b) O Código Brasileiro de Proteção do Consumidor. Revista de Direito do Consumidor, vol 7

Benjamin AH, Marques CL (2012) Relatório-Geral da Comissão de Juristas-Atualização do Código de Defesa do Consumidor. President of the Senate, Brasilia

Benjamin AH et al (2013) Comentários ao Código de Defesa do Consumidor, 4th edn. Ed. RT, São Paulo

Benjamin AH, Marques CL (2014) Extrato do Relatório-Geral da Comissão de Juristas do Senado Federal para atualização do Código de Defesa do Consumidor (14.03.2012). Revista de Direito do Consumidor, vol 92, Mar-Apr

[135]Bauman, Zigmunt, Trabajo, consumismo y nuevos pobres, (Trad. Victoria de los Ángeles Boschiroli), 1. Rep., Barcelona: Gedisa, 2003, p. 63: "Como afirma Bauman: "en una sociedad de consumo, la 'vida normal' es la de los consumidores, siempre preocupados por elegir entre la gran variedad de oportunidades, senaciones placenteras y ricas experiencias que el mundo les ofrece. Una 'vida feliz'. . ."

[136]Bauman, Zigmunt, Trabajo, consumismo y nuevos pobres, (Trad. Victoria de los Ángeles Boschiroli), 1. Rep., Barcelona: Gedisa, 2003, pp. 64–65: "los pobres de la sociedad de consumo no tienen acceso a una vida normal; menos aún, a una existencia feliz. . .consumidores manqués. . ., expulsados del mercado. . .En la sociedad de consumidores, esa incapacidad es causa determinante de degradación social y 'exilio' interno. Esta falta de idoneidad, esta imposibilidad de cumplir con los deberes del consumidor, se convierten en resentimineto: quien la sufre está excluido del banquete social que comparten los demás."

Benjamin AH, Marques CL, Bessa LR (2014) Manual de direito do consumidor, 6th edn. Ed. RT, São Paulo
Bessa LR (2009) Relação de consumo e Aplicação do Código de Defesa do Consumidor, 2nd edn. Ed. RT, São Paulo
Dan W (2012) A Protecção do Turista através do Direito do Consumidor: Efeitos da Globalização e o Estudo Empírico da China. Revista de Direito do Consumidor, vol 83
Dan W (2014) Tourist-consumer protection in Macau SAR of China as a world tourism destination. Revista de Direito do Consumidor, vol 92
Dan W (2016) Breves Notas sobre a Aplicação da Nova Lei do Consumidor na China: Novos Direitos e Novas Responsabilidades. Revista de Direito do Consumidor 103:129–142
Fiechter-Boulvard F (2000) La notion de vulnérabilité et sa consécration par le droit. In: Cohet-Cordey F (org.) Vulnérabilité et droit: le développement de la vulnérabilité et ses enjeux en droit. Presses Universitaires de Grenoble, Grenoble, pp 14 et seq
Garcia L (2007) Direito do Consumidor – Código comentado e Jurisprudência. Ed. Impetus, Niterói
Grinover AP et al (2007) Código Brasileiro de Defesa do Consumidor comentado pelos autores do anteprojeto, 9th edn. Forense, Rio de Janeiro
Gsell B (2014) Wohnraunmietrecht als Verbraucherrecht, in WuM, Juli
Jayme E (1995) Identité culturelle et intégration: le droit internationale privé postmoderne. Recueil des Cours de l'Académie de Droit International de La Haye, Kluwer, Doordrecht
Jayme E (1999) Visões para uma teoria pós-moderna do direito comparado. Revista dos Tribunais, vol 759, Jan
Klausner EA (2015) "A globalização e a proteção do consumidor brasileiro" (Globalization and protection of Brazilian consumers). In: Revista de Direito do Consumidor. N. 97. Jan./Feb
Lacour C (2007) Vieillesse et vulnérabilité. Presses Universitaires d'Aix Marseille, Marseille
Lipovetzky G (2006) Los tiempos hipermodernos. Anagrama, Barcelona
Lorenzetti RL (2006) Teoría de la decisión judicial: Fundamentos de derecho. Rubinzal-Culzoni, Buenos Aires
Marques CL (2001) A proteção do consumidor: aspectos de direito privado regional e geral. In: XXVII Curso de Derecho Internacional-OEA/CIJ, Ed. Secretaría General- Subsecretaria de Asuntos Jurídicos, Washington, pp 657–780
Marques CL (2002) A proteção do consumidor de produtos e serviços estrangeiros no brasil: primeiras observações sobre os contratos a distância no comércio eletrônico. Revista de Direito do Consumidor 41:39–64
Marques CL (2006) Consumer Protection in Private International Law Articles: the need for an Interamerican Convention on the law applicable to some consumer contracts and consumer transactions. In: Bourgoignie T (Dir.) Regards croisés sur les enjeux contemporains du droit de la consommation. Blais
Marques CL (2007) Modificações trazidas pela decisão da ADIn 2.591 sobre a constitucionalidade (e imperatividade) da aplicação do CDC aos contratos bancários, financeiros, de crédito e securitários. Processos repetitivos. Diálogo entre o Código de Defesa do Consumidor, o Código Civil de 2002, as leis bancárias aplicáveis aos contratos bancários com pessoas físicas, consumidores, sob a luz da Constituição Federal. Revista de Direito do Consumidor 68:289–398
Marques CL (2010) Brésil-Rapport national. In: Fernández Arroyo DP (ed) Consumer protection in international private relationships. CEDEP, Asunción
Marques CL (2012a) O 'diálogo das fontes' como método da nova teoria geral do direito: um tributo a Erik Jayme, in Marques, Claudia Lima. Diálogo das Fontes – do conflito à coordenação de normas no direito brasileiro. São Paulo
Marques CL (2012b) Towards a global approach to protect foreign tourists: building governance through a new cooperation net in consumer and tourist issues. In: Sierraltra A, Marques CL (orgs.) Derecho internacional, mundialización y gobernanza. Cedep, Assumption
Marques CL (2013) Esforços para incluir o tema da proteção do turista na Agenda de Trabalho da Conferência de Haia e a proposta brasileira de "Convenção de Cooperação em Matéria de

Proteção dos Visitantes e Turistas Estrangeiros". Revista de Direito do Consumidor, vol 90, Nov–Dec
Marques CL (2014a) Contratos no Código de Defesa do Consumidor. Ed. RT, São Paulo
Marques CL (2014b) sobre a vulnerabilidade dos analfabetos na sociedade de consumo: o caso do crédito consignado a consumidores analfabetos. Revista de Direito do Consumidor, vol 95
Marques CL (2015a) Cap. 4. In: Marques CL, Benjamin AH, Bessa LR (eds) Manual de Direito do Consumidor, 6th edn. São Paulo
Marques CL (2015b) Mulheres, Idosos e o Superendividamento dos Consumidores: cinco anos de dados empíricos do Projeto-Piloto em Porto Alegre. Revista de Direito do Consumidor, vol 100
Marques CL (2016) 25 anos de Código de Defesa do Consumidor e as sugestões traçadas pela Revisão de 2015 das Diretrizes da ONU de proteção dos consumidores para a atualização. Revista de Direito do Consumidor 103:55–106
Marques CL, Gsell B (2015) Novas Tendências do direito do consumidor: Rede Alemanha-Brasil de Pesquisas em Direito do Consumidor. São Paulo, Ed. RT
Marques CL Lima CCde (2013) Extratos dos substitutivos dos Projetos de Lei 281, 282 e 283 de 2012 authorship Senator Ricardo Ferraço. Revista de Direito do Consumidor, vol 90, Nov–Dez
Marques CL, Miragem B (2012) Anteprojetos de lei de atualização do Código de Defesa do Consumidor. Revista de Direito do Consumidor, v. 82 and FF. RT, April-June, São Paulo
Marques CL, Miragem B (2014) O Novo Direito Privado e a proteção dos vulneráveis. São Paulo
Marques CL, Miragem B, Lixinski L (2010) Development and consumption: foundations for a consumer protection as a human right analysis. In: Piovesan F, Smith AVP (eds) Right to development. Forum, Belo Horizonte
Martins PL (2002) O abuso nas relações de consumo e o princípio da boa-fé. Forense, Rio de Janeiro
Martins FR, Ferreira KP (2012). A contingente atualização do Código de Defesa do Consumidor: novas fontes, metodologia e devolução de conceitos. Revista de Direito do Consumidor, vol 83, RT, from July to September, São Paulo
Micklitz H-W (2014) Unfair commercial practices and misleading advertising. In: Reich N, Micklitz H-W, Rott P, Tonner K (eds) European consumer law. Intersentia, Cambridge
Miragem B (2003) A defesa administrativa do consumidor no Brasil – Alguns aspectos. Revista de Direito do Consumidor 46, pp 120–164, Apr-jun
Miragem B (2012) Direito do consumidor e ordenação do mercado o princípio da defesa do consumidor e sua aplicação na regulação da propriedade intelectual, livre concorrência e proteção do meio ambiente. Revista de Direito do Consumidor 81:41 et seq
Miragem B (2013) Serviços turísticos, espetáculos esportivos e culturais no mercado de consumo: a proteção do consumidor nas atividades de lazer e entretenimento. Revista de Direito do Consumidor 85
Miragem B (2014) Curso de Direito do Consumidor. 5. Ed. RT, São Paulo
Miragem B et al (2015) O volume 100 da Revista de Direito do Consumidor – Passado, Presente e Futuro. Revista de Direito do Consumidor 100:13–15
Morato AC (2008) Pessoa jurídica consumidor. Ed. RT, São Paulo
Nishiama AM (2010) A proteção constitucional do consumidor, 2nd edn. Forense, Rio de Janeiro
Pasqualotto A (1992) Os serviços públicos no Código de Defesa do Consumidor. Revista de Direito do Consumidor. 1
Reich N (2014) General principles of EU civil law. Intersentia, Cambridge
Schmitt CH (2014) Consumidores hipervulneráveis – A proteção do idoso no mercado de consumo. Atlas, São Paulo
Senado F (2010) Relatório vinte anos de vigência do Código de Defesa do consumidor: Gráfica do Senado Federal, Brasília
Senado F (2012) Atualização do Código de Defesa do Consumidor – Relatório. Presidência do Senado Federal, Brasília
Sodre MG (2009) A construção do direito do consumidor. Atlas, São Paulo
Yiing Y (2016) Chinese approaches to reform consumer protection law: substantive law and conflict law. Revista de Direito do Consumidor, vol 103

Chapter 10
Regional Integration and Consumer Safety: An Emerging Concern in the Gulf Region

Thierry Bourgoignie

10.1 The Need for Consumer Safety: Overall Policy Considerations

On any consumer market, being national, regional, or international, three major concerns are driving interventions by the legislator designed to increase consumers' protection against the risks linked to the use of products or services that may prove to be defective or dangerous:

- Reducing the risk of having products or services appear on the market that are defective or constitute a danger to their users; this objective is being pursued by strengthening upstream controls. The action is a preventive one: it relates to the quality and safety of the products brought into the marketplace; it is the responsibility of several stakeholders, i.e., the State authorities, standardization bodies, and economic operators themselves.
- Reducing the vulnerability of the individual user or his inability to avoid the occurrence of a defect or an accident: efforts are being made in order to increase the consumer's information about the nature, composition, properties, and instructions for use of the product or about the dangers associated with the use of the said product (informative certification and labeling, comparative tests, warnings and instructions, labeling requirements, etc.).
- Granting compensation to the victims of a product-related accident: the goal is to repair any damage caused by a safety defect that could not be avoided despite of the preventive controls made and the information made available.

The paper was previously published at Revista de Direito do Consumidor, Vol. 108.

T. Bourgoignie (✉)
Research Group on International and Comparative Consumer Law, Université du Québec à Montreal, Montreal, QC, Canada
e-mail: bourgoignie.thierry@uqam.ca

C. Lima Marques, D. Wei (eds.), *Consumer Law and Socioeconomic Development*,
DOI 10.1007/978-3-319-55624-6_10

Both individual and collective interests are at stake:

- Any individual consumer has a fundamental right to be protected against risks of death, personal injury, or damage caused by a product or service that is put into circulation on the marketplace. Notably, the right to safety has been proclaimed as one of the fundamental rights of consumers by the United Nations General Assembly Resolution "Guidelines for consumer protection" of April 1985, as amended in 1999 and recently revised in 2015.
- In a mass consumption society, that same right is shared by millions of consumers as it can be expected that one single product-related accident will cause damage to a high number of, if not all, buyers or users of the same product.
- Product-related accidents and damage will severely undermine the consumers' confidence in the marketplace and therefore interfere with the good functioning of the market system itself.
- Product-related accidents will have an immediate harmful impact on the perception of this country as a safe place for tourism, leisure, or shopping excursions. At a time when tourism is becoming the main source of revenues for several countries in the Gulf region, this policy consideration is of utmost importance.
- External costs that are linked to product-related accidents, such as social security payments, losses of income, compensation for unemployment, and damage to the environment involve society as a whole; hence, there is a fully justified rationale for not leaving the contracting parties alone to decide or to bargain on the ways to allocate risks, and also to involve the State authorities as representing public and social policy interests.

10.2 The Need for a Regional Response

While consumer safety should be a well-confirmed policy goal in each country, the building of a common market in the Gulf region and the opening of borders between Gulf Cooperation Council (GCC) States[1] call for policy responses to be defined at the regional or GCC level and responsibilities to be clearly allocated among national and regional competent authorities.

10.2.1 Gulf Region: An Emerging Common Market

Under the *Economic Agreement between the Gulf Cooperation Council States* adopted by the GCC Supreme Council on December 31, 2001, the "elimination

[1]GCC States are the United Arab Emirates, the Kingdom of Saudi Arabia, the Sultanate of Oman, the Kingdom of Bahrain, the State of Qatar and the State of Kuwait.

of all tariff and non-tariff barriers as well as rules regarding prohibited and restricted goods" is stated as a key segment of the customs union and common market to be established among the Contracting Parties (Articles 1 and 3). National laws, rules, and practices in the areas of consumer protection, product safety, and market surveillance may constitute measures equivalent to such obstacles to trade.

As known, some general interests protected under public national policies do constitute legitimate exemptions from the strict application of free-trade rules, as long as they are duly justified and not discriminatory. This is the case with the "protection of human life and health," which has been most commonly admitted as a legitimate exemption under bilateral, regional, or international free-trade agreements, including WTO rules.[2] While the Gulf Economic Agreement does not explicitly refer to such an exemption,[3] it can be expected that safety, including consumer safety, will be admitted as a valid exemption from the strict application of the Agreement's free-trade principles.

The Economic Agreement also confirms the importance of law approximation as a tool for limiting trade irritants between the Gulf States. Chapter III of the Economic Agreement requires GCC States to achieve a "high level of harmonization between Member States" in all relevant areas. These will include consumer protection and consumer safety. Namely, Article 5 of the Agreement calls for Member States "to take the steps to adopt unified standards and specifications for products."

Besides, the planned economic integration process shall be accompanied by the creation of regional institutions in charge of taking initiatives, including legislative ones, aiming to develop and to consolidate the common market under construction. Institutional systems and mechanisms shall be established in order to monitor the actual implementation by the Member States of the policies adopted and legislation enacted by the regional (Gulf) competent authorities (Chapter VIII of the Economic Agreement).

The regional institution that has been designated as competent in the area of product safety is *the GCC Standardization Organization* (GSO). While GSO's tasks mainly relate to standardization, its functions by far exceed voluntary standard setting and include the adoption of mandatory standards and technical regulations, market surveillance, conformity assessment, accreditation, and even consumer protection.[4]

---

[2]Conway (2012).

[3]The only exemption explicitly made under the Economic Agreement is for environment protection measures (Article 10).

[4]See GSO By-laws on www.gso.org.sa.

10.2.2 Consumer Safety as a Regional Policy Concern

Market regionalization, i.e. the emergence and development of economically integrated zones at regional levels, such as the GCC Common Market, brings obvious benefits to consumers in terms of increased choice, more competition, and hence reduced price on the marketplace.

However, it also entails risks of additional market gaps in the protection of consumers on national marketplaces:

- Increased circulation of goods and services and less border controls between GCC States increase the risk that dangerous products freely circulate in the region.
- The multiplication of ports of entry increases the risk that dangerous or nonregulated products imported from other countries enter the territory of the region.
- Dumping of dangerous products from higher regulated countries within the Gulf region to less regulated member States is highly probable.
- Transborder consumer markets may create additional market failures or unbalances between consumers and economic operators with respect to consumer information, negotiation of contract terms, and redress mechanisms. Namely, cross-border transactions do create complex issues regarding the jurisdiction designated as competent to handle consumer complaint and the law declared applicable to the case.

Besides, the application of different consumer protection and product safety rules and/or market surveillance practices throughout the Gulf region is hardly compatible with the objective of building up an open and single market between the GCC States. Lack of uniformity creates distortions of competition and disparities between the Gulf States. Such disparities entail different levels of constraints for economic operators within the region, as well as different levels of protection for consumers residing in the Gulf or visitors to the Gulf countries.

There is also a need to approximate the level of safety that is granted to consumers within the economically integrated region to the level of protection granted on foreign markets, in order to avoid that the products recalled, prohibited, or restricted from high-regulated markets outside of the Gulf region be exported to and admitted into the region. Simultaneously, exports from the Gulf region to foreign markets will become increasingly dependent upon the conformity of Gulf products with safety and quality standards applicable on higher-regulated markets.

Market globalization makes the approximation of regional frameworks for consumer safety with internationally accepted regulations and standards unavoidable and urgently needed. This is especially true for the Gulf region, where both consumer protection and product safety remain far less regulated areas than in other world regions.

Consumer protection is a recent policy concern in the Gulf countries. To date, only the Sultanate of Oman has defined a broad consumer protection strategy and adopted a comprehensive law on consumer protection;[5] in the other Gulf countries, Consumer Protection Acts, while in the process of consolidation,[6] remain very limited in scope and poorly enforced. Moreover, one major GCC State, i.e. the Kingdom of Saudi Arabia, has not adopted any law on consumer protection yet.

The same is true with product safety legislation. None of the GCC States has adopted an umbrella legislation on product safety, nor is there any law on market surveillance. Product safety is mainly, if not exclusively, based on the adoption of sector-by-sector mandatory standards and technical regulations by State standardization bodies. There is no such concept as general product safety or commonly accepted definition of a safe product. The interpretation of safety remains restricted to the lack of conformity of the product with existing standards and regulations. The main institution responsible for product safety, market surveillance, and even consumer protection is the standardization authority. As to market surveillance activities, they remain by far less developed in the nonfood sector, mostly reactive, limited to products for which mandatory standards exist, not clearly defined, and poorly enforced.

This limited and piecemeal approach is not compatible anymore with the more comprehensive and detailed policies and legislation developed in the area of product safety and market surveillance by the main trade partners of the Gulf States. Legal initiatives recently taken worldwide in the area of product safety and market surveillance are indeed numerous. Let us quote, as for example:

- at the level of the European Union: *Directive 2001/95 of 3rd December 2001 on General Product Safety*, *Regulation 765/2008 of 9th July 2008 setting out the requirements for accreditation and market surveillance relating to the marketing of products*, *Commission Decision 768/2008 of 9th July 2008 on a common framework for the marketing of products*, and the proposal submitted in 2013 for a so-called "Product Safety and Market Surveillance Package," likely to improve the safety of products circulating in the Single Market and to step up market surveillance concerning all nonfood products;
- in the United States: the *Consumer Product Safety Improvement Act* of 2013;
- in Canada: the Federal *Product Safety Act* of 2010;
- in Australia: the *Australian Consumer Law* of 2010;
- in China: several important legislation on food and product safety adopted in the past several years, as well as increased cooperation between EU, US, and China authorities (*Trilateral Summits*).

[5]*Sultani Decree 66/2014 promulgating the Law on consumer protection.*

[6]Bahrain: *Law 35/2012 on consumer protection*; Kuwait: *Law 39/2014 on consumer protection*; Qatar: *Law 8/2008 on consumer protection* and *Ministerial Decree 68/2012*; United Arab Emirates: *Federal Law 24/2006 on consumer protection*; Yemen: *Law 46/2008 on consumer protection*.

10.3 Ongoing Initiatives

The Gulf region, under the leading role of GSO, is moving in the direction of a more integrated and harmonized legal framework for product safety, consumer protection, and market surveillance, which recognizes internationally accepted standards and laws.

A quick reference to the following recent developments illustrates this new policy trend in the region:

- At the national level—
  - United Arab Emirates: draft of a *Federal Law on Product Safety*, as submitted to the Cabinet of Ministers;
  - Emirate of Dubai: draft of *Law on Public Safety*, as approved by the Executive Council of Dubai Municipality;
  - Bahrain: draft of *Law on Standardization*, pending;
  - UAE, Bahrain, Kuwait, Oman, Qatar, and Yemen: laws on consumer protection recently adopted or revised.
- At the regional level—
  - Draft of *Law on Product Safety and Market Surveillance*, as prepared and finalized by GSO;
  - Draft of *Model Law on Consumer Protection*, as prepared and finalized by the GCC Consumer Protection Committee;
  - GSO Strategy on Product Safety and Market Surveillance for 2016–2020, adopted;
  - GSO Sectoral Technical Regulations for Low Voltage Electrical Equipment and Appliances (2014), for Children's Toys (2013), on G Marking (2008), and on General Product Safety (2008):
  - guidance documents and recommendations adopted by GSO (for example, on conformity assessment modules and notified bodies);
  - intensive training programs run by GSO.

Reference

Conway E (2012) La protection du consommateur à l'épreuve de l'Organisation mondiale du commerce. Éditions Yvon Blais, Cowansville (Québec, Canada)

Part II
Financial Crisis and Consumer Protection

Chapter 11
Consumer Credit Regulation and International Financial Markets: Lessons from the Mortgage Meltdown

James P. Nehf

11.1 Introduction

According to estimates from the International Monetary Fund, worldwide banking losses resulting from the mortgage meltdown and ensuing financial crisis were approximately $1 trillion U.S., of which $500M+ was represented by a decline in home values and foreclosures (a trend that continues today as losses continue to grow) and $400M+ in other categories of loans and securities related to real estate, consumer credit, and corporate debt.[1] Later estimates, looking at a broader range of peripheral losses, totaled more than $4 trillion.[2] Balance sheets of multinational financial institutions were severely weakened (e.g., the collapse of Wall Street titan Bear Stearns). Market liquidity dried up, with curtailed credit availability for banks; business, small and large; and consumers. In the aftermath, unemployment doubled, economic growth halted, and a prolonged recession settled in and has continued for several years in most of the developed world.

Much of the political reaction to the crisis focused on the impact of the subprime housing market on Wall Street investment firms and multinational banks that were deemed "too big to fail." Little attention was given to the reasons why the subprime housing market failed in the first place: the weakening of consumer protection laws that could have prevented the rampant fraud and predatory lending practices in the subprime market if they had been maintained (or strengthened) and rigorously

---

[1]Morris (2008).

[2]*I.M.F. Puts Bank Losses From Global Financial Crisis at $4.1 Trillion*, New York Times, Apr. 21, 2009. Other estimated losses went as high as $14 trillion. *See* Tyler Atkinson, David Luttrell, and Harvey Rosenblum, *How Bad Was It? The Costs and Consequences of the 2007-09 Financial Crisis,* (Federal Reserve Bank of Dallas, July 2013).

J.P. Nehf (✉)
Robert H. Mckinney School of Law, Indiana University, Indianapolis, IN, USA
e-mail: jnehf@iupiu.edu

C. Lima Marques, D. Wei (eds.), *Consumer Law and Socioeconomic Development*,
DOI 10.1007/978-3-319-55624-6_11

enforced. This chapter reviews the historical development and purpose of those laws, chronicles the economic forces that caused them to be modified or ignored, and examines the repercussions that followed. It concludes by summarizing the key elements of the "Dodd-Frank Wall Street Reform and Consumer Protection Act" and the role that the newly created and still controversial Consumer Financial Protection Bureau will play in preventing a similar crisis from crippling the world economy in the future.

11.2 The Root Cause: Subprime Lending in the U.S.

Although many conditions contributed to the crisis, or heightened its severity, the subprime lending market in the United States was at the root of the problem. Subprime lending is the extension of credit to consumers that do not qualify for the best rates and credit terms because their income or assets are too low or they have a relatively weak credit history.[3] During the early part of the twenty-first century, subprime lending in the home mortgage market was characterized by higher up-front costs (high application fees, high appraisal fees, mandatory credit insurance, etc.), low or no down payments (money often borrowed for the entire purchase price and associated transaction fees, little or no verification of a borrower's income or ability to pay, interest-only loans or adjustable rate mortgages (ARMs) to keep payments affordable for the first few months or years, misleading disclosures of basic loan terms, and bait and switch tactics to generate business revenue.[4]

The subprime market grew exponentially during this period for several reasons. First, home prices in many markets (particularly on the East and West coasts) were skyrocketing, in some markets rising at 20% or more per year. Many individuals in those markets, even many with good credit, could not afford the down payments and monthly installment payments on relatively small homes under traditional underwriting standards. Second, the U.S. Congress passed laws that encouraged lending to lower-income individuals to help them attain home ownership in ways that previously were not available. Third, the mortgage broker industry flourished, and small businesses sprang up offering to find creative and affordable mortgages for people at low cost. Because mortgage brokers typically would sell the mortgage without recourse in a secondary market as soon as it was issued, the brokers assumed none of the risks if the mortgage failed. Thus, they had little incentive to ensure that the mortgage was suitable for the individual long term or that the individual could pay the monthly payments when the initial low interest rate expired.[5] The combination of these factors flooded the market with buyers bidding

---

[3]Donna (2000), p. 4, (quoting Interagency Guidance on Subprime Lending, March 1, 1999).

[4]Shelby (2009).

[5]Nestor and Rashmi (2010), pp. 1607, 1626.

up prices on houses and saddling consumers with large mortgage debts and inflated values of their homes.

This dynamic continued for several years, and all was well while home prices continued to soar. If a temporary (adjustable rate) mortgage was about to expire, a homeowner could find another broker (or often the same broker) to refinance the mortgage under another temporary, adjustable rate. Success of this model depended on an inflationary housing market, so borrowers in short-term mortgages could either refinance or sell at a profit. While predictions of a decline were heard for years, few in the banking industry heeded the warnings until it was too late.[6]

If the only problem was a marginal increase in the number of home foreclosures, many banks and mortgage lenders would have lost money, but the losses would have been manageable and bank failures relatively few. The risks compounded, however, by the expansion of the securitization of mortgages and their importance in the investment community. In the aftermath of the September 11 attacks on the United States, the stock market collapsed, causing investors to look for "safe" investments with good returns. To spur the economy, however, the Federal Reserve Board lowered interest rates, so investments in traditional bonds and other debt instruments yielded low returns.[7] The creation of collateralized mortgage obligations (CMOs) with government guarantees (facilitated by Fannie Mae and Freddy Mac) offered investors good returns, but traditional CMOs with government guarantees were less lucrative than many private CMOs without government guarantees. In an effort to increase the yields on CMOs, Wall Street banks created complex hybrid securities that promised stable maturities and cash flows.[8] To increase the returns, subprime mortgages were mixed into the hybrids because they were usually at higher interest rates, up to 20% of the assets in some of these CMOs. Largely due to securitizations transactions, the dollar value of subprime loan originations rose from $96.8 billion in 1996 to approximately $ 600 billion in 2006.[9] These investments even attracted Fannie Mae and Freddy Mac (shorthand references to entities that underwrote home mortgage loans with government guaranties) as an investment option because of their higher returns.[10]

While there was nothing wrong with mixing in higher-risk mortgages with lower-risk mortgages in a CMO, success of the investments depended largely on rating agencies valuing the risks accurately. They did not do so for a variety of reasons, and they underestimated the rate of default on the risky mortgages.[11] One

[6]Jo (2008).

[7]Robert (2009), pp. 113–137 . ("Through most of 2003 and into 2004, the federal funds rate stood at 1%-the lowest it had ever been.").

[8]Andrew (2010), p. 1383.

[9]Ashcraft and Schuermann (2008).

[10]The quasi-government mortgage underwriter Freddie Mac created the first CMO's in 1983, but its foray into the subprime market was a foreshadowing of dangerous times ahead. Anna and Adam (2009), p. 1075.

[11]See U.S. Sec. & Exch. Comm'n, *Summary Report of Issues Identified in the Commission Staff's Examinations of Select Credit Rating Agencies* 34–35 (2008), available at http://www.sec.gov/

reason for the underestimation was the assumption that the mortgages were issued in compliance with applicable laws and underwriting standards in the states where they were issued. But mortgage brokers and other issues had taken shortcuts and issued mortgages under terms that were destined to fail. Rating agencies took shortcuts of their own and did not perform the required due diligence to make an accurate assessment of the risks.[12]

11.2.1 What Caused the Crisis?

To summarize these events, as U.S. housing prices soared, mortgage originators created new products and approved subprime mortgages on terms that many debtors could not afford for long. Securitization of mortgages removed originators from default risk and spread risk among the investor class. Rating agencies underplayed the default risks to securities investors, and when home prices flattened, as was inevitable, borrower default rates increased more than expected. They increased for many reasons, but two of the primary reasons were the adjustment of temporary rates to much higher rates that mandated monthly payments that many homeowners could not afford and the inability to refinance at lower rates because flattened or reduced home values would not support a refinancing without a large down payment. Compounding the problem, since many people paid little or no money down on their homes, they had no equity in the home. After a few months in arrears, there was little incentive to try to keep the home. Keys were turned over to the bank in foreclosure.

Default rates were not drastically higher than expected. Most banks could absorb a marginal decrease in returns and survive. However, the relaxing of regulations governing investment banks during the first decade of the twenty-first century allowed banks such as Lehman Brothers and Bear Stearns to leverage their holdings by as much as 35 or 40 to 1,[13] meaning that for every $1 million they held in assets they were borrowing $35–40 million. When holdings are leveraged to such a great extent, if returns are only slightly higher than expected, Wall Street bankers make billions, but if they are slightly lower than expected, they lose billions and cannot cover their debts. Once the house of cards began to fall, banks everywhere shored up their positions to protect their assets, short-term lending among banks came to a shrieking halt, and firms in overleveraged positions either failed because they could not repay what they owed or had to be rescued by the Federal Reserve Bank

---

news/studies/2008/craexamination070808.pdf (finding that rating agencies underestimated risks associated with subprime mortgage-backed securities); Carrick Mollenkamp et al., *Behind AIG's Fall, Risk Models Failed to Pass Real-World Test,* Wall St. J., Nov. 3, 2008, at A1 (discussing the failure of AIG's risk models and quoting Warren Buffett: "All I can say is, beware of geeks ... bearing formulas.").

[12]Devine (2011), p. 177.

[13]Jonathan and Christopher (2010), p. 647; Curt (2010), p. 889; Robert (2003), p. 765.

virtually overnight if they were deemed "too big to fail." This led to the tightening of credit markets worldwide, unemployment as businesses hesitated to expand (or could not find capital to finance expansion), and the great recession that has lingered for years.

11.2.2 The Role of Consumer Credit Laws in the Financial Crisis

The weakening of consumer credit laws in the home mortgage market was not the sole cause of the financial crisis, but it was certainly a contributing cause. For many years, state consumer laws protected against deceptive practices and unfair terms in the mortgage market, particularly with respect to subprime lending. Beginning in the 1990s, changes in federal law preempted many state consumer laws that were designed to protect consumers against unfair lending practices. Then credit rating agencies pressured states to weaken consumer laws further to increase efficiencies in securities markets nationwide. And mortgage brokers found loopholes in the remaining state and federal consumer protection laws (legally in many cases) and issued mortgages under terms that were likely to fail. Mortgage-backed securities (CMOs) then included these mortgages in the investments that precipitated the financial meltdown.

As examples of consumer protection laws before the crisis, at the federal level the Home Ownership and Equity Protection Act (HOEPA)[14] gives consumers in many mortgage transactions a right to cancel, prohibited balloon payments, requires lenders to consider a debtor's ability to repay, and banned negative amortization (with loss of equity) and prepayment penalties. However, HOEPA was not applicable to an initial purchase money mortgage (only refinancing of existing mortgages), and it was not applicable to open-end lines of credit (traditional home equity lines). It also applied only when the initial APR is very high or upfront fees are very high. State laws often filled the gaps. They added important protection such as interest rate ceilings, limits on negative amortization, prohibitions against prepayment penalties, deceptive practices, etc.[15]

All of these terms became common in subprime mortgages because the state laws were modified in many states under pressure from securities rating agencies. Rating agencies (such as Fitch, Standard & Poor's, and Moody's) lobbied to standardize and weaken state lending laws to create more uniformity nationwide and simplify the securitization of mortgage products. Rating agencies threatened that they would not rate CMOs (or would require costly "credit enhancements") if state borrower protection laws were deemed too strict.[16] Many states capitulated

---

[14]Codified in Federal Reserve Board Regulation Z (2011), 12 C.F.R. 226.32.

[15]Patricia et al. (2009), p. 1327.

[16]Daniel (2009), p. 447.

and changed their laws to avoid the flow of mortgage capital away from their states and into states where laws were weaker.[17] Investors were not told that laws had changed or that payments on mortgages (and investment returns) depended on debtors whose credit risk had not been evaluated under diligent underwriting practices. Compounding the problem, mortgage brokers were evading the consumer laws that remained, with few consequences because once they sold the loans in the secondary market, they were out of the picture. Investors were not told that brokers were skirting the laws that remained on the books, increasing the investment risk.

11.2.3 What Might Have Been

If state and federal consumer credit laws had not been weakened, in all likelihood mortgage rates for many borrowers would have been higher, some applicants would not have qualified for mortgages under normal underwriting standards, and home values would not have increased at such a rapid pace because there would have been fewer buyers bidding up prices. More importantly, there also would have been fewer defaults, fewer consumer credit records damaged, fewer losses to investors and securities firms, and less calamitous impact on the U.S. and world economies.

Politicians, regulators, and voters should understand that there are good reasons for consumer protection laws: (a) they help ensure that consumers are well informed about the benefits, risks, and options when deciding whether to enter into a transaction and under what terms; (b) they channel consumers that probably should not be entering into a transaction away from transactions they are not well suited for, or if they are not channeled away the consumers at least go forward fully aware of the risks; and (c) they foster efficiencies in the investment markets that depend on transparency and accurate valuation of the assets that support the investment.

11.3 Moving Forward

In July 2010, President Obama signed into law the "Dodd-Frank Wall Street Reform and Consumer Protection Act," a mammoth piece of legislation totaling over 800 printed pages.[18] Among its many provisions, the law called for the creation of a new, independent consumer protection agency, Consumer Financial Protection Bureau (CFPB), which was created to protect consumer borrower interests in financial transactions. Dodd-Frank also reformed mortgage laws,

[17]Kingo (2010), p. 335.

[18]Dodd-Frank Wall Street Reform and Consumer Protection Act, Pub. L. 111–203, H.R. 4173 (2010), at http://www.sec.gov/about/laws/wallstreetreform-cpa.pdf.

created new rules for securities rating agencies, and made other changes designed to insulate financial markets from "systemic" risks in the future.

The CFPB was a key part of President Obama's plan to reform the financial system in the United States. In its early drafting stages, it was a proposal for an entirely new agency, similar in structure to the Federal Trade Commission, but a political compromise made it a "bureau" under the Federal Reserve Board. The CFPB, however, does have independent rulemaking and enforcement authority in well-defined areas of its jurisdiction. The justification for the bureau was succinctly stated by its most prominent advocate, Elizabeth Warren, a Harvard law professor (and later U.S. Senator) who became the interim chief of the bureau shortly after it was created:

> It is impossible to buy a toaster that has a one-in-five chance of bursting into flames and burning down your house. But it is possible to refinance an existing home with a mortgage that has the same one-in-five chance of putting the family out on the street... Similarly, it's impossible to change the price on a toaster once it has been purchased. But long after the papers have been signed, it is possible to triple the price of the credit used to finance the purchase... The difference between the two markets is regulation.[19]

Advocates for the CFPB argued that there was little transparency in complex consumer credit products (particularly in the home mortgage market), hidden costs could trap consumers in expensive mortgage plans, and conflicts of interest existed with current bank regulators because bank solvency (not consumer protection) was their primary mission. Thus, over time the laws protecting consumer borrowers became weaker across the board.

Compounding these problems, regulator "shopping" by financial institutions inhibited the development of strong consumer rules as banks and other credit grantors structured themselves so they would fall under the regulatory authority of the agency that would best serve their goals, which usually meant less strict consumer borrower rules. To illustrate, the following regulators of financial institutions existed at the time Dodd-Frank became law: the Office of Comptroller of Currency (OCC), which regulated national banks and foreign bank branches; the Federal Reserve Board (FRB), which regulated banks that are members of the federal reserve system and bank holding companies; the Office of Thrift Supervision (OTS), which regulated federal savings and loan associations; the National Credit Union Administration (NCUA), which regulated federal (and some state) credit unions; the Federal Deposit Insurance Corporation (FDIC), which regulated state-chartered banks that are not members of the federal reserve system; and the Federal Trade Commission (FTC), which regulated creditors not regulated by other federal agencies. In addition, numerous state agencies regulated credit grantors to some extent. Under this system, any agency that imposed strict borrower protection rules would see credit grantors restructuring so they would be regulated by a less strict agency. The result was a "race to the bottom" with respect to consumer rules,

[19]Elizabeth Warren (2007), p. 8; Bar and Elizabeth (2008), pp: 98–100.

as none of the agencies had adopted or enforced rules to prevent the type of practices that led to the mortgage crisis.

11.3.1 *Hope for the Future*

There is some reason to hope that history will not repeat and that reforms are now in place that will prevent a similar financial crisis in the future. The CFPB is empowered to address most forms of consumer credit products. It must "consult" with bank regulators in rulemaking, but it has independent authority to create more effective borrower protection rules.[20] Most importantly, unlike the bank regulators, the primary mission of the CFPB is consumer protection. The bureau has power to determine that financial products and practices are unfair or deceptive, and it can require that disclosures to borrowers be clear, simple, and concise so people can make better-informed decisions about the credit agreements they make. The CFPB also has enforcement and examination powers over most large lenders in the United States, will take a lead role in educating consumers about all credit matters, will review mandatory contract clauses in consumer financial contracts to assess fairness, and has jurisdiction over debt collectors, debt buyers, and other players in financial markets.[21]

There is a significant risk, however, that the powers of the CFPB will be weakened by efforts of the Republican Party in the U.S. Congress, which now has majorities in both the House of Representatives and the Senate, although this could change with the elections in November 2016. Republican members of Congress tend to favor market solutions over mandated government norms, and many seek to abolish or weaken the CFPB. They fear that the bureau will burden financial institutions with additional costs, threaten bank solvency with unnecessary rules, increase cost of credit to consumers, and create credit restrictions that will hurt small businesses that rely on credit to fund their businesses, resulting in job losses.

11.3.2 *Mortgage Law Reforms*

Even if the CFPB is abolished or its powers curtailed, other reforms in Dodd-Frank may help prevent another financial crisis, although many critics say that the bank reforms did not go far enough in this regard. Mortgage lenders must make a

---

[20]For a list of final rules issued by the CFPB through August 2016, see the CFPB website on "Final Rules" at http://www.consumerfinance.gov/policy-compliance/rulemaking/final-rules/?formid=1&filter1_title=&filter1_topics=Mortgages.

[21]John and Kristin (2010).

"reasonable determination," based on verified and documented information, that the borrower can repay the loan, and they must make reasonable efforts to verify a borrower's income.[22] They cannot steer consumers into loans that are against the customer's interests. The law prohibits incentive pay to mortgage originators based on the type of loan taken (compensation must be tied to the amount of the loan principal regardless of mortgage type), and there can be no more "yield spread premiums" (bonuses to brokers just for getting borrowers to accept higher interest loans when they actually qualified for lower rates).[23] The law also limits prepayment penalties on conventional mortgages and prohibits such penalties completely on more complex loans. It creates stricter requirements for property appraisals, which may prevent lenders from overvaluing properties and lending more against the property than is prudent.[24]

11.3.3 New Rules for Securities Rating Agencies

In an effort to improve the critical role that credit rating agencies play in securities markets, Dodd-Frank introduces a strict regulatory framework for credit rating firms to improve quality of ratings, objectivity, and accountability. It imposes limits on "shopping" for good ratings among rating firms, calls for new rules on conflicts of interest, creates an Office of Credit Ratings at the SEC with its own compliance staff and authority to fine agencies, and creates a private right of action for investors against rating agencies for a "knowing or reckless" failure to conduct a reasonable investigation during rating process.[25]

11.3.4 "Stress Tests" Imposed by the Federal Reserve Board

Dodd-Frank also required the Federal Reserve Board to ensure the safety of the largest financial institutions, as well as the overall strength of the financial system. The Federal Reserve has adopted regulations to enhance the capital strength and liquidity of several systematically important financial institutions that are deemed "too big to fail."[26] Capital and liquidity standards are now determined by

[22]These rules took effect in January 2014. *See* 12 C.F.R. 1026.43.

[23]*See* Federal Register, Vol. 75, No. 185, Friday, September 24, 2010.

[24]*See* Wall Street Reform: The Dodd-Frank Act, https://www.whitehouse.gov/economy/middle-class/dodd-frank-wall-street-reform; and H.R.4173—Dodd-Frank Wall Street Reform and Consumer Protection Act111th Congress (2009–2010) https://www.congress.gov/bill/111th-congress/house-bill/4173.

[25]*See* "Credit Rating Agencies," Securities Exchange Commission, at https://www.sec.gov/spotlight/dodd-frank/creditratingagencies.shtml.

[26]Mark et al. (2016).

internationally accepted norms (the "Basel III" accord), but the Fed raised these standards higher for the largest U.S. banks. Similar standards were imposed by banking regulators in other countries.[27] Banks are also required to conduct "stress tests,"[28] which are designed to verify whether they can operate in conditions similar to those that occurred during the financial crisis. In addition, large banks are required to develop plans (often referred to as "living wills") to manage potential failure and reduce their chances of needing a government bailout. In April 2016, however, federal regulators said that five of the country's largest banks, including JPMorgan Chase and Bank of America, still did not have credible plans in place.[29]

11.4 Conclusion

Although the memories of politicians (and voters) can be short, the most important lesson to be learned from the financial crisis is that while consumer protection laws may impede some market transactions, some transactions should not be made in the first place and effective laws can help ensure that they do not occur, or if they do occur, at least informed consumers know what they are getting into and the market operates more efficiently. In addition, allowing lenders to evade or ignore consumer laws without fear of enforcement can have far-reaching, systemic impact beyond harm to borrowers, especially when loans are securitized in highly leveraged transactions. For securities markets to work efficiently, there must be market transparency and reliable ratings, which effective consumer laws can help facilitate. In sum, while businesses may view consumer protection laws as a nuisance or impediment to the pursuit of short-term profits, they are essential to sustaining economic growth and stability over the long term.

References

Andrew JK (2010) The home mortgage crisis: protecting absent stakeholders in foreclosure litigation: the foreclosure crisis, mortgage modification, and the state court responses. Loyola Los Angel Law Rev 43:1383

Anna G, Adam JL (2009) Rewriting Frankenstein contracts: workout prohibitions in residential mortgage-backed securities. South Calif Law Rev 82:1075

Ashcraft A, Schuermann T (2008) Understanding the Securitization of Subprime Mortgage Credit, Working Paper. Federal Reserve Bank of New York

Bar O, Elizabeth W (2008) Making credit safer. Univ Penn Law Rev 157:98–100

Curt H (2010) Mortgage forgiveness debt relief act of 2007. Cap Univ Law Rev 38:889

---

[27] Stijn and Laura (2014).

[28] *See* the Federal Reserve stress test guides at http://www.federalreserve.gov/bankinforeg/dfa-stress-tests.htm.

[29] Renae (2016).

Daniel I (2009) Private risk, public risk: public policy, market development, and the mortgage crisis. Fordham Urban Law J 36:447
Devine E (2011) The collapse of an empire? Rating agency reform in the wake of the 2007 financial crisis. Fordham J Corp Fin Law 16:177
Donna T (2000) Predatory Lending. Raises Default Risk, Mortgaging Serv. News, June 16
Kingo H (2010) Preying on the American dream: the argument for HOEPA reform amidst predatory lending's dire effects on the elderly poor. Geo J Poverty Law Policy 17:335
Jo C (2008) Dangerous loans: consumer challenges to adjustable rate mortgages. Berkeley Bus Law J 5:1
John EV, Kristin AM (2010) What You Need to Know About the Consumer Financial Protection Bureau, 10-2 Antitrust Src. 1, December
Jonathan CL, Christopher MD (2010) The SEC in Bankruptcy: past, present and future: controlling the market for information in reorganization. Am Bankr Inst Law Rev 18:647
Mark H, Tim S, John RW (2016) Understanding the new liquidity coverage ratio requirements. Richmond Federal Reserve Board, January
Morris G (2008) The subprime and credit crisis. Peterson Institute, April 3
Nestor MD, Rashmi D-C (2010) Property in crisis. Fordham Law Rev 78:1607, 1626
Patricia AM, Andrey DP, Susan MW (2009) Systemic risk through securitization: the result of deregulation and regulatory failure. Conn Law Rev 41:1327
Renae M (2016) Regulators Reject Plans of 5 Big U.S. Banks for Preventing Another Taxpayer Bailout, Washington Post, 13, April
Robert BC (2003) The Bankruptcy of Haig-Simons? The inequity of equity and the definition of income in consumer Bankruptcy cases. Am Bankr Inst Law Rev 10:765
Robert TM (2009) Morals in a market bubble. Dayton Law Rev 35:113–137
Shelby DG (2009) Disquiet on the home front: disturbing crises in the nation's markets and institutions. Pace Law Rev. 30:7, n. 14
Stijn C, Laura K (2014) The Regulatory Responses to the Global Financial Crisis: Some Uncomfortable Questions. IMF Working Paper, Research Department and Institute for Capacity Development, March
Warren E (2007) Unsafe at any rate: if it's good enough for microwaves, it's good enough for mortgages. Democracy 8

Chapter 12
The International Financial Crisis and the Protection of the Brazilian Consumer

Héctor Valverde Santana

12.1 Introduction

The financial crisis that has originated in the United States in September 2008 has as a consequence the so-called bubble in the American house market. In just a few terms, the mortgage loan of almost all the world was impaired, and the crisis became global.

During the time of the crisis, the main focus of the protected measures adopted by governments around the world was the protection of the market and the inner industry, to stimulate industrial production and avoid bankruptcies.[1] This concern, on the other side, is also implicated in some protected policies that need to be limited by international rules, like the General Agreement on Trade in Services[2] and the World Trade Organization rules, with a view to ensuring the maintenance of the international trade.[3] The inner protected measures had as collateral effect the restriction of the international trade in view of the growth of the "protectionist incentives, that intensified the 1930's crisis and stimulated the economical and political nationalism."[4]

The main policies implemented by governments around the world were implied—or, at least, they tried to—in the reduction of interest rates, stimulating

[1]Naidin et al. (2012), p. 1. Available in: www.fgv.br/direitogv/projetopontes. Access in: 25 jun. 2012.

[2]Sigla em Inglês: GATS.

[3]Naidin et al. (2012), p. 3. Available in: www.fgv.br/direitogv/projetopontes. Access in: 25 jun. 2012.

[4]Naidin et al. (2012), p. 1. Available in: www.fgv.br/direitogv/projetopontes. Access in: 25 jun. 2012.

H.V. Santana (✉)
Faculty of Law, University Center of Brasília, Brasília, Brazil
e-mail: hectorvsantana@gmail.com

C. Lima Marques, D. Wei (eds.), *Consumer Law and Socioeconomic Development*,
DOI 10.1007/978-3-319-55624-6_12

consumption by facilitating credit, the injection of public money in financial institutions to prevent bankruptcy, and providing the supporting of the consumption market. Suppliers of products were also protected by stimulating production and employment; especially, they can take advantage of government procurement, and investment and production subsidies by the state.[5]

In Brazil, the crisis has a weight different from that of the rest of the world. As highlights Luiz Ricardo ChagasAmorim, Brazil had a "path of economic growth and increased rate of inward investment."[6] Despite the instability of the global market, Brazil has reasonable internal economic condition that result in relative stability when compared with other countries.

However, the international financial crisis also reached Brazil. Despite statements by the then President of the Republic Luis Inacio Lula da Silva, the international financial crisis certainly affected Brazil. As pointed out by Perla Buenrostro, "there was in December (2008), a decrease of 12.4% of its industrial production, the worst since 1991. Likewise, according to the Brazilian Central Bank, exports were reduced by 26% in January 2009."[7] The letter of juncture of the Brazilian Institute of Applied Economic Research (IPEA, in Portuguese), dated March 2010, describes in detail the arrival of the international financial crisis in Brazil: "With the deepening of the international financial crisis, from the fall of Lehman Brothers Bank, which occurred in September 2008, the international situation has undergone great shock. The risk of a systemic crisis caused a sharp drop in liquidity in financial markets, accompanied by a sharp rise in risk aversion of investors. Thus, the global demand also dropped, causing a strong negative impact on commodity prices. In this first stage, the crisis hit the Brazilian economy through two mechanisms, namely the interruption of funding sources and the fall in global demand for our products exported. These two factors, coupled with an internal situation in which the level of stocks reflecting an expectation of growing demand, caused a strong reduction in the level of industrial production. On the demand side, both investment and the quantities exported and imported were also greatly affected by the crisis, reflecting not only the fall in production, but the increase in uncertainty and downturn in external demand. (...) Given the severity of effects triggered by the financial crisis, the trajectory of the Brazilian economy in 2009 has shown a great capacity for recovery, and a significant reduction of vulnerability to external shocks."[8]

Leane Cornet Naidin, Maria Fernanda Gadelha, and Marta Calmon Lemme observed that the Brazilian government took as major steps the creation of "funding programs and production subsidies to specific sectors, as well as reducing the tax

[5]Naidin et al. (2012), p. 1. Available in: www.fgv.br/direitogv/projetopontes. Access in: 25 jun. 2012.

[6]Amorim (2012), p. 20. Available in: www.fgv.br/direitogv/projetopontes. Access in: 25 jun. 2012.

[7]Buenrostro (2012), p. 12. Available in: www.fgv.br/direitogv/projetopontes. Access in: 25 jun. 2012.

[8]Cardoso et al. (2012). Available in: http://www.ipea.gov.br/portal/index.php?option=com_content&view=article&id=2483&Itemid=3. Access in 03jul. 2012.

burden." Also, the IPEA Survey Charter states: "In this context, the easing of monetary policy coupled with tax relief measures created the necessary conditions for the resumption of credit demand associated with the consumption of durable goods."[9]

According to the article published by the Getulio Vargas Foundation, "the automotive, steel and footwear industries have been the main targets of the support measures taken by governments of various countries." The other focus is also, on civil construction and agriculture, as in Brazil.[10]

In this scenario, is highlighted the importance of careful state action, which in Brazil has historically had role "decisive moments like this. The weight, size and ability of the state to legislate may be the key lever for that Brazil does not stop and prductive-industrial intensification capable of, at the end of international problems, put us in a very superior position which we enter in the crisis."[11]

In other words, when it stimulates and protects the supplier, it is also protecting the consumer; this is well exemplified in the article *Desemprego: fasesocial da crise*, of the Review Pontes: entre o comércioe o desenvolvimentosustentável: "In general, recovery plans, as well as other isolated measures, seek to promote both production and consumption. Thus, for example, the injection of funds should provide greater availability of consumer credit in order to drive purchases and reinvigorate the market. However, there is no effective guarantees that the ease of access to credit to take place, as indeed there was not in relation to private banks, both the U.S. and in other countries."[12]

The creation of jobs and stimulus to employment, even temporary, is another form of action in order to maintain the purchasing power of consumers. In Japan, for example, "the granting of state subsidies to local governments to increase the temporary hires, as well as assistance for companies become formal informal workers. There are governments that have chosen to primarily act as mediators between the representative bodies of employers and employees."[13]

In these measures, the consumers were not always considered but have not been completely forgotten. Even so, albeit indirectly, they give priority to the protection of trade.

---

[9]Cardoso et al. (2012). Available in: http://www.ipea.gov.br/portal/index.php?option=com_content&view=article&id=2483&Itemid=3. Access in: 03jul.2012.

[10]Naidin et al. (2012), p. 2. Available in: www.fgv.br/direitogv/projetopontes. Access in: 25 jun. 2012.

[11]Amorim (2012), p. 21. Available in: www.fgv.br/direitogv/projetopontes. Access in: 25/06/2012.

[12]Desemprego (2009), p. 3. Available in: www.fgv.br/direitogv/projetopontes. Access in: 25/06/2012.

[13]Desemprego (2009), p. 3. Available in: www.fgv.br/direitogv/projetopontes. Access in: 25/06/2012.

12.2 Measures Adopted by Brazil to Protect the Consumer

Since the beginning of the 2008 crisis, Brazil has stood out on the world stage as one of the countries that resisted the economic crisis. Economists point out that this was due to "internal market growth."[14]

However, this does not mean that the country has not been affected by the crisis. Just as the world's major economies, Brazil also showed a significant increase in interest rates. Brazil had others problems as raising the value of the american dollar and the difficult access to consumer credit.[15]

The Brazilian government applied measures such as tax reduction, the implementation of housing programs for low-income persons, and credit guarantee in combating the crisis. According to Arlete Sampaio, "these measures form [formed] a whole to confront the economic crisis. The goal is [was] the same: to avoid recession and the deterioration of the living conditions of the population."[16]

It was observed that the goal of the government was to encourage consumption. It tried to ensure that the consumer and the supplier of credit making massive investments in the financial system. It also worked on tax reduction for specific sectors, especially due to the country's concern for civil construction and agriculture. Another action of the government was the control of interest rates by the Central Bank of Brazil in order to ensure financing and credit. Recently, public banks lowered interest rates on loans and financing, which reflects the government's concern in maintaining the purchasing power of the consumers.[17]

According to Gilson Luiz Eusébio, the investment made by the Brazilian government in the consumer market, ensuring the disadvantaged livelihood assistance programs, guarantees the income of the population, circulation in trade, and economic stability. In this sense, the government said that there is "a direct relationship between economic development and social development."[18]

12.3 Governmental Sector

The coordination of public policy relating to consumer protection is the responsibility of the Consumer National Secretary (Senacon) established by Decree 7738, of May 29, 2012, of the Ministry of Justice, a body of the Federal Executive. It aims to

---

[14]Association of housewives, consumers and the citizenship.Available in: http://www.adocontb.org.br/index.php?codwebsite=&codpagina=00020849Access in: 25 jun. 2012.

[15]Association of housewives, consumers and the citizenship. Available in: http://www.adocontb.org.br/index.php?codwebsite=&codpagina=00020849Access in: 25 jun. 2012.

[16]Euzébio (2012).

[17]Association of housewives, consumers and the citizenship.Available in: http://www.adocontb.org.br/index.php?codwebsite=&codpagina=00020849Access in: 25 jun. 2012.

[18]Euzébio (2012).

ensure the protection and exercise of the rights of consumers, promote harmonization in consumer relations, and encourage the integration and joint action of the members of the National System of Consumer Protection (SNDC).

Article 105 of the Consumer Protection Code states that the National System of Consumer Defense (SNDC) is composed of Federal, state, Federal District, municipal bodies, and private consumer protection entities. Brazil has a successful experience in the administrative organization, in conjunction with private entities, of consumer protection. The direct service to the consumer is done through the Procons, entities linked to the government (executive bodies, legislature, or the public prosecutor). The Procons have as assignments administrative monitoring and sanctioning of providers' activities and promotes the care of consumers, providing them with information. Finally, Procons also does an important job in the reconciliation of interests between consumers and suppliers.

Before the crisis, Brazil also had to adopt measures to protect credit and the market, among which may be cited "funding programs and production subsidies to specific sectors, as well as reducing the tax charge."[19]

With regard to taxes, for example, reduction of taxes may represent a greater purchasing power of consumers, especially if done in order to directly affect the price paid by the consumer, as in the past—and again in the current month—in the case of tax on industrialized products (IPI). However, the sources pointed out that there was the expected outcome in view of the difficulty of maintaining the loan and financing.[20] Furthermore, the falling of new cars prices also reflected proportionally in the used cars, which in practice also generated loss to the consumer, so that even if the supplier transfers the charge reduction in the final price, the consumer will have pay almost the same difference as before (if not more).

During this period of crisis, observing the need to also protect the consumer investor, the Securities and Exchange Commission (CVM) signed a Technical Cooperation Agreement with the Department of Consumer Protection and Defense (DPDC) to promote the exchange of information and improvement of regulatory, inspector, and educational activities for investors, as described by the Securities and Exchange Commission. The organization also emphasizes the importance of the agreement for joint action in the protection of the investor consumer.[21] It is noteworthy in this context the importance of this agreement for handling the extremely volatile area, where the consumer has little or no knowledge and is very vulnerable.

Exports have a significant importance in the stability of the internal market; therefore, as reported in the Review Pontes, of the Getulio Vargas Foundation, the

---

[19]Naidin et al. (2012), p. 1. Available in: www.fgv.br/direitogv/projetopontes. Access in: 25 jun. 2012.

[20]Desemprego: a fase social da crise. *Pontes – entre o comércio e o desenvolvimento sustentável.* March/2009, vol. 5, n. 1, p. 3. Available in: www.fgv.br/direitogv/projetopontes. Access in: 25 jun. 2012.

[21]*Comissão de ValoresMobiliários.* Available in: http://www.cvm.gov.br/port/infos/Comunicado %20acordo%20de%20cooperação%20CVM%20DPDC.asp.Access in: 03 jul. 2012.

country had to take large steps to ensure the maintenance of exports and sustain the market. It should be noted, among others, that the "injection of liquidity through the sale of 276 million to repurchase agreements in January the signing of a loan agreement with the World Bank in February, which was expected to grant additional 60 million to Unibanco, in order to meet the needs of exporters. Since October, Lula's government ordered the National Development Bank to increase by 5 billion the lines of financing."[22]

12.4 Financial Sector

The main concern of the consumer as an active actor in the financial sector is the lack of information. It was therefore necessary to develop a policy for financial education and state policies that would be appropriate for the Consumer Protection Code, especially in the face of the Agreement signed between the Securities and Exchange Commission and the Department of Consumer Protection and Defense. It created a public policy aimed at financial education, involving the Ministry of Education, Ministry of Finance, the Central Bank of Brazil, and the Securities and Exchange Commission.[23] Luciana Casemiro describes that "the goal is to give citizens tools so you can make informed choices of consumption, savings and investment. The information is also on the basis of the partnership of the Securities and Exchange Commission with the Department of Consumer Protection and Defense, which prepare in 'four hands' a second newsletter for the consumer."[24]

12.5 Civil Entities for Consumer Protection

Given the economic crisis, civil entities for consumer protection also expressed that they were trying to avoid measures unfavorable to the consumer. Brazilian entities linked to Consumers International, such as Brasilcon (Brazilian Institute of Policy and Consumer Rights) and IDEC, worked with hundreds of organizations around the world in favor of consumer protection policies. Information rights, investment protection, and the need for standardization stand out as the main objectives of this

[22]Desemprego: a fase social da crise. *Pontes – entre o comércio e o desenvolvimento sustentável.* Março/2009, vol. 5, n. 1, p. 12. Available in: www.fgv.br/direitogv/projetopontes. Access in: 25 jun. 2012.

[23]Casemiro (2012). Available in: http://oglobo.globo.com/economia/mercado-financeiro-defesa-do-consumidor-se-aproximam-apos-abalo-da-crise-global-de-2008-2703190. Access in: 25 jun. 2012.

[24]L. Casemiro (2012) Available in: http://oglobo.globo.com/economia/mercado-financeiro-defesa-do-consumidor-se-aproximam-apos-abalo-da-crise-global-de-2008-2703190. Access in: 25 jun. 2012.

action, especially with regard to financial products and services. Authorities struggle to obtain more fairer financial services and to establish, more clearly, the rules and discipline of protection of consumers.[25]

Even knowing that Brazil maintained its market well before the crisis, the task of the Brazilian Institute of Consumer Defense (IDEC) is to see to it that the government did not concern itself only with the encouragement of consumption but also with the development of policies of awareness to avoid overindebtedness. As seen so far, consumption is essential for the maintenance and balance of the internal market and therefore the national economy. However, if the actors—consumer and supplier—are reckless, incurring excessive debt on one hand and charging abusive interest rates on the other, the market weakens, inflation rises, and the economy is destabilized.[26]

Besides the awaken to the importance of state action and acting socially demanding these actions, the Brazilian Institute of Consumer Defense (IDEC) understood to be necessary a consumer's own awareness to act cautiously in the consumer market. Accordingly, it proposed some protective attitudes on how to avoid investment risk or low-liquidity investment, such as avoiding long financing and the purchase of real estate during the crisis, choosing to pay in cash and getting the maximum discount, avoiding buying U.S. dollars and imported products, and, generally, avoiding debts, loans, and interests.[27]

The European Coalition for Responsible Credit (ECRC) is an organization that promotes responsible lending. In 2008, this organization published the "Declaration on the Credit Crisis," which addressed its concern on credit amid the then impending global crisis. Brasilcon (Brazilian Institute of Consumer Policy and Rights) continues to evaluate the effects of irresponsible lending policies, the relationships existing in an indebted society, and the instability of the monetary system. The paper examines the causes of the crisis and suggests possible solutions to the problem by encouraging fair practices and transparency in trade and investment policies.[28]

Brasilcon (Brazilian Institute of Consumer Policy and Rights) further reports that "since June 2007 this context has been presented as compulsory agenda in discussions in the Council of Europe that has stated that as indecent and regrettable practices such as: (i) credit card debt secured by borrowers' residences, (ii) expensive renewable credits with interest charges, (iii) offers of loans combined with insurance products with hidden bonus clauses (iv) conversion of loans with fixed rates on loans variable rates, before increases in interest rates or deceptive

[25]Gunn (2012).

[26]Association of housewives, consumers and the citizenship.Available in: http://www.adocontb.org.br/index.php?codwebsite=&codpagina=00020849Access in: 25/06/2012.

[27]Association of housewives, consumers and the citizenship.Available in: http://www.adocontb.org.br/index.php?codwebsite=&codpagina=00020849Access in: 25/06/2012.

[28]Brasilcon. Available in: http://brasilcon.org.br/?pag=destaque&id=1988. Access in: 03jul.2012.

loans on favorable initial conditions, (v) usurious loans and loans too expensive for the poor, among others."[29]

Given this scenario, Brasilcon reports that "the ECRC intends to provide full disclosure to the Declaration, which may be signed by all coalition partners, among them, consumer organizations, welfare organizations, anti-poverty groups, and scientific groups and social activists."[30]

12.6 Financial Regulation of Brazil

12.6.1 Legislative Competence

The 1988 Federal Constitution provides for the exclusive jurisdiction of the Union to legislate on credit policy, foreign exchange, insurance and transfer of securities (Article 22, VII), saving systems, and obtaining and guaranteeing popular savings (Article 22, XIX). Moreover, the Federal Constitution of 1988 also provides for concurrent jurisdiction among Federal, the state, and Federal District to legislate, among others, on financial law (Article 24, I).

Thus, the state and Federal District have legislative jurisdiction only as to the financial law, without forgeting that the Union lays down general rules on the matter. Besides, in matters relating to the financial market, the legislative competence of the Union is evident, and because of that, a federal control as to the enactment of laws on the financial markets, the performance of banks, insurers, entities that extend credit or institutions that finance the acquisition of goods in the consumer market is done.

12.6.2 Central Bank of Brazil

The Central Bank of Brazil is a federal agency created by Federal Law 4594 of December 13, 1964, whose duties are, among others, to exercise control of credit in all its forms, exercise control over foreign capital, oversee financial institutions, and apply the penalties provided by law. The historical evolution of the Central Bank of Brazil reveals the changes observed in its decisive role in regulating the financial system and consumer protection: "after the creation of the Central Bank sought to provide the establishment of mechanisms aimed at playing the role of 'bank of banks.' In 1985, it was promoted to government financial reorganization with the

[29]Brasilcon. Available in: http://brasilcon.org.br/?pag=destaque&id=1988. Access in: 03 jul. 2012.

[30]Brasilcon. Available in: http://brasilcon.org.br/?pag=destaque&id=1988. Access in: 03 jul. 2012.

separation of accounts and functions of the Central Bank, Bank of Brazil and the National Treasury. In 1986, the moviment account was closed and it was eliminated automatic supplies that hampered the work of the Central Bank. The government financial reorganization process lasted until 1988, when the functions of monetary authority were progressively transferred from the Bank of Brazil to the Central Bank, while the atypical activities carried on by it, such as those related to the promotion and administration of federal debt, were transferred to the Treasury. The Federal Constitution of 1988 provides important tools for the Banco Central, among which are the exclusive exercise of Union competence to issue currency and the requirement for prior approval by the Senate, by secret ballot, after public hearing, the names appointed by the President of the Republic for the posts of president and directors of the institution. In addition, prohibited the Central Bank to grant loans directly or indirectly to the National Treasury."[31]

12.7 Legal Protection of the Consumer

12.7.1 Consumer Defense Code (Material Plan)

Consumer protection in Brazil was elevated to a fundamental right by the Constitution of 1988 through Article 5, item XXXII, which determines the state's duty to promote, according to the law, consumer protection. In the same constitutional level, consumer defense was also accepted as a principle of the economic order, pursuant to Article 170, section V.[32]

Federal Law 8078, of September 11, 1990 (Consumer Defense Code), regulates the Federal Constitution of 1988 regarding consumer protection in the infraconstitutional plan. It is a legal autonomous microsystem that has as its main purpose the regulation of the legal relation of consumption, with cross-sectoral approach in civil protection, especially in the recognition of basic consumer rights, the regulation of consumer contract, and compensation for damage caused by the product and service providers in the consumer market; administrative protection, which involves the actions of the state in monitoring and sanctioning suppliers that violate the standards of consumer protection; criminal protection, which creates specific criminal figures in the consumer market; and procedural protection of the consumer, with emphasis on the regulation of class action.

The Consumer Protection Code introduces the concepts of the subjects (consumer and supplier) and objects (products and services) of the legal relation of consumption. The concept of standard consumer is referred to in Article 2, caput, which considers all natural or legal persons as a consumer, provided they purchase or use products and services as an end user.[33]

[31] http://www.bc.gov.br/?HISTORIABC. Access in 03jul.2012.

[32] Miragem (2010), pp. 39–46.

[33] de Almeida (2006), pp. 37–42.

In addition to the standard concept of consumer, the Consumer Protection Code cites three other cases falling under the term consumers.[34] In Article 2, sole paragraph, of the Code of Consumer Protection, a community of people, even if indeterminate subjects, that intervenes in any consumer relation is treated as a consumer. The community is protected in its manifestation in consumer relations, in terms of diffuse, collective in the strict sense or homogeneous individual rights. The accident victim of consumption, i.e., a person that cannot be classified as a standard consumer but suffers moral or material damages due to a harmful event committed by the supplier, is also treated as a consumer, pursuant to Article 17 of the Consumer Defense Code. Also, it is considered consumer by equalization all the people that are identifiable or not exposed to business practices or to the consumer contract, pursuant to Article 29 of the Code of Consumer Protection.[35]

The activity of financial institutions in Brazil is classified as a consumer service, pursuant to Article 3, § 2, of the Consumer Defense Code.[36] The entities that grant credit or grant funding do not provide any product but provide paid service in the consumer market.

Therefore, the activity of credit granting or providing financing in Brazil is a matter regulated by Consumer Law, once set remains the legal relationship of consumption, since these subjective and objective elements provided by law: (a) consumer: is the final recipient of the activity provided in the consumer market, the one who gets the credit or acquires an asset through financing, (b) supplier: is the financial institution that develops the activity of granting credit or grant funding, (c) object: it is characterized by paid service of granting credit or grant funding that takes place in the consumer market.

12.7.2 Small Claims Courts (Procedural Plan and Access to Justice)

The Article 98, I, Federal Constitution, has created the Small Claims Courts to promote reconciliation, trial, and execution of civil suits of lesser complexity, instituting the accelerated rite and the prevalence of the principle of orality. Federal Law 9099, of September 26, 1999, confers on the Civil Small Claims Courts the power of conciliation, prosecution, and trial of civil suits of lesser complexity not exceeding 40 times the minimum wage.[37]

[34]Casado (2000), pp. 33–37.

[35]Santana (2009), pp. 56–80.

[36]Consumer Defense Code. Art. 3°, § 2°: Service is any activity provided in the consumer market, for remuneration, including the nature of banking, financial, credit and insurance, except those resulting from labor relations.

[37]The value of the minimum wage in Brasil was fixed in R$ 622, 00 (six hundred twenty-two reals) from 01 jan. 2012.

This is great progress in protecting the rights of citizens in general and consumers in particular. Also noteworthy is the fact that access to the Small Claims Courts does not require payment of costs, and there is no condemnation in legal fees in the first instance, except in cases of bad faith. Thus, it is shown often the bringing of actions against financial institutions that do not respect the rights of consumers. Many offenses against the legal rights of consumers by financial institutions are presented to the judiciary, which sets the public policy for the appropriate treatment of conflicts, encouraging the search for consensual methods of conflict resolution, especially conciliation and mediation, according to Resolution n. 125, of 29 November 2012, of the National Council of Justice.[38]

12.8 Brazilian Jurisprudence on the Protection of the Consumer in Financial Issues

The Consumer Defense Code, through Article 3, § 2, expressly included contracts concluded by banks, financial institutions, and credit institutions with their clients as typical legal relations of consumption. However, despite the clear legal provision, there was always a significant resistance from member institutions of the national financial system to consumer protection in Brazil. After 11 years of the Consumer Defense Code, the Confederation of National Financial System (CONSIF) promoted direct action of unconstitutionality before the Supreme Court, aiming to be declared unconstitutional Article 3, § 2, of the Consumer Defense Code and, therefore, intending to exclude the impact of the protective standard of consumer to the activities undertaken by institutions belonging to the national financial system.

The Supreme Court rejected the request made in ADIn 2591-1, reaffirming the constitutional basis of consumer law and the necessary and proper submission of the activities of Brazilian financial institutions to protective standards of the Consumer Protection Code.[39] It is worth mentioning the important lesson drawn up by Minister Celso de Mello, in these terms: "... Look, therefore, that the Consumer Defense Code just cannot dispose, nor affect, on matters concerning the structure and functioning national financial system (topics that are not regulated by cited standard), these matters—now considered the art. 192 of the Constitution, the text amended by Constitutional Amendment. 40/2003—are propers of disciplining by a complementary law. I understand, therefore, that in the Consumer Defense Code there isn't unconstitutionality, sustained by CONSIF, author of this direct

[38]http://www.cnj.jus.br/atos-administrativos/atos-da-presidencia/323-resolucoes/12243-resolucao-no-125-de-29-de-novembro-de-2010.

[39]Marques (2011), pp. 531–548.

action. Instead, and under this aspect, the Consumer Defense Code has full constitutional validity, especially if we consider the principles that standard, conditionate and inform the proper formulation and implementation of national policy of the consumer relations, whose primary objective—recognized the vulnerability of consumers in the consumer market—is to facilitate the attending of the needs of consumers, respect for their dignity, health and safety, protecting their economic interests, improving their quality of life, as well transparency and harmonization of consumer relations."[40]

The Superior Court of Justice has jurisdiction, among others, to judge in special appeal when the contested decision is contrary to a treaty or federal law, denying them effective, judging valid act of local government contested under federal law or gives to federal law differing interpretations of which there are assigned another court (art. 105, III, "a," "b," and "c" of the Federal Constitution of 1988). Thus, issues on consumer protection law, including on the financial aspects, are judged ultimately by the Superior Tribunal of Justice, which promotes understanding of consolidation activity through edition of summaries.

With reference to consumer right at the level of national financial activity, it should be recorded summary 297, which states unequivocally the role of the Code of Consumer Protection in financial activities, in these terms: "The Consumer Protection Code is applicable to financial institutions." Other summaries of the Superior Court of Justice relating to the financial system can be recorded: (a) summary 247: "the contract of credit availability in the current account, accompanied by the statement of debt, is able document for filing the monitoring action"; (b) summary 258: "the promissory note tied to contract credit facility does not enjoy autonomy because of the illiquidity of the title that originated"; (c) summary 259: "the action of accountability may be proposed by the bank account holder"; (d) summary 285: "in the bank contracts subsequent to the Consumer Protection Code applies the top of 2% penalty"; (e) summary 286: "The renegotiation of the bank contract or the confession of the debt does not preclude the possibility of discussion on possible illegalities of the previous contracts"; (f) summary 287: "the Financing Basic Rate (TFB) can not be used as an index for indexation in contracts with banks"; (g) summary 288: "The Long Term Interest Rate (TJLP) can be used as an index for indexation in contracts with banks"; (h) summary 294: "It is not facultative contractual clause that provides for the commission of staying, calculated by the mid-market rate calculated by the Central Bank of Brazil, limited the rate of contract"; (i) summary 296: "the compensatory interest, not cumulative with the commission of staying are due in the period of default, with a mid-market rate stipulated by the Central Bank of Brazil, limited to the percentage employed"; (j) summary 381: "in the bank contracts, it is forbidden to the judge to know, ex officio, of unfair clauses."

---

[40]http://redir.stf.jus.br/paginadorpub/paginador.jsp?docTP=AC&docID=266855. Access in 03 jul. 2012.

Register also the recent edition of summary 497, which is concerned about the civil liability of financial institutions, in these terms: "Financial institutions respond objectively by the damage caused by 'unforeseeable circumstances internal' relating to fraud and offenses committed by others in banking operations." This is a subject of consolidation of understanding coherent with the legal nature adopted by the Consumer Protection Code regarding the liability of the supplier; in other words, the verification of the fault of the financial institution for damages suffered by consumers is dispensable.

Article 52 of the Consumer Defense Code determines that the supplier of credit or financing must provide the following prior and adequate information to the consumer: (1) price of the product or service in local currency, (2) amount of interest and the actual annual interest, (3) additions provided by law, (4) number and frequency of installments, (5) total amount payable, with and without funding.

Besides the aspects mentioned above, Brazilian jurisprudence supports several other consumer rights, particularly in the international financial crisis. Cite as an example the various judgments that recognize the abusive business practices of financial institutions, declare the nullity of the abusive clauses in granting of credit contracts and grant funding contracts, impose damages by way of moral damages in cases of violation of personality rights of consumers, among others.[41]

12.9 Update of the Consumer Defense Code

The Brazilian Consumer Defense Code is considering a model in Latin America to protect the weaker party, especially consumers. While incorporating many legal advances, it should be noted that this is a law drafted in the early nineties. The passing of more than two decades led to the emergence of several themes in consumption in the face of new requirements imposed by market dynamics.

The Senate, supporting the premise of effective change in the market for the last 20 years, created on November 30, 2010, the Commission of Jurists composed of Antonio Herman Benjamin, Ada Pellegrini Grinover, Claudia Lima Marques, Leonardo Roscoe Bessa, Roberto Augusto Castellanos Pfeiffer, and Kazuo Watanabe, which is intended to provide support for the updating of the Consumer Defense Code. After several technical meetings, public hearings, and open opportunity for suggestions and criticisms of civil society in general, the Commission of Jurists presented on March 14, 2012, a final report to the Senate proposing to update the Consumer Defense Code on three main points: (a) e-commerce, (b) overindebtedness,[42] (c) collective actions.

It is worth to note that beyond the three main axes, the Commission of Jurists also proposes general changes with the purpose of emphasizing consumer

[41]de Almeida (1982), pp. 97–103.

[42]Bertoncello and de Lima (2006), pp. 191–210.

protection, among which are more consumer-friendly interpretation and integration, knowledge *ex officio* by the judiciary and public administration regarding violation of the standards of consumer protection, protection of personal data of consumers, creating of the figure of "harassment of consumption," extension of the extension of the statute of limitations for 10 years, and the setting of the home consumer as competent for bringing action against the supplier.

It is recognized that the changing economy and society in Brazil allows the incorporation of relevant legislative issues into the balance of the consumer market. Thus, there is a proposal to strengthen the constitutional dimension of the Consumer Defense Code in order to highlight the option of our Constitution for the protection of the consumer, this person being recognized as the weakest in the consumption process. It is proposed to enhance the ethical-inclusive and solidarist dimension of the Consumer Defense Code, recognizing that the consumer law has an important function or dimension of social inclusion and is an effective tool to combat social exclusion. Finally, there is effort to increase the trust, efficiency, and legal certainty of the Consumer Defense Code, updating it as an effective instrument to regulate the market, prevent conflicts, and enhance the confidence of Brazilian consumers.[43]

Finally, it is worth to note that the work of the Commission of Jurists has resulted in the presentation of three draft legislation that currently proceeds through the Senate.

12.10 Conclusion

The international financial crisis that began in the United States of America in 2008 reached the Brazilian financial market and, consequently, weakened consumer protection. The harmful effects of the breach of international financial market, especially from some rich countries, echoed to a lesser degree in Brazil because the country was booming in economy and did not fully embrace the theory of free and unregulated market. Indeed, radical liberalism has always been viewed with suspicion in Brazil, which is rightly concerned with controlling the financial market within the limits necessary. Therefore, in Brazil there was not a "bubble" in stock exchanges, and the country got to minimize the disastrous consequences, especially on mortgage.

The Brazilian government has promoted the reduction of taxes, implemented housing programs for the poorest people, and guaranteed lending grants as measures to combat the international financial crisis. The Brazilian consumers have a mixed system of protection for their rights: administrative and judicial. At the administrative level, there is a constant activity for improving the National System of Consumer Defense, coordinated by the newly created National Secretary of

[43]Federal Senate (2012), pp. 19–26.

Consumer, and financial market regulation by the Central Bank of Brazil, a federal agency with many attributions, including monitoring and sanctioning of financial institutions that operate in opposition to the established rules on the market.

The performance of civil entities for consumer protection must be registered, especially in the National Congress, to ensure a policy option that would best suit the interests of Brazilian consumers in the financial market, preventing credit shortage or the adoption of a recessive economic orientation.

In Brazil, there is adequate legal instruments to tackle the financial problems arising from the crisis, but it should be noted the great political strength of financial institutions at the federal executive and legislative powers, without a corresponding consumer power to interfere in the formulation of public policies, a factor that systematically leads to conflicts of interest in channeling of the financial problems characteristic of the national reality.

The updating of the Consumer Defense Code is the most important landmark for the protection of consumers in the twenty-first century, as well as the most effective measure to prevent the harmful actions of market participants that may violate the rights of consumers.

Finally, the current challenge comes from the understanding of society that we now live in a new time with new demands and a greater dependence on different countries, whether rich or poor. The incorporation of new consumer protective rules, especially regarding the regulation of overindebtedness and the change of attitude of state powers (executive, legislative, and judicial) are some suitable means to overcome the serious problems caused by the financial crisis, whose consequences we cannot measure accurately.

References

Amorim RLC (2012) O Brasil e os seus investimentos: quais são os impactos da crise? Pontes – entre o comércio e o desenvolvimento sustentável. June/2009, vol. 5, n. 2. Available in: www.fgv.br/direitogv/projetopontes. Access in: 25 jun

Bertoncello KRD, de Lima CC (2006) Tratamento do crédito ao consumo na América Latina e superendividamento. In: Cavallazzi RL, Marques CL (coord.) Direitos do consumidor endividado: superendividamento e crédito. Revista dos Tribunais, São Paulo

Buenrostro P (2012) O financiamento ao comércio em tempos de crise. Pontes – entre o comércio e o desenvolvimento sustentável. March/2009, vol. 5, n. 1. Available in: www.fgv.br/direitogv/projetopontes. Access in: 25 jun

Cardoso et al (2012). Available in: http://www.ipea.gov.br/portal/index.php?option=com_content&view=article&id=2483&Itemid=3. Accessed 3 July 2012

Casado M d M (2000) Proteção do consumidor de crédito bancário e financiamento. Revista dos Tribunais, São Paulo

Casemiro L (2012) Mercado financeiro e defesa do consumidor se aproximam após o abalo da crise global de 2008.Available in: http://oglobo.globo.com/economia/mercado-financeiro-defesa-do-consumidor-se-aproximam-apos-abalo-da-crise-global-de-2008-2703190. Access in: 25 jun

de Almeida CF (1982) Os direitos dos consumidores. Almedina, Coimbra

de Almeida JB (2006) A proteção jurídica do consumidor, 5th edn. Saraiva, São Paulo

Desemprego (2009). p 3. Available in: www.fgv.br/direitogv/projetopontes. Accessed 25 June 2012

Euzébio GL (2012) Proteção social faz a diferança - Bolsa família e outros programas ganham relevância em tempos de crise. Desafios do desenvolvimento: a revista mensal de informações e debates do IPEA. Available in: http://www.ipea.gov.br/desafios/index.php?option=com_content&view=article&id=1229:reportagens-materias&Itemid=39Access in: 25 jun

Federal Senate (2012) Relatório da comissão de juristas: atualização do código de defesa do consumidor – antepro jetos. Gráfica do Senado Federal, Brasília

Gunn L (2012) Para Idec e Consumers International, G-20 tem de atacar verdadeiras causas da crise. Available in: http://www.idec.org.br/em-acao/artigo/para-idec-e-consumers-international-g-20-tem-de-atacar-verdadeiras-causas-da-crise. Access in: 25 jun

Marques CL (2011) Contratos no código de defesa do consumidor: o novo regime das relações contratuais, 6th edn. Revista dos Tribunais, São Paulo

Miragem B (2010) Curso de direito do consumidor, 2nd edn. Revista dos Tribunais, São Paulo

Naidin LC, Gadelha MF, Lemme MC (2012) A crise econômica, as políticas governamentais e o comércio internacional. Pontes – entre o comércio e o desenvolvimento sustentável. June/2009, 5(2):1. Available in: www.fgv.br/direitogv/projetopontes. Access in: 25 jun

Santana HV (2009) Dano moral no direito do consumidor. Revista dos Tribunais, São Paulo

Chapter 13
Free Trade Agreement and Investment Treaty Innovations to Promote More Sustainable Financial Markets for Consumers

Luke Nottage

13.1 Introduction

Bilateral and regional trade and investment treaties (FTAs and BITs) have proliferated worldwide, including within the Asia-Pacific region, along with double-tax treaties (DTTs). But countries like Australia have recently become more concerned about FTAs and BITs. This chapter examines processes that states can agree to, especially through commitments made in treaties before disputes arise, that are likely to minimize claims being filed or escalated and therefore to promote sustainable cross-border trade and investment in the field of financial services. It also considers adding commitments requiring or encouraging treaty partners to introduce new obligations on credit suppliers to notify national regulators where they detect unusually high levels of financial stress among borrowers and then for the regulators to share that information as an "advance warning" system for financial market stability.

13.2 Hybrid Dispute Resolution Mechanisms for Investment Treaties

BITs traditionally aim to protect foreign investors from illegal interference by the host state, for example, through direct expropriation (nationalization) or indirect expropriation (such as discriminatory taxes on foreign investors). Investment

Most of the author's works cited in this chapter (or related manuscript versions) are freely downloadable via http://ssrn.com/author=488525.

L. Nottage (✉)
University of Sydney Law School, Sydney, NSW, Australia
e-mail: lukenottage@gmail.com

C. Lima Marques, D. Wei (eds.), *Consumer Law and Socioeconomic Development*,
DOI 10.1007/978-3-319-55624-6_13

chapters in bilateral and now some regional FTAs typically combine such protections with liberalization of foreign investment, going beyond commitments made by host states under the World Trade Organization (WTO) regime—which essentially only covers cross-border investments in listed service sectors. BITs and FTA chapters have proliferated since the collapse or economic liberalization of communist regimes from around 1990, followed by the stalemate in 2000 towards a new WTO round of trade and investment liberalization at the multilateral level. An increasingly common feature of these investment treaties has been a dispute mechanism that allows foreign investors from the home state to bring an international arbitration claim against the host state, rather than having to persuade its home state to bring an interstate claim (as under customary international law or the WTO system).[1]

In the wake of the global financial crisis (GFC), concerns have escalated about the scope of investment treaties, especially the investor-state arbitration (ISA) mechanism. Some argue that this system goes too far in protecting foreign investors' interests,[2] encouraging the worldwide spread of reckless providers of financial services.[3] After the GFC, the Australian government also became concerned about its regulatory capacity being overly constrained, albeit primarily regarding capacity to tax mining companies and to regulate tobacco—particularly after it was subject to its first-ever ISA claim, brought by a Philip Morris subsidiary under an old investment treaty with Hong Kong.[4] An advisory body also suggested that ISA commitments anyway may not necessarily attract additional inbound foreign direct investment (FDI), or even help much Australia's outbound investors.[5] In April 2011, Australia announced a significant policy shift, eschewing ISA provisions in all future treaties—even with developing countries.[6]

However, various commentators suggested that Australia's new direction represented an overreaction and that various alternatives remain available to address public interest concerns about ISA and investment treaties more generally.[7] For example, more exceptions can be added to treaties regarding prudential regulation of financial markets, or ISA can be excluded regarding investments in certain

[1]See generally Bath and Nottage (2011), p. 1; Bath and Nottage (2016).

[2]See generally e.g. Sornarajah (2012), via http://www.vcc.columbia.edu/content/fdi-perspective. See also e.g. Lazo (2014). www.transnational-dispute-management.com/article.asp?key=2037.

[3]See e.g. Kelsey (2010), p. 3.

[4]See Nottage (2013), pp. 452–474; https://www.ag.gov.au/tobaccoplainpackaging. The claim was eventually dismissed on jurisdictional grounds, for abusive 'forum shopping' under general international law principles, in 2015.

[5]Productivity Commission, *Bilateral and Regional Trade Agreements: Research Report* (13 December 2010), http://www.pc.gov.au/projects/study/trade-agreements/report. But see now Armstrong and Nottage (2016), http://ssrn.com/abstract=2824090.

[6]Department of Foreign Affairs and Trade, Australian Government, *Gillard Government Trade Policy Statement: Trading our Way to More Jobs and Prosperity*, archived at http://blogs.usyd.edu.au/japaneselaw/2011_Gillard%20Govt%20Trade%20Policy%20Statement.pdf.

[7]Nottage (2011a), http://ssrn.com/abstract=1860505; Trakman (2012), p. 83; Kurtz (2012), p. 65.

financial market sectors (leaving only an interstate dispute resolution process).[8] After a (more center-right) Coalition Government won the general election on September 7, 2013, Australia has reverted to including ISA on a case-by-case assessment. It ratified major FTAs with China and Korea and signed the Trans-Pacific Partnership FTA that links twelve regional economies, including ISA with a range of procedural and substantive safeguards.[9] An "anti-ISA" private member's Bill introduced by a Senator from the Australian Greens was opposed, as going too far, by Coalition and also opposition Labor Party Senators in a Report issued in 2014.[10]

This chapter argues that further scope for settling disputes effectively within an ISA framework can be created by extending features already found in some treaties. For example, in the sensitive area of taxation policy, where states have long been concerned to retain a greater degree of national sovereignty and discretionary power,[11] investment treaties quite often have special provisions relating to possible claims by foreign investors that host state's tax measures amount to expropriation. Specifically, if an investor initiates such a claim, its host state can agree with the impugned host state that the latter's measures are *not* expropriatory, thus suspending the investor's ISA claim.[12] Such an agreement might anyway be sought and obtained between states even after the investor has filed a claim because they created the investor's ISA rights in the first place. But it seems fairer to put investors clearly on notice, through treaty provisions included prior to any disputes arising, that their claims are subjected to this sort of state control.[13]

Such provisions encourage both states to negotiate and cooperate with a view to agreeing on whether the tax measure is appropriate. However, this does assume that

[8]Cf. e.g. the *Japan-Korea BIT*: Hamamoto and Nottage (2010), http://ssrn.com/abstract=1724999.

[9]Nottage (2016), http://ssrn.com/abstract=2767996.

[10]Nottage (2015a), p. 245.

[11]Burch and Nottage (2011), p. 128.

[12]See, e.g., *Japan-Indonesia Economic Partnership Agreement* (art 73(4)). A watered-down variant can be found in Chapter 11 of AANZFTA, which provides in Art 25 (emphasis added):

> 6. Where an investor claims that the disputing Party has breached Article 9 (Expropriation and Compensation) by the adoption or enforcement of a taxation measure, the disputing Party and the non-disputing Party shall, upon request from the disputing Party, hold consultations with a view to determining whether the taxation measure in question has an effect equivalent to expropriation or nationalization. Any tribunal that may be established pursuant to this Section shall accord *serious consideration* to the decision of both Parties under this Paragraph.

[13]Rather similarly, domestic and international contract law protects 'third party beneficiaries' of agreements between parties who subsequently wish to alter rights accorded to such third parties. See, e.g., UNIDROIT Principles of International Commercial Contracts art 5.2.5 ('The parties may modify or revoke the rights conferred by the contract on the beneficiary until the beneficiary has accepted them or reasonably acted in reliance on them'); *Property Law Act 1969* (WA) s 11(3), *Property Law Act 1974* (QLD) s 55(3)(d); Draft Proposal [3.2.16.09] of the Japanese Civil Code (Law of Obligations) Reform Commission, http://www.shojihomu.or.jp/saikenhou/English/draftproposals.html#Book3ch6.

the host state is notified and kept informed (by the investor and/or the host state) about the ISA claim. Also, if the home state agrees with the host state that the measure (like an additional tax or levy on financial services providers) is not expropriatory, it may expect a reciprocal acknowledgement should it introduce a similar measure in its own jurisdiction that generates an ISA claim by investors from the other state. States should consider extending this type of provision first to encompass other types of measures (e.g., relating to financial services or public health), as well as other types of claims (e.g., alleged breaches of the "fair and equitable treatment" obligation also commonly found in investment treaties).[14] Some of Australia's other recent FTAs do allow interstate agreements on interpretations of other provisions, which then bind ISA tribunals. Its FTA with China went as far as clarifying that this applies to pending as well as future claims and introduced moreover an innovative "public welfare notice" procedure that triggers early consultations with the home state if the host state believes its impugned measure is in the public interest.[15] Second, treaties could add an express reciprocity commitment. If one state (A) agrees with the other (B) that an ISA claim initiated by an investor of A over a measure (X) introduced by B should be suspended because X does not violate the treaty, then an investor of B should be expressly precluded from initiating a similar claim if A then also introduces a measure substantively identical to X.

This approach therefore generates another mechanism that can result in states "trading up" to higher agreed regulatory standards,[16] rather than the "race to the bottom" often feared by critics of FTAs and BITs. If managed well, greater transparency by involving the host state in this way can effectively mediate the bilateral dispute between its investor and the host state. Admittedly, for the investor, this risks "re-politicising" the dispute because its home state may block its claim, whereas one of the major benefits of a treaty-based right to bring direct ISA proceedings against the host state has been seen as the "de-politicisation" of the dispute—by cutting out the investor's home state as gatekeeper to claims against the host state. But at least under this proposed approach, the foreign investor can initiate the ISA claim; its home state only becomes formally involved after that, in dealings with the home state.

In addition, future investment treaties can add requirements for the home state to consult formally with the foreign investor before agreeing with the host state that a measure does not breach protections against expropriation or other substantive rights. This requirement can draw inspiration from the tax treaty dispute resolution system. Since 2008, the *Model Tax Convention on Income and on Capital* published by the Organization for Economic Cooperation and Development (OECD), the

---

[14]Burch and Nottage (2011), p. 128. On FET, see generally e.g. Gallus (2011), p. 223.

[15]See Nottage (2015b), p. 185.

[16]Cf. generally Vogel (1995). For another example of how consumer protection law is improving despite greater liberalization of trade and investment, see Nottage and Thanitcul (2016), p. 1 (manuscript at http://ssrn.com/abstract=2703130).

primary template for a multitude of DDTs worldwide, has added new provisions. If a taxpayer finds itself taxed by both tax treaty partners, it can trigger an interstate arbitration if 2 years have elapsed without interstate negotiations resolving the issue under the traditional "mutual agreement procedure."[17]

13.3 International Cooperation to Regulate "Unsafe" Consumer Credit

Another proposed mechanism to address contemporary concerns about investment treaties, in the context of globalizing financial service markets, has no precedent yet in treaty practice. Since the GFC, however, renewed attention has been paid to the many analogues between unsafe tangible consumer goods and risky financial services, especially unsecured consumer credit, yet gaps in the regulatory framework covering the latter.[18] A recent trend in developed countries over the last decade or so involves requiring suppliers of consumer goods to disclose accident information to safety regulators. The aim is to provide regulators with product and market information so as to engage in better dialogue with suppliers about potential or actual safety problems and then (if necessary) to escalate the regulatory response through product recalls, bans, mandatory safety standards or public warnings about certain goods.[19] FTAs could add requirements for regulators in treaty partners to share such accident information, to further develop an "advance warning" system for dangerous goods.[20] The treaties could even require each state to implement duties on product suppliers to disclose product-related incidents—or at least to consider introducing such duties.

Similarly, national regulators of consumer credit should first consider introducing an obligation on credit suppliers to disclose problems experienced by their borrowers that are abnormally high—compared to past experience of the individual supplier as well as the industry sector.[21] Indicia of such "unsafe credit" could include default rates, insolvencies, and even suicides among borrowers. Admittedly, such problems may not necessarily be caused directly by the features of the consumer credit services provided. However, this could be addressed by exempting suppliers from disclosure where the incidents can be shown to be clearly unrelated to the services in question—as under Japan's amendments in 2006 adding a disclosure duty on suppliers of tangible consumer goods. Causation difficulties

[17] See further Burch et al. (2012), p. 1013.

[18] See e.g. Bar-Gill and Warren (2008), p. 1; Denahy (2015), p. 56. For an insightful European precursor to the idea of extending consumer product safety regulation design and implementation to consumer credit regulation, see also Huls et al. (1994).

[19] Nottage (2011b), p. 3.

[20] Nottage (2014), p. 114 (with a longer version at http://ssrn.com/abstract=1509810).

[21] Nottage and Kozuka (2012), p. 129. But see Pearson (2012), p. 266.

also diminish if the disclosure obligation is tied to past experience of the service provider, as well as overall industry sector trends—which can be publicized by the regulators, thanks to better information flows created by disclosure duties imposed on all suppliers. After all, financial institutions already spend large sums to develop sophisticated information technology aimed at "profiling" their borrowers.[22] Compliance costs involved in this new disclosure obligation should therefore be quite low.

Next, financial market regulators in each treaty partner state should commit via FTAs to share such "incident" information collected from their respective credit suppliers and then should collaborate in identifying problematic trends. Financial institutions, even suppliers of unsecured consumer credit, increasingly invest and operate on an international scale,[23] so national regulators should respond accordingly. Of course, such information sharing could be achieved instead by ad hoc Memoranda of Understanding between financial markets regulators, as we see already being signed between regulators charged with securing the safety of tangible consumer goods. But adding such obligations to cooperate into FTAs themselves would help defray growing concerns that these treaties lack adequate regulatory safeguards, despite the collapse of global financial markets in 2008.

13.4 Conclusion

The GFC has understandably heightened fears that financial markets worldwide have been excessively liberalized, fueled by cross-border investment underpinned by trade and investment treaties. However, rather than simply abandoning such treaties or core features such as ISA protections, this chapter has demonstrated considerable scope to add innovative mechanisms to rebalance the interests of both private firms and sovereign states charged with protecting the wider public interest. Novel treaty mechanisms directed at financial service markets are particularly promising, given the limited progress in enhancing regulatory frameworks through multilateral initiatives, for example, via the Group of Twenty (G20) and the OECD.[24]

---

[22]See Harrison and Gray (2012), p. 15, http://www.consumeraction.org.au/downloads/ProfilingforProfit-final-formatted.pdf; and more generally Sexton (2012), http://www.smh.com.au/business/every-click-you-make-theyll-be-watching-you-20120713-221ay.html.

[23]For example, the growth of Japan's unsecured credit market (until re-regulation in 2006) was partly fueled by large-scale investments by US firms such as GE Money and their 'sweat box' business model. See Kozuka and Nottage (2009), p. 199.

[24]Williams (2012). Compare also Davis (2011), http://www.apec.org.au/docs/11_CON_GFC/Regulatory%20Reform%20Post%20GFC-%20Overview%20Paper.pdf. For significant reforms in national law and administration across several developed countries, however, see Fairweather et al. (2017).

Acknowledgments The original version of this chapter drew on research for the project entitled "Fostering a Common Culture in Cross-Border Dispute Resolution: Australia, Japan and the Asia-Pacific," supported by the Australian Commonwealth through the Australia-Japan Foundation which is part of the Department of Foreign Affairs and Trade. The present version draws on an Australian Research Council Discovery Project grant (DP140102526) into international investment dispute management. The views remain personal to the author.

References

Armstrong S, Nottage L (2016) The impact of investment treaties and ISDS provisions on foreign direct investment: a baseline econometric analysis. Sydney Law School Research Paper 16/74

Bar-Gill O, Warren E (2008) Making credit safer. Univ Pa Law Rev 157:1

Bath V, Nottage L (2011) Foreign investment and dispute resolution law and practice in Asia: an overview. In: Bath V, Nottage L (eds) Investment law and dispute resolution law and practice in Asia. Routledge, London, p 1

Bath V, Nottage L (2016) Asian investment and the growth of regional investment agreements. In: Antons C (ed) Routledge handbook of Asian law. Routledge, London (forthcoming)

Burch M, Nottage L (2011) Novel treaty-based approaches to resolving international investment and tax disputes in the Asia-Pacific region. Aust Int Law J 18:128

Burch M, Nottage L, Williams B (2012) Appropriate treaty-based dispute resolution for Asia-Pacific commerce in the 21st century. UNSW Law J 35(3):1013

Davis K (2011) Regulatory reform post the global financial crisis: an overview. Report prepared for the Melbourne APEC Finance Centre, March

Denahy M (2015) Expanding the regulatory toolkit: banning financial products on product safety grounds. Competition Consum Law J 23:56

Fairweather K, O'Shea P, Grantham R (eds) (2017) Credit, consumers and the law: after the global storm. Routledge, London

Gallus N (2011) The "Fair and Equitable Treatment" standard and the circumstances of the host state. In: Brown C, Miles K (eds) Evolution in investment treaty law and arbitration. Cambridge University Press, Cambridge, p 223

Hamamoto S, Nottage L (2010) Foreign investment in and out of Japan: economic backdrop, domestic law, and international treaty-based investor-state dispute resolution. Sydney Law School Research Paper No 10/145

Harrison P, Gray CT (2012) "Profiling for Profit": a report on target marketing and profiling practices in the credit industry. Consumer Law Action Centre, Melbourne, p 15

Huls N, Reifner U, Bourgoinie T (1994) Overindebtedness of consumers in the EC Member States: facts and search for solutions. Centre de droit de la consommation, Leuven

Kelsey J (2010) How the trans-Pacific partnership agreement could heighten financial instability and foreclose government's regulatory space. N Z Yearbook Int Law 8:3

Kozuka S, Nottage L (2009) The myth of the careful consumer: law, culture, economics and politics in the rise and fall of unsecured lending in Japan. In Niemi-Kiesilainen J, Ramsay I, Whitford W (eds) Consumer credit, debt and bankruptcy: comparative and international perspectives. Hart, Oxford, p 199

Kurtz J (2012) Australia's rejection of investor-state arbitration: causation, omission and implication. ICSID Rev 27:65

Lazo RP (2014) Is there a life for Latin American countries after denouncing the ICSID convention? TDM 1

Nottage L (2011a) The rise and possible fall of investor-state arbitration in Asia: a skeptic's view of Australia's "Gillard Government Trade Policy Statement". Transnational Dispute Manag J 8(5)

Nottage L (2011b) Suppliers' duties to report product-related accidents under the New Australian consumer law: a comparative critique. Commercial Law Q 3

Nottage L (2013) Investor-state arbitration policy and practice after *Philip Morris Asia v Australia*. In: Trakman L, Ranieri N (eds) Regionalism in international investment law. Oxford University Press, New York, pp 452–474

Nottage L (2014) Asia-Pacific regional architecture and consumer product safety regulation for a post-FTA era. In: Lewis MK, Frankel S (eds) Trade agreements at the crossroads. Routledge, London, p 114

Nottage L (2015a) The 'Anti-ISDS Bill' before the senate: what future for investor-state arbitration in Australia? Int Trade Bus Law Rev 18:245

Nottage L (2015b) Investment Treaty Arbitration Policy in Australia, New Zealand – and Korea? J Arbitration Stud 25:185

Nottage L (2016) The TPP investment chapter and investor-state arbitration in Asia and Oceania: assessing prospects for ratification. MJIL (forthcoming)

Nottage L, Kozuka S (2012) Lessons from product safety regulation for reforming consumer credit markets in Japan and beyond. Sydney Law Rev 34(1):129

Nottage L, Thanitcul S (2016) Introduction. In Nottage L, Thanitcul S (eds) ASEAN product liability and consumer product safety law. Winyuchon, Bangkok, p 1

Pearson G (2012) Suitable for an individual or acceptable for all? A response to Nottage and Kozuka. Aust Prod Liability Rep 22(8):266

Sexton E (2012) Every click you make, they'll be watching you. Sydney Morning Herald, 14–15 July 2012. http://www.smh.com.au/business/every-click-you-make-theyll-be-watching-you-20120713-221ay.html

Sornarajah M (2012) Starting anew in international investment law. Columbia FDI Perspectives, No. 74, July 16

Trakman L (2012) Investor state arbitration or local courts: will Australia set a new trend? J World Trade 46(1):83

Vogel D (1995) Trading up: consumer and environmental regulation in a global economy. Harvard University Press, Cambridge, Mass

Williams T (2012) Continuity not rupture: the persistence of neoliberalism in the Internationalisation of Consumer Finance Regulation. In: Wilson T (ed) International responses to crisis: credit, over-indebtedness and insolvency. Ashgate, Dartmouth

Chapter 14
Financial Consumer Protection in China: Country Report

Dan Wei

14.1 Introduction

Financial services in the People's Republic of China (PRC) refers to the services provided in PRC by the finance industry: banks, investment banks, insurance companies, credit card companies, consumer finance companies, government sponsored enterprises, and stock brokerages.

As China is improving constantly its financial service legislation, financial consumer protection has become an important concern for Chinese regulators. The ratio of consumer lending to total loans outstanding made from all banks increased from 1% in 1998 to 12% in 2008; by the third quarter of 2009, RMB 4.99 trillion (or $730.4 billion) of outstanding bank loans were extended to consumers. The size of housing mortgages, now the largest component (87% as in the third quarter of 2009) of consumer credit, grew more than 200 times between 1997 and 2008, reaching a total of RMB 4.35 trillion ($637.2 billion).[1]

As a consequence of the impact of global financial crisis, in recent years, the rate of return of more and more financial wealth management products sold by commercial banks in China has turned out to be zero or negative. Many complaints raised by financial consumers have focused on unfair clauses contained in standard contracts, misleading statement, and insufficient information disclosure. The number of complaints and judicial actions related to financial consumer interest has been constantly increasing since 2008. According to one investigation of Chinese financial consumer, 54.7% will only read their contracts briefly, and even 11.1%

[1]This chapter is a part of research project "Global Governance and International Protection of Consumers" (MYRG2015-00100-FLL) sponsered by the University of Macau. See Allen et al. (2012), available at http://www.nber.org/chapters/c12071.pdf.

D. Wei (✉)
Faculty of Law, University of Macau, Macau, China
e-mail: danwei@umac.mo

C. Lima Marques, D. Wei (eds.), *Consumer Law and Socioeconomic Development*,
DOI 10.1007/978-3-319-55624-6_14

never read it when they choose financial products or services.[2] In 2014, there was more than one-third of the new form P2P, the congregation raised platform, that was suspected of violating the law; however, only 72 companies were charged by judicial authorities.[3]

As a direct response, Chinese financial regulatory agencies have elaborated some normative acts with a particular attention to strengthen financial consumer protection. One example is the promulgation of the Guiding Opinions of the General Office of the State Council on Strengthening the Protection of the Rights and Interests of Financial Consumers in 2015. The State Administration for Industry & Commerce of the PRC is collecting suggestions on the draft of Implementing Regulation of Law on Protection of Consumer Rights and Interests in 2016; China Insurance Regulatory Commission adopted "The Administrative Measures for the Information Disclosure of New-Type Personal Insurance Products" on September 18, 2009 (which came into force on October 1, 2009); China Banking Regulatory Commission promulgated "The Measures for the Administration of the Sale of Wealth Management Products of Commercial Banks" on August 28, 2011 (which came into force on January 1, 2012) and "Notice on Improving the Client Complaint Handling Mechanisms of Banking Financial Institutions to Effectively Protect Financial Consumers" on March 23, 2012.

14.2 Sources of Law for Regulation of Financial Services and List of Relevant Legislation

The legal system for regulation of financial services of China is composed of the following parts:

At the level of national laws, there are the following laws, including:

- Law on Protection of Consumer Rights and Interests (1993, amended in 2009 and 2013),
- General Principles of Civil Law (1986, revised in 2009),
- Law of Contracts (1999),
- Law on the People's Bank of China (1995, amended in 2003),
- Law on Commercial Banks (adopted in 1995 and amended in 2003 and 2015),
- Law on Banking Regulation and Supervision (2003, amended in 2006 and 2007),
- Insurance Law (1995, amended in 2002, revised in 2009, amended in 2014),
- Securities Law (1998, amended in 2005 and 2007), etc.

---

[2]Financial Consumer Protection Bureau of the People's Bank of China, Investigation on the Accomplishment of Chinese Financial Consumer 2015, Available at: http://www.pbc.gov.cn/jingrxfqy/145720/145761/2958801/2015092818585691706.doc, accessed on 7, August 2016.

[3]Xu (2016), pp. 71–80.

At the level of administrative regulations, several regulations have been published, including the following:

- Regulation on the Administration of Savings (1992, amended in 2011),
- Regulation on Foreign Exchange Management (1996, revised in 1997),
- Guiding Opinions of the General Office of the State Council on Strengthening the Protection of the Rights and Interests of Financial Consumers (2015), etc.

At ministerial level, the People's Bank of China, China Banking Regulatory Commission, China Insurance Regulatory Commission, and China Securities Regulatory Commission have elaborated and released numerous administrative norms, namely:

- Notice on Improving the Client Complaint Handling Mechanisms of Banking Financial Institutions to Effectively Protect Financial Consumers (2012);
- China Banking Regulatory Commission: Pilot Administrative Measures for Consumer Finance Companies (2013);
- the People's Bank of China, Implementing Measures of the Operations Office of the People's Bank of China for the Protection of Financial Consumption Rights and Interests (2013);
- Guiding Opinions of the People's Bank of China and the China Banking Regulatory Commission on Stepping up Financial Support for New Consumer Fields (2016).

If one looks at the legislation and regulation dated before 2012, it shows that those legal provisions provide to some extent a protection of financial consumers' rights and interests. Except the Securities Law, which begins with the protection of legitimate rights and interests of investors as one of the objectives, other legal texts have not paid much attention to protect financial consumers' rights. For example, Article 1 of Law on Commercial Banks provides that "the present Law is hereby formulated for the purpose of protecting the legal rights and interests of commercial banks, depositors and other clients..." and protects equally the interests of commercial banks and consumers. Even though Article 1 of Law on Banking Regulation and Supervision mentions the protection of the interests of depositors and other customers, it aims mainly to improve banking regulation and supervision, standardize banking supervisory process and procedures, prevent and mitigate financial risks in the banking industry, and promote a safe and sound banking industry because according to Chap. 3 "Regulatory and Supervisory Responsibilities", no specific provisions on consumer protections can be found. The Insurance Law and other regulations do not provide any special protection for financial consumers.

Since 2012, more attention has been given to protect financial consumers' rights. A breakthrough is the Guiding Opinions of the General Office of the State Council on Strengthening the Protection of the Rights and Interests of Financial Consumers (2015).

14.3 Regulatory Structure

The domestic financial regulators in China are as follows.

The People's Bank of China: as a central bank, it will play an even more important role in China's macroeconomic management. The amended Law of the People's Republic of China on the People's Bank of China (PBC), adopted by the sixth meeting of the Standing Committee of the 10th National People's Congress on December 27, 2003, provides that the PBC performs the following major functions: (1) drafting and enforcing relevant laws, rules and regulations that are related to fulfilling its functions; (2) formulating and implementing monetary policy in accordance with law; (3) issuing the renminbi and administering its circulation; (4) regulating financial markets, including the interbank lending market, the interbank bond market, foreign exchange market, and gold market; (5) preventing and mitigating systemic financial risks to safeguard financial stability; (6) making payment and settlement rules in collaboration with relevant departments and ensuring normal operation of the payment and settlement systems; (7) administering credit reporting industry in China and promoting the building up of credit information system; (8) engaging in financial business operations in line with relevant rules, among others.

In 2012, the People's Bank of China established the Financial Consumer Protection Bureau. The Operation Office of the People's Bank of China also promulgated a Draft for Comments "Implementing Measures for the Protection of Financial Consumption Rights and Interests" in 2013.

The *Financial Consumer Protection Bureau* shall perform the following duties to protect consumption rights and interest, namely, to guide and urge financial institutions to fully perform the obligations of protecting the rights and interests of financial consumers, to publicize the knowledge on financial consumption and carry out financial consumer education, to carry out research and draft policies and regulations on financial consumers' protection, and to set up regulatory rules of financial services.

The *China Banking Regulatory Commission* has the responsibilities (1) to formulate supervisory rules, (2) to conduct on-site examination and off-site surveillance of the banking institutions and take enforcement actions against rule-breaking behaviors; (3) to provide proposals on the resolution of problems of deposit-taking institutions in consultation with relevant regulatory authorities; etc.

The *China Insurance Regulatory Commission* is authorized to ensure the following major responsibilities: (1) formulates policies, strategies, and plans regarding the development of the insurance industry; drafts relevant laws and regulations regarding insurance supervision and regulation; and makes relevant rules for the insurance industry; (2) examines and approves the clauses and premium rates of insurance lines related to the public interests, statutory insurance lines, and newly developed life insurance lines; files the insurance clauses and premium rates of the other insurance lines; (3) supervises the business operation of public-policy-oriented insurance and statutory insurance; supervises organizational forms and operations such as captive insurance and mutual insurance; conducts administration of societies and organizations such as China Insurance Association and China Insurance Society; (4) conducts investigation into the following irregularities and imposes penalties accordingly: unfair competition and other irregularities by insurance organizations and practitioners and direct engagement or disguised engagement in insurance business by noninsurance organizations; (5) lays down standards for the information system of the insurance industry; establishes insurance risk-assessment, risk-warning, and risk-monitoring systems; follows, analyzes, and predicts the operation of the insurance market; compiles the statistics and report forms of the insurance industry and discloses them in accordance with relevant regulations of the State.

China Securities Regulatory Commission is dedicated to protecting investors' rights and interests in stock markets.

Respectively, these three commissions have also set up their consumer protection departments since being approved by the State Council in 2011.

14.4 Definition

In accordance with Article 2 of Law on Protection of Consumer Rights and Interests, "The rights and interests of natural persons in purchasing and using commodities or receiving services for daily consumption shall be under the protection of the present Law, or under the protection of other relevant laws and regulations in absence of stipulations in this Law." In terms of the definition given by the Law on Protection of Consumer Rights and Interests, a consumer must be a natural person whose act is to purchase or use commodities or to receive services, with an aim to satisfy his/her daily consumption needs. The amended Law on Protection of Consumer Rights and Interests in 2013 in Article 28 mentions for the first time "financial services" for consumers.

"Financial consumer" is not yet a legal term, and its definition is far from uniform. One view is that "financial consumer" is a natural person who receives services offered by financial institutions or purchases and uses products provided by financial institutions, with an aim to satisfy his/her personal or family daily needs. Another opinion holds that any natural person (such as depositor, mortgagee, insurance counterpart, portfolio investor) with contractual relations with financial institutions can be considered as financial consumers. Another view considers that the weaker or inferior party in financial transactions is a "financial consumer"; not only natural persons but also legal persons and other unincorporated associations and bodies are all financial consumers as long as they rely heavily on information disclosure by financial institutions.

According to the Draft for Comments "Implementing Measures of the Operations Office of the People's Bank of China for the Protection of Financial Consumption Rights and Interests" in 2013, financial consumer refers to natural persons who purchase and use financial products or accept financial services. Nevertheless, this particular draft has not been adopted so far.

In China, it seems urgent to define the notion of "financial consumer," considering its vulnerability and unprofessionalism. As a matter of fact, "financial consumer" is an extension and a specification of the notion of consumer in the financial areas. Depositors with bank accounts aiming to pay for daily expenses, personal loan lenders for the purchase of durable goods or real estate, insurance applicants with an intention to avoid uncertain risks in the future, and any individual and institution that receives fee-based financial products provided by financial institutions are qualified to be financial consumers.

Nevertheless, the term "financial consumers" has been adopted and incorporated formally by the China Banking Regulatory Commission in the Notice on Improving the Client Complaint Handling Mechanisms of Banking Financial Institutions to Effectively Protect Financial Consumers.

Paragraph 3 of the Guiding Opinions of the General Office of the State Council on Strengthening the Protection of the Rights and Interests of Financial Consumers confirms the following rights of financial consumers: the rights to personal safety and asset security, the right to be informed, the right to personal privacy and consumption information security, the right to make independent choices, the right to fair trading, the right to seek recourse, the right to be educated, and the right to be respected.

It should be noted that the Regulation for Implementing the Law of the People's Republic of China on the Protection of Consumer Rights and Interests (Consultation Paper), published in August 2016, incorporated more detailed obligations to protect financial consumers and specified situations that are considered as the violation of lawful interests of financial consumers.[4]

14.5 Obligations of the Provider Before Entering Into the Contract with the Consumer

In 2005, the China Banking Regulatory Commission promulgated "Guidelines for the Risk Management of Personal Financial Management Services Provided by Commercial Banks" and outlined some obligations for financial product providers.

First of all, a commercial bank shall classify the customers according to the features of different types of personal financial management, customers' economic conditions, risk understanding capacities, and risk affordability and clarify customer groups for which each type of personal financial management consulting service is suitable.[5]

---

[4]Chinese version is available at http://www.chinalaw.gov.cn/article/cazjgg/201611/20161100482105.shtml.

[5]Article 16 of Guidelines for the Risk Management of Personal Financial Management Services Provided by Commercial Banks, September 29, 2005.

In addition, when providing a customer with services such as financial planning, investment consulting, or investment product recommendation, a commercial bank shall review and inquire about the customer's financial status, investment experiences, investment purpose, and his/her understanding and affordability of the relevant risks and shall evaluate whether the customer is suitable for purchasing the recommended product. The relevant evaluation opinions shall be signed by both parties.[6] As far as the investment products with high-market risks are concerned, particularly the investment products related to derivative trading, a commercial bank shall not recommend or sell such a product on its initiative to the customers that have no relevant transaction experiences or that are evaluated to be unsuitable for purchasing this product.

In 2011, the China Banking Regulatory Commission issued "Measures for the Administration of the Sale of Wealth Management Products of Commercial Banks," which further highlighted the risk-matching principle, according to which a commercial bank shall maintain a match between the risk rating of a wealth management product and the assessed risk tolerance of clients and specify in the sales documentation the scope of clients suitable for the sale of the product and set sales restriction measures in the sales system.[7]

In China, the assessment of the risk tolerance of a financial consumer shall be conducted when he/she purchases a wealth management product for the first time. The assessment is based on the age, financial status, investment experience, investment purpose, expected return, risk appetite, liquidity requirement, risk knowledge, and risk loss tolerance of the consumer. When a financial consumer reaches the age of 65, a commercial bank shall take into full account the age, investment experience, and other factors.[8] The assessment result of suitability shall be signed by the financial consumer for confirmation.

In order to better protect financial consumer's interests, the assessment of the risk tolerance shall be made regularly or from time to time. Where a consumer has not received a risk tolerance assessment for over 1 year or any event that may affect his/her risk tolerance has occurred, he/she shall accept a risk tolerance assessment at the sales office or through the online banking service of a commercial bank before purchasing a wealth management product again. Without such assessment, the commercial bank shall not sell any wealth management product to the consumer.[9]

[6]Article 22 of Guidelines for the Risk Management of Personal Financial Management Services Provided by Commercial Banks, September 29, 2005.

[7]Article 25 of Measures for the Administration of the Sale of Wealth Management Products of Commercial Banks.

[8]Article 28 of Measures for the Administration of the Sale of Wealth Management Products of Commercial Banks.

[9]Article 29 of Measures for the Administration of the Sale of Wealth Management Products of Commercial Banks.

The Measures for the Administration of the Sale of Wealth Management Products of Commercial Banks further provide that before handling the subscription formalities of a wealth management product for a consumer, a salesperson shall effectively identify the consumer; introduce the sales process, fee rates, methods of fee payment, and other matters on the wealth management product to the consumer; know the consumer's risk tolerance assessment result, term of investment, and liquidity requirements; remind the consumer to read the sales documentation, especially the risk disclosure and important information on rights and interests; and ensure that the consumer has copied the risk confirmation sentences.[10]

From a comparative view, one can see that unlike the experiences of European and North American experiences, generally speaking, a financial consumer suitability system in China has not been established yet. Despite some rules, it is still necessary to improve hierarchical and dynamic management and fine-tune the systems in order to only offer appropriate financial products and services to suitable consumers.

14.6 Public Policy Expectations of the Consumer

So far, financial literacy programs have been largely promoted by financial regulatory bodies and financial associations in China. Financial education activities take mainly the following forms: financial knowledge exhibitions, launching of public service websites, publishing warning information, delivering financial knowledge to the communities and countryside.

14.7 Information Disclosure That Consumers Must Receive Before Entering Financial Services Contracts

Consumers must receive risk disclosure before entering financial service contracts. According to the Guidelines for the Risk Management of Personal Financial Management Services Provided by Commercial Banks, the disclosure of risks shall be sufficient, clear, and accurate and guarantee the consumer to be able to correctly understand the said contents on the disclosure of risks. All the materials provided by a commercial bank to consumers, which might affect the consumers' investment decisions, the introduction on various investment products sold by the commercial bank, and the evaluation and analysis, made by the commercial bank on consumer' investments, shall include corresponding contents on the disclosure of risks.[11]

---

[10]Article 53 of Measures for the Administration of the Sale of Wealth Management Products of Commercial Banks.

[11]Article 29 of Guidelines for the Risk Management of Personal Financial Management Services Provided by Commercial Banks, September 29, 2005.

Meanwhile, the China Banking Regulatory Commission adopted some interim Measures for the Administration of Commercial Banks' Personal Financial Management Services,[12] namely, the advertising and introduction materials on a financial management plan of a commercial bank shall include the disclosure of the product risks and shall be expressed with eye-catching and exoteric words. With respect to a financial management plan not guaranteeing proceeds, the commercial bank shall, before concluding a contract with a customer, provide the estimated data of the forecasted rate of proceeds from the financial management plan, the estimation method, and the main basis of estimation.

More recently, in accordance with the Measures for the Administration of the Sale of Wealth Management Products of Commercial Banks, commercial banks shall not publicize specific wealth management products on TV or radio. In a conspicuous position of the publicity and sales documentation of a wealth management product, there shall be an alert to financial consumer, which reads: "Wealth management is not equal to deposit. Please be aware of the risks associated with the product and make prudent investment decisions."[13]

Besides including some important risk alerts and statements for financial products with or without safeguarded principal and floating income, the publicity and sales documentation shall include the type, term, risk-rating result, and suitable consumers of the product, with an example on the investment results in the worst-case scenario.[14]

14.8 Information Disclosure That the Consumer Must Receive in the Course of the Contract

14.8.1 Information Disclosure from General Perspective: Provisions in Some Laws

Article 19 of Law on Protection of Consumer Rights and Interests establishes the obligation of disclosing information for business operators and prohibits false and misleading propaganda: "Business operators shall provide consumers with authentic information concerning their commodities or services, and may not make any false and misleading propaganda. Business operators shall give truthful and definite replies to inquiries from consumers about the qualities of the commodities or

[12]Article 40 of Interim Measures for the Administration of Commercial Banks' Personal Financial Management Services, adopted by China Banking Regulatory Commission on September 29, 2005.

[13]Article 17 of Measures for the Administration of the Sale of Wealth Management Products of Commercial Banks.

[14]Article 18 of Measures for the Administration of the Sale of Wealth Management Products of Commercial Banks.

services they supply and the operation methods thereof. Shops shall mark clearly the prices of the commodities they supply."

Nevertheless, financial consumers are at a disadvantageous position in terms of professional knowledge, financial transaction experiences, and learning ability. In this sense, Article 19 of the Law on Protection of Consumer Rights and Interests seems to have no much scope to exercise its abilities in financial transactions.

The Law on Commercial Banks (adopted in 1995 and amended in 2003 and 2015) does not request any obligation of disclosure except for interest rates and business hours. Article 31 provides that commercial banks shall determine its own interest rates in accordance with the upper and lower limits for deposit interests set by the People's Bank of China and make announcement. Article 49 requests that commercial banks publicize their business hours for the convenience of clients and work at the business hours announced; "no commercial bank may stop business or shorten the business hours without permission."

The Measures for Information Disclosure of Commercial Banks (2007) state the minimum requirements for commercial bank's information disclosure. Commercial banks may disclose more information at their own discretion and be conducted in a standardized way in line with the principle of authenticity, accuracy, completeness, and comparability. Commercial banks shall disclose financial and accounting reports, management of a variety of risks, corporate management, and annual major events.

The Insurance Law (adopted in 1995 and amended in 2002, 2009, and 2015) reinforces the protection for the insured and the beneficiary's legal rights and interests by demanding insurance company's obligation of disclosing information. According to Article 17 of the Insurance Law, where an insurance contract is entered into by using the standard clauses of the insurer, the insurer shall provide an insurance policy with the standard clauses attached and explain the contents of the contract to the insurance applicant. For those clauses exempting the insurer from liability in the insurance contract, the insurer shall sufficiently warn the insurance applicant of those clauses in the insurance application form, the insurance policy, or any other insurance certificate and expressly explain the contents of those clauses to the insurance applicant in writing or verbally. If the insurer fails to make a warning or express explanation thereof, those clauses shall not be effective.

The Securities Law (adopted in 1998 and amended in 2005 and 2014) includes a section entitled "On-going Disclosure of Information" in the chapter of "Trading of Securities" and provides very detailed rules on the obligation of information. The information as disclosed by issuers and listed companies according to law shall be authentic, accurate, complete, and timely and shall not have any false record, misleading statement, or major omission. If an issuer applies for an initial public offer (IPO) of stocks, he/she must, after submitting the application documents, disclose the relevant application documents in advance according to the provisions of the securities regulatory authority under the State Council (Article 21). An issuer shall not issue any securities before making an announcement of the relevant financing documents of public issuance (Article 25). In accordance with Article 71, "the securities regulatory authority under the State Council shall carry out supervision over the annual reports, midterm reports, temporary reports of listed companies as well as their announcements, over the distribution or rationing of new shares of such listed companies, and over the controlling shareholders and information disclosure obligors of the listed companies. The securities regulatory body, stock exchange, recommender or securities company involved in underwriting as well as the relevant personnel thereof shall not, before an announcement is made by the company according to the provisions of the relevant laws and administrative regulations, divulge any content concerned before making the announcement."

14.8.2 Information Disclosure from Financial Consumer's Perspective: Ministerial Norms

It should be noted that financial institutions shall use words easy to understand in information disclosure to accurately describe the product information. Financial institutions shall be responsible for the objectiveness and authenticity of the information disclosed by them and may not omit any important information. The Administrative Measures for the Information Disclosure of New-Type Personal Insurance Products, promulgated by the China Insurance Regulatory Commission on September 25, 2009, contain such requirement.[15] Aiming to protect the interests of the insurance consumers, on March 27, 2015, the China Insurance Regulatory Commission further requested insurance companies to reinforce information disclosure of the investment accounts; in particular, when the assets include infrastructure investment plans and real-estate-related financial products, the insurance companies shall disclose the investment proportions, valuation methods, underlying assets, and major investment, according to the Notice on Matters Concerning Regulating the Investment Accounts for Investment-Linked Insurance. In relation to disclosure forms, information can be disclosed in forms, including but not limited to explanations and introductions on media or company websites, explanations and introductions in product presentations, explanations and introductions made by sellers, return visits made by customer service staff, and reports sent on a regular basis.[16]

The Measures for the Administration of the Sale of Wealth Management Products of Commercial Banks request commercial banks to follow the principles of good faith, due diligence, and true information disclosure.[17]

---

[15]Article 5 of Administrative Measures for the Information Disclosure of New-type Personal Insurance Products.

[16]Article 2 of Administrative Measures for the Information Disclosure of New-type Personal Insurance Products.

[17]Article 5 of Measures for the Administration of the Sale of Wealth Management Products of Commercial Banks.

The Measures for the Administration of the Sale of Wealth Management Products of Commercial Banks further provide that sales documentation of a wealth management product shall include one page dedicated to important information on rights and interests of the consumer, at least containing the process for the consumer to purchase the product, the process for rating the risk tolerance of the consumer, the specific meaning of each rating, the suitable wealth management products, and other relevant information, methods, channels, and frequency of information disclosure made by the commercial bank to the consumer; ways and procedures for the consumer to make complaints to the commercial bank and contact information on the commercial bank; and other matters needing explanation to the consumer.[18]

The sales contract of a wealth management product shall specify the scope of investment, type of investment assets, and investment proportion of different types of investment assets and ensure reasonable floating according to the ratio stipulated in the sales documentation during the continual existence of the product. If any significant market change makes the investment proportion temporarily exceeds the floating range and may have a major impact on consumers' expected return, timely information disclosure shall be made to consumers. To adjust the scope of investment, type of investment assets, or investment proportion according to market conditions, a commercial bank shall make information disclosure according to the relevant provisions before adjustment; if a consumer refuses to accept the adjustment, it shall allow the consumer's early redemption of the product according to the contract.[19]

The sales contract shall at the same time specify the items, conditions, rates, and methods for charging sales fee, custody fee, investment management fee, and other fees. In case there is a need to adjust the agreed fees but a consumer refuses to accept the adjustment, it shall allow the consumer's early redemption of the product according to the sales documentation.[20]

In short, the recent ministerial guidelines and norms in China contain similar requirements on information disclosure in the European Union's (EU's) Markets in Financial Instruments Directive, EU's financial instrument directive, USA's Dodd-Frank Wall Street Reform and Consumer Protection Act, and Japan's Financial Instruments and Exchange Law. Nonetheless, the obligation of information disclosure for financial consumers has not been addressed by any law yet; the existing regulatory norms are at a rather low level of legal effects. On the other hand, there is still a need to strengthen relevant legal liability in Chinese regulations.

[18] Article 19 of Measures for the Administration of the Sale of Wealth Management Products of Commercial Banks.

[19] Article 20 of Measures for the Administration of the Sale of Wealth Management Products of Commercial Banks.

[20] Article 21 of Measures for the Administration of the Sale of Wealth Management Products of Commercial Banks.

14.9 Other Protections for a Consumer in the Course of the Contract

So far, in addition to the abovementioned points, no other important protection (such as reopening, hardship) can be found for a financial consumer in the course of the contract.

14.10 Consumer Disputes

Generally speaking, in case of disputes with business operators over consumer rights and interests, consumers may settle the disputes through the following approaches: (1) consult and conciliate with business operators; (2) sent a request to consumer associations for mediation; (3) appeal to relevant administrative departments; (4) apply to arbitral organs for arbitration according to the arbitral agreements with business operators, and (5) to institute legal proceedings in the people's court.[21]

Before lodging complaints to the Operations Office of a financial institution where his/her rights are infringed upon, a financial consumer shall first complain to the same level or higher level institution.[22] After prior handling, if the consumer still has an objection, he/she may lodge an oral or written complaint to the relevant departments of the Operations Offices. Where no consensus can be reached or where the parties are unable to reach a mediation agreement, the consumer may also request other institutions to conduct mediation or arbitration or bring a lawsuit.[23]

The China Banking Regulatory Commission has requested all policy banks, state-owned commercial banks, joint-stock commercial banks, and financial asset management companies; the Postal Savings Bank of China; all provincial rural credit cooperative unions; and trust companies, enterprise group finance companies, and financial leasing companies to designate one senior manager responsible for protecting the lawful rights and interests of financial consumers in the head office and branch offices.

In accordance with the Notice on Improving the Client Complaint Handling Mechanisms of Banking Financial Institutions to Effectively Protect Financial Consumers, banking financial institutions shall improve their client complaint handling mechanisms, formulate complaint handling procedures, specify the responsibilities of each position, resolve client complaints in a timely and appropriate manner, and actively prevent compliance risks and reputational risks;

---

[21]Article 34 of Law of the People's Republic of China on Protection of Consumer Rights and Interests.

[22]However, in practice, the effectiveness of such mechanism remains to be observed. More comments see Gao and Chen (2015), pp. 80–90.

[23]Li (2016), pp. 138–145.

banking financial institutions shall enhance their capabilities of handling on-site complaints at business outlets, standardize the procedures for handling on-site complaints at business outlets, specify the responsibilities of complaint handling personnel, and strictly implement the initial consultation accountability system to effectively enhance their capabilities of handling on-site complaints. Where a banking financial institution causes any loss to a financial consumer, it shall compensate or indemnify the financial consumer in accordance with the relevant legal or contractual provisions. One of the improvements regarding the time frame for handling complaints is that all client complaints shall be handled within 15 working days, which may be extended appropriately under complex circumstances or for particular reasons but shall not exceed 60 working days, and clients shall be notified of the extension and reasons for extension by text message, e-mail, or letter.

In May 2016, under the direction of the Shanghai headquarters of the People's Bank of China, the Shanghai Financial Consumption Dispute Resolution Center cooperated with local financial institutes and set up a pilot of the fast-track on small claim disputes.[24]

14.11 Extent of Consumer Complaints/Litigation

The existing Chinese legislation has not defined yet the extent of consumer complaints or consumer litigation.

However, according to one investigation of the Financial Consumer Protection Bureau of the People's Bank of China, 69.9% of the consumers believe that if one local bank went bankrupt, the government should compensate their deposits instead of themselves taking the responsibilities.[25]

14.12 Concluding Remarks

Generally speaking, with the impact of global financial crisis, China, as the largest emerging economy in the world, began to pay more attention to reinforce its financial service regulation and legal framework on financial consumer protection. In particular, in recent years, Chinese financial regulators and agencies have promulgated a number of secondary legislation that adopts foreign countries'

[24]The People's Bank of China, http://shanghai.pbc.gov.cn/fzhshanghai/113598/3060002/index.html, accessed on 7, August, 2016.

[25]Financial Consumer Protection Bureau of the People's Bank of China, Investigation on the Accomplishment of Chinese Financial Consumer 2015, http://www.pbc.gov.cn/jingrxfqy/145720/145761/2958801/2015092818585691706.doc, accessed on 7, August 2016.

legislative experiences on financial consumer protection. Chinese supervisory bodies have been trying to improve the transparency of transactions by imposing the obligation of information disclosure.

However, the secondary legislation usually takes the form of ministerial guidelines and notice, which seems to lack binding force and applicability. In this sense, it is necessary to adopt the form of laws instead of secondary legislation to better protect financial consumer's rights and interests. There is an urgent need to adopt the Implementing Rules of the Law on Protection of Consumer Rights and Interests by expanding its scope of protection to financial consumers, incorporating provisions on legal liability of finance industry, and establishing an efficient dispute mechanism for financial consumers. Finally, financial consumer protection in China requires, in the near future, a coordinated approach (or an integrated approach) through incorporating the separate regulations on banking, insurance, and securities currently in force.

International exchange and cooperation is beneficial for China to improve financial consumer protection. During China's G20 Presidency for 2016, China hosted several workshops and several events of Global Partnership for Financial Inclusion and supported to continuously implement G20 Financial Inclusion Action Plan, with a special focus on financial consumer protection and financial literacy.[26]

References

Allen F, "QJ" Qian J, Zhang C, Zhao M (2012) China's financial system: opportunities and challenges. In: Fan J, Morck R (eds) Capitalizing China. University of Chicago Press, Chicago

Gao T, Chen C (2015) Financial consumer protection: theoretical analysis, government functions and policy suggestions. Comp Econ Social Syst pp 80–90, No. 1, 2015

Li C (2016) On the construction of financial dispute mediation mechanism to protect financial consumers. Legal Forum No. 3(vol. 31. Ser. No. 165):138–145

Xu Y (2016) Empirical legal studies of the protection of internet financial consumer rights. Rev Ind Econ pp 71–80, 25, May

[26]http://www.gpfi.org/sites/default/files/documents/Global%20Partnership%20for%20Financial%20Inclusion%20(GPFI)%20China%202016%20Priorities%20Paper.pdf.

Chapter 15
Current Issues for Consumer Protection Law in Australia

Gail Pearson

The Australian Consumer Law (ACL) is being reviewed in 2016. The review is being undertaken by the Commonwealth Department of Treasury pursuant to an intergovernmental agreement at the time of the new national framework.[1]

There was a review of the Australian financial system in 2014 chaired by a prominent former banker. This included consumer protection outcomes.[2]

The ACL (Schedule 2 to the *Competition and Consumer Act 2010* (Cth)) came into effect at the beginning of 2011. It is second-generation national legislation and replaced the first Commonwealth national consumer protection legislation, the Trade Practices Act 1974 (Cth) (TPA). The TPA rested on the 'corporations power' in the Commonwealth Constitution. The ACL is based on an 'application model' whereby the Commonwealth makes the legislation and this is adopted as State legislation.[3] It applies as both Commonwealth and State law but is Commonwealth law only to the extent of Commonwealth legislative power, that is in this case the 'corporations power'.

The ACL does not apply to financial services.[4] Consumer financial protection is in three statutes: the *Corporations Act 2001* (Cth), the *Australian Securities and*

[1]Intergovernmental Agreement for the Australian Consumer law July 2009 para E. www.coag.gov.au/sites/default/files/ICA-australian-consumer-law.pdf.

There are now documents to support this Review: A national Consumer Survey to assess consumer and business perceptions and the effectiveness of the laws and regulatory framework. http://consumerlaw.gov.au/australian-consumer-survey/; An Issues Paper, March 2016 and a Comparative analysis of Overseas Consumer Policy Frameworks, April 2016 http://consumerlaw.gov.au/review-of-the-australian-consumer-law/about-the-review/.

[2]Commonwealth of Australia (2014).

[3]See Standing Committee of Officials of Consumer Affairs (2009).

[4]*Competition and Consumer Act 2010* (Cth) s 131A. The TPA used to apply to the whole of the economy including financial services. Financial services were carved out in 1989.

G. Pearson (✉)
Business School, University of Sydney, Sydney, NSW, Australia
e-mail: gail.pearson@sydney.edu.au

C. Lima Marques, D. Wei (eds.), *Consumer Law and Socioeconomic Development*,
DOI 10.1007/978-3-319-55624-6_15

Investments Commission Act 2001 (Cth) and the *National Consumer Credit Protection Act 2009* (Cth).

15.1 Objectives of the ACL

The ACL was introduced with a number of objectives:

To Reduce the Regulatory Burden on Business[5] The Australian Commonwealth is a federation with specified powers accorded to the Commonwealth government and residual powers with the six State governments. Prior to the ACL, consumer protection laws in the market for goods and most services were both Commonwealth and State. State Fair Trading Acts complemented the TPA by echoing its provisions but in time began to diverge from it and from each other.

An Efficient National Market[6] Strong competition policy measures were in place, but there were still shortcomings. The retail market was still only approximately a 50% national market. Any ineffective consumer protection measures could fetter an efficient market.

Greater Economic Integration Between Australia and New Zealand[7] While recognising that there were costs in greater integration, there was also a recommendation that harmonisation of the non-excludable warranties in consumer contracts should be considered. It was envisaged that New Zealand may even be able to adopt legislation in the application model.[8]

Seamless National Rules[9] The detail in some different rules between States still inhibited activity in the market for goods and services. There was a piecemeal approach to national consumer policy through consultation between governments. There was no uniform approach to initiating or amending legislation.

---

[5]Australian Government (2006).

[6]Committee of Inquiry into National Competition Policy (1993), Australian Government Productivity Commission (2005).

[7]Australian Government Productivity Commission (2004), Australian Government Productivity Commission Review of the Australian Consumer Product Safety System Productivity Commission Discussion Draft July 2005; Productivity Commission (2005), Review of National Competition Policy Reforms Productivity Commission Inquiry Report No 33; Parliament of the Commonwealth of Australia, House of Representatives Standing Committee on Legal and Constitutional Affairs (2006), Productivity Commission (2008b).

[8]Standing Committee of Officials of Consumer Affairs (2009), p. 9.

[9]Australian Government Productivity Commission (2005).

Integrated Consumer Product Safety[10] This was important in the context of developing a more integrated national market, relations with New Zealand, reduction of tariffs in Australia, and import of products from emerging economies.

Improving Consumer Well-Being, Including That of the Vulnerable[11] While not always observed, there is a long Australian legal tradition of protection for all.[12] Technology, product complexity and an ageing population may be creating more vulnerable consumers.[13]

Concern for Small Business[14] Since the ACL came into effect, there have been further changes, including incorporation of small business contracts within the unfair contract terms provisions,[15] and changes to the statutory unconscionability provisions to eliminate the distinction between consumer- and business-related factors that inform a finding of unconscionability.

Shared Responsibility of Consumers, Business and Government[16] A condition of the involvement of one State in the ACL process was that the ACCC should give a greater priority to consumer policy. An important regulatory focus is seeking business compliance with consumer laws. A court may take into account past behaviour, contrition and cooperation and the culture of compliance within the business when imposing sanctions.[17] In some sectors, there are strong self-regulatory systems. The ACL gave government-enhanced regulatory powers, including the ability to require businesses to substantiate their claims.[18]

15.2 Some Matters for Review[19]

Improvement of the Multi-Regulator Model[20] There is a multi-regulator framework for the ACL. This is a 'one law, multiple regulator' model. It encompasses the national regulator, the Australian Competition and Consumer Commission (ACCC) and the state fair trading agencies. The ACL regulators meet together in Consumer

[10] Australian Government Productivity Commission (2005), Review of the Australian Consumer Product Safety System Productivity Commission Discussion Draft, July.

[11] Productivity Commission (2008b).

[12] *Cable v. Sinclair [1788] NSWKR 7; [1788] NSWSupC 7 http://www.law.mq.edu.au/research/colonial_case_law/nsw/cases/case_index/1788/cable_v_sinclair/.*

[13] Commonwealth of Australia (2015), p. 300.

[14] Australian Government Productivity Commission (2005), p. XX1.

[15] ACL s 23. The amendments come into effect in November 2016.

[16] Productivity Commission (2008b). See especially Terms of Reference.

[17] *Australian Competition and Consumer Commission v Woolworths Limited* [2016] FCA 44.

[18] ACL s 219.

[19] Pearson (2016); See *Australian Consumer Law issues Paper*, March 2016.

[20] Productivity Commission (2016).

Affairs Australia and New Zealand (CAANZ). Although they have the same powers under the ACL, the state regulators may have additional enforcement powers. The ACCC is concerned with competition and overall consumer detriment.[21] It rarely deals with individual consumer complaints. When the ACCC litigates a consumer issue, it does so with a view to enforcing against larger companies as this will have the greatest impact on consumer detriment. It may litigate to clarify the law. The State Fair Trading and Consumer Affairs agencies are responsible for individual complaints and enforcement. There is a major issue of comparability between regulators. There is no nationally aggregated consumer complaint data or enforcement data.

There is also a question of regulatory distribution between the ACL regulators and the financial service regulators. There is one national regulator for financial services, including consumer credit, the Australian Securities and Investments Commission (ASIC). ASIC is responsible for both market and consumer regulation. The idea of a super consumer regulator encompassing the consumer protection function of ASIC has been floated but does not have much traction.

Access to Justice[22] Access to justice is portrayed as not limited to individual consumer well-being but as reinforcing social and economic benefits and in particular norms of conduct. Consumers are encouraged to first try to resolve a complaint with a trader. The state agencies may sometimes assist this process. If this fails, consumers may take a complaint to one of the State administrative tribunals that have specialist divisions for consumer complaints, such as the Victorian Civil and Administrative Tribunal (VCAT) and the New South Wales Civil and Administrative Tribunal (NCAT). Other options are small claims courts such as the Magistrates Court. It is also possible to take a matter to the Federal Court. The tribunals are low cost and emphasise mediation, though in the case of a decision there are limited rights of appeal to the superior state court, the Supreme Court. There is no Retail Ombudsman, though there are developed Ombudsman schemes for other sectors of the economy. A Consumer Survey associated with the review of the ACL suggests an increase in consumer satisfaction in resolving complaints, a decrease in awareness of consumer dispute resolution services and an increase in consumers taking action to resolve problems.[23] The ACCC can bring representative actions.[24]

An Increase in the Quantum of Civil Pecuniary Penalties This is on the table. Many of the ACL contraventions are either a civil matter or a criminal offence, the

---

[21]https://www.accc.gov.au/about-us/australian-competition-consumer-commission/compliance-enforcement-policy; Renouf and Balgi (2013), http://consumeraction.org.au/wp-content/uploads/2013/04/CALC-Regulator-Report-FINAL-eVersion.pdf.

The Productivity Commission is currently undertaking an assessment of the multi-regulator framework: http://www.pc.gov.au/inquiries/current/consumer-law.

[22]Productivity Commission (2014), *Access to Justice Arrangements* Report No 72.

[23]*Australian Consumer Survey*, 2016 http://consumerlaw.gov.au/australian-consumer-survey/.

[24]ACL ss237, 238.

differences being in the standard of proof and the penalty.[25] The purpose of civil pecuniary penalties is to secure compliance and facilitate enforcement while maintaining a distinction between civil and criminal penalties because conviction carries a stigma.[26] A problem arises because there can be a significant quantitative disjunction between the revenue of a firm that engages in conduct that contravenes the ACL and the maximum penalty that can be imposed per contravention.[27]

A Better Mechanism to Incorporate Trusted International Safety Standards Into Australian Law[28] The ACL harmonised the national product safety system. In addition to bans, compulsory recall and voluntary recall of unsafe goods, suppliers must now report any consumer goods associated with death, serious injury or illness.[29] The question is a mechanism for bringing international standards into Australian law and updating mandatory Australian standards. The government Minister makes or declares safety standards.[30] Standards from the organisation Standards Australia can be 'declared' standards.[31] When the relevant Standards Australia standard changes, it is currently not possible to automatically update this as a mandatory standard. Due to copyright, it is not possible to reference an international Standard as a mandatory Australian Standard.[32]

A General Unfair Business Practices Rule? If so, should it encompass business-to-consumer practices only or also embrace business-to-business practices? An unfair commercial practice rule was earlier considered and rejected.[33] Amendments to the ACL to protect small businesses are a step in this direction.

Clarification of 'Major Failure' in Relation to the Consumer Guarantees The mandatory non-excludable consumer guarantees in the ACL signalled a shift away

---

[25]The legislation is structured to create separate but identical obligations with either civil or criminal consequences. On civil penalties in Australia, see Australian Law Reform Commission (2001).

[26]*Commonwealth of Australia v Director, Fair Work Building Industry Inspectorate; Construction, Forestry, Mining and Energy Union v Director, Fair Work Building Industry Inspectorate* [2015] HCA 46 at [16], [17], [22], [24].

[27]See, for instance, *Australian Competition and Consumer Commission v Coles Supermarkets Australia Pty Ltd* [2014] FCA 1405.

[28]ACCC Consultation Paper *International Standards Associations: Consumer product safety* May 2016 https://consultation.accc.gov.au/product-safety/international-standards/supporting_documents/Consultation%20paper%20%20International%20standards%20associations%20%20April%202016.pdf; Commonwealth of Australia *Competition Policy Review Final Report* March 2015 (Harper Review) Recommendation 10.

[29]ACL s 131. *Australian Competition and Consumer Commission v Woolworths Limited* [2016] FCA 44.

[30]ACL s 104, s 105.

[31]ACL s 105 (1). On the role of Standards Australia, see Commonwealth of Australia (2015), Box 10.8 p. 136.

[32]Standards Australia *Forum on AS/NZS 1698: 2006 Protective helmets for vehicle users* February 19 2015; Rod Sims, Chairman ACCC(2015), *Keynote Presentation: Australasian Consumer Law Roundtable 2015* 1 December.

[33]See Paterson (2013), Productivity Commission (2008a), p. 141.

from contract and implied terms to protect consumers towards a performance standard that is more akin to a tort norm of conduct.[34] The statutory-implied terms no longer exist in the national legislation.[35] The standards in the consumer guarantees reflect the defunct implied terms as they concern acceptable quality, fitness for purpose, description and others. Prior to the introduction of the consumer guarantees, Australian legislation used the language 'merchantable quality'. In addition, express warranties become consumer guarantees.[36] Warranties against defects (also known as extended warranties) are also regulated.[37]

Since these performance standards are not contracts, they are not enforced as breach of contract. The legislation distinguishes between minor failure and major failure, and this has implications for the remedial regimes. A consumer may reject the goods only for a major failure or if a non-major failure cannot be remedied.[38] There has been no superior court decision on the consumer guarantees or on the remedial regime. Since the introduction of the ACL, the ACCC has been an active litigator, but in relation to the consumer guarantees it has concentrated on representations about the guarantees rather than failure to comply with the guarantee.[39] Decisions in the Tribunals (both NCAT and VCAT) indicate some misunderstanding of the distinction between a consumer guarantee and an implied term and inconsistent understanding of what constitutes a major failure, along with the remedial consequences.

Digital Products and Platform Liability The ACL is digital neutral. For the purposes of the ACL, computer software is 'goods'. A platform that is simply a conduit for information notwithstanding that an algorithm can target the recipients of information is unlikely to be held liable for the information.[40] The questions of whether and, if so, in what circumstances and how to construct platform liability are being considered. There are further issues about the information and algorithms on comparison websites and the veracity of online reviews. Platforms often incorporate reputation rating, and this is sometimes put forward as a substitute for more effective regulation. The ACCC provides information for consumers about online shopping scams via a webpage.[41]

The Sharing Economy Much of the application of the ACL is predicated on the provider being a business or conduct that is undertaken in trade or commerce. In the

---

[34]*Competition and Consumer Act 2010* (Cth) Schedule 2 s 64. But note s 64A.

[35]The state of Sale of Goods Acts retain implied terms.

[36]ACL s 59.

[37]ACL s 102; *Australian Competition and Consumer Commission v Fisher & Paykel Customer Services Pty Ltd* [2014] FCA 1393.

[38]ACL ss 259–263.

[39]ACL s 29. See, for example, *Australian Competition and Consumer Commission v Avitalb Pty Ltd* [2014] FCA 222.

[40]*Google Inc v Australian Competition and Consumer Commission* [2013] HCA 1.

[41]http://www.scamwatch.gov.au/types-of-scams/buying-or-selling/online-shopping-scams.

sharing economy, which includes some peer-to-peer lending and crowd funding, accommodation sharing and transport ride sharing, the service is not provided by a business, though in some instances, particularly if repetitive, the conduct involved is in trade and commerce. The nature of sharing transactions raises questions of the statutory definition of a consumer. Much of the sharing economy is facilitated by platforms, and the issue is the extent, if any, of platform liability.

Consumer Access to Data Held by Firms About Them Firms use individual and aggregated consumer data to make commercial decisions. Such data are said to be critical for innovation.[42] Usage data are collected and in some instances provided to individual consumers. It is suggested that consumers should have such information to make better decisions and for a more competitive economy.[43]

The Interaction of the ACL and the ASIC Act and Particularly in Regard to the Implied Terms of the ASIC Act and the Consumer Guarantees of the ACL The objective of seamless national rules suggests that conduct rules should be the same, irrespective of the product or service being sold. The ASIC Act was partially amended at the time of the ACL to incorporate unfair term provisions. The Australian High Court has recently decided that late payment fees in credit card contracts are not unfair contract terms.[44] There was no change from implied contract terms to the performance standard of consumer guarantees. There is little litigation on the ASIC Act's implied terms that do include fitness for purpose but that do not include a quality obligation.

A recent amendment to the *Competition and Consumer Act 2010* (Cth) is a new part to ensure that surcharges for particular methods of payment, eg credit cards, are not excessive.

Consumers have access to low-cost tribunals in the market for goods and services governed by the ACL. There is no Retail Ombudsman. Consumers have access to the Financial Ombudsman Service in the market for financial services.[45] There is no tribunal. The possibility of a Retail Ombudsman has been flagged, and the possibility of a Banking Tribunal has been raised in the media.

A New Obligation Concerning the Suitability of Financial Products and Services[46] There is an existing suitability obligation for consumer credit imposed on advisers and providers. There is another somewhat analogous standard of appropriateness for financial advice. The Murray review of the Australian financial system discussed the possibility of a suitability standard for sales of products and services to individuals. It left this aside for the future. Instead, it

---

[42]Commonwealth of Australia (2014), p. 188.

[43]Commonwealth of Australia (2015), p. 303.

[44]*Paciocco v Australia and New Zealand Banking Group Limited* [2016] HCA 28.

[45]This is a self-regulatory industry funded service. Membership of an ADR scheme is a condition of holding an Australian Financial Services License.

[46]Commonwealth of Australia (2014), Recommendation 21.

said that basic products should be suitable for most people and recommended a high-level principle-based targeted product design and distribution obligation.

15.3 The International Reach of the ACL

The ACL may apply to practices and transactions that emanate externally from Australia and reach into Australia. It also applies to practices and transactions from Australia that reach out of Australia.[47] The ACL extends to conduct outside Australia of corporations doing business in Australia, persons resident in Australia, and Australian citizens.[48] Outside Australia, they cannot, for instance, engage in misleading or deceptive conduct or sell goods that do not meet the standard of the consumer guarantees. A 'corporation' also includes a foreign corporation.[49] If a person engages in conduct in Australia or carries on business in Australia, it will be amenable to the ACL. This has been interpreted to include a company incorporated in the USA that had servers in Australia, had subscribers in Australia and provided support services from outside Australia to subscribers in Australia.[50] The ACL has a provision to protect Australian jurisdiction. Neither a 'choice of law' clause nor an analysis of the proper law of the contract resulting in that law being the law of another jurisdiction will be effective to oust the operation of the consumer guarantees division of the ACL.[51] This means that representations about the consumer guarantees, if made by a person otherwise amenable to the ACL, are still justiciable under the ACL.[52] The policy of the statute "has been made part of the [Australian] ordre public interne and ordre public international".[53]

The significance of *Australian Competition and Consumer Commission v Valve Corporation (No 3) [2016]* FCA 196 discussed above is that it establishes the application of consumer law in Australia to goods and services supplied across borders to consumers in Australia when Australia was not the proper law of the contract yet, due to the statute, the ACL applied. It is likely that the width of this application to digital services will continue to be tested. There is a problem with

---

[47] See ACL s 2; *Competition and Consumer Act 2010* (Cth) s 4(1), s 5. This is similar to the situation with the old Trade Practices Act.

[48] *Competition and Consumer Act 2010* (Cth) s 5.

[49] *Competition and Consumer Act 2010* (Cth) s 4(1).

[50] *Australian Competition and Consumer Commission v Valve Corporation (No 3)* [2016] FCA 196.

[51] ACL s 67; *Australian Competition and Consumer Commission v Valve Corporation (No 3)* [2016] FCA 196.

[52] *Australian Competition and Consumer Commission v Valve Corporation (No 3)* [2016] FCA 196.

[53] *Akai Pty Ltd v People's Insurance Company Limited* [1996] HCA 39; 188 CLR 418 at 433; *Australian Competition and Consumer Commission v Valve Corporation (No 3)* [2016] FCA 196 at [117].

platforms operating in Australia whose standard form contracts being used internationally do not conform with Australian law.[54]

15.4 International Cooperation

Both consumer protection agencies, ASIC and the ACCC, cooperate internationally. The ACCC website lists its MOUs with regulatory agencies in other jurisdictions.[55] The ACCC is an active member of the International Consumer Protection and Enforcement Network (ICPEN), constituted by 50 consumer protection agencies.[56] ASIC has issued principles to guide cross-border regulation and assist in lowering regulatory barriers.[57]

References

Australian Government (2006) Rethinking Regulation Report of the Taskforce on Reducing Regulatory Burdens on Business January (Red Tape Report)

Australian Government Productivity Commission (2004) Australian and New Zealand Competition and Consumer Protection Regimes, Productivity Commission Research Report, 16 December

Australian Government Productivity Commission (2005) Review of National Competition Policy Reforms, Productivity Commission Inquiry Report No 33

Australian Law Reform Commission (2001) Principled Regulation Civil and Administrative Penalties in Australia, ALRC 95

Committee of Inquiry into National Competition Policy (1993) Review of the Committee of Inquiry into National Competition Policy, Hilmer Report

Commonwealth of Australia (2014) Financial System Inquiry Final Report, Murray, November

Commonwealth of Australia (2015) Competition Policy Review Final Report March (Harper Review)

Parliament of the Commonwealth of Australia, House of Representatives Standing Committee on Legal and Constitutional Affairs (2006) Harmonisation of legal systems within Australia and between Australia and New Zealand, November

Paterson J (2013) A general prohibition on unfair commercial practices? In: Malbon J, Nottage L (eds) Consumer law and policy in Australia and New Zealand. Federation Press, Sydney

Pearson G (2016) Further challenges for Australian consumer law, in National Law School Delhi, National Seminar on Consumer protection New Age Challenges, in collaboration with IIPA New Delhi and Government of India Department of Consumer Affairs, February

Productivity Commission (2005) Review of National Competition Policy Reforms Productivity Commission Inquiry Report No 33

---

[54]Deloitte Access Economics *The sharing economy and the Competition and Consumer Act*, ACCC 2015 p vii.

[55]https://www.accc.gov.au/about-us/international-relations/treaties-agreements.

[56]http://www.icpen.org/.

[57]ASIC *Regulatory Guide 54 Principles for Cross Border Regulation* June 2012.

Productivity Commission (2008a) Review of Australia's Consumer Policy Framework v 2
Productivity Commission (2008b) Review of Australia's Consumer Policy Framework Final Report (2 vols) Canberra
Productivity Commission (2014) Access to Justice Arrangements Report No 72
Productivity Commission (2016) Consumer Law Enforcement and Administration July, www.pc.gov.au/inquiries/current/consumer-law/issues/consumer-law-issues.pdf
Renouf G, Balgi T (2013) Consumer Action Law Centre Regulator Watch The Enforcement Performance of Australian Consumer Protection Regulators, Consumer Action Law Centre
Standing Committee of Officials of Consumer Affairs (2009) An Australian Consumer Law Fair Markets–Confident Consumers, Cth of Australia

Part III
National and Regional Consumer Law Issues: Helping the Economic Development

Chapter 16
Relations Between International Law and Consumer Law in the Globalized World: Challenges and Prospects

Claudia Lima Marques

16.1 Introduction

The first Report of the ILA's Committee on International Protection of Consumers has stated: "Issues of consumer law are no longer national. Market globalization has changed not only the way we produce, but also the way we consume. The new 'global citizen' is also a 'global consumer', a circumstance that adds new complexities to the area of international consumer protection."[1]

Indeed, consumers are key players of the new globalized world.[2] However, the internationalization of consumer's day-to-day lives has not always been followed by the updating of rules and mechanisms to prevent and to settle the new international disputes that arise.[3] It is interesting that the first academic efforts to protect consumers through (private and public) international laws are now 40 years old.[4] The works of ZWEIGERT, LANDO, and NEUHAUS became famous, suggesting, firstly, that private international law should include social values[5] and, secondly, that party autonomy should be abandoned in contracts between weak and strong parties as the consumers and the domicile of the consumers should be preferred.[6]

[1]See Discussion Paper at www.ila-hq.or/en/committees/index.cfm/cid/1030.

[2]Ramsay (2001), p. 45.

[3]So Fernández Arroyo (2010).

[4]Early academic contributions, as Gisela Rühl reminds, include Lando (1972), Maulaurie (1973) and Von Hoffmann (1974), so Rühl (2011), p. 570. Digital copy in http://ssrn.com/abstract=1816641.

[5]See also the pioneer work of Pocar (1986) and Leclerc (1995), p. 330.

[6]See Von Hoffmann (1974), p. 398ss; Kropholler (1978), p. 634.

C.L. Marques (✉)
Faculty of Law, Federal University of Rio Grande do Sul, Porto Alegre, Brazil
e-mail: cmarques.ufrgs@gmail.com

C. Lima Marques, D. Wei (eds.), *Consumer Law and Socioeconomic Development*,
DOI 10.1007/978-3-319-55624-6_16

Despite the efforts of Professor Arthur VON MEHREN with the projected Hague Convention on Consumer Sales in 1979[7] and the supranational efforts with the European Conventions of 1968 (Brussels Convention on conflicts of jurisdiction, now replaced by Brussels I Regulation 44/2001) and 1980 (Rome Convention on the law applicable to contracts, now replaced by Rome I Regulation 593/2008), a truly international hard law rule on international consumer protection does not exist until today.[8] The UN Guidelines for Consumer Protection from 1985 (1999) remains the only international (universal) instrument dealing with the national (and international) protection of consumers.

The paradox is that the international protection of consumers is made mainly by national law.[9] The question is if this is enough for an effective protection in the globalized market. Supranational and regional laws (at the European Community, in Mercosur, in CARICOM, at the OAS) are now attempting to fill this gap.[10] Scarcely, soft law and universal declarations have some guidelines about the international dimension of consumer protection.[11]

Jean Michel Arrighi, examining the international legal instruments of Mercosur, has once stated that the consumer was "the forgotten protagonist" of the global market.[12] Today, many international organizations (the OAS with CIDIP-VII, the UNCITRAL with online arbitration, the Mercosur, the CARICOM) and academic institutions (like the International Law Association, the International Academy of Comparative Law, the International Association of Consumer Law, the

---

[7]Von Mehren (1982).

[8]Fernández Arroyo (2010), p. 216. Existing international instruments tended to expressly exclude consumers from their scope, like the 1980 UN Convention on Contracts for the International Sale of Goods, the 2005 UN Convention on the Use of Electronic Communications in International Contracts, and the 2005 Hague Convention on Choice of Court Agreements. The Soft law does the same. The soft law normally exclude consumer contracts or does not have special rules for then, treating B2B and B2C contracts at the same standards. Examples included the UNCITRAL Model Law on E-commerce and the UNCITRAL Model Law on arbitration.

[9]Especially outside European Community, in Japan, Korea, Russia Federation, Switzerland, Canada and the USA, so Rühl (2011), in http://ssrn.com/abstract=1816641. It is also to mention the long-awaited first Act of China Private International Law, "*Law of Application of Law for Foreign-related Civil Relations of People's Republic of China*" (LALFCR), adopted on October 28 2010, in force on April 1 2011 with an especial rule (Article 42) on consumer protection. "Article 42: *Consumer contract shall be governed by the law of the place of the consumers' habitual residence; if the consumer has chosen the law of the place of the provision of commodities or services as applicable, or if the entrepreneur has not been engaged in relevant business activities at the place of the consumer's habitual residence, the law of the place of the provision of commodities or services shall be applied.*" So Weizo (2011), p. 176.

[10]See Perez (2008).

[11]See for example, the 1999 OECD Guidelines for consumer Protection in the context of electronic commerce and the 2010, *Consumer Policy Toolkit,* Available from www.oecd.org/sti/consumerpolicy/toolkit.

[12]Arrighi (1992), p. 126.

International Academy of Commercial and Consumer Law) are working on the international protection of consumers.[13]

The question is why the progress is so insignificant. The relation between international law and consumer law in the globalized world is not without tensions; for example, the economic analyses do not accept the rationale that consumers are the weaker party in international contracts.[14] Also, the way to protect consumers in international contracts, through private international law or regarding conflict of jurisdictions, is not settled[15]; soft law or hard law is not enough;[16] international conventions, for example, are needed.[17] On the other hand, there is a worldwide consensus that consumer law is a strong instrument to globalize the rule of law and also to assure not only free trade but also global governance in our contemporary world.

This article aims to analyze these tensions as challenges to international consumer law (Part I) and these consensuses as future prospects to building universal guidelines and principles to the international protection of consumers and tourists (Part II).

16.2 Current Challenges and Approaches to the International Protection of Consumers

As Montesquieu wrote, "...the natural effect of commerce is to achieve peace ... but if the spirit of commerce can bring together Nations, it cannot do the same with individuals."[18] Indeed, globalization and the interdependence of markets have enhanced not only cross-border choices and possibilities of consumers but also the international disputes involving business and consumers.

Highlighting the important role of international law to protect consumers nowadays and to face the global financial crisis by enhancing consumer protection, the ILA's Committee on International Protection of Consumers decided to make a Statement on the Working Session held at the 74th Conference of the ILA in The Hague, *De Jure Humanitates*, in August 2010, as follows:

1. Consumer protection must be a part of the international agenda of both public and private international law, taking account of the fact that consumers are the weaker parties.

---

[13]See the survey of all these efforts in Fernández Arroyo (2010), pp. 9 et sq. Bourgoignie (2009), pp. 3 sq.

[14]So Rühl (2011), p. 570. Digital copy in http://ssrn.com/abstract=1816641.

[15]See Teitz and Stewart (2011).

[16]See Fernández Arroyo (2010), pp. 659 sq.

[17]See Bourgoignie (2009), 9 ff.

[18]Montesquieu, L' esprit des lois, XX, 2, quoted by Kessedjian, Catherine. Codification du droit commercial international et droit international privé, in Recueil des cours, 2002, tome 300, p. 93: "*l'effet naturel du commerce est. de porter à la paix...Mais si l'esprit du commerce unit les nations, il n'unit pas de même les particuliers.*"

2. Therefore, the consumers have the right to the application of minimum mandatory rules and should be able to take advantage of the most favorable law.
3. Considering the consequences of the global financial crisis, triggered by inadequate regulation of consumer credit, there is a need to ensure effective, fair and transparent regulation of consumer financial services which recognizes the central role for consumers throughout the world.

This statement enshrines answers to the two questions we want to pursue: why protecting consumers in international contracts and how to do that.

16.2.1 Consumers as the Weaker Party at International Contracts

Not long ago, consumer protection was a matter of domestic law, and the country legislator could consider consumers as weaker party in contracts and torts. Today, some theories, like law and economics, consider that consumers are not "weaker" as such, but they have an information deficit. The rationale of consumer protection should be information asymmetries and behavioral anomalies. In the international scenario, there are also other asymmetries, like a very imperfect competition market, language difficulties, small value of consumption, and high costs of an eventual litigation and also performance of the warranties.

Indeed, to deal with increasing global "fusion of societies and markets"[19] in the twentieth century, private international law doctrine has proposed initially a "commercial approach."[20] Consumer contracts are not seen as different to other international business-to-business contracts, and the same conflict of law rule could apply, normally allowing choice of law. This doctrine hoped to create a transnational and global law, a new *lex mercatoria*.[21] In many cases, this laissez-faire approach has posed serious problems.

Since the Internet made consumer distance contracting easier in the end of the '90s,[22] since tourism contracts increased and became more and more complex, as demonstrated by time-sharing and package travel contracts, with real and substan-

[19]Van Loon (2005), p. 33.

[20]Cf. Kronke (2005), p. 62.

[21]The Germans are calling this new doctrine, *Theorie transnationaler Rechtsprozesse*, see Buckel et al. (2006), 347 ff.

[22]See Geist, Michel. Y a-t-il un 'là' là? Pour plus de certitude juridique en rapport avec la compétence judiciare à l'égard d'Internet, Étude commandé par la Conférence pour l'harmonisation des lois au Canada et Industrie Canada, 2001, p. 1 of the original, quoted *Digital Equipement Corp. C. Altavista Technology, Inc. 1997*, Judge Nacy Gertner: "Internet n'a pas de frontières territoriales". OCDE, Recommendation of the OECD Council Concerning Guidelines for Consumer Protection in the Context of Electronic Commerce (Paris, 9 December 1999), http://oecd.org./dsti/sti/it/consumer/prod/CPGuidelines_final.pdf.

tial contracts with more than two countries,[23] the "interests" on consumer protection lead to strong responses, in the national laws (i.e., Article 120 (2) Suisse PIL restraining choice of law clauses and the 2011 Brazilian Draft on the Revision of the Consumer Code restraining international binding arbitrations and choice of forum clauses in consumers contracts),[24] in the case law (see *Panasonic do Brasil* case),[25] and has frozen the work of international organizations (i.e., 10 years of unsuccessful discussions about the *destination forum* and *origin forum* rules in the Hague Conference).[26]

In my opinion, here it is necessary to establish the differences of the B2C contracts vis-à-vis the B2B contracts. At this moment, it is important to establish the differences or characteristics of the international consumer transactions and contracts when compared to the international trade relations.

It is certain that in international trade, there are also language barrier, the lack of information, different law rules and uses, difficulties and insecurity about delivery and payment, warranty difficulties, different quality levels and post-sale services,[27] but these difficulties gain a special meaning when the contractual partner is a non-expert, acting outside of his main professional activity, a consumer.[28]

One difference of international consumer transactions is, therefore, the inherent informational and specialization imbalance between the international contractual partners, if one has a vulnerable *status* of consumer, with an informational deficit.[29] The international trade, sales, or service-rendering relations between people domiciled in different countries usually occur between legal persons or professionals, dealers, and entrepreneurs, thus experts and professionals able to move in the international business scenario. In the context of international consumer contracts, the reality is different. The consumer-partner is attracted either through aggressive marketing (for example, mass advertising, telemarketing and shopping, emotional time-sharing sales, special sales for tourists, etc.) or by reduced prices

---

[23]See about this problems Jayme (2000), p. 118ss.

[24]See about this nullification of the choice of law clause in consumer contracts and the critical remarks from Siehr, that proposes a *favor consumatoris* approach, in Siehr (2002), p. 279.

[25]Brazil, Superior Tribunal de Justiça, RESP. 63.981—SP j. 11.04.2001, Rel. Sálvio de Figueiredo Teixeira.

[26]See position of governments, in Conférence de la Haye de droit international privé: avant-projet préliminaire de Convention sur la compétence et les jugements étrangers en matière civile et commerciale, 30 Octobre 1999, htpp://www.hcch.net/f/conventions/draft36f.html (31.05.2001), and in Consumer Protection in the Global Marketplace: Looking Ahead, US Federal Trade Commission, Bureau of Consumer Protection, September 2000, in , http://www.ftc.gov/bcp/icpw/lookingahead/electronicmkpl.pdf. And position of the NGO's in Global Business dialogue on electronic Commerce, http://www.gbde.org (31.05.2001) and Consumers International, http://www.consumersinternational.org (31.05.2001).

[27]On the difficulties of international commerce see Feldstein (1986), 9 ff. See also Jaudad et al. (1991), p. 1.

[28]In this sense European Commission, *Guía del consumidor europeo en el mercado único*, Comisión Europea, Bruxelas (1995), pp. 15 and 16.

[29]See on the vulnerability of the consumer, my book, Marques (2012), 140 ff.

(discounts, tax reduction, free shipping, etc.), by the adventure sense (games, bets, prizes), or by his own ignorance concerning the difficulties in the transnational contracts (little knowledge of the language to understand the offer or the advertising, imported products with superior quality myth, new products, products unknown in emerging countries, lack of legal advice or of a legal department to assist the negotiation, expectation that the brand will have post-sale services in his country, etc.). International trade rules, private international law (choice of law) rules, in general, are built on the basis of professionalism and specialty of the partners involved, to protect the one who sells, who supplies the product and the service, not the one who only pays for it (buyer, service receiver, or "consumer").

Another specificity of an international consumer contract is its lack of "continuity" or its "discontinuity." Trade contracts are characterized by repetition, and even international contracts tend to open new markets in very cooperative and long-lasting trade relations. International consumer contracts, on the other hand, usually involve a single exchange, are not of long term, does not benefit from the international financial system or from transfer of technology in the strict sense of the word.[30] For example, being a tourist is an isolated seasonal phenomenon. To buy through e-commerce a piece of software or a book expert, one is acting, on the contrary, outside of his profession. The consumer buys because of a special price or the advertised qualities, trusting, sometimes, on a non-existing legal protection and undertaking enormous risks when disclosing his credit card number on the Internet.

The other characteristic is the small value of the transaction. It is very difficult repeating the performance and the existence of an effective "global warranty." Nowadays, the international consumer contract is a mass-like phenomenon, if considered, for instance, seasonal tourism, time-sharing, its circles of international exchanges, holiday packages, air transportation, maritime cruises, etc.[31] Individually considered, the international consumer contract has, however, a small value, whether it is for the economy of a country or for a supplier. This small value makes it very difficult for the consumer to have access to justice; therefore, a potential claim of the consumer can be repressed (also by imposing a choice of forum or a binding arbitration). All this makes it difficult for the implementation of the consumer's rights, whether the consumer is to fill out a claim, to go back to the supplier to complain, to enforce his warranty, etc.

The international consumer still has another specificity, which is common for services in general: to perform the consumer contract again, in case of breach of the contract, is very difficult. In case of tourism, it is almost an impossible task to have a substitute performance. For instance, in the case of an excursion for a few days in a polluted beach, there is no way to recover the comfort of a hotel in a distant country

[30]A rare exception would be the time-sharing contract or multi-property, which is a long-lasting relation, by times national or international (with exchange circles), see on the subject the Brazilian scholar, Tepedino (1993).

[31]see, for all, Lete Achirica (1997), pp. 32–34.

and so on. The remedy will be only economical. In the matter of distance contracts, the eventuality of the wastage of time, the loss of a chance, and the pain and suffering related to the defective performance of the international consumer contract are almost constant as well. So it is best to prevent these damages and to minimize them.

It must be given emphasis, at last, that there is a strong political-economic component in the national and international consumer protection rules. An exporting country, like Germany, which maintains a high level of its consumer protection, will raise the quality of its products, which will thus find greater international acceptance. If a tourist country, like Brazil, increases the level of tourist protection and makes it easier the access to justice, it ensures better tourist conditions and favors the development of this important sector of the economy. In other words, rules of consumer law foster competition of the internal market and promote international competitiveness, as well as contribute to the creation of an internal market with loyal competition and the achievement of governmental policies.[32]

The protection of the consumer, as a person[33] and as a weaker party, in an era of globalization, is the one new trend in international law.[34] If consumer law has traditionally been an internationalized area of law, since many consumer problems are similar all over the world and cross-border solutions are sought, now there is a new internationalization of the global responses. In other words, the globalization process has put new pressure on consumer law, on the wake of the liberalization of the global economy, and also on international law, to develop innovative ways to face new demands for regulation on consumer law. The challenge is how to do that.

16.2.2 How to Protect Consumers in International Transaction: Can Private International Law Help?

In theory, consumer must not be harmed, be it on the aspect of safety, quality, and warranties or on the access to justice only because he acquires a product or uses a service from another country or is supplied by a company or businessman established abroad.[35] Moreover, the tourist consumer, the traveler, the one who acquires products and services in another country must have the possibility to count on a minimal protection of his interests, as well as the one who, watching publicity

[32]Ghersi (1993), 30 ff.

[33]Jayme (2003b), p. 186.

[34]See OCDE, Recommendation of the OECD Council Concerning Guidelines for Consumer Protection in the Context of Electronic Commerce (Paris, 9 December 1999), http://oecd.org./dsti/sti/it/consumer/prod/CPGuidelines_final.pdf. And OECD, Draft High Level Principles on Financial Consumer Protection (2011), http://www.oecd.org/dataoecd/31/9/48473101.pdf.

[35]So Marques (2011), 132 ff. Stiglitz (1995), p. 20.

from a manufacturer placed abroad, decides to enter into a distance contract or a contract through electronic means. There has been, after all, a substantive change in the market structure,[36] a globalization also in the private consumer transactions,[37] which brings into light the market faults and the limits of the idea of consumer "sovereignty" in the current market, as we saw.[38] His position is more and more vulnerable, and the imbalance of the consumer transactions is inherent,[39] urging an effective protection and a positive intervention of states and international bodies.[40]

Yuko Nishitani[41] considers that there are four models to protect consumers in international contracts today worldwide: (a) some countries, like Brazil, have no special rule on conflict of laws to protect consumers,[42] but case law normally use the substantive existing consumer protection rules as "lois de police" or mandatory rules (see *Panasonic* case)[43]; (b) some countries, like Switzerland, create a special rule (Article 120 (2) of the Swiss Act on Private International Law) excluding party choice of law.[44] This model calls for the application of the law of the consumers' residence in all cases and can bring some predictability but is considered too radical[45]; (c) the 2003 *Groupe Européen de Droit International Privé model* allows the party choice of law, with a subsidiary use of the mandatory rules of the country of the consumer's habitual residence[46]; (d) the European model from the former Article 5 (2) of the 1980 Rome Convention, today Article 6 (1) of the Rome I Regulation, limits party choice of law.[47] According to this model (also Article 11 (1) of the Japanese Private International Law Act), the parties may choose the applicable law even if one of the parties is a consumer; however, the choice may not deprive the consumer of the protection afforded to him by the mandatory provisions of the law of his habitual residence. This European model requires an issue-by-issue comparison between the chosen law and the mandatory law of the consumer's habitual residence to decide if the chosen law provides for more or less protection. It is a preferential law approach because if the chosen law provides for less

---

[36]According to Botana García and Ruiz Muñoz (1999), p. 8.

[37]See, for all, Ghersi (1995), 139 ff.

[38]So Bourgoignie (1988), p. 64.

[39]Calais-Auloy (1992), p. 1, considers that this unbalance has always existed, only now it is qualified in such a way that one of the social goals of our time is to protect the consumer in a structurally weaker position.

[40]Also Botana, p. 8 mentions the current "degradación de la posición del consumidor".

[41]Nishitani, Yuko. Party autonomy and its Restrictions by Mandatory Rules in Japanese Private International Law, in Basedow et al. (2008), pp. 94–95.

[42]Nishitani, p. 94.

[43]Stj, Resp. 63.981—SP j. 11.04.2001, Rel. Sálvio de Figueiredo Teixeira.

[44]Nishitani, p. 95.

[45]Nishitani, p. 95.

[46]Nishitani, p. 94.

[47]Nishitani, pp. 94–95.

protection to consumers, the contract is governed by a law mix consisting of the chosen law and the mandatory provisions of the law at the consumer's habitual residence. The mandatory provisions are substantial rules providing a minimum standard, normally given by directives and should apply also when the contract is governed by a non-EU state law (see Article 46b (3) Germany EGBGB). In the absence of a party choice of law, the law of the consumer's habitual residence governs the contract.[48]

Gisela Rühl[49] considers that there are only three models: excluding party choice of law, like the Swiss PIL Act; limiting party choice of law, like the American model, which requires a connection to the chosen law (reasonable relationship, see Par. 187 (2) of the Restatement (Second) of Conflict of Laws); and curtailing party choice of law, like the European Model.

The European Model is interesting because it tries to answer the actual challenge of an effective consumer protection through private international law classical and innovative tools and through substantive policy-making rules, like the directives providing mandatory rules.

Because the use of internationally mandatory rules are not so common in the Latin American countries, the Brazilian-Argentinean-Paraguayan proposal to the OAS CIDIP-VII efforts calls for the application of the law most favorable to the consumers (without the European mix application of the mandatory rules and the chosen law).[50] The Brazilian-Argentinean-Paraguayan proposal at the OAS Inter-American Convention CIDIP-VII Part II proposes to overcome the current situation of a legal gap in private international law on consumer protection in international contracts in the Latin American countries by replacing the current international trade law approach *favor offerentis* to more flexible conflict of law rules and a new *favor consumatoris* approach.[51] So far, here is a fifth model to be seen: allowing but limiting party choice of law to the most favorable law to consumers (a most favorable law test).

In 2004–2005 began the process toward the choice of a subject for the Inter-American Conference, known as CIDIP-VII on consumer protection. Taking note of the increase in international consumer contracts and transactions, especially through e-commerce[52] and mass tourism,[53] in the three Americas and being aware that Free Trade Agreements, bilateral and multilateral, in the region are becoming more common and that the development of distance-selling techniques

[48]Nishitani, p. 97.

[49]Rühl (2011), p. 570. Digital copy in http://ssrn.com/abstract=1816641.

[50]See, for all, Fernández Arroyo and Mastrángelo (2005), 3 ff.

[51]About the need of an Inter-American Convention on consumer protection with special and more favorable conflict of law's rules to consumers, see my 2000 OAS-CIJ Cours, Lima Marques, Cláudia, A proteção do consumidor: aspectos de direito privado regional e geral, *XXVII Curso de Derecho Internacional-OEA/CIJ*, Ed. Secretaría General—Subsecretaría de Asuntos Jurídicos, Washington, 2001, pp. 657–780.

[52]See Boiteux (2003), p. 104.

[53]See *Revista PROCON-SP*, julho, agosto e setembro 2007, p. 38.

and marketing are open in the national market of all OAS countries, without a natural counterparty in developing new and more efficient instruments to consumer protection, the countries agreed to think about the role of international law to achieve a more effective consumer protection and a fair globalization of the American markets.

In 2005, the General Assembly of the OAS determined two topics for CIDIP-VII—Consumer Protection and Secured Credit: Electronic Records for the implementation of the Inter-American Model Law on Secured Credit (AG/RES 2065, XXX-O/05). In March 2006, the discussion was started in a Virtual Expert Forum coordinated by John Wilson (AG/RES 2217, XXXVI-O/06).[54] In December 2006, at the Federal University of Rio Grande do Sul, in Porto Alegre (Brazil), the Preparatory Expert Meeting for CIDIP-VII (OAS) took place, organized by the Brazilian Ministry of Justice and Ministry of Foreign Affairs and the OAS, being coordinated by the Federal University of Rio Grande do Sul and BRASILCON, Brasilia.[55]

The negotiations at the OAS on an Inter-American Conference on Consumer Protection began with a preparatory Meeting at the Federal University of Rio Grande do Sul, Porto Alegre, Brazil. In this meeting, Canada presented a contra-proposal to the Brazilian Convention. The Canadian government had its former Proposal for a Model Law on conflict of jurisdiction and on conflict of laws withdrawn. So there are two major approaches for consumer protection through international law currently under consideration at the OAS.[56] Brazil's initial proposal, now converted into an Argentinean-Paraguayan-Brazilian Joint Proposal, focuses on choice of law and requires the use of the "the most favorable law to the consumer" and mandatory rules of the country of the consumer's domicile. Three optional protocols are dealing with definitions, international mandatory rules, and conflict of jurisdiction. The U.S. proposals focus on mechanisms for redress in

[54]Wilson (2006), pp. 28–31.

[55]The invitation was the following: "La Presidencia de la Comisión de Asuntos Jurídicos y Políticos tiene el honor de dirigirse a las Misiones Permanentes y a la Misiones Observadoras Permanentes de la OEA con respecto a los trabajos preparativos para la Séptima Conferencia Especializada Interamericana sobre Derecho Internacional Privado (CIVIP-VII) y se permite informar que, con el objetivo de proporcionar la continuación de los trabajos preparatorios para la CIDIP-VII, cuya metodología fue establecida por el Consejo Permanente de la OEA (documento CP/CAJP-2309/05), el Departamento de Protección y Defensa del Consumidor de la Secretaría de Derecho Económico del Ministerio de Justicia de Brasil (DPDC/SDE/MJ), con la colaboración de la Universidade Federal do Rio Grande do Sul (UFRGS) y el Instituto Brasileño de Política y Derecho del Consumidor (BRASILCON), organizan una reunión preparatoria. Dicha reunión tratara los siguientes documentos de trabajo aprobados: 1) la propuesta de los EUA de una "Ley Modelo sobre Mecanismos de Restitución Monetaria para los Consumidores"; 2) la propuesta de Brasil respecto "una Convención Interamericana sobre la Ley Aplicable a Algunos Contratos y Relaciones de Consumo" y 3) la propuesta de Canadá de "una Ley Modelo sobre Jurisdicción y Reglas de Conflictos de Leyes para Contratos de Consumo". La reunión se llevará acabo en la Universidade Federal del Rio Grande do Sul en la ciudad de Porto Alegre, Brasil, los días 2, 3 y 4 de Diciembre de 2006."

[56]See Fernandez Arroyo and Moreno Rodriguez (2007), p. 10; Howells et al. (2010), p. 15.

national and international consumer contracts, rather than choice of law. The U.S. proposals for Model Laws include small claim procedures, government agency claims, online dispute resolution (ODR), and chargeback mechanisms for credit cards.

These varied approaches to consumer protection have not helped to form a consensus. Brazil, Argentina, and Paraguay consider that Model Laws should be the "the best available rules on consumer protection" and prefer a convention that will be binding and submitted to a judicial and legislative constitutional control since these countries have all the rules in their national constitutions dealing with consumer protection. The US government prefers nonbinding rules. In 2010, after the drafting negotiations, the Brazilian government wanted to call the Inter-American Conference on consumer protection, but it was not possible. A new round of negotiations was called, but with less interest, since the Latin American countries have not enjoyed support from the industrialized countries on a subject that interest them.

The current situation is that some Latin American countries want to keep working on the topic of consumer protection and want to call the CIDIP-VII Part 2 conference on consumer protection, and others prefer to change the subject of study and shift to a CIDIP-VIII process. This situation has frozen the negotiations. CIDIP-VII Part 1 was a model law on securities, and it is done. The OAS negotiations on consumer protection remain at the same footing in 2012 as in 2010. Brazil, Argentina, Paraguay, Uruguay, and Venezuela are now negotiating a small Mercosur Convention on consumer protection with the same principles and rationale. Brazil and Argentina are also changing the Consumer Protection Code and the Civil Code to include special conflict of law rules to protect consumers in distance contracts.[57] UNASUL, which brings together 13 Latin American countries, could also be the next forum. It remains open if the OAS negotiations will bring some fruits.

16.3 Future Prospects to Building Universal Principles to the International Protection of Consumers and Tourists

The increased use of the *lex fori*, mandatory rules, and the *ordre public* concepts to protect the consumers in each national or supranational market—for example in Brazil[58] and the European Union[59]—is only the tip of the iceberg of this silent revolution to end the so-called "neutrality" of private international law.[60] The

[57] See Geib (2012), 177 ff.

[58] Lima Marques and Jacques (2005), p. 127.

[59] See, for all, Mayer (1996), 513 ff.

[60] Jayme (1996), p. 259.

future changes in the methodology of private international law can be foreseen in matters of consumer protection.[61] The crisis of the private international law method can only be solved by new ideas and courage to propose a return to the social values of conflict of law rules, such as the protection of the weaker party.[62] Here is to consider the growing symbolic of consumers in the globalized market (A) and new developments and efforts to establish core consumer protection principles also in private international law and to advance the protection of international tourists (B).

16.3.1 *The Growing Symbol of Consumers in the Globalized Market and the Lessons of the Global Financial Crises: The Rise of the* homo oeconomicus et culturalis

In another article,[63] I claimed that the global consumer is the *Menschenbild* of the twenty-first century. My thesis is that consumers could be the *homo novus* of the global market, the *Menschenbild* of the twenty-first century, the archetype of the sociological man of our times; therefore, private international law, as well as public international law, should focus on this new man.[64] The global financial crisis has begun with the deregulation of the consumer market in the US, and the bankruptcy of consumers in one country led to a global bankruptcy from banks and financial institutions.

The lesson here is that consumer protection is one of the bases of global governance, and the access to global consumption can be seen as the symbol of this new era of citizenship.

Gustav Radbruch stated that the concept of person shows the level of development of a national legal order.[65] Although the sociological archetype of the *homo novus*,[66] as Dahrendorf pointed out,[67] has its limits, I am not convinced that is without significance, and, in that sense, 11 countries in Latin America included consumer rights in their constitutional law system.[68] The Brazilian Constitution, for example, has included it in its list of main liberties (Article 5 XXXII Brazilian Federal Constitution, 1988)[69] as a fundamental right: "The State must provide consumer defense through the law."[70] In emergent countries, consumer rights

[61]CF. Jayme (2003a), p. 85ss.

[62]Medeiros (2004), p. 67ss.

[63]Marques (2011), pp. 363–389.

[64]Marques (2011)366 ff.

[65]Radbruch (2003), pp. 124 a 127. See also about the Radbruch (2003), p. 182.

[66]See Kirchgässner (2008), pp. 1 sq.

[67]Dahrendorf (2006), p. 25.

[68]See also Pinard (1996), p. 315.

[69]See Alexy (1996), p. 179.

[70]Official translation of the See Ministry Of Justice, *Consumer Defense in Latin America-Geopolitical Atlas*, English version, Editor Ideal, Brasília, 2005, 16.

appear to be as important as civil rights.[71] The reason for this can be that consumer protection is central to trade and development,[72] but perhaps there is a more symbolic reason.[73]

16.3.1.1 Access to Consumption as a Symbol to the Technological Global Society

In 1795, Kant's *Zum ewigen Frieden* proposed that a person's (*Menschen*) three circle of basic rights includes the following: for the citizen of a nation, the *ius civitatis*; in relation to other nations, the *ius gentium*; and for the world citizen, the *Weltbürgerrecht* or "global law," the *ius cosmopoliticum*.[74]

As Thierry Bourgoignie stated, consumer law has an inherent "international character" (*vocation international*).[75] In our postmodern times, the consumers are more active and are considered as an important economic agent of integrated markets.[76] The importance of consumer protection is highlighted, especially by the growing international transport, the exponential development of electronic commerce business to consumer (B2C), and the mass tourism in our times.[77]

The protection of the consumer, as a person and as a weaker party, in the globalization era, is the new trend in international law.[78] Erik Jayme in his 1995 Hague Course about postmodern conflicts of law had already alerted that the different cultural views of society and of free market in the world; the increasing need for respect of the new human rights of the *homo oeconomicus*; the need for protection of the weaker parties, especially consumers, in mass contracts and torts; and the different governmental interests and policies could create a new divide of values in international law.[79]

Since the Internet made consumer distance contracting easier at the end of the '90s[80] and since tourism contracts increased and became more and more complex, such as time-sharing and package travel contracts, involving real and substantial contracts with more than two countries,[81] the different "interests" on consumer

---

[71] See Tepedino (2010), pp. 83 sq.

[72] Perez (2008), p. 699.

[73] See about the social organization of symbols, Baudrillard (2000), pp. 57 sq. And Marques et al. (2006), pp. 145–190.

[74] See analysis of Jayme (2003b), pp. 102 sq.

[75] Bourgoignie (1988), p. 215ss.

[76] Jayme (1995), II, p. 60s.

[77] Marques (2002), pp. 1503–1622. See also Araújo (2007), p. 130s.

[78] See OCDE, Recommendation of the OECD Council Concerning Guidelines for Consumer Protection in the Context of Electronic Commerce (Paris, 9 December 1999), http://oecd.org./dsti/sti/it/consumer/prod/CPGuidelines_final.pdf. And doctrine:

[79] Jayme (1995), II, p. 33ss.

[80] See Geist (2001).

[81] See about this problems Jayme (2000), p. 118ss.

protection lead to strong responses in the national legislature, i.e., Article 120 (2) Suisse PIL,[82] and, more recently, in China.[83] Perhaps it is time to propose a third approach, which we can call—following Erik Jayme—new humanism.

For Zygmunt Baumman, for those living in the consumer society, the "normal life" is to be a consumer, not anymore to be a "producer": our capability or aptitude to consume is more important today than our employment or class in the society.[84] Very critical to this reality, Zygmunt Bauman alerts that in the global society, the new "poorest" are the ones excluded from the consumer society.[85] Indeed, the struggle to have access to consumption, to participate in the globalization in an active manner, especially in the emergent economies, seem to be more important today than the myth of the consumer's sovereignty in the market.

My thesis is that the "sociological and academic archetype"[86] of "consumers" can be more important in international law, as the new global actor in the twenty-first century, more than we normally assume.[87] Consequently, consumer protection should be in the agenda of both private and public international laws.

16.3.1.2 From *homo politicus* to *homo oeconomicus et culturalis*

If you follow the evolution of private international law, you can consider that in the nineteenth century, as the discipline was systematized by Savigny, and also Story (1834) and Mancini (1865),[88] the *Menschenbild* was directly linked with the nation-state: the citizen. The *homo politicus* as part of a forming country, state, or nation was the focus of the discipline. The connecting factors were his citizenship, domicile, or locale of establishment. Their human rights were from the first generation: civil rights, surging freedom against the state. This *homo politicus* needs in Kant's conception a *ius civitatis*: a national or local law.

As Hannah Arendt[89] states, the *Menschenbild* of the twentieth century was different: the *homo faber*. This archetype of the sociological man of the past century was an *animal laborans*, an active man (with *vita activa* in opposite to the middle

---

[82]See about this nullification of the choice of law clause in consumer contracts and the critical remarks from Siehr (2002), p. 279.

[83]See the "*Law of Application of Law for Foreign-related Civil Relations of People's Republic of China*" (LALFCR), 28.10.2010, in force since 1.04.2011: "Article 42: *Consumer contract shall be governed by the law of the country of the consumers' habitual residence. The law of the country where the products/commodities and services be supplied should govern the contract, provided that it was chosen by the consumer or there is no related business activities of supplier/professional in the country of the consumer's habitual residence.*"

[84]Bauman (2007), p. 126.

[85]Bauman (2003), p. 10. See also de Bauman (2007); apud Antoniolli (2007), p. 227, note 53.

[86]See about the limits of this archetype, Dahrendorf (2006), p. 25.

[87]See about this importance, Simmel (1995), S. 9–10.

[88]See Jayme (2003b), pp. 102 sq.

[89]Arendt (2009), p. 147.

age *vita contemplativa*),[90] an entrepreneur, a worker (also a consumer) who changed the national and international economies and brought to us the divide between capitalists and employees.[91] Their human rights were of a second generation: labor rights, surging equality, and protection through the law. In the international scenario, the struggle was to be equal and to have freedom to do business. This *homo faber* has built the international society. This *homo faber* needs, according to Kant's idea, a *ius gentium*: an international respected and effective law.

In my opinion,[92] the *Menschenbild* of the twenty-first century is a *homo economicus et culturalis*,[93] an active hyperconsumer,[94] conscious of his culture and local identity,[95] and also conscious of the freedom, limits,[96] standardization[97] dimensions, and the potentials of the global information society[98]: a *confident* consumer.[99] In contrast to Adam Smith's conception, this is no longer a rational consumer[100] but an egocentric, non-expert, and sentimental *homo consumens*,[101] an economic actor,[102] but not no more a constructive one.[103] The question is whether this *homo oeconomicus et culturalis*[104] is really global. Kant had foreseen that this *homo novus* needed a *ius cosmopoliticum* or a global/transnational law.

I can conclude by saying that this *homo economicus et culturalis* is already a part of the agenda of private international law.[105] Once again, not only the global enterprises of the *homo faber* but also the protection of the individuals (as consumers) and the role of the human rights are the focus of this discipline. Various initiatives are ongoing. There is ample opportunity for the approaches and

---

[90]So the title in German: Arendt (2007), pp. 375 sq.

[91]In French, the same book, Arendt (1983), p. 301: "Nous avons vu que l'animal laborans, prisionnier du cicle perpetual du processus vital, éternellement soumis à la nécessité du travail et de la consummation, ne peut échapper à cette condition quén mobilisant une autre faculté humaine, la faculté de faire, fabriquer, produire, celle de l'homo faber qui, fabricant d'outils, non seulement soulage les peines du travail mais aussi édifie un monde de durabilité."

[92]Veja Marques (2011), pp. 302 sq.

[93]Marques (2016), pp. 42 e seg.

[94]Cova (2005), pp. 201 sq. And about the "post-moderne individual", Rosenau (1992).

[95]Jayme (1995), v. II, p. 239ss.

[96]Burkatzki (2007), p. 244ss.

[97]Höffe (2000), pp. 172.

[98]See Losch (2006), pp. 145sq.

[99]About the paradigm of the confident consumer and it abuse (Wilhellsom), see Micklitz et al. (2010), pp. 18 sq.

[100]See Manstetten (2004), p. 268.

[101]See Antoniolli (2007), p. 227, nota 53.

[102]Rolle (2005), p. 373ss.

[103]See the person as commodity, Bauman (2007), p. 52ss.

[104]See Marques (2011).

[105]See Bourgoignie (2009), pp. 3sq.; Jaeger (2008), pp. 307 sq.

methodologies of private international law to make significant contributions to the development of special rules to protect consumers, nationally and internationally.

16.3.2 Toward an Effective Protection of Consumers and Tourists: New Developments on the International Scenario

In two areas, new developments can be seen: in the protection of international tourists and in the development of new authoritative guidelines or principles on international protection of consumers.

16.3.2.1 The Increase of the Participation of Developing Countries and ASADIP's New Interest on the Protection of International Tourists

International tourism has a growing attention in crisis times.[106] According to the *2012 UNWTO Tourism Highlights*, despite occasional shocks, international tourist arrivals have shown virtually uninterrupted growth—from 277 million in 1980 to 528 million in 1995 and 983 million in 2011. International tourism receipts for 2011 are setting new records in most destinations despite economic challenges in many source markets. According to monthly and quarterly data for 2012 included in the *UNWTO World Tourism Barometer*, international tourist arrivals worldwide grew at a rate of 5% in the first 4 months of 2012. Forecasts prepared by the UNWTO in January 2012 point to a growth of 3–4% in international tourist arrivals for the full year of 2012. Total international arrivals are expected to reach one billion in 2012 for the first time.[107]

Considering the unanimous decision of the General Assembly of ASADIP, which occurred on November 26, 2011, in Costa Rica, that proactive measures would be taken in the formulation of an Agenda of the Americas in Private International Law, on the topic of interest to the states of the region, ASADIP's members and other participants of the II ASADIP's Preparatory Meeting of the Hague Conference Council, which occurred on March 23rd, 2012, at the Pontifical Catholic University of Rio de Janeiro, PUC-Rio, have manifested their full support to add to the Hague Conference Work Programme the topic of tourist protection, with an emphasis on international administrative cooperation. The Explanatory Declaration stated:

[106]See Soares (2012), 113 ff.

[107]See https://s3-eu-west1.amazonaws.com/storageapi/sites/all/files/docpdf/unwtohighlights12enlr_1.pdf.

According to the **World Tourism Organization**, tourism is a positive activity for countries, for mutual understanding and intercultural respect, contributing to world peace.[108] Tourist is the visitor who status longer than 24 hours,[109] and who participates in this movement of persons to places different from their place of origin.[110]

Considering that the **activity of providing tourism services is responsible for a significant share of the production of wealth globally**, the topic is socially and economically important. Its considerable growth is noteworthy, especially in developing countries that import and export these services. According to the World Tourism Organization, from 1975 to 2000, tourism has grown 4.6% each year and, in 2009, tourism ranks **fourth** among exports, behind only fuels, chemicals and motor vehicles.[111] Despite the global financial crisis, the flow of tourists has grown continuously, but it has experienced a fragmentation.[112] According to the World Tourism Organization, the influx of tourists into **developing countries** has grown from 31% in 1990 to 45% in 2008.[113] This new phase is marked also by an **increase in the complexity** of their activities, either in relation to the expansion of the chain of providers, or even the increasing sophistication of the nature of the services provided.[114]

---

[108]See 'Global Code of Ethics for Tourism', UNWTO: "Art. 1. Tourism's contribution to mutual understanding and respect bet ween peoples and societies 1. The understanding and promotion of the ethical values common to humanity, with an attitude of tolerance and respect for the diversity of religious, philosophical and moral beliefs, are both the foundation and the consequence of responsible tourism; stakeholders in tourism development and tourists themselves should observe the social and cultural traditions and practices of all peoples, including those of minorities and indigenous peoples and to recognize their worth;...".

[109]"2.9. A visitor is a traveler taking a trip to a main destination outside his/her usual environment, for less than a year, for any main purpose (business, leisure or other personal purpose) other than to be employed by a resident entity in the country or place visited. These trips taken by visitors qualify as tourism trips. Tourism refers to the activity of visitors. 2.13. A visitor (domestic, inbound or outbound) is classified as a tourist (or overnight visitor), if his/her trip includes an overnight stay, or as a same-day visitor (or excursionist) otherwise." http://unstats.un.org/unsd/statcom/doc08/BG-TourismStats.pdf.

[110]"Tourism is a social, cultural and economic phenomenon related to the movement of people to places outside their usual place of residence pleasure being the usual motivation. The activities carried out by a visitor may or may not involve a market transaction, and may be different from or similar to those normally carried out in his/her regular routine of life. If they are similar, their frequency or intensity is different when traveling. These activities represent the actions and behaviors of people in preparation for and during a trip in their capacity as consumers." http://unstats.un.org/unsd/statcom/doc08/BG-TourismStats.pdf.

[111]http://www.dadosefatos.turismo.gov.br/export/sites/default/dadosefatos/estatisticas_indicadores/downloads_estatisticas/Estatxstica_e_Indicadores_de_turismo_no_Mundo_-_2009_1__3_.pdf.

[112]See *Travel and Tourism Competitiveness Index*, **TTCI. 2009**: the 10 top-ranked in tourism competitivity in the Americas are: Canada 5.32 (5th in the world), USA 5.28 (8th in the world), Barbados 4.77 (30th), Costa Rica 4.42 (42nd), Brazil 4.35 (45th), Mexico 4.29 (51st), Puerto Rico 4.27 (53rd), Panama 4.23 (55th), Chile 4.18 (57th), Jamaica 4.13 (60th). In 2009, Brazil occupied the 45th position, in a total of 139 countries, but dropped to 52nd 2 years later, in a total of 133 countries, in 2011, behind the United States, Canada, Barbados, Mexico, Costa Rica, and Puerto Rico.

[113]http://www.dadosefatos.turismo.gov.br/export/sites/default/dadosefatos/estatisticas_indicadores/downloads_estatisticas/Estatxstica_e_Indicadores_de_turismo_no_Mundo_-_2009_1__3_.pdf.

[114]See, Hippel (1986), pp. 255 e seg.

The protection of tourists is **addressed today primarily through soft law instruments**, among which are the "Manila Declaration on World Tourism of 10 October 1980" and "Manila Declaration on Social Impact of Tourism of 22 May 1997" of the **World Tourism Organization**,[115] and the Global Ethics Code for Tourism of the World Tourism Organization (1999),[116] endorsed by the **United Nations Organization** ("Global Code of Ethics for Tourism", UN Resolution adopted by the General Assembly 21 December 2001, A/RES/56/212),[117] **and by conventions about specific contracts,** such as the **UNIDROIT Convention on tourist travel contracts**[118] of 1970 ("*International Convention on Travel Contracts* –CCV', April 23, 1970),[119] ratified by few countries[120] (and denounced by Belgium in 1994 and Argentina in 2010), which has influenced a number of domestic laws,[121] and several conventions about **transportation contracts**,[122] of great success and use, but it is not addressed by any norm globally. The **OECD** has a Tourism Committee (*OECD Tourism Committee*), that gathers statistics and studies about tourism policies in developed countries.[123] **It appears to us that two factors** stemming from societal changes, that impact tourist protection today, could engender the need for a "**renewal of international instruments on tourism**" ("***renovación de los textos internacionales sobre turismo***")[124]:

a) **The growth of mass tourism and the increase of the participation of developing countries: a quantitative and destination change of globalized tourism**. There is more time for leisure nowadays, for consumption and tourism as a means of self-realization,[125] just as there are means of financing in order to make tourism accessible to nearly all classes of the population, resulting in decentralized mass tourism, and turning today to developing countries, less prepared for the influx of visitors. If in 1950 tourism destinations concentrated in industrialized countries in Europe and North

[115] http://www.univeur.org/CMS/UserFiles/65.%20Manila.PDF.

[116] http://ethics.unwto.org/en/content/global-code-ethics-tourism.

[117] See also guidelines on sustainable tourism, http://hqweb.unep.org.

[118] http://www.unidroit.info/program.cfm?menu=convention&file=convention&lang=en&msid=46.

[119] Garcia Rubio (1999), p. 29:"*En 1966 el Instituto [UNIDROIT] emprendió la tarea de elaborar reglas uniformes para las relaciones jurídicas entre las agencias de viaje y sus cleintes, que concluyeron con la redacción de un Convenio internacional relativo al contrato de viaje (CCV), finalmente firmado en Brusela el 23 de abril de 1970…[de] escaso éxito…*".

[120] http://www.unidroit.org/english/implement/i-70.pdf, more specifically: Italy, China, San Marino, Togo, Cameroon, Benin. Entry into force: 26 February 1976.

[121] See Tale (2005), p. 17, on the Argentinean Law (Ley 18.829 y Decr. 2182/72) and the Spanish Law of 1963. On the inclusion in the German BGB of the Reisevertrag, see Garcia Rubio (1999), p. 38; Minervini (1974), pp. 443 e seg.

[122] Aguirre Ramírez and Fresnedo (1999), pp. 11 e seg.

[123] http://www.oecd.org/document/63/0,3746,en_2649_34389_1932863_1_1_1_1,00.html. The website states that: "…the OECD Tourism Committee is in a unique position to serve as an international forum for co-ordinating policies and actions. The OECD is the only global forum for discussions of tourism policies among industrialised countries."

[124] Borrowed from TUDELA, Tueda (2006), p. 251.

[125] Bauman (2007), pp. 52 e seg.

America, now 45% of tourism in the world has developing countries as a destination. Concerns over sustainable tourism, climate change,[126] security and quality of tourism services, as well as access to justice and enforceability of judgments in tourists' countries of residence have since occupied center stage. In 1999, in Chile, the World Tourism Organization approved the Global Code of Ethics for Tourism, approved two years later, in 2011, also by the United Nations General Assembly, containing clauses on the right to tourism, non-discrimination, sustainable tourism and accessibility.

b) **Changes in the tourist's profile, the increasing complexity of tourist contracts and the use of new technologies: the insufficiency of tourist protection solely as a consumer**. According to scholars in the area, there is no consensus on the definition of tourist between the World Tourism Organization and the World Trade Organization[127]; instead, there are over 40 codes and guidelines, and economic integration processes like the European Union and MERCOSUR have become increasingly concerned with the protection of tourists-consumers, particularly with regard to some contracts and their position as a consumer, particularly in European Directives on travel contracts combined with tourist packages[128] and time-sharing,[129] but not always with respect to conflicts of laws.[130] It is important to highlight the early efforts of UNIDROIT about travel contracts, such as the 1970 Convention, ratified by five countries, but denounced by Belgium (1994) and Argentina (2010) because of their difficulties with new developments in the field and the idea of objective liability.[131] The **World Trade Organization**, in the Uruguay Round, included tourist services in the GATS as one of the four "means and forms of service provision" expressly as "consumption abroad",[132] imposing the principles of "non-discrimination and flexibilizing the principle of national treatment and access to markets".[133] Spanish scholars highlight there was a cultural change in tourism in the twenty-first century,[134] including activities that were not considered consumption before (and are still not considered that in some countries), such as tourism for conferences, professional or religious training, as well as long-term student travel beyond one year.[135] Domestic research shows that, with the development of new technologies on distance contracts, many tourists no longer use travel agencies[136] but use instead other public and private intermediaries, or hire the

[126]See OECD and United Nations Environment Programme (UNEP) study titled "*Climate Change and Tourism Policy in OECD Countries*".

[127]Pezzutti (2010), pp. 16–17.

[128]See Garcia Rubio (1999), pp. 12 e seg.

[129]See Lete Achirica (1997), p. 46 and following. On the new Directive on the topic of 2008 and the Framework Directive of 2011, see Paisant (2010), p. 303; Gest (2010), p. 13 e seg.

[130]Micklitz et al. (2010), p. 563, that on the Rome I Regulation and its article 6 says that: *"This declaration is by no means clear and needs interpretation. Problematic is the case of the so-called 'active consumer' who travels abroad and should at least be protected by the mandatory provisions of the law of the country of his temporary stay; this seems to be excluded by Article 6, according to Garcímatin a 'loophole of the text' which would allow unlimited free choice under Article 3(1).*"

[131]D'Archivio, María e., Otro vulnerable entre nosotros ... el consumidor turista, in *Microjuris.com*, doc. 5652-AR.

[132]Labandera (2006), pp. 41–42.

[133]Labandera (2006), p. 43 y nota 17.

[134]Tueda (2006), pp. 256 e seg.

[135]In Argentina student tourism is considered to be consumption and is expressly regulated, see Del Busto (2006), pp. 282 e seg.

[136]Atheniense (2002), pp. 17 e seg.

services directly.[137] Hence, the protection of consumer only in that role and upon return to their country of origin no longer seems sufficient, wider protection being necessary, only in the role of tourist, without discrimination between national and foreign tourists, without prejudice to the protection guaranteed to consumer of access to courts in their country of origin, but developing methods of rapid and facilitated protection to tourists as visitors and greater cooperation among national consumer protection bodies in this respect.

The number of case scenarios is large[138] outside the European Union,[139]that has harmonized legislation on the matter.[140] These problems appear already in the **country of destination of tourists**, but they are not addressed in light of the **inexistence of fast and efficient channels** for these visitors. On the other hand, there is a **great demand for litigation in the tourists' countries of residence.**[141] These are fairly inefficient and expensive cross-border litigation cases, or litigation with the trip organizers (even if, with electronic means, hiring these services is increasingly done directly), litigation that could be avoided with better information,[142] more administrative cooperation in the prevention and creation of conciliatory and urgent measures, as attested by leading cases found in Brazil, Argentina and the United States.

The current models of tourist protection in private international law are essentially four: 1. Establishment of **substantial special uniform rules** for contracts of interest to the sector, such as the UNIDROIT Convention on Travel Contracts of 1970 or the conventions on air transport; 2. The **creation of special conflict rules** to **protect the consumers**, applicable - sometimes - to tourists, such as the Regulation (EC) n. 593/2008 on the law applicable to contractual obligations (Rome I) of the European Union, but that most of the laws of the region nothing mention about special protection of tourists; 3. Establishment of **channels of administrative cooperation of fast conciliation**, such as the MERCOSUR Agreement on consumer visitors of 2005, indication of administrative or judicial bodies to perform fast conciliations as in the case of Brazil and the Special Small Claims Courts, available 24 hours at airports, and 4. **Guarantee of privileged access to the forum** of his

---

[137]A research from the Brazilian government in preparation for the 2014 World Cup says that "most tourists visiting Brazil in 2010 did not use travel agencies (65,4%)." http://www.turismo.gov.br/export/sites/default/turismo/o_ministerio/publicacoes/downloads_publicacoes/Documento_Referencial_Turismo_no_Brasil_2011-2014.pdf.

[138]See the research on the Province of Mendoza, Argentina, showing an increase of 80% in problems with international destinations (Brazil), Benitez (2006), p. 233.

[139]See on Directive 90/314/CEE of the Council, of 13 July 1990, Miranda (2000), p. 22 and following. And the leading case, CJCE, 26.2.1992, Mme. Hacker c. Euro-Relais, Recuiel Dalloz, nr. 37, 29.12.1992, p. 454. And Lopez (2009), pp. 160–161.

[140]See Poillot (2006), pp. 87 e seg.

[141]See UFRGS research on the Brazilian case law (and information system of consumer litigation in Brazil, SINDEC, www.mj.org.br), Argentinean, Uruguayan and North American, attached to the research on the Province of Mendoza, Argentina, showing an increase of 80% in the problems with international destinations (Brazil), Benitez (2006), pp. 232–233:"*Tipo de quejas de los turistas: 1. Transporte aéreo 40% (retraso en vuelos) 2. Alojamiento 17% (alojamiento de alquiler) 3. Agencia de Viajes 13% (incumplimiento de servicios) 4. Trsporte automotor 11% (demora) 5. Precios diferenciados a turistas extramjeros 8% (hotelería y entradas en parques nacionales) 6. Alquiler de autor 3¨(calidad de los vehículos) 7. Gastronomía 2% (sobrefacturación) 8. Otros 6%.*"

[142]See Achirica (1987), p. 277.

domicile, even when the consumer is a tourist and the plaintiff of the claim, for cross-border disputes upon their return from the trip, which does not always ensure success in the claim, as the research of American, Brazilian, Uruguayan and Argentinian leading cases has demonstrated, by the difficulties of enforcement and liability of the supply chain, the small amount of the claim and existence of "*forum non conveniens*" in some legislations. Having examined the models in detail, the initial suggestion is to *prioritize the new methods of cooperation, whether legal (with the central authorities), or administrative*, and the methods of alternative dispute resolution such as conciliation and judicial methods adapted to the urgency (and speed of stay of the tourist in that country) in order to facilitate access to justice and the methods of alternative dispute resolution, such as the example of the MERCOSUR and the emergency conciliations at the airports in Brazil.

It is to be noted that **the MERCOSUR has a successful experience with administrative agreements of cooperation for the protection of visitors** (Inter-Institutional Letter of Understanding among the agencies of consumer protection of MERCOSUR member states for the protection of **consumer visitors** of 2005)[143] and the Technical Chambers of discussion and assessment between the tourism sectors and these bodies, and that **the European Union drew some guidelines with regard to conflict of laws protecting the tourist, as a consumer, in its Regulation** (EC) n. 593/2008 on the law applicable to contractual obligations **(Rome I) and** Regulation n. 44/2001 on jurisdiction and the recognition and enforcement of judgments in civil and commercial matters **(Brussels I)**, that can serve as a model, including with respect to the necessity or not of special rules of conflict of laws and taking into account that in most of the legislations of conflict of laws of the countries of ASADIP the tourist is not protected in a special way, either as consumers or as a visitor, it seems important to further study the issue and share experiences, especially the experience of the administrative cooperation of MERCOSUR, the experience of the European Union and the conciliations at the airports in Brazil, among others, to verify the convenience of more general and universal measures on the topic.

Whereas in the preparatory meeting in Rio de Janeiro in 2012, the research on the current state of protection of tourists in the region was presented by the Group "MERCOSUR and Consumer Law", UFRGS, under the coordination of Professor Dr. Claudia Lima Marques, and that the Brazilian members of ASADIP, with support from the Brazilian Society of International Law, **concluded that the tourist, whether domestic or foreign-but especially the latter-, is in a situation of special vulnerability, deserving special protection**, and other measures to prevent injury, especially information and quick access to assistance channels, as well as the facilitation of solutions to their problems and disputes.

It was concluded that, **in the current context, the tourist emerges in a particularly vulnerable way before these complexities, both in national and international contexts, as a natural evolution of the concept of subject of rights and foreigner**. Accordingly, there remain clear risks to those involved in this chain, given the potential for proliferation of conflicts that result in a reduction of social and economic efficiency. In a scenario of strong investment and sustainable development it would be essential to establish international standards domestically and globally to reduce risks, provide guarantees for the new subject, the tourist and also the investment, making the normative activity a global dialogue between various interests to ensure the development with confidence and legal certainty for all stakeholders. The debate on the issue of protection of tourists could allow a new dialogue among the interested states and developing states, the sector involved and the

[143]See www.mj.org.br and previous problems, in Fellous (2004), p. 155 and following.

World Tourism Organization, as well as processes of economic integration, MERCOSUR and the European Union, with the common goal of protection of tourists.

Whereas **one of the objectives of ASADIP** (Asociación Americana de Derecho Internacional Privado) is to "*cooperate with ... universal institutions ... in charge of the elaboration and development of Private International Law*", such as the Hague Conference and "*exchange experiences in all matters relative to Private International Law.*"[144] Given that its **objective** is not only to "*disseminate the work of international bodies in the area of Private International Law*" but also "*to promote studies and research towards the development*" of private international law and that in 2011 and 2012, ASADIP groups conducted exhaustive research on the issue of protecting the tourist-consumer, **noting that there is a legislative gap** in this area and the suitability of treating the subject in Private International Law. ASADIP members gathered in Rio de Janeiro concluded that the protection of tourists has its own characteristics and **is an important part of protecting weaker parties in these days of globalization, growing mass tourism, decentralization of tourist destinations increasingly located in developing countries and subject to disasters and accidents, thereby considering it positive to begin more detailed studies on the feasibility and necessity of the Hague Conference work towards the development of a global instrument for protection of tourists**, which could prioritize administrative cooperation and use of existing conventions such as the one on access to justice to allow the protection of tourists.

Whereas there was **strong support for the issue of protecting tourists** in the ASADIP meeting in Costa Rica in November 2012, especially from the representatives of some states, which was repeated at the meeting in Rio de Janeiro, culminating in the drafting of the Rio de Janeiro Charter **proposing the theme for the Hague Conference and urging states' performance in this regard**.

Indeed, the UWTO efforts to organize a new convention are directed toward the emergency measures in case of a crisis, like the one created by volcanoes or other natural catastrophes (tsunamis, earthquakes, etc.). The protection of tourists as consumers is a new subject and could be an interest for the future. Better international administrative and judicial cooperation is a need on the subject also.

16.3.2.2 Core Principles and Rights for the International Protection of Consumers

The adoption of protective rules, regulation, even conventions, and their enforcement by governmental agencies in a scenario of better international administrative and judicial cooperation is a need—and a very important step—for the effective protection of consumers in the globalized market, but as David Stewart notes, "one cannot look to the government for all solutions."[145]

So initiatives, like the efforts of the ILA's Committee on International Protection of Consumers, can help to enhance the role of international law in the protection of

[144] ASADIP website, www.asadip.org.py.

[145] Teitz and Stewart (2011), p. 100.

consumers. The first Statement of the Committee in 2010 is a good example,[146] but the Committee could work in the future toward the development of universal principles or guidelines to countries, businessmen, and parties willing to engage in international contracts with consumers.[147] So these principles will be formulated by the input from existing international organizations, members of different legal backgrounds, and with the basis of other accepted principles developed today.[148] The principles should be subject to substantial international review and comments before established, like other ILA Guidelines.

The most important factor is the acknowledgement that consumers, as individuals, whenever engaging in an international contract, they should be treated as a weaker party and be not deprived of the minimum consumer protection rules that exist in their country of habitual residence or domicile.

In other words, it is important that consumers should not be treated as experts on the products or services or as professionals who are used to complex and sophisticated contracts and clauses and to international litigation and arbitration processes. Consumer protection should begin from the contractual business partner, taking account of the imbalance of power, information, language knowledge, and time and economic resources between consumers and suppliers. At its heart, the need for consumer protection arises from an imbalance of power, information, and resources between consumers and their providers, placing consumers at a disadvantage, especially in cross-border transactions, when language, distance, and small value can make it impossible to prevent and solve disputes. Here, cooperation and loyalty between contractual partners can avoid disputes and help to build trust in the global market.

In my opinion, there are 10 core consumer rights that should be assured in international contracts:

1. *Right to be treaty as weaker party and not as expert or businessman;*
2. *Right to be informed and to have a proper disclosure of the contract terms, the product or service characteristics and risks and about the chosen law;*
3. *Right to safety and privacy in the data informed and by international payments;*
4. *Right to the application of minimum mandatory rules and to be able to take advantage of the most favorable law;*
5. *Right to redress of economic and moral damages suffered in international contracts, inclusive to be able to take advantage of collective redress, if provided in one of the laws connected with the case*
6. *Right to take advantage of cooling-off-period, if is provided in one of the laws connected with the case*
7. *Right not to be discriminated by its domicile or nationality*

146 See www.ila.org.

147 See similar initiative by the Pace University New York, in www.pace.edu.us. The goal seems to be to established common universal substantial principles on consumer protection that can be used as a contract "law" by the parties, similar to the unified sales contract law now proposed in Europe (COM 2011 635).

148 See COM (2011)635 final, Proposal of a new Regulation on a Common European Sales Law for consumers.

8. *Right to take advantage of the longest time or period of extinctive prescription provided in one of the laws connected with the case*
9. *Right to indicate errors, misuse of data, abuse, unfair or deceptive trade practices and to have it charged back*
10. *Right to be heard by a domestic judicial body, if binding international ODR, arbitration or other ADR mechanisms are considered unfair or are caring in a foreign language.*

The ILA's Committee on International Protection of Consumers could develop principles and guidelines to help consolidate these consumer rights in our globalized market, and so taking the lead on global consumer protection efforts. The idea is launching a work to develop best practices, rules, or principles to guide enterprises and businessmen to rethink their practices and to join this effort to build international contract guidelines that assure effective and real consumer protection.

16.4 Conclusion Remarks

As the former member of the Inter-American Juridical Committee of the Organization of American States (OAS), nominated by the U.S., Antonio Perez stated: "effective consumer protection is . . . central to trade and development . . . [and] . . . have important political, economic, and social benefits." And as David Steward stated, consumer protection can help the development of the rule of law in all countries worldwide.[149] In this line of thinking, international protection of consumers can be a chance to enhance more trust and confidence in a globalized market.

Erik Jayme in his 1995 Hague General Course about postmodern conflicts of law had already warned that the different cultural views of societies about the free market on one hand and on the other hand the increased need of protection for the weaker parties in the global market, especially for the consumers—representing the call for a new kind of human rights—could create a new division of values in private international law.[150] The actual tensions existing about international protection of consumers can be seen as a chance for innovative thinking and to renew the important role of private international law to provide answers for international relationships.

Let us hope that the future work of the ILA's Committee on international protection of consumers can help to avoid this situation (division of values/culture divide) and may provide new responses for consumer protection; be a new global platform for experts and stakeholders to exchange views and experiences, to learn the lessons from the actual difficulties on establishing a universal guideline to consumer protection in international contracts; and establish an effective international dialogue on this important subject.

[149]Teitz and Stewart (2011), pp. 81, 82.

[150]Jayme (1995), p. 33ss.

References

Achirica JL (1987) El contrato de multipropiedad y la protección de los consumidores. CEDECS, Barcelona

Aguirre Ramírez F, Fresnedo C (1999) Curso de Derecho del Transporte – Transporte Aereo. FCU, Montevideo

Alexy R (1996) Theorie der Grundrechte. Suhrkamp, Frankfurt

Antoniolli L (2007) The Italian consumer code: a milestone or a monument. In: Boele-Woelki K, Grosheide W (eds) The future of European contract law-essays in honour of Ewoud Hondius. Wolters Kluwer, Austin

Arendt H (1983) Condition de l'homme moderne. Calman-Lévy, Paris

Arendt H (2007) Vita activa (The Human condition, 1958), 5th edn. Piper, München

Arendt H (2009) A condição humana, 10th edn. Forense Universitária, Rio de Janeiro

Arrighi J (1992) La Protección de los Consumidores y el Mercosur. In: Revista Direito do Consumidor, n. 2. São Paulo

Atheniense L (2002) A responsabilidade jurídica das agências de viagens. Del Rey, Belo Horizonte

Baudrillard J (2000) A sociedade de consumo. Edições 70, Lisboa

Bauman Z (2003) Trabajo consumismo y nuevos pobres. Gedisa, Barcelona

Bauman Z (2007) Consuming life. Polity Press, Cambridge

Basedow J, Baum H, Nishitani Y (2008) Japanese and European private international law in comparative perspective. Möhr, Tübingen

Benitez D (2006) Informe del Derecho del turismo en Argentina. In: Facal J (Coord.) Derecho del Turismo. FCU, Montevideo

Boiteux B (2003) Legislação de turismo. Campus, Rio de Janeiro

Botana García G, Ruiz Muñoz M (Coord) (1999) Curso sobre protección jurídica de los consumidores, Ed. Ciencias Juridicas, Madrid, p. 8

Bourgoignie T (1988) Eléments pour Une théorie du droit de la consommation. Story, Bruxels

Bourgoignie T (ed) (2009) L'intégration économique régionale et la protection du consommateur. Ed. Yvon Blais, pp 3sq

Buckel S, Christensen R, Fischer-Lescano A (2006) Neue Theorien des Rechts. UTB, Stuttgart

Burkatzki E (2007) Verdrängt der Homo oeconomicus den Homo communis? – Normbezogene Orientirungsmuster bei Akteuren mit unterschiedlicher Markteinbindung. DUV, Wiesbaden, p 211ss

Calais-Auloy J (1992) Droit de la Consommation, 3rd edn. Dalloz, Paris

Cova B (2005) L'hiper-consomateur: entre immersion et sécession. In: Aubert N (ed) L'individu hypermoderne. Sociologique Clinique, Paris

Dahrendorf R (2006) Homo sociologicus – ein Versuch zur Geschichte, Bedeutung und Kritik der Kategorie der sozialen Rolle, 16 Aufl. VS Verlag, Wiesbaden

Del Busto E (2006) Regulatorio del turismo estudiantil en la República Argentina. In: Facal Julio (Org.) Derecho del Turismo. Ed. FCU, Montevideo

Feldstein S (1986) Contratos Internacionais. Abeledo-Perrot, Buenos Aires

Fellous B (2004) Proteção do consumidor no Mercosul e na União Européia. Ed. RT, São Paulo

Fernández Arroyo D (2010) Preface, Consumer protection in International Private Relationships (CEDEP-ASADIP, Asunción) 9

Fernández Arroyo D, Mastrángelo F (Org) (2005) El Futuro de la codificación del Derecho internacional privado en América- De la CIDIP VI a la CIDIP VIII, Org. Ed. Alveroni, Córdoba, 3 ff

Fernandez Arroyo D, Moreno Rodriguez JA (eds) (2007) Protección de los consumidores en America-trabajos de la CIDIP VII (OEA). Le Ley-CEDEP, Asunción, p 10

Garcia Rubio MP (1999) La responsabilidad contractual de las agencias de viaje. Ed. Montecorvo: Madrid

Geib G (2012) A necessidade de regras específicas de direito internacional privado no contrato de consumo internacional eletrônico: principais aspectos quanto ao foro competente e à lei aplicável. In: Revista de Direito do Consumidor, vol. 82. Revista dos Tribunais, São Paulo, pp 185–188
Gest J (2010) La négociation de la Directive relative aux droits des consommateurs. In: Mazeaud D, Schulze R, Wicker G (ed) L'amorce d'un droit europeen du contrat – La proposition de directive relative aux droits des consommateurs. Société de Législation Comparée, Paris
Geist M (2001) Y a-t-il un 'là' là? Pour plus de certitude juridique en rapport avec la compétence judiciare à l'égard d'Internet, Étude commandé par la Conférence pour l'harmonisation des lois au Canada et Industrie Canada
Ghersi CA (1993) Razones y fundamentos para la integración regional. In: Mercosur - Perspectivas desde el derecho privado, Ghersi (Coord), 30 ff
Ghersi S (1995) La posmodernidad jurídica – Una discusión abierta. Gowa, Buenos Aires
Hippel E (1986) Verbraucherschutz. Mohr, Tübingen
Höffe O (2000) Derecho intercultural. Barcelona, Gedisa
Howells G et al (2010) Handbook of research on international conumer law. Edward Elgar, Chelteham
Jaudad B et al (1991) Droit du commerce international. Dalloz, Paris
Jayme E (1995) Identité culturelle et intégration: Le droit internationale privé postmoderne. Recueil des Cours de l'Académie de Droit International de la Haye. Kluwer, Doordrecht
Jayme E (1996) Identité culturelle et intégration: Le droit international privé postmoderne. RCADI 251:259
Jayme E (2000) Langue et Droit. Rapport général-Bristol 1998, Rechtsvergleichung-Ideengeschichte und Grundlagen von Emerico Amari zur Postmoderne. C.F. Müller, Heidelberg, p 118ss
Jayme E (2003a) O Direito Internacional Privado do Novo Milênio: a proteção da pessoa humana face à globalização, Cadernos do Programa de Pós-Graduação em Direito da Universidade Federal do Rio Grande do Sul – PPGDir./UFRGS, vol 1, n. 1, març, p 85ss
Jayme E (2003b) Gesammelte Schriften- Internationales Privatrecht und Völkerrecht, Band 3. C.F. Müller, Heidelberg, pp 102 sq
Jaeger Jr A (2008) Impasses do Direito Processual Civil Internacional do Mercosul e a oportunidade para o revival das CIDIPS. In Grudmann S, Dos Santos M (ed) Direito Contratual entre liberdade e proteção dos interesses e outros artigos alemães-lusitanos. Coimbra, Almedina
Kirchgässner G (2008) Homo oeconomicus, 3rd edn. Mohr Siebeck, Tübingen
Kropholler J (1978) Das Kollisionsrechtliche System des Schutzes der Schwächeren Vertragspartei, 634–661
Kronke H (2005) Herausforderungen internationaler Privatrechtsmodernisierung. In: Kieninger E-M (ed) Denationalisierung des Privatrechts? Symposium anlässlich des 70. Geburtstages von Karl Kreuzer. Mohr Siebeck, Tübingen
Labandera P (2006) Marco jurídico multilateral del turismo y su regulación nacional. In: FACAL, Julio (Coord), Derecho del Turismo, Montevideo, FCU, pp 41–42
Lando O (1972) Consumer contracts and party autonomy in the conflict of laws. NITR 15:2008–2219
Leclerc F (1995) La protection de la partie faible dans les contrats internationaux. Bruylant, Bruxelas p 330
Lete Achirica J (1997) El contrato de Multipropriedad y la Protección de los consumidores. Ed. Cedec, Barcelona, pp 32–34
Lopez V (2009) El Libro Verde de 2007 desde una perspectiva regional. In: Bourgoignie T (Org.) L'intégration économique et la protection du consommateur (Regional economic protection and consumer protection). Yvon Blais, Cowansville (Québec)
Losch B (2006) Kulturfaktor Recht. UTB, Colônia, pp 145sq

Manstetten R (2004) Das Menschenbild der Ökonomie – Der homo economicus und die Anthropologie von Adan Smith. Karl Alber, Freibug
Marques CL (2011) Contratos no Código de Defesa do Consumidor. RT, São Paulo, 132 ff
Marques CL (2012) Contratos no Código de Defesa do Consumidor. RT, São Paulo, 140 ff
Marques CL (2016) Manual de Direito do Consumidor, 7 edn. São Paulo, RT, pp 42 e seg
Marques CL, Almeida JB, Pfeiffer R (coord.) (2006) Aplicação do Código de Defesa do Consumidor aos bancos – ADin 2.591. Ed. RT, São Paulo
Marques CL, Jacques D (2005) Normas de aplicação imediata Como um método Para o direito internacional privado de proteção do consumidor no Brasil, Estudos em Memória do Professor Doutor António Marques dos Santos, Coimbra, Almedina I 127
Maulaurie P (1973) La protection du consommateur en droit international privé. Travaux de l'Association Henri Capitant 24:389–397
Mayer P (1996) La protection de la partie faible en droit internacional privé, in La protection de la partie faible dans les rapports contractuels: comparaisons franco-belges. Paris, LGDJ, 513 ff
Medeiros APC (2004) Perspectivas contemporâneas do Direito. Ed. Universa, Brasília
Minervini G (1974) Le contrat touristique. In: XIe. Congrès International de Droit Comparé – Teheràn. Bruylant, Bruselas
Micklitz H, Stuyck J, Terryn E (2010) Consumer law. Hart, London
Miranda M (2000) O contrato de viagem organizada. Almedina, Coimbra
OECD (2011) High-level principles on financial conumer protection. Available at https://www.oecd.org/g20/topics/financial-sector-reform/48892010.pdf. Accessed 3 April 2017
Paisant G (2010) Direito comunitário europeu do consumo: estado, problemas atuais e desenvolvimento. Revista de Direito do consumidor 76
Perez AF (2008) Consumer protection in the Americas: a second wave of American Revolutions? 5 U. St. Thomas L. J. 698 Spring
Pezzutti M (2010) Algunas consideraciones sobre el régimen administrativo de la actividad turística en el Uruguay. In: Facal Julio (Org.) Derecho del Turismo. Ed. FCU, Montevideo
Pinard G (1996) Los Derechos HUmanos en las constituiciones del Mercosur. Ciudad Argentina, Buenos Aires
Pocar F (1986) La protection de la partie faible en droit international privé. Recueil des cours de l'Academie de droit international de la Haye, t. 188. Martinus Nijhoff Publishers, Dordrecht/Boston/London, p 400
Poillot É (2006) Droit Européen de la consommation et uniformisation du droit des contrats. LGDJ, Paris
Radbruch G (2003) Rechtsphilosophie, 2nd edn. C. F. Müller, Heidelberg
Ramsay I (2001) Consumer protection in the era of informational capitalism, consumer law in the information society. Hague, Kluwer Law International, p 45
Rolle R (2005) Homo oeconomicus – Wirtschaftsanthropologie in philosophischer Perspektive. Königshausen & Neumann, Würzburg, p 373ss
Rühl G (2011) Consumer protection in choice of law. Cornell Int Law J 44:570
Siehr K (2002) Internationales Privatrecht. C.F. Müller, Heidelberg
Simmel G (1995) Gesamtausgabe, Philosophie der mode, band 10, Suhrkamp: Frankfurt, S. 9–10
Soares A (2012) A tutela internacional do consumidor turista. Revista de Direito do Consumidor 82
Stiglitz G (1995) El derecho del consumidor en Argentina y en el Mercosur. In: Derecho del Consumidor (Buenos Aires), vol 6, p 20
Tale C (2005) Contrato de viaje. Hammurabi, Buenos Aires
Tepedino G (1993) Multipropriedade Imobiliária. Saraiva, São Paulo
Tepedino G (2010) Comentários ao Código Civil. Saraiva, São Paulo
Tueda J (2006) Madurez y insuficiencia del derecho del turismo español: su presente y sus incertidumbres. In: Facal J (Org) Derecho del Turismo. Ed. FCU, Montevideo
Teitz L, Stewart D (2011) International consumer protection and private international law. In: Marques CL, Arroyo D, Ramsey I, Pearsons G (eds) The global financial crisis and the need for

consumer regulation: new developments on international protection of consumers. Orquestra Ed., Porto Alegre/Asunción

Van Loon JH (2005) Unification of private international law in a multi-forum context. In: Denationalisierung des Privatrechts? Symposium anlässlich des 70. Geburtstages von Karl Kreuzer, Kieninger, Eva-Maria, Tübingen: Mohr Siebeck, 33

Von Hoffmann B (1974) Über den Schutz des Schächeren bei internationalen Schuldvertragen, 396–420

Von Mehren A (1982) Rapport explicatif - Loi applicable à certaines ventes aux consommateurs. In: Actes et Documents de la Quatorzième session (1996), t. II, Ventes aux consommateurs, Bureau Permanent de la Conférence de la Haye, La Haye, p 6ss

Weizo C (2011) Chinese civil procedure and the conflict of laws. Tsinghua Press, Beijing

Wilson J (2006) En Cadernos do Programa de Pós-Graduação em Direito-PPGDir. UFRGS, N. V, March, pp 28–31

Chapter 17
Economic Development, Capitalism, and Consumer Law in Brazil: Rejecting the Argument for "Legal Paternalism"

Amanda Flávio de Oliveira

17.1 The Triumphant Religion of the Twentieth Century: Economic Growth

The observation is Robert F. Samuelson's, in his text *The Spirit of Capitalism*: to the author, it was not Christianity or Islam the religion that prevailed in the last century *but the ideal of economic growth.*[1]

The teasing makes sense. Beyond the daily evidence identified in the highlighted headlines of the newspapers, and that shows the long-lasting "battles" waged by national governments for positive economic indicators, the official record found in constitutions fully reveals the priority of the theme.

It could not be any different. As the nation-states are submitted to the phenomenon of "constitutionalism"—and when one has in mind the democratic model that prevails today—state objectives, in order to be considered legitimate, should be clearly identified in the basic law of the country, as well as the tools available for their achievement. Not everyone, however, believes so. The opinion of the US Supreme Court Justice Oliver Wendell Holmes, in the case *Lochner* vs. *New York*, is famous in this respect. In Holmes's view, the constitution of a people must be neutral with regard to economic policy, without opting for a paternalistic or liberal system since it was created for people of different ideologies. Nevertheless, his opinion was the subject of considerable criticism, in which one sees the influence of Adam Smith, the most important liberal theorist to date, on James Madison, Alexander Hamilton, and James Wilson, regarded as some of the "fathers" of the

---

The Portuguese version of this paper was published at Revista do Direito do Consumidor, Vol. 108.

[1]Samuelson (2001), p. 205.

A.F. de Oliveira (✉)
Faculty of Law, Federal University of Minas Gerais, Belo Horizonte, Brazil
e-mail: amanda@afdeoliveira.com.br

C. Lima Marques, D. Wei (eds.), *Consumer Law and Socioeconomic Development*,
DOI 10.1007/978-3-319-55624-6_17

US Constitution. It is more likely that the possible neutrality of the Constitution of that country as to the economic fact was an *ideological* option and not a choice, according to the reasons given by Holmes.[2]

Specifically in Brazil, the current Constitution of 1988, which resulted from a movement of reconstruction of democratic ideals in the country, includes, in numerous provisions, the discipline of the economy. At the very beginning of the text, Article 3 lists the following *objectives of the Republic*, among others: "to guarantee national development" and "to eradicate poverty and substandard living conditions and to reduce social and regional inequalities."

To realize this desideratum, the Constitution makes choices, some crystal clear, others less so: (1) it states that the social values of work and free enterprise are the fundamentals of the Republic; (2) it regulates the economic order, to which it dedicates a title (Articles 170–192) and indicates its guiding principles: *national sovereignty, private property, the social function of property, free competition, consumer protection, environment protection, reduction of regional and social inequalities, pursuit of full employment and preferential treatment for small businesses constituted under Brazilian laws having their head-office and management in Brazil*; (3) it determines the exceptionality of direct exploitation of economic activity by the state (Article 173) and establishes the modes of indirect state intervention in the economy, in the forms of *control, incentive and planning.* Added to this scenario is the important reference to the *domestic market* as part of the national patrimony, and which "shall be supported with a view to permitting cultural and socio-economic development, the well-being of the population and the technological autonomy of the country" (Article 219).

This set of options and tools has led scholars to clearly perceive in Brazilian constitutionalism the option for *capitalism* as an economic system,[3] although they differ on a more liberal or more social feature of the enshrined economic model. Being the Constitution of 1988, the seventh Brazilian constitutional text in a short time span of 150 odd years, it can be said that from a historical-economic standpoint, it is in a context of a *wavelike movement*,[4] which favored the absence of the state at one time and its strong presence in the economy at another. In other words, the analysis of the theme shows that, since the undoubtedly liberal model of the first Constitution (1824, a time when Brazil was still an Empire), one has noticed a departure from the model of classical economic liberties. However, there were episodes of stronger intervention (Constitution of 1937, for instance) and episodes of text considered neoliberal (Constitution of 1946, for example). Some may regard

[2]About this topic: Ely, pp. 27–35. For this author, "the framers anticipated a substantially free market resting on private property". *Id.* ibid., p. 35.

[3]In this sense, de Souza (2002), p. 459. Alberto Venâncio Fillho understands that capitalism was reflected directly on "the legal and political thought with the drafting of the various constitutions which began to regulate the political life of European states in the nineteenth century and were imitated by Latin American countries upon conquering their independence" (translation mine), Venancio Filho (1988), fl. 7.

[4]de Souza (2002), p. 102.

this "wavelike movement" as instability with respect to the Brazilian government's relationship with the national economy, at least formally. Even if it is so, it is necessary to stress, however, that it would mean a "slight" instability since it is not possible to identify brutal breaks among the various templates analyzed. In its still short existence (the independence of Brazil occurred in 1822), the Brazilian state distanced itself from or approached the economic phenomenon from conjunctural needs, and always because of some political instability.

Nonetheless, it seems undeniable that the Brazilian Constitution in effect (and all the previous ones) chose *capitalism* as the economic system. The same cannot be said for the adoption of *economic liberalism* as a shaper of economic relations. In this apparent contradiction lies the source of much misunderstanding on the part of legal scholars, which has given rise to improper criticism against the national Consumer Law.

17.2 Nonliberal Capitalism?

Liberalism and capitalism are ideas united by their historical genesis but should not be confused. Liberalism, as ethics, emerged in a context of struggle for individual freedom, human equality, a context entirely consistent with the historical moment during which it arose. Such moment, especially fertile for the development of its bases, was the French Revolution. Liberalism represented, at that moment, the fight against absolutism, authoritarianism, aristocracy, and privileges. It represented a kind of "humanism," in the sense that protecting human persons entailed the recognition of such persons as individuals, granting them the right to be free to lead their lives and individual progress according to their qualities and will. These ideas, taken to the political level, meant the defense of personal freedom against the state. From the economic point of view, they signified the recognition of the rights to free enterprise, freedom of contract, freedom of trade and private property.[5] Capitalism was thus the economic core of liberalism. Among the characteristics of capitalism itself, and which distinguish it from socialism, are the private property of the means of production, wage labor, and profit-geared production.[6]

It must be emphasized, nonetheless, that liberalism should not be confused with capitalism. The liberal logic is only properly understood and interpreted if seen in the context of the struggles against oppression of which it was part originally. At that moment, it meant much more than only ensuring free market, freedom of contract, and economic freedom. Its great ideal, its *raison d'etre*, was the rescue of human dignity.

From the viewpoint of its economic achievement, liberalism drew on capitalism. But it should definitively be highlighted that *the foundational arguments of the*

[5] About this topic, see: Courl (2001).

[6] Nunes (2007).

liberal ideal never intended for the defense of absolute individual freedom (or absolute market freedom). Theoretical examples and factual historical evidence for this statement abound.

As for theoretical examples, all know Adam Smith's authority as the greatest theorist of liberalism of all times. The famous professor from Glasgow is, even today, an undeniable influence on all defenders of liberty, in light of the arguments developed in his classic book "The Wealth of Nations." Yet, although his ideas are still today celebrated and referred to, few have been his real readers. Much is said; little is known.

Adam Smith never advocated full economic, absolute, and unrestricted freedom. On the contrary, he admitted the state's presence in hypothetical situations where there is omission, disinterest, or inability to act on the part of the private sector. One should add to this the caveat of the Portuguese Professor Fernando Araujo, a great expert in Smith's views on freedom. Araujo describes the "wilting" of Smith's enthusiasm for the "era of trade" from his "initial findings on the type of excessive practices that unrestricted economic freedom can produce."[7] The same author points out the fact that Smith condemned market "speculators."

Similarly, it should be emphasized the highly subjective nature of Smith's moral ideas and social philosophy. On the basis of his theoretical conception, human beings could be classified as (1) hardworking, sparing, frugal, industrious on one hand and (2) indolent, lazy on the other.[8] In modern times, this Manichean classification can be easily regarded as *simplistic*, as well as subjective and nonempirical. However, it was adequate in the historical period in which it was published (eighteenth century). This theory sounds innocent or, for some, optimistic[9] when its bases are studied in today's context of market and of the development of sciences (economics, anthropology, psychology, among others).

Smith's historical importance and relevance in having served as a developer of discussions that have lasted centuries after his death are undeniable. But to bring his ideas to the current context and conjuncture, and, worse, without having read them, is absolutely inadequate.

The same misunderstanding occurs regarding the ideas of John Stuart Mill, who is also hailed as one of the greatest historical defenders of human freedom. Mill's thoughts are often mentioned incompletely. In his book "On Liberty," the thinker makes a clear distinction between the portion of the life of an individual that concerns only himself and the share of the life of an individual that relates to others. In numerous passages, he shows concern for the exercise of freedom in society, in which one is "obliged to observe a certain line of conduct towards

[7]Araujo and Adam (2001), p. 1193. Still on the same topic, I recommend: de Souza (2002).

[8]About this topic, see: Nunes (2007).

[9]Avelãs Nunes addresses Smith's classic work as a manifestation of optimistic anthropology. According to him, the theory of the "invisible hand" which states that each person seeking individual progress necessarily contributes to universal progress, must be so classified. *Op. Cit.*, p. 338.

others," in which an individual has to recognize the interests of others as "rights," and where persons who, by their actions, produce harmful effects on others should be punished severely. Mill even classifies society as the "protector of all its members."[10] Likewise, when rereading his work, one should take into consideration the fact that the book was published in 1859, a period when celebrating freedom was the keynote of the time. Still, it should be noted that Mill did not defend a broad and unrestricted individual freedom.

In the legal field, it is essential to verify the ideas of Hans Kelsen, the greatest legal theorist of all time, on the theme of freedom. The Austrian philosopher, who developed a "Pure Theory of Law," studied the consequences of the conception of justice based on freedom as the highest value in his work *The Problem of Justice*, published more recently (twentieth century). To him, freedom is a basic presupposition in the legal science. But he distances himself from the ideas of existential metaphysical freedom, which make no sense to law.[11] According to Kelsen, "the idea of freedom as a principle of justice must undergo transformation." In other words: "Freedom (= liberation) *from* the normative order has to become freedom *under* the normative order and individual freedom has to be transformed into social freedom."[12]

As if it were not enough the fact that, in laying the foundations of liberal doctrine, the fundamental authors themselves made, in their theories, obvious concessions to situations where a broad and unrestricted liberty should be rejected, the truth is that, in the field of factual and historical evidence, capitalism and liberalism have always coexisted with some level of state intervention in the economy, in all cases. Even though the option for the liberal state was relativized, capitalism was not decharacterized as the chosen economic system.

Given the abundant evidence of this fact found in the constitutions of so-called liberal states, for example, already heavily studied by the doctrine of economic law, some theorists have concluded that capitalism without any intervention[13] is inconceivable. Even from the point of view of its essence, capitalism will only be legitimate as a self-restraining option of the state, set forth in the national legal system.[14] But it is not only for that reason. What is verified is that even in hypotheses of stronger state intervention in the economy its purpose has always been, in constitutions opting for the capitalist system, the preservation of market economy, which is precisely the essential basis for capitalism. In other words, a portion of economic freedom is waived in favor of the very preservation of

[10]This idea is specifically found in Mill (2000), p. 122.

[11]In this sense, Legaz y Lacambra (1960), p. 143.

[12]Kelsen (1996), p. 49.

[13]Venancio Filho (1988), p. 6.

[14]Legaz Y Lacambra explains this issue in the following terms: "el ordenamiento jurídico es un sistema de limitaciones de La libertad que tiene su contrapartida em La creación de otras tantas esferas de libertad; es, pues, la organización positiva de la libertad." Legaz Y Lacambra. *Op. cit.*, p. 146.

capitalism.[15] Therein lies the tension between capitalism and liberalism. A state may adopt the capitalist model with a robust intervention in the economy without decharacterizing capitalism.

It is not the aim of this paper to describe the reasons that led to the inclusion of social concerns (state intervention in the economy and therefore in economic freedom) for the preservation of capitalism. This theme has already been thoroughly developed in works of political economy.[16] However, it is important to stress the concept that reflects the contradiction that has gradually emerged between liberalism and capitalism since their common origin. In this sense, scholars point out the dissociation that occurred between the moral/political core and the economic core of liberalism: the humanist inspiration that was the motto for the development of its theories soon found itself confronted with the resulting consequences of the logic of the accumulation of wealth advocated by capitalism.[17] But capitalism will never exceed or deny liberalism since the latter provides the means of realization of the former.

17.3 Generations of Human Rights?

A dear topic of contemporary law, both internationally and nationally, is the subject of human rights. The purpose is noble. For some time, humanist thinkers have claimed the main role of the individual in the production, application, and interpretation of law. Many approaches exist under the label "humanist"; some have the clear purpose of ideological confirmation; others voice an honest and high philosophical concern.[18]

Despite all the tragedy and human suffering, Edgar de Godoi Mata-Machado notes, as a positive effect of the trauma caused by the two world wars of the early twentieth century, the "irruption of the Person in the legal world through a new declaration of Human rights, now and for the first time in history, with the express imprint of universality."[19]

---

[15]This is what Cabral Moncada understands: "In fact, public intervention in the economy aims, more often than not, to reach the proper functioning of the market." (Translation mine) De Moncada (2007), pp. 35–36.

[16]In a very brief summary, one can say that the crisis of the classic economic liberalism is related to the Industrial Revolution, the phenomenon of large concentrations of enterprises, the poor material conditions of workers in the early twentieth century, the crisis of 1929, the economic consequences the two World Wars. Venancio Filho, Alberto. Op. Cit., p. 9 and following.

[17]About this topic, see: Courl (2001).

[18]About the topic of humanism, see: Legaz y Lacambra (1960); Lima (1965); Luckesi (1994), pp. 270–289; Maritain (1999); Mata-Machado (2000); Moix (1968); Mondin (1998); Mounier (1964); Nogare (1994); Perine (2001), pp. 28–47; de Lima Vaz (2001).

[19]Mata-Machado (2000), p. 84.

In fact, the recognition of human rights, especially the international initiatives in this area during the twentieth century, had an obvious impact on national constitutions and represents the greatest revolution ever experienced by positive law.[20]

The good doctrine has pointed out the inadequacy of the treatment of human rights that has become vulgarized in the legal literature, and is based on the supposed existence of "generations" of rights. For these authors, the classification of "generations of human rights" has an exclusively historical meaning and never a normative one[21] and, in fact, has provided a "disservice to the cause of international protection of human rights."[22] This is because the essential characteristic of human rights is their indivisibility, the result of human indivisibility, the sole holder of those rights.[23] The segmentation in generations has allowed for an interpretation of their contents as if the possibility of denial of a category by the others were admissible or as if the possibility of opposition, competition, or conflict between them were acceptable. Such circumstances are absolutely unreasonable and were not part of the debates that led to the international recognition of human rights.

It was not by chance that the rights to liberty were the first types of human rights recognized by international forums and then posited in constitutional texts. Their legitimacy occurred primarily through their enshrinement in the Declaration of the Rights of Man of 1789, and their generalization may be attributed to the global postwar period, when they were highlighted by the Universal Declaration of Human Rights and the American Declaration of the Rights and Duties of Man, in 1948. These rights are mainly the fruits of a liberal conception of the state, and their recognition is consistent with the historical moment during which to defend freedom meant prioritizing the human person with regard to law.

As human history and international institutions evolved; the rights to liberty (also known as *civil and political rights*) were the first to receive attention. However, the same evolution of historical events led to the imperious necessity of recognizing another kind of human rights, the so-called *economic and social rights*. That is because the exercise of the rights to liberty demonstrated their limitations and shortcomings. The economic and social rights stemmed, therefore, from the exercise of political and civil rights and signify the search for a real humanism, not a fictional one.

At that moment, it was understood that to preserve people's well-being did not mean only to value their personal freedom and the resulting freedoms of market, of contract, among others. To that level of rights, other rights should be added. These ones, after all, would ensure the *real* liberty of persons, a de facto liberty, which has been classified as "the best citizenship."[24]

---

[20]To Lorenzetti, human rights have been responsible for totally transforming law, p. 320.

[21]Lorenzetti (2006), p. 38.

[22]Trindade (2000), p. 126.

[23]*Id.* Ibid.

[24]de Moncada (2007), 5. edn.

Social rights represent a "historic response to a very concrete traditional deficit in the basic democratic rights."[25] However, it is important to highlight that *they do not imply the overcoming of the rights to equality and liberty, which remain preserved in International Treaties and constitutional texts, albeit now conformed to a new reality*. Peter Haberle summarized the issue: "'Se trata de lograr eficiência en y a través de La libertad pero siempre acompañada de igualdad'. He aqui nuestra gran oportunidad. Ni más ni menos."[26]

Social and economic rights are compatible with the new state that emerged after the classical liberal state. Their realization requires the presentation [provision] by the state, and they presuppose some form of control or regulation of freedom. They are therefore a manifestation of the overcoming of classical liberalism, but they cannot be referred to as an anticapitalist policy.[27] Even with the enshrinement of these rights in the legal system of a country that has opted for capitalism as an economic system, private property, wage labor, the private ownership of the means of production, and their exercise with a view to profiting remain safeguarded.

17.4 "Legal Paternalism": That Unknown Institution

If legal and economic concepts have been used systematically in order to denote misunderstanding or ignorance, the inadequate use of the term "legal paternalism" has also been frequent. On almost every occasion, the use of the term occurs in a subjective and biased manner[28] based on a common sense understanding. Almost always protective actions with which one disagrees receive the label "paternalistic." In this sense, paternalism always represents an affront to liberty and competitive society.[29]

Norberto Bobbio, in his *Dictionary of Politics*, had already identified the elements with which the term is confused: paternalism, in ordinary language, is a manifestation of authoritarianism, even if it is benevolent.[30] The same author, elsewhere in his work, also warns of the lack of neutrality of all political terms, "each of which can be used based on the user's political leanings to generate emotional reactions, for approval or disapproval of a certain behavior, to cause,

---

[25] Haberle (2002), p. 202.

[26] Id. ibid., p. 226.

[27] In the same sense see, Cabral De Moncada, *op. cit.*, p. 184.

[28] In their *Dicionário básico de filosofia*, Japiassú and Marcondes mention the sense, almost always derogatory, with which the term is used. Japiassu and Marcomdes (1996), p. 208.

[29] Prado (2014), pp. 29–30.

[30] This situation is not foreign to Bobbio, to whom: "The political language is notoriously ambiguous. Most of the terms used in the political discourse have several meanings. This variety depends on the fact that many terms have gone through a long series of historical changes (. . .) Most of these terms derive from the common language. (Translation mine) Bobbio (1998), p. V.

finally, consensus or dissent."[31] Bobbio also mentions the "threat" that liberal thought historically identified in the paternal state and elaborates on the numerous thinkers responsible for relating the paternal power to the divine power of kings rejected by liberals.[32] If monarchy was the manifestation of a paternal state, to fight it was the mission of the advocates of liberalism.

An attempt to transpose these circumstances to the present day makes it possible to recognize traces of political paternalism in contemporary Brazil, even though it is a republic under the rule of law. However, it is not the way and direction that the term has been employed. Today, paternalism is identified more clearly with patriarchalism and *coronelismo* (**Translator's note:** *the political, social and economic power held by rich landowners (colonels), especially in the northeast of Brazil*), which, unfortunately, can be identified in Brazilian society more clearly in some regions and in a softer and limited way[33] in others.

Paternalism also represented, in human history, a real threat to the capitalist model implemented in the set of bases of the liberal state. In the following decades, even when the capitalist system was adopted, paternalism was constantly identified as "the socialist threat." On the topic, Otto H. Kahn published in the US, in 1919, the work *The menace of paternalism*, in which he stated forcefully: "Government, in its very essence, is the negation of competition"; "From governmental paternalism to socialism is not a very long step"; "Nor, indeed, can paternalism and liberty exist side by side."[34] Kahn stated that the paternalistic ideas would always have the support of those who seek popularity, the opportunists, the envious ones, and even those desirous of social justice, but that do not examine critically and in the light of reason the experience that shows that in this way society will sustain more harm than good.[35]

It should be recognized, however, that Kahn commits the same mistake he sees in the position of socialism advocates: the use of highly subjective arguments, almost emotional, to support his ideas. The contradiction of his speech against the lack of rational basis for the paternalistic belief is evident in the foundation he used to support liberal ideas: "I have complete confidence in the sober common sense of the American people."[36]

Whatever the ideological conviction of the researcher is, it is his duty to contextualize the problem on which he intends to reflect at the more contemporary stage of the development of sciences. Specifically in relation to the theme of this

---

[31] *Id.* ibid., pp. V–VI.

[32] *Id.* ibid., p. 908.

[33] Retired Ambassador José Osvaldo de Meira Pena refers to the "immemorial tradition of respect for the father, the husband, the elder, the grandparents, the lords over their household servants, the prince over his vassals, the patrimonial chief, the master of the *Casa Grande* over his clientele. In this conception, the state authority is based on its most distant hierarchical roots. "Later, he adds: "In Brazil, we note that (...) paternalism contaminates the whole structure of our political life." (Translation mine) Pena José Osvaldo de Meira, pp. 68–69.

[34] Kahn (1919), pp. 6–9.

[35] *Id.* ibid., p. 13.

[36] *Id.* ibid., p. 6.

paper (Brazilian Consumer Law), from a scientific standpoint, it is not correct to conduct an assessment of its framing in a liberal or paternalistic state model, disregarding all that has been built since Adam Smith and Stuart Mill about human behavior in the market. Nor can one face the "socialist threat" with the same eyes and the same arguments once the historical experience has provided many other elements to form a serious criticism. It is again Bobbio, in another work, who accurately notes that in the face of fear or weakening of confidence in progress, everyone is able to make diagnoses. The problem arises at the time of the choice of the remedies to be prescribed.[37]

In Brazil, the untechnical use of the expression "legal paternalism" to refer to the domestic Consumer Law, or to specific aspects of its effectiveness, is common. This use is totally inadequate. The Brazilian Consumer Protection Code, the fruit of a constitutional provision, consists of a law created under a democratic legislative process and seeks to give efficacy to a globally recognized fundamental right. The application of the Code always occurs through specifically identified authorities with that competence. These authorities' decisions will always be subject to procedural appeals that ensure the guarantee of a fresh look at the case and allow for correction of any excesses committed by a judge that, in a reprehensible fashion, has exceeded the protection limits allowed by law.

As to the basis for protection of the subject of rights, the law sets forth literally that "consumers' vulnerability" is the reason for the protective treatment given. Objectively, it is noteworthy: (1) consumers are all, without distinction, who are in an economic relationship as an acquirer or a receiver of a product or service, which makes them a universal and nondiscriminatory category; (2) the condition of "vulnerability," which makes one party worthy of protection at the expense of the other, applies to all who are consumers, without distinction; and (3) other fields of knowledge, in contemporary times, have already identified, tested, and produced robust research that proves the situation of vulnerability in which human persons are in different circumstances of life, even if sometimes they honestly believe they are making rational decisions. The condition of vulnerability can no longer be referred to as a mere "claim" without empirical support. Compelling studies demonstrate the limited human rationality and its "biased" behavior in the market. To posit the principle of consumer vulnerability in the legal text is fully consistent with the recognition of economic and social human rights and their claim arising out of the protection of the real freedom of people.[38]

---

[37]Bobbio (2002), pp. 200–201.

[38]The topic of consumer vulnerability according to recent studies of psychology and economics was better developed by us in: de Oliveira and dos Santos Ferreira (2012), pp. 13–38; and in de Oliveira and de Castro Ferreira (2014), pp. 231–249.

17.5 Brazil: Market Economy, Consumer Law, and the Unavoidable Socioeconomic Reality of Its Population

If economic growth is the "engine" and "religion" of our times, it is not any different in Brazil. Having made a clear option for capitalism, as previously mentioned, the 1988 Constitution, in force, can only be understood within the economic reality it was created and to which it relates.

Brazil, which is still a young nation, has opted for market economy since its first Constitution of 1824. The departure from the classical liberal assumptions occurred definitively in the third Brazilian Constitution of 1934[39] and has been evident in all subsequent constitutional texts.[40]

At present, the constitutional rules governing economic activity coexist with principles derived from classical liberalism and principles stemming from a welfare state. This circumstance does not unsettle the reigning capitalism. With regard specifically to positive human rights, the first time that economic and social rights appeared in Brazilian constitutionalism was in 1988. This means the national legal system recognized the insufficiency of civil and political rights for the achievement of the ideal of human dignity.

Among the social and economic rights enshrined, prominent space has been reserved for consumer rights. That is because, in addition to recognizing *consumer rights* (Article 5 shows the human person as the clear recipient of this new right), the Constitution also included *consumer protection* as a restrictor of the free exercise of the economic activity (Article 170 regards the economic agents as clear addressees of the norm). These provisions coexist (and must be interpreted), along with the principles of free enterprise, free competition, and private property, among others.

In turn, the national consumer protection policy had arisen and developed in the country, even before the [1988] constitutional recognition of the related law. Even in a hostile normative scenario (the Civil Code of 1916, clearly inspired by liberal ideals, regulated contracts), civil society was organized into consumer protection associations (the first association was in Porto Alegre in 1975). The Public Ministry created specialized offices (1980s), and other consumer protection public agencies were organized (the first Procon [Consumer Watchdog] in São Paulo dates back to1976). The reason for the celebrated success of the policy that would be institutionalized at the constitutional level years later may be the spontaneous origin of the consumerist movement within civil society. Effectively, consumer protection in Brazil arose from a clear social yearning[41] and contains elements that make it

[39]In the same sense, see de Souza (2002), p. 86.

[40]About this topic Sérgio Couri states: "The divorce between capitalism and liberalism is more sensitive in developing countries, where the maintenance of one demanded, starkingly, the suppression of the other."(Translation mine) Courl (2001), p. 68.

[41]I elaborated on this topic in: de Oliveira (2002), pp. 97–105.

unique when compared with consumer protection policies adopted and implemented in other capitalist countries.

From the viewpoint of the irrefutable reality, Brazil is a country with more than 205 million inhabitants and has a glaring functional illiteracy rate of 20% of the people.[42] More than 11 million people live in substandard settlements, such as shantytowns and stilt houses, in precarious living conditions.[43]

With regard specifically to the respect for fundamental rights, the 1988 Constitution has been accused of having caused the litigation "boom" because it generously broadened the spectrum of fundamental human rights and included in its text many economic and social rights. This fact has given rise to an alarming growth in the number of cases for the Brazilian judiciary to consider in recent decades.

Data on lawsuits regarding consumer law are instructive: the theme is notably one of the most sought-after subjects in the national judiciary. According to the official 2015 Report of the Judiciary (base year 2014), the current judiciary caseload shows over *two million* cases for trial on "Suppliers' Liability/Compensation for Moral Damages," which makes this topic the *third* most demanded subject in the country, taking into account the universe of 79 courts.[44] The highlights are the figures for the most demanded subjects in the *Small Claims Courts* and the *Appellate Panels* in which "Consumer Law" is the most discussed topic: at least 22% of the actions for trial deal with some aspects of consumer law.

In the year that marks the 25th anniversary of the Brazilian Consumer Protection Code, the numbers are well worth a reflection. One should not argue that the staggering number of lawsuits on consumer law demonstrates a positive datum, the result of a possible growing conception of citizenship, because they represent an overwhelming evidence of the effective access to justice ensured in the country regarding this matter or they show the norm recipients' trust in their rights and in the judiciary. Can't be that. *A state in which fundamental rights are effectively respected cannot present high rates of litigation on these rights.*

---

[42]These are official numbers detailed in the Demographic Census 2000/2010. Available at: http://seriesestatisticas.ibge.gov.br/series.aspx?t=taxa-analfabetismo&vcodigo=PD384. Last access on 01/22/2016, at 5:23 pm.

[43]IBGE [Brazilian Institute of Geography and Statistics], Pesquisa Nacional por Amostra de Domicílios [National Household Sample Survey] 2011.

[44]The numbers refer to the following Courts: 3 Superior Courts (TST [Superior Labor Court], STJ [Superior Court of Justice] and TSE [Superior Electoral Court]), 25 Courts of Appeals, 20 TRTs [Regional Labor Courts], 5 TRFs [Regional Federal Courts], 23 TREs [Regional Electoral Courts] and 3 Courts of State Military Justice. For more information: *Justiça em Números 2015: ano-base 2014*/Conselho Nacional de Justiça. Brasília: CNJ, 2015, fl. 49.

17.6 Final Thoughts: Lack of Knowledge, Misunderstandings, and Ideology

Professor Washington Peluso Albino de Souza, a pioneer researcher in economic law in Brazil, warned, some time ago, about the fact that the economic agents[45] had not yet understood in its proper dimension the high concept of market introduced by the 1988 Constitution.

Indeed.

The 1988 Constitution is the result of a historical, legal, specific social and economic movement. Furthermore, it should be interpreted and understood in full compliance with the reality of the country and from Brazil's insertion in the international economic context. Consumer law and the national consumer protection policy must be interpreted and understood similarly. To insert Brazilian constitutional and legal norms that govern economic activity in closed compartments, in rigid and/or foreign doctrines; to label them; and thereafter to conduct study and criticism or draw conclusions only produce reflections that are *distorted* or *impaired in their validity*.

On the other hand, if human rights are indivisible, their practice around the world has shown a wide disparity between the methods of implementation of the rights of liberty compared with the economic and social rights.[46] A striking proof of this is the inconceivable social disparity that still exists in Brazil.

If one moves the concern over the economic model (liberalism versus paternalism, capitalism versus socialism) or its theoretical reflections (civil and political rights versus economic and social rights) to the *human person*,[47] his needs and intrinsic dignity, the various ideologies eventually converge on a common goal and then a particularized legal system for the most different global realities of growth and development arises. If the religion of the moment is economic growth, its sacred purpose can only be the human person.

References

Araujo F, Adam S (2001) O conceito mecanicista de liberdade. Almedina, Lisboa
Bobbio N (1998) Dicionário de política. Editora UNB, Brasilia
Bobbio N (2002) Elogio da serenidade e outros escritos morais. Editora Unesp
Courl S (2001) Liberalismo e societalismo. Editora UNB, Brasilia
de Lima Vaz HC (2001) Humanismo hoje: tradição e missão. Puc-Minas, Instituto Jacques Maritain, Belo Horizonte

---

[45] de Souza (2002), p. 464.

[46] This caveat is found in: Trindade (2000), p. 150.

[47] This is what Edgar de Godoi da Mata-Machado proposes. Mata-Machado (2000), p. 128. Cançado Trindade also points out the "centrality of victims" as the legacy of the Second World Conference on Human Rights (1993–2013). Trindade (2014), p. 105.

de Moncada LSC (2007) Direito Económico, 5th edn. Coimbra Editora, Coimbra
de Oliveira AF (2002) O sistema Nacional de Defesa do consumidor -Histórico. Revista de Direito do Consumidor, v. 44
de Oliveira AF, de Castro BB (2014) Proteção do consumidor de crédito: uma abordagem a partir da economia Comportamental. Revista de Direito do Consumidor, v. 93
de Oliveira AF, dos Santos Ferreira FM (2012) Análise econômica do Direito do Consumidor em períodos de recessão. Uma abordagem a partir da Economia Comportamental. Revista de Direito do Consumidor, v. 81
de Souza WPA (2002) Teoria da Constituição Econômica. Del Rey, Belo Horizonte
Haberle P (2002) Pluralismo y Constitución. Editorial Tecnos, Madrid
Japiassu AH, Marcomdes D (1996) Dicionário básico de filosofia, 3rd edn. Jorge Zahar Editor, Rio de Janeiro
Kahn OH (1919) The menace of paternalism. Constit Rev 3(114)
Kelsen H (1996) O problema da justiça. Martins Fontes, São Paulo
Legaz y Lacambra L (1960) Humanismo, estado y derecho. Casa Editorial Bosch, Barcelona
Lima AA (1965) Pelo humanismo ameaçado. Editora Tempo Brasileiro, Rio de Janeiro
Lorenzetti RL (2006) Teoría de La decision judicial. Fundamentos de derecho. Rubinzal-Culzoni, Santa Fe
Luckesi CC (1994) O humanismo no Brasil. In: Nogare PD (ed) Humanismos e anti-humanismos. Introdução à antropologia filosófica, 13th edn. Vozes, Petrópolis
Maritain J (1999) Por um humanismo cristão. Ed. Paulus, São Paulo
Mata-Machado EG (2000) Contribuição ao personalismo jurídico. Prefácio da professora Elza Maria Miranda Afonso. Del Rey, Belo Horizonte
Mill JS (2000) A Liberdade/Utilitarismo. Martins Fontes, São Paulo
Moix C (1968) O pensamento de Emmanuel Mounier. Tradução Frei Marcelo L. Simões. Paz e Terra, Rio de Janeiro
Mondin B (1998) O humanismo filosófico de Tomás de Aquino. EDUSC, Bauru
Mounier E (1964) O personalismo. Tradução João Bénard da costa, 2nd edn. Livraria Duas Cidades, São Paulo
Nogare PD (1994) Humanismos e anti-humanismos. Introdução à antropologia filosófica, 13th edn. Vozes, Petrópolis
Nunes AJA (2007) Uma introdução à economia política. Quartier Latin, São Paulo
Perine M (2001) Um conflito de humanismos. In: de Lima Vaz HC (ed) Humanismo hoje: tradição e missão. PUC-Minas, Instituto Jacques Maritain, Belo Horizonte
Samuelson RF (2001) The spirit of capitalism. Foreign Aff 80(01)
Trindade AAC (2000) A proteção internacional dos direitos humanos e o Brasil, 2nd edn. Editora Universidade de Brasilia, Brasília
Trindade AA (2014) A proteção dos vulneráveis Como legado da II Conferência Mundial de direitos humanos (1993–2013). IBDH/IIDH/SLADI, Fortaleza
Venancio Filho A (1988) A intervenção do Estado no domínio econômico. Renovar, Rio de Janeiro. Edição fac-similar de 1968

Chapter 18
The Illegal and Abusive: Proposals for a Systematic Interpretation of Abusive Practices in the 25 Years of the Consumer Defense Code

Bruno Miragem

18.1 Introduction

The record of 25 years of the existence of the Consumer Defense Code and its contribution to the development of private law and change—for the better—of the practices and negotiating customs in Brazil has been made, with justice, with enthusiastic praise. It is not without reason, considering that there were rare times in which a law mobilized such in the private law doctrine and jurisprudence,[1] making its impact felt on the rereading of classical concepts and discipline of the new realities.[2] Examples abound, such as resignification of the law, which gave affirmation to the principles of good faith and gave balance to the institutes of contract and civil liability, as well as attention to the new phenomena in consumer society—which is of growing importance until today—such as the legal discipline of advertising, of databases, and of other advances that are not within the limits of substantive law.

The Portuguese version of this article was published by Revista do Direito do Consumidor, Vol. 104, pp. 99–127.

[1]Due tribute should be noted, without prejudice to other important magistrates, to the original contributions, in the first decade of the Code, of Ruy Rosado de Aguiar junior, Salvio Figueiredo Teixeira, Carlos Alberto Menezes Direito and Fátima Nancy Andrighi originally members of the respective State courts and that amounted to the Superior Court of Justice in the period, without prejudice to dozens of other judges, Judge Sergio Cavalieri , the Court of Justice of Rio de Janeiro.

[2]It should be noted as a repercussion of the consumer law on the general law system, the gradual recognition and theoretical elaboration on the protection of the vulnerable by private law, as explained in: Marques and Miragem (2014), p. 17 and ss. In European law, the recognition of the principle of protection of *weaker parties*, as a kind of principle that emerges from the consumer law and receives an "*upgrade*" to the General civil law in: Reich (2014), p. 37 and ss.

B. Miragem (✉)
Faculty of Law, Federal University of Rio Grande do Sul, Porto Alegre, Brazil
e-mail: bmiragem@uol.com.br

C. Lima Marques, D. Wei (eds.), *Consumer Law and Socioeconomic Development*,
DOI 10.1007/978-3-319-55624-6_18

This renewal of law did not occur without attention to the own sense that consumer protection takes on Brazilian law, of a fundamental right provided for expressly in the Constitution of the Republic (art. 5, XXXII) and animated by the principle of dignity of the human person (art. 1, III).[3]

The potential update that fostered the studies, application, and development of the concepts of the Consumer Defense Code in Brazilian law has been subject to little exploration[4] as to its potential in promoting the effectiveness of consumer law and, in particular, for the own sorting of the consumer market, the so-called *abusive practices*. Contemplating a series of related conducts by the legislator in art. 39 of the CDC, it originally expressed, in its, the command "It is forbidden to the supplier of products and services." After the legislative alteration promoted by the older Brazilian Antitrust Law (Law 8.884 of June, 11, 1994), realizing the character of example of conduct and situations that are mentioned, it started referring that "It is forbidden to the supplier of goods or services, among other abusive practices," following its specific enumeration.

Regarding abusive practices, this concept is the equivalent, in Brazilian law, of what comparative law refers to as *unfair practices* in American law, as enshrined in European law—a kind of *unfair practices*. It was presented in the explanatory reasons of the Code—second-known lesson of Antonio Herman Benjamin—as "a series of behaviors, whether or not contractual, which abuse the consumers' good faith, as well as of their inferior economic or technical situation." The jurist proceeds in stating that "It is understandable, therefore, that such practices are considered unlawful per se, regardless of the occurrence of damage to the consumer."[5]

Turns out from the technique of illustrative enunciation of various conducts of supplier prohibited by law, as well as its dissociation of previous existence of consumer contract, or moved for the purpose of simultaneous protection of the interests of the consumer and of free competition, the various related behaviors by the legislature must be interpreted according to a common sense. Hence, the expression pointing out to *abusive* conduct—and in this sense returning to the traditional concept not only of *abuse of right* but also of *abuse of legal position* by the supplier[6]—has the virtue of promoting certain *conceptual unit* on the conducts expressly validated in legal norm. Likewise, it facilitates the identification of others that bear similar characteristics in relations between suppliers and consumers established in the consumer market.

There is an equivalent effect between *abusive*—that is, how the exercise of rights or freedom in compliance with the limits established by law is done—and *illegal*—which occurs when the law simply prohibits certain conduct. The concept of abuse,

---

[3]Miragem (2014), p. 50. In the same sense, Miragem (2002), p. 111 and ss.

[4]It should be noted, one of the specific studies on the subject, articles: Sayeg Ricardo Hasson, p. 37 and ss; Lisbon (2001), pp. 199–204; Pfeiffer Roberto c, p. 131 and ss. Similarly the book: da Silveira (1999).

[5]Benjamin (2005), p. 361.

[6]Miragem (2013a, b), pp. 242–243.

however, points, in Brazilian law, to the violation of established limits, whether done through good faith or not—as supported, among others, by Gabriel Stiglitz,[7] Héloïse Carpena,[8] and Plinio L Martins[9] and as also recognized most recently by economic or social theories or by customs.[10] This, in fact, was the reason established by the text of art. 187 of the Brazilian Civil Code of 2002: "Art. 187. The holder of a right who, while exercising it, manifestly exceeds the limits imposed by its economic or social order, by good faith or by morals also commits tort."[11]

Nevertheless, the interpretation and application of the various legal assumptions provided for in the items in art. 39 of the Consumer Defense Code do not always observe the mentioned sense of unity among the various situations described there. The same is said due to the open nature of the standard in relation to the description of the conduct prohibited and the plasticity of sanctions aimed at curbing and suppressing such permitted practices. It is, most of the times, to isolate the interpretation of one or other conducts according to the particular circumstances of the facts concerned, without joining the legal notion of abuse as an instrument of consumer protection, whether considered individually or collectively, and also of the very stability and proper functioning of the consumer market.

It is essential to promote a systematic vision of abuse and its frequency of the use of the concept in order to establish safe criteria for the interpretation and realization of many of the conducts described in art. 39 CDC, purposely written with the use of indeterminate concepts. The definition of the expressions "just cause" (art. 39, subparagraphs I and X), "according to habits and customs" (art. 39, item II), "avail themselves of weakness or ignorance of the consumer" (article 39, subparagraph IV), or "manifestly excessive advantage" (art. 39, item V) requires common sense in the interpretation of the concept of abuse and its repercussions on the consumer and the consumer market. The absence of criteria reasonably defined and recognized, questions the effectiveness of the standard, but once present, their interpretation and application are to be subject to the judgment of authorities—administrative or judicial—and, in turn, subject to the appeals provided for in our system—to the detriment of the purpose of repression of the malfeasance of vendors who abuse of their position.

The present study has the objective of proposing the criteria for a systematic interpretation of the abusive practices, such as those set out in art. 39 of the Consumer Defense Code, in order to identify the common sense of the various conducts listed in the norm, from the legal notion of abuse. With this objective, first

[7]Stiglitz (1992), pp. 27–35.

[8]Carpena (2001), p. 71 *et seq.*

[9]Martins (2002), p. 51 *et seq.*

[10]Miragem (2013a, b), p. 142 and ss.

[11]The Civil Code of 2002, to divide into two unlawful clauses indicated, beside the traditional wrongful unlawful clause (art. 186 of the CC/02, playing in part art. The Civil Code of 1916 159), a new unlawful clause, by abusive exercise of rights (art. 187). For the subject, I refer you to: Miragem (2013a), cit.

will be examined the characteristic situations of application of the prohibition norms of abusive practices in Brazilian law and, in a second part, the proposition of common criteria for their identification.

18.2 The Situation of Abusive Practices in Consumer Law

The provision on abusive practices in Brazilian law, by means of art. 39 CDC, covers a series of prohibited conducts of the supplier that are considered unfair in light of his position of power in relation to the consumer. Suppliers approach, without identifying themselves fully, with unfair competition practices, even if some of their conducts may cause both injury to free competition and injury to consumer interest.

The technique of non-exhaustion of the hypotheses provided by law is due to the recognition of creativity in negotiating, whether in a positive aspect—for the formatting of different business models—or, in the specific case, in a negative sense, the adoption of different conducts susceptible of being qualified as abusive practices.[12] Strictly speaking, the various hypotheses provided for by law, as we say, "seek to preserve certain situations or qualities that represent consumer advantage, as in the case of the possibility of reflection to formation of negotiating will, the guarantee of formation of consensus, its clarification and information, among other species of clauses for the protection of effective contractual freedom of the vulnerable part."[13]

Brazilian jurisprudence will develop the concepts set out in the norm, with higher incidence in some situations, as the chances of tying[14] or unsolicited submission of product or service.[15] On the other hand, the prohibition of certain practices of the activities of the supplier involves delimitation of the exercise of freedom of negotiating of the supplier, provided in art. 170 of the Constitution, which establishes as the basis of economic order the social values of labor and free initiative. The exercise of this freedom has as its basis the principle of consumer protection (art. 170, V).

[12]Benjamin (2005), p. 362.

[13]Miragem (2014), p. 283.

[14]REsp 384.284/RS, Rel. Min. Herman Benjamin, 2ª Turma, j. 20/08/2009, DJe 15/12/2009; REsp 969.129/MG, Rel. Min. Luis Felipe Salomão, 2ª Seção, j. 09/12/2009, DJe 15/12/2009; REsp 1,397,870/MG, Rel. Min. Mauro Campbell Marques, 2ª Turma, j. 02/12/2014, DJe 10/12/2014.

[15]Regarding the unsolicited sending of credit cards, the abusive practice referred to in art. 29, III, of the CDC, was even object of the Superior Court of Justice: "It is unfair commercial practice sending credit card without express consumer's request and is set up for compensable tort and is subject to the application of administrative fines". See also on sending various unsolicited products: REsp 1,102,787 / PR, Rel Min Sidnei Beneti, 3rd Class, j. 16/03/2010, 29/03/2010 Dje.

18.2.1 Legal Prohibition and Restriction on the Freedom of the Supplier

The legislative technique chosen by the legislature was to establish a prohibition of conducts, which is set out in the provisions of art. 39 CDC, making them illegal, qualifying them as species of abusive practices. It is clear that there is a limitation to party autonomy of the vendor as an economic agent, drawing limits to the exercise of freedom of initiative and creativity that characterizes the economic activity in a market economy system.

The choice of the legislator of what are abusive practices, in this way, was over all pertinent. In European law, subsequent to the CDC, Policy 2005/29/EC systematized unfair commercial practices prohibited by provisions made in a series of norms, in which specific practices were established, such as in respect of comparative advertising (Directive 84/450/EEC), distance selling (Directive 97/7/EC), inhibitory actions on consumer protection (Directive 98/27/EC), and distance marketing of financial services (Directive 2002/65/EC), among others.

The *unfair commercial practices*, in the European standard, are classified into two categories: *misleading* and *aggressive* commercial practices. The *misleading commercial practices* (arts. 5 and 6 of Directive 2005/29/EC), with greater detail, refer to conducts that the Brazilian CDC had more general forecast, from the moment of supply (arts. 30–35) and advertising (arts. 36–38)—and, in the same way, the so-called illegal advertising—up to the imposition of duties of contractual information and effects of breach (art. 46).

On the other hand, the *aggressive commercial practices* laid down in Directive 2005/29/EC coincide in part with the several conducts deemed abusive by art. 39 CDC. Article 8 of the Directive defines aggressive commercial practices: "if, in this case, taking account of all its features and circumstances, it harms or is likely to impair significantly, due to harassment, coercion, including the use of physical force—or undue influence, the freedom of choice or the behavior of the average consumer with respect to a product, and therefore drives or is susceptible to drive the consumer to make a decision that this transaction would not have taken in another manner."

In part, the consumer's freedom of protection is preserved in Brazilian law by the provisions of art. 39, IV, CDC, which defines prohibited abusive practices: "to rely on the weakness or ignorance of consumers, given their age, health, knowledge or social condition, to impinge him your products or services." The precise definition of how this *predominance* is characterized, however, deserves interpretations in accordance with the circumstances of the case and also the specific conditions of the consumer. This is an important norm in the protection of consumers with aggravated vulnerability;[16] however, this does not exhaust its meaning and scope. In this regard, we observe the same orientation of Directive 2005/29/EC, which, as

---

[16]Miragem (2014), p. 290.

the exact observation of Norbert Reich, did not try to mention "vulnerable consumers" but "consumers whose characteristics make them particularly vulnerable" to abuse.[17] The definition is also not easy in European law. So refers the German master, "the vulnerable consumer concept is considered alongside the concept of informed consumer,"[18] which is useful above all to make sense of and to determine the impact of consumer definition with heightened vulnerability, hence the convenience of an even better accuracy of the growing prevalence of conditions from the identification of concrete conducts of the supplier, which reveals itself as the task of doctrine and jurisprudence.[19]

There is a need for safe boundaries for the interpretation of the limits to autonomy for negotiation set out in law. Its generality can serve, as to stop to identify and to restrain harmful conducts to consumers, as to define itself by excessive distinction of the judicial or administrative authority, in a level of intervention and judgment on the conducts of economic agents in a diverse sense than the norm intends to offer.

18.2.2 The Dynamics of Sanctions on Abusive Practices in Brazilian Law

In addition to the nonexhaustive enumeration of the conducts typified as banned, another feature is identified with regard to the discipline of abusive practices set out by the CDC, that is, penalties for the infringement of the prohibition by the suppliers. In this respect, it should be noted that the prohibition rule was an economic measure. It merely establishes the fence for the conduct that it defines, among others that may be added by interpretation and judicial concretization of an indeterminate concept of abuse. Nothing is mentioned about sanctions in cases of violation of the prohibition. And, in this regard, there are two possibilities of interpretation of the rule: a first, more restrictive, interpretation would indicate the impossibility of making a provision of sanctions in the face of the absence of an express forecast. Second possibility, more comprehensive—and received properly in Brazilian law—is that the absence of specific sanctions, at the same time which define itself as conducts that are prohibited, characterizes the illegal aspect of violation of the prohibition. In this case, when the tort is recognized, all the penalties that reject it are admitted.

Thereby, the unlawful causing of damage raises the duty to compensate. The same applies when, due to an abusive practice, a contract is concluded—for

[17]Reich (2014), p. 56.

[18]Reich (2014), p. 56.

[19]See: STJ, REsp 1,329,556/SP, Rel. Min. Ricardo Villas Bôas Cueva, 3ª Turma, j. 25/11/2014, DJe 09/12/2014; TJRS, ApCiv N° 70,066,551,318, 23ª Câmara Cível, Rel. Ana Paula Dalbosco, j. 24/11/2015.

example, in case a contract has been concluded by a conduct typified in art. 39, IV, namely, the prevailing weakness or ignorance of the consumer, this will be invalidated if it is demonstrated that there was no conscious, or partially ineffective, consent of the consumer, in the case of preserving advantages secured by law. For example, art. 46 CDC provides: "the contracts that govern the relationship of consumption will not force consumers, if not given the opportunity to have prior knowledge of its contents, or if the respective instruments are drafted in such a way as to impede the understanding of its meaning and scope."

In fact, the only chance of special sanction in relation to unfair practices of art. 39 CDC—in this case, in its only paragraph—leads to the partial ineffectiveness of the obligation celebrated by abuse of the supplier. The norm in question sets that "the services provided and the products sent or delivered to the consumer, in the case provided for in paragraph III, are regarded as free samples, so there is no obligation for payment." The solution of the legislature was wise. After all, in the event of an unsolicited sending of a product or service, if it were to be rejected by the consumer, the natural consequence would be the recognition of the absence of a contract (absolute absence of consent), which could evoke, even if not requested, a duty of restitution by the consumer. The legislator thus defined legal cause so that the consumers can keep the product or service through their comparison to a free sample, avoiding payment. The effect of the rule comprises the granting of a benefit to the consumer and, at the same time, a sanction to the vendor because of abusive practice of sending a spam.

The sanction of invalidating the contract or rendering it ineffective is by reason of the unlawful act. Article 166, VII, of the Civil Code is didactic: the negotiation is null when "the law explicitly declares null, or prohibits him to practice without imposing a sanction." The same goes with the duty to repair the damages caused by the unlawful act. If the abusive practice causes damage to the consumer, the supplier has a duty to compensate.

The right to claim will be individual; if harmed by a combined sale (art. 39, I), for example, the consumer can plead for the nullity of one of the contracts. Or when the practice spreads reaching consumers that are not determinable, it calls for the application of art. 82 of the CDC and the role of legitimate entities for the collective custody of the legitimate consumers. Administrative bodies also have the duty to curb infractions to the rule on prohibition of abusive practices.

Besides the sanctions made under a judicial process and the deduction of pretension of the prejudiced, directly or through their representatives, the Administration also acts through the exercise of its police power. In this case, the Administration has the power to impose sanction of a repressive character, which is provided for in art. 56 CDC (in particular, pecuniary penalty).

It is to be noted, in this regard, as discussed in the National Congress' legislative proposal, the extension of the competence of administrative authorities for consumer protection, giving them the power to enforce specific performance against the supplier on behalf of the injured consumers, especially in the case of vices.

The legislative proposal, originating from the claims and from the intelligence of organizations for consumer defense coordinated by the National Secretariat of the

Consumer (Senacon), was originally sent by the President of the Republic to the National Congress. Its text, however, was also incorporated in the project of updating the Code of Consumer Protection, approved by the Federal Senate and forwarded to the Chamber of Deputies (currently Bill 3514/2015, of the Chamber of Deputies). Article 60-B, which is suggested to be introduced in the Code, gives the administrative bodies the power to impose corrective measures, without prejudice to other sanctions, consistent with the set deadline for compliance with and the implementation of a daily fine for delay: "I—replace or repair the product; II—return of that has been paid by the consumer through misappropriation; III meeting of the offer by the supplier, when there is express record in writing; IV—return or chargeback, by supplier, of the amount paid by the consumer, when the product delivered or the service provided does not correspond to what has been expressly agreed by the parties; V—providing appropriate information requested by the consumer, whenever such application is related to the product purchased or to the contracted service." However, the question is, are sanctions intended for violations of consumer rights also applicable to situations caused by abusive practices of suppliers?

The variability of the penalties for the commission of abusive practices contributes decisively to the effectiveness of the prosecution of the many legal assumptions concerning what can be classified as prohibited conduct. However, it is true that the increased activities of the administrative bodies, by other material measures of achievement when rights are violated, and the corresponding authority to impose a specific penalty in consequence of this breach promote the effectiveness of the legal protection of consumers.

18.3 Are Uniform Criteria for the Interpretation of the Abusive Practices Possible?

Is it possible to define uniform criteria for the interpretation and application of art. 39 CDC, in particular when they comprise indeterminate concepts? The answer is in the affirmative. There are criteria that pertain to the entirety of the Code, featuring its norms that reveal specific consumer protection purposes. So is the case of the principle of material equivalence and its protection in consumer relations. The same applies in relation to the recognition of vulnerability as the basis and purpose of the rules of consumer law or the collective character of the prohibition and repression of unfair practices, which do not focus on the exclusive examination of the existence of reparable damage on a consumer individually but on its collective impact.

The following are three criteria for interpreting the conducts specified in the norms that typify the abusive practices in the CDC: first, the *abnormality* or *excess* of the negotiating freedom of the supplier; then the *collective impact* that characterizes the abusive practice, without prejudice to causing concrete effects to the individual consumer; and, finally, the *treachery* and *violation of good faith* that characterize the abusive practice, as learned from comparative law, taking as an example the so-called consumer harassment.

18.3.1 Abnormality and Excess: The Example of the Practice of Raising Prices Without Just Cause (Art. 39, X, CDC)

A first useful criterion to the appropriate identification and sanctioning of abusive practices is *abnormality* or *excess* in the exercise of the freedom of negotiations by the supplier. In other words, it identifies that the role of the supplier in their relationships with consumers do not follow the course which would be considered reasonable, or could be assumed due to the nature of the activity, that the products and services provided and the characteristics of the market in which it is inserted.

A good example of the application of this criterion concerns the abuse referred to in art. 39, X, CDC, which prohibits the conduct of "raising, without just cause, the price of products or services."

Frequently, situations are brought to public knowledge where suppliers of products and services, considering certain factual circumstances, raise the prices they charge to offer products and services in the consumer market, generating huge social disapproval, especially when egotistical purposes are identified, or even certain opportunism, in view of the difficulty or dire need of consumers for access to these goods. Just to cite recent examples, the marketers of tarpaulins and shingles, in the face of an increased demand therefor caused by natural disasters (storms and windstorms) and the damage they cause (especially the unroofing of houses), multiply the price or fuel resellers who, anticipating the increase of tribute that has not been applied yet, increase the price charged to consumers in a percentage far above from that which results from the impact of new tax rates on the value until then practiced. In these situations, and in many others where the increase of prices charged to the consumers doesn't keep a relation of proportion direct with the increase in costs, arise always the question about the regularity of this conduct faced with the law.

The examination of the subject is not as simple as it may seem at first sight. Initially, the obvious can be inferred: our economic system is based on free enterprise, so that state intervention in the economic domain can only be done upon constitutionally permitted situations, observing the principle of proportionality.[20] It is necessary to consider the rationality of the known economic law of supply and demand. It is necessary to be careful, however, about employing extreme liberal interpretation, condemning per se any state intervention in the market.

[20]Similarly, identifying in particular the proportionality as a new principle of European law, applicable to both corporate, civil and contract, see: Reich (2014), pp. 182–183.

Most of the times, it is more an expression of a legitimate political will than an invocation of the contents of the right itself. Any approach to the issue should consider both the constitutionally defined intervention for the protection of the consumer (arts. 5, XXXII and 170, V, of the Constitution) and the free competition (arts. 170, IV, and 173 of the Constitution).

18.3.1.1 Rising of Prices and Arbitrary Increase of Profits Without Just Cause

The text of art. 39, item X, was not foreseen in the original writing of the CDC. It was introduced by the former Antitrust Law (art. 87 of Law 8884/1994). In fact, in long tradition established in the Brazilian law of repression to the so-called *arbitrary increase of profits*. Article 2, item II, of Law 4371, of September 11, 1962, already established as a form of abuse of economic power "to raise prices without just cause, in the case of any type of monopoly, with the objective of arbitrarily increasing profits without increasing production." Any form of raising of prices without just cause and the exercise of a monopolistic position are contrary to the command of art. 148 of the Brazilian Constitution of 1946, which entrusted to the law the task of repressing all forms of abuse of economic power, including those that had the objective of "arbitrarily increasing profits." The same was present in art. 157 of the Constitution of 1967.

Delegated Law No. 4, of September 26, 1962, approved by the Constitution of 1988,[21] already gave the state the power to establish price limits in order to prevent excessive profits (art. 6, IV). Law 8884/1994 had introduced item XXIV to its art. 21, defining as breaking economic order "to impose excessive prices, or increase without just cause the price of a good or service."

The Antitrust Law currently in force (Law of November 30, 2011, 12,529) preferred to define in its art. 36, subparagraph III, as breaking the economic order, by which economic agents should be responsible regardless of fault, the acts that have as their goal "to arbitrarily increase profits," even if such outcome has not been achieved.

The concepts of competition law and consumer law are common in various factual situations, to a certain extent, although with the natural difficulties in demonstration in the concrete case.[22] The question is whether the definition provided for the consumer protection legislation conquered autonomy in relation to the evolution of competitive norms.

There are important distinctions that should be considered. In art. 39, section X, of the CDC, the *elevation of prices without just cause* is prohibited. Its current application allows consumer protection against the practice of high prices even in

---

[21]STF, AI 268,857—AgR, Rel. Min. Marco Aurélio, 2ª Turma, j, 20/02/2001, DJ 4/05/2001.

[22]STJ, REsp 1,296,281/RS, Rel. Min. Herman Benjamin, 2ª Turma, j. 14/05/2013, DJe 22/05/2013.

the absence of prior agreement between the parties.[23] A distinction is made from *arbitrary increase of profits*, whose reasons can be others, which even includes excessive profit, remembering that a company can be inefficient or increase the prices charged to the consumers for other reasons, not only to increase their profits.[24] Although there is not a loss of sight of a possible or probable relationship of cause and consequence, it cannot be asserted adamantly that because of a price increase *without just cause* there is an *arbitrary* increase of profits.[25]

The raising of prices without just cause is not unknown in the competition law concept. The old Law 8884/94 includes useful criteria to determine the occurrence of chance. The sole paragraph of art. 21 set among the criteria for the imposition of excessive or unjustified increase in prices, in addition to other relevant economic and market circumstances, the behavior of the cost of inputs or the introduction of quality improvements; the price of the product, when it was substituted without substantial amendments; the price of similar products and services or its evolution, in comparable competitive markets; and the existence of adjustment or agreement involving the increase of prices or costs (cartel).

The law brought nothing more than elementary lessons of economics. And it established a distinction between *imposition of excessive prices* and *unjustified price increases*. The imposition of excessive prices was necessarily a species of the abusive exercise of dominant position. There is a power to impose, on the basis of a dominant position, and its exercise characterized the abuse. Already the unjustified rise in prices can also be associated with the dominant position in the market, but not only.

The absence of this distinction is what makes many jurists just admit the infringing character of price increase without just cause, if practiced by the holder of a dominant position, in order to characterize its abusive exercise. That is, the autonomy of the offensive type of elevation without just cause for not only prices is not only in the competitive legislation but also in the Code of Consumer Protection itself. The examination of art. 39, X, of the CDC, however, allows a distinction. One cannot identify as synonyms *excessive* increase and increase *without just cause*. There are regulated markets in which the price increase takes place only within the limits in which regulatory standards allow,[26] by price fixing. On the other hand, the natural evolution of prices, due to the economic climate, will not be considered high without just cause. The most common is the situation in which high costs make up the price. It is natural that before this fact, one cannot require the supplier to maintain a stable or reduced profit, which can only be adopted in rational limits, voluntarily, as a strategy for attracting customers.

---

[23] Miragem (2014), pp. 296–297.

[24] Filho (1998), p. 86.

[25] TJRS, ApCiv e Necessary Reexamination n. 70,059,453,456, 17ª Câmara Cível, Rel. Liege Puricelli Pires, j. 25/09/2014. In the same sense: Ap Civ n. 70062718671, 18ª Câmara Cível, Rel. Pedro Celso Dal Pra, j. 26/02/2015.

[26] STF, RMS 28.487, Rel. Min. Dias Toffoli, 1a Class, j. 26/02/2013, Dje 15/03/2013.

The interpretation and application of art. 39, X, CDC must also recognize the basic rules of formation of prices, such as the costs of production and their application, index, or percentage (*mark up*), allowing the coverage of other costs not considered in production costs, such as taxes, fees, and the desired profit in order to arrive at a price benchmark.[27] Similarly, the indirect costs allotted for the entire production, whose impact will depend on the scale the products are produced, should be considered in order to get the unit cost and the so-called nonstandard costs; for example, in the case of shops, in accepting multiple cards as a means of payment, each transaction is paid with distinct rate.

In the case of the formulation of the price of services, there are still other elements to be considered, such as uncertainty of the runtime, mobilization and demobilization costs, possible withdrawal of customers, and investments made.

This does not mean that the supplier should merely pass along the costs. Strictly speaking, its purpose must be to offer quality products and services with competitive prices, that is to say, which has the ability to attract consumers.

In this way, the increase of price without just cause reveals an abnormality. The concept of just cause, in this case, is decisive. Can the cause of increase of high prices be demanded? In ordinary terms, yes. The question, however, is whether there is a limit to this escalation of price in view of the reasons that give cause to an increase in demand. Returning to the example of the construction material salesman, he takes advantage of a hailstorm to increase the price of tiles to 1000%, in view of the demand of those whose roof had been damaged. An ethical-social judgment will tend to condemn the "undue exploitation" of the situation. A strictly economic judgment, however, will consider the opportunity of maximizing profits from the event.

It can be contended that the market autoregulates itself. If a supplier increases its prices excessively, it will lose consumers. In a perfectly competitive market, it is possible. The hypothesis of art. 39, X, of the CDC seems to apply only to those situations in which the supplier raises prices excessively, in order to keep clients, especially in view of their captivity or dire need. In the case of provision of services, long-term contracts should be considered, in which the consumer faces certain obstacles for shifting from a competitor to another, such as the grace period for fruition of the services, loyalty clauses or simply common red tape, endless links, or a series of successive measures that should be adopted to end the engagement. Is it dependence or captivity that will make part of the consumers, even those who have realized the excessive increase, stay linked to the original contract?

The concept of increase of prices without just cause, an abusive practice provided for in art. 39, X, of the CDC, cannot be confused with the arbitrary increase of profits provided in competition law rules, nor can the existence of abuse of a dominant position be assumed as it maintains a certain line of interpretation in competition law. The imposition of high prices without just cause is kind of an abuse in the exercise of the freedom of negotiation of the supplier, according

[27]Martins (2003), Fama (2009), p. 282.

to the dogma of abusive practices in consumer protection legislation. This does not cause any price increase—even if it is for maximization of profits—to be *in itself* abusive. After all, you are in a market economy. However, there are limits that should be considered, such as the good faith and the vulnerability of the consumer in a given specific situation.

Although originating from the legislative tradition of the competition law in Brazil and initially associated with notions of increase without just cause and increase of profits with arbitrary abuse of dominant market position, the definition of abuse provided for in the Code of Consumer Protection takes on autonomy, in view of the interests of consumers. This makes the identification and sanctioning of the increase of the price of products and services without just cause provided for in the CDC not necessarily dependent on the identification of the abuse of a dominant position or the increased profits of the supplier.

What is asked is what criteria will make it possible to identify—in a market economy with free enterprise—the situations in which the increase of prices of products and services by the supplier surpasses the limits of private autonomy and be considered abusive practice due to the absence of just cause.

18.3.1.2 Material Equivalence and Fair Price

The legal definition of *just cause* and *fair price* has a long tradition in western law. The notion of cause, in private law, although it has double sense, deserved greater acceptance in our system from the objective, functional notion—especially in the examination of the question of contracts.[28] In order to identify itself as the objective reason for which recognizes given legal solution, or the adjustment of installments of the parties in the contracts (sinalagmatic cause). In this sense, the cause of the contracts is identified according to their function. The notion of a *just cause*, in terms of high prices, however, will join the formation of the principle of equiva lence, which accompanies the whole development of private law, with phases of greater or lesser prominence throughout history.[29]

The origins of the principle of equivalence associate its philosophical development (especially in Aristotle and his notion of distributive justice), and the recognition by the law itself. In Roman law, from the third century A.D., Emperor Mark recognizes abnormal harm (*laesio enormis*) for the protection of sellers regarding the commitment to the price of the thing, taking in to consideration the concept that every good has its fair price (*iustum pretius*).[30] This notion is developed in the Middle Ages[31]—especially from the influence of the Christian doctrine on the law,

---

[28]We develop better the subject about the cause of the contracts in: Miragem (2013a, b), p. 269.

[29]See about his contemporary Wieacker (1993), p. 599.

[30]Kaser and Knutel (2014), p. 244.

[31]According to Jacques Le Goff the price system in the middle ages, alongside claims of social solidarity, also watches the growing influence of the formation of State bureaucracy and its effort to collect taxes. Le Goff (2010), p. 148.

serving as a vehicle of hatred of the Church to activities aimed at profit and usury.[32] In conceptual terms, it is stated by the need to keep an equivalence relation between the value of the product and the value of what one can buy with the money for which it was sold, an esteemed common among the parties.

Currently, infringement of the principle of equivalence in contracts is associated with the notions of *exaggerated disadvantage* or *significant imbalance*.[33] This idea of significant imbalance admits two understandings: moral and economical. The first will require an abuse of position of the part that has the power to impose the price, usually, in an unfair behavior, and violator of good faith. The economic understanding, in turn, focuses on identifying the imbalance centered on the costs and risks of the operation.[34]

In consumer law, at first sight, the absence of just cause, which characterizes the banned abusive practice, in the increase of prices is not justified by the increased costs of the activity. As Antonio Herman Benjamin said, "in principle, a stabilized economy, high above the inflation index raises a presumption—relative, it's true—of lack of just cause."[35]

In a system of free enterprise, however, because of a lack of direct control on prices, the supplier cannot, a priori, be deprived of the possibility of readjusting the prices of its products and services, including—to be well understood—increase of profit margin. The abuse will be present when it is done covertly or where there is clear exploitation of a dominant position that is being extended to the consumer (here, of course, it is considered in the sense that it recognizes consumer law and contracts in general—contract position inequality—not that one exactly developed in competition law). The vendors' behavior evidences the disloyalty in its relationship with the consumer. In fact, abusive practices generally involve grounds of disloyalty in relation to the consumer, whether individually or collectively.[36]

The price increases that are justified by the differentiation between consumers motivated by goals of tax policy (whether to bear higher costs/investments or to promote goals of social solidarity) cannot, equally, be considered abusive.[37]

---

[32]The nucleus of the Christian conception of fair price remains valid according to Catholic thought, especially in the so-called social doctrine of the Church. About, see: de Avila (1993), p. 376.

[33]Martins (2009), p. 356.

[34]Stoffel-Munck (2000), pp. 330–332.

[35]Benjamin (2005), p. 381.

[36]See the definition of article 5 of Directive 2005/29/EC: "A commercial practice is unfair if: a) is contrary to the requirements of professional diligence; b) distorts or is likely to distort substantially the economic behavior, in respect of a product, the average consumer that is intended, or affecting, or of the average member of a group when a commercial practice is aimed at a particular group of consumers."

[37]STJ, AgRg no REsp 1,121,617/PR, Rel. Min. Castro Meira, 2ª Class, j. 14.04.2011, *DJe* 27.04.2011.

In a proposal for a systematization of the criteria for the interpretation of the increase without just cause, one must take into account the abnormality of the suppliers' conduct that leads to the infringement of the principle of equivalence.

This abnormality is revealed as follows: (a) by the *quantitative excess* of the increase, which is verified by its extension and decoupling of increased costs for the production of the goods or performance of services and (b) by *qualitative excess,* revealing the unfair practice of concealment of the price increase under false justifications or taking advantage of a dependency or captivity of the consumer in relation to a particular product or service. He who uses passing-on of certain costs and taxes as a percentage significantly higher than effectively impact on the formation of the final price dissimulates. It is considered as taking advantage of a situation of dependency or consumer captivity, taking science or even giving cause obstacles to obtain resolution of the contract or impossibility of getting another product or service that meets his interests, if it serves to increase their prices. In both cases, there is an act that modifies the system of prices until then practiced, topping them. One should not, however, examine the motivation of these acts, but the objectivity of the conduct of the supplier.

It is not at a loss of sight the fact that another function of price is also to make attractive activity to those who undertake it at a legitimate profit. The prior control of prices is only admitted in view of well-delimited social interests and in the interest of balance and stakeholder access to certain products or services—with the known risks of causing dysfunctions in the market in the face of mistakes. In the case of a posteriori control, the incidents of art. 39, X, of the CDC will establish the necessary precautions so that the interpreter, as it fulfills that norm, does not exceed in its discretion. It is not, of course, a case where one tries to find out whether or not the increase is too large or if he supports or not the sustained motivations in economic sense in order for the increase to be recognized by the law.

Brazilian jurisprudence is concerned, correctly, with the proper demonstration of the absence of just cause in terms of lifting prices. Many judgments signal the need for the production of expert evidence for the identification of excess, beyond just identifying the profit margin.[38] However, it does not move far from the possibility of reversal of the burden of proof, present in the hypotheses of art. 6, VIII, of the Consumer Defense Code.[39] In the case of the supervisory activities of the State, it evidences the existence of the breach by the supplier.

The situations in which there is the practice of lifting price without just cause arise from the change of the normal course in a vendor's activity. However, it does not contain all the situations in which there is material equivalence. In addition to the chance of control of unfair terms that impose excessive disadvantage to the consumer (art. 51, IV c/c § 1, CDC), in the list of abusive practices there are others that steer in the same direction, such as in the case of item V, art. 39, which

[38]As an example: TJRS, appeal and Review Necessary Necessário 70,067,235,796, 20ª Câmara Cível, Rel. Carlos Cini Marchionatti, j. 16/12/2015.

[39]Benjamin (2005), p. 381.

prohibits the conduct of "demanding from consumer manifestly excessive advantage." Although there are certain distinctions as to the possibility of raise without just cause (section X), in both practices the idea of excess is present, thus a common element for interpretation and application. And, above all, share to delimit what is considered excessive, given the absence of just cause.

A good example is the possibility of collection of different prices for cash payment or through credit card. On one hand, it is argued that the credit card reduces the risk of default for the supplier and serves as a means of expanding the clientele, by facilitating payment, negotiating advantages whose costs cannot be transferred directly to the consumer who is willing to pay through this mode—hence the impossibility of differentiated prices. On the other hand, the argument that prevails is that the adoption of differentiated prices, properly notified to the consumers, allows higher costs of credit card payment—represented especially by the amount payable by the supplier to the administrator of that means of payment—to be transferred only to consumers effectively making use of this facility. Although contradictory, both are defensible arguments according to rational assumptions. It is about determining if one pays only in case of use or whether the cost should be internalized by the supplier and distributed to the price of all its products and services. It should be noted that the Superior Court of Justice leans by the recognition of the existence of abusive practice in the case of differentiated prices charged by invoking the hypothesis of art. 39, sections V and X, under the ground that it is an improper transfer of consumer costs, considering the benefit obtained by the supplier.[40]

A ideia de anormalidade e excesso, portanto, guarda relação com a quebra de parâmetros de razoabilidade e boa-fé, revelando um aproveitamento da situação do consumidor pelo fornecedor—abuso de posição dominante (*Mächtposition*), útil critério para definição de prática abusiva.

The idea of abnormality and excess is related to the breach of the parameters of reasonableness and good faith, involving abuse of the situation by the supplier—that is, abuse of a dominant position (*Mächtposition*), a useful criterion for the definition of abuse.

18.3.2 The Collective Dimension of Abusive Practices

Another relevant issue concerns a situation permitted by the legislative technique adopted by the legislator of the CDC, and here we call for the objective of well explaining it, as there is a possibility of "double qualification." As is acknowledged by all, the CDC, especially its rules on substantive law, reveals itself as a law governed by

---

[40]In this sense: REsp 1,479,039/MG, Rel. Min. Humberto Martins, 2ª Turma, j. 06/10/2015, DJe 16/10/2015; e REsp 1,133,410/RS, Rel. Min. Massami Uyeda, 3ª Turma, j. 16/03/2010, DJe 07/04/2010. The topic is sensitive. It should be noted that the Minister Humberto Martins, in the most recent decision, changed their understanding signed in AgRg decision in REsp 1,178,360/SP, in 2010.

principles. The use of the expression—already consecrated may not be the best, given the strict definition of principle in law—serves to indicate that they took the legislatures' details or specific situations, or traced broad lines for action of suppliers, deducted from the duties that were imposed, compared with the rights granted to consumers. This means to say that there is in the Code, excluding exceptions,[41] situations in which it is defined in detail the fulfilment of a particular duty by the supplier or the detailed content of this duty. This implies, especially in the case of contractual situations, for example, that the violation of any duty by the supplier can characterize breach of the contract and can also configure as a vice of the product or service or as a violation of the offer, of advertising, such as abuse and so on.

Examples abound. It has already been discussed in Brazil, at the initiative of a number of manufacturers that have reduced the amount of their packaging products without highlighting this consumer information (the so-called makeup); it is argued whether this would be a violation of the duty to inform in the offer, labeling, or advertising or an abusive practice of increase without just cause (quantity of the product is reduced the price remains the same). To this day, noting that a vice of a product and service is susceptible of justifying a claim of damages of the consumer (art. 18, paragraph 1, II and art. 20, II), there are cases in which it is difficult, in practice, to determine what the exact distinction is between this situation and a real product. Reproduced the general formula, that the addiction is characterized by the violation of a duty of adequacy and the fact that the product or service is a scheme which arises from breach of a duty of security, it must be considered that, as it has this duty of safety associated to the psychophysical integrity of consumer, no major difficulties. It turns out that the interpretation given to the duty of security is more comprehensive, including also the heritage integrity of the consumer. In this case, economic losses are also susceptible to claim for compensation as "product or service". This will have important practical effects as, for example, the incidence stated in art. 27 of the CDC and its statute of limitations.[42]

In the case of abusive practices this can also occur, in addition to the fact that, in situations in which there is a fault in the contract of consume by the supplier, when the situation is characterized an express way as those of art. 39 or another situation that is identified as an abusive practice, because of the character purely illustrative of the norm, being possible to subject the supplier to two sanctions: The one in reason of the fault, and another one due to abusive practice. It is clear that in these

[41] With legal mention—if the detailed definition of the duty of information regarding in the supply and presentation of products referred to in article 31 of the code: "the offer and presentation of products or services shall ensure correct information, clear, precise, and now in Portuguese language about its features, quality, quantity, composition, price, warranty, terms of validity and origin, among other data, as well as on the risks they pose to the health and safety of consumers." One must not lose sight of this standard, despite their level of accuracy, intense regulatory activity object by relevant administrative bodies, such as, for example, in the case of food and medicines, for example, through ANVISA—national health surveillance Agency. With any luck, health risks and consumers measures, regarding its intensity for the purposes of consumer information, or other data referred to in the standard, will be the subject of specific exam for each type of product or service.

[42] On the subject I refer to Miragem (2014), pp. 528–529.

situations, exist the need to recognize the repression defined by the law to the abusive practices stemmed from a collective dimension of their effects.

Note that there are situations in which the breach occurs not by abusive conduct but by simple mistake that gives cause to a breach of contract, such as a case of simple nonfulfillment of obligation. In other situations, however, the conduct defined as abuse generates damage to the consumer, which can even represent an individual benefit. However, in this case, the prohibitions are explained by their effects to the collective consumers—thus, the balance between the individual consumer and the collectivity of consumers or between current and future consumers (future generations).

Once again, examples abound. The practice of tying (art. 39, I) is illustrative. It can even be advantageous in certain situations to the individual interest of the consumer. However, it will be improper since the conditioning of the sale of a product to the purchase of another reveals the inefficiency of one of them, so that the practice is harmful to free competition between economic agents and products that compete for market.[43] It is not possible to refer to individual damage or advantage, but simply to preserve the interests of the collectivity.[44]

In European law, the doctrine recognizes two basic criteria for the identification of unfair practices: on one hand, an objective criterion, which implies the commitment of autonomy and, one the other, a subjective criterion, through wrongful conduct or intent to harm or prevent a legitimate consumer decision.[45] Directive 2005/29/EC, however, shall be guided by the objective criteria, which makes sense considering the goal of protecting the consumer. Thus, in the case of deceptive practices, they shall be deemed to be harmful to the consumer per se, regardless of whether they cause damage to one or more consumers.[46] In case there will be a violation of good faith, a disloyalty, the same will be sanctioned.

---

[43]Miragem (2014), p. 102.

[44]On the subject, the known decision of the SUPREME COURT, the rapporteur min. Herman Benjamin on the topic, in which referred to: “the standard is clear: there is lawlessness when the supply of a product or service is conditional upon the acquisition, by the consumer, of another well or unjustified quantitative limits. In the first situation, the abuse is configured by the lack of relevance (or natural necessity) in the sale of products or services, i.e. by the requirement, whatever the reason, combined purchasing of consumer goods which, as a rule, are offered or supplied separately.” And continues: “In other words, the sale (or rather,) tied sale is averse to just cause; put another way, is inexorably abusive practice, no matter how much you seek pretexts to legitimize it. Thus, the fact that the tying was imposed only for the payment time limit detracts abuse and the misuse of acquisition product conditioning objectified by the consumer”. (STJ, REsp 384,284/RS, t., j. 20.08.2009, rel. Min. Herman Benjamin, *DJe* 15.12.2009).

[45]Micklitz Haus –W. The general clause on unfair practices. In: Howels et al. (2006), pp. 104–105.

[46]So the recent decision of the Court of Justice, C-388/13, 16.04.2015: “the policy 2005/29/EC of the European Parliament and of the Council of 11 May 2005 concerning unfair business-to-consumer negotiation in the internal market and amending Directive 84/450/EEC, directives 97/7/EC, 98/27/EC and 2002/65/EC of the European Parliament and of the Council and Regulation (EC) No 2006/2004 of the European Parliament and of the Council (“unfair commercial practices directive”), must be interpreted as meaning that the reporting by a professional to a consumer, of a wrong information, such as that at the issue in the main proceedings, must be described as “misleading” commercial practice in this policy, even though this communication only concerns a single consumer”.

The existence of abuse in situations that restrict a simple breach of a specific contract by the supplier cannot be mistaken. In other words, one must distinguish between the setting of the abuse and its sanctions, and the assumption of responsibility of the supplier for breach toward consumers who fulfill the contract, whose solution is given according to the rules of breach of contract. Hence why if you recognize a collective dimension, which implies the identification of abuse with a conduct by the organization or specific reiteration of a conduct, which has consequently also defined and implemented effective judicial and administrative sanctions the purpose of suppression of conduct and its modification. In order to benefit from the collective of consumers and, even, promote the improvement of the market itself.

18.3.3 Disloyalty, Violation of Good Faith: The Siege of Consumption

The definition of abusive practices carries with it the breach of the duty of loyalty by the supplier toward the consumer. That is clear in many of the events contemplated in art. 39 of the CDC since it highlights a position of leverage of the supplier and the power to enforce certain consumer behavior. There is, in these cases, a violation of the duties of loyalty, collaboration, and respect for legitimate expectations arising out of the good-faith objective.[47]

The concrete experience of market practices, as well as the lessons of comparative law in relation to the conduct of negotiations of certain suppliers, through the adoption of various strategies to enforce (the use of the verb by the legislator in art. 39, IV, of the CDC is illustrative) products and services, suggests the convenience of detailing these unfair conducts. That was the option of Directive 2005/29/EC when dealing with aggressive commercial practices, identifying those that characterize harassment, coercion, or undue influence.

Article 9 of the Directive establishes the following: "Article 9—Use of harassment, coercion and undue influence: in order to determine whether a commercial practice uses harassment, coercion—including the use of physical force—or undue influence, the following elements are taken into account: a) the time and place in which the practice is applied, its nature and persistence; b) the use of threatening or abusive language or behavior; c) the use by any misfortune or circumstance of such gravity that harms the ability of consumer decision, of which the trader is aware, to influence the consumer's decision; d) Any onerous or disproportionate non-contractual barriers imposed by the trader, when the consumer wishes to exercise their contractual rights, including to settle the contract or to change product or professional; e) and any threat to take action, where this is not legally possible."

---

[47]Miragem (2014), p. 283. Marques Claudia Lima. Contracts in the Code of consumer defense. 7ª ed. São Paulo: RT, p. xx.

The European solution impresses by the level of detail and objectivity of criteria, assisting in the activity of the interpreter. It can be verified in the mentioned conducts the violation of the duty of loyalty and good faith, through actions of the supplier that intimidate the consumers or simply seek to deceive or take advantage of a situation of weakness. Such criteria, although not foreseen normatively in Brazilian law, are equally useful in the interpretation of art. 39, IV, of the CDC. The duty of loyalty, to respect the consumer, implies positive attitudes of the supplier, clarifying the decision of the consumer to buy and advising him with transparency. And also implies the duty of abstention from a use of the specific situation of the consumer, which can impose such sensations, given certain condition of vulnerability, affecting the exercise of his freedom.

This concept of consumer harassment did not pass unnoticed in the improvement initiatives and update of the Code, in progress in recent years. However, its prediction was made within the scope of the changes planned for the CDC at work in The Legal Experts Commission designated in the Federal Senate, which focused on the discipline of specific phenomena, such as e-commerce and the prevention and treatment of superdebt of consumers. Thus, consumer harassment update projects that today are handled in the Brazilian Parliament are established in accordance with the scope of the work of the Commission, on the topics of e-commerce and superdebt.

Senate Bill project 281/2012 (currently Mayor Bill 3514/2015), which provides for the discipline of electronic commerce, provides for its inclusion in art. 6 of the CDC, item XII, predicting how basic consumer law "freedom of choice, especially in the face of new technologies and data networks, prohibited any form of discrimination and harassment of consumption."

On the other hand, Senate Bill 283/2012 (currently Mayor Bill project 3515/2015), among other measures for the prevention of consumer superdebt, proposes the inclusion of art. 54-C in the text of the CDC, which establishes specific abusive practices in the provision of consumer credit, covering, in item (IV) of the text under discussion, the following act: "harassing or pressuring consumers to hire the supply of product, service or credit, even from a distance, by electronic means or by telephone, especially if consumers are elderly, illiterate, sick or in a state of heightened vulnerability or if premium is involved."

In both cases, the law in passing incorporates the prohibition of consumer harassment in e-commerce, as well as in the provision of credit, which may be given even before any kind of relationship between the consumer and the credit provider begins—like initial offering or advertising—or, as occurs in many situations, in the course of a business relationship that already exists, in which the supply of credit, under distinct arrangements, is held successively in which I have already referred to as *current business relationship*[48] (in particular, between the consumer and a financial institution, which are bound, by time, in a series of successive or concomitant contracts).

---

[48]Miragem (2013a, b), pp. 253–254.

In the case of art. 6, paragraph XII, of the current Mayor Bill project 3514/2015, the text chooses to adopt a generic prediction of prohibition of discrimination and consumer harassment as a means of protecting the freedom of choice of consumers in electronic commerce. The proposed solution is comprehensive and offers opportunity for fulfillment of the concept by the interpreter.

Regarding the text of art. 54-C, subparagraph IV, to be included in the CDC (PLC 3515/2015), harassment refers to a particular purpose (employment of service or credit), regardless of the means (in person or at a distance by electronic means or by phone), seeking to protect consumers in general but, above all, those who have exacerbated vulnerability. It similarly focuses on contracts where there is credit offer by offering a premium. In this last case, one realizes that this is not simply the right offer of a premium but also the possibility to get it through events or raffles, which in any case undermines the purpose of stimulus to credit charge, to which the norm is associated.

Aware of these hypothesis, and even considering doctrinal and jurisprudential construction that can be developed from this category called consumer harassment, on the basis of criteria associated with the violation of the duty of loyalty and good faith, serve also to give density to art 39, IV, of the CDC itself. They assist the interpreter in the exact definition of what is understood by "avail themselves of weakness or ignorance of the consumer, in view of their age, health, knowledge or social condition, to sell them their products or services."

That is, the category of consumer harassment and the criteria that are given by comparative law (especially in art. 9 of Directive 2005/29/EC), although it is estimated by its legislative existence in the legislative projects proceeding in the Brazilian Parliament, it is useful, independent of these, to guide the interpretation and application of rules already made in art. 39, the CDC, in particular its subparagraph (IV). Strictly speaking, in the category of consumer harassment, the generality of violations by the supplier of their duty of good faith in freedom of consumer choice in accordance with the recognized principles of morality in the consumer market is contemplated.

18.4 Final Considerations

Among the reasons for the success of the Consumer Defense Code in Brazilian law is the sophisticated interpretation of its rules of case law and doctrine. Since the origin of the Code, one can see the inspiration on innovations from the comparative law perspective and the development of original solutions, as well as the recognition of new sources of formation of legal links (placing of the product on the market, information, sales, advertising) and its effects, as well as the definition of a list of duties of suppliers, associated with a general duty of quality.

In respect of abusive practices, the heterogeneous character of the conduct referred to in art. 39 CDC points out some common criteria, derived from good faith and the protection of consumer's vulnerability, that are helpful in the interpretation and realization of their concepts. Thus, abusive practices are associated with the concepts of abnormality and excess in the exercise of the freedom of negotiation of the supplier.

A collective dimension is also recognized in the characterization of the abusive practices, identifying a way to act with the supplier in disregard of its express or implied duties on consumer relationship, characterized by a purpose or reiteration in prohibited conduct and the ability to achieve consumers individually or collectively. Also, the violation of good faith, taking advantage of the vulnerability of the consumer or of the need for/dependence on a given product or service, qualifies as an abusive practice, by disregard of the duties of cooperation inherent in a contractual relationship.

The precision of the criteria for the definition of abusive practices, in this way, at the same time as it serves the interpretation of the types set out in the norm, it sets standards for identification of other kinds of conduct that consider themselves as violating the paradigm of quality (duty of quality of suppliers) required in a relation of consumption. They are also useful, given the nonexhaustive character of the norms, in the identification and examination of new conducts not provided originally or renew the *modus operandi* established, as is characteristic of the transformations in the consumer goods market and business strategies of vendors.

References

Benjamin AH (2005) Brazilian Consumer Defense Code reviewed by the authors of the draft, 8th edn. Forense universitária, São Paulo

Carpena H (2001) Abuse of law consumer contracts. Renovar, Rio de Janeiro

da Silveira RA (1999) Market practices in consumer law. Juruá, Curitiba

de Avila FB (1993) Little encyclopedia of social doctrine of the church, 2nd edn. Loyola, São Paulo

Fama R (2009) Cost management and pricing, 5th edn. ATLAS, São Paulo

Filho S (1998) Calixto. *Direito concorrencial.* As estruturas. Malheiros, São Paulo, p 86

Howels G, Micklitz HW, Wilhelmsson T (2006) European fair trading law. The unfair commercial practices directive. Ashgate, Hampshire

Kaser M, Knutel R (2014) Römisches Privatrecht. 20. Auflage. Verlag C.H. Beck, München

Le Goff J (2010) Lo sterco del diavolo. Il denaro nel medievo. Laterza, Roma

Lisbon RS (2001) Unfair commercial practice. Consum Law Rev 39. RT, jul-Sept, São Paulo

Marques CL, Miragem B (2014) The new private law and the weaker parties protection. RT, São Paulo

Martins PL (2002) The abuse in consumer relations and principle of good faith. Forensics, Rio de Janeiro

Martins E (2003) Cost accounting, 9th edn. ATLAS, São Paulo

Martins FR (2009) Principle of contractual justice. Saraiva, São Paulo

Miragem B (2002) Consumer protection as a fundamental right: legal consequences of a concept. J Consum Law 43. RT, São Paulo

Miragem B (2013a) Abuse of law, 2nd edn. RT, São Paulo

Miragem B (2013b) Banking law. RT, São Paulo

Miragem B (2014) Course of consumer law, 5th edn. RT, São Paulo

Reich N (2014) General principles of civil law I. Intersentia, Cambridge

Stiglitz G (1992) The consumer law and abusive practices-reality and perspectives in Argentina. Consum Law Rev 3. RT, jul-Sept, São Paulo

Stoffel-Munck P (2000) L'abus dans le contrat. Essai d'une théorie. LGDJ, Paris

Wieacker F resurgence (1993) History of modern private law, 2nd edn. Calouste Gulbenkian Foundation, Lisbon

Chapter 19
Children, Consumption, and Advertising: Brazil's Point of View

Adalberto Pasqualotto

19.1 Introduction

Life is responsible for bringing new challenges to people and their relationships. Not so long ago, mothers used to take care their children at home while fathers went out to work. The professionalization of women changed this scenario. Children started to be looked after by day care providers, whether at home by nannies or at a nursery. Meanwhile, technology has transformed human communications. At first, television crossed borders. Then the Internet left in the past the separation caused by distance. A third factor was added for the emergence of a true new world: the political-economic fact of the fall of the Berlin Wall and the globalization of capitalism. In this new scenario, powerful companies began to dispute the market with sophisticated tools, constantly innovated by technology. The dispute intensifies competition while uniting converging forces. This is the case of advertising, a conciliation point among the interests of suppliers of products and services and media companies.

Advertising creates artificial needs, stimulating sumptuary consumption and expanding market boundaries by creating new consumers. In this universe, we can find children. The absence of mothers most of the day found in television and, more recently, in tablets true electronic nannies. Children consume and induce consumption. Therefore, children have become strategic targets of advertising. Children are, however, human beings in development. Although in an increasingly early way, accelerated by the impetuosity of the lifestyle and by the technological vortex, children remain fragile, thus becoming an easy prey for marketing. This is the context in which a debate is developed with several areas: neuropsychological,

A. Pasqualotto (✉)
Law School, Pontifical Catholic University of Rio Grande do Sul, Porto Alegre, Brazil

Law School, Federal University of Rio Grande do Sul, Porto Alegre, Brazil
e-mail: pasqualotto@pucrs.br

C. Lima Marques, D. Wei (eds.), *Consumer Law and Socioeconomic Development*,
DOI 10.1007/978-3-319-55624-6_19

interested in the form of absorption of advertising stimuli by the child; educational, questioning what is the role of parents and sufficiency as well as insufficiency of guidance and supervision; and legal (to mention only three), debating the amount of State intervention and its regulatory role.

This paper aims to approach the three areas present in the title, with special emphasis on the legal issue and from a Brazilian perspective.

19.2 Controversy in Brazil: Advertising Between Satire and Political Correctness

Brazil is an emerging market and practices an economic system based on free enterprise, competition, and consumer protection. These are, among others, principles enshrined in the Economic Order chapter of the Brazilian Federal Constitution (article 170). Since there is no hierarchy among the principles, the proportionality shall be considered to overcome any problems existent, mainly with regard to the consumer protection front to the others.

Consumer protection is an innovation of the Brazilian Federal Constitution of 1988. Previously, the concept did not exist in the Brazilian legal system. Capitalism has, however, always been practiced. In the '50s, the country has joined the mass society. We can consider the implementation of the automobile industry as a starting point. In 1960, Brasilia, the capital of Brazil, was created. Brazil was going through the JK years, a synthesis of the developmental era stimulated by the work of President Juscelino Kubitschek. Soon, however, his policy would upset the national scene. In 1964, Brazil began the military regime, which was a culmination of a crisis initiated in 1961 with the resignation of President Jânio Quadros, successor of JK, after only 7 months in office at that time. The military government curtailed civil liberties but continued the economic development. It implemented, however, a system of censorship that affected the freedom of the press and reached commercial advertising. The advertisers are required to undergo prior analysis of their texts and productions. In order to react against such measure, a National Code of Advertising Self-Regulation was drafted and gave rise to the creation of the National Council for Advertising Self-Regulation (Conar).

The military regime ended in 1985, and in 1988 the new Brazilian Federal Constitution was enacted, definitely making Brazil a democracy again. Consumer protection was established as an individual guarantee, a State duty, and a principle of economic order by the Constitution. In 1990, in view of the express provision of the Constitution, the Consumer Protection Code was enacted. Among other issues, the Code addresses basic rules on advertising: it imposed as one of its principles the identification (advertising should be easily and immediately identified as such) and the truth (the advertiser must enable consumers to know factual, technical, and scientific data that support the advertising message) and established misleading advertising (able to mislead the consumer) or abusive advertising (advertising that goes against certain values, including taking advantage of the lack of judgment and experience of children) as unlawful.

Conar did not welcome the Consumer Defence Code because self-regulation was enough to regulate advertising. Meanwhile, with the enactment of the Code, Conar launched an institutional advertising campaign, self-nominating itself as the controller of misleading and abusive advertising. At the same time, a consumer defense association filed a suit accusing Nestlé of doing abusive advertising of its products toward children. The suit was filed against the advertising company, the filmmaker, and Conar. Conar was considered liable due to its self-called fiscalization role. Conar alleged to be unlawfully suited and affirmed that because of its civil association nature it has no coercive power over advertising companies and it could only suggest the interruption of the advertising message. The judge found for Conar but considered that the Council used to do misleading advertising of them. Such decision showed the limits of self-regulation in Brazil.[1]

This early conflictual coexistence between Legal Consumer Protection and the Council never ended. On the contrary, it has increased. In 2014, the National Council for the Rights of Children and Adolescents (Conanda), a deliberative body of the Secretary of Human Rights from the Presidency, which is responsible for promoting policies to protect and to promote children's and adolescents' rights, issued a Resolution (n. 163) providing for abusive practices in advertising aimed at children and young audiences. Forthwith, the Council reacted strongly, with the adherence of corporate bodies of the media and entrepreneurs, alleging that the Conanda Resolution was illegal because only laws from Congress could provide for that matter.

19.3 The Constitutional Parameters: Freedom of Speech and Free Enterprise vs. Full Protection and Consumer Defense

The legal discussion on advertising to children is based on the Constitution. The Brazilian Federal Constitution guarantees free expression of thoughts (article 5, IV), free expression of intellectual, artistic, scientific, and communication activities, regardless of censorship or license (article 5, IX), as well as freedom of creation, expression, and information without restriction "subject to the provisions of the Constitution" (article 220, "caput"). Such reservation immediately indicates

[1]Decision from September 22, 1991, published on the journal *Direito do Consumidor*, vol. 1, São Paulo [1991?], pp. 222–228.

that communicative freedom[2] is not absolute[3] and shall be in conformity with other constitutional provisions. There are several ones, starting from paragraph 4 of article 220, which allows advertising restrictions to tobacco, alcohol, pesticides, medicines, and therapies.

Regarding children, article 227 of the Brazilian Federal Constitution assures them "absolute priority" on matters such as life, health, education, and other rights, safeguarding them from "all forms of (...) exploitation." Safeguarding means understanding the children's vulnerability to communicative freedom, as article 221 determines that radio and television stations (as well as the Internet, which did not exist in 1988) respect the "ethical and social values of the person and the family" in their programs and productions (item. IV, article 221).

Broadly speaking, the communicative freedom can also be controlled to protect consumers to the extent that the restrictions on advertising provided for in paragraph 4 of article 220 are concerned, since commercial advertising is directed to consumers and they shall be protected against harmful and inherently dangerous products and services. If such provision provides for adults, let alone children.

Another important question in this debate is whether advertising should effectively be considered a direct representation of freedom of speech. There is no doubt that any human manifestation can be traced back as a form of expression and understood as a manifestation of intelligent life. However, the nature of a determined manifestation will concern the interest that it immediately affects. In the history of civilization, freedom of speech has allowed citizens to speak publicly.[4] The affected interests were, and still are, civil liberties of essentially political nature. The concept of freedom of speech has expanded to other areas such as artistic, intellectual, and scientific creation, all of them present in the same political interest as they all express critical thinking. The concept has also been expanded to the freedom of press, with the proper rights to inform and to be informed; once this perspective also preserves man's freedom of citizens.

Otherwise, commercial advertising affects primarily interests of the market and of free enterprise. The Brazilian Federal Constitution finds in the free enterprise and in the exploitation of the human labor the two principles of economic order, which

---

[2]The expression "communicative freedom" is used by Jonatas Machado, referring to the right to freedom of speech as a mother right (Machado 2002, pp. 416–417). Under Brazilian Law, Ingo Sarlet agrees with the complex of communicative liberties in Machado's line of thought, although he has highlighted the singularities of the Brazilian Constitution compared to others by refusing to use the term "freedom of speech" as a gender (Sarlet et al. 2012, pp. 435 e 440). The expression is appropriated in light of the article 220 of the Brazilian Constitution because this section concerns media.

[3]In light of the habeas corpus 82.424, the Supreme Court provided that freedom of speech is not an absolute constitutional guarantee, following moral and legal limits (HC 82.424-RS).

[4]"No man may be disturbed for his opinions, even religious ones, provided that their manifestation does not trouble the public order established by the law." "The free communication of thoughts and of opinions is one of the most precious rights of the man: any citizen thus may speak, write, print freely, except to respond to the abuse of this liberty, in the cases determined by the law" (Articles X and XI of the Declaration of the Rights of Man and of the Citizen, 1789).

follow a series of other principles, including consumer protection. Therefore, the legitimate interests of consumers[5] can justify restrictions to commercial advertising, especially if it is considered that it is an immediate and essential result from the economic activity, only remotely integrating the rights to freedom of speech. This statement is not affected by paragraph 4 of article 220 of the Brazilian Federal Constitution; once that provision only characterizes a special regime of advertising of products and services and does not deal with the advertising activity in general terms.

19.4 Legal Grounds: Abuse and Major Vulnerability

Subject to the Federal Constitution, substantive law embodies the parameters of the protection of children and consumers in general.

The Statute of Child and Adolescent (Law n. 8.069/1990) provides that "by law or other means," the child and the adolescent are entitled to "physical, mental, moral, spiritual and social development, in conditions of freedom and dignity" (article 3) and assigns to the family, community, society in general, and the public authorities the duty to "ensure, with absolute priority" their inherent rights (article 4). Then the Statute states that "no child or adolescent will be subject to any form of negligence, discrimination, exploitation, violence, cruelty and oppression" (article 5) and that the social ends toward which this Law is directed, the requirements of the common good "and the peculiar condition of children and adolescents as persons in development will be given due consideration" (article 6). These four articles are a true declaration of principles in favor of child protection, leaving no doubt that, although one cannot affirm that there are absolute rights, the force that arises from them is extremely important in any consideration of proportionality facing possible conflicting interests.

The combination of two of these four principles is particularly relevant when considering the commercial interests of advertising: the prohibition of any form of exploitation of children and their special condition of a person in development.

However, what implementation power could be drawn from such pragmatic texts? This is an important question for a person who is analyzing the contrast between Brazilian social reality and the social norm theory. Indeed, children (and many adults too) are neglected in poor sanitary conditions where they live, on the streets where they wander, in the absence of schools or appropriate schools, in the impoverished health posts. Does this iniquitous reality not destroy the legal project?

A good answer to this question was provided by Judge Wilson Carlos Rodycz in 1991 in the above-mentioned award where he, in other words, decided that the

[5] Among consumers' basic rights are safeguard of life, health and safety, education and communication as to the proper use of products and services and the protection against misleading and abusive advertising (Article 6, Consumer Defense Code).

Council was making misleading advertising of itself. The Council stated that children are capable of distinguishing fiction from reality. With such arguments, the Council was trying to mischaracterize abusive advertising using a video of a theft: children entering into a closed supermarket at night to get the desired sweets and candies. The judge accepted the opposite argument, alleging that the scene in the advertising video, which was performed by boys from privileged social classes, would reverberate "in younger and more miserable children, without the same experiences in the world," as a "way to obtain happiness."

The ruling addressed a particularly sensitive issue for a country with such a big level of social inequality as Brazil. Advertising stimulates consumption and should not change values by leading to misleading conduct. Therefore, it can be better understood the meaning of the legal concept of "taking advantage on the lack of judgement and experience of the child" and is completed by analyzing what the Constitution states. The Constitution was made as a social construction project, aimed to "eradicate poverty and substandard living conditions and to reduce social and regional inequalities"[6] and is intended to "ensure everyone a life with dignity, in accordance with the dictates of social justice." It cannot be considered a mere piece of rhetoric. The horizontal effect of the Constitution means that its rules are also applicable in relations between individuals, being mandatory in everyday life.

Some of the problems of the applicability of laws are the general clauses and the undetermined legal concepts, which allow for an interpretive spectrum that is often sensitive to rhetoric. Therefore, the debate on the Conanda Resolution started. The reaction was the argument that the Resolution was illegal; some legal experts affirmed that it only provided interpretation criteria to the judge to define in which concrete situations the advertising message was taking advantage on the lack of judgment and experience of the child.[7] The Resolution mentions persuasive tools that are used in advertising aimed at children: the use of child language, supersaturated colors, children's soundtracks, real and fictional characters of childhood, among others. These are resources that take advantage of the "lack of judgment and experience of the child" or that "avail themselves of the consumer's weakness or ignorance in view of age, health, knowledge or social condition, in order to force the consumer to accept their products or services" (article 39, IV, from the Consumer Defense Code, defining a kind of abusive practice).

The social condition, as one may see in written form, is also a criterion of definition of abuse, which brings us to the conclusion that the application of the laws—not only the ones awarded by courts but also the ones that the citizen must

[6]Brazilian Constitution Art. 3. The fundamental objectives of the Federative Republic of Brazil are: I—to build a free, just and solidary society; II—to guarantee national development; III—to eradicate poverty and substandard living conditions and to reduce social and regional inequalities; IV—to promote the well-being of all, without prejudice as to origin, race, sex, color, age and any other forms of discrimination.

[7]In this sense, Bruno Miragem's legal opinion to Alana Institute on the Resolution: Miragem (2014), pp. 459–495. Still on the Conanda Resolution: Pasqualotto and Barreto (2014), pp. 89–104.

respect—cannot disregard the condition of the others. Therefore, the reference patterns in an activity of such social impact as advertising must remain aware of the heterogeneity of the country.

The child, in his peculiar situation as a person in development, has been treated as vulnerable, as well as others in distinct situations such as the elderly, the illiterate, the immigrants, and so on.[8] The vulnerability of the child is demonstrated by neurology. According to Jaderson Costa da Costa, director of the Brain Institute at the Pontifical University of Rio Grande do Sul, the child's brain development occurs in waves that correspond to age groups. Brain activity is stimulated by excitation or inhibition mediated by contacts (synapses). Excitatory and inhibitory stimuli occur at different times: excitatory synapses arise earlier, and its peak occurs at around 5 years old and will prevail until adolescence. Inhibitory activities will be developed later, at around 16 or 17 years old, bringing then the balance. Therefore, the predominance of excitatory synapses enables children to make impulse choices until adolescence.

The nefarious persuasion of advertising on children was addressed in a recent decision of the Supreme Court of Justice, in which it was recognized the practice of abusive advertising by a food company that offered children's watches as a gift with the purchase of their products. The award has not yet been published,[9] but it signals an important trend of precedent that is more consistent with the constitutional principles.

19.5 What Should Be Done?

The premises for the debate are as follows: (a) the child is vulnerable, and (b) the Brazilian Constitution assures them absolute priority; on the other hand, (a') television and other media, including advertising, contribute to the child's socialization, and (b') the Constitution guarantees freedom of speech broadly and free enterprise.

The question is relevant to advertising regulation forms: self-regulation (adopting the current nomenclature in Brazil) or state regulation? The latter includes a possible prohibition of advertising to children, which derives from the application of the rule mentioned in the Consumer Defense Code (abusive adver-

[8]For everyone: Marques and Miragem (2012). About vulnerability of children in face of advertising: Gonçalves (2009).

[9]News about the judgment are available on the website of the Supreme Court of Justice: http://www.stj.jus.br/sites/STJ/default/pt_BR/Comunicação/Not%C3%ADcias/Not%C3%ADcias/Segunda-Turma-mantém-condenação-de-empresa-por-publicidade-infantil-indevida. Accessed on April 9, 2016.

tising that takes advantage of the lack of judgment and experience of the child), together with the child's proven vulnerability.[10] The opposite of this position is to understand that any legal intervention is a form of unacceptable paternalism because the State should let parents take care of the education of their children, leaving them to decide what children can watch on television.

These extreme positions find obstacles. The former (without considering axiological aspects) because its enforcement is virtually impossible.[11] Banning advertising on television, on the Internet, and in other media will not prevent children from the effects of advertising, and they will be eventually affected by other means. Forms of advertising nowadays are not only conventional, as one can see in programming and in reaching its target indirectly, for example, by licensing products and brands: superheroes will be waiting for children at the shopping malls, giving rise to an atmosphere of enchantment and excitement. Paternalism, on the other hand, is not a relevant argument in Brazil in light of the Constitution. One can just recall the general duty of the family, community, society in general, and the public authorities to protect the child as the Constitution states.[12]

Self-regulation, as practiced in Brazil, is grossly insufficient. Conar proudly announces that it has already judged more than 8000 cases of wrong advertisement with its code of ethics since 1980, when it was implemented, which indicates a steady average of 30 decisions per year. In the same period, the investment in advertisement in Brazil has grown exponentially. Considering the period between 2013 and 2015, the total investment in advertisement in Brazil has grown from 18 billion dollars to 22 billion dollars.[13] This shows how comfortable self-regulation is because it is not credible that such a huge increase in the advertising budget is not accompanied by a proportional increase in cases of infringement of ethical and legal rules.

---

[10] In this sense, Alana Institute, the main Brazilian NGO on children's rights and adolescents, states that the Conanda Resolution affirmed the illegality of advertising aimed at children. According to http://criancaeconsumo.org.br/wp-content/uploads/2014/02/Publicidade-Infantil-é-ilegal.pdf. Accessed on April 10, 2016. The Court of Justice of São Paulo decided on March 11, 2016 and cited the Conanda Resolution as an inhibitor of advertising aimed at children (Appellate Judge Moacir Peres), although the subject matter of the dispute was another. The dispute was about the abuse—which was recognized by the majority of the Court—of beer advertising that discriminates women (TJSP. 7ª Public Law Chamber. Civil Appeal n. 0005431–07.2010.8.26.0053. Rel. Appellate Judge Luiz Sérgio Fernandes de Souza. Trial date: March 11, 2016. Available on: http://esaj.tjsp.jus.br/cjsg/resultadoCompleta.do;jsessionid=C671F6C379934C88CE9D4452434D2EC9.cjsg3. Accessed on April 10, 2016.

[11] Also, making a review of the forms of control of child advertising in several countries: Marques and Bertoncello (2014).

[12] Mutatis mutandis, the difference between constitutional contexts was argued by Judge McCombe to reject comparisons with the precedents of the Supreme Court of the United States in the judgment of a UK High Court on the ban of tobacco advertising brought in *Tobacco Advertising and Promotion Act 2002* (*Apud* Howells (2015). While in other societies the paternalism is relevant, this does not apply in Brazil from a constitutional legal point of view.

[13] Data available on: http://blog.mediaresponse.com.br/content/post/previsoes-de-investimentos-em-publicidade-no-brasil-ate-2018. Accessed on April 10, 2016.

Another comparison is quite illustrative. In France, the body that is responsible for regulating advertising—*Autorité de Régulation Professionnelle de la Publicité - ARPP*—has examined 20,646 television messages, besides 15,273 other messages related to all forms of media.[14] This does not show that offenses to the code are so high in France, but the analysis is prior to the release of the message. Would it be considered censorship? Certainly not, because the control system was created with the agreement of all parties involved. In fact, France practices coregulation, a system in which the State, professionals, and entities representing society (such as nongovernmental organizations and consumer associations) practice regulation with consensus. Undoubtedly, it is a model to be followed.

In Brazil, good news came from the private sector. The Brazilian Association of Soft Drinks and Non-Alcoholic Beverage has announced that its associated companies—which represent the largest manufacturers in the country and international brands—will stop advertising for children under the age of 12. This is another good model to be followed.

19.6 Conclusion

In a polemic subject such as advertising and law, it is difficult to reach consensus, but it is inevitable to take into consideration the constitutional and legal framework of the country where the debate is happening. The Brazilian Constitution protects consumers and children and constitutes a project of society to be built in accordance with its values. Constitutional rules not only bind the government but are also imposed on private relations. Therefore, advertisers, companies, and the media cannot ignore them.

On the other hand, any idea or regulation system in such a dynamic and innovative activity as advertising must not fail to consider the possibilities of effective implementation. Between pure self-regulation and radical government intervention, the best way is possibly in coregulation made from a directive legislative command in conjunction with all parties involved, the stakeholders, including appropriate social representations.

References

Gonçalves TA (2009) A proteção à vulnerabilidade infantil frente à comunicação mercadológica. In: Pereira TS, Oliveira G (eds) Cuidado e vulnerabilidade. Atlas, São Paulo

[14]Data available on: http://www.arpp-pub.org/IMG/pdf/Commentaires_STATS_2015.pdf. Accessed on April 10, 2016.

Howells G (2015) European and UK controls on regulation of tobacco advertising. In: Pasqualotto A (org.) Publicidade de tabaco: frente e verso da liberdade de expressão comercial. Atlas, São Paulo

Machado J (2002) Liberdade de expressão: dimensões constitucionais da esfera pública no sistema social. Coimbra Press, Coimbra, pp 416–417

Marques CL, Miragem B (2012) O novo direito privado e a proteção dos vulneráveis. Revista dos Tribunais, São Paulo

Marques CL, Bertoncello KRD (2014) Publicidade e infância: sugestões para a tutela da crianças consumidoras. In: Pasqualotto A, Alvarez AMBM (eds) Publicidade e proteção da infância. Livraria do Advogado, Porto Alegre

Miragem B (2014) Proteção da criança e do adolescente consumidores: possibilidade de explicitação de critérios de interpretação do conceito legal de publicidade abusiva e prática abusiva em razão de ofensa a direitos da criança e do adolescente por resolução do Conselho Nacional da Criança e do Adolescente - Conanda: parecer. Revista de Direito do Consumidor 95:459–495. São Paulo

Pasqualotto A, Alvarez AMBM (eds) (2014) Publicidade e Proteção da Infância. Livraria do Advogado, Porto Alegre

Pasqualotto A, Barreto MAM (2014) A comédia da publicidade: entre a sátira e o politicamente correto, vol 96. Revista de Direito do Consumidor, São Paulo, pp 89–104

Sarlet I et al (2012) Curso de Direito Constitucional. Revista dos Tribunais, São Paulo, pp 435 e 440

Chapter 20
Further Challenges for Australian Consumer Law

Gail Pearson

20.1 Prospective Review

20.1.1 The Review of the ACL

The Australian Consumer Law (ACL) was reviewed in 2016 following an Issues paper produced by Commonwealth Treasury in March 2016. It adopted a behavioural economics approach rather than a pure efficient market standpoint. There will be another national Consumer Survey as a follow up to the 2011 Survey.

The ACL was put in place following a report of the Productivity Commission (PC).[1] Its concern was to enhance productivity through efficient enforcement outcomes for a national market (particularly in the area of product safety). It recognised the importance of competition for an efficient economy and stated the overarching objective: 'improve consumer wellbeing by fostering effective competition and enabling the confident participation of consumers in markets in which both consumers and suppliers trade fairly and in good faith'.[2] The PC said that the enforcement regime should be reviewed no less than 10 years after the new national law was implemented.[3] When the Council of Australian Governments (COAG) agreed to the ACL, they agreed to a review within 7 years.[4]

---

[1]Since this paper was written the ACL Review process has continued. It can be consulted at consumerlaw.gov.au/review-of-the-australian...law/about-the-review/. See Productivity Commission, *Review of Australia's Consumer Policy Framework Final Report* 2008 (Australia).

[2]Ibid at vol 2, 27.

[3]Ibid at vol 1, 23.

[4]The Intergovernmental Agreement was signed in July 2009, http://consumerlaw.gov.au/review-of-the-australian-consumer-law/, last seen on 14/1/2016.

G. Pearson (✉)
Business School, University of Sydney, Sydney, NSW, Australia
e-mail: gail.pearson@sydney.edu.au

C. Lima Marques, D. Wei (eds.), *Consumer Law and Socioeconomic Development*,
DOI 10.1007/978-3-319-55624-6_20

The review took place in 2016.[5] It followed a national survey of consumers, which found a high awareness of the existence of consumer laws and a broad awareness of dispute resolution.[6] However, a large proportion could not articulate what rights they have.[7] About three-quarters recalled problems with goods or services. The cost to consumers of dealing with problems was estimated at A $14.2 billion and for businesses A$6.6 billion (not taking into account costs to repair or replace products).[8] The products of greatest concern were utility services, mobile phones, electronic goods, and Internet service providers.[9] About 33% had a problem with a banking or financial service, many relating to scams and rip-offs.[10] The survey identified few limitations of the law.[11] An earlier stakeholder survey indicated that a regulator did not investigate breaches of the law quickly enough or communicate clearly, there was too much red tape compliance and it was not sufficiently resourced.[12] Consumers and investors were less confident than providers believed them to be.[13]

20.2 Regulatory Philosophy and Architecture

20.2.1 The Australian Architecture of Consumer Law

Regulation of the economy from a consumer perspective is divided between financial services and the rest. Australia pioneered the 'twin peaks' model of financial services regulation, adopted some years later in the UK, which distinguishes between prudential regulation and conduct regulation. This paper is primarily about conduct regulation for consumer transactions, both financial and otherwise. There are two conduct regulators—the Australian Securities and Investments Commission (ASIC), responsible for all financial services, including consumer credit, and the Australian Competition and Consumer Commission (ACCC). The main legislation administered by ASIC is the *Corporations Act 2001* (Cth), the *Australian Securities and Investments Commission Act 2001* (Cth) (ASIC Act) and the *National Consumer Credit Protection Act 2009* (Cth) (NCCPA). The ACCC administers the *Competition and Consumer Act 2010* (Cth) (CCA). The Australian

[5]See http://consumerlaw.gov.au/review-of-the-australian-consumer-law/terms-of-reference/, last seen on 14/1/2016.

[6]Commonwealth of Australia (2011).

[7]Ibid, at 14.

[8]Ibid, at ix, x, 35,46, 68f.

[9]Ibid, at 36, 50f.

[10]Ibid, at 55.

[11]Ibid, at 101.

[12]ASIC *ASIC Stakeholder Survey 2013*, –/9/2013 at ii.

[13]Ibid at 23.

Consumer Law (ACL) is in Schedule 2 of the latter Act, and there is a rough identity between the ACL and the consumer protection part of the ASIC Act. All this is complimented by a co-regulatory system and, in particular, an industry-financed external dispute resolution (EDR). The ACL is a multi-regulator system, and the state Fair Trading Departments and state-based tribunals play an important role in enforcement and disputes.[14]

20.2.2 The Regulators

There is a high level of cooperation between the two regulators, ASIC and the ACCC, both of which have business regulation and consumer protection functions.[15] Commissioners of one agency have sometimes been commissioners of the other. A major difference is the single regulator framework of ASIC and the multi-regulator framework of the ACCC. Although the ACL is Commonwealth legislation, it operates in cooperation with State Fair Trading agencies. An example of cooperation between the ACCC, ASIC, Consumer Affairs Western Australia and NSW Fair Trading is the action taken against individuals and 'We Buy Houses'. The scheme involved rent to buy, advertising and paid training camps for consumers who were encouraged to believe that they could build wealth through certain property strategies.[16] Another area of cooperation, between the ACCC and the state fair trading regulators, has been private colleges offering vocational education to students.[17]

No amount of cooperation can overcome legislative duplication. The once 'simple and comprehensive' prohibition against misleading and deception has been judicially described as a 'plethora of pointlessly technical and befuddling statutory provisions scattered over many Acts' in a 'morass of dense, difficult to understand legislation' whose application depends on 'mind boggling' definitions. 'The cost to the community, business, the parties and their lawyers, and the time for courts to work out which law applies have no rational or legal justification.'[18] This is not the only statutory provision at issue.

---

[14]See *Maintaining Consistency with the Australian Consumer Law A guide to maintaining a harmonised and consistent approach when developing and reviewing legislation*, –/7/2013, http://consumerlaw.gov.au/files/2015/09/Guide_Maintaining_consistency_with_the_ACL.pdf, last seen on 14/1/2016.

[15]Memorandum of Understanding Between the Australian Securities and Investments Commission and the Australian Competition and Consumer Commission, December 2004.

[16]*Commissioner for Consumer Protection v Susilo* [2014] WASC 50 (Supreme Court of Western Australia); *Coordinated Investigation Results in ACCC Taking action against We Buy Houses and Rick Otton regarding property strategies* ACCC, Media Release MR 23/15, 3/3/2015.

[17]See *ACCC takes action against education services broker Acquire Learning* ACCC Media Release MR 265/15, 17/12/2015 2015.

[18]*Wingecarribee Shire Council v Lehman Brothers Australia Limited (in Liq)* [2012] FCA 1028 (Federal Court of Australia) per Rares J in 'Summary'.

Are the consumer protection functions of ASIC and the ACCC best served in separate regulatory bodies, or should they be combined in one super-regulator for consumers? Until 1998, consumer protection for financial services (apart from credit, which was then a state matter) was not administered separately.[19] The bifurcation followed federal court decisions imposing liability on statements in a prospectus and the fallout from the collapse of a major insurance company.[20] The financial system reforms following the Wallis report,[21] which put in place the 'twin peaks' regulation of the market for financial services and split prudential and conduct regulation, consolidated this separation. Consumer credit was rolled into ASIC after it became nationally regulated.

There are two important rationales given for separate regulators. The first is consolidating expertise in complex financial products and services and how the market for them works. This presupposes a market for goods and services quite distinct from financial products and services. The second is the advantage in co-locating competition and consumer protection regulation as matters of uncompetitive behaviour will often have a consumer dimension. For instance, agreements between travel agents and airlines[22] or between mortgage brokers and banks,[23] if anti-competitive, impact on services and prices for consumers. A further argument is the expertise and success of one regulator, the ACCC, in litigation.[24] Recently, it has been very successful in claims that retailers falsely represented the effect of the consumer guarantees under the ACL.[25] By contrast, ASIC has been mired in a series of corporate collapses linked to mis-selling and bad financial advice scandals. Consumers have lost significant amounts of money, and there has been a series of parliamentary inquiries.[26]

[19]The then Trade Practices Act 1974 (Cth) (Australia) applied to all sectors of the economy. The then Trade Practices Commission became the Australian Competition and Consumer Commission in 1995.

[20]*Fraser v NRMA Holding Ltd.* (1995) 55 FCR 452 (Federal Court of Australia); The HIH Royal Commission, Commonwealth of Australia, *The Failure of HIH Insurance* Volumes 1–3, 2003.

[21]Commonwealth of Australia, *Financial System Inquiry Final Report*, (Wallis) –/3/1997.

[22]*Flight Centre Limited v Australian Competition and Consumer Commission* [2015] FCAFC 104 (Full Court, Federal Court of Australia).

[23]*Australian Competition and Consumer Commission v Australia and New Zealand Banking Group Limited* [2015] FCAFC 103 (Full Court, Federal Court of Australia) (held not anti-competitive).

[24]The ACCC famously has lost a number of high profile cases e.g. *Australian Competition and Consumer Commission v C G Berbatis Holdings Pty Ltd.* [2003] HCA 18, (2003) 214 CLR 51 (High Court of Australia); *Google Inc. v Australian Competition and Consumer Commission* [2013] HCA 1, (High Court of Australia) but it is an active litigator and generally successful.

[25]*Australian Competition and Consumer Commission v Bunavit Pty Ltd.* [2016] FCA 6 (Federal Court of Australia) at [69].

[26]Commonwealth Parliamentary Joint Committee on Corporations and Financial Services, *Inquiry into Financial Products and Services in Australia* (*Ripoll*), –/11/2009; Commonwealth Parliamentary Joint Committee on Corporations and Financial Services, *Inquiry into the Collapse of Trio Capital*,–/5/2012; The Senate Economics References Committee, Commonwealth of

Both ASIC and the ACCC put the market first. ASIC's highest priority is promoting investor trust and confidence in markets that will fund the real economy and lead to economic growth. It self-reports on engagement with stakeholders, surveillance, guidance by setting standards and expectations, education, enforcement (divided into punitive and protective) and policy advice and implementation.[27] The ACCC states its purpose as making markets work for consumers now and in the future. Protecting the interests and safety of consumers is its second goal; its first is maintaining and promoting competition.[28] It subtly emphasises enforcement more than compliance.[29] The objectives of ASIC and the ACCC are established in legislation.[30] The first emphasises confident and informed consumer participation, the second welfare. Since all Australians are participants in the market for goods and services and all working and most retired Australians in the market for financial services, this seems an odd mismatch for consumer protection legislative responsibilities, which echo each other.

The argument for a super-consumer protection regulator might be to combine specialist financial services and litigation expertise. It would also overcome gaps such as advice about investment in housing, which falls outside financial advice.[31] It could deal with credit for sales of goods and services in an integrated fashion. It would overcome any consumer confusion about which protective agency to approach and consolidate a unified approach.

20.2.3 Shifts in the Philosophy of Australian Consumer Law

Australian consumer protection law is moving from protective models based on notions of the autonomous rational individual making free choices to one recognising the limits of rational choice based on the economic theory of efficient markets and aims to protect individuals from their own cognitive biases. The model of enforcement has long since moved from private action by the individual for damages to escalating 'responsive' regulatory action building up from the base of

---

Australia, *Performance of the Australian Securities and Investments Commission*, –/6/2014; Commonwealth Parliamentary Joint Committee on Corporations and Financial Services, *Inquiry into Proposals to Lift the Professional Ethical and Education Standards in the Financial Services Industry*, –/12/2014. The Senate Economics References Committee, Commonwealth of Australia, *Scrutiny of Financial Advice*, to report by 1/2/2016.

[27] *ASIC Annual Report 2014–2015* at 34ff.

[28] *ACCC and AER Annual Report 2014–2015* at 15, 25.

[29] See ACCC *2015 ACCC Compliance and Enforcement Policy* February 2015 at 5.

[30] S 1 (2) *ASIC Act*; S 2 *CCA*.

[31] It does not fall within S 961 *Corporations Act 2001* (Cth) as without more the advisee would not be a retail client but is governed by S 12 DC ASIC Act.

the regulatory pyramid. It has been described as a convergence of the deterrence and accommodative models of regulation.[32] An important component is seeking voluntary compliance from firms. In addition to enforcement litigation, the regulator can require firms to substantiate claims they make about products,[33] take enforceable undertakings (including compliance programs),[34] and issue public warning notices[35] and can bring actions for compensation on behalf of consumers.[36] In addition to the regulator, courts and tribunals, there is an extensive system of self-regulation notably through codes of conduct and external dispute resolution.[37]

Like the rest of the common law world, Australian consumer protection laws have been predicated on modifying freedom of contract by ensuring that those with whom consumers deal are qualified, licensed or otherwise reputable and by mandating information disclosure so that consumers have information about the product or service prior to the contract in order for them to make rational choices.

These two prongs of protection, the vetted provider and deliberate disclosure, have been complemented by a third measure, the search for sustained fair market conduct by prohibiting a multitude of activities such as high pressure sales and conduct or representations described as false, misleading or unjust. These build on common law and equitable doctrines of misrepresentation, duress, mistake and unconscionability.

Added to these is a fourth, the earliest form of protection, modification of the contract. The first of these is the implied term. Terms implied in fact or implied in law have a long history in contract law and in particular in the Indian Contract Act, 1872, and subsequently the English Sale of Goods Act 1893. Australian states adopted English sales legislation passing their own legislation from the late nineteenth century and later modifying the implied term for consumer protection purposes. In Australia, this was done first by making the implied terms non-excludable in consumer contracts and then circumventing privity of contract by making manufacturers liable, if liability would otherwise arise by reason of an implied term. Since the introduction of the ACL, Australia has shifted away from the use of contractual terms for consumer protection. Similar protection is now provided by consumer guarantees. These are not terms in a contract. They establish

---

[32]On responsive regulation in the Australian context see The Senate, Economics Reference Committee "Regulatory theories and their application to ASIC" in *Performance of the Australian Securities and Investments Commission* Cth of Australia, –/6/2014 at 28.

[33]S 219 ACL.

[34]S 218 ACL.

[35]S 223 ACL.

[36]S 239 ACL.

[37]There are voluntary codes of conduct and Ombudsman schemes in both the goods and services and financial services sectors. On a particular sector see Howell (2015), p. 544. There is currently problem with unpaid compensation following determinations made against financial advisers by the Financial Ombudsman Service see The Senate Economics References Committee, Commonwealth of Australia, *Scrutiny of Financial Advice* Submission No 14.

performance standards for goods and services whose content is similar to that required of an implied term. The contract may also be modified post formation if a term is unfair[38] or if the conduct associated with it is unjust or unconscionable.

The fifth measure of protection involves regulation of the standards for products and services. These may concern the goods or services irrespective of the buyer, or they may require a match between the goods and services and the buyer. This involves product information standards, product safety standards, and liability for defective goods, that is, those that are not as safe as what consumers generally are entitled to expect, if they cause harm. Standards of performance linked to the characteristics of the buyer or acquirer are present in the term of fitness for purpose. They are also required for consumer credit, which must be assessed as 'not unsuitable' for the debtor. There is a current debate as to whether other financial service products should also be suitable for the acquirer.

The sixth measure of protection, relevant to those saving for their retirement, those investing and those needing credit for housing, purchase of goods and services or everyday consumption, is financial literacy.[39] There is a link between levels of financial literacy and the ability to make use of information disclosed to consumers.

The 2014 Financial System Inquiry explored the limits of freedom of contract based on disclosure. It concluded that there were shortcomings in disclosure as a regulatory tool, much disclosure was ineffective, behavioural biases challenge the notion that individuals are rational and this further limits the utility of disclosure.[40] It also said that financial literacy is not the sole answer.[41] Nevertheless, it recommended more innovative forms of disclosure while at the same time increasing product issuer and seller liability for product design and distribution.[42]

---

[38] If a term is unfair, the contract stands if it can operate without the term and the term is void. This was the decision in *Australian Competition and Consumer Commission v ACN 117372915 Pty Limited (in liq) (formerly Advanced Medical Institute Pty Limited)* [2015] FCA 368 (Federal Court of Australia). This case involved the sale of nasal spray to men with erectile dysfunction. At [954], the following term was held void as unfair: *Termination. Sexual dysfunction is a chronic condition and treatment can take some time. For this reason we stipulate that your contract with us for* [sic] *the period decided in the first consultation with the AMI doctor. You may cancel your treatment program with AMI at any time by giving AMI not less than 30 days notice. Cancelling your treatment program you will be entitled to a refund for the unexpired period of your treatment program less an administration fee of 15% and less the cost of any medication already provided to or prepared for you. No refund will be provided for the expired period of the treatment program or the 30 day notice period. All cancellation must be communicated to AMI in writing signed by you. Oral cancellation will not be accepted in any circumstances.*" The conduct of targeting vulnerable men was also held unconscionable.

[39] Australia has significant financial literacy programs sponsored by regulators, notably ASIC and by the private sector, notably banks. See e.g. *ANZ Survey of Adult Financial Literacy in Australia*, –/5/2015.

[40] Commonwealth of Australia, *Financial System Inquiry Final Report*, November 2014 (Murray) at 9, 94.

[41] Ibid at 193.

[42] Ibid at 194.

The 2015 Competition Review squarely endorsed a consumer choice model.[43] It leavened this with references to the 'right' information on which to base a choice, the importance of comparison for choice, including comparator websites, and recommended that governments should use the insights of behavioural economics to regulate presentation of 'information and choices in ways that allow consumers to access, assess and act on them'.[44] Financial calculators are also a choice aid.[45]

There will be an ongoing tension between residual notions of freedom of contract, rational choice theory and different varieties of closer protection through tests of fair conduct, safety and suitability. It will be testing to devise regulatory strategies that account for individuals' cognitive biases. A further challenge, particularly in the light of widespread non-compliance in some sectors of the financial service market, is whether complete faith in responsive regulation should be sustained.

20.3 Some Agenda Items for the ACL Review

20.3.1 A General Unfair Business Practices Rule?

Should there be a general unfair business practices rule? If so, should it encompass business to consumer practices only or also embrace business-to-business practices? There is currently a live debate on amending the rules on anti-competitive behaviour to more closely regulate big business.[46] Australia already has prohibitions against misleading or deceptive conduct, unconscionable conduct and unfair contractual terms. There is a long-standing prohibition against conduct that is or is likely to be misleading or deceptive.[47] This is complimented by a prohibition against false representations.[48] There is a highly developed equity jurisprudence and statutory prohibition against unconscionable conduct.[49] The prohibition against unfair contractual terms applies to standard form contracts with a consumer or small

---

[43]Commonwealth of Australia (2015), p. 293.

[44]Ibid at 305 Recommendation 21. On comparison websites and their regulation, see also *ACCC and AER Annual Report 2014–2015* at 51; ACCC *The Comparator Website Industry in Australia*, –/11/2014.

[45]ASIC/Latitude Insights Report 455 *Consumer testing of the Choice product dashboard* –/9/ 2014; ASIC Consultation Paper 249 *Remaking ASIC Class Order on generic financial calculators: [CO 05/1122]*, –/12/2015.

[46]M. Han, *Former ACCC head slams successor's plan Sims power push runs into trouble*, Australian Financial Review 1, (12/1/2016). The proposal is to amend s 46 CCA to eliminate the requirement that the prohibition on use of monopoly power requires the company to 'take advantage'.

[47]S 18 ACL; S 12DA ASIC Act.

[48]S 19 ACL; S 12DB ASIC Act.

[49]Ss 20, 21, 22ACL; Ss 12CA, 12CB, 12CD ASIC Act.

business.[50] There are many further specific prohibitions such as prohibitions against pyramid selling and harassment and coercion.[51] An unfair commercial practices rule was considered prior to the ACL and rejected.

20.3.2 Penalties

It is likely that in the review of the ACL, the ACCC will argue that the maximum civil penalty for a contravention of the Act should be increased.

The structure of the ACL and the ASIC Act is that a contravention may be either a civil matter or a criminal offence, the differences being in the standard of proof and the penalty.[52] There are some exceptions to this such as the contravention of the prohibitions against misleading or deceptive conduct.[53] Civil penalties may also be imposed under the *National Consumer Credit and Protection Act* 2009 (Cth).[54]

The civil penalty regime was at issue in *Australian Competition and Consumer Commission v Coles Supermarkets Australia Pty Ltd.* [2014] FCA 1405. In this case, Coles accepted that it had contravened the unconscionability provision of the ACL by deliberately using its stronger bargaining position to make threats of commercial consequences to five smaller suppliers if they did not pay an ongoing rebate to Coles and if they did not make payments outside the supply contracts for profit gaps and wastage. The ACCC and Coles asked the Court to impose ACL s 224 penalties in respect of the two sets of contraventions against the five suppliers. In the judgment, Gordon J said: 'it is a matter for the Parliament to review whether the maximum penalty of $1.1 million for each contravention of Pt 2-2 of the ACL by a body corporate is sufficient when a corporation with annual revenue in excess of $22 billion acts unconscionably. The current maximum penalties are arguably inadequate for a corporation the size of Coles'.[55] The total civil penalty imposed on Coles was $6,300,000.[56] The Court examined the quantum of the penalties under different headings: the amount of loss caused and profit gained; whether Coles had engaged in similar prior conduct; the size of the contravener Coles, including its

[50] S 23 ACL; S 23 ASIC Act.

[51] Ss 44, 50 ACL; Ss 12DK, 12DJ ASIC Act.

[52] On civil penalties in Australia see Australian Law Reform Commission, *Principled Regulation Civil and Administrative Penalties in Australia* [2001] ALRC 95; ASIC Report 387 *Penalties for Corporate Wrongdoing* March 2014.

[53] S 224(1) ACL.

[54] S 167 NCCPA. The first proceeding was a contravention by a person advertising that he could provide credit when he was not licensed to do so. *Australian Securities and Investments Commission v ACN 092879733 Pty Ltd.* [2012] FCA 923 (Federal Court of Australia).

[55] *Australian Competition and Consumer Commission v Coles Supermarkets Australia Pty Ltd.* [2014] FCA 1405 (Federal Court of Australia) at [106].

[56] Ibid at [229].

market share and financial position; the deliberateness of the conduct; the involvement of senior employees or management; the culture of compliance and corrective measure in response to the contravention; cooperation with the regulator; maximum penalties; the one transaction principle; and the totality principle. It will be noted that the penalties imposed were for each particular contravention but were not the maximum that could be imposed as the Court did not consider these the gravest of contraventions.

GE Capital was likely to lose about $6 million as a result of changes to the law prohibiting unsolicited credit limit extension offers and in response deliberately made misrepresentations that activating a credit card would give consent to receiving such offers. There were three contraventions, and the total amount that could be imposed was $3.3 million. The Court opined that the contraventions should not be assessed at the lowest end and imposed penalties of $1.5 million, taking into account the absence of a compliance program.[57]

Since *GE Capital* and *Coles*, the High Court has commented on pecuniary penalty regimes in Australian law. Their purpose is to secure compliance and facilitate enforcement while maintaining a distinction between civil and criminal penalties, because conviction carries a stigma.[58] Typically, legislative regimes with civil penalties have 'a range of enforcement mechanisms including injunctions, compensation orders, disqualification orders and civil penalties', and in choosing an enforcement mechanism, the regulator must 'balance considerations of compensation, prevention and deterrence'.[59] The issue before the High Court was whether the Court could receive submissions on penalties that had been agreed between the regulator and the contravener. The Full Bench agreed that it could, saying: 'there is an important public policy involved in promoting predictability of outcome in civil penalty proceedings and that the practice of receiving and, if appropriate, accepting agreed penalty submissions increases the predictability of outcome for regulators and wrongdoers'.[60] This decision means that a business and regulator will be able to negotiate agreed facts and penalties, and if the Court is persuaded that this is accurate and appropriate, this can be the penalty. The Court can still give the parties the opportunity to withdraw consent if the penalty is not appropriate.

---

[57] *Australian Securities and Investments Commission v G E Capital Finance Australia, in the matter of GE Capital Finance Australia* [2014] FCA 701 (Federal Court of Australia) at [96], [100].

[58] *Commonwealth of Australia v Director, Fair Work Building Industry Inspectorate; Construction, Forestry, Mining and Energy Union v Director, Fair Work Building Industry Inspectorate* [2015] HCA 46 (High Court of Australia) at [16], [17], [22], [24].

[59] Ibid at [24].

[60] Ibid at [46].

20.3.3 The Vulnerable

There are fears that technology, product complexity and an ageing population are creating more vulnerable consumers.[61] Australian consumer laws contain numerous protections of the vulnerable. The equity and equity-based prohibitions against unconscionable conduct require a finding that the plaintiff be at a special disadvantage vis-à-vis the defendant, who must know of that disadvantage. The courts have adopted an expansive view of what constitutes a special disadvantage, including emotional vulnerability,[62] but not so far as to protect those able to protect themselves.[63] The test for the general prohibition against misleading and deceptive conduct directed towards sections of the public rather than a particular person takes into account the 'target audience', which would capture an audience with vulnerable characteristics.[64] There are special protections for the vulnerable in consumer credit transactions. All consumer loans must be suitable for the borrower, that is, the borrower must have the capacity to repay without substantial hardship, and the loan must meet their objectives and requirements.[65] The special protections include banning short-term loans, restricting loans to social security recipients and special provisions for reverse mortgages, usually taken out by the elderly.[66] In 2015, substantial civil penalties were imposed on a consumer leasing company that dealt with social security recipients and had breached its disclosure and suitability obligations. While acknowledging that commercial operators may supply valuable services to vulnerable consumers, the Court said: 'Commercial behaviour leveraged off the vulnerability of others will be closely scrutinised and disciplined where it departs from the normative standards enshrined in legislation.'[67]

Since 2005, there have been special strategies to protect indigenous consumer rights. The objectives of the 2005–2010 plan were improving indigenous knowledge of rights and obligations, improving trader behaviour to reduce indigenous detriment and promoting partnerships between consumer agencies and indigenous organisations. The 2010–2013 plan had three strategic objectives—trading practices, housing and consumer literacy.[68] There is particular concern about door-to-door

---

[61] Harper, Supra Note 43 at 300.

[62] *Louth v Diprose* [1992] HCA 61 (High Court of Australia); on the elderly see *Australian Competition and Consumer Commission v Lux Distributors Pty Ltd.* [2013] FCAFC 90 (Full Court Federal Court of Australia).

[63] *Kakavas v Crown Melbourne Ltd.* [2013] HCA 25 (High Court of Australia).

[64] For a comparison of this test as recently applied in consumer protection and investor protection. See Corones (2014), p. 281.

[65] S 115, S 128 NCCPA.

[66] Burns (2013), p. 611.

[67] *Make it Mine Finance Pty Ltd., in the matter of Make it Mine Finance (No 2)* [2015] FCA 1255 (Federal Court of Australia) at [19], [122].

[68] Ministerial Council of Consumer Affairs, *Taking Action, gaining Trust* National Consumer Strategy Plan 2010–2013 p 2.

selling, misleading marketing, debt collection and 'book-up', particularly where traders control bank accounts.[69] The 2014–2016 plan includes a 'Be Smart – Buy Smart' resource for indigenous communities. In 2015, there was a national campaign to prevent indigenous consumers entering funeral plan contracts that they do not understand and are unsuitable.[70]

Substantive legislative requirements have limited effect if the vulnerable are unable to access determination of their rights. There is a highly developed network of Financial Counsellors who assist the vulnerable with debt.[71] There are consumer law centres and pro-bono activity by large law firms. State-based tribunals have very small fees compared with courts. Ombudsmen Schemes such as the Financial Services Ombudsman are free for consumers. One proposal might be a Retail Ombudsman, funded by retailers.

20.3.4 The Sharing Economy

Much existing regulation is predicated on the provider being a business. For instance, in Australia, the prohibitions on misleading or deceptive conduct and unconscionable conduct require the conduct to be in trade and commerce. The unfair terms prohibition requires a standard form contract, a boiler plate contract generated by business. The consumer guarantees require the goods or services to be supplied. The regulation of consumer credit requires the credit provider to be lending as a business. The provision of a financial product or service will be in business. This is antithetical to the sharing or collaborative economy, usually predicated on platforms that might be information publishers, marketers, price setters or payment processers.[72] Platforms also present a competition issue.[73]

A clear example of the sharing economy is peer-to-peer lending. A platform allows lenders that are not banks (and may not be in the business of lending) and potential borrowers to interact. The biggest peer-to-peer lenders in Australia are SocietyOne and Ratesetters.[74] Loans are at lower rates of interest than bank rates. This will benefit consumers. However, if the lender is not in the business of lending,

---

[69]Ibid at 4, 5. On unsolicited sales in indigenous communities see *Australian Competition and Consumer Commission v Titan Marketing Pty Ltd.* [2014] FCA 913 (Federal Court of Australia); see also http://www.accc.gov.au/media-release/accc-takes-action-against-fdra-for-alleged-consumer-law-breaches-in-aboriginal-communities January 2016, last seen on 14/1/2016.

[70]Avoid a funeral rip-off campaign to protect indigenous consumers NSW Fair Trading, Media Release 27/7/2015. See the Avoid a funeral rip-off video on the NSW Fair Trading YouTube channel at http://bit.ly/1KsG2V4, last seen on 14/1/2016.

[71]Financial Counsellors Australia.

[72]Deloitte Access Economics, *The sharing economy and the Competition and Consumer Act*, ACCC 2015 at v, 1ff.

[73]Harper, Supra Note 43 at 135.

[74]https://www.societyone.com.au/; https://www.ratesetter.com.au/, last seen on 6/1/2016.

the protections in the *National Consumer Credit Protection Act 2009* (Cth) based on disclosure of information about the credit contract, assessment of suitability and hardship provisions will not apply.[75] A further example might be crowd-sourced funding.[76]

Uber, the ride sharing platform, and Airbnb, the share room or accommodation platform, have a presence in Australia.[77] Uber is slowly being legalised in Australia as the ACT has been followed by NSW and Western Australia.[78] In Victoria, it is illegal.[79] It nevertheless operates with fierce opposition from the taxi industry. Taxis and hire cars must be licensed; their drivers must pass examinations and be accredited.[80] They are subject to safety inspections, and civil penalties may be imposed. This protects consumers. By contrast, Uber drivers are not automatically covered by their personal insurance policies, so they may be completely uninsured.[81] Real estate agents who assist in the rental of holiday accommodation must be licensed.[82] There is a Property Services Compensation Fund established by the Act to which licensees must contribute,[83] and professional indemnity insurance requirements.[84] The Compensation Fund protects persons if a real estate agent fails to account for monies held by him.[85] This gives a measure of protection to consumers. By contrast, those renting via accommodation platforms such as Airbnb enter into a contract with the accommodation provider, who may or may not be insured and who may or may not return any deposit or bond monies.

Questions arise as to the extent to which private persons who offer services such as loans, rides and accommodation should be treated as businesses for consumer protection purposes and whether facilitative platforms should share some liability with these service providers.

A different perspective would emphasise self-regulation, reputational rating, and certification rather than occupational licensing, permitting platforms to develop their own regulation and insurance.[86]

---

[75]The Act requires the credit provider to provide credit in the course of a business of providing credit in this jurisdiction or as part of or incidentally to any other business of the credit provider carried on in this jurisdiction: S 5 (1) (d) NCCPA.

[76]The Corporations Amendment (Crowd-sourced Funding) Bill 2015 (Cth) is currently the subject of an inquiry by the Senate Economics Legislation Committee.

[77]On the sharing economy. See Kaplan and Nadler (2015), p. 103; In less than 2 years Uber transactions increased from 1 to 22% relative to electronic taxi transactions, Deloitte Access Economics, Supra Note 73 at 9.

[78]Sier (2015) and McDuling (2015).

[79]Butler (2015).

[80]E.g. *Passenger Transport Act 2014* (NSW).

[81]Khadem (2015).

[82]See *Property, Stock and Business Agents Act 2002* (NSW).

[83]Ss 3, 17A(2), s 165 *Property, Stock and Business Agents Act 2002* (NSW).

[84]S 22 *Property, Stock and Business Agents Act 2002* (NSW).

[85]S 173 *Property, Stock and Business Agents Act 2002* (NSW).

[86]Allen and Berg (2014).

20.3.5 Consumer Access to Data

To what extent should consumers have access to data held about them by bodies that collect data? Consumer data, aggregated and individualized, are used for commercial decision-making and for marketing. The supermarket needs to understand what products to stock, in what quantities and which dates particular products are in high demand. We receive advertising individualised to our perceived needs on our phones and computers. Wider access to private sector data is said to be a key to innovation and competition.[87]

In *Google Inc. v Australian Competition and Consumer Commission* [2013] HCA 1, the High Court of Australia rejected an argument that Google was liable for misleading advertisements created by advertisers (not Google) that appeared as 'sponsored links' when consumers entered certain search terms. 'Sponsored links' are different from organic links thrown up by consumer search terms. Advertisers participated in Google's Adwords program, which allowed them to specify the keyword that would generate a 'sponsored link'. The High Court found that Google had not made the statements in the advertisements, nor had it endorsed them. It had not engaged in misleading or deceptive conduct. Google was like other intermediaries such as newspapers, passing along information.[88] This link between searches and advertising raises the question of data that search engines have and whether consumers should have access to it.

Consumers have access to their data held by credit reference bureaux. They can ensure that it is accurate.[89] This is important as credit checks have become important for lenders in establishing whether a loan is 'not unsuitable' for the potential borrower. One part of the three-pronged suitability test is that the borrower has the capacity to repay the loan without substantial hardship. The consequences of inaccurate data might prove detrimental to a consumer wrongly denied or granted credit.

Detailed usage data for services such as credit cards, phones, Internet connections, water, gas and electricity are regularly provided with accounts requiring payment. Numerous service and product providers have loyalty schemes that reward individuals for repeat usage. These include Frequent Flyer points for airline travel, FlyBuy and discount schemes (including for petrol) at supermarkets and loyalty cards with associated discounts at outlets as diverse as bookshops, sporting wear stores and fashion stores. If consumers had access to this data, would they be able to use it? Would they be able to check its accuracy? Is there an over-riding principle that they should have such access?

---

[87]Murray, Supra Note 40 at 188.

[88]*Google Inc. v Australian Competition and Consumer Commission* [2013] HCA 1 (High Court of Australia) at [68]–[70].

[89]Part 111A *Privacy Act 1988* (Cth). There is also voluntary comprehensive credit reporting to share positive credit data. The FSI Report recommended there should be a review of this in 2017 Murray, Supra Note 40 at 190.

International online platforms such as Amazon can predict what particular items (which book by which author, which CD by which obscure composer) a consumer might buy. Amazon uses first-, second- and third-party data.[90] Banks have large investments in data about consumer buying habits through digital finance and financial information about their customers.[91] With suitable algorithms, they can target individuals who have made one purchase with offers of related purchases. For instance, an individual buys an international flight with a credit card; the bank can almost instantly offer foreign exchange or travel insurance. In 2015, the Commonwealth Bank of Australia released an app to recognise when customers enter a shopping centre and send offers from retailers to the customers' smart phones.[92]

Should consumers have access to this data about themselves? Under Australian Privacy Principle 12, if an individual requests information about their personal information, in general, it should be given to them.[93] Given the limits of information disclosure as a strategy for optimum consumer choices, will possibly unprocessed data that consumers receive about themselves be any more helpful? The US Smart Disclosure Report asserts that such information can help consumers make 'dramatically easier' choices and promote efficiency, innovation, economic growth.[94] This view is supported in the Competition Review, which concluded that businesses and consumers should benefit from information about individuals who if they receive information about their own consumption should change their behaviours, which would lead to innovation and competition, provided that the information is useable.[95]

20.3.6 International Safety Standards

In 2014, the Federal Court ordered Alpha, which operated in-flight sales for Qantas on international flights, and Qantas to publish adverse publicity orders, pay pecuniary penalties, pay full refunds to buyers and destroy and dispose of nanodots, that is, small high-powered magnets that were banned in Australia for being dangerous to children, who might swallow them.[96] Even safety is not immune from scammers. In 2015, the Federal Court declared that a firm, Safety Compliance Pty Ltd., had contravened the ACL by falsely representing that small businesses need safety wall

[90]Accenture (2015), p. 9.

[91]Ibid at 6, 7.

[92]Yeates (2016).

[93]S 12 *Privacy Act 1988* (Cth) Schedule 1. There are restrictions on this: s 12.2; s 12.3.

[94]Executive Office of the President (2013), pp. 8, 9.

[95]Harper, supra Note 43 at 303.

[96]*Director of Consumer Affairs Victoria v Alpha Flight Services Pty Ltd.* [2014] FCA 1434 (Federal Court of Australia).

charts and first aid kits, sold by the firm, to comply with workplace safety requirements.[97]

Australia has extensive regulation of product safety. In addition to tort law, now partially codified in the state-based Civil Liability Acts, there are detailed provisions in the Australian Consumer Law. The Minister may make or declare safety standards for goods and for services.[98] Declared standards can be those prepared or approved by Standards Australia.[99] There may be either civil or criminal consequences if goods or services subject to a safety standard are supplied and do not comply with that standard.[100] There may be warnings about unsafe goods, and they may be recalled or banned.[101] Important new reporting provisions were introduced in the ACL to require suppliers to report goods or product-related services that may have caused death, serious injury or illness by use or foreseeable misuse.[102]

A major generator of safety standards is the International Standards Organisation (ISO).[103] Common standards for products have an important role in trade facilitation and harmonisation. Standards can both enhance and inhibit competition.[104] The United Nations Economic Commission for Europe (UNECE) also generates standards. In February 2015, Standards Australia held a forum to consider motorbike helmet standard regulation. This highlighted two regulatory problems. ACCC mandatory standards could not be automatically updated with changes to the pertinent Australian Standard, and referencing an international Standard as a mandatory Australian Standard created copyright problems.[105] In some cases, individuals needed special exemptions for larger motorcycle helmets that complied with international standards, and NSW was considering altering its laws so that an approved motorcycle helmet would include those complying with the Australian Standard and with the UNECE Standard. The Harper Report recommended a review of all standards and whether international standards can be adopted.[106] Supported by the Council of Australian Governments (COAG), the ACCC appears keen to find a way to reference well-established international standards.

---

[97] *Australian Competition and Consumer Commission v Safety Compliance Pty Ltd. (in liq) (No 2)* [2015] FCA 1469 (Federal Court of Australia); *Safety Compliance Pty Ltd. and individuals ordered to pay penalties for misleading small businesses* ACCC MR 274/15, 23/12/2015.

[98] S 104, S 105 ACL.

[99] S 105 (1) ACL. On the role of Standards Australia see Harper supra Note 43 at 136, Box 10.8.

[100] S 194 ACL.

[101] Products recalled in 2014–2015 include frozen berries, infinity electrical cable and vehicle airbags.

[102] S 131, S 132 ACL.

[103] For instance ISO/TS 20245:2014 is a standard for cross border exchange of second hand goods.

[104] Harper, Supra Note 43 at 135f.

[105] Standards Australia *Forum on AS/NZS 1698: 2006 Protective helmets for vehicle users* February 19 2015; R. Sims, Chairman ACCC, *Keynote Presentation: Australasian Consumer Law Roundtable 2015* 1/12/2015.

[106] Harper Supra Note 43 at 139, 140 Recommendation 10.

20.3.7 International Law, Cooperation, and Consumers

While Australia is an active participant in trading blocs, there is no equivalent to the EU and its Directives on matters going to consumer protection. The ACL is part of gradual harmonisation of Australian and New Zealand laws.[107] The ACL does not apply if a buyer buys from an overseas seller or from a private seller. Regulator websites carry warnings about online sales. The ACCC has an online shopping scam webpage.[108] Online international shopping remains a major challenge for domestic regulators.[109]ASIC cooperates internationally and issued principles directed in part to lowering regulatory barriers between jurisdictions.[110] A problem with platforms operating in Australia is standard form contracts used internationally that do not conform with Australian law.[111]

The ACCC is an active member of the International Consumer Protection and Enforcement Network (ICPEN), constituted by 50 consumer protection agencies.[112] It promotes global cooperation and shares information about cross-border activities. One of its initiatives is econsumer.gov, a site for consumers to report international scams. As part of this international cooperation, the ACCC recently swept websites and apps looking for drip pricing.[113] Drip pricing is when a site advertises one price and then successively adds on additional charges as part of the purchasing process, so there is a discrepancy between the advertised price and the ultimate price. This has been particularly rife in travel, accommodation and ticketing services. In *Australian Competition and Consumer Commission v Jetstar Airways Pty Limited* [2015] FCA 1263, the Federal Court found that Jetstar and Virgin Australia Airlines had engaged in drip pricing, sucking consumers, through progressive disclosures on its online booking site, into the seller's marketing web. This was misleading and in contravention of ACL s 18. The Court followed the High Court of Australia in *Australian Competition and Consumer Commission v TPG Internet* [2013] HCA 54, where it was held that the general thrust of information may mislead even if it is later corrected.[114] Add-ons are one important issue in cross-border consumer transactions. Safety standards are another. There is potential

---

[107]Both Australia and New Zealand are also members of the OECD Committee on Consumer Policy.

[108]http://www.scamwatch.gov.au/types-of-scams/buying-or-selling/online-shopping-scams, last seen 12/1/2016.

[109]Gawith (2006), p. 115.

[110]ASIC *Regulatory Guide 54 Principles for Cross Border Regulation* –/6/2012.

[111]Deloitte Access Economics, Supra Note 73 at vii.

[112]http://www.icpen.org/, last seen 8/1/2016.

[113]*Internet sweep shows improvements to disclosure in online booking processes* ACCC MR 258/15, 16/12/2015.

[114]*Australian Competition and Consumer Commission v Jetstar Airways Pty Limited* [2015] FCA 1263 (Federal Court of Australia) [33]–[41].

for much greater alignment and harmonisation of laws to protect consumers in the Indo-Pacific region.

20.3.8 Some Tidying Up

Inevitably in a review process, there is legislative tidying up. This can involve shifts in policy or simply the search for consistency. Some of the matters on the agenda are whether the consumer guarantee regime should be extended to financial services as the ASIC Act has retained implied terms rather than consumer guarantees,[115] inconsistent liability of linked credit providers for goods under the ACL and the NCCPA, the extension of the prohibition on unfair contractual terms to insurance contracts, whether unfair term prohibitions should apply more widely than standard form contracts.[116]

20.4 Conclusion

Robust consumer protection can enhance an efficient and competitive market economy and drive productivity. The review of the ACL is an opportunity to reflect on legislation and current regulatory challenges. Regulatory architects have built two market citadels. In reality, some activities fall between each. More importantly, this has led to overlapping statutory constructs, which even senior judges find challenging. A review of the ACL should identify all gaps and inconsistencies between the Competition and Consumer Act and the ASIC Act. Many of the items identified have a competition dimension. There should be greater focus on eliminating definitional problems. Both the ACCC and ASIC put substantial resources into education and persuasion. It is clear that some economic actors do not wish to comply with the law. It may be time to put less emphasis on responsive regulation and even more on enforcement. While consumer choice must be maintained, it is too easy to manipulate cognitive biases, particularly in rapidly changing digital and international environments.

[115]It was held that extended warranties are financial services in *Australian Competition and Consumer Commission v Fisher & Paykel Customer Services Pty Ltd.* [2014] FCA 1393 (Federal Court of Australia) at [26].

[116]There is a wide interpretation of standard form contract. In *Australian Competition and Consumer Commission v Chrisco Hampers Australia Limited* [2015] FCA 1204 (Federal Court of Australia) a contract which had an opt out term and under which consumers could select items from a catalogue was a standard form contract.

References

Accenture (2015) North America consumer digital banking survey – Banking shaped by the customer

Allen D, Berg C (2014) The sharing economy – how over-regulation could destroy and economic revolution. Institute of Public Affairs December. www.ipa.org.au. Accessed 10 Jan 2016

Burns F (2013) The evolving statutory regulation of reverse mortgages in Australia's 'risk society'. Monash Univ Law Rev 39(3):611

Butler B (2015) Double trouble for Uber as it faces court cases the Australian, 26 September

Commonwealth of Australia (2011) Australian Consumer Survey 2011, June

Commonwealth of Australia (2015) Competition Policy Review Final Report, March, (Harper)

Corones S (2014) Australian competition and consumer commission v TPG internet; Forrest v Australian securities and investments commission. Melb Univ Law Rev 38(1):281

Executive Office of the President (2013) National Science and Technology Council Smart Disclosure and Consumer Decision Making: Report of the Task force on Smart Disclosure, Washington, May

Gawith D (2006) Non litigation based redress for international consumer transactions in not cost-effective – a case for reform? Macquarie J Bus Law 3:115

Howell N (2015) Revisiting the Australian banking code of practice: is self-regulation still relevant for improving consumer protection standards? Univ N S Wales Law J 38(2):544

Kaplan RA, Nadler ML (2015) Airbnb: a case study in occupancy regulation and taxation. Univ Chicago Law Rev Dialogue 82:103

Khadem N (2015) Are Airbnb and Uber Creating a New Black Economy? Sydney Morning Herald, 12 February

McDuling J (2015) Uber is winning its war with the Australian taxi lobby. Sydney Morning Herald, 21 December

Ministerial Council of Consumer Affairs, Taking Action, Gaining Trust National Consumer Strategy Plan 2010 2013

Sier J (2015) The Untold Story of Uber's arrival in Australia. Australian Financial Review, 2 December

Yeates C (2016) Banks use big data to fight competition The Sydney Morning Herald 3, 2–3, January

Chapter 21
The Emergence and Development of Chinese 3.15 Anticounterfeiting

Shan He

21.1 The Meaning of 3.15 Anticounterfeiting

The 3.15 anticounterfeiting measure is a special phenomenon in China. Its core originates from the punitive damages in the Law of the PRC on the Protection of the Rights and Interests of Consumers in 1993. After the Supreme People's Court had formulated the Provisions on Several Issues Concerning the Application of Law in the Trial of Food and Drug Dispute, 3.15 anticounterfeiting damages showed the trend of the outbreak.

As opposed to official anticounterfeiting, 3.15 anticounterfeiting is a broad concept, which includes anticounterfeiting damages from customers who are defrauded or suspected to be defrauded, unofficial professional persons, trademark owners, ordinary citizens and legal persons that report to the administrative department, the media, and the social organizations that support anticounterfeiting, so unofficial professional person is only one of them. The core of 3.15 anticounterfeiting is 3.15 anticounterfeiting damages. 3.15 anticounterfeiting damages are punitive compensation; the punitive compensation contains the meaning of sanctions, which constitutes 3.15 anticounterfeiting damages. Ordinary civil compensation that has not the meaning of sanctions does not constitute 3.15 anticounterfeiting damages.

The draft of the chapter was translated by Wang Yinhuan.

S. He (✉)
Association of Consumer Law, China Law Society, Beijing, China
e-mail: hs1213@npc.gov.cn

C. Lima Marques, D. Wei (eds.), *Consumer Law and Socioeconomic Development*,
DOI 10.1007/978-3-319-55624-6_21

21.2 Social Origins of 3.15 Anticounterfeiting

The system of 3.15 anticounterfeiting appeared at the beginning of the Chinese market economy. At this time, its appearance has deep social origins.

The third plenary session of the 11th party implementing reform and opening up established the development of a socialist market economy. For 30 years, earth-shaking changes have taken place in China, commodity economy developed rapidly, the living standards of the masses of the people are improved greatly.

Market economy is so good, why did it cause 3.15 anticounterfeiting?

Firstly, the basic rule of market economy operation is competition. The competition among business operators seems to be a good method to give the market the best supply and to protect the customers, even the economic interests of the whole society. Competition promotes the development of the commodity economy; meanwhile, the competition caused the survival of the fittest. To the business operators, it is the live-death issue at stake. The weak operators would rack their brains, even take all kinds of means to live, in order not to be eliminated in the fierce competition of the market. Therefore, if the competition exists, the confusion of counterfeits, the misleading of false propaganda, the slander of making up a lie, and even commercial bribe, infringement of trade secrets, tying, dumping, win sales, abuse of monopoly, and business with power come out one by one.

Secondly, market economy is commodity economy; its instinct is to pursue maximum profit. Earning money is the inner power of the businessman. Profit is neither commentary nor derogatory but a neutral word. Illegal operators seek profits through fraud and deception above the law. Marx is quoted from the quarterly review: "with adequate profit, capital is very bold. A certain 10% will ensure its employment anywhere; 20%, certain will produce eagerness, 50%, positive audacity; 100%, will make it ready to trample on all human laws, 300%, and there is not a crime an which it will scruple nor a risk it will not run, even to the chance of its owner being hanged."

This is the origin of "counterfeiting" of commodity economy. The tree wants to be quiet, but the wind is blowing. It is not transferred by people's will. It is the unity of opposites that there is counterfeiting, that there is anticounterfeiting. The official team consisting of the public security, the court, the Procuratorate, and the Administration for Industry and Commerce takes the responsibility of anticounterfeiting; they have more success, which makes illegal operators within earshot discouraged. But it is not a united team; some of them collapsed themselves in the "sugar-coated bullets" and drifted into the umbrella of counterfeiting. The more the administrative organs strike, the more the fake appeared in some place. Someone from the custom said: "We will catch nine vessels and set one free. If we catch ten vessels all, what will we do and how to get our achievements. This is ecological balance." This is Chinese reality, so we need to start 3.15 anticounterfeiting besides the official anticounterfeiting.

21.3 The Law of the PRC on the Protection of the Rights and Interests of Consumers Establishing Punitive Compensation

We cannot start 3.15 anticounterfeiting without the legislation of the Law of the PRC on the Protection of the Rights and Interests of Consumers and without the punitive compensation in it.

Why did the Law of the PRC on the Protection of the Rights and Interests of Consumers come into being? In the primary stage of socialism, it is the basic and the main contradiction between people's increasing material and cultural needs and the backward productive forces. Protecting rights and interests is the focal point of the contradiction. Only, we protect consumers; the producers would supple the more and the better food, which is conducive to production and harmonious to the society. Just as the UN Guidelines for Consumers said: "remember that the customers should have right to obtain a harmless product and promote fair and equitable and sustainable economic and social development." Based on this idea, in 1983, the International Consumer Union established the 15th of March as International Day for Customer's Rights and Interests. After China takes the road of market economy, protecting the customers' rights and interests would greatly promote the development of social production. At this time, 3.15 began in China; meanwhile, the establishment of the Chinese market economy bred the Law of the PRC on the Protection of the Rights and Interests of Consumers.

In the early 1990s, the Law of the PRC on the Protection of the Rights and Interests of Consumers was formulated; meanwhile, fake commodities are everywhere, in the state-owned enterprise and in the flea market, which infringed the customers. In this situation, how did the Law of the PRC on the Protection of the Rights and Interests of Consumers do? The law is not empty; it needs to solve realistic problems. How can the Law of the PRC on the Protection of the Rights and Interests of Consumers be formulated well? We need to fight against counterfeit goods, not only by the official administrative organs but also by the consumers. How can consumers be mobilized? The mechanism of using economic level is a good method—China folk "lack one, punish ten," which is formulated as the law is the punitive compensation. The customers who was cheated or who had known the counterfeit food and bought it can use this regulation to fight against illegal operator. For example, the customer buys a bottle of fake Mao Tai; besides the bottle belonging to the customer, the seller will give 10 times compensation to the customer. This will cause the customers to rush to buy the fake Mao Tai, and thus no seller dares to sell the counterfeit goods. The customers who are given the legal weapon "lack one, punish ten" and who are promoted to fight against counterfeit goods will get benefits. The fake one is just like a mouse; whenever it goes, vituperation follows. So there is nowhere to hide.

Appointed to draft the law, I spent half of the year considering and researching the problem of anticounterfeiting in the winter of 1991. In the Fu Zhou meeting in 1992, I put forward the idea of punitive compensation to fight against anticounterfeiting and had warmly approved reaction from colleagues of industrial and commercial Circles and Customers association. In the same year, I wrote the paper "Discussing the idea of 'lack one, punish ten.' in punitive damages," which set up the theoretical foundation to formulate the law of punitive damages. The idea is consistent with the new development of civil compensation theory. There is evolution process in the theory of civil compensation. In the early days of civil law, tort claims abide by the principle of liability for fault. It means if someone has fault, he/she needs to compensate, and vice versa. The development of commodity economy adds the principle without fault; it means if food causes personal injury or property damage and the customer suffers, he/she may claim for compensation from the seller and producer of the product. The country in chaos uses severe punishment; the murderous behavior intending to damage the customers' rights and interests must be punished ten times; these punitive damages include the compensation of the property and spirit.

After the hard work, the fourth session of the Standing Committee of the Eighth National People's Congress passed on Oct. 31, 1993, the Law of the PRC on the Protection of the Rights and Interests of Consumers with unanimous support. The article of punitive damages was finally written in the law. Article 49 provided: "If a business operator provides goods or services with fraud, it shall, in accordance with the requirements of consumer, increase compensation for the losses incurred, the amount of compensation for the consumers has doubled the price of purchasing goods, or the cost of receiving services." This regulation developed the punitive principles of the general rules of civil law; it is originated from civil law countries, which constitutes the core clause of the Law of the PRC on the Protection of the Rights and Interests of Consumers. Disability compensation, death compensation, and punitive damages jointly draw up "one fed flower, two blue leaves" in the Law of the PRC on the Protection of the Rights and Interests of Consumers, which are sharp legal weapons. The shining punitive compensation article provides a legal basis for customers' anticounterfeiting.

21.4 The Development of Punitive Compensation

Chinese punitive compensation indomitably developed deeply after the Law of the PRC on the Protection of the Rights and Interests of Consumers regulated it

21.4.1 10 Times Compensation in the Food Safety Law

On Feb, 28, 2009, the seventh session of the Standing Committee of the Eleventh National People's Congress passed the Food Safety Law. The provisions of paragraph 2 of Article 96 provide: "Besides claiming damages, a consumer may require the producer, who produced food which does not conform to the food safety standards, or the seller who knowingly sells food which does not conform to the food safety standards, to pay 10 times the money paid."

It added to pay two times the money paid in the punitive compensation through amending the Law of the PRC on the Protection of the Rights and Interests of Consumers. This regulation was written in the provisions of paragraph 2 of Article 55. It is agreeable to promote the development of punitive damages.

How should "10 times compensation" in the Food Safety Law be evaluated? I think "10 times compensation" developed our punitive compensation. Although "10 times compensation" needs to be improved if the consumer suffered extra damage, it increases fivefold compared with "2 times compensation." It has taken an important step forward in the system of Chinese punitive damages.

After the Law of the PRC on the Protection of the Rights and Interests of Consumers was amended, the Food Safety Law followed, the provisions of Article 148 provide: "Besides claiming damages, a consumer may require the producer, who produces food which does not conform to the good safety standards, or the seller who knowingly sell food which does not conform to the food safety standards, to pay 10 times the price paid or 3 times the damages paid, if that increase of compensation is less than 1000 yuan, to pay 1000 yuan paid." It adds the regulation of "3 times the damages paid."

21.4.2 Writing Punitive Compensation in Tort Law

The draft of the Tort Law did not have punitive compensation.

Under the joint efforts of everyone, on December 26, 2009, the 12th session of the Standing Committee of the Eleventh National People's Congress passed the Tort Law, which used the phrase "punitive compensation." The provisions of Article 47 provide: "where a manufacturer or seller knowing any defect of a product continues to manufacture or sell the product and the defect causes a death or any serious damages to the health of another person, the victim shall be entitled to require the corresponding punitive compensation." The punitive compensation can only be used on defective products, so it is written in Chapter V titled Product Liability.

The punitive compensation is applied widely, not only in product liability. On March 15, 2013, the Chinese law society on the protection of the Rights and Interests of Consumers held a seminar on the topic of "Management of illegal SMS and unauthorized commercial message." I also proposed to use punitive compensation to manage illegal SMS and unauthorized commercial message. The operator, who sends one message, will be punished 100 yuan. Who dares to send it? The customers will mobilize and eliminate the illegal SMS and unauthorized commercial message.

21.4.3 Punitive Compensation in Tourism Law

The Tourism Law covered punitive compensation, which was passed by the fourth session of the Standing Committee of the 12th National People's Congress. The provisions of paragraph 1 of Article 70 provide: "if the travel agency fails to perform its obligations agreed in the package tourism contract or perform its contracted obligations in a way that does not conform to the agreement, it shall take the responsibility for breach of contract like continuing to fulfill the contract, adopting remedy measures, making compensation, etc.; in case it causes personal damage or property loss to the tourists, the travel agency shall honor its liability. In the event that the travel agency is competent to fulfill its contracted obligations, yet refuses to do so even upon the request of the tourists, which then causes such serious consequences like harming the tourists' personal health or retaining the tourists, the tourists may also request the travel agency to pay a sum of compensation between one time and three times the amount of the travel costs."

21.4.4 Punitive Compensation in Trademark Law

The Trademark Law, which was amended according to the decision adopted at the fourth session of the Standing Committee of the 12th National People's Congress on August 30, 2003, added punitive compensation. The provisions of Article 63 provide: "The amount of damages for infringing the exclusive right to use a trademark shall be actual losses that the right owner has suffered as a result of the infringement during the period of the infringement; where the losses suffered by the right owner cannot be determined, the amount of damages for trademark infringement shall be the profits that the infringer has earned as a result of the infringement during the period of the infringement; where the losses suffered by the right owner, or the profits earned by the infringer, cannot be determined, the amount of damages shall be determined based on a reasonable amount that would be paid for a licensing royalty for the trademark right. If there is malicious infringement and an existence of serious circumstances, the amount may be more than one up to three times the aforesaid determined amount. The amount of damages will also include reasonable expenses the right owner has suffered to prevent the infringement. For the purpose of determining the amount of damages, where the account books and information related to the infringement are held by the infringer, and where the rights owner has presented as much proof of its claims as is practically possible, a People's Court may order the infringer to submit such account books and information. If the infringer refuses to submit such account books and information, or submit a false version thereof, a People's Court may determine the amount of damages with reference to the right owner's claims and proof. Where the actual losses suffered by the right owner, the profits earned by the infringer, or the licensing royalties of trademark infringement cannot be determined, a People's Court shall award damages up to RMB 3,000,000, depending on the facts of the case."

Most of the trademark owners are legal persons; the punitive compensation must cause the legal person to fight for the counterfeits. In 1996, I had published the paper "Further Studies on the Punitive Compensation." In this paper, I appealed to formulate a legal person anticounterfeiting regulation because legal persons are powerful; if they organize people to buy the counterfeits intentionally and claim to add compensation, if anticounterfeiting companies appear, who would dare to sell the counterfeit goods? This is anticounterfeiting by economic levels; it is more powerful than administrative behavior. After 20 years, the law of legal person appeared in the field of anticounterfeiting.

However, very few people knew about this article; it is difficult to find a case of anticounterfeiting by trademark owners. In order to further the punitive compensation of the amended Trademark Law and to promote anticounterfeiting of legal persons, cooperating with the Chinese law research society on intellectual property rights, the Chinese law research society on customers held a symposium for advocating and implementing punitive compensation on August 30, 2015, on the anniversary of the Trademark Law. The symposium aimed to promote the appearance of the trademark over "Wang Hai," to show the anticounterfeiting of legal persons to the Chinese people and to clarify the market by punitive compensation with more power.

21.4.5 The Amended Law of the PRC on the Protection of the Rights and Interests of Consumers Increasing the Amount of Compensation

On October 25, 2013, the fifth session of the Standing Committee of the 12th National People's Congress amended the Law of the PRC on the Protection of the Rights and Interests of Consumers secondly. The law raised the punitive compensation from one time to three times and regulated the double compensation for losses in the provisions of Article 55.

Aiming at the dishonesty with bluffs and deceits, punitive compensation developed in more fields. Under the regulations of punitive compensation, 3.15 anticounterfeiting constantly reached high tide. Roughly, there were six instances of upsurges; the first one was when the press in BTV took the lead in propagating the punitive compensation of Article 49 in the Law of the PRC on the Protection of the Rights and Interests of Consumers. The sign is broadcasting "Offering reward for Anti-counterfeiting" in 1995. The second one was when Wang Hai bought fake goods and claimed successfully in the winter of 1995. The third one was when the Court supported to claim compensation for the buyer. There are two cases: one was when a couple of Ren Xiaohui was cheated by fake furniture and claimed for double compensation; the other was XI Cheng Court's decision of Xu Beihong's fake drawing, which was the first case in which the customer bought a fake product while suspecting it. The fourth one was when the former vice director of Technical Supervision Bureau of Long Yan Municipality in Fu Jian province was prosecuted for a telephone fee worth "1.1 yuan." The fifth one is when the two-level courts of He Bi in He Nan condemned a fraud real estate developer to pay double purchases. The sixth one is when the Primary Court, the Intermediate Court, and the High Court gave a sentenced of double compensation for the price of a new car.

Six upsurges of anticounterfeiting caused great repercussions in society and promoted the movement of consumer protection vigorously. According to the statistics from China Consumers Association, ever year the amount of punitive compensation that the consumers obtain is millions of yuan. The huge figure constitutes a beautiful landscape.

21.5 Implementation of the Punitive Compensation

The Supreme Court supported the conclusion that the consumers bought fake products while knowing it in the Provisions on Several Issues Concerning the Application of Law in the Trial of Food and Drug Dispute more than a year after the Supreme Court formulated the judicial interpretation, so many problem need to be resolved regarding 3.15 anticounterfeiting. For example, some people defamed and committed prejudice against unofficial anticounterfeiting persons, who were hurt from time to time. And another claims excessive rights and damages. We need to research, demonstrate, and guide 3.15 anticounterfeiting in order to incorporate it into the legal track. My opinions are as follows:

1. Realize that the 3.15 anti-counterfeiting claims is the original intention of the 1993 law article 49 of punitive damages. The Supreme People's court established it on Several Issues concerning the application of law in the trial of disputes food and drug regulations clearly. The persons who fight against counterfeits seems like Woodpeckers, the Law of the PRC on the Protection of the Rights and Interests of Consumers Breeds of them, eats insects, guards the forest for the service of the green market. The behavior of defaming and having prejudice against unofficial anti-counterfeiting persons is wrong and illegal.
2. Realize that the 3.15 anti-counterfeiting claims must be the rational claim in accordance with the law. The Law of the PRC on the Protection of the Rights and Interests of Consumers regulated 3 times compensation, and the Food Safety Law regulated 10 times compensation. We should claim according to this amount, which is the line of the law impassably. Don't claim for hundreds of millions of yuan and ignore the law limits claim rights, that will lead to protect rights excessively.
3. Draw the boundaries of anti-counterfeiting claims and blackmail. it means that the excessive claim is not equal to the blackmail.

4. Remember that anti-counterfeiting can't do without the National administrative enforcement and Judicial organs. Without the official anti-counterfeiting, 3.15 anti-counterfeiting is a meaningless word with no result. Administrative enforcement and judicial organs is the main forces and the 3.15 anti-counterfeiting is the guerrilla units. The official organs and 3.15 anti-counterfeiting cooperate hand in hand, to fight a people's war, to wipe out the fake goods.

In 1993, the punitive compensation of Article 49 of the Law of the PRC on the Protection of the Rights and Interests of Consumers came out. In 1995, Wang Hai emerged. In 2015, thousands of anticounterfeiting persons stood out. The punitive compensation will continue to develop. The Law of the PRC on the Protection of the Rights and Interests of Consumers and the Food Safety Law will be perfect with time. Let us hold the banner of anticounterfeiting. Let us forge ahead on the road of counterfeiting rights protection according to law. Let us contribute as the woodpecker to purifying the market and to protecting the customers' rights.

Chapter 22
Real Estate Under Construction, Consumer Law and Development

Roberto Augusto Castellanos Pfeiffer

22.1 Introduction

The purchase of buildings under construction is a subject of extreme relevance to millions of Brazilian consumers because it is the most common way of acquiring new properties in Brazil and has assumed even greater importance on account of public housing policies that encourage loans for the purchase of real estate by the lower-income population, in particular the program "my house, my life."[1]

The theme has economic and social relevance. The construction is an organizer of the economy, with high participation in the gross domestic product, with strong impact on employment of labor, and in the generation of taxes.[2] And the demand for

The Portuguese version of this article was published at Revista de Direito do Consumdior, Vol. 105, pp. 81–101.

[1]According to art. 1 of law No 11,977/09, My House, my Life Program aims to establish mechanisms to encourage the production and acquisition of new housing units or refurbishment of urban real estate and rural housing production or reform, for families with monthly income of up to R$ 4650.00 (equivalent to US$ 1500.00 dollars).

[2]The participation of the sector in the Gross Domestic Product of Brazil is more than 5%. Source: http://www.cbicdados.com.br/home/.

R.A.C. Pfeiffer (✉)
Faculty of Law, University of São Paulo, São Paulo, Brazil
e-mail: roberto.pfeiffer@usp.br

C. Lima Marques, D. Wei (eds.), *Consumer Law and Socioeconomic Development*,
DOI 10.1007/978-3-319-55624-6_22

housing is strong due to the high housing deficit existing in Brazil.[3] It is an important vector for social and economic development.[4]

If the vulnerability is an integral part of the relationship, it appears so intensified on the acquisition of real estate under construction: firstly, by the complexity of the contract of sale, which is often related to a real estate financing operation, with the consequent acquisition of credit, and, secondly, because of the emotional factor, since the acquisition of property for housing represents the realization of the great dream of life, which causes him to be psychologically more prone not to observe details of the contract.

This scenario is favorable to the supplier, who makes use of unfair terms and practices, increasing the imbalance in its relationship with the consumer.

The scope of the article is precisely the analysis of the main issues of the important dialogue between the Brazilian real estate law and consumer law on the protection of purchasers of buildings under construction.

22.2 Application of the Brazilian Consumer Defense Code

The purchase and sale of real estate under construction is submitted to the Brazilian Code of Consumer Protection only if there is a simultaneous presence of a supplier as a vendor and a consumer as a buyer. In other words, it is not any real estate transaction that will be governed by the Brazilian Code of Consumer Protection.

For example, if an individual alienates his property to another, the relationship is **civil** in nature. The supplier being an absent figure, we face a consumer-to-consumer relationship (C2C), which is governed by the Brazilian Civil Code.

If a construction company is hired by an investment fund for the construction of a shopping mall, we face a business-to-business relation (B2B) because the buyer would not be considered a consumer, since the project will be aimed at an economic function (the lease of space to third parties).[5]

On the other hand, if a seller that alienates buildings under construction to a consumer is a **developer**, who is responsible (directly or through the contraction of another company) for the construction and sale of real estate, he would be

[3]Housing shortage means the stock necessary to replace the substandard housing, the excessive burden on rent (commitment greater than 30% of household income on rent between families who earn up to three minimum wages) and the excessive density in rented homes (source: http://www.forumdaconstrucao.com.br/conteudo.php?a=33&Cod=507. Accessed on 02.10.1016). It is estimated that in 2012 such deficit in the Brazil would be 5.2 million households (source: http://www.valor.com.br/brasil/3733244/fgv-Brazil-needs-to-r-76-bi-to-year-to-zero-deficit-housing, access at 02.10.2016).

[4]On the various meanings of development see: Pfeiffer (2011), pp. 17–29.

[5]On the importance of rigorous distinction between corporate contracts, civilians and consumption see: Forgioni (2010).

considered as a supplier, as described by article 3 of the Brazilian Consumer Defense Code, and thus subject to its provisions.

This is also the understanding of the Brazilian Superior Court of Justice, as demonstrates the following fragment of a recent court statement:

> 2. In spite of the incorporation contract be governed by Law number 64/4591, incidence of the Brazilian Consumer Defense Code, and should be observed the General principles of the right to seek justice, the equivalence of the benefits and the objective good faith, sealing the illicit engorgement.
>
> 3. The developer, as real estate condo development booster, attracts the liability for damages that may result from the non-performance or improper performance of the contract, including damage arising from faulty construction.[6]

But, accordingly with Brazilian law, the purchaser is considered a **consumer** only if he is the end user. That is the case, for example, of the acquisition of residential property for the establishment of housing of the buyer and their relatives, which corresponds to the vast majority of purchases of real estate under construction.

I understand the fact that the buyer person renting the property or reselling it after the acquisition does not denature its originally established consumer relationship, and it remains possible to apply the Brazilian Consumer Defense Code, firstly, on the ground that the original intention of the consumer was to acquire the real state for his personal use and, subsequently, on account of the further reasons that he decided (or was required) to resell the property or assign it or lease it. This is what happens, for example, in the cases in which the buyer changes town or has no more financial conditions to continue paying the benefits.

However, even if this argument were not accepted, the possibility of application of the Brazilian Consumer Defense Code would persist as the Brazilian Superior Court of Justice adopts the **mitigated finalist theory**, which allows the application of the Brazilian Consumer Defense Code to **intermediate consumption** (that is, the purchase of supplies or services within the framework of an economic activity) if the **vulnerability** of the buyer is demonstrated.[7] Normally, consumers face a strong vulnerability in their relationship with the developer, which has technical and legal domain of their business, as well as high economic power.

Of course, there will be no consumer relationship if the buyer is an entrepreneur that acquires significant amount of real estate in order to effect the rental or sale of real estate, so organized and in the framework of the economic activity. In this case, the acquirer would not be considered a consumer, given the corporate character of the activity.

Another exception is the legal person that buys a commercial property with the intent to install itself to develop a business activity. In this case, the purchaser is not

---

[6]AgRg in REsp 1,006,765-Rel. Min. Ricardo Villas Bôas Cueva-3rd t.-j. in 18.03.2014.

[7]This is the understanding of Brazilian Superior Court of Justice. For example: AgRg in REsp 687,239-rel. Minister Nancy Andrighi-t.-DJ 02.05.2006, p. 307. Here are the abstract of judgment: "civil law. Consumer. Further in the special feature. Concept of consumer. Legal person. Specialness. Not finding. The case law of the Superior Court of Justice has evolved in order to only admit the application of CDC to exceptionally legal entrepreneur, when shown their vulnerability in this case; or by assimilation, in the situations provided for in arts. 17 and 29 of the CDC".

the final economic user, not fitting in the definition of consumer of the finalist theory. Exceptionally, if there is evidence of vulnerability in this case, the finalist mitigated theory can be used and the Brazilian Consumer Defense Code would be applied to govern the relationship. An example is a microenterprise that acquires commercial room to develop its activities.

22.3 Improper Transfers of Third-Party Costs

In the alienation of buildings under construction, it is common that the developer requires the buyer to pay the costs of third parties whose services are developed for the benefit of the vendor, and so his payment would be originally the responsibility of the supplier.

However, consumers usually pay such expenses without discussions, since otherwise the sale will not be performed.

In this item, I will discuss the validity of the transfer of the following costs: (1) Technical Advisory Service real estate (SATI), (2) brokerage commission, and (3) cost of condo prior to the possession of the consumer.

The Brazilian Superior Court of Justice has analysed the developer's conduct to transfer to the consumer the payment of SATI-Technical Advisory Service real estate and with the payment of brokerage Commission. The rapporteur is the Minister Paulo de Tarso Sanseverino, and the interpretation adopted is a judicial precedent to guide the solution of all other causes with the same object (REsp 1599511, Rapporteur Judge Paulo de Tarso Sanseverino, DJe 2016.09.06).

22.3.1 Imposition of Payment of SATI

There are several arguments to demonstrate the unlawfulness of the payment by the consumer of the cost called "technical advisory service real estate," which remunerates the making of the contract and other legal services necessary for the conclusion of the contract of sale.

First of all, there is a lack of **adequate information** because the consumer only has science of the need to pay such expense at the time of completion of the contract, which violates articles 6, paragraph III, and 31 of the Brazilian Consumer Defense Code. The buyer has not previously been informed of the existence of the service or the price to be paid, which will increase the final value that will be paid for the acquisition of the property.[8]

[8]The Court of Justice of the State of São Paulo has interpreted that the supplier's failure in give appropriate information is able to rule out the validity of the imposition on payment of SATI. See in this respect: Appeal No. 152536–70.2012.8.26.0100-rel. Des. Élcio Trujillo-10th Board of private law-j. in 5/28/2015.

However, even though it was informed from the beginning, the collection of SATI would be abusive because it is contracted by the developer and hired for their benefit. Indeed, the contract of buying and selling—whose writing and filling is the main result of the provision of the SATI—has the nature of a contract of adhesion,[9] being drawn up according to what is specified by the developer.

It is the typical contract of adhesion and disciplined by article 54 of the Brazilian Code of Consumer Protection: the consumer does not negotiate the content of the contractual arrangements, and the completion of the drafting of the contract is effected with the simple filling of consumer data and of the property and the form of payment of the price, and the remaining provisions conform to the standard stipulated by the developer.

The autonomy of the will of the consumer is completely disregarded: the consumer does not have the prerogative to choose whether or not he will hire the service whose payment is charged. Furthermore, he did not choose the company providing the SATI, which is imposed by the developer and which normally belongs to the same group of the legal entity that coordinates the process of sale of real estate, which reinforces the contention that their services are targeted to satisfy the interests of the supplier.

Therefore, it is hiring service imposed on the consumer by professional who was not chosen by him and whose end result of greater relevance—the redaction of the contract of sale—results in profit mainly to the supplier. It offends the principle of objective good faith[10] to require the consumer to pay for developing a membership agreement, whose content was previously determined by the supplier.

Finally, I might point out that the developer incurs in **tying** because he imposes the hiring and payment of SATI as a condition to sign the contract of sale. Tying is considered an abusive conduct by article 39, subparagraph I, of the Brazilian Consumer Defense Code.[11]

22.3.2 Brokerage Commission

Most Brazilian real estate developers in construction require the purchasers, as a condition for signing the commitment of buying and selling, the obligation to pay the Commission of brokers hired to intermediate the sale.

The first objections to be pointed out is the **absence of adequate information**, because only at the time of signature of the contract is the buyer informed that he

[9]Marques (2014).

[10]On the concept of objective good faith view: Martins-Costa and Branco (2002).

[11]The Court of Justice of the State of São Paulo pacified the understanding that the imposition of the SATI configures tying. Among other precedents see: Appeal No. 0146519–52.2011.8.26.0100 4th Board of private law-rel. Des. Milton Carvalho-j. in 11/8/2012. Brazilian Superior Tribunal of Justice decided that is abusive the vendor charge of technical advisory service real estate (SATI), or similar activity (REsp 1599511, Reporter Minister Paulo de Tarso Sanseverino, DJe 06/09/2016).

has to pay such expense, a condition that is omitted in marketing announcements as in other stages of negotiation. There is, thus, a violation of articles 6, paragraph III, and 31 of the Brazilian Consumer Defense Code.

However, even if the consumer would have been informed from the moment of the offer, the imposition of payment of a broker fee would not be valid, for misrepresenting the nature of the brokerage contract, which is disciplined by article 722 of the Brazilian Civil Code as follows: "by the brokerage contract, a person, not connected to each other by virtue of the provision of services or for any dependency relationship, is obliged to get to the second one or more business, according to the instructions received."

The contract of real estate brokerage has as its constituent elements: a prior procurement (written or oral) of a person (physical or legal) unrelated to the other (whether acting as agent or service provider with any dependency relationship).

The main desideratum is the intermediation, where a person requests the broker to approach another to commit the transaction. The brokerage commission is payable by the party that hired him, as long as there is the completion of the purchase and sale of the property.[12]

The observance of the dynamics of the process of sale of real estate under construction allows the conclusion that it is not the consumer who effectively hires the intermediation of the alienation of the property but the developer.

Indeed, normally, the developer hires a brokerage firm to plan and execute the sale of real estate under construction. The firm is responsible not only for the sale but also for the marketing project conception. And usually there is a sales stand conceived and installed by the broker firm, which is the main point of attraction and reception of potential buyers. There is thus a strong relationship between the developer, the broker firm, and the broker agents.

It is clear that it is not the consumer who hires the brokerage service but the developer. In this context, it is an abusive conduct to transfer responsibility for the payment of the broker fees to the consumer.[13]

Furthermore, the price to be paid by the service of brokerage fee is not defined by the consumer but by the seller and the broker firm. It remains unclear the suppression of free will of the consumer: the intermediation is not his choice but the developer's, and also he could not choose the broker (which is imposed by the seller) and does not set the price that will be paid.

If the developer hired the broker firm, he must be responsible for the payment of the commission. This responsibility cannot be transferred to the consumer, who did not opt to hire the broker firm, did not choose the broker, and did not negotiate the price.

---

[12]Article 725 of Brazilian Civil Code stipulates: "the remuneration is payable to the broker once you have achieved the result provided for in the contract of mediation, or even if this is not effective by virtue of repentance."

[13]This is the understanding of The Court of Justice of Federal District: TJDFT-Judgment No 849298, 20130110206447APC, Rapporteur Des. Gilberto Pereira de Oliveira-3rd Class-j. in Civil 2/4/2015–2/24/2015 DJ.

One argument used by developer defendants is that even if the seller pays the broker fee, he will transfer this cost to the final price. So the broker fee, direct or indirectly, is paid by the consumers. In this context, there is no reason for debate as to who has the original responsibility to pay the broker fee for the reason that at the end of the day, it will be the consumer who will pay this cost.

However, strong arguments could be offered against this statement. First of all, from an economic point of view, it is much more efficient if the broker fee is paid by the developer because he has opted to sell the real estate using a broker firm, instead of internal sales. In this context, it is important that the responsibility for the payment of broker fee would be assigned to the developer because he will be more careful in the cost-benefit analysis (that is, whether it would be better to hire a broker firm or make the sale directly, without an intermediation). On the other hand, if the developer could easily transfer this cost to the buyer, he will not be very careful and could make the most expensive decision. So it is more efficient from an economic point of view to allocate such costs directly to the developer.[14]

Second, is not correct the argument that such costs would be passed on to the price anyway. It is not always possible to transfer all costs to the final price. Depending on the situation, the supplier has to decrease his profit margin, absorbing such costs. This is what happens, for example, in situations of economic recession, with retraction of demand for real estate and less supply of home loans, in which there is stabilization or price drop, paring down of costs, and less profit margin. So if the demand is weak, the supplier cannot pass directly to the final price cost increases, having to absorb them and decrease their profit margin; otherwise, he runs the risk of not attracting the consumer and keeping high inventory of homes for sale.

Third, if the developer does not advise at the beginning of the negotiation that the consumer will have to pay an extra cost (the broker fee), he is making a **misleading offer** since he offers to the buyer a price that does not match the final value that will be paid by him. It is a fenced practice by articles 31 and 37 of the CDC. The **objective good faith** imposes transparency, requiring that the supplier inform appropriately the consumer the value that will be effectively paid. If he fails to inform correctly the price that will be paid, he practices misleading offer, a conduct that violates articles 6, III, 31, and 37 of the Brazilian Consumer Defense Code. In this context, the transfer of such costs allows the **masking of the final price**, something that is forbidden by Brazilian consumer law.

Finally, when the developer refuses to sign the contract of sale if the consumer does not pay the broker fee, he is making a **tying**, a practice that is considered abusive pursuant to article 39, I, of the Brazilian Consumer Defense Code.[15]

---

[14]On the optimal allocation of costs between economic agents view: Cooter and Ulen (2008).

[15]There are several judgments of the Court of Justice of São Paulo State judging abusive transfer of brokerage fees. Among them: Appeal No. 1003177-27.2015.8.26.0196-Rel. Des. José Rubens Queiroz Gomes-7th Chamber of private law-j. in 1/18/2016. I quote the following excerpt from his statement: "the transfer values relating to consumer spending on brokerage. Membership agreement. Imposing as a condition to consummate the purchase of the property. Sale married. Article

22.3.3 *Condo Common Charges Before Delivery of the Keys*

A clause that is normally inserted in contracts of purchase and sale of real estate under construction stipulates that the consumer has the responsibility for the payment of expenses of a condominium even though the provider has not given him the effective possession of the property with the corresponding delivery of home key. In other words, the construction of the main building is over, but the specific unit of the buyer was not delivered. But the developer imposes that consumer pay the condo common charges, even if he has not delivered yet the specific consumer unit.

This occurs, for example, in situations where there are still finishing works to be made in the unit belonging to the consumer, which prevents its delivery. Another usual problem is the difficulty in the scheduling of inspection on the property, which could take excessive time because the developer designates for such a task a few employees.

But the biggest problem focuses on bureaucratic procedures that delay the drawing up of the deed to the unit. Often the developer does not send the necessary documentation, delaying the finalization of the loan contract and, in consequence, also delaying the signature of the property deed and its consequence registry. Despite this delay, the developer refused to give the possession of the house to the consumer until the completion of the bureaucratic process because he understands that it runs less risk of consumer default if he does not deliver the unit before the signature of property deed. If he makes his own warranty, he cannot force consumers to pay the condo common charges.

The Brazilian Superior Court of Justice has established the thesis that "the effective possession of the property, with the delivery of the keys, sets the moment from which arises for the condominiums the obligation to make payment of condominium expenses."[16]

Therefore, it is improper to include a clause that requires the purchaser to pay the condominium expenses before its effective ownership in the property, for generating an excessive advantage to the developer and countering the nature of the contract, being entirely null pursuant to article 51, subparagraph IV, of the Brazilian Code of Consumer Defense.

39, of the CDC". However, Brazilian Superior Court of Justice has adopted the understanding that is valid the contract which transfers to the purchaser the obligation to pay the brokerage Commission on contracts of selling of real estate under construction, since that was previously informed the total price of the unit, with the highlight of the value of the brokerage Commission (REsp 1599511, Reporter Minister Paulo de Tarso Sanseverino, DJe 06/09/2016).

[16]EREsp 489,647, Segunda Secção, Rel. Min. Luis Felipe Salomão, DJe 15/12/2009.

22.4 Consent Fee: An Abusive Contractual Clause

The commitment of buying and selling is a preliminary contract[17] that generates real rights pursuant to article 1225, VII, of the Brazilian Civil Code.[18] Many complications focus during its term, would take place several years before the granting of the deed to the property. For example, the buyer would have to live in another city, or if he loses his job, he could not have enough money to continue the payment and might need to sell the real state to another person.

So many factors can cause the consumer's interest in alienating the property rights before its delivery. The assignment of rights is, in this context, an instrument on freedom of contract[19] and has a relevant economic function as it allows the movement of contracts, being beneficial to both the buyer and the seller.

The buyer has an opportunity to capitalize to acquire a property in another city. The developer can sell the property to a person who has financial health to pay off debt (unlike the primitive purchaser).

The purchase and sale of real estate under construction usually include a clause that imposes the seller's consent as a condition for the validity of the transfer of the rights. That provision seems reasonable. Indeed, at the time the assignment is carried out, there usually still exists a considerable debit balance. So the seller needs to search whether the transferee has the financial capacity to perform the installments.

Furthermore, with the contractual assignment, the assignor transfers to the transferee not only his rights but also his obligations. Thus, it is salutary that the proposal be imposed as a condition for the validity of the transfer.

The Brazilian Superior Court of Justice has stated that "it's not abusive clause prohibiting the promissory purchaser of the property to cede his contractual position to third parties without prior consent of the promissory vendor."[20]

There is another precedent of the Brazilian Superior Court of Justice interpreting that "the transfer of mortgage do not have against the wishes of the financial agent; the correlation of this depends on application instructed by proof that the transferee meets the requirements of the housing system."[21]

The Brazilian Superior Court of Justice considers, therefore, that the purpose of the imposition of the consent lies in the possibility of analysis, by the seller, of the economic and financial capacity of the assignee, so as not to run the risk of eventual default.[22]

[17]Simao (2005).

[18]Venosa Sílvio de Salvo. Compromisso de compra e venda com eficácia real: direito do promitente comprador. In: http://www.professorsimao.com.br/artigos_convidados_venosa.htm.

[19]Article 421 of the Brazilian Civil Code, which holds that "the freedom to hire will be exercised on the basis and within the limits of the social function of the contract".

[20]REsp 1,027,669-Rel. Min. António Carlos Ferreira-4th Class-j. in 12/2/2014-DJe 5/18/2015.

[21]REsp 783,389-Rel. Min. Ari Pargendler-Corte Especial-j. em 21/05/2008-DJe 30/10/2008.

[22]REsp 1,036,530-Rel. para o acórdão: Min. Luis Felipe Salomão-4ª Turma-j. em 25/03/2014-DJe 15/08/2014.

On the other hand, I understand that is abusive the contractual clause that charges the developer consent. This kind of clause establishes that the developer consent will be done only if the consumer pays in advance a value denominated as "consent fee" (sometimes called "assignable contract rate" or "transfer fee").

There is no basis to support the imposition of a value to the provision of the consent. The imposition of the vendor consent reverts primarily in its favor since it allows the measurement of the financial conditional of the transferee. It offends the principle of objective good faith to require the buyer to pay for an analysis that reverts to the benefit and exclusive warranty of the seller.[23]

There is, still, to get away from the argument that the consent fee is a way to recover costs incurred by the seller in making the instrument of transfer of rights and the analysis of the financial capacity of the assignee.

The work to be developed by the seller in rendering consent is extremely simple, limited to the making of a new record with the name of the transferee and the analysis of its credit capacity. The credit transfer agreement, whose content does not exceed one page and is a standard form, is composed of uniform clauses.

Thus, the so-called consent fee pays activities easily performed by the business structure of the developer, already included in the price of the contract and reverts in its sole benefit, being thus abused in its collection.

Finally, it is usually charged an exorbitant value, being common to insertion of rates that correspond to a percentage that ranges between 1 and 4% of the updated value of the contract at the time of the sale, which is completely disproportionate, generating unreasonable enrichment of the supplier.

So the consent fee is a disproportionate value charged without reasonable foundation. In this context, the clause provided for is abusive, for establishing an exaggerated consumer disadvantage (article 51, IV, paragraph 1, items II and III, of the CDC).[24]

If the consumer has paid the value of the rate of consent to the developer at the moment of the transfer of the contract, he shall be entitled to a return of the amount paid, as established by the Brazilian Consumer Defense Code and by article 884 of the Brazilian Civil Code.[25]

---

[23]As recognized by the following precedent of the Court of Justice of the State of São Paulo: n. 0010295 Appeal-03.2012.826.0576, 10th Board of private law-Rel. Des. Carlos Alberto Garbi-j and 27.01.2012.

[24]View, beyond the precedent cited in note 8 the following judgment of the Court of Justice of the State of São Paulo: Appeal No-4, 2nd 61,809 Chamber of private law-Rel. Des. Antonio Cesar Peluso-j. in 1999.

[25]Article 884 of Brazilian Civil Code has the following wording: "The person who, without just cause, has enriched at the expense of others, will be required to repay the unduly received, made the updating of currency values".

22.5 Compensation for Construction Delay

The purchase and sale of real estate under construction stipulate a time limit for the construction of the condo units, usually about 36 months from the signing of the contract.

However, in several cases, the developer has various works in progress, and by inadequate management, it delays the termination of the construction, delivering the consumer unit after the passing of the deadline stipulated in the contract.

The construction delay is disrespect to the stipulation in the contract, such as a violation to the rule of the **binding offer**, since the term of completion of work is stipulated in the publicity material of the enterprise.[26]

The first consequence of nonobservance of the time limit is the payment of a fine stipulated in the contract as a penalty for the delay. Thus, if the contract contains fine for the delay, the developer shall pay the prescribed amount to the consumer. Such a sanction will serve as the basis of calculation of the fine to be imposed on the developer.

If the contract has not established a penalty clause for the construction delay, it is possible to insert it in the contract, with support in the good faith doctrine and in the rule of interpretation most favorable to the consumer laid down in article 47 of the CDC: apply to the supplier the same fine that would be charged to the purchaser for breach of contract.

In addition to the fine, the consumer has the right to receive compensation for damages suffered as a result of the delay in the delivery of the property.

The main damage that typically occurs is that the consumer cannot use the condo unit as planned. So, for example, he will have to continue to support the cost of rent of his former residence. Or if the consumer wants to rent the unit to a third party, the construction delay means postponing income.

It is clear that the construction delay generates loss of money that must be repaired, according to article 927 of the Brazilian Civil Code[27] and article 6, item VI, of the Brazilian Consumer Defense Code. These norms stipulate the right to full compensation of the damage, which covers the lost profits.

The Brazilian Superior Court of Justice has decided many cases in the sense that there is a presumption on the occurrence of lost profits in the event of construction delay, which thus should be repaired cumulatively with the contractual penalty. I quote the following court statements:

> 1. This Superior Court already signed understanding that failed to fulfill the deadline for delivery of the immovable object of sale and purchase commitment, is applicable to conviction for loss of profits, with presumption of prejudice to the promissory purchaser.[28]

---

[26]The binding offer is stipulated in art. 30 of the CDC, then transcribed: "Art. 30. All information or advertising, sufficiently precise, conveyed by any form or means of communication regarding products and services offered or presented, obliges the supplier that the vehicle or use do and integrates the contract to be concluded".

[27]On the interpretation of article 927 of Brazilian Civil Code view: Goncalves (2015).

[28]AgRg in Ag 1,319,473-Rel. Minister Ricardo Villas Bôas Cueva-third Class-tried in 6/25/2013-DJe 12/2/2013.

> In accordance with the settled case law in this Court, the non-performance of the contract of sale, for example, in the absence of delivery of the property on the date agreed upon, entails corresponding to compensation beyond the criminal clause moratorium, the payment of compensation for lost profits for the non-enjoyment of the property during the time the lives of promissory sales. Precedent.[29]

Thus, if the seller delays the performance of the contract and delivers the unit after the passing of the deadline stipulated in the contract of sale, the consumer must pay not only the fine stipulated in the contract but also the corresponding value that the damage effectively caused.

The Brazilian Superior Court of Justice has already signed understanding that during the period of delay, the consumer must pay regular benefits; it is not valid, for example, the legal determination of no incidence of monetary correction of the value of benefits. Applying such kind of provision would change the economic-financial balance of the contract, not keeping economic equivalence with the prejudice caused to the consumer, which disrespects him according to the precepts of articles 395 and 944 of the Brazilian Civil Code.[30]

On the other hand, in the event that the supplier proves that he is not responsible for the construction delay, he can avoid the burden of paying the contractual penalty and compensating the consumer for loss of profits.[31]

Which are the causes that avoid the developer's responsibility for construction delay? The first of these is the claim of force majeure,[32] such as a natural disaster (e.g., a cyclone that hit the construction works).

Also exempt is the duty of repairing the chance of occurrence of **unforeseeable circumstances**, i.e., the third action outside to the consumer relationship that causes the delay. An example is a disaster involving a helicopter that interferes with the work in progress, which requires reconstruction of part of the building, delaying delivery of the condo units.

Only unforeseeable circumstances that are unpredictable and oblivious to the supplier caused by a third party outside of the consumer relationship are able to exclude the payment responsibility of the developer.

On the other hand, the responsibility to repair a claim will not be subject to the exemption of the supplier if the damage was caused, for example, by a company hired by him since it is part of the production chain. Also must be rebutted the allegation (very common in years in which there was a *boom* in real estate in Brazil) that the delay resulted from labor shortages or lack of building materials because the correct planning of input acquisition is part of the developer's activity.[33]

---

[29]AgRg no AREsp 525,614-Rel. Ministro Luis Felipe Salomão-4ª Turma-julgado em 19/08/2014-DJe 25/08/2014.

[30]REsp 1,454,139-Rel. Ministra Nancy Andrighi-3ª T. -j. em 03/06/2014-DJ 17/06/2014.

[31]This is the interpretation of the Brazilian Superior Court of Justice case-law. See: REsp 808,446-Rel. Minister Castro Filho-3rd t.-j. in 8/24/2006-DJ 10/23/2006.

[32]Regarding force majeure and unforeseeable circumstances as excluding the responsibility of the supplier, even without your expressed at the CDC forecast view: Denari (2005), pp. 190–191.

[33]Superior Court of Justice-AgRg no AREsp 388,439-Rel. Min. Paulo de Tarso Sanseverino-3ª T. -julgado em 28/04/2015-DJe 07/05/2015.

It can occur that the delay is the **fault of the consumer**,[34] for example, if the consumer did not offer specifications for customization of his unit, leading subsequently to a delivery delay. In this case, he will not be able to blame the developer for construction delay.

Normally, entering a period of grace in the clause can regulate the consequences of construction delay. For example, the contract stipulates that the work will last for 30 months, being acceptable a grace period of six months. This clause does not appear to be abusive.[35]

However, the period of grace to be valid must be worded clearly and prominently, allowing the consumer to plan his future in an appropriate manner. Obscure clauses are considered invalid by articles 46 and 47 of the Brazilian Consumer Defense Code.

Furthermore, if the advertising of the project only mentions the deadline, without highlighting the grace period, I understand that its subsequent inclusion in the contract will not be valid. Indeed, there will be a **misleading advertising by omission** (article 37, § 3, of the Brazilian Consumer Defense Code), obliging the entrepreneur to deliver the unit within the time limit set in the advertising material, without being able to use the grace period eventually placed in the contract, under the rule of the binding offer (article 30 of the CDC). One of the most important elements taken into consideration by the consumers in their decision to acquire property is the construction deadline. It is not reasonable, offending the principle of objective good faith, that the developer advertises a deadline without the mention of a grace period and subsequently putting in the contract the possibility of postponement of the deadline.

Concerning punitive damages, Brazilian Superior Court of Justice case law understands that the mere contractual nonperformance, punishable by penalty clause established in the contact, does not generate an opportunity for moral damages. There are legal precedents to the effect that if there is failure to comply with a contractual disposition already sanctioned by a penalty clause, there is no opportunity to claim compensation for moral damage.[36]

But there are some cases of contractual breach that result in intense personality offense, reaching the honor or the intimacy of the contractor.[37]

In a recent judgment, the Brazilian Superior Court of Justice stated that on account of a very long delay, the plaintiff has to support a strong anguish. So it is

---

[34]Article 12, § 3°, III and Article 14, § 3, III of Brazilian Consumer Defense Code.

[35]The dominant interpretation in the Courts of Justice is not to be abusive, in theory, the grace period clause. By way of example see: TJSP-0185092 Appeal-62.2011.8.26.0100-Rel. Des. Percival Nogueira-Camara of private law-tried in 11/1/2012. MIN.AS-AI 10,024,132,800,889,001-Rel. Des. Square milk-17th Civil Chamber-tried in 12/5/2013. TJRS-AC 70,058,181,421-Rel. Des. Eduardo João Lima Costa-19th Civil Chamber-tried in 2/27/2013.

[36]Resp 202,564-Rel. Min. Savio de Figueiredo Teixeira-4th Class-j. on 02.08.2001–01.10.2001 DJ.

[37]Resp 1,072,308-Rel. Minister Nancy Andrighi-third Class-j. in 5/25/2010-DJe 6/10/2010.

reasonable that the developer compensate him, paying a value as moral damage. I quoted the following excerpt of the Court's statement:

> 2. The enforceability of contract of promise of purchase and sale of housing unit, due to the absence of real estate development construction by the incorporator, 09 (nine) years after the due date for delivery, cause serious and founded anguish in the spirit of the acquirer, not of mere embarrassment arising from breach of contractual clause commonplace, allowing the compensation of moral damage.[38]

In conclusion, depending on the circumstances of each case, a construction delay would be able to generate a duty of the developer to compensate the consumer for moral damage.

References

Cooter R, Ulen T (2008) Law & economics. Pearson, Boston
de Salvo Venosa S Compromisso de compra e venda com eficácia real: direito do promitente comprador. http://www.professorsimao.com.br/artigos_convidados_venosa.htm
Denari Z (2005) Código de Defesa do Consumidor comentado pelos autores do anteprojeto
Forgioni P (2010) Teoria Geral dos contratos Empresariais. Revista dos Tribunais, São Paulo
Goncalves CR (2015) Responsabilidade civil. Saraiva, São Paulo
Marques CL (2014) Contratos no Código de Defesa do Consumidor. Revista dos Tribunais, São Paulo
Martins-Costa J, Branco GLC (2002) Diretrizes teóricas do novo Código civil brasileiro. Saraiva, São Paulo
Pfeiffer RAC (2011) Desenvolvimento. In: Rodrigues José Paulo (Org.). Saraiva, São Paulo
Simao JF (2005) Direto civil: contratos. Atlas, São Paulo

[38]REsp 830,572-Rel. Ministro Luis Felipe Salomão-4ª Turma-j. em 17/05/2011-DJe 26/05/2011.

Chapter 23
Real Estate Consumer Credit: A New Side to Vulnerability

Walter José Faiad de Moura and Leonardo Roscoe Bessa

And you think you have to want more than you need
Until you have it all you won't be free
(...)
And when you think more than you want
Your thoughts begin to bleed
I think I need to find a bigger place
Because when you have more than you think
You need more space
(. . .)
Society, you're a crazy breed.
Hanna Jerry and Vedder, Eddie, "Society". Into the wild, 2007.

23.1 Introduction: Vulnerability in the Consumer Market

The establishment of modern private law is based on the paradigms of freedom and equality and, consequently, of individuals' autonomy in all sorts of interpersonal relations. It works based on the idea that right holders are rational and free and have the necessary conditions to self-rule their lives. From another perspective, *the new private law* seeks to value human rights and new social and economic roles. It aims at the equalitarian protection of the most vulnerable individuals in legal relations.[1]

[1]Marques and Miragem (2014), pp. 24–29.

W.J.F. de Moura
Brasilcon Board, Brasília, Brazil

University Center of Brasília (UniCEUB), Brasília, Brazil
e-mail: secretaria@wmaa.com.br

L.R. Bessa (✉)
Brasilcon Board, Brasília, Brazil

University Center of Brasília (UniCEUB), Brasília, Brazil

Brasilcon, Brasília, Brazil
e-mail: roscoe@mpdft.mp.br

C. Lima Marques, D. Wei (eds.), *Consumer Law and Socioeconomic Development*,
DOI 10.1007/978-3-319-55624-6_23

In this new *era* of private law, consumers' legal protection granted by the state is justified in view of their fragility—vulnerability—in the consumer market.[2] Consumers are the most fragile party in all sorts of legal relations established in the consumer market. The consumer market, especially considering its current mass conformation, raises potential and constant offences with different emphases against consumers' material and existential interests, which have become legally governed by modern acts.

Before attending information purposes or real needs, sophisticated marketing and advertising strategies, individuals' increasingly closer contact with gadgets and their hyper-connectivity to online life create successive consumption needs, thus stimulating consumption in an incessant manner. Business practices that not only affect the ideal competitive environment but also detrimentally interfere with consumers' interests through decreased product and service quality, and price raise is common.[3]

Products that are manufactured and marketed in series can lead to serial defects, causing material and possible moral damages. The constant public recalls made by companies in order to repair products show the scale of this issue.[4] In the virtual environment, the number of digital sales by means of electronic commerce grows alongside consumer privacy offences related to personal data.[5]

The sensitive distance in the relationship between consumers and suppliers before and after the sale should also be emphasised. The disregard towards

---

[2] As noted in another source, "the legal protection of consumers is included in the historical context in which the Civil Code lost its centralising character in the regency of private relations and, at the same time, norms considering the real characteristics of individuals—concrete subjects with their own particularities—were multiplied. This stepped away from Nineteenth Century paradigm of abstract men and formal equality. Regarding the first point, the Twentieth Century removes the exaggerated centrality and completeness pretention of the Civil Code. After the 1930s, a series of extravagant laws were issued in Brazil. Due to their scope, they put into question the absolute and central role of the Civil Code of 1916. Following that, the Code lost its exclusivity character in regards to private property relations. Special laws—and no more extravagant ones or exceptions—are issue in order to give effect to the state's welfare intervention. Bessa Leonardo Roscoe (2009), p. 27.

[3] Despite the normative prohibition and the actions of the Administrative Council for Economic Defence. Law 12529 of 30 November 2011 establishes the Brazilian System for the Defence of Competiveness and advocates the prevention from and repression of violations against the economic order. The aforementioned legal act establishes a series of administrative infractions (article 36) which invariably affect the collective interests of consumers. This is the case of the agreement between companies to establish the final price of a particular product (cartel)—and such prices may be more than double the price resulting from free competition.

[4] The so-called recall is envisaged by article 10 of the Consumer Code. The goal is to avoid consumption accidents in situations where one finds a defect after placing the product in the market. "Article 10. The supplier cannot put the products or services that they know (or should know) are heavily harmful or hazardous to health and safety. §1 The supplier of products that become aware, after placing a product or service in the consumer market, of the risks they pose should immediately report their concerns to the competent authorities and to consumers through public advertisements. §2 The aforementioned advertisements will be conveyed by the press, radio and television and all costs shall be paid by the supplier of the product or service. §3 Whenever they become aware of the risks products or services pose to the health and safety of consumers, the union, states, the Federal District, and the municipalities should inform the population about it".

[5] On the current meaning and legal relevance of privacy, especially with regards to personal data. Danilo Doneda (2006).

consumers after services have been agreed and products have been purchased is noticeable. Other issues such as behaviours that offend consumers' personality rights, such as abusive debt collection (honour offence), queues longer than one hour, delayed and misinformed call centre customer services and difficulties and misuses related to the exercise of their rights to cancelation—denunciation—of long term contracts, etc, should also be considered.

The recognition of consumer vulnerability in the market has led to the issuing of specific rules that protect such individuals, particularly since the 1970s.[6] Resolution 39/42 of the United Nations (UN) reflects the existence of a certain consensus on the need for consumer protection by the state. The resolution was issued in 1985. It recommended that governments develop and strengthen strict policies for the protection of consumers with the following purposes: health and safety protection, promotion and protection of consumers' economic interests, proper provision of information in order to enable consumers to make the right choices, consumer education, effective possibility of consumer compensation and freedom to create groups and associations that can take part in political decisions that affect consumers' interests.

Brazil has structured consumer normative protection through its Federal Constitution of 1988, which states that consumer protection is a fundamental right (article 5, XXXII), thus implicitly recognising the existence of material inequality (which should be corrected) between consumers and suppliers. Furthermore, the constitution makes it explicit that consumer protection is a principle that should be considered by any economic activity (article 170, V).[7]

---

[6]Several countries, especially from the 1970s on, have issued rules for the protection of consumers' interests. Some examples of that are the German Law 09.12.1976 known as AGB-Gesetz on the general conditions of contracts, the French Law from 22.12.72 on housing sale, and the Fair Credit Reporting Act of 1970, which currently still rules the database for credit protection in the United States. However, the "birth" of Consumer Law took place in the previous decade. Law doctrine points out that a symbolic moment for the emergency of consumer protection was a message from the President of the United States, John Kennedy on 15 March 1962 to the US congress which emphasised the need for the protection of consumers' interests, principally in regards to the need for product quality, adequate information, fair prices, consumer participation in governmental decisions which might affect their interests. Precisely due to this event on the 15th of March the world now celebrates the day as Consumer Day. In Brazil, the National Consumer Day was established by Law n. 10504 from 08 June 2002. Article 2 establishes that on the 15th of March "federal, state and municipal agencies for the defence of consumers will promote festivals, debates, lectures and other events in order to disseminate consumer rights".

[7]Still from a constitutional perspective, the dignity of human beings, which is expressed by the Federal Republic of Brazil (article 1, III of the Brazilian Federal Constitution), justifies their protection in the consumer market. In fact, "consumer protection should be studied as a particular and essential moment of a broader type of protection: the protection of human personality". Gustavo Tepedino correctly posits that article 5, XXXII, and article 170, V, must be analysed together with the arrangements of article 1, III and 3, III, of the Brazilian Federal Constitution: "Thus, the Constituent Assembly not only included consumers under the umbrella of individual rights and guarantees, but also established that consumer protection must be carried out from an instrumental perspective, i.e., with the instrumentalisation of their patrimonial interests protecting their dignity and existential values. This is therefore a normative perspective to protect human beings in consumer relations, not just the consumer as a category per se". A responsabilidade civil por acidentes de consumo na ótica Civil-constitucional, in *Temas de Direito Civi* l, Rio de Janeiro, 2004, Renovar, pp. 279–281.

In compliance with the provisions of article 48 of the transitional constitutional arrangements,[8] Law n. 8078 (commonly known as the Consumer Protection Code[9]) was established in September 1990. Item I of article 4 states that the need for consumer protection is due to their fragility, which is technically addressed as *vulnerability*.

The importance of the discussion and the meaning of vulnerability have not decreased with the advent of the Consumer Protection Code (Law n. 8078). This is due to the fact that this concept does not only call for norm establishment—which would then lose force once the law was enacted—but also calls for a hermeneutical criterion for the good enforcement of the Consumer Protection Code[10] and the establishment of public policies.

In the 25 years that the Consumer Protection Code has been in effect, the debate on the extension of the meaning of consumer vulnerability still stands, and it tackles the issue from different angles according to the activity developed in the market and the personal characteristics of individuals.

This paper seeks to analyse specific aspects of the vulnerability of consumers who want home ownership, especially highlighting the lack of specific regulations regarding real estate contracts. The paper posits that the market has certain features that can justify not only a specific sub-category of vulnerable individuals but also other theoretical and regulatory propositions.

---

[8]Article 48. Within a hundred and twenty days after the promulgation of the Constitution, the National Congress will elaborate the consumer defence code.

[9]The Consumer Defence Code was inspired by important legislative models from other countries. The greatest influence came from the Projet de Code de la Consommation. The basic consumer rights were taken from Resolution 39/248 UN. Other models were the Lei General para la Defensa de los Consumidores y Usuarios from Spain, Lei 29/81 from Portugal, Lei Federal de Protección ao Consumidor of 5 February 1976 from Mexico, and the Loi sur la Protection du Consommateur, issued in 1979 in Quebec. In relation to specific issues, the Code was inspired by the European Community Law: Policy 84/450 (advertising) and 85/374 (civil responsibility for consumer accidents). Regarding the contractual protection of consumers, the examples followed were Decreto-lei 446-85 from Portugal and the Gesetz zur Regelund des Rechts des Allgemeinen Geschaftsbedingungen—AGB Gesetz of December 1976 from Germany. The influence of the US law was directly through the Federal Trade Commission Act, the Consumer Product Safety Act, the Truth in Lending Act, the Fair Credit Reporting Act, and the Fair Debt Collection Practices Act. There was also a direct influence, as the most modern European rules for consumer protection were inspired in US cases and statutes. GRINOVER, Ada Pellegrini *et al. Código de Defesa do Consumidor comentado pelos autores do Anteprojeto*. 8. ed. rev. and ampl. Rio de Janeiro, Forense Universitária, 2004, p. 10.

[10]For example, in this case the concept and meaning of vulnerability are crucial for determining whether the legal entity that operates in the market can be considered a consumer. This is a doctrinal approach called informed finalism (*finalismo aprofundado*) which is based precisely on the notion of vulnerability of small businesses so to justify their legal protection as consumers. Bessa, Leonardo Roscoe. *Relação de consumo...*, cit., pp. 59–66. Following this same line, Cláudia Lima Marques stresses that vulnerability can work for the good enforcement of norms, "it is an instrumental notion which guides and sheds light to the enforcement of the protective and rebalance norms for and equal basis and equitable justice". *Contratos no Código de Defesa do Consumidor*, 6 ed., São Paulo, Revista dos Tribunais: 2011, p. 323.

23.2 Different Aspects of Consumer Vulnerability

On the basis of Western capitalism, the nineteenth century patrimonial tradition implies that individuals are able to make valid decisions as they are able to freely exercise their will.[11] The very concept of the 'individual' was established from a liberal perspective of patrimonial legal relations. It thus shaped the idea that individuals are those who 'have rights to property and credit, which protects their interests in benefiting from some things excluding others'.[12] The reflection of this historic choice reinforced protections focusing on patrimony in classic private law, which comes from the idea that the order should be maintained by the state by focusing on recovering property damages.

After the bourgeois revolution—the era of volunteerism[13]—individuals' capability to act according to their freedom of choice was recognised as a precondition for civil life and as a personality attribute. This was translated into the 'necessary discernment for the practice of some or all legal acts'.[14] However, the approach to capability during that period was statistical and only considered individuals' ability to be or to be not bound to something in light of established legal impediments or openings. Capability was universally measured considering factors such as the age of the individual. It was presupposed that every individual in society—regardless of having formal education—was able to fully administer the rational managing of their assets.

Even nowadays, after the transformation of obligations and with new paradigms for protection from consumer vulnerability in the market, there are still those who believe that every purchase or debt is a result of a presumably well-thought decision of consumers. However, freedom of choice and access to sufficient information for a well-thought decision have been deeply compromised, especially from the twenty-first century onwards. The massive use of marketing strategies in the stages prior to the contract has been crucial to lead consumers to purchase in an increasingly more automatic manner without any reflection or rationality, focusing basically on leaving the anonymity created by mass economic relations.[15]

To better understand consumer vulnerability in the market, law doctrine has sought to analyse it from different angles. Firstly, the proposition by Cláudia Lima Marques should be stressed. The author sees vulnerability from four perspectives: technical, legal, factual and informational.[16]

---

[11]Souza (1999a), p. 25. While individualism is not an evil feature, whether or not in agreement with the positions of Hobbes or Montesquieu, it was a crucial factor for unleashing absolute state intervention in private life management.

[12]Barassi (1955), p. 43.

[13]Rodrigues (1979), p. 9.

[14]Monteiro (2003), p. 9.

[15]Benjamin et al. (1999), p. 226.

[16]Contratos no Código de Defesa do Consumidor, 6 ed., São Paulo, Revista dos Tribunais: 2011, p. 323.

Technical vulnerability concerns consumers' lack of specific knowledge regarding the features of the product or service that they are purchasing or hiring. Information deficit increases by the day, considering how fast products and services that incorporate innovations and technological advances emerge. On the other hand, the lack of knowledge about product features creates difficulties for the exercise of consumers' right to choose and can also more intensely induce mistakes.[17]

According to Cláudia Lima Marques, legal vulnerability 'is the lack of specific legal, accounting, or economic knowledge'.[18] The legal superiority of suppliers, which makes them customary litigants, should also be considered as companies structure and organise themselves with legal sectors and advisors so they can take disputes to court. These sectors are included in the companies' costs. One legal demand does not make a huge difference for the regular performance of the companies' business activities. In fact, it is actually necessary to justify the resources invested in that area. For consumers (casual litigants), regardless of their legal knowledge, taking a case to court inevitably entails emotional stress, hassles and time dedication to the process. The inequality is obvious and has explicit reflections on the attitude of both parts when making settlements and removing conflicts of interest.[19]

Factual or socio-economic vulnerability is a result of the economic superiority of suppliers or superiority due to monopoly or essentiality of services: 'the point of concentration is another contractual party, which, due to monopoly position (be it factual or legal), and due to great economic power, or the essentiality of a service, imposes its superiority to those who make agreements with it'.[20]

Finally, informational vulnerability is related to the importance of appearance, communication and information in an increasingly visual, fast and risky market. 'One of consumers' distinguishing features is precisely their information deficit, and it would not be necessary to stress that this is a new kind of vulnerability, once it would already be encompassed as a type of technical vulnerability.' Nowadays, however, 'information is not missing, it is abundant, manipulated, controlled, and at times unnecessary when provided'.[21]

The classification of consumer vulnerability or the different perspectives about it—with its clear didactic nature—meet their aim of improving understanding about consumer inequality in the market and, thus, of finding means to rebalance this relationship. It assists the hermeneutic work of consumer protection norms and induces (or should induce) the proposition of public policies.

---

[17]Contratos no Código de Defesa do Consumidor, 6 ed., São Paulo, Revista dos Tribunais: 2011, pp. 324–326.

[18]Contratos no Código de Defesa do Consumidor, 6 ed., São Paulo, Revista dos Tribunais: 2011, p. 327.

[19]Leonardo Roscoe Bessa, *Relação de consumo...*, cit., pp. 42–43.

[20]Contratos no Código de Defesa do Consumidor, 6 ed., São Paulo, Revista dos Tribunais: 2011, p. 325.

[21]Contratos no Código de Defesa do Consumidor, 6 ed., São Paulo, Revista dos Tribunais: 2011, p. 329.

Without rejecting the proposition of Claudia Lima Marques,[22] the authors of this paper have sought to highlight different aspects that demonstrate and reinforce consumer vulnerability. In his dissertation on this subject, Paulo Valerio Morais views consumer vulnerability from six aspects. One of the highlights is the so-called psychological or biological vulnerability. The author posits that the idea that consumers are free in the consumer market is fallacious since biological or psychological vulnerability makes them slaves of the desires created by advanced marketing resources, as, considering the knowledge regarding human nervous system, 'those who are interested in its stimulation will make use of techniques to bring out needs, create desires, and manipulate will demonstrations, thus generating indefinite circumstances which can result in increased consumption and, in a more perverse way, force the consumption of inadequate products or services'.[23]

Diógenes Faria de Carvalho emphasises the direct connection between consumerism and over-indebtedness. Based on authors and studies from the areas of psychology, sociology and anthropology, he posits that vulnerability is forged by the consumerism environment and its respective values:

> Consumerism is carried out not only by immediate necessity, but also by the contentment caused by the widespread use of advertising by social media channels which generalise information and stimulate purchases. Not having the object of desire triggers furtive reactions which result in uncommon, incontrollable and utopic thoughts and feelings. They are often irrational shortcuts caused by vulnerability and cognitive limitations. Also, facility to acquire an asset in an increasingly globalised economy results in exaggerated consumption, which reaches large scales once they are driven by product trends in the market.[24]

[22]The Brazilian Superior Court of Justice examines consumer vulnerability alongside the same lines of the propositions of Cláudia Lima Marques. One example of that can be the following trial: "(...) doctrine traditionally indicates the existence of three types of vulnerability: technical (lack of specific knowledge on a product or service that is the object of consumption), legal (lack of legal, accounting or economic knowledge and its reflections on consumer relation), and factual (situations in which consumers' economic, physical, or psychological insufficiency makes them unequal in comparison to suppliers). More recently, informational vulnerability (insufficient data on the product or service, which can influence the decision process of the purchase) is also being considered. 5. Despite the *in abstracto* consideration of such types of vulnerability, other examples can present new forms of vulnerability that can call for the Consumer Protection Code in a consumer relation. In an inter-company relationship, aside from the vulnerability hypotheses considered by the doctrine and court decisions, the dependency relationship of one of the parties in relation to the other can, depending on the case, constitute vulnerability, which would then entail the legitimate enforcement of Law n. 8078/90. This would thus mitigate the rigidity of the finalist theory and allow the equalisation of the condition of the buyer legal entity to that of a consumer". (REsp 1195642/RJ, Rel. Ministra Nancy Andrigui, j. on 13/11/2012, DJe 21/11/2012).

[23]Moraes (1999), p. 152.

[24]Carvalho Diógenes Faria de (2015), p. 16. Following that, the author states that: "consumerist culture is full of constant quality pressures which demand the acquisition of refined and luxury goods. Nowadays, added values have come to mean wealth accumulation and prestige. This new behaviour pattern adopted by individuals has resulted in rampant (hyper) consumerism".

Following this same line, studies on behavioural economics (BE) have incisively criticised the 'rational decision theory' developed by the economic analysis of law (EAL). As pointed out by Amanda Flávio de Oliveira and Bruno Braz de Castro, consumers—far from following the rationality ideal—purchase products and services by impulse driven by their emotions. They have a series of irrational cognitive characteristics: limited rationality, limited self-interest and limited willpower.[25]

In relation to credit and over-indebtedness, the authors of this paper support the importance of adequately informing consumers, although they argue that there is a need to go beyond that by establishing a format that takes the cognitive peculiarities of the interested parties into account. They point out that when it comes to obtaining credit, there is an issue with inter-temporal decisions—immediate interests vs. future interests—once consumers in general do not conduct a cold analysis of short- and long-term outcomes. There is a cognitive tendency to value immediate benefits at the expense of future gains, as well as a preference for postponing costs, and dissatisfactions. Also, consumers have issues with properly comparing the dynamics between long term and short term.[26]

Clarissa Costa Lima also points out consumer fragility in relation to credit. Among other factors that lead to over-indebtedness, impulsivity,[27] information asymmetry, lack of financial education, consumers' incomplete heuristics (which leads them to poorly evaluate the risk of excessive indebtedness) and irresponsible credit granting[28] can be highlighted.

Based on the theoretical approaches analysed so far, it is possible to observe that theories related to vulnerability have improved the understanding of this legal phenomena through multidisciplinary perspectives in sociological, economic and psychological approaches. These outlines demonstrate that addressing vulnerability leads one to seek to understand individuals and their particular vicissitudes, which thus confirms that new private law lines in fact use a humanist approach to legal relations. Technological and environmental factors, as well as specific business practices, can also exacerbate consumers' difficulties in finding a balance between suppliers, which confirms the need for state intervention.

Home ownership purchase seems to be one of those base relations that brings together in one single circumstance factors that are characteristic of consumers'

---

[25]Oliveira and Castro (2014), p. 235.

[26]*Revista de Direito do Consumidor*, cit., p. 243.

[27]Incidentally, an observation made by Diogenes Faria de Carvalho should be considered: "The illusions which culminate in desires and desired objects are believed to put men in a situation of considerable vulnerability and suffering. When individuals surrender to immediate pleasures instead of making sacrifices for the sake of their future, this is conditioned to economic debt and momentary satisfaction. Such unruly behaviour will be a legacy for future generations—a cultural debt, and a legacy of exhaustion and compulsory contamination which annihilate healthy and rational consumption practices". *Consumo e (super) endividamento: vulnerabilidade e escolhas intertemporais*, cit., p. 18.

[28]Lima (2014), p. 178.

exacerbated vulnerability. The historic Brazilian housing deficit[29]—particularly from the 1950s on—gave rise to a series of policies to attract public and private investments. These are now established in a relevant sector of the Brazilian economy,[30] which organised itself industrially by offering mass residential products supported by practice matrices and contracts that are not considerate of the norms of protection of borrowers. This phenomenon is relevant and should be addressed by an approach that considers the particularities of the real estate market and emerging problem-situation categories that have had disturbing social, economic and legal effects.

23.3 From the House Ownership Dream to the Real Estate Industry

Brazilians are familiar with the popular thought that 'Brazilian people are always looking to fulfil their dream of house ownership'. The thought itself demonstrates the realisation that there are a number of challenges to housing access in the country. Despite its large territory, which has continental proportions, the country has failed to conduct a desirable land distribution.[31] The use of the word 'dream' itself, and the designation of a non-driven mental activity, indicates the desire to accomplish a project whose implementation seems difficult or utopic.[32] Commonly speaking, selling houses is not far from dealing with dreams since it explores a basic familiar need that, despite its economic aspects, appeals to citizenship, status and social desirability.[33]

From the data retrieved from history and geopolitics,[34] it is possible to notice that the simple act of buying a house does not represent a simple relationship

[29]According to the João pinheiro Foundation (in partnership with IDB/UNDP/and the Ministry of Cities), the Brazilian housing deficit has little drop variance, with an average of almost five million families without conventional houses (considering the historical series involving metropolitan regions and other areas measured since 1995). Available at http://www.fjp.mg.gov.br/index.php/produtos-e-servicos1/2742-deficit-habitacional-no-brasil-3. Accessed 08 February 2016.

[30]According to the Brazilian Chamber of Construction Industry, civil construction activity constitutes about 8.0% of the Gross Domestic Product of Brazil, and it operates with a considerable amount of consumer capital. Available at http://www.cbicdados.com.br/menu/pib-e-investimento/pib-brasil-e-construcao-civil. Access 08 February 2016.

[31]Furtado et al. (2013), Estimativas do déficit habitacional brasiliero (2007–2011) por municípios (2010).

[32]Ferreira (2004).

[33]Bonduki (2008), pp. 70–104.

[34]Looking back, the collapse of the self-sufficient rural economy lead to (especially in Western countries—each one at their time) rural exodus migration trajectories with migrants landing in cities with something in mind: the dream of owning their houses. After the Twentieth Century, population flows are no longer from farms to cities, but in between increasingly populous cities (states and countries) which are challenged by environmental preservation, land order issues, and

between the constructor and the resident for conventional economic sake. When it comes to housing (especially when speaking of mass commercial launches), it is important to consider the elements of this complex relationship in which consumers are surrounded by strong marketing campaigns, sophisticated financing, registration acts, ancillary contracts, engineering and architecture models, etc. Also, there is a constructed social stereotype that posits that individuals are meant to be born, grow up, work, build a family and live at home. In this context, buying a house (or renting it) is a crucial task for citizens and leaves place to few alternatives.

In the classic essay written by Thomas Marshall,[35] the first state interventions that provided public policies on housing meant a legitimate expectation for individuals: that there should be a house to accommodate each family once several legislators chose housing as a basic right of their people.[36] Socialist systems worked with the idea that property would be a common good but one that would still be accessed through work. In capitalist systems, however, private real estate ownership, which is destined for familiar residences, has come to represent one of the crucial material components for the condition of citizenship provided by the private sector by means of visibly expensive contracts.[37]

Like Marshall, when it comes to *homo economicus*, economists and sociologists have captured the relatively standardised behaviour of individuals searching for capital in order to maximise their dreams, projects and life achievements, including properties and housing.[38] History seems to have confirmed Marshall's thesis once; as argued by Lizabeth Cohen, after the Second World War, the so-called Consumer Republic structured itself under the perspective that each family would establish themselves as a social cell when occupying their own houses, which would be preferably purchased.[39]

In this context, the civil housing construction market has apparently developed itself in an isomorphic manner, taking advantage of the growing demand for residences in urban centres, of the high volume of state capital that subsides constructors, and of very similar models of contractual obligations (mortgages, elongated real estate credit and seemingly advantageous interest rates).[40]

Building and selling houses gained relevance in the world economy in the end of the twenty-first century, when it gave rise to increasingly bigger division scales,

---

the search for a balance between housing supply and demand (Johnson and Beale 1998, p. 18; Batty 2008, p. 770).

[35]Marshall (1950), p. 60.

[36]And so did (p.e.) the German Constitution, the Italian constitution (1947), and the Spanish one (1978). The US Constitution, as well as the Brazilian (1934) and the French (1958) ones gave established the inviolability of private from the perspective of house ownership, aiming at family peace and tranquillity.

[37]Kong (1992), pp. 147–161.

[38]Schumpeter and Hausman (1994), p. 228, 1949 Foucault et al. (2010).

[39]Parallel to the acquisition of property, there is the no less important relation of home leasing, not analysed in this study.

[40]Cohen (2004), p. 237.

redesigning supplier chains with industrial-like features. Ever since then, this sector started adopting sophisticated supply techniques and mass financing. Together with the promises of high profitability and land appreciation, this situation attracted financial investors, bank institutions and capital market actors who saw the 'dream' of home ownership as a powerful niche to be explored in an increasingly intense and aggressive manner.[41]

Up to the 2010s, this market niche consolidated into a truly good business model that brought about high rates of employment, an increase in payment of taxes, the union of large corporate groups and growing family debt due to profit (payment of interest) in real estate credit. During this last stage, private capital interest in real estate investment for families evolved through very aggressive commercial and financial practices, focused on fast return rates and lacking adequate preventive regulation. This sector of the economy, however, hitherto overstimulated, performed catastrophically, resulting in the historic 2008 global crisis. Hundreds of thousands of North American consumers found themselves unable to afford real estate credit payments, losing their jobs, income and their homes.[42]

Since then, notwithstanding the fact that real estate contracts and transactions were an established business modality, with a seemingly well-established regulation,[43] international authorities have been reviewing rules for granting baking credit and housing loans to consumers[44] who are known to be in extremely vulnerable conditions. The path of the post-2008 real estate market showed that all its refinement was not sufficient to beget legal or contractual instruments capable of protecting families from economic fluctuations and from speculation.

The precepts of modern private law were harshly put to the test, with its principles of residents who are free, self-determining and fully rational in their choices, when an astonishing number of consumers lost their homes overnight, victims of disloyal trade practices, from all across the northern hemisphere. Between the government and the housing production sector, there arose a need for the reformulation of public policies and the perception that citizens need a *new* protection system,[45] recommending the utmost care in acquiring their own homes.

[41]Stone (1983), p. 49.

[42]Kotz (2009), p. 16.

[43]Samuel and Lewis (1920), Coviello (1924).

[44]Turner et al. (2009).

[45]Schwartz (2012), pp. 35–58.

23.4 Dwelling: A Reflected Economic Need or an *Easy Dream*?

The business environment for the supply of real estate property is not as conservative as the twentieth century perception of a society described by Zygmunt Bauman as a 'producer society of solid modernity'. The times have changed, and the suppliers of the real estate sector work with a new psychological and behavioural understanding of consumers, exploiting what Bauman calls a 'liquid modernity' in capitalism.[46] The market does not sell homes but dreams, life projects and financial investments.

During the solid phase of capitalism, it was believed that consumer choices were steered towards precepts related to security, durability, stability and even a measure of ruggedness. The main values were moderation in spending and the desire to provide future generations with material goods, savings, and, naturally, to trade a life of renting for owning a home. The most common payment method for acquiring economic goods was done all at once and with accrued savings. The contracts so far had a character of immediate obligations, not long-lasting, and the most far-sighted people recommended that long-term payments be avoided so that the bond with creditors could be broken as soon as possible.[47]

Workers new to the urban scene would tend to limit their expenses to their monthly income, especially because providers and financial institutions seldom gave opportunities for instalment payment or payment through loans.[48] One of the few planned long-term debts acquired by the families was the mortgage for the purchase of a home, a protracted choice influenced by the conservatism stemming from much bureaucracy and the debtor's personal analysis, as well as political-economic instabilities, high inflation rates, freezing of prices and not very elastic income.

From the solid phase of capitalism to the following one, named by Bauman 'liquid modernity', marketing and other political-economic factors gradually introduced a change in consumer behaviour regarding purchase decisions. From the 1970s, individuals began to play the economic role of the estuary of industrial production, now integrated into market strategies and policies aiming at the maintenance of consumption proportionally to the growing supply. The means through which this economic goal was achieved was the exposure of individuals to unending publicity, in the context of a false notion of ease and legal security in contracts,

[46]The categories proposed by Bauman were not established based on sociopolitical conjectures, but take into account the choices and desires of social groups relating to their own consumption. Bauman (2008), p. 49.

[47]Bauman (2008), p. 42.

[48]Bauman (2008), p. 32.

based on the idea that, in the market, desire is enough to possess what the market offers unceasingly in fashion cycles.[49]

The consumer society, in the phase of liquid modernity, is frequently urged to replace the old with the new, acquiring the newest releases of the industry, in search of expanding their estate with increasingly fast cars, modern computers and ever-larger houses or apartments.[50] The lifestyle sought by people is no longer defined by their state of mind,[51] but by their clothes, shoes, accessories or hairstyles.[52]

The market has ceased to be an environment for the satisfaction of basic needs in life, as it was in the solid modernity of subsistence and security, to become a field for the realisation of every consumer's desires and aspirations. To experience this socio-economic model while dealing with low-economic-value goods and services is a possible scenario, aggravated when the short-sighted *liquidity* of the consumerist buying frenzy involves a residence whose financing is expensive, complex and of extremely long duration.

In this context, it is worrying to disfigure a home as an economic good of a merely residential use. To reside somewhere has become a lifestyle, an expression of personality and a social status shaped into neighbourhoods, condominiums and buildings custom built to generate a maximum sensation of well-being in consumers, the receivers of multi-services, design, comfort and safety. The value added to real estate has naturally been reflected by prices, interest and the extension of real estate contracts, with a steady increase in family debt due to real estate credit, characterised by high financial values and payments spanning almost entire lifetimes.[53]

[49]Bauman, Zygmunt. *Op. Cit.*, pp. 51–52. "Accordingly, in a society of consumers the pursuit of happiness – the purpose most often invoked and used as bait in marketing campaigns aimed at boosting consumers' willingness to part with their money (earned money, or money expected to be earned) – tends to be refocused from making things or their appropriation (not to mention their storage) to their disposal – just what is needed if the gross national product is to grow. For the consumerist economy, the previous focus, now by and large abandoned, portends the worst of worries: the stagnation, suspension or fading of buying zeal. The second focus, however, bodes rather well: another round of shopping. Unless supplemented by the urge to get rid of and discard, the urge for mere acquisition and possession would store up trouble for the future." Perhaps through a fault in translation, consumerism described the solid modernity of capitalism, it being patent in the Portuguese language that the word itself is associated with exaggerated consumption, which is, paradoxically, more in line with the characteristics of the liquid modernity of the second phase.

[50]After all, as illustrated by the song in the epigraph, *when you have more than you think, you need more space*.

[51]Jayme (2003), p. 60.

[52]Frade and Magalhaes (2006), p. 24.

[53]Souza (1999b).

23.5 Aspects of Aggravated Vulnerability in Debtors of Real Estate Contracts and Traces of the Brazilian Market

In Nabil Georges Bonduki's study,[54] the Brazilian reality reveals that, since the Vargas administration, the state has constantly worked to stimulate the acquisition of homes by the population, especially within the low-income classes. Such policies, however, have been established in direct connection with the productive sector, with its formulation and structural definition being done without the participation of the population, which normally assumes a passive stance.[55] The profile of the public intervention in this market has for a most distinctive characteristic the granting of legal and subsidiary benefits to the productive and financial sector with a direct impact on the system of bonds to be provided by debtors, in the models of real estate contracts with no room for negotiation, as well as in severe charges upon lack of payment.[56]

At first, the granting of real estate credit had a conservative character and was aided by the state,[57] but it eventually initiated a period of strong financial losses to Brazilian borrowers, affected by hyperinflationary interests linked to contracts that did not establish any protection to the debtors.[58] From the 1990s, the stabilisation of the Brazilian currency, together with greater levels of economic growth, enabled a more sophisticated real estate market, in which the interests and participation of actors from the private sector, disseminating more aggressive trade practices in property sale, especially concerning marketing. Despite the creation of the Consumer Protection Code, borrowers were still subjected to a very abusive set of trade practices and contract clauses.[59]

As an example, between the 2000s and the 2010s, the Brazilian real estate market saw the arrival of business (and contract) models hitherto unknown to the Brazilian legal framework. Dwelling units became available as investment funds, projecting financials, shared ownership properties, housing bonds, time sharing, rental pool and built to suit, not counting the intervention of bonds and resources

---

[54]Bonduki (2004), p. 192.

[55]Aigner et al. (2001), pp. 493–507.

[56]An example is Federal Law no. 5,107, of 13 September 1966, admitting and limiting the use of mandatory savings—of the Government Severance Indemnity Fund (FGTS)—for the acquisition of homes. Law no. 5,107/1966 was revoked by Law no. 8,036/1990. From the Vargas administration, Caixa Economica Federal bank began specialising in real estate credit, afterwards incorporating the National Housing Bank and becoming the largest Brazilian financial institution to subsidize credits for home acquisition. De Azevedo (1988), pp. 107–119.

[57]Feijo (2007), p. 466. Regarding John Maynard Keynes' *general theory*, practiced by capitalist economies since 1930, recommending government intervention in the economy to stimulate production, which, in turn, generated a rise in employment.

[58]Rolnik and Nakano (2009), p. 09.

[59]Santos Cláudio (1999).

from the capital market. In such models, builders' operational costs were maximised, with growing spending on publicity, brokerage and civil registry formalities.

Marketing has exacted a considerable change in the conception and cognitive function of real estate products from the consumer's point of view,[60] leaving aside the caution expected of one who engages in an expensive and lengthy commitment and making it seem ephemeral and fleeting so as to enhance the senses and the mood changes. Residential condominiums have gone from mere engineering projects to truly multifunctional enterprises, in which people's sensitive points are exploited, as in the case of the warlike surveillance apparatus that wholly exploits the fear brought on by urban violence to attract insecure residents.

Hundreds of publicity campaigns are divulged through papers and even on the television, as well as by text messages on mobile phones, advertising residential real estate units as simply as one would advertise any household appliance. The nuances of real estate financing and the complexities of civil construction (especially high rises) are subjected to oversimplification, in which *excessively easy* credit accelerates immediate and ill-considered acquisition processes, disregarding the idea of limited income and the particular long-term engagement.[61]

The idea of advanced purchase and immediatist consumption is materialised into units decorated before the building is delivered, set up in sumptuous and extremely luxurious sale stands. The sacred moment of researching and comparing prices and financing interest is disregarded when financial institutions already work in exclusive partnerships with building companies, advancing a pre-made joint financing proposal. The solemn act of delivering the keys, when it would be advisable to look closely at the physical and documental details of the unit, is replaced by festivities set to music and toasts that cloud the purchaser's judgment.

Common sense dictates how impressive it is that real estate brokers manage to bring value to homes by offering full leisure facilities, air conditioning, CCTV systems, posh decoration, etc. The consumer is rarely informed with transparency, however, about what is included in the real estate unit (especially the common area), as well as relevant items such as title clearance certificates, descriptive memoranda, attention to building regulations (such as the Brazilian Association of Technical Standards (ABNT)), the reach of home insurance cover, clarity in the payment of brokerage commissions, composition of the interest rates and their different application, etc.

Immediatist and impulsive purchasing behaviour, combined with the creation of shallow needs surrounding the consumption of products and services, make up the profile of liquid modernity consumers. The growth in the rate of sales, if Bauman's

[60]Benjamin Antonio Herman de Vasconcelos et al., *Op. Cit.*, p. 264.

[61]Caixa Econômica Federal has recently increased its real estate credit to periods of up to 35 years, obviously with interest that far surpasses the initial value of the acquired resource. Available at: http://www1.caixa.gov.br/imprensa/noticias/asp/popup_box.asp?codigo=6911946. Access on 8 February 2016.

idea[62] is taken into consideration, causes the consumer to lose sight of the concerns regarding planning, investment returns and savings in the so-called society open to credit.[63]

Based on the observation of the characteristics of the real estate market, it is possible to define this segment as having high absorption of capital, a considerable governmental participation to stimulate investors, constant changes in contract models and intense marketing stimulation of consumers. On the other hand, the market's current profile is also not transparent as to practices and obligations, obscure regarding charges (on payment and lack thereof) and evasive on the risks that an immediate and inconsiderate decision can bring to the family budget.

It must be stressed that the vulnerability of the consumer in real estate contracts is aggravated both in the models of supply (inputs) and in the practices and products offered (outputs). One can consider as inputs the regulatory framework of financing (norms for housing financing), types of contracts (and interest) on offer, the concept of the real estate product relayed to the consumer and the asymmetry of information. The outputs encompass the trade practices employed, the final quality of the products and services, and the asymmetry of information.[64]

Regarding all things hitherto considered, the harmony legally recommended between consumers and suppliers, as set out in article 4, item III, of the Consumer Protection Code, depends on the balance between inputs and outputs of the real estate market. It is necessary to reduce the flaws perceived not only from an economic standpoint but mainly in the legal protection to the most vulnerable party, the consumer, so that Brazil does not repeat the collapse observed in the northern hemisphere, especially during the 2008 economic and financial crisis, which had the real estate market for an epicentre.

23.6 Current Legal and Jurisprudential Aspects: The Vulnerability of the Real Estate Borrower Must Be Identified and Mitigated

On a legislative level, public policies do not seem to have evolved to increase specific protection to consumers of real estate products and services in their new situations of aggravation. From the consumer's standpoint, the Brazilian legal framework has been much the same since 1990, with the publication of the Consumer Protection Code. However, under the perspective of real estate suppliers, there are several recent norms regulating financing—whose wording puts

[62]Bauman (2008), p. 49.

[63]Marques et al. (Coord.) (2000), p. 3. In the United States, opening to credit began increasing in the 1970s. In some European countries, such as Portugal, the opening started in the 1990s. In both cases, the expansions were preceded by an organisation of the financial system.

[64]Sealey and Lindley (1977), pp. 1251–1266.

borrowers at a disadvantage, moving in the opposite direction of the public real estate policies currently practised in developed countries.

The models for public incentive to real estate credit in Brazil broadened the granting of bonds overlapped with the financial institutions. The classic incentive model is set out in Law no. 4,380/1964, which instituted the Real Estate Financing System, aimed at 'facilitating and promoting the construction and acquisition of homes, especially by the lower-income classes' (article 8, Law no. 4,380/1964). Its main characteristic is drawing upon the FGTS and savings accounts, which has relatively lowered the costs of real estate transactions, despite not reducing the interests paid by consumers. Financing operations based on this contract model flooded the Brazilian judicial branch with a wide variety of suits filed by borrowers who could not pay their debts. The law underwent alterations (in 2001 and 2009) that broadened the guarantees for real estate creditors.

The main questions of the consumers pointed out the disparity between the rate chosen for the escalation of the contracts' outstanding balance and the evolution of the borrower's income, as well as the practice of capitalised interest (anatocism). In practice, they are long-term contracts that could not be paid on time, particularly due to incomprehension of the duties brought on by the contract at the time of its signature. Having as basis the rulings of the Superior Court of Justice (constitutionally competent to be the last instance of interpretation of Brazilian federal law) regarding such contracts, interest is reviewed in favour of good faith. However, incomprehensibly, the Consumer Protection Code has a different application in some cases (such as contracts covered by the Credit Guarantee Fund (FCVS)).[65]

A second model was built with Law no. 9,154/1997, around the Real Estate Financing System and shaped to seek more openness and competitiveness in the granting of real estate products, adopting the strategy of attracting investors to the real estate sector. The incentive granted by the norm worked not only with the flexibility of interest rates but also with the overlapping of contract bonds, with emphasis on the modality of the out-of-court auctioning of the property, hitherto non-existent in the country (articles 24 to 27 of Law no. 9,514/1997, with alterations by Law no. 10,931/2004). In face of the new model, a new batch of lawsuits is filed in the judicial branch, questioning the abusive position of real estate creditors when auctioning debtors' residences, especially concerning disrespect to the property's commercial value and the refusal to return the difference already paid by the consumer.

Consumers who used to deal solely with a construction company and a bank now discuss their debt with securitisation companies, investment funds and even parties

[65]See the following rulings by the Superior Court of Justice (STJ): AgRg no REsp 902.555/SP, Rapporteur: Minister ANTONIO CARLOS FERREIRA, FOURTH PANEL, ruled on 18/12/2012, DJe 04/02/2013; AgRg no AREsp 438.106/RS, Rapporteur: Minister HERMAN BENJAMIN, SECOND PANEL, ruled on 12/08/2014, DJe 25/09/2014; AgRg no AREsp 527.456/RS, Rapporteur: Minister RAUL ARAÚJO, FOURTH PANEL, ruled on 03/02/2015, DJe 18/02/2015; REsp 954.588/RS, Rapporteur: Minister HUMBERTO MARTINS, SECOND PANEL, ruled on 06/03/2012, DJe 14/03/2012.

not mentioned in the original contract, if they are acquiring property through Law no. 9,514/1997. The auction run by the creditors, in these situations, takes place through a simple notification, outside the legal suit, and thus without the possibility of refuting the value at which the property was appraised, and with an even smaller spectrum for debtors to have their say. When it comes to defending the value paid by consumers in face of the aforementioned auction, the Superior Court of Justice has upheld the enforcement of Law no. 9,514/1997, with no aid whatsoever to borrowers, who frequently have no knowledge of contracting or authorising this form of auction.[66]

Apart from the concept of the contract models and regulatory framework itself, matters such as the possibility of applying more onerous interest before delivering the keys[67] and the right for judicial suits discussing insurers' responsibilities for perceived damages in low-income housing to be tried by ordinary courts (as opposed to federal courts) have been treated favourably to the financing companies.[68]

In such circumstances, legal solutions in Brazil seem to be moving towards the protection of the capital invested by the real estate sector and not the protection of the market's consumers, affecting sensitive topics both in its inputs and its outputs. This perception of government intervention is out of sync with other economies and legal systems, such as the North American, in a worrying discrepancy with the protection of this possible category of vulnerable consumers. A few years ago, the National Commission created to assess and present the causes of the economic and financial crisis of the United States (GPO) published the Financial Crisis Inquiry Report, stating that:

> The US Government public real estate policies contributed the most to the 2008 financial crisis. Such policies fed an enormous real estate bubble between 1997 and 2007 and fostered the granting of 27 million low-income loans, many of which were ready to fail as soon as the bubble began to inflate.[69]

If the robust North American economy identified a market flaw in the public real estate policy that deregulated the protection of consumers of real estate credit, considering the due proportions, it does not seem a safe path for less-structured economies and legal systems—such as the Brazilian one—to tend towards greater

[66]MC 20.135/SC, Rapporteur: Minister LUIS FELIPE SALOMÃO, FOURTH PANEL, DJe 22/10/2012; AgREsp 638.441/SP, Rapporteur: Minister LUIS FELIPE SALOMÃO, FOURTH PANEL, DJe 19/05/2015.

[67]AgRg no AREsp 262.706/RJ, Rapporteur: Minister LUIS FELIPE SALOMÃO, FOURTH PANEL, ruled on 11/02/2014, DJe 17/02/2014; **EREsp 670.117-PB, Original Rapporteur: SIDNEI BENETI, Rapporteur for appellate ruling: Minister Antonio Carlos Ferreira, 2nd Section, STJ, ruled on 13/6/2012.**

[68]AgRg no AREsp 363.451/PE, Rapporteur: Minister HUMBERTO MARTINS, SECOND PANEL, ruled on 08/09/2015, DJe 16/09/2015; EDcl no AgRg no REsp 1519713/MG, Rapporteur: Minister HUMBERTO MARTINS, SECOND PANEL, ruled on 13/11/2015.

[69]Available at: https://www.gpo.gov/fdsys/pkg/GPO-FCIC/pdf/GPO-FCIC.pdf. Access 8 February 2016.

flexibility in consumer vulnerability regarding home acquisition contracts. On a legislative and jurisprudential level, there are clear signs that consumers have not been given adequate protection, and these decisions tend to affect them in their capacity to maintain their contractual commitments balanced and on time. In such circumstances, legal solutions in Brazil tend towards the protection of the capital invested by the real estate sector, leaving consumers unprotected in this market.

23.7 Conclusion

Vulnerability is a key concept in the *new private law* that, despite the existence of studies to better understand it, remains open and to be complemented by research works that consider new market realities, the analysis of the practical trade and contract differences that represent unknown vulnerabilities to consumers' good faith, trust and security. The humanisation of private law relations has attracted—to studies and legal concepts—multidisciplinary approaches that allow for the broadening of the generalist understanding of the individual, replacing it with the search for individual legal protection, capable of adjusting the jurisdictional application to the needs of each consumer, considering their peculiarity and particularity.

The market niche and real estate transactions with consumers currently represent a peculiar context of legal relationship, in which vulnerability is aggravated in relation to borrowers purchasing homes. The value of contracts is high and generally represents the highest debt of the family unit that uses real estate financing. However, the perceived trade practices do not adopt the preventive measures recommended by the doctrine and consumer protective legislation, revealing an undue oversimplification of the engagement in large long-term debt. Real estate products are advertised in a massive and unceasing manner, in publicity campaigns that give housing a *liquid* and fleeting character, more concerned with status and satisfaction than with the build quality or the ability to make payments.

To enter a real estate deal is no everyday act, in spite of the image shown by the civil construction industry to consumers, forsaking the legal responsibilities of information and warning. There is parsimony on the state's part not only in controlling this publicity but especially in the deregulation of real estate contracts, which ends up leaving the consumer unprotected in relation to real estate suppliers. The laws that regulate real estate financing, on their part, have allowed for greater encumbrance on borrowers, imposing increasingly excessive payments upon consumers. The enforcement of the Consumer Protection Code has been neglected for some modalities of financing, as well as to admit that consumers pay compound interests or lose their homes without due right to reply or defence.

The lessons learned by more experienced economies and legal systems, such as the North American one (in 2008), seem to recommend that government intervention recognises the vulnerability of the borrower in real estate, avoiding more liberties to real estate investors. Such as banking, real estate is afforded a high level of protection for stimulating the country's economic growth, as well as due to the sensitivity of the systemic balance of economy. However, there seem to be no doubts that the role of real estate credit has been overestimated, and its protection does not justify treading on consumers' rights and bonds.

Working with the concept of vulnerability specifically applied to real estate contracts seems to allow insights and solutions that re-establish clearer boundaries in legal security to borrowing consumers, as well as the readaptation of the publicity, the contract models and the practices employed. The legal system that implements real estate credit (both the SFN and SFI) also has social purposes, which will only make sense if the consumer is protected in all stages of this specific economic relation. It does not seem to be the right path to abandon the protection of the borrowing consumer, considering that public policies should broaden the concept of incentive beyond the simple notion of facilitated real estate credit, that is, perceiving the consumer's vulnerability as a key factor to be tackled, providing the sector with sustainability.

References

Aigner SM, Flora CB, Hernandez JM (2001) The premise and promise of citizenship and civil society for renewing democracies and empowering sustainable communities. Sociol Inq 71 (4):493–507

Barassi L (1955) Instituiciones de Derecho Civil. Trad. Ramon Garcia de Haro de Goytisolo. JMB, Barcelona, vol. 1

Batty M (2008) The size, scale, and shape of cities. Science 319:5864

Bauman Z (2008) Modernidade Líquida. Translation by Plínio Dentzen. Zahar, Rio de Janeiro

Benjamin AH de V et al (1999) Código Brasileiro de Defesa do Consumidor: comentado pelos autores do anteprojeto. 6th edn. Forense Universitária, Rio de Janeiro

Bessa LR (2009) Relação de Consumo e aplicação do Código de Defesa do Consumidor. Editora Revista dos Tribunais, São Paulo

Bonduki N (2004) Origens da habitação social no Brasil: arquitetura moderna, lei do inquilinato e difusão da casa própria, 4th edn. Estação Liberdade, São Paulo

Bonduki N (2008) Política habitacional e inclusão social no Brasil: revisão histórica e novas perspectivas no governo Lula. Revista eletrônica de Arquitetura e Urbanismo 1:70–104

Cohen L (2004) A consumers' republic: the politics of mass consumption in postwar America. J Consum Res 31(1):236–239

Coviello N (1924) Della trascrizione. Marghieri, Napoli

De Azevedo S (1988) Vinte e dois anos de política de habitação popular (1964–1986): criação, trajetória e extinção do BNH. Revista de Administração Pública 22(4)

De Carvalho DF, Dos Santos N (2015) A vulnerabilidade psíquica e o superendividamento do consumidor. Diretoria-Conpedi, p 111

Doneda D (2006) Da privacidade à proteção de dados pessoais. Renovar, Rio de Janeiro

Feijo R (2007) História do pensamento econômico: de Lao Zi a Robert Lucas, 2nd edn. Atlas, São Paulo

Ferreira ABdeH (2004) Novo dicionário Aurélio da língua portuguesa. Editora Positivo

Foucault M, Ewald F, Fontana A (2010) The birth of biopolitics: lectures at the Collège de France, 1978–1979. Palgrave Macmillan, Basingstoke

Frade C, Magalhaes SS (2006) A outra face do crédito. In: Maeques CL, Cavallazzi RL (Coord.) Direitos do consumidor endividado: superendividamento e crédito. RT, São Paulo

Furtado BA, Limaneto VC, Krause C (2013) Estimativas do déficit habitacional brasiliero (2007–2011) por municípios (2010)
Jayme E (2003) Direito Internacional Privado e Cultura Pós-Moderna. Cadernos do Programa de Pós-Graduação em Direito – PPGDir./UFRGS, Porto Alegre: PPGDir./UFRGS, 1(1), March
Johnson KM, Beale CL (1998) The rural rebound. Wilson Q 22(2)
Kong K (1992) The cransformation of a 'Real-Socialist' administrative system into a conventional Western European System. Int Rev Adm Sci 58(2)
Kotz DM (2009) The financial and economic crisis of 2008: a systemic crisis of neoliberal capitalism. Rev Radical Polit Econ, p 16
Lima CCde (2014) O tratamento do superendividamento e o direito de recomeçar dos consumidores. Revista dos Tribunais, São Paulo
Marques CL, Miragem B (2014) O novo direito privado e a proteção dos vulneráveis, 2nd edn. Revista dos Tribunais, São Paulo, pp 24–29
Marques MML et al (Coord.) (2000) O endividamento dos consumidores. Almedina, Coimbra
Marshall TH (1950) Citizenship and social class, vol 11. Cambridge University Press, Cambridge
Monteiro WB (2003) Curso de Direito Civil: direito das obrigações, 32nd edn. Saraiva, São Paulo
Moraes PVDP (1999) O Código de Defesa do Consumidor: princípio da vulnerabilidade no contrato, na publicidade, nas demais práticas comerciais. Síntese, Porto Alegre
Oliveira AFde, Castro BBde (2014) Proteção do consumidor de crédito: uma abordagem a partir da economia comportamental. Revista de Direito do Consumidor 93. Revista dos Tribunais, São Paulo
Rodrigues S (1979) Dos vícios de consentimento. Saraiva, São Paulo
Rolnik R, Nakano K (2009) As armadilhas do pacote habitacional. Le monde diplomatique Brasil 5(3)
Samuel W, Lewis CM (1920) The law of contracts. Voorhis & Company, Baker
Santos Cláudio HM (1999) Políticas federais de habitação no Brasil: 1964/1988. IPEA, Brasília
Schumpeter JA, Hausman DM (1994) Science and Ideology
Schwartz H (2012) Housing, the welfare state, and the global financial crisis what is the connection?. Polit Soc 40(1)
Sealey CW, Lindley JT (1977) Inputs, outputs, and a theory of production and cost at depository financial institutions. J Financ 32(4):1251–1266
Souza HMde (1999a) A Natureza, o Homem e a Economia: considerações, leis e mecanismos de interação e equilíbrio. UnB, Brasília
Souza HMde (1999b) The overspent American: why. New York
Stone PA (1983) Building economy: design, production, and organization: a synoptic view, 3rd edn. Oxford Press, Oxford
Turner A et al (2009) The turner review: a regulatory response to the global banking crisis. Financial Services Authority, London

Chapter 24
Consumer Protection in E-Commerce in Brazil: The Updating of the Consumer's Protection Code

Antonia Espíndola Longoni Klee

24.1 Introduction

The globalization and the international commerce resultant from the cultural, social, and economic development of mankind do bring worries.[1] One of the most characteristic results of globalization is the creation of the Internet,[2] a fact that links the global community together in a virtual world by means of the communication provided by the international network, which has extinguished the space, as mentioned by Jayme,[3] and has represented a real rupture with the past.[4]

---

[1]Jayme (2003), p. 85.

[2]Lorenzetti teaches that "The Internet is 'an international network of interconnected computers, allowing tenths of millions of people to communicate among themselves, as well as the access to a huge quantity of information all over the world'. Some legally interesting features can be observed: it is an open network, as anyone can access it; it is interactive, as the user generates data, navigates, and establishes relations; it is international, in the sense that it allows transcending the national barriers; there is a multiplicity of operators; it has a self-referring system configuration which lacks a center that may called 'authority', operates in a decentralized way, and builds the order as of chaotic rules; has the aptitude of generating its own rules on base of custom; presents an acceleration of the historic time; allows communication in 'real time', and a 'de-territorialization' of the legal relations; decreases drastically the cost of transactions". Lorenzetti (2004), pp. 24–26.

It is said that the Word Internet has been first utilized in 1974. Mercosul.com (Org.) (2000), p. 6.

The Internet can be also defined as follows: "[...] international interconnected computers network, that allows its users a quick and dynamic exchange of matters [. . .] Motta et al. (2005), p. 242.

Martins asserts that the Internet is one of the most emblematic faces of globalization. Martins (2010), p. 3.

[3]Jayme (2003), p. 86. In that text the author points out the feature of ubiquity inherent to the E-commerce. The text has been also published in Jayme (2005), pp. 3–20.

[4]Wald (2003), p. 61.

A. Espíndola Longoni Klee (✉)
Faculty of Law, Federal University of Rio Grande do Sul, Porto Alegre, Brazil
e-mail: antoniaklee@hotmail.com

C. Lima Marques, D. Wei (eds.), *Consumer Law and Socioeconomic Development*,
DOI 10.1007/978-3-319-55624-6_24

Such communication, facilitated by the Internet, determines a greater vulnerability of those who communicate.[5] Among those are the consumers who relate to suppliers of products and services,[6] entering into remote contracts, connecting themselves by the Internet, which is a new environment of interpersonal relationship.

The Internet has come about in a system of interconnected computer networks in the United States of America, in the Cold War period, along the 1960s, for military and industrial protection purposes.[7] The world computer network had and has the feature of assuring the quick access to information, not having a unique center for data issuing and receiving. It has appeared as a necessity for distributing information in a decentralized way. In a war time, that was especially important due to the possibility of any attack that would destroy the center of command of the military operations. With the Internet, data might go on being retransmitted, irrelevant of the specific communication points that could be obliterated. Subsequently, the computer interlinking network started to be utilized in the American universities and research laboratories. In a third moment, it has spread around the world. Thus, a great amount of information has become available to people and institutions that could access the network.

The Internet is a world computer network operated by people interacting and communicating, exchanging messages, files and texts, data, images, sound, and voice. Once utilized by companies, the Internet has enabled negotiation without

---

[5]Marques (2004), p. 72.

[6]The concept of supplier is in art. 3rd of the CDC. Marques says of the concept of supplier in Marques (2006), pp. 393–426.

See also, Pasqualotto (1991), p. 52, abr.

For the comments on art. 3rd of the CDC, see Nunes (2007), pp. 108–124.

In the same way, see Filomeno (2007), pp. 46–50.

Bessa explains the concept of *equated supplier*, beside the *generic concept* of supplier of art. 3rd of the CDC. The author explains that the Consumer's Defense Code indicates and details in other parts, other than in art. 3rd, activities carried out by suppliers of products and services that are subject to the law. Therefore, the definition of *equated supplier* takes into consideration the preponderance of the supplier's activity, and not the configuration of a supplier with all the requirements of the *caput* of art. 3rd. Bessa (2007), pp. 84–87.

[7]Martins asserts that the origin of the Internet "dates back to the 1960s, during the Cold War, when the North American government started the Arpanet project (precursor of the Internet, created by ARPA—Advanced Research Projects Agency, in the sense of a connection among military and industrial computers, in 1969, via the telephone network, so as to prevent a possible nuclear attack, and, in face of such preoccupation, not one only control center to be destroyed existed"—Martins (2010), p. 33.

The same way, it is asserted that the creation of the Internet occurred in in 1960s, in the United States of America, although being recognized as a global phenomenon only in the 1990s, with the creation of the World Wide Web, or simply www, which basic idea has been created by Tim Berners-Lee in 1989. Mercosul.com (Org.) (2000), p. 5 e 7.

frontiers, both in the business-to-business (B2B)[8] and in the business-to-consumers (B2C) relationships.[9]

More than an effective change in the relationship systems, the Internet requires a necessity of transposing and adapting concepts and, wherever applicable, making adequate the existing law,[10] to be complemented by the specific regulation of the innovative aspects of the computer world network, in a civil-constitutional approach, pursuant to the principle of prohibiting retrogression (or of no regression), considered implicitly by the Brazilian Constitution of 1988.[11]

Under such approach, a Jurists Committee has been instituted by the Federal Senate Presidency,[12] with the purpose of supplying subsidies for the updating of the Consumer's Protection and Defense Code, among other aspects, in the e-commerce subject matter. Such Committee has elaborated a Draft Bill, which on August 2, 2012, has gone through the Federal Senate, identified as Senate's Bill n° 281 of 2012, which "Amends Act n° 8078 of September 11th, 1990 (Consumer's

---

[8]The *B2B* is also known as *e-biz*, defined as "the exchange of products, services, or information between companies, more than between companies and consumers". Mercosul.com (Org.) (2000), p. 34.

[9]Ballarino refers that, besides the *B2B* and the *B2C* contracts, there are the *P2P (peer to peer)*, which "are those entered between subjects of the 'degree', mainly known by the exchange of music files according to the modalities of *Napster"*. Ballarino (2006), p. 203.

[10]Professor Doctor Cesar Viterbo Matos Santolim, a Pioneer in the treatment of the legal aspects of E-commerce, in his excellent Master's Dissertation, defended at the School of Law of UFRGS in 1993, subsequently published as a book, *Formação e eficácia probatória dos contratos por computador*. São Paulo. Saraiva, 1995, sustains that the consumer's protection in E-commerce can occur by applying the principles already enshrined in that sphere, i.e. objective good faith, transparency, confidence, probity, vulnerability, obligational solidarity, and private autonomy. Santolim (2005) p. 55, jul./set.

We can say that Santolim has been inspired by the magnificent Clovis do Couto e Silva, *magister emeritus* at the School of Law of UFRGS, who pondered: "Certainly, the legal world has shortcomings, but this means that it is in a constant evolvement, making its principles dynamic, in contact with the social necessities, so as to comprehend situations not foreseen before". Couto e Silva (1976), p. 113.

Junqueira asserts that to the electronic contracts are also applicable the principles of obligatoriness, autonomy of the will, consensualism, and good faith. Junqueira (1997), p. 111.

Following the steps of Santolim and Junqueira, Elias affirms that to those contracts entered via the Internet are applicable, besides the already mentioned principles, the one of loyal cooperation, and the one of information. Elias (2008), p. 70.

[11]On such theme, Sarlet (2009).

[12]The Jurists Committee has been created on December 2, 2010 by Act n° 305 of the Chairman, who has been reelected until March 31, 2012, by Acts of Chairman n° 308 of 2010, n° 115 of 2011, and n° 206 of 2011. In such period, the Jurists Committee has been presided by the Minister of the Superior Court of Justice (STJ) Antonio Herman de Vasconcellos e Benjamin, and as members Professor Doctor Claudia Lima Marques (Relater-General), and by the professors doctors Ada Pellegrini Grinover, Leonardo Roscoe Bessa, Roberto Augusto Castellanos Pfeiffer and Kazuo Watanabe, and has been advised in the technical-legal area by the legal-technician Wellerson Miranda Pereira. The Report-General of the Committee may be read at Brasil. Senado Federal. Atualização do Código de Defesa do Consumidor: anteprojetos: relatório. Brasília, DF, [2012]. See, mainly p. 27 et seq.

Defense Code), for to improve the general provisions of Chapter I of Title I, and provide on E-commerce."[13]

The synopsis of Bill n° 281 of 2012 on e-commerce shows the following explanation:

> [. . .] establishing that the legal rules and businesses should be construed and integrated in a manner more favorable for the consumer, and provide on general rules for the consumer's protection in the E-commerce, so as to reinforce their trust and guarantee an effective defense, preserving the safety in transactions, protection to self-determination and privacy of personal data; the rules apply to those activities developed by suppliers of products and services by electronic means, or similar; establishes that consumers can cancel remote contracting within seven days as of accepting an offer, or receipt or availability of a product or service; provides that should a consumer exercise the right to cancel, the accessory credit contracts are automatically terminated, without any cost to consumer; typifies as a penal infringement the act of publishing, hosting, exhibiting, disposing, utilizing, sharing, donating, or in any way assign or transfer personal data, information or identifiers, without the express authorization of their owner and informed consent, save legal exceptions.[14]

On March 14, 2012, on the eve of the Consumer's World Day, the Minister of the Superior Court of Justice Antônio Herman de Vasconcellos e Benjamin has handed to the Senate's President, Senator José Sarney, the Report-General of the Jurists Committee for the Updating of the Consumer's Defense Code, with the propositions passed by the members of the Jurists' Committee to be analyzed by the Environment Committee, Consumer's Defense and Inspection & Control (CMA). The main themes approached by the jurists in the three bills were e-commerce, overindebtedness, and class actions. Minister Benjamin has then affirmed: "The proposed updating is surgical. The CDC is a landmark of citizenship, although, after 20 years, it needs to be renewed."[15]

Since August 15, 2012, Bill n° 281 has been going through Congress. It was approved by the Plenary of the Senate and was sent to the House of Representatives in November 2015. During its processing, Bill n° 281 went through several changes, and many provisions are quite different from its original proposal. However, the main objective remains the same.

Bill 281/2012 comes to reinforce the aspect of a more favorable protection of the consumer, not only in the general consumption relations but also in regard to e-commerce.

---

[13]Senate Bill n° 281/2012 amends Act n° 8078, of September 11, 1990 (Consumer's Defense Code), so as to improve the general provisions of Chapter I of Title I, and provide on E-commerce. Available at: http://www.senado.leg.br/atividade/rotinas/materia/getPDF.asp?t=177192&tp=1. Access on: 7 April 2016.

[14]Senate Bill n° 281/2012 amends Act n° 8078, of September 11, 1990 (Consumer's Defense Code), so as to improve the general provisions of Chapter I of Title I, and provide on E-commerce. Explanation on synopsis. Available at: http://www.senado.leg.br/atividade/rotinas/materia/getPDF.asp?t=177192&tp=1. Access on: 7 April 2016.

[15]Brazil. Federal Senate. Jurists Committee presents report on the CDC updating. Available at: http://www12.senado.gov.br/noticias/materias/2012/03/14/comissao-de-juristas-encerra-primeira-etapa-do-cdc. Access on: 30 Jul. 2012.

From among the rights assured by the CDC, regarding electronic contracts, are the provisions of article 31.[16] That is so because, certainly, one of the main functions of the Internet is to provide the means of presenting and offering products and services. Therefore, the offer and presentation of products via the Internet must assure correct, clear, precise, and ostensive information about the features, qualities, quantity, composition, price, guarantee, terms of validity, and origin, among other information, as well as the risks they present to the consumers' health and safety. Such rights should be also assured in contracts by the Internet.

Regarding safety, Bill 281/2012 has added subparagraphs XI and XII to article 6 of the CDC, as follows:

> Art. 6th. The basic rights of consumers are:
>
> [...]:
>
> XI – self-determination, privacy, and safety of personal information and data provided or collected by any means, including electronic;
>
> XII – freedom of choice, mainly in face of new technologies and data networks, being prohibited any form of discrimination and harassment to consumption.[17]

In a seminar in Rio de Janeiro about e-commerce regulation in Brazil, dealing with subparagraph XII of article 6 of the Consumers Defense Code, Guilherme Magalhães Martins[18] provoked the audience with the following questions: freedom of choice of whom? Freedom of expression of whom? There is a need to discuss these principles and to apply them always in the perspective of the protection of the consumers' rights. By the time discussing the end of net neutrality, it is important to think about it.

Santolim ponders that "By mentioning, besides the 'privacy' and the 'safety', also the 'self-determination' of information, as a 'basic right' of consumers, the Bill focuses exactly on the dynamic perspective of the utilization of the acquired information by the supplier."[19] With such, the author wants to say that "any application of such information for producing new information should be the object of a previous authorization by consumer."[20]

[16]See comments on art. 31 of CDC by Benjamin, Antônio Herman de Vaconcellos e. Das práticas comerciais. In: Grinover, Ada Pellegrini et al. *Código Brasileiro de Defesa do Consumidor*: comentado pelos autores do anteprojeto. 9. ed. rev., atual. e ampl. Rio de Janeiro: Forense Universitária, 2007. pp. 282–289. See also, Nunes (2007), pp. 396–411.

For an analysis on the application of art. 31 of the CDC by the courts, see Marques, Claudia Lima; Benjamin, Antônio Herman de Vasconcellos and; Miragem (2006), pp. 482–494.

[17]Senate Bill n° 281/2012 amends Act n° 8078, of September 11, 1990 (Consumer's Defense Code), so as to improve the general provisions of Chapter I of Title I, and provide on E-commerce. Available at: http://www.senado.leg.br/atividade/rotinas/materia/getPDF.asp?t=177192&tp=1. Access on: 7 April 2016.

[18]Martins, Guilherme Magalhães. Information and Safety (Lecture). Consumer's protection in E-commerce (Pannel). Seminar on regulation of E-commerce in Brazil. Rio de Janeiro and Palácio (2012).

[19]Santolim (2012), p. 73 et seq.

[20]Santolim (2012), p. 73 et seq.

In those two subparagraphs added by the Committee, "There is a strengthening in the consumer's protection,"[21] based on trust, and yearning for all phenomena of remote distribution. The idealizers of the Bill have provided an equalization of purchases made outside the business place, at home, and remotely so as to impart more safety to relations,[22] thus purchases made by the site, being the consumer or not in the supplier's place.

24.2 Innovations Brought by Senate Bill n° 281/2012 to the Consumer's Rights in Brazil: The E-Commerce

The main change wanted by Senate Bill n° 281/2012 includes regulation of e-commerce to the Consume's Defense Code. The addition of art. 44-A to the text of CDC inaugurates Section VII of Chapter V (The Commercial Practices) of Title I (The Consumer's Rights). This Section VII is called "The Electronic Commerce" and it aims to regulate consumer protection in e-commerce in Brazil.

Article 44-A determines that Section VII "provides general protection rules of the consumer in the E-commerce, aiming at reinforcing their confidence and assuring an effective protection, reducing the asymmetry of information, the preservation of safety in transactions, the protection to self-determination and privacy of personal data," more or less repeating the provisions of article 6, XI, of the Bill.

Article 44-A provides the confidence, freedom of the other party, the weaker party, and mentions good faith. It is a rule of overture and aims at reinforcing such confidence, guaranteeing the effective consumer's tutelage, providing the application of the rules of the CDC to the electronic media or similar media, foreseeing the technological advancement, which is a positive thing.

Article 44-B determines the minimum information for the consumer to be given access to the supplier. Such provision dialogues with articles 31 and 33 of the CDC, bringing them over to its core, incorporating them; considering that article 44-B will be applied jointly with articles 31 and 33 of the CDC, always by legal determination, in contracts entered into by electronic means, article 44-B imposes a series of requirements to be fulfilled by the supplier of the products and services that they wish to market with consumers by electronic means. Such requirements are information that should be made available in a clear place, of easy viewing, in the supplier's webpage.

Article 44-B is inspired by the general good faith clause and the supplier's duty to inform. It is qualified information that the supplier must give to consumers so as to impart safety on the business to be entered by the parties: the information about the supplier that uses an electronic or similar means.[23]

---

[21]Santolim (2012), p. 73 et seq.

[22]Marques (2012).

[23]Marques (2012).

Santolim points out that the proposed article 44-B "considers a set of information about the supplier, in the E-commerce, that should be made available to the consumer."[24] The author points out that it is about the "application of the principle of good faith (objective), in its sub-principle of transparency, and that it is good for to impart a minimum necessary of certainty about the very existence of the other party."[25]

Article 44-C provides for the specific information that should be presented about the features of the products and services offered by electronic or similar means.

Such provision goes on imposing a series of obligations to the supplier of products and services utilizing electronic or similar means: "it means the application of trust [. . .], emphasizing the necessity that the electronic means be not only efficacious as an instrument for accessing the market for the supplier's profit, but for preserving the possibilities of protection to the consumer's interests."[26]

The contents of the proposed article 44-D also point out the protection of trust in the e-commerce. Such provision governs the conducts imposed on suppliers in the sense of enlarging the consumer's access to the whole business carried out. One should emphasize the preoccupation of the Jurists Committee in the sense of supporting the characteristic of integrity of the electronic registration, "requirement without which one could not recognize the effectiveness evidence of a 'document', in its legal sense," as emphasized by Santolim.[27] The contextual preoccupation, which is the basis for such provision, is the question of a contract's lasting support.

Article 44-E imposes a list of supplier's obligations when contracting electronically with consumers: (1) before signing the contract, the supplier must send the content of the contract (its clauses) to the consumer, written in Portuguese, in an accessible language, and can be easily viewed on the supplier's webpage; (2) the supplier must send immediate confirmation of receipt of acceptance of the offer; (3) the supplier must offer a contract via a durable medium, understood as any instrument, including electronic, that offers guarantees of reliability, intelligibility, and conservation of contractual data while still allowing ease of reproduction (printing or copying); (4) the supplier must provide a form or a facilitated and specific hyperlink to consumer fulfillment in case of exercise of the right to retract. Article 44-E also provides that if the supplier does not fulfill these obligations, the cooling off period should be extended for another 14 days.

Article 44-F aimed at forbidding the practice of spamming. Such provision proposes to ban the sending of nonrequested electronic message to certain addressees.

The Committee has adopted the *opt in* model, which means that "the consumer who wishes receiving the messages should say in advance in that sense, nevertheless recognizing also the *opt out* modality [. . .]."[28]

---

[24] Santolim (2012), p. 73 et seq.

[25] Santolim (2012), p. 73 et seq.

[26] Santolim (2012), p. 73 et seq.

[27] Santolim (2012), p. 73 et seq.

[28] Santolim (2012), p. 73 et seq.

Thus, a supplier should not send electronic messages to consumers unless the consumer has already opted for receiving them or has already entered into a contractual relationship with the company. In other words, a supplier cannot send over electronic messages to consumers if there is no previous relationship and must stop sending them if consumer says he does not want to receive the e-mails anymore.

Behind such discussion lays the subject of prohibiting the sale of costumers' records and the "follow the money" rule, which is a way of reinforcing the safety of consumers' data.

That is, if the supplier can send e-mails over to the consumer, the messages stop being nonrequested, stop being illegal, either because there has been a previous consumption relationship or because the consumer has authorized them. The text is not clear.

Article 44-G provides that the supplier of product or service through the Internet or any other electronic commerce mode will only ask the consumer to provide the information necessary for the completion of the contract; any other information in addition to the indispensable one will be optional, and the consumer must be given advance notice of this condition.

The same way, it is important to point out the guarantee provided in article 49 of the CDC, where there is a provision for right to retract, which purpose is protecting the consumer's will,[29] for such will to be calmly decided and reflected, protected from the aggressive techniques of home sales, out of the business place and remote. Such right, expressly guaranteed by the CDC, influences positively the protection of a consumer who contracts by electronic means, as Internet contracting is deemed a remote contracting. Article 49 is the subject of an updating by the Senate Bill n° 281 and deserves to be applauded.

Article 49 of the CDC mentions expressly those contracts celebrated out of the business place, or celebrated by the telephone, and it provides a seven-days cooling off period to the consumer. The Bill cared about not holding itself just for the electronic means idea for it is a concept that is widening itself.[30] Communication through the Internet is similar to the one by telephone. Therefore, one may say that the legal relations established in a virtual environment are also regulated by such rule,[31] because they are remote contracting, entered into out of the business place. However, there being an updating of the provision, should the Congress pass the text of Senate Bill n° 281/2012, the mentioning in electronic contracts will become clear and express, and there should remain no doubt that article 49 will be applicable to contracts celebrated by electronic means.

---

[29] See the comments on art. 49 of the CDC in Nery Junior (2007), pp. 559–564. See also Nunes (2007), pp. 565–572. For an analysis of the application of art. 49 of the CDC by the courts, see MARQUES, Claudia Lima; BENJAMIN, Antônio Herman de Vasconcellos and; MIRAGEM, Bruno Nubens Barbosa. *Comentários ao Código de Defesa do Consumidor*: artigo por artigo. 2. ed., rev., updated & enlarged. São Paulo: Revista dos Tribunais, 2006. pp. 670–683.

[30] Marques (2012).

[31] Marques (2006), p. 856.

According to its present text, article 49 sets two cumulative requirements for a consumer's contract right to retract: (a) the seven-day term has been complied with, and (b) the contracting has been held out of the business place. By such provision, the Code's elaborator aimed at safeguarding the situations where a consumer who did not have access to the product or service and, therefore, the term is designed to verify the correspondence between the consumer's expectation and the real product purchased due to its increased vulnerability, resulting from the distance between the contracting parties.

By the light of the doctrine and jurisprudence, a contract out of the business place is being deemed as entered into when (a) the product is delivered at the consumer's home and (b) the contracting of the product or service is carried out by telephone.

Assuring the rights to retract in e-commerce is a way of protecting the consumer and preventing abusive practices by suppliers.[32] This is because, according to Almeida: "Under the name of cancellation rights, are comprehended all the hypotheses where the law assigns one of the contracting parties (consumer) the ability to, in a certain time period and without consideration, be released from a contract, by means of a unilateral and unmotivated declaration."[33]

The rationale of article 49 of the CDC is that the supplier assumes the risks of the commercial practice out of the business place,[34] and mainly when it is e-commerce. This does not escape the purpose of the whole CDC's microsystem of protecting the weakest party, more vulnerable in the consumption relation. In other words, "if the physical contact with the product, by its delivery, arises a feeling like cancelling the purchase act, the consumer's right to cancel the contract must be acknowledged when the contract is cancelled."[35]

One may say that, in e-commerce, there is an extrinsic vulnerability linked to the consumer's technical fragility. The intrinsic vulnerability is related to psychical aspects. They are incidental vulnerabilities, unfavorable circumstances that make consumers even more susceptible of enduring damages, deprived of the full real capability of deciding what is best for them, because of the nonpersonalized and nondialogued conduct of the e-commerce.

About the application of article 49 of the CDC to contracts entered into by the Internet, the Court of Justice of Rio Grande do Sul has decided that "There being a purchase made out of the business place—via Internet—the consumer's right of cancellation is applicable, as provided by art. 49, caput, of the CDC."[36]

---

[32]Marques (2006), p. 870.

[33]Almeida (2005), p. 105.

[34]Carvalho (2001), p. 106.

[35]Coelho (2006), p. 34, dez.

[36]See the synopsis of judgment: Synopsis: Consumer. Purchase and sale outside the business place. Exercising the right of cancellation. Payment by debit on the credit card. Cancellation. Persistence of collections. Passive legitimacy of seller, once it is impossible to identify the true causer of damage. Exegesis of art. 7, paragraph, of the CDC. Purchase made by the Internet. As the right of cancellation of the business has been rightfully exercised, by reason of its characteristics

To exemplify, let us mention a judgment of the Court of Justice of Rio Grande do Sul that applied article 49 of the CDC to a contract entered into via the Internet based on the fact it was carried out outside the business place: "Redressing of damages. Consumer. Purchase and sale of cell phone made via Internet. Right of cancellation exercised as per art. 49 of the CDC. Nuisance for confirming the contract cancellation. Collection of payment installments in the credit card invoice which lasted up to the phone withdrawal. Right of restitution of paid values. Inexistent pain & suffering. Judgment maintained. Appeal not provided."[37]

Nery Junior says that the right to retraction exists *per se*, "without the necessity of any justification for the consumer's attitude."[38] That is, the cancelation clause should focus fully on those cases where the consumption contract is entered into outside the business place. The consequence of exercising the right of cancelation is the client's satisfaction,[39] which should increase the volume of consumption transactions held in the net.

Santolim has a different opinion; he examines the question of the consumer's right of cancelation in contracts entered into via the Internet and concludes that it is not necessarily a relationship "outside" the business place "as this must be

---

(art. 49 of the CDC), the collection of the parts related to the undone business is undue. Right to declaration of extinction of contract and unenforceability of installments. Judgment confirmed by its own fundamentals. Appeal not provided. Rio Grande Do Sul. Civil Appeal Panel. *Civil appeal n° 71000955773, of the 3rd* Civil Appeal Panel. Appellant: Terra Networks Brasil S.A. Appealed Party: Luciane Ávila. Relator: Eugênio Facchini Neto. Porto Alegre, 3 de outubro de 2006. Available at: http://www.tj.rs.gov.br/site_php/jprud2/ementa.php. Access on: 30 Aug. 2008.

There are cases where art. 49 is applied to contracts entered via Internet. See: Synopsis: Consumer. Preliminary rejected. Purchase of air conditioner via Internet. Exercising the right of cancellation of purchase (art. 49 of the CDC) after 15 minutes of its concretion. Installments credited in credit card invoice. Request of returning the values not answered by respondent. Ordered to reimburse the unduly collected amount in double. Hypothesis of bad contractual execution, which, in general, does not give raise to indemnification for moral damages. Such amount estranged from condemnation. Appeal partially provided. RIO GRANDE DO SUL. Civil Appeal Panel. *Civil appeal n° 71001388974*, of the 1st Civil Appeal Panel. Appellant: Ameri canas.com. Appealed: Marcelo Ramos Azevedo. Relater: Heleno Tregnago Saraiva. Porto Alegre, March 27, 2008. Available at: http://www.tj.rs.gov.br/site_php/jprud2/ementa.php. Access on: 30 Aug. 2008.

Synopsis: Consumer. Purchase of home theater device via Internet. Exercising the right of cancellation (art. 49 of the CDC). Requesting replacement of purchased item for another of higher quality. Complementation of value by deposit into current account. Item delivery delayed. Business undoing requested. Necessity of returning the amount demonstrably paid for such title. Hypothesis of bad contractual execution, which, in general, does not give raise to indemnification for moral damages. Appeal partially provided. RIO GRANDE DO SUL. Civil Appeal Panel. *Civil appeal n° 71001116813*, of the 1st Civil Appeal Panel. Appellant: Globex Utilidades S.A. – Ponto Frio. Respondent: Patrick Jan Georg Klemt and Aline Leal Fontanella. Relater: Ricardo Torres Hermann. Porto Alegre, April 19, 2007. Available at: http://www.tj.rs.gov.br/site_php/jprud2/ementa.php. Access on: 30 Aug. 2008.

[37]Rio Grande (2010).

[38]Nery Junior (2007), p. 560.

[39]Almeida (2005), p. 109.

approached for its existence in the computers network, and not physically."[40] The author defends the restricted application of article 49 of the CDC in contracts entered into by the Internet; he sustains that such provision should be employed in electronic contracts only when a deficit of reflection and/or deficit of consumer's information is proven.[41] That is, according to Santolim, not every supplier who offers his products and services via the Internet instigates a consumer to buy by impulse. Therefore, the application of article 49 of the CDC would not be justified in all and any electronic contracts.

During a public hearing held in the Court of Justice of Rio Grande do Sul, in Porto Alegre in 2011, organized by the Jurists Committee for the Updating of the Consumer's Defense Code,[42] Santolim has mentioned that such debate will be surpassed in case the Congress accepts the modification proposed by the Jurists Committee in the text of article 49 of the CDC.

The new text of article 49 of the CDC, as appearing in Senate Bill n° 281/2012, proposed by the Jurists Committee, is the following:

> Art. 49. A consumer may cancel the remote contracting, within seven days as of accepting the offer or receipt or availability of a product or service, whichever occurs the last.
>
> Par. 1st. If the consumer exercise the right of cancellation foreseen in this article, the eventually paid amounts, at any title, during the reflection term, should be returned at once, monetarily indexed.
>
> Par. 2nd. By remote contracting it is understood the one carried out outside the business place, or without the simultaneous physical presence of consumer and supplier, mainly at home, by telephone, by mail order, by electronic means, or similar.
>
> Par. 3rd. It is equated to the contracting foreseen in Par. 2nd hereof, that one where, although carried out at the business place, the consumer did not have the previous opportunity to know the product or service, for not being on display, or for the impossibility or difficulty of accessing its contents.
>
> Par. 4th. The withdrawal formalized within the period provided for in the *caput* implies the return of the product with all accessories received by the consumer and invoice.
>
> Par. 5th. If the consumer exercises the right of cancellation, including withdrawal of funds or financing transaction, credit ancillary contracts shall be automatically terminated and must be returned to the credit provider the total amount financed or granted supplied to him, plus any interest due until the effective date of return, taxes and fees, which are charged only when applicable.
>
> Par. 6th. Without prejudice of the consumer's initiative, supplier should communicate at once the manifestation of the exercise of cancellation to the financial institution of credit card administrator, or similar, so that:
>
> I – the transaction should not be entered into consumer's invoice;
>
> II – the amount should be reversed, in case the invoice has been already issued at the moment of communication;
>
> III – if the price is fully or partially paid, be entered as a credit of the respective amount of the invoice immediately after the communication;

[40]Santolim (2004), pp. 93–94.

[41]Santolim, Cesar Viterbo Matos. The principles of consumer's protection and E-commerce in the Brazilian Law. *Revista de Direito do Consumidor*, São Paulo, v. 14, n. 55, p. 79, Jul./Sep. 2005.

[42]Santolim (2012), p. 73 et seq.

Par. 7th. Should the products supplier fail to comply with the provisions of par. 1st or par. 6th, the paid value should be returned in double.

Par. 8th. Supplier should inform clear and ostensibly, the adequate, facilitated and efficacious means available for the exercise of the right of cancellation of the consumer, which must contemplate, at least, the same ways used in the contracting.

Par. 9th. The supplier should send over to consumer an individuated and immediate confirmation of receipt of the notice of cancellation.[43]

In a different positioning from Marques,[44] who sustains the unrestricted application of article 49 of the CDC, because of the distance between the supplier and the consumer, which emphasizes the consumer's vulnerability, Almeida affirms on the fundamentals of the right to cancelation: "The most common of the indicated fundamentals is the granting of the time necessary for a reflected consent, a cooling off period, that protects consumers against the risk of rushing provoked by the psychological persuasion and pressure, by surprise and seduction of the aggressive methods of marketing. As a cumulative or alternative fundamental to the protection of reflection, it is invoked the neutralization of the deficit of information of consumer, in situations that make difficult seeing the product and check its quality, of the institutional unbalance inherent to the circumstances of situational monopoly. Acting as a compensation for the psychical and informative inferiority, and safeguarding the formation of a will free of influences, the right of cancellation would work as an instrument for the realization of the material and effective contractual freedom. [. . .] Thus, the right of cancellation appears as a substitute, either of coaction, or of willfulness, depending on how one keeps more in view, the protection of reflection, or of information."[45]

Coelho presents a criterion of thoughtfulness as to the application of article 49 of the CDC to contracts entered into via the Internet. Says the author: "Such disposition (art. 49 of the CDC), should we remain in its literality, would be applicable to the E-commerce. But it is not appropriate to establish that any consumption act made via Internet could be cancelled by a repenting consumer, within 7 days. Think of any financial operation made by Internet-banking, such as a fund application, money transfer, or loan contracting. It is not reasonable supposing that, 7 days after, a consumer could unilaterally undo the operation just because he repented of his act. On the other hand, it is undeniable that the physical contact (visual or tactile) of consumer with a product he intends to buy transmits him information that no Internet page is capable of supplying. The most true an electric appliance photo can be, and presents details; however much he turns it 360°, the physical contact of

[43]Art. 49 of the Senate Bill n° 281/2012. Amends Act 8078 of September 11, 1990 (Consumers Defense Code), for improving the general provisions of Chapter I of Title I and provide on E-commerce. Available at: http://www.senado.leg.br/atividade/rotinas/materia/getPDF.asp?t=177192&tp=1. Access on: 7 April 2016.

[44]Marques (2004), p. 259.

[45]Almeida (2005), pp. 107–108.

the product displayed in a store permits the consumer to have a more complete idea of what he is purchasing, should he conclude the purchase."[46]

And the author concludes: "In general, art. 49 of the CDC can be applied to E-commerce whenever there is less information on the product or service to be bought in such sales channel, than in the physical commerce. That is, there is no right of cancellation if consumer may have, by the Internet, strictly the same information about the product or service he would have if the consumption act would have been practiced in the physical and not virtual environment. That is, if the site permits consumer to listen to the CD tracks and presents all information appearing on the cover and back (that is, permits rigorously all the same consumer would be entitled to access if he would have been examining the product in a physical store), then there are no reasons to recognize the right of cancellation. On the other hand, however more information provided by the site, the Internet user has no chance to open the fridge's door or feel the size of a TV set. In this case, if the physical contact with the product, by the delivery, causes a feeling of cancellation of the purchase act, the consumer's right of cancelling the contract must be recognized."[47]

The inclusion of paragraph 5 of article 49 by Senate Bill n° 281 in the Brazilian Consumer's Protection and Defense Code addresses some of Coelho's problematics, trying to solve them.

One of the latest amendments introduced was the one that included article 49-A in Senate Bill n° 281, to specifically deal with the purchase and sale of air tickets on the Internet:

> Art. 49-A Notwithstanding the right to termination of the air transport contract before the start of the journey (Art. 740, § 3° of the Civil Code), the exercise of the right to retract from the purchase of airline tickets may have its cooling off period differentiated, because of the peculiarities of the contract, by standard based on regulatory agencies regulation.
>
> Single Paragraph. The regulation mentioned for in the *caput* should be held no later than one hundred and eighty days after the entry into force of this Act.

Article 49-A clearly restricts the consumer's right to retract, in the case of purchase of air tickets.

Trying to increase the consumer's protection before the work of the Jurists Committee, in her excellent book "Trust in the E-commerce and consumer protection: a survey of the legal businesses of E-commerce consumption," Marques had suggested some complementing to the Consumer's Defense Code, to expressly mention the contracts entered into via the Internet and other electronic means. Among them is the inclusion of an article 49bis, with the following text:

---

[46]Coelho, Fábio Ulhoa. Direitos do consumidor no comércio eletrônico. Available at: http://www.ulhoacoelho.com.br/pt/artigos/doutrina/54-direitos-do-consumidor-no-comercio-eletronico.html. Access on: 1 Aug. 2010.

[47]Coelho, Fábio Ulhoa. Direitos do consumidor no comércio eletrônico. Available at: http://www.ulhoacoelho.com.br/pt/artigos/doutrina/54-direitos-do-consumidor-no-comercio-eletronico.html. Access on: 1 Aug. 2010.

Art. 49bis. When a supplier uses, either for the conclusion, or execution, total or partial, of a contract with consumers, an electronic means, of telemedia, teleshopping, or similar means of mass media, he should organize a technical mean so that the consumer may have a previous access to the contract's text, and the information imposed by articles 31, 33, 40 and 52 of this law; and may inform, quick and definitely, the occurrence of error or failure in the order or prompt cancelling of the contracting, without financial cost for such.

Par. 1st. In such cases, he should also organize a technical mode so that the consumer may keep and file the text of the contract and be given a confirmation, individuated and automatic, about the contracting success, its time and place.

Par. 2nd. When the duties of the caput hereto are fulfilled, the supplier should organize a technical mode so that the consumer may – by the same mode – communicate his repentance, in fourteen days, pursuant to the regime imposed by art. 49 of the law hereto, and be given a confirmation on the contract's termination. Should consumer not receive the information foreseen in n° 1, his term of repentance, according to art. 49, should be extended to thirty days, as of the moment he identifies the physical address of supplier.[48]

Marques' inspiration for writing article 49 is in the European law, with a longer term of reflection so as to safeguard the consumers' rights; the author's suggestion was in the sense that the consumer can desist from contracting at once, realizing repentance from contracting, and increasing the term for exercising the right of cancelation.

On October 25, 2011, the European Union has adopted Directive 2011/83/EU[49] of the European Parliament and the Council, regarding the consumers' rights, which amended Directive 93/13/EEC[50] of the Council and Directive 1999/44/EC[51] of the European Parliament and the Council and which has revoked Directive 85/577/EEC[52] of the Council and Directive 97/7/EC[53] of the European Parliament and the Council. Such European Directive has modernized the European law.

Thus, looking for a dialogue between the concept of business place set by the Civil Code and the rule of article 49 of the CDC, both should enter into effect,

[48]Marques (2004), pp. 468–469.

[49]Directive 2011/83/EU of the European Parliament and the Council, of October 25, 2011. Available at: http://eur-lex.europa.eu/LexUriServ/LexUriServ.do?uri=OJ:L:2011:304:0064:088:PT:PDF. Access on: 3 Aug. 2012. A deeper analysis of this European Directive will be made in a further opportunity.

[50]Directive 93/13/EEC of the Council, of April 5, 1993, ref. abusive clauses in contracts entered with consumers. Available at: http://eur-lex.europa.eu/LexUriServ/LexUriServ.do?uri=CELEX:31993L0013:PT:HTML. Access on: 3 Aug. 2012. As amended.

[51]Directive 1999/44/EC of the European Parliament and the Council, of May 25, 1999, on certain aspects on the sale of consumption goods and the guarantees thereto. Available at: http://eur-lex.europa.eu/LexUriServ/LexUriServ.do?uri=OJ:L:1999:171:0012:0016:PT:PDF. Access on: 3 Aug. 2012. As amended.

[52]Directive 85/577/EEC of the Council, of December 20, 1985, ref. the protection of consumers in the case of contracts negotiated outside the business places. Available at: http://eur-lex.europa.eu/LexUriServ/LexUriServ.do?uri=CELEX:31985L0577:pt:HTML. Access on: 3 Aug. 2012. Revoked.

[53]Directive 97/7/EC of the European Parliament and the Council, of May 20, 1997, ref. protection of consumers rel. remote contracts. Available at: http//ec.europa.eu/consumers/policy/developments/dist_sell/dist01es.pdf. Access on: 3 Aug. 2012. Revoked.

observing that a site is a mere representation of the physical place and can be understood in the legal context as "at a distance" and/or "outside the business place." The virtual place of business and the physical place are one and only legal reality, differing in the aspect of their representation and the means where they are inserted.

As demonstrated above, there is no consensus in the doctrine about the fundamentals of the application of the consumer's right of cancelation to the electronic contracts. While some jurists sustain its application for being contracts celebrated outside the business place, others affirm that it is necessary because of the insufficient information or lack of information provided to the consumer on on-line contracts that justifies the reflection period or the cooling off period provided to the consumer, so he can think about the need to contract.

The proposed amendment in the text of article 49 of the CDC, made by the Jurists Committee for the CDC's Updating, is in perfect consonance with the technologic advances of the contracting means and the necessary adaptation of our consumerist law. The Committee has kept the term of reflection in 7 days, as they considered that it was not the opportune moment to widen the term to 10 or 15 days, as in Europe.

The Committee has kept the 7-day term of reflection, while in Europe it is 14 days, since 2002, for financial services, and since October 2011, by Direction 83/2011.

Bill n° 281/2012 on e-commerce still foresees punctual amendments in some more articles of the CDC:

- in article 56, with the insertion of subparagraph XIII, which will provide the "temporary suspension or prohibition of offer and electronic commerce," more polemic, based on the precautionary principle;
- in art. 59, with the addition of paragraph 4, which will determine that "Should a supplier, by electronic or similar means fails to fulfill the penalty of suspension or prohibition of offer, and of E-commerce, without prejudice of other administrative or legal measures of prevention of damages, the Judiciary will determine, by request of the administrative authority or the Public Attorney Office, within the limit strictly necessary for guaranteeing the effectiveness of sanction, that the performers of financial and payment services used by supplier, alternatively or jointly, under payment of a daily fine: I – hold the payments and financial transfers to a supplier of E-commerce; II – block the banking accounts of supplier";
- the insertion of article 60-A imposing that the reiterated breach of the supplier's obligations set forth in this law may give rise to the application by the judiciary of a civil penalty in an appropriate amount to the seriousness of the conduct and sufficient to inhibit further violations, without prejudice to applicable criminal and administrative sanctions and the compensation for damages, material and moral, caused to consumers; it also determines that the degree and the allocation of the civil fine must observe the provisions of article 57 of the CDC;

- the inclusion of article 60-B, stating that "Without prejudice to the sanctions provided for in Chapter VIII, based on formalized complaint by consumers, the administrative authority in their respective area of expertise and competence, may commence administrative proceedings, secured contradictory and full defense to apply, individually or cumulatively, in case of proven violation of consumer protection rules, the following corrective measures, establishing a deadline for compliance: I - replacement or repair of the product; II - return than any paid by consumers through misappropriation; III - offer compliance by the supplier, where it is included in writing and expressly; IV - return or chargeback, the supplier, the amount paid by the consumer when the delivered product or service does not correspond to what expressly agreed by the parties; V - adequate provision of information required by the consumer, where such application store relationship with the purchased product or service contracted. § 1° In the case of fixed-term failure by the administrative authority for corrective measure imposed a daily fine shall be charged in the sole paragraph of molds of art. 57. § 2° The daily fine mentioned in § 1° will be reversed, as appropriate, to the Defense Fund of Diffuse Rights or the state or local funds to consumer protection";
- in article 72-A, in which the Committee adds a penal type, characterizing a crime against the consumption relations for a supplier who utilizes the e-commerce to "Publish, host, exhibit, license, dispose, utilize, shares, donate, or in any way assign personal data, information, or identifiers, without the express authorization of their owner and informed consent, save legal exceptions. Penalty – Imprisonment, from one to four years, and fine";
- finally, the Committee's amendment of the text of article 101 of the CDC, which deals with the actions of contractual and extracontractual liability, including remote supply, national and international. The international dimension of the Consumer's Defense Code appears, and an international contract adapted to a globalized consumption society. The same way, article 101 tries to fight the clause of choice of court and arbitration in the consumption relations.

24.3 Final Considerations

In face of a diversity of factors that lead to the appearance of new contracts, and different modes of contracting, the law cannot remain tied to inert dogmas that were adequate for a certain historical period and a specific economic, political, and social order. The multiplication of contracts, as observed in the entering of contracts of adhesion, by telephone, by computing; the contract entered into by the Internet; the international contracts; and the consumption contracts illustrate that the way of thinking of law in the twenty-first century must transform into a stronger and more complete one, becoming an efficient tool in the dealing with the legal relations that are being set by the Internet.

The Brazilian society has changed from 1990 to date, the economy has changed, we have a new Civil Code, and the Consumer's Defense Code must be updated. Therefore, it has been of extreme importance the updating work of the Consumer's Defense Code carried out by the Jurists Committee, elaborating the Bill of updating on the e-commerce theme.

The legal regulation of this novel technique imposes the reexamination of traditional concepts, as always occurs when new technological developments are created. The jurist ought to, on one side, carry out the reinterpretation of the system in effect, deepening the analysis of values and principles inscribed in the core of the traditional concepts, and betake an interpretation by the light of the Constitution, remaining always attentive to new challenges; on the other side, it ought to be the mediator between the multiple interests, sometimes contradictory, that the utilization of such technology generates in face of the different categories of actors, either suppliers or consumers.

It is also for the jurist to conciliate the classical contractual principles to the postmodern, multiple, and pluralist conception of contract, overcoming the existing impasses and catalyzing the true cultural revolution that is occurring, started by the coming of the Internet. The new society requires, therefore, a new law, a new legal dogmatism.

Finally, one cannot forget to recognize the important role to be played by the judiciary in the interpretation of the consumers' protection rules so as to adapt them to the consumption carried out via the Internet. It will not be different, after the updating of the CDC: it will be up to the judges and the materializing action of precedents to contribute in a decisive way to the definition of the limits and the reaching of the provisions contemplated by the Consumer's Defense Code, dialoguing with the Civil Code and aiming at the protection of the dignity of the human being and the protection of the more vulnerable ones, by analyzing the contractual relations of consumption by the Internet.

References

Almeida CF (2005) Direito do consumo. Almedina, Coimbra

Ballarino T (2006) A Internet e a conclusão dos contratos. In: Posenato N (Org.). *Contratos internacionais*: tendências e perspectivas: estudos de direito internacional privado e direito comparado. Unijuí, Ijuí, p 203

Bessa LR (2007) Aplicação do Código de Defesa do Consumidor: análise crítica da relação de consumo. Brasília Jurídica, Brasília

Carvalho RBde (2001) A Internet e as relações de consumo. In: Schoueri Luís Eduardo (Org.). Internet: o direito na era virtual, 2 edn. Forense, Rio de Janeiro

Coelho FU (2006) Direitos do consumidor no comércio eletrônico. Revista do Advogado 26(89):34, dez, São Paulo

Couto E Silva CV (1976) A obrigação como processo. J. Bushatsky, São Paulo

Elias PS (2008) Contratos eletrônicos e a formação do vínculo. Lex, São Paulo

Filomeno JGB (2007) Disposições gerais. In: Grinover AP et al (eds) Código Brasileiro de Defesa do Consumidor: comentado pelos autores do anteprojeto, 9th edn. rev., atual. e ampl. Forense Universitária, Rio de Janeiro, pp 46–50

Jayme E (2003) O direito internacional privado do novo milênio: a proteção da pessoa humana face à globalização. Cadernos do Programa de Pós-Graduação em Direito PPGDir/UFRGS 1(1):85, mar, Porto Alegre

Jayme E (2005) O direito internacional privado no novo milênio: a proteção da pessoa humana face à globalização. In: Marques CL, Araujo N (Org.) O novo direito internacional: estudos em homenagem a Erik Jayme. Renovar, Rio de Janeiro, pp 3–20

Junqueira M (1997) Contratos eletrônicos. Mauad, Rio de Janeiro

Lorenzetti RL (2004) Comércio eletrônico. Translated by: Fabiano Menke. Notes by Claudia Lima Marques. Revista dos Tribunais, São Paulo

Marques CL (2004) Confiança no comércio eletrônico e a proteção do consumidor: um estudo dos negócios jurídicos de consumo no comércio eletrônico. Revista dos Tribunais, São Paulo

Marques CL (2006) Contratos no Código de Defesa do Consumidor: o novo regime das relações contratuais, 5th edn. rev., atual. e ampl. Revista dos Tribunais, São Paulo

Marques CL (2012) The updating of the Consumer's Defense Code (Lecture). E-commerce and its implications (Panel). Seminar on the regulation of E-commerce in Brazil. Rio de Janeiro, RJ, Palácio do Comércio, Auditório da Associação Comercial do Estado do Rio de Janeiro (ACRJ), 14 September

Martins GM (2010) Formação dos contratos eletrônicos de consumo via Internet, 2nd edn. rev. e atual. Lumen Juris, Rio de Janeiro

Mercosul. Com (Org.) (2000) B2B: uma alternativa para a expansão de seus negócios na Internet. Cia. Latino-Americana de Negócios On-Line, São Paulo

Miragem BNB (2006) Comentários ao Código de Defesa do Consumidor: artigo por artigo, 2nd edn. Revista dos Tribunais, São Paulo

Motta FP, Guelmann KR, Castilho WM (2005) Reflexões sobre o direito do consumidor e a Internet. In: Capaverde AdoC, Conrado M (Org.). Repensando o direito do consumidor: 15 anos do CDC: 1990–2005. Ordem dos Advogados do Brasil, Seção do Paraná, Curitiba

Nery Junior N (2007) Da proteção contratual. In: Grinover AP et al (eds) Código Brasileiro de Defesa do Consumidor: comentado pelos autores do anteprojeto, 9th edn. rev., atual. e ampl. Forense Universitária, Rio de Janeiro

Nunes LAR (2007) Comentários ao Código de Defesa do Consumidor, 3rd edn. rev. e atual. Saraiva, São Paulo

Pasqualotto AdeS (1991) Conceitos fundamentais do Código de Defesa do Consumidor. Revista dos Tribunais 80(666):52, abr, São Paulo

Rio de Janeiro RJ, Palácio doC (2012) Auditório da Associação Comercial do Estado do Rio de Janeiro (ACRJ), 14 September

Rio Grande SS (2010) Civil Appeal Panel. Civil appeal n° 71002071918, of the 2nd Civil Appeal Panel. Relater: Vivian Cristina Angonese Spengler. Porto Alegre, February, 24

Santolim CVM (2004) A aplicação dos princípios de proteção do consumidor ao comércio eletrônico no direito brasileiro. 2004. 123 f. Thesis (PhD Law) – Graduation Program; School of Law Universidade Federal do Rio Grande do Sul, Porto Alegre

Santolim CVM (2005) Os princípios de proteção do consumidor e o comércio eletrônico no direito brasileiro. Revista de Direito do Consumidor 14(55):55, jul./set, São Paulo

Santolim CVM (2012) Annotations by the Jurists Committee for the updating of the Consumer's Defense Code in the part related to E-commerce. Revista de Direito do Consumidor 83:73 et seq., Jul, São Paulo

Sarlet IW (2009) A eficácia dos direitos fundamentais: uma teoria geral dos direitos fundamentais na perspectiva constitucional, 10th edn. Liv. do Advogado, Porto Alegre

Wald A (2003) A evolução do contrato no terceiro milênio e o novo Código Civil. In: Alvim Neto JMdeA, César JPC, Rosas R (Coord.). Aspectos controvertidos do novo Código Civil. Revista dos Tribunais, São Paulo

Chapter 25
The Right to Be Forgotten and the Indirect Control of Consumer Databases

André de Carvalho Ramos

25.1 Introduction: The Direct and Indirect Controls of Consumers' Data

In 2005, I wrote an article about the consumers' right to privacy and the credit reporting agencies' databases,[1] with emphasis on civil actions in public interest filed by the Federal Prosecution Office and the work of the Parliamentary Committee of Investigation on the credit reporting agencies. Ten years later (2015), the proliferation of consumers' databases is still a current issue. In a globalized world where information is the key to profit, Brazil faces the challenge of regulating and preventing abuses in the (successful) market of consumers' databases.

There are two models of regulation of consumers' databases: (1) direct control and (2) indirect control. On one hand, direct control is exercised by the administrative bodies (such as the consumer protection bureau) and by the judiciary when charges are filled by the aggrieved consumer himself. Indirect control, on the other hand, consists of monitoring the action of entities not directly related to the consumers' databases, such as Internet web browsers, to prevent the overexposure that affects consumers' rights.

In Brazil, the legal approach regarding the direct control has received few innovations since the edition of the Brazilian Consumer Protection Code in 1990

The Portuguese version of this article was published by Revista de Direito do Consumidor, Vol. 104, pp. 131–147.

[1]de Carvalho Ramos (2005).

A. de Carvalho Ramos (✉)
Faculty of law, University of São Paulo, São Paulo, Brazil

Ana Cândida Muniz Cipriano Faculty of Law, University of Buenos Aires, Buenos Aires, Argentina
e-mail: andredecarvalhoramos@gmail.com

C. Lima Marques, D. Wei (eds.), *Consumer Law and Socioeconomic Development*,
DOI 10.1007/978-3-319-55624-6_25

(Law No. 8078). The consumer can only rely on generic provisions to be protected against the abuses, and there is not an administrative body for the private database management. In this sense, the new Brazilian Law 12.414 of 2011, which regulates the maintenance of credit history, did not create new institutions since it has only referred the credit inspection to the existing bodies of consumer protection.

It is worth it to make a reference to the article C*onstitutional right to privacy and investigative consumer reports: little brother is watching you* published in 1974 since it still reflects the reality on the issue. In the article, authors McLaughlin and Vaupel explain that the consumer databases, called little brother in an allusion to the Orwell's big brother, have more data on the population than the government itself.[2]

The power of the information of the private databases is clear as they can serve as a form of coercion for the consumers to pay abusive debts in order not to have their names inserted in the system. Also, ironically, there is no equality between private and public uses of databases as the insertion of tax liability information ordered by the judiciary on the databases is considered an unfair constraint.[3]

In contrast with the direct control, the indirect control reflects the Internet society. Nowadays, the overexposure of information makes it possible to analyze virtually every detail of an individual's life, what gradually reduces the sphere of private life, making everything accessible and permanent. In this regard, the Court of Justice of the European Union has already ruled that the Google search engine should withdraw from the Internet the results that were offensive to the right to be forgotten. It is important to mention that the Court's decision did not order the removal of the information from the Internet itself (what would be impossible, considering the Internet capillarity) but only the removal of the information from the most popular search engine.

In this context, this article aims to analyze the impact of the right to be forgotten as an instrument to limit the consumers' data control by web browsers. Initially, the species of databases and its impact on everyday life are examined, followed by the right to privacy and its relation to the right to be forgotten. Last but not least, the article focuses on the impact of the right to be forgotten as an additional protection to consumers in Brazil.

25.2 Origin and Development of Consumer Databases in Brazil

The credit databases, also known as consumer files, are not a novel feature in Brazil. Its origins go back to the 1950s, along with the expansion of the credit sales practice. At the time, the risk of default stimulated the creation of informal records of consumer information to be used by the stores before the business transaction was completed, as well as to facilitate the methods of debt collection.[4]

---

[2]Mclauglin and Vaupel (1974–1975), pp. 773–828.

[3]de Paula (2013).

[4]Grinover (2000), p. 340; Bessa (2003).

The importance of consumers' databases increased alongside the growth of companies specialized in organizing information and selling it to traders interested in data regarding the local debtors. The cycle of acquiring and searching information was organized as follows: the traders bought information from each store regarding debtors; then all the data was gathered in one complete archive that was sold back to the stores. Gradually, the exchange of debtors' information has expanded impressively, generating the contemporary consumers' databases, a huge network that consists of the collection and the exchange of consumer information for the purpose of monitoring financial activities and consumption habits of individuals and legal entities.[5]

Following this global tendency, nonprofit entities of local businessmen that gathered debtors' information emerged in Brazil in the second half of the 20th century. The idea was to make fewer manual checks and to reduce debt collection costs, making it possible to access consumers' information more easily. Nowadays, the information is mainly in the hands of the credit reporting agencies, which collect data from all around the country and run it through an efficient exchange system, creating a catalog of information about consumers in almost all the national territory. It is to bear in mind, however, that the credit reporting agencies in Brazil do not have one centralized database.[6]

25.3 Species of Databases in Brazil

The nature of the data regards the credit status of an individual or legal entity and can contain positive information (such as the record of payment and shopping habits) or negative information (such as credit protests, nonsufficient-fund checks and debts). Also, the databases gather information regarding credit commitments, such as loans and leases, to manage the repayment of debt. The information is collected by the notary public, the clerk of court, the registry of commerce, the Central Bank, the public records, among other sources.[7]

It is to distinguish the databases as a product that contains negative or positive information about individuals and legal entities from the information exchange tools that allow the constant update of these databases. As the information is collected, processed, and interchanged with other companies, a true profile of each consumer is created.

With the technological advances, new information regarding the consumers' life is aggregated, crossed, and transmitted instantly to the databases. Thus, the impact of this database activity can be easily seen in everyday life. The disclosure of a debt

[5]The two main credit reporting agencies in Brazil are the SPCs and the SERASA. More information is available at: http://www.serasaexperian.com.br/ and https://www.spcbrasil.org.br/.

[6]Stürmer (1992), pp. 35–94.

[7]Stürmer (1992), pp. 35–94. Also, see Efing (2002).

inserted in a consumers' database can cause loss of property to a company or pecuniary and personal loss to an individual. Also, the positive information concerning the consumers' habits is a sample of the worlds' reduction of the protected sphere of intimacy.

In this context, the Posner dilemma arises: all the information, including the personal consumers' information, has economic value, and hence the desire for profit from this data collides with the consumers' right to privacy. As a consequence of the tremendous economic value of the information on the consumer, a whole sector of the Brazilian economy has developed a monitoring system of individuals' activities and habits.[8]

25.4 General Aspects Regarding the Right to Privacy

The right to privacy is the power that the individual has to choose to be alone and not to be disturbed in his private life, forming a sphere of autonomy and exclusion of others who can only intrude with consent. In this sense, article 5, X, of the Brazilian Constitution stipulates that "the privacy, private life, honor and image of persons are inviolable, guaranteeing the right to compensation for property or personal loss resulting from this violation."

The right to privacy is a fundamental right that allows its holder to prevent that certain aspects of his life are subjected to public opinion against his will.[9] This right includes, according to main scholars, the right of the individual to keep a domain with his subjective thoughts and feelings, family relationships and friendships, as well as his private life, which involves all social, work, and study relations.[10]

Privacy was consecrated in 1890, in the article *Right to Privacy*. Authors Warren and Brandeis gave a new meaning to the right to be alone that encompasses the various manifestations of the being, as letters, drawings, gestures, and conversations, which deserved to be protected.[11] Since this initial study, there has been an intense development of the privacy protection, bringing debates about its scope and content, especially when faced with the constant increase of the information flow in the current globalized world.

To understand the dynamics of privacy protection, the theory of spheres was developed. This theory provides that the privacy broadly covers three concentric circles: (1) the circle of the private life, (2) the circle of familiarity, and (3) the circle of secrecy.[12]

[8]Posner (1977–1979), pp. 423–428.

[9]de Carvalho Ramos (2015), p. 536.

[10]de Moraes (2009), p. 53.

[11]Warren and Brandeis (1890), pp. 193–220.

[12]da Costa (1995).

The circle of private life is the set of relations between the holder and other individuals containing information (e.g., data on one's wealth) and also feelings with less impact on familiarity, such as common acquaintances. In this circle are contained, among others, the confidentiality of tax information, data, and phone records.

The circle of familiarity is composed of a set of events (information, images, writings, and gestures) that are only shared with close friends and family and, at most, with professionals subject to attorney–client privilege or doctor–patient privilege. This circle includes the provision of the Brazilian Constitution prohibiting the intrusion of third parties in the individual's home (article 5, IX), as well as the protection of unauthorized access and publication of the content of communications.

Finally, in the circle of secrecy, there are all manifestations and intimate preferences that are sensitive components of the holder's personality, involving his personal options, opinions, and feelings that, by his decision, should be safe from third-party curiosity.

The theory of the spheres assumes that the protection of privacy depends on the conduct of the holder, which, from personal choices, decide what will or will not be shared with the public. On this regard, the Brazilian Civil Code stipulates that "the private life of the individual is inviolable, and the judge should take the necessary steps to prevent or terminate an act contrary to this provision" (article 21).

In the Brazilian Constitution and the human rights treaties, the right to privacy coexists with the right to information and with freedom of the press. Therefore, the right to privacy is restricted by the proper conduct of the holder. If the holder exposes his image to the public, he cannot refuse to disclose its image in the public scenario that he participates in (a rally, a popular demonstration, etc.). Moreover, those with a public image (celebrities) or those engaged in a political life accept greater exposure and cannot claim a right to privacy to prevent the disclosure of discreditable facts concerning their image.[13]

Another limitation to the right to privacy relates to the preponderance, in a judgment of proportionality, of the right to information over the right to privacy. The *murder of Lebach soldiers case*, decided by the Federal Constitutional Court of Germany in 1973, is a classic example of this restriction. The ruling of the Court examined the prohibition of the release of a documentary about a massacre that occurred in Lebach (where four soldiers were killed in an ammunition theft) on the verge of the discharge of one of the convicted criminals.

The Court decided that, in general, the right to information regarding serious crimes has a social interest that prevails over the right to privacy, authorizing the disclosure of the name, photo, and other identification of the convict in a documentary. However, in the view of the Court, the right to privacy and image could prevail in a different situation, as the elaboration of a subsequent documentary, years later, would jeopardize the reintegration of the convict into the society, being

[13] de Carvalho Ramos (2015), p. 538.

prohibited. Finally, in 1999, two decades after the original ruling, the Court allowed the broadcast of another program on the *Lebach case* with the argument that the long period of time had fostered the rehabilitation of those involved in the crime.[14]

Another aspect of the issue under discussion in Brazil is whether the disclosure of a mere suspicion of a criminal action or administrative corruption not yet final and unappealable consists in a violation of the right to honor and privacy. In several judicial precedents, Brazilian courts have considered that there is no violation of the right to honor and privacy if the information disclosed meets two criteria: (1) the information seems credible at that time, and (2) its content is relevant to the public interest, being excluded from the privacy protection level.

On the matter, the Brazilian Superior Court of Justice has decided that the honor and the image of citizens are not violated when true and reliable information are disclosed and, more importantly, when the information is of public interest. Thus, the media is not liable if it seeks reliable sources and exercises its investigative activity hearing various stakeholders to withdraw doubts as to the veracity of the information. In spite of that, the duty of veracity should be evaluated in the journalistic context where the news must be quickly disclosed. If the suspicion on the individual really existed and the news reported that it were indeed suspicious without appointing the person as a convicted felon, the Brazilian Supreme Court considers that there is no violation of the honor or privacy, even if, years later, the person is acquitted of all charges.[15]

25.5 The Right to Be Forgotten in Consumers Relations

25.5.1 General Aspects of the Right to Be Forgotten

As seen above, the right to privacy has limits that lead, in certain situations of conflict of rights, to the prevalence of the right to information. In today's information society, where past facts can be easily collected by search engines, a discussion arises: is it possible that the course of time turns a fact that once was of public interest into a fact encompassed now by the right to privacy?

This question concerns the right to be forgotten as a development of the right to privacy. The right to be forgotten balances the right to privacy and the right to information as it consists in the faculty of the rights' holder of requesting the removal from the public access of an information that has lost the public interest by the course of the years. It is relevant to point out that the right to be forgotten is exercised in a context that differs from that of the *Lebach case*: on the latter, public interest and, consequently, the right to information prevail over the right to privacy;

---

[14]Martins (2005), p. 540.

[15]Brazilian Superior Court of Justice. Appeal n° 984,803, judge-rapporteur Nancy Andrighi, judgment of 19 ago 2009.

in the former, differently, there is no longer public interest, being the information only of private interest after some time.

The right to be forgotten (*droit à l'oubli, el derecho al olvido* or *direito ao esquecimento*) has two aspects: (1) the right to oblivion, which does not allow the disclosure of information, and (2) the right to erasure, which seeks the elimination of the recorded fact that, given the past, can no longer be considered public, requiring the holder's authorization to be kept in databases.

One of the first cases regarding the right to oblivion was the *Landru case*, decided by the French Court of Cassation in 1967. The Court analyzed if the right to oblivion applied to the companion of the *Landru* serial killer, as her name had been associated with *Landru's* in a movie made by Claude Chabrol (*Landru's* criminal behavior has become famous as he seduced several widows and, after he was given access to their assets, killed them and burned their dismembered bodies). The Court rejected the claim, arguing that the claimant herself had made the information regarding her relationship with the serial killer public by publishing book on the topic.[16]

Moreover, at the time, the right to be forgotten was debated without the current characterization, only in cases of criminal convictions in which the discharged convicted saw his rehabilitation hampered by the resurgence—from time to time—of the case in the media.[17] It was the *Filipacchi et Cogedipresse case* of the Paris' *Tribunal de Grande Instance*, in 1983, that the right to oblivion was recognized as a right to every individual involved in public events after the passage of years, which enables preventing the disclosure of the individuals' involvement on an event, if its participation is not indispensable to historical facts.[18]

It is to be quoted that the Court of Justice of the European Union established the right to be forgotten in the judgment of the *Costeja González case* in May 13, 2014. In the case, a Spanish national claimed the elimination of his name from the search results of a web browser (Google) regarding a debt in the Spanish social security since the payment of the debt, although correct, had occurred more than 15 years ago and the maintenance of his name on the database damaged his current good-payer image. The Court gave preference to the respect for private and family life and to the protection of personal data (mentioned in articles 7 and 8 of the Charter of Fundamental Rights of the European Union) over Google's right of freedom and third parties' rights to information, emphasizing that its decision was justified by the lack of public interest in the contested information. As a result, the Court

[16]*Tribunal de Grande Instance*, Seine, 14 de outubro de 1965. Mme S. c. Soc. Rome Paris Film, confirmado: Cour dA Paris 15 de march 1967.

[17]This concern with the rights of discharged convicts was seen in the *Lebach case* of the Federal Constitutional Court (mentioned above),

[18]*Tribunal de Grande Instance,* Paris, 20 de april 1983, *Mme. M. c. Filipacchi et soc. Cogedipresse.*

ordered the web browser (Google) to remove the personal information of the claimant from the search results.[19]

Also in Brazil, the right to be forgotten related to consumers' relations was advocated as being one of the aspects of the right to privacy, and the data can be saved only during a given time but not forever.[20] Besides, a 2013 nonbinding precedent guidance to the Brazilian judges stated that "the protection of human dignity in the information society includes the right to be forgotten," as well as it has been stressed out that "the right to be forgotten does not imply the right to delete facts or rewrite the story, but only provides the possibility to discuss the use that is given to past facts, specifically the manner and purpose for that they are remembered."[21]

The Brazilian Superior Court of Justice has recognized the right to be forgotten in the *Slaughter of the Candelaria case* (a massacre of eight children in Rio de Janeiro in 1993). The Court ruled that the individuals acquitted by the jury for their involvement in the slaughter had the right to not see their names included in a television show that reconstructed the tragedy years later.[22] In turn, the same Superior Court of Justice did not recognize the right to be forgotten in the *Aida Curi case*, where the relatives of a murder victim in the 1950s sought to prohibit a television program about the murder in 2013. The Court decided that since the famous murder had occurred more than 50 years ago, the crime had become historical and the facts related to the event had entered the public domain, being impossible to disclose a program about the murder without information about the victim.[23]

It is to be emphasized that the decision in the *Slaughter of the Candelaria case* balanced the rights involved—the right to be forgotten and freedom of information—in the light of the current Brazilian paradigm of democracy and independence of the judiciary, where the arbitrary restrictions once imposed on privacy and freedom at the time of military dictatorship are no longer accepted.

---

[19]In this regard: *"As the data subject may, in the light of his fundamental rights under Articles 7 and 8 of the Charter, request that the information in question no longer be made available to the general public by its inclusion in such a list of results, it should be held, as follows in particular from paragraph 81 of the present judgment, that those rights override, as a rule, not only the economic interest of the operator of the search engine but also the interest of the general public in finding that information upon a search relating to the data subject's name. However, that would not be the case if it appeared, for particular reasons, such as the role played by the data subject in public life, that the interference with his fundamental rights is justified by the preponderant interest of the general public in having, on account of inclusion in the list of results, access to the information in question."* Court of Justice of the European Union, C-131/12, judgment of 13 may 2014, paragraph 97. http://curia.europa.eu/juris/document/document.jsf?docid=152065&doclang=ES.

[20]Limberger (2002), pp. 247–271, 266, Available at http://www.amprs.org.br/arquivos/revista_artigo/arquivo_1274905702.pdf.

[21]The whole precedent guidance is available at: http://www.cjf.jus.br/CEJ-Coedi/jornadas-cej/enunciados-vi-jornada.

[22]Brazilian Superior Court of Justice, Appeal n.1.334.097/RJ, judge-rapporteur Luis Felipe Salomão, judgment of 28 may 2013.

[23]Superior Court of Justice, Appeal no. 1335153/RJ, judge-rapporteur Luis Felipe Salomão, judgment of 28 may 2013.

25.5.2 The Brazilian Consumer Protection Code Provisions and the Right to Be Forgotten

The Brazilian Consumer Protection Code has a provision (article 43, § 1°) that states that "records and consumer data should be objective, clear, truthful and in an easy to understand language and can not contain negative information for a period exceeding five years."

Even without an express mention, it is clear that this provision relates to the privacy of consumers' information. The article stresses the temporary character of consumers' records and data and, by preventing the maintenance of negative information, gives back to the consumer the control over the information regarding his life. As Fried affirmed: "Privacy, thus, is control over knowledge about oneself."[24]

The possibility of keeping information for five years in consumers' databases comes from the need of preserving the interests of those companies that grant credit. It is considered that five years after the insertion of the information in the database, the reason that once justified the maintenance of the data in the system is mitigated by the need to respect the privacy of the consumer. The reasoning of the provision is that a consumer who once avoided paying his debts cannot be perpetually tied to his past default.

As the article is directed to the credit reporting agencies and their consumers' databases, the question that remains is whether it is also possible to require that third parties who are not the managers of such databases (Internet web browser, for example) comply with the command of removing consumers' information after five years.

The consumer interest on an expansive interpretation of the duty of removal of data after a period of time is obvious: to prevent negative information—which was wrongfully inserted in or which should already be removed from consumers' databases but which could still be searched online—to be used as a way of permanent embarrassment. The idea is to avoid the creation of an online *parallel and perennial consumers' database* driven by Internet web browsers.

The *Costeja González case* of Court of Justice of the European Union could be easily adaptable to the consumers' situation if the unpaid debt is replaced by a consumers' debt. In both situations, the maintenance of the information in Internet web browsers has the potential of generating negative consequences on individuals' private lives.

Since there is no express provision that imposes the duty to remove from the Internet information regarding consumers' debts, the consumer himself has the alternative of appealing to the right to be forgotten in order to prevent that Internet web browsers continue to disclose negative information. It is to be highlighted, however, that the application of the right to be forgotten to the consumers' information available at the Internet is not free from criticism, requiring an analysis of the main arguments regarding this issue.

First, it is argued that the freedom of information could prevail over the right to privacy and the right to oblivion, making it unnecessary to remove consumers'

---

[24]FRIED, Charles. Privacy in Yale Law Journal, v. 77, 1967–1968, pp. 475–493, cit. p. 483.

information from Internet web browsers. Although there is, indeed, a situation of conflict of rights, one cannot assume that the freedom of information would prevail in abstract over any other right. It is essential to consider that in a democratic society without state censorship, there are economic interests that value consumers' information and profit from their image.

Second, there is the supposition that the right to be forgotten would violate the right to memory. In fact, the right to oblivion is not capable of summoning before historical facts or public domain situations where the right to memory reigns. In spite of that, when the information is merely private, the right to privacy should contemplate the possibility of removal of data from the Internet after a period of time. In a globalized society where information is the key to profit, the mitigation of privacy should apply only when oriented to relevant public interest.

The third argument focuses on the freedom of the press, questioning whether it is possible for the judiciary decide if certain information consists of a social relevant fact or if it could be removed from the Internet at the individual's request. From another perspective, the critics point to the prevalence of the freedom of information. Also in this case, it is to be stressed that the freedom of information cannot be used to prevent access to justice to enforce the right to privacy.[25]

Fourth, there is the argument that if information was relevant in the past and its disclosure was lawful, the passage of time cannot turn this disclosure into an illicit act. Nevertheless, time is an important factor in assessing the legal status of a given fact. The above-quoted article 43 of the Brazilian Consumer Protection Code, prescribing the removal of information from consumers' databases after a period of five years, is a good example of the relevance of time as a factor to decide the lawfulness or unlawfulness of a certain conduct. The same reasoning applies to article 748 of the Brazilian Code of Criminal Procedure, which provides that, given the rehabilitation, the previous convictions will not be mentioned in the criminal records of the discharged convicted, except when required by a criminal judge.

25.6 Conclusion: The Right to Hope in Consumers Relations

Article 43 of the Brazilian Consumer Protection Code paved the foundation of consumers' protection against abusive practices of the credit reporting agencies. The interpretation of this provision should be guided by the contemporary society of information, where data are launched instantaneously as well as have the potential to become perennial in the Internet.

[25]The precedents of the International Human Rights Courts reaffirm that the freedom of information could, in some situation, make room to the right to privacy. On the topic, see de Carvalho Ramos (2015), pp. 538 e 539.

In this context, the national and international precedents, as well as main scholars, point toward the use of the right to be forgotten as a way of broadening the scope of the right to privacy. The implementation of the right to be forgotten in consumers' relations concerned about the removal of personal data from Internet web browsers after a period of time avoids that negative debt information is endlessly perpetuated, which, in a global consumer society, has harmful consequences to the consumers' image.

In the final analysis, the right to be forgotten is in line with the *right to hope*, preventing that negative or discreditable facts from the past influence the daily life of individuals. To sum up, it is the application of the right to be left alone to consumer relations.

References

Bessa LR (2003) O consumidor e os limites dos bancos de dados de proteção ao crédito. Ed. Revista dos Tribunais, São Paulo

da Costa PJ Jr (1995) O direito de estar só: tutela penal da intimidade, 2nd edn. Revista dos Tribunais, São Paulo

de Carvalho Ramos A (2005) O pequeno irmão que nos observa: os direitos dos consumidores e os bancos de dados de consumo no Brasil. Revista de Direito do Consumidor, v. 53, pp. 39–53. São Paulo

de Carvalho Ramos A (2015) Curso de direitos Humanos, 2nd edn. Saraiva, São Paulo

de Moraes A (2009) Direito constitucional, 24th edn. Atlas, São Paulo

de Paula B (2013) Protestar contribuinte de ICMS no SPC é inconstitucional. Available at: http://www.conjur.com.br/2013-mar-09/breno-paula-protestar-contribuinte-icms-spc-inconstitucional. Accessed 27 Dec 2015

Efing AC (2002) Bancos de dados e cadastro de consumidores. Ed. Revista dos Tribunais, São Paulo

Fried C (1977–1979) Privacy: economics and ethics – a comment on Posner. Georgia Law Rev 12:423–428

Grinover AP et al (2000) Código de brasileiro de defesa do consumidor: comentado pelos autores do anteprojeto, 6th edn. Forense Universitária, Rio de Janeiro

Limberger T (2002) O direito a intimidade do cliente bancário - Uma proposta de interpretação conjugando a sistemática constitucional, costumeira e civilista. Revista do Ministério Público do Rio Grande do Sul 48:247–271. Available at http://www.amprs.org.br/arquivos/revista_artigo/arquivo_1274905702.pdf

Martins L (ed) (2005) Cinquenta anos de jurisprudência Do Tribunal constitucional federal alemão. Konrad Adenauer Stiftung, Montevidéu

Mclauglin M, Vaupel S (1974–1975) Constitutional right of privacy and investigative consumer reports: Little Brother is watching you. Hastings Constitut Law Q 2:773–828

Posner RA (1977–1979) The right of privacy. Georgia Law Rev 12:393–422

Stürmer BA (1992) Banco de Dados e 'habeas data' no Código do Consumidor. Revista de Direito do Consumidor 1:35–94

Warren SD, Brandeis LD (1890) The right of privacy. Havar Law Rev 5:193–220

Chapter 26
Regulation and Supervision of Internet Finance and Consumer Protection in China

Yixian Zhao

Recent years, Internet finance in China witnessed a rapid development in a way that financial services constantly innovate by the support of information and communication technology. This pattern includes not only the innovation of the convenience of financial services, thanks to the Internet and trading terminal or other technological progress, such as online sale of monetary funds, and also the change of trading channels like equity crowdfunding. In 2015, ten ministries, including People's Bank of China (referred to as PBOC hereafter), promulgated the *Guiding Opinions for Promoting Healthy Development of Internet Finance* (2015), in which six legitimate Internet finance patterns are prescribed: online payment, online loan, equity crowdfunding, online sale of monetary funds, online insurance, online trust, and consumption finance.[1]

[1]According to *Guiding Opinions for Promoting Healthy Development of Internet Finance*, Article 7 to Article 12 in Part 2: Online payment is a service to launch payment orders and transfer monetary funds by computers, mobile phones or other apparatuses on the Internet; Online loan includes personal online loan (that is P2P online loan) and online small loan. P2P is the direct loan between individuals on the Internet platforms. Personal online loan institutions should insist the function of platforms and clarify its nature of information intermediaries. These institutions mainly provide information services for direct loan between lenders and borrowers and are prohibited to provide assurance services and illegally absorb funds. Online small loan is that small-loan companies controlled by Internet companies offer small loan to clients by using the Internet. Equity crowdfunding financing mainly refers to public small equity crowdfunding on the Internet, which is completed on the Equity crowdfunding financing intermediaries' platforms (Internet websites or similar electronic medias; Online sale of funds refers to funds sale institutions cooperate with third-party payment institutions to sell funds or other financial products; Online insurance refers to insurance companies operate online insurance business; Online trust and online consumption finance refer to trust companies and consumption finance companies operate online businesses.

Y. Zhao (✉)
East China University of Political Science and Law, Institute of BRICS Legal Studies, Shanghai, China
e-mail: evaaiw@outlook.com

C. Lima Marques, D. Wei (eds.), *Consumer Law and Socioeconomic Development*,
DOI 10.1007/978-3-319-55624-6_26

As a financial consumer in China, his or her daily life may unconsciously evolve in the above six fields. For example, someone pays the water and electricity bills online (online payment) and selects a commodity in an online store and then applies for installment (consumption credit finance and online payment); purchases goods, as well as refund insurance in case of dissatisfaction with the goods (online insurance); subsequently checks the refund of last consumption and conveniently deposits the refund into *Yu'e Bao* (purchasing online monetary funds); when finding out that a familiar restaurant is launching an equity crowdfunding online thus clicks the "I want to be an owner" (equity crowdfunding); lends 300 yuan to a five-day P2P (peer-to-peer) program online, which is recommended by a friend via a social network, in expectation of a 1.5 yuan interest.[2] Internet finance, becoming more and more popular, has a profound effect on people.

The high-speed development of the Internet finance in China depends on several factors: first, due to the popularization of infrastructure and application technology, on the one hand, China now has 1.104 billion mobile phone subscribers, which represents 84% of total population.[3] Meantime, Internet and mobile technology spread rapidly among population both in rural and urban areas, and the popularity rate has reached 42%.[4]

Second, since electronic commerce market in China becomes well-fledged and Chinese consumers attach importance to the recommendation of social nets, consumption behavior is easily affected. Popularity of online consumption largely motivates the development of third-party payment platforms. Some reports claim that China has become the biggest electronic commerce market in the world; registration accounts have reached 1.089 billion, and over 0.5 billion active users complete payment online. In 2009, the ratio of cash to GDP was reduced to 11.4%. Online payment reached to 130.4 billion dollars in 2013, and transaction volumes had been reported to reach 619.4 billion dollars.[5] At the same time, close contact among acquaintances in social nets (some leading social nets like *WeChat*, *QQ*, *Sina microblog*, etc.) and demonstration effect of groups, especially the behavior of "grab a red envelope" in recent years during the Spring Festival, make more and more people join in the online payment. By means of the recommendation of online groups of the same kind (such as schoolmates, colleagues, fellow villagers, etc.) and

[2]Reference to Internet financial institutions' websites for products promotion, such as http://8.wacai.com/detail/10070775-0.htm etc.

[3]Butani (2012). http://www.fonearena.com/blog/59613/mobile-subscriber-base-in-chinacrosses-1-104-billion-with-revenues-over-116-26-billion-in-2012.html; Ericsson. 2013."Ericsson Mobility Report." Ericsson, August. http://www.ericsson.com/res/docs/2013/emr-august-2013.pdf.

[4]Xinhuanet (2013).

[5]Fei'er (2013). http://www.globaltimes.cn/content/788360.shtml#.Uybq6_mSwuc; International Monetary Fund, "Financial Sector Assessment Program of the People's Republic of China." IMF Country Report No. 12/81. Washington, D.C.: IMF. P7.

strong impulsion by word of mouth in family relationship, people have quickly become familiar with Internet finance.[6]

The third factor is that traditional financial pattern cannot satisfy loan requirements for those medium and small enterprises and also for rural areas, which prevents their financial needs for a long time. Internet finance, however, comes into existence in a competitive way, attempting to analyze big data to refine the problem of costly communication between borrowers and lenders so that the capital can be offered accurately and really meet their developmental requirements. Meanwhile, facing with inflation, interest rate of bank deposit accounts, averaging 3.5% or so, seems unattractive; plus, with other economic factors' influence, consumers who have spare capital to purchase financial products or invest gradually divert to Internet finance, especially when online platforms publicize that their investment can earn 8 to 20% annual profits. With a high spreading speed, there have been more than 200 P2P platforms since 2006, continuing to increase at a 300% rate each year.[7] This pattern encourages a number of people to offer loan to acquire higher profits.

Governmental policies and attitude to Internet finance is another factor that plays a crucial role in its development. Governments now hold an open view on Internet finance, encourage innovation, and positively promote the innovation of Internet financial platforms, products, and services by various policies. China is one of few countries that allow third-party payment platforms to provide electronic services, and 233 business licenses were issued by the end of 2012.[8] In spite of the recent *E'zu Bao*, an online financing platform that is involved in illegally absorbing public funds, and other similar accidents, with more and more banks and formal financial institutions' participation, as well as constantly published regulations and rules to refine the governmental supervision on Internet finance, the developmental trend of Internet finance is optimistic as a whole. It can be estimated that increasingly low-income groups will be connected to Internet finance and contact with the market, financial services and information by those existing online payment platforms, well-developed electronic commerce and strong social nets, which can be ascribed to the support and technological innovation by several Internet giants like *Alibaba*, *Tecent*, and so on.

This article focuses on the risk that consumers are faced with under the new Internet finance and its regulatory framework. Then it will analyze and conclude the varied protection extent offered by different Internet financial patterns in accordance with the existing legal rules and finally illustrate the methods to establishing a better legal regime to protect Internet financial consumers' rights and interests.

---

[6]Leesa Shrader and Eric Duflos, China: A New Paradigm in Branchless Banking, Working Paper CGAP. http://www.cgap.org/publications/china-new-paradigm-branchless-banking.

[7]Leesa Shrader and Eric Duflos, China: A New Paradigm in Branchless Banking, Working Paper CGAP. http://www.cgap.org/publications/china-new-paradigm-branchless-banking.

[8]Butani (2012). http://www.fonearena.com/blog/59613/mobile-subscriber-base-in-chinacrosses-1-104-billion-with-revenues-over-116-26-billion-in-2012.html.

26.1 Legal Framework

26.1.1 Definition of Financial Consumer

According to the current legal framework, China now neither includes the financial consumer protection in the comprehensive *Law on the Protection of Consumer Rights and Interests* nor sets up a single special law for financial consumer protection but continues to publish relevant rules by different supervision agencies pursuant to the spread and development of financial services. These rules can be perceived from various lower-level authorities and sources. Therefore, even though in 2006 the China Banking Regulatory Commission (referred to as the CBRC hereafter) issued the *Guidelines for Financial Innovation of Commercial Banks*, in which the "financial consumer" was firstly mentioned, the accurate definition of financial consumer was not described by the amendment of the *Law on the Protection of Consumer Rights and Interests* in 2014. Furthermore, this Code with its aim to protect nationwide consumers, emphasizes the protection for consumption behavior with the purpose of satisfying personal or family needs. Thus, it does not give a clear answer whether the behavior of purchasing financial products and services can be protected or not. It just prescribes in Article 28 that "...business operators providing securities, insurance, banking, and other financial services shall provide consumers with information on their business addresses and contact methods, the quality, quantity, and prices or fees of commodities or services, the duration and manner of performance, safety precautions and risk warnings, after-sales services, and civil liability."

Administrative Measures of the People's Bank of China for the Protection of Financial Consumers' Rights and Interests (for Trial Implementation), 2013, defines "financial consumer" as meaning natural persons who purchase and use the financial products sold by financial institutions or receive the financial services provided by financial institutions within the territory of the People's Republic of China. However, normative legal documents issued by China Securities Regulatory Commission (referred to as CSRC hereafter) do not use the concept of "consumer," so the question here is whether those "investors" participating in Internet equity crowdfunding can be protected as a consumer. Similarly, *Commercial Bank Law* and *Banking Supervision Law* or other financial supervision laws do not mention the concept of financial consumer but simply indicate the necessity for protecting the legal rights and interests of depositors and other clients.

Guiding Opinions of the General Office of the State Council on Strengthening the Protection of Financial Consumers' Rights and Interests (2015) and *Guiding Opinions for Promoting Healthy Development of Internet Finance* (2015) also give no indication of the concept of financial consumer. Thus upper-level laws should clarify the concept of financial consumer and offer a clear definition of ordinary investor.

As far as academics are concerned, excluding institutional investors and professionals whose jobs are dealing with financial investment, the following groups should be treated as falling within the scope of consumer protection: most retail clients lacking financial expertise and people who apply for and use credit consumption in daily life, purchase profitable but lower-risk financial products like fund and others, or accept deposit, insurance services offered by financial institutions to secure their properties are safe, value added, or under the risk control.[9]

Throughout the legislative trend of developed countries and the publication of international universal practices, protecting financial consumers is increasingly emphasized. At the same time, more and more countries incorporate nonprofessional individual investors (retail clients) into the scope of financial consumer and grant them the same rights as an ordinary consumer.[10] Because of separated supervision by different agencies, continuous innovation of Internet finance, and the development of new financial products that break the boundary of traditional division, lacking of definition of financial consumer will result in legislative basis being insufficient, the power of supervision agencies unclear and the enforcement of law ineffective. So how to make these normative legal documents match with each other is a huge work, which still needs to be thrashed out.

26.1.2 Regulatory System

What legislative pattern China now adopts on financial supervision is based on the separated operations, which means that PBOC, together with CBRC, CSRC, and CIRC (commonly referred as *one bank and three commissions*) supervise traditional financial operation based on the division of bank, securities, and insurance. Local financial offices set by local governments are part of supervision agencies. Another relevant Internet financial supervision agency includes the Ministry of Industry and Information Technology, the Ministry of Finance, the State Administration of Industry and Commerce, the State Internet Information Office, etc. This pattern highlights supervision on financial organizations, and it is the legal nature of enterprises that determines the corresponding supervision agency, which distinguishes from the supervision pattern that takes financial products as division basis, called "block supervision." PBOC also sets Financial Consumer Protection Bureau, and local "*one bank and three commissions*" (*Yihang Sanhui*) set branches at local level. This pattern is so-called hierarchical supervision. Financial consumers' rights and interests' protection websites and protecting consultation telephones are also established as the protection platforms.[11] It seems that local consumer protection associations have felt powerless to cope with financial consumption featuring as strong specialty. In particular, Internet financial organizations usually are involved in comprehensive operations, and like what this article mentioned at the beginning,

[9]Wei and Zhao (2016).

[10]Yang (2013), pp. 118–127.

[11]Website is www.12363.org, consultation and complaint telephone number is (0086)-12363.

their operation crosses different fields, including banking, securities, insurance, and trust. Multi-regulatory agencies will easily cause poor communication, lower efficiency, and difficulties in cooperation. So it is questionable for such an arrangement to match with each other and provide effective protection for financial consumers. According to the report launched by the World Bank aiming to evaluate the financial consumer protection in more than 100 countries, supervision regime in China still has much room to promote and longer distance to catch up with the developed countries. Meanwhile, compared with those developing countries with emerging market economies, China's defects are obvious.[12]

26.1.3 The Risk of Internet Finance and Current Legal Framework

From the aspect of legal nature, current Internet finance assumes certain function of branchless banking and belongs to the bank-led model,[13] which means that relying on the POS terminal and mobile phone technology to deliver specific transaction information, the third party will act as the main service channel for its clients and complete delivery outside bank branches. Therefore, the risk that consumers encounter under the branchless pattern will readily come into existence in our Internet finance, and the main risk largely stems from using the third-party payment platforms and mobile phones or other technological assistance apparatuses.

(1) Given their own interests, providers are unwilling to hold activities benefiting financial consumers most. (2) Providers do not completely conform to laws and regulations that prescribe consumer protection and diligence obligation. (3) Privacy and capital security cannot be guaranteed. All of these risks have appeared during the development of Internet finance, for example, illegally absorbing funds with a claim of online loan or using the new clients' capital to repay the old ones' interest. According to incomplete statistics, nationwide, there were 27 problematic online loan platforms in the first four months of 2014, with 0.6 billion *yuan* involved. And by July, 2014, 150 of them ran away. Additionally, many online electronic platforms launch credit loan for consumption, which brings risk of excessive credit loan. It is reported that 49% netizens applied for loan in 2014. Without checking original ID cards and no requirement for signature, 72.3% applications are admitted and over 60% accounts acquire loan without offering mortgage. But for 73.8% of the total surveyed netizens, their individual incomes each month range from 2000 to 8000 *yuan*, and for a less proportion of 57.7%, their available allowance is only about 500–1500 *yuan*.[14] Furthermore, due to technological risks and potential

---

[12]Dias (2013).

[13]One of indicators of judging bank-led Model is that the third-party payment institutions are not allowed to provide cash services according to current laws and regulations.

[14]iResearch, "Research Report on Online Credit Loan Clients", 2015. www.iresearch.cn.

threats, it is difficult for Internet finance to ensure security. Accounts information, ID card information, and credit reports are stolen and then sold out on a large scale; stealing capital in others' accounts and falsely using someone else's credit line are not a novelty; and the leaking channels and scope, as well as the speed, are extensive and rapid.[15] Moreover, taking the current development of Internet finance in China into consideration, another potential risk relating to coordination with other legal systems is that according to our *Electronic Signature Law*, the procedure of acquiring electronic evidence is complex. It is hard to perform burden of proof without special technological methods, which will leave consumers at an adverse position once disputes come out.[16] At the same time, since the Internet finance is a kind of online transaction, jurisdiction is another factor that should be considered, especially when consumers resort disputes to the court. All of these will increase the cost of protecting rights.

26.2 The Type and Supervision of Internet Finance

Since the formulation of legal rules on Internet finance is slower than the practice and the risk that different types of Internet finance is faced with is varied, the protection for financial consumers has various emphasis. Thus, this article will selectively choose several types of Internet finance services and analyze the supervision on Internet financial institutions and protection for financial consumers under the current legal regulations and rules so that it provides some guidance for those readers who need to fully understand Internet finance in China.

26.2.1 Online Payment

Aiming for online payment, on December 28, 2015, PBOC issued *Administrative Measures on Online Payment Business of Non-banking Payment Institutions* (referred to as "Measures" hereafter), which was implemented on July 1, 2016. This regulation, with a relatively comprehensive prescription of the rules to protect online payment, mainly includes the following.

[15] Yin (2014), pp. 75–76.

[16] Reference to *Electronic Signature Law of the People's Republic of China* (2015Amendment), http://www.miit.gov.cn/n11293472/n11294912/n11296092/16817369.html.

26.2.1.1 Conform to the Principle of "Knowing Your Clients"

If a payment institution opens payment accounts for clients, it shall conduct real-name system management of clients, register and take effective measures to validate clients' basic identity information, verify their valid identity certificates as required, retain copies or photocopies of the valid identity certificates, and establish unique identification codes for clients.

Non-banking payment institutions with licenses to conduct online payment businesses (referred to as "payment institution" hereafter) can offer two types of accounts: (1) accounts are on the basis of banking accounts, and (2) accounts needing clients pay transaction capital in advance and then can launch order of payment, but clients cannot overdraft, lend, lease, or sell their accounts. All accounts will be categorized into three groups pursuant to the checking channels and strictness degree, and the scope of financial services ranges from different levels: consumption, transfer, and balance payment transaction within 1000 yuan; balance payment transaction within 100,000 yuan; balance payment transaction within 200,000 yuan and allowing to purchase financial products. Besides, a payment institution shall, according to the safety degree of trading verification methods, conduct limit management of individual clients that make payments with the balance of payment accounts.

26.2.1.2 Standard Form Contract, Notice Obligation, and Risk Warnings

A payment institution shall sign service agreements with clients to agree on the responsibilities, rights, and obligations of both parties, which shall at least specify the business rules (including but not limited to business functions and workflow, identity recognition and trading verification methods, and fund settlement methods, among others), charging items and standards, service flow and rules for inquiry, disputes and complaints, among others, measures of preventing and handling business risks and illegal activities, the division of liabilities for clients' losses and compensation rules, etc. The payment institution shall ensure that the content of the agreement is clear and easy to understand and remind, in a conspicuous manner, the client to pay attention to matters with material interest to him or her.

Where a payment institution opens a payment account for a client, it shall, in a conspicuous manner, inform the client in the service agreement and take valid means to confirm that the client has been fully aware of and clearly understood the following content: "the balance of funds in the payment account is not equal to the client's bank deposits, and is not protected by the *Deposit Insurance Regulation*, and it is, in nature, the prepaid value owned and authorized by the client for custody by the payment institution. Although the monetary funds with prepaid value belong to the client, they are deposited in the bank in the name of the payment institution, instead of the client, and the fund transfer orders shall be issued by the payment institutions to the bank."

A payment institution shall fully warn clients of the potential risks of the online payment business, disclose in a timely manner new means of committing crimes by offenders, offer necessary safety education to clients, and give risk warnings on high-risk businesses before and during operations.

26.2.1.3 Information Disclosure and Report System

The payment institution shall, before January 31 each year, announce on its website the risk incidents that occurred in the previous year, the occurrence of and compensation for clients' losses caused by risks, the number and type of clients' complaints that occurred in the previous year, the proportion of complaints that have been handled, the complaint handling speed, etc. The payment institution shall faithfully report the aforesaid content, the provision, use and balance of risk reserve, and other information in the annual supervision report.

Where a payment institution needs to suspend its online payment services due to system upgrading, debugging, or any other reason, it shall make an announcement at least five working days in advance. The payment institution shall, before modifying the clauses of its agreement, raising its service charging rates or increasing any new charging item, publicize on the website or any other service channel for 30 consecutive days in a conspicuous manner and confirm that clients have been aware of and accepted all details to be adjusted before clients handle the relevant businesses for the first time.

To provide innovative products or services on online payment, cease the provision of products or services, or cooperate with any overseas institution in providing online payment services within China, a payment institution shall report to the PBC branch office at the place where the legal person is located at least 30 days in advance. Where the payment institution has any serious risk incident, it shall report to the PBC branch office at the place where the legal person is located in a timely manner, and if it finds any suspected violation of law or crime, it shall report to the public security authority at the same time.

26.2.1.4 Ensuring the Security of Data and Privacy

A payment institution shall not falsify or conceal any trading information. Especially for those core data like trading amount, bank accounts, a payment institution shall retain operational records for at least five years as of the date when the operation comes into force. The payment institution shall collect, use, save, and transmit clients' information under the "minimum" principle and inform clients of the use, objective, and scope of the relevant information. The payment institution shall not provide clients' information to any other institution or individual unless it is otherwise prescribed in any law or regulation and confirmed and authorized by clients item by item. A payment institution shall agree in agreements to prohibit franchised merchants from saving the magnetic stripe information or chip information of clients' bank cards, verification code, validity term, password, or any other sensitive information and, in accordance with the law, bear the losses caused by and liabilities for the leakage of relevant information.

26.2.1.5 Consumer Protection System

- Advance compensation: a payment institution shall establish and improve risk reserve rules and trading compensation rules, make advance compensation for fund losses in full amount in a timely manner if clients' reason cannot be proved in an effective manner, and protect clients' lawful rights and interests. Where a payment institution sends a payment order to the bank where the client opens the account to withdraw funds from the client's bank account, the payment institution and the bank shall expressly agree on the applicable scope of withdrawal and trading verification methods and make an undertaking on unconditional assumption of advance compensation for the losses caused by the risks of such type of transactions in full amount.
- Dispute resolution: a payment institution shall provide clients with trading information inquiry services within at least one year free of charge via websites, uniform service hotline, and other channels; establish and improve error dispute and complaint-handling rules; and assign professional departments and personnel to handle trading errors and client complaints in an accurate and timely manner based on facts.
- Protection for consumers' rights and interests: a payment institution shall fully respect clients' independent right of choice, shall not force clients to use the payment services it provides, and shall not obstruct clients from using the payment services provided by any other institution. The payment institution shall fairly display all kinds of fund receipts and payment methods available to clients, shall not induce or force clients to open payment accounts or handle fund receipt and payment through payment accounts in any form, and shall not set any additional unreasonable conditions. Payment institutions shall join the Payment & Clearing Association of China, accept the administration of industry self-disciplinary organizations, and promote the level of consumer protection at appropriate times.

According to the law, if it fails to establish as required management rules, such as clients' real-name system management, handling of error disputes and complaints, risk reserves and trading compensations, or fails to give risk warnings or discloses the relevant information as required or fails to perform its reporting obligation as required, it will be imposed a fine of 10,000 *yuan* up to 30,000 *yuan* in accordance with the provision of the *Measures for the Administration of Payment Services Provided by Non-financial Institutions.* If it provides payment services for any illegal transactions; fails to reflect the information on online payment transactions in a truthful, complete, and accurate manner; falsifies or conceals trading information or is guilty of information leakage; interferes in the clients' independent selection of payment service providers or fund receipt and payment methods; or discloses any false information to the public, it will be imposed a fine of 30,000 *yuan* or its illegal gains, if any, will be confiscated; if the circumstances are serious, the PBOC shall withdraw its Payment Business Permit. However, whether the above legal responsibilities are too slight to function well and provide effective protection is still questionable. As a whole, this new *Measures* follows the international universal practice for protecting financial consumers, establishes the lowest supervision requirement, and tries its best to protect this new pattern of Internet finance so that it can develop the idea of branchless banking and inclusive finance and enhance competition with traditional financial institutions. As a result, people, in particular low-income groups, will receive better services.

26.2.2 Online Loan

At the end of 2015, the notorious illegal absorbing funds case of *E'zu Bao* became one of severe vicious cases reported by the Supreme Peoples' Procuratorate to the National People's Congress during the 2016 annual session. *E'zu Bao* took the way of online loan and illegally absorbed over 50 billion yuan and finally left about 0.9 million victim investors from 31 provinces. The accused claimed to the public that its business pattern was "Financing lease company would contract with the project company, and then launch financing by the way of credit assignment on the their platform. After financing, project companies would pay the rent to financing lease companies and the latter would pay principal and profits." Taking an extremely high interest rate as enticement, fabricating financing lease project, continuously borrowing money to repay the existing debts, and self-guaranty, *E'zu Bao* illegally absorbed a great deal of funds. At the same time, *Yucheng Group* also kept control of three guarantee companies and one factoring company to offer guaranty for projects on *E'zu Bao* platform.[17]

As a new pattern of Internet finance, online loans in the P2P form appear to have a rapid, strong, and abnormal development trend and thus receive widespread attention both from academics and industries. According to the statistics provided by an independent institute, by the end of July, 2014, there are around 1300 P2P online loan platforms in operation, and during the first six months of 2014, approximately 16.7 billion dollars (about 100 billion *yuan*) transaction volume was completed. Western countries, however, only have a few online loan platforms, and the scale of online loan is around two billion dollars (about 12 billion *yuan*).

[17]Yang Bai, Ji chen, "Facts Research of Ezubao Illegally Absorbing Funds Case". Reference to the Supreme People's Procuratorate of the People's Republic of China's website: http://www.spp.gov.cn/zdgz/201602/t20160201_111982.shtml.

Strictly speaking, P2P in China is mainly used to satisfy financing needs for those medium and small enterprises, not the real peer to peer but peer to business.[18] Now, it is hard to identify whether these medium and small enterprises that acquire financing by online loan can fall within the scope of the service objects of inclusive finance, the loans they get are really used for products, and the threshold to access to financial services should be enhanced. This prosperous development, in fact, reflects that the traditional finance cannot meet those medium and small enterprises' and low-income groups' financing needs, especially the ignorance of big state-owned financial institutions about small and microfinance, and financial consumers with affluent capital lack reasonable investment channels. As a result, different changes come into existence when the aggressive informal folk finance combines with Internet technology.

The promoter of online loan actually tempts unspecified online groups to raise capital and thus with a public feature. Some scholars think that if regulatory authorities simply regard the operators of online loan platforms as information agencies and not taking part in capital transference, the concessionary access will not function well.[19] However, if the role the operator plays oversteps the boundary of information agency and becomes the credit intermediary, it will give rise to more legal problems. When an online loan platform offers guaranty for the borrower, the credit risk will be transferred to the institution that provides guaranty and public lenders will lose motivation to verify the credit quality of borrowers.[20] On the other hand, like *E'zu Bao*, the platform itself controls a third-party guarantee company, which largely increases the possibility of being deceived. Similar methods also include this: the platform directly or by a related party takes those long period and large amount borrowing needs apart and converts them to some short period and small amount credit and then sell them to financial consumers. In this way, the platform can change the period, divide creditor's rights as loan transfer, but also easily bring liquidity risk. By selling credit, establishing capital pool, and releasing loans to the public, online loan platforms factually assemble deposits, settlements, and loans in themselves and become the shadow banking.

In accordance with the existing laws and regulations, online loan platforms can only be defined as information agencies and cannot provide guaranty, establish capital pool, and illegally absorb public deposits. According to related requirements of criminal law and from the aspect of supervision, an individual can borrow no more than 0.2 million *yuan* and the number of lenders is not over 30 people, while

[18]Ranran Zhao, "The "Helping Hand" of Internet Financial Supervision". http://mp.weixin.qq.com/s?__biz=MzI2OTA5MjQ0NQ==&mid=400574136&idx=2&sn=bac6a5c356ced2564c8b00df71d42dab&scene=23&srcid=032679qBfCE6DTh8wZXOy42D#rd.

[19]Zhao and Luo (2014), pp.118–126.

[20]Ranran Zhao, "The "Helping Hand" of Internet Financial Supervision". http://mp.weixin.qq.com/s?__biz=MzI2OTA5MjQ0NQ==&mid=400574136&idx=2&sn=bac6a5c356ced2564c8b00df71d42dab&scene=23&srcid=032679qBfCE6DTh8wZXOy42D#rd.

for medium and small enterprises, requirements are 1 million *yuan* and 150 people respectively. In practice, if lenders' capital is accumulated in the P2P platforms instead of transferring to borrowers directly or financing projects acquire capital from temporary advances by platforms and platforms later absorb these capital back from the social public or platforms do not perform their checking obligations, keep silent, or fail to find out that borrowers are illegally absorbing public funds or other criminal activities, platforms will be likely to violate the above prescriptions and offend the crime of illegally absorbing the public deposit, crime of establishing a banking institution without authorization, crime of illegal business operations, etc. Besides, if the debtor cannot repay the loan on time and the Internet platform advances interests even to principals, the platform cannot claim recovery from the borrower as an intermediary service institution.

Under the existing legal framework, online loan in a non-P2P form also has great risks adverse to financial consumers. For example, if the original lender offers loan to the borrower and later transfers the principal and interest between the first payment and second payment to a new investor, then it is questionable whether the unproduced interest can be transferred. The original lender transfers credit to a new investor without notifying the debtor, which has no binding effect on the debtor. So the debtor still repays the loan to the original lender rather than the new investor, and finally the new investor may not fulfill his credit. Even if the transferred credit has created guaranty, the new investor is still faced with the above risk because of absence of information to the debtor and the difficulty in completing transference registration in practice in terms of online transaction. In addition, once the borrower breaches the contract, the question is whether and how to take legal action. In any matter, arbitration or litigation will be extremely difficult, especially when lenders come from all over the country.[21]

In December 2015, CSRC published the *Interim Measures for Administration of Online Loan Information Intermediary Activities* (Exposure Draft), and now it is still in the phase of public consultation. According to this Draft, Internet information intermediaries are supervised by CSRC, together with local financial supervision agencies. Apart from these mentioned legal rules, this Draft gives more specific responses to the legitimacy of certain practices, such as prohibiting offering assurance service, prohibiting offering financing to platform itself or related third parties, prohibiting releasing loan, prohibiting providing borrowers guaranty or commit to repay principal and interest, prohibiting taking the financing projects apart, prohibiting operating offline (nonelectronic channel) business, etc.

In terms of financial consumer protection, the Draft emphasizes the real-name system and necessary verification of the borrower's and lender's qualification and the financing project; asks platforms to take action to prevent fraudulence; and

[21]Xueli Cheng etc., "The Main Problems of Internet Financial Platform Trading of Credit Assignment", http://www.chinalawinsight.com/2015/03/articles/finance/%E5%80%BA%E6%9D%83%E8%BD%AC%E8%AE%A9%E7%B1%BB%E4%BA%92%E8%81%94%E7%BD%91%E9%87%91%E8%9E%8D%E5%B9%B3%E5%8F%B0%E4%BA%A4%E6%98%93%E5%B1%82%E9%9D%A2%E7%9A%84%E4%B8%BB%E8%A6%81%E9%97%AE%E9%A2%98/.

prohibits false propaganda and concealing the defects and risks of financing projects or using confusing language and other deceptive methods to promote and mislead the public. The draft also demands that the platform should evaluate with due diligence the age, health condition, financial condition, investment experience, risk preference, and risk endurance of lenders; otherwise, transaction services should be unavailable. Meantime, the draft mandatorily asks that the lender should have non-break-even investment experiences and be familiar with the Internet and highlights that the online loan platform cannot substitute the lender to make decision and should remind the lender to notify online loan risks and forbidden behaviors in an obvious way, and each item should be identified by the lender. The Draft also asks Internet credit loan platforms to fully disclose the information about borrowers and financing projects and the outcome of risk evaluation on the platform. Besides, the platform need not only disclose the transaction volume, loan amount, bad debt rate, the number of lenders and borrowers, consumer complaints, and other operation and management information but also to spread knowledge on online loan and develop risk education.

Legislators do not use the concept of financial consumer in this Draft but attempt to rectify frequently emerging risks in practice by legal rules and underline the protection for lenders. But from the view point of inclusive finance, low-income groups are likely to become borrowers in an online loan. Faced with all kinds of services and fees, they should be incorporated into the financial consumer protection system. Additionally, online platforms usually offer lengthy contracts and ask lenders to click "The lender here is a qualified lender, has non-break-even investment experiences and is familiar with the Internet." In this way, platforms avoid their checking obligations. For those consumers who have little contact with financial services, have lower education background, and are appealed to invest purely for high profits, it is hard to fully understand the content of the contracts. Therefore, we are looking forward to the formal publication of the Draft, as well as to pay close attention to the enforcement of law in the future.

26.2.3 Equity Crowdfunding

CSRC is responsible for the supervision on Internet equity crowdfunding, and it published the *Exposure Draft of Measures for Administration of Private Equity Crowdfunding Financing (for Trial Implementation)* at the end of 2014, and now this Draft is still in the phase of public consultation. This Draft gives an indication of the direction of the future supervision on private equity crowdfunding financing and the extent of consumer protection. This Draft, again, does not use the concept of financial consumer but substitutes it with "investor." On management, this Draft demands that the Internet crowdfunding platforms should conform to the threshold of net assets and requirements of professional staff and set special accounts to manage the funds they raise. Similarly, platforms cannot finance for themselves, provide guaranties, hold shares on behalf of someone else, transfer shareholder's rights, or promote financing projects to those non-real name registration accounts. This Draft also asks that the financing party should meet the requirement of scale of medium and small enterprises and obey the *Securities Law*. Another mandatory requirement is that platforms cannot issue securities publicly or by advertisement or temptation or in a disguisedly public way, and they also cannot issue securities to unspecified people. After financing, the total number of shareholders should be not over 200 people. To conform to this prescription and convert those unspecified objects to specified ones, the Draft suggests qualified investors—individuals who have more than three million financial assets (renminbi) or over 500,000 annual incomes during the recent three years and have abilities to recognize, judge, and assume corresponding investment risks. In practice, operation modes of some platforms are as follows: transferring their own legal obligations of checking investors to those individual investors, asking investors to represent themselves as qualified investors, and then launching equity crowdfunding. Compared with the law and regulations of online payment and online loan, this Draft weakens consumer protection, which acts in cooperation with the idea mentioned in this article that lack in clear definition of financial consumers may result in some problems.

26.3 Protection for Financial Consumer's Rights and Interests

At present, financial consumers in China have the following characteristics: poor security awareness and financial abilities needed to be enhanced, particularly since Internet finance reduced the threshold to allow consumers to access financial services. Consumers with lower education background, less experience in financial services, and easily peer-affected decision-making typically underestimate risks, fail to select appropriate financial products or take effective action to protect themselves. Meanwhile, financial consumers often encounter costly rights protection and lack experiences in dispute resolution.

In November 2015, the State Council issued the *Guiding Opinions of the General Office of the State Council on Strengthening the Protection of Financial Consumers' Rights and Interests*, which highlights that the protection of financial consumers' rights and interests plays a crucial role in preventing and resolving financial risks and also has a positive effect on consolidating financial consumers' confidence, sustaining the security and stability of finance, and promoting social fairness and justice. This Opinion mentions eight rights, including the following:

(1) Right of property safety—this includes strictly distinguishing assets of institutions and assets of clients and not misappropriating or occupying the capital of clients.
(2) Right of information—financial institutions shall, in plain language, disclose information that may affect their decision-making to financial consumers in a timely, true, accurate, and complete manner and fully alert risks and shall not

issue any fraudulent information that is exaggerated in product revenue or conceal product risks or conduct false or misleading publicity.

(3) Protecting financial consumers' right of choice—financial institutions shall not force any client to purchase or sell products or services, conduct tie-in sale of products or services against the will of financial consumers, attach any unreasonable conditions, or take any misleading means to entice consumers to buy any other products.
(4) Right of fair trade—financial institutions may not aggravate financial consumers' responsibilities, restrict or eliminate financial consumers' lawful rights in the standard form of contracts, restrict the approaches of financial consumers seeking legal remedy, or mitigate or exempt their civil responsibilities for damaging financial consumers' lawful rights and interests.
(5) Right of claim according to the law—financial institutions shall establish internal multilevel complaint-handling mechanisms, improve complaint-handling procedures, establish a complaint-handling information inquiry system, and improve the quality and efficiency of handling of financial consumers' complaints.
(6) Right to education—financial institutions shall further strengthen financial consumer education, actively organize or participate in financial knowledge dissemination activities, carry out extensive and continuous routine education of financial consumer, and help financial consumers with improving the cognitive competence for financial products and services and self-defensive ability.
(7) Right to be respected—financial institutions shall not discriminatorily or differentially treat financial consumers due to difference in gender, age, race, ethnicity, nationality, or other factors.
(8) Right of information safety—financial institutions shall take effective measures to strictly prevent and control financial consumers' information disclosure risks.

The eight rights constitute a right framework that is identical to the right category in the comprehensive *Law of Protection of Consumers' Rights and Interests*, which sets a unified system for the current comprehensive *Law of Protection of Consumers' Rights and Interests* and future single financial consumer protection and promotes the connection between general law and special law. At the same time, this *Opinion* comes up with a framework of consumer protection to Internet institutions and platforms. On the one hand, under the current supervision pattern, it leaves some room for different supervision agencies to conduct specific requirements on financial products; on the other hand, it reflects government' choice of policy inclination between consumer protection and encouragement of financial innovation, which is a subtle balance.

Therefore, financial consumer protection can set some basic and urgent bottom line. For example, we can choose two important starting points among eight rights.

26.3.1 Comprehensive and Transparent Information Disclosure

This principle requests, when opening an account, that the disclosure includes not only the interest rate and fee rate but also the information and account change or other significant matters. Disclosure methods can take the form of "key matters within one page" and use concise language to make consumers easily understand the core matters. For example, when offering online loans, equity crowdfunding, online funds, online insurance, or other financial services, three elementary points should be clarified within one page before consumers purchase financial products:

(1) Who is the provider of financial products and services? Who is the opposite party in contract? Especially when the Internet finance just acts as the third party, it should explain to consumers that it is an agency, not the direct financial provider.
(2) Is the product a guaranteed fund or other types of investment? What are the maximum losses under the worst condition?
(3) What are the product cycle and service fees? Comprehensive and transparent information disclosure will help consumers to understand the risks that they may meet and urge Internet financial institutions to fairly compete by offering economical prices transparently and better services under the open conditions.

26.3.2 Providing Accessible and Effective Mechanism for Complaints and Resolving Disputes

Ensuring the channel of complaints accessible is one of key points of financial consumer protection. Given the nature of the Internet, compensation at a great distance will be a challenge. Most financial consumers typically belong to "have-nots" under the Galanter's Model, because the time and expenses are costly and consumers have less experience in using formal financial institutions and judicial recourse. For example, according to the *Administrative Measures for the Online Payment Business of Non-banking Payment Institutions*, demanding Internet financial institutions to offer simple complaint mechanisms, as well as exerting the function of Financial Consumer Protection Bureau, is important for consumer protection. If the law can authorize the Financial Consumer Protection Bureau to perform more regulatory supervision, including the power of formulating rules and power of supervision and enforcement, the Bureau can promulgate regulations and guiding opinions or other legal documents to conduct supervision on regulated organizations and will have authority to make executive punishment and handle consumers' complaints, which will establish a complete and unified protection mechanism. Nevertheless, since China now supervises on the basis of different financial fields, whether the decentralization of the supervision authorities will influence the final effect of the formulation and enforcement still needs further observation. Similarly, with the United States and other developed countries where problems and conflicts of cross-supervision exist before the special legislation of financial consumer protection but by analyzing and concluding 26 laws and regulations issued during the past 30 years, the framework of consumer rights finally is set in the law of consumer financial protection. Therefore, when China formulates its own supervision rules, it should strike a balance between advanced experience and current local conditions.

The development of supervision on Internet finance in China follows the common experiences associated with the early phases of financial markets: no detailed rules and regulations during its market cultivation period; considering setting market access conditions for service providers in accordance with market development—like the *Administrative Measures for the Online Payment Business of Non-Banking Payment Institutions* and two regulations that are still in the phase of public consultation for full consideration, the *Interim Measures for Administration of Online loan Information Intermediary Activities* (Exposure Draft) and *Exposure Draft of Measures for Administration of Private Equity Crowdfunding Financing (for Trial Implementation)*; and supervising potential threats to consumer protection at the same time. The speed of innovation of Internet finance is faster than laws and policies, and sometimes it is no supervision that results in its "prosperous" development. In a long term, with the expansion of financial markets, it becomes necessary for the legislation, especially when some people use Internet finance to illegally absorb funds or engage in other criminal cases. The success and security of Internet financial services finally depend on supervision and governance in an appropriate and coordinated way. If the drafting financial statutes and regulations are defective or are promulgated untimely, it is likely to prevent the new-born Internet finance from entering into the market and cannot ensure that financial service fees make profits under a fairly competitive environment. Meanwhile, the costs of enforcement, other related institutions, as well as the feasibility of supervision methods should also be taken into account,[22] particularly the enforcement of laws and regulations. Under the current regulatory pattern, it needs further research whether each supervision agency has necessary abilities and can coordinate with each other. Striking a balance between the goal of protecting consumers and the goal of promoting financial services, especially evaluating the possible risks resulting from the new financial service pattern is always an important direction for legislation in China.

References

Butani D (2012) Mobile subscriber base in China crosses 1.104 billion with revenues. Fonearena, 25 December 2012

CGAP (2012) A guide to regulation and supervision of microfinance. The World Bank

---

[22]CGAP (2012).

Dias D (2013) Implementing consumer protection in emerging markets and developing economies. CGAP
Fei'er W (2013) New payment rules from PBC. Global Times, 12 June 2013
Wei D, Zhao Y (2016) O crédito para consumo e os direitos do consumidor financeiro na China
Xinhuanet (2013) China drafting regulation for mobile payment: report. Xinhuanet, 11 December. http://news.xinhuanet.com/english/china/2013-12/11/c_132959171.htm
Yang D (2013) The theory of construction of financial services integration law. J Renmin Univ China (3)
Yin Y (2014) Protection for internet financial consumers' rights and interests. China Finance (12)
Zhao Y, Luo P (2014) The theory of internet financial supervision. Law Rev (6)

Chapter 27
Overindebtedness in Mercosul Countries: An Overview

Káren Rick Danilevicz Bertoncello and Clarissa Costa de Lima

27.1 Introduction

In Mercosul[1] countries (Brazil, Argentina, Paraguay, Uruguay, and Venezuela), the opening of the credit market started in the last decade, modifying the subconsuming scenario of the low-income households, which are incapable of accessing credit, which is exclusively, at that time, for the medium class. In Brazil, for example, Lula's popular credit stimulation politics was responsible for increasing consumption among low-income households, which absorbed 17 billion reais offered in the market. In 2005 and 2006, 2.15 million families left the D/E consumer class and turned to class C.[2] The type of credit called "payroll loans" captivated all the social classes and was responsible for the increase in the evolution of credit with real growth of 760%, compared to January

[1]Founded at Treated of Assunção, in 1991, which establishes that its mission is to increase goods and services offers available in order to ameliorate its inhabitant's life. See: Souza (1996), p. 155.

[2]According to a study realized by the Latin Panel, the biggest research company about domestic consumption in the Latin America, there has been a reduction of five points of the population that belongs to the D/E groups (families with incomes up to 4 monthly salaries—salário mínimo is a monthly minimum wage). This segment represented 44% of the total in 2005 and has passed to 39% this year. The C group has moved up to 37% of the population in the country. According to the analysis done by its CEO Ana Cláudia Fioratti this changes happened due to the buying of durable goods favored by the increase of the money and access to the credit. Research done 11/22/2006 at http://br.news.finance.yahoo.com/22112006/25/financas-classes-d-ampliam-consumo-nao-duraveis.html.

K.R.D. Bertoncello (✉) • C.C. de Lima (✉)
Department of the Consumer Law at the Center of Studies of AJURIS, School of Magistracy of the State of Rio Grande do Sul, Porto Alegre, Brazil
e-mail: Krdb@tj.rs.gov.br; Clarissalima@tj.rs.gov.br

C. Lima Marques, D. Wei (eds.), *Consumer Law and Socioeconomic Development*,
DOI 10.1007/978-3-319-55624-6_27

2004 and January 2011, representing the movement of R$ 139.7 billion[3] and R$ 274 billion in December 2015.[4]

In Europe, it took place in the 60s, bringing along problems related to prevention and treatment of overindebted families. That explains the existence of legislation in many countries of the European Union that designs a system of treatment of consumers' insolvency or overindebtedness.

Despite analysis referring to Mercosul, the internationality[5] of the overindebtedness theme imposes a study of already existent models, as well as practice observed before in studies such as abusive commercial practices, publicity, quality safety of products and services, control of abusive contract clauses.

In this overindebtedness domain, we understand relevant the comparison with the French legislation model because of its evolution regarding the combat of social exclusions originated with the credit approval. This legislation dedicates special attention to consumers' protection regarding credit operations since 1798, with the 78-22 law that said in its article 2:

> Les dispositions de la présente loi s'appliquent à toute operations de crédit, ainsi qu'à son cautionnement éventuel, consentie à titre habituel par des personnes physiques ou morales, que ce soit à titre onéreux ou gratuit. Pour l'application de la présente, loi, la location-vente et la location avec option d'achat ainsi que les ventes ou prestations de services dont le paiment est échelonné ou differé sont assimilées à des opérations de crédit.

The overindebtedness problem is not restricted to developed countries' consumers, and it can also create devastating effects in developing countries due to the absence of legal support and the subsistence consuming or subconsuming reality. This lack of attention, according to Antônio Herman Benjamin, "is ironic as well, because it is exactly in poorer countries that, due to the economical and psychological fragility of consumers the respect of these basic rights is paramount.[6]

The overindebtedness phenomenon was the object of an empiric research, unedited in Rio Grande do Sul, Brazil; coordinated by Prof. Cláudia Lima Marque; and developed in the Law Post-Graduation Program of the Federal University of Rio Grande do Sul, together with the Civil Department of the Public Defense in the same state, with 100 cases of individuals' overindebtedness. Results showed that the overindebted profile in Rio Grande do Sul was very similar to the lower class overindebted in Canada, where similar research took place.[7]

---

[3]Source: Banco Central do Brasil *in*: http://www.bcb.gov.br/pec/boletimregional/port/2011/04/br201104b2p.pdf.

[4]Source: https://www.fazenda.gov.br/noticias/2016/janeiro/fgts-como-garantia-do-credito-consignado-privado.

[5]The internationalization of the Consumer Rights Code has been identified by Antônio Herman Benjamin when he affirms that "transnational companies utilize industrial standards and uniform commercial techniques and international scale", having as consequence the fact that "the consumer in this side of the planet faces problems very similar to those of the Asiatic e do Pacific consumers". For this matter, see: Benjamin (1993), In: http://www.bdjur.stj.gov.br.

[6]Benjamin (1993), In: http://www.bdjur.stj.gov.br.

[7]See: Marques (2006), pp. 255–309.

Therefore, it is the necessity to analyze, in the second part of this research, the Brazilian judiciary's experience with the pilot project for the treatment of consumer overindebtedness situations, even before the creation of a special law that takes care of this subject.

27.2 Legislative Treatment of Consumers' Credit and Overindebtedness in Mercosul

27.2.1 Legal Framing of the Consuming Credit

Mercosul countries own "economical, political and cultural identity, which includes language (Spanish except for Brazil where Portuguese is spoken), European colonization, religion (mainly catholic), culture (iberic), a major urban population, a continental Law (civil law, based in codes), and, in a certain way, routinary economical-political crisis."[8]

Uruguay is the only MERCOSUL country that does not have a specific regulation about consumer rights in Federal Constitution, and it was the last one to legislate this subject through Law number 17.189 of 1999.[9] Although the approval of a consumer rights law in a country of scarce consumerist culture is an advance, an article about consumer credit and information responsibility foresees:

> Artículo 15: El proveedor deberá informar, en todas las ofertas y previamente a la formalización del contrato respectivo:
>
> a) El precio, incluido los impuestos.
> b) Em las ofertas del crédito o de financiación de productos o servicios, el precio de contado efectivo, según corresponda, el monto del crédito otorgado o el total financiado en su caso, y la cantidad de pagos y su periodicidad. Las empresas de intermediación financiera, administradoras de créditos o similares también deberán informar la tasa de interés efectiva anual.
> c) Las formas de actualización de la prestación, los intereses y todo outro adicional por mora, los gastos extras adicionales, si los hubiere, y el lugar de pago.
>
> El precio difundido en los mensajes publicitarios deberá indicarse según lo establecido en el presente artículo. La información consignada se brindará conforme a lo que establezca la reglamentación.

This law was structured in two parts: the first one, dedicated to the regulation of the consuming relationship in its substantial aspects and, the second one, destined to the administrative organization. Of the first 39 articles, 17 refer to information responsibility, and article 21 regulates specifically the obligation of information in financial services.[10]

---

[8] Benjamin (1993), In: http://www.bdjur.stj.gov.br.

[9] Fellous (2003), p. 171.

[10] Castilla (2000), pp. 45–77.

Paraguay, on the other hand, states in article 72 of its Constitution a simple state obligation of taking care of the quality control of food, drugs, chemical, and biological products, without referring specifically to the term consumer. The constitutional reform of 1992 includes consumer protection in article 38, which foresees the individual or collective consumer rights of demanding from public authorities protective actions for their interests, as well as the environment, public health, and living defense, related to life quality and the collective assets.[11]

Law 1334, of 1998, designed disposition similar to the Uruguayan one, establishing the obligation of credit information, as well as anticipated payment:

> Artículo 29: En las operations de crédito para la acquisition de productos o servicios deberá consigners, banjo Pena de unladed, canto segue: a) el precio al contado del been o service en question, b) el monto de los intereses, las tasks annuals o manuals a que stops se calculi as Como la tasa de interés moratoria, c) calqued recharge sober el precio por commission, gastos administrative, tasks, etc, d) el numerous de pagos a effectual, as Como su periodicidad, la sumac total a pager por el product o service, la que no podia superior al precio al contado mass los intereses, y f) los drenches u obligations de las parts en caso de incumplimiento.
>
> Artículo 30: En toda venta o prestación de service a crédito, el consumidor tendrá derecho a pager antecipadamente la totalidad de lo adeudado. En ambos casos, se procederá a la consiguiente reducción proporcional de los intereses.

The Argentinian Constitution entered the international current[12] establishing this new right in article 42, saying:

> Los consumidores y usuarios de bienes y servicios tienen derecho, en la relación de consumo, a la protección de su salud, seguridad e intereses económicos; a una información adequada y veraz, a la libertad de elección y a condiciones de trato equitativo y digno.
>
> Las autoridades proveerán a la protección de esos drenches, a la educación para el consumo, a la defensa de la competencia contra toda forma de distorsión de los mercados, al control de los monopolios naturales y legales, al de la calidad y eficiencia de los servicios públicos, y a la constitución de asociaciones de consumidores y de usuarios.
>
> La legislación establecerá procedimientos eficaces para la prevención y solución de conflictos, y los marcos regulatorios de los servicios públicos de competencia nacional, previendo la necesaria participación de las asociaciones de consumidores y usuarios y de las provincias interesadas, en los organismos de control.

Argentinian Consumer Rights Law n. 24.240, of September 22,1993, does not talk directly about bank services, although the doctrine tends to frame bank operations under this law. In the same sense, jurisprudence provides: "Si been la norma no hace mención expresa a las entidades bancarias (salvo en lo referente a los créditos para consumo, art.36) ha de considerarse que éstas se encuentram abarcadas, ya que se trata de aquellas personas jurídicas a que refierem el art. 2, que en forma profesional prestan servicios a consumidores o usuarios; no tratándose de los servicios excluidos Como los que prestan los profesionales liberales"(CCCom. de Rosario, sala III, "Moriconi, Marcelo y outra c/Banco

[11]Fellous (2003), pp. 169–170.

[12]Sabsay and Onaindia (2000), p. 157.

Argencoop Ltdo.", L. L. del 6-3-99).[13] In 2009, a change in the Law has expressly included bank contracts with consumers.

Article 36 regulates the information obligation in credit operations:

> In credit operations for goods or services acquisition there will be consignation, under risk of annulation: cash payment, balance at terms, total interests to be paid, annual effective rate, amortization form of interests, other existing expenses, payments and their periodicity, extra expenses or existing additional, total financed amount to be paid.

Recently, in 2015 was approved the Civil and Comercial Code of Argentina, which brings express rules on bank contracts with consumers and users (articles 1384 to 1389), reinforcing the duty to inform. Note that the breach of the duty to inform the consumer leads to the nullity of the contract (article 1389). The consumer protection law has been kept in force and must be applied in conjunction with the Civil and Commercial Code. Argentina also passed a special law for credit cards (Ley 25.065 de Tarjetas de Credito).[14] Law 26.684, Ley de concursos y quiebras of 1995, of Argentina was modified in 2008 to create a "small contest" that can be used by consumers, if civil servants.[15] In March 2012, it was introduced in the Senate Chamber Argentina [a] bill pertaining to family insolvency, reinforcing the need for state intervention on the subject to mitigate the difficulties resulting from excessive credit consumption.

In Brazil, the amendment seeks the highest protection level in Mercosul, bringing in its Federal Constitution consumer protection as a fundamental right and as a principle of economic order:

> Article 5, XXXII: The State will promote, under the forms of law, the consumer rights.
>
> Article 170: The economical order, founded in human work valorization and free initiative, has as function to ensure all existence worthy of human dignity, according to the social justice values, observing the following principles: (...)
>
> V) consumer rights.

The Brazilian Consumer Rights Code, Law 8.078, September 11, 1990, was the first consumer's protective legislation in Mercosul, and that accelerated efforts to the harmonization of legislation in other countries in the block. Also, the Brazilian

[13] Lorenzetti and Marques (2005), p. 417.

[14] Mosset and Wajntraub (2008), p. 201.

[15] The original texto of the Bankruptcy Law: "*CAPITULO IV - De los pequeños concursos y quiebra - ARTICULO 288.- Concepto. A los efectos de esta ley se consideran pequeños concursos y quiebras aquellos en los cuales se presente, en forma indistinta, cualquiera de estas circunstancias: 1- que el pasivo denunciado no alcance la suma de CIEN MIL PESOS ($100.000.-) 2- que el proceso no presente más de VEINTE (20) acreedores quirografarios. 3- que el deudor no posea más de VEINTE (20) trabajadores en relación de dependencia. ARTICULO 289.- Régimen aplicable. En los presentes procesos no serán necesarios los dictámenes previstos en el artículo 11, incisos 3 y 5, la constitución de los comités de acreedores y no regirá el régimen de supuestos especiales previstos en el artículo 48 de la presente ley. El controlador del cumplimiento del acuerdo estará a cargo del síndico en caso de no haberse constituido comité de acreedores. Los honorarios por su labor en esta etapa serán del 1% (uno por ciento) de lo pagado a los acreedores.*"

law elaboration coincided with the end of its dictatorship period[16] and external market opening. This legislation included bank, financial, or credit activities in the "consuming services" concept, according to article 3, § 2[17], which initially generated some discussion and strong resistance from the bank sector, which intended to keep out of the protective rules.

In this step, looking forward to preventing the incidence of the Consumer Rights Code in bank contracts, because of the quoted article above, the Financial System National Confederation (CONSIF) adjudicated at the Federal Supreme Tribunal the Unconstitutionality Direct Action (ADIn 2.591). In effect, the Confederation intended to declare unconstitutional formally and materially the mentioned legal provision in order to see purged from the Consumer Rights Code the normative provision that gives to banks and financial and insurance services their evident consuming relationship character. This lawsuit was decided on June 7, 2006, declaring the full constitutionality of the Consumer Rights Code and its application to bank, credit, financial, and insurance services and operations by nine votes favorable and two against.[18,19]

Moreover, the Brazilian statute provided specific rules when it established primordially the responsibility to give information on credit operation conditions

---

[16]First Presidential direct elections occurred in the end of the 80s.

[17]Article 3rd §2nd Brazilian Consumer Rights Code: "Service is any activity offered in consuming market, upon payment, including bank, financial, credit and insurance nature operations, except for the ones resulting of work relationship."

[18]Cláudia Lima Marques embraces the STF decision because it recognizes the values of the Constitution and it is based on the Consumer Defense Code teaching us: "The consumer's right is more than before recognized and granted as a fundamental right in Brazil (art. 5°, XXXII) and connects the State (vertical efficacy in the relations of Public Law, in the consumer relations and the Judge-State, in the relations state as legislator and in the relations of the state as Executive power). The ADIn 2.591 decision also opens a new moment to the Drittwirkung, for the so called horizontal efficacy of the fundamental rights in the banking relations, amongst bank consumers, amongst financial corporations and credit companies and securities companies on Brazil." See more about the effects of the decision of the STF in the article "The Victory of the ADIn 2.591 and the Reflexes on the Bank Consumer Law of the Decision of STF Granting Constitutionality to the Defense Consumer Code" (MARQUES, Cláudia. Aplicação do Código de Defesa do Consumidor aos bancos: ADIn 2.591. São Paulo: Revista dos Tribunais, 2006, pages 363–395).

[19]"Ação Direta De Inconstitucionalidade 2.591-1; Proced. : Distrito Federal; relator originário : min. Carlos velloso; relator para o acórdão :min. Eros grau; reqte. : confederação nacional do sistema financeiro – consif. Advdos. : ives gandra s. Martins e outros. Reqdo. : presidente da república. Reqdo.: Congresso Nacional.

"Art. 3°, §2°, Código De Defesa Do Consumidor – Art.5°, xxxii, Da Cb/88 – Art.170, V, DA CB/88 – Ação Direta Julgada Improcedente.

1. The financial institutions are all of them under the incidence of the rules of the Consumer Defense Code.
2. The Consumer Defense Code reaches under its incidence all the financial institutions. "Consumer", to the effects of the Consumer Defense Code is any person or company that uses as its final destination the banking, financial and insurance activities.
3. The conditions imposed by the article 3°, §2° of the Consumer Defense Code should be interpreted according to the Brazilian Federal Constitution."

and the abrogation of the obligatory pact or the total loss of payments made by the defaulting consumer. So establish the articles 52 and 53 of the Brazilian CDC (Consumer Rights Code):

> I-When providing products or services that involve credit approval or financial concession to the consumer, the provider must, amongst other requirements, inform the consumer previously and properly about:
>
> II-product or service price in national currency;
> III-total interests to be paid and annual effective rate;
> IV-additional provided for in law;
> V-number and frequency of installments;
> VI-total amount to be paid, with and without financing.
>
> In contracts of goods and real estate purchases and sales, under installment payments, as well as in chattel mortgage, consider abrogated the full right of provisions that establish the total loss of paid installments, in creditors advantage that, because of inadimplence, plead the end of the contract and the repossession of the alienated good.

27.2.2 Overindebtedness of Countries in Mercosul

In Brazil, although we do not have official data about the main causes of overindebtedness, unemployment and microcredit stimulation did not leave Brazilians unscathed by this worldwide phenomenon. The arguments are convincing: easy and fast credit approval, without consulting credit protection entities, accessible to those with credit restrictions.

Credit expansion occurs among low-income households with few education, as well as among the retired, who became the new load of bank loans through consigned credit zero risk operation to banks, because it allows the National Social Security Institution (INSS)[20] to deduct the installments direct from the retired person's salary or from his/her pension. Since May 2004, when this modality of credit started to be offered, more than five million retired people appealed to banks to contract loans with monthly deductions from their pensions, reaching an amount of more than 13 billion in April 2006.[21]

Regarding Argentinian reality, overindebtedness is related, among other causes, to monetary depreciation and unemployment. This is also caused by international

[20]The National Social/Previdência Social plan is a social security plan for those who contribute to it. It's a public institution that seeks to recognize and concede rights to its members. The money transferred to the Previdência Social is used to replace the worker's income when he is unable to work due to illness, physical permanent incapacity, high age, death or involuntary unemployment and maternity leave.

[21]News available at Brasil website. Ministério da Previdência Social. The loans giving in consignment achieved R$ 470 million in April 2006. See: http://www.previdencia.gov.br. Searched on 5/26/2006.

phenomena such as information technology development, which reduces human resource needs, and economic globalization, which makes possible massive introduction of products coming from countries where production costs are lower because of weak or inexistent social protection of salaried workers.[22]

Although it is possible to affirm that consumer protection laws are an unequivocal advance in favor of consumer interests, reality demonstrates its inefficiency in holding the rising number of indebted consumers who, due to most various reasons, have no conditions to reimburse the contracted credit. Despite that, none of the Mercosul countries have a specific overindebtedness prevention and treatment regimen for their consumers.

It is true that in Brazil the Civil lawsuit (articles 748 to 786) foresees the civil insolvency hypothesis of the individual and not the businessman debtor when debts exceed the value of the debtor's assets. However, it is not an overindebtedness treatment system, as is configures a procedure of execution by amount against the debtor, not establishing an investigation of personal and social insolvency causes and neither a negotiation scheme that allows the consumer to overcome this situation, as it seems to be the French legislation objective.[23,24,25]

Therefore, whatever is the content of the legislation adopted in Mercosul countries regarding overindebtedness, it must contain prevention rules related to the information responsibility as a way of clarification to the layman about his credit risks and the future compromising of his earnings, ensuring a balance between the parties since the beginning of the contract and assuming the legitimate ignorance of the consumer who contracts with a professional.

Regarding this matter, Professor Cláudia Lima Marques suggests that the structure of the provision contains "specific rules for good faith, information, concern and cooperation responsibilities, in order to avoid overindebtedness in Brazil, a project of law that treats material subjects, imposing a control of publicity and information about consuming credit to lower income households, imposing format rules, making easier the right of regretting in the consumer credit, imposing limits to the personal guarantees, imposing the legal vinculation amongst payment, subcontract and principal consuming contract, as well as regarding processual or administrative subjects, as in the French law."[26]

---

[22]Andorno and Argentin (1997), p. 58.

[23]See Jose Reinaldo de Lima Lopes first reflection about the consuming credit problematic in Brazil, in "Crédito Ao Consumidor e Superendividamento- Uma problemática Geral". Revista de Direito do Consumidor n.17, pp. 57–64.

[24]Regarding this matter, see interesting research done by PEIC (Pesquisa de Endividamento e Inadimplência do Consumidor—Consumer Indebtedness and Inadimplence Research) launched by Fecomércio in February 2004, collected monthly with around 1.000 consumers in São Paulo's metropolitan area, having as goal the diagnosis of the level of earnings compromising, indebtedness and inadimplence of individuals through special checking, credit cards, personal loan or installments in general.

[25]For this matter, see: Kilborn (2006).

[26]Marques (2006), p. 308.

In this regard, the Commission of Jurists appointed by the Senate formulated Senate Bill n. 283/2012, covering measures for the prevention and treatment of overindebtedness of the natural person consumers. The text was inspired by comparative law, notably French law, and consolidated the practice of voluntary renegotiations carried out under the coordination of the judiciary since 2006, through conciliation hearings with the presence of the debtor and its creditors with aim of obtaining payment of debts and preserving the existential minimum.[27]

27.3 Pioneer Project: Brazilian Judiciary's Power

27.3.1 Exposition of Reasons

Since Brazil does not have a special legislation about the treatment of the situations of overindebtedness, the pioneer project, and by the exclusive initiative of the state judges, proposes a proceeding based on the voluntarism of the parts involved. It has as its basis the "Conciliation Project" of the National Council of Justice/Conselho National de Justiça. This project presents identical fundaments with those mentioned by the "Conselho Nacional de Justiça" on its motif exposition:

> The proposal treats about the mechanisms destined to make agreements in cases already taken to the Judiciary or on disputes not yet transformed in law suits.
>
> The strategy aims to diminish substantially the duration of the process and to create solutions for it through simplified proceedings. The goal is to reduce the number of cases that only grow in the judiciary, waiting to be decided. This would be an easy-access mechanism to every citizen confronting the serious problem of disputes and would create a more engaged justice taking its instruments to the communities.
>
> This initiative depends not on the edition of new laws or a constitutional reform, like the notion presented in article 5°, II, of the Brazilian Federal Constitution, and it presents zero cost to the Federation using a material structure that is already existent and/or easy to rearrange, such as conciliators and lay judges aiming to install conciliation centers in their actual jurisdictions and mainly bringing justice to the countryside where there are no offices of the judiciary, establishing in this way true alternatives for the population and the means capable of solving the cases that it has to face.[28]

The pioneer project in the jurisdictional environment has been developed in the jurisdictions of Charqueadas and of Sapucaia do Sul under the responsibility of the judges who are authors of this paper and those who created the project and are not restricted to the consumers that live in those two cities. Today, this project has been developed in five states of Brazil (Rio Grande do Sul, São Paulo, Paraná, Pernambuco, and Sergipe) and the federal district (Brasília).

---

[27] http://brasilcon.org.br/arquivos/arquivos/a1f170d24b1918166696a03adf6aa56e.pdf.

[28] See on website: http://www.conciliar.cnj.gov.br/conciliar/arquivos/ProjetoConciliar.doc.

The justification to the execution of the pioneer project is based on the consumers' and their creditors' independent wish to participate in hearings and renegotiations. We registered also the presence of the duty to renegotiate as one of the authorizing fundaments of the mediation, and it has to be conducted by a judge.

In this sense it can be mentioned the study of the "general duty of renegotiation of the long term contracts" according to the present European doctrine that has been drawing the duties of cooperation, *bona fides*, and the old exception of ruin as teaches Cláudia Lima Marques.[29] This is one of the functions of the *bona fide*, according to the German doctrine would be " to correct and to adapt in case of change of circumstances"[30] and as a result the fundament of the duty of renegotiate facing the negotiation's broken base.

As for the treatment of overindebtedness in countries where there are already existing laws about the topic, the distinct philosophies that give base to it can be divided in two conceptual categories of systems: the "fresh start policy" and the "system of reeducation." The first faces the "overindebtedness as a risk associated to the expansion of the financial market and, for that believes in the socialization of the risk of credit development conceiving a limited responsibility to the consumer." In this system, the debtor's patrimony is sold to pay the debt that it covers and the rest is forgiven. The second is founded "in the idea of the consumer has failed and need to be educated again. This is a conservative social model where the individuals are seen as responsible beings and citizens and less as economical agents." In this way, the overindebted person is forced to pay the debts with his patrimony at the moment and through a payment plan that will take money from the income to be received; this will have to be agreed upon by the creditors.[31]

The proceeding elaborated for the pioneer project took into consideration the European model of reeducation and its emphasis on a pedagogical approach as the form to prevent and to treat overindebtedness. We understand that for the Brazilian case, this is the model to implement the principles of the National Policy for Consumer Relations described in article 4° of the Consumer Defense Code, especially the principle in part IV of the article that refers to the respect to education and information, recognizing that suppliers and consumers should know about their rights and duties to improve the consumer market.

Furthermore, this system requires from the debtors an active learning about the consequences, the costs, and the responsibility of taking too many loans. This will also stimulate the creditors to settle amicably the disputes if the effort of the debtors are valued to fulfill their obligations.[32] This active learning finds its peak at the negotiation hearing, to which all the creditors and the consumers are invited, and

---

[29]Mmarques (2002), p. 245.

[30]Mmarques (2002), p. 186.

[31]Leitao and Maria et alii (2000), pp. 214–217.

[32]Kilborn (2006), p. 66.

which explained about the social phenomenon of overindebtedness and its repercussions. All the presents are instigated to find an alternative for the debtor to honor the obligations within their possibilities.

As for the procedural characteristics, it can be conciliation before a lawsuit exists or within an existing lawsuit.

The type of conciliation done before a lawsuit is filed starts by a standard form containing all the information about the consumer, who should voluntarily fill out the data and submit them to the proper office of the judiciary. In this case, the procedure takes place when the consumer does not have pending lawsuits with creditors; the renegotiation of the debts will occur before a lawsuit is filed, where eventually the creditors may start to see their credit money.

On the other hand, the type of conciliation within an existing lawsuit can only occur in the cases where there is a pending suit between the consumer and the creditors (action to revise, action to collect, action to have the credit paid, and an action called "monitória," among others).

The total of debt can be a result of consignment credit, of consumer credit in general, of contract on services (essential services or not); these could be already due, and there is no limitation to its amount. The excluded debts are alimony debts, fiscal debts, mortgage debts, and those that are originated from civil or criminal compensation—because they are not originated from a consumer relation. In the case of mortgage credits, it is due to its contractual complexity and legislation.

As for the conditions to be accepted, the consumer cannot be a company, he/she has to come with bona fide status, and he/she can have any level of family income. Another important requirement is that the credit taken cannot be for the support of his/her profession for this is part of the requirements of the bankruptcy law.

Also admitted are the consumers identified as "unconscious active overindebted," and the passive type that is being excluded only is the conscious type of consumer.

The doctrine clarifies that the conscious active overindebted type is the person that has acted without any intention to pay, trying to defraud creditors; the unconscious active type is the debtor that has acted under an impulse or did not formulate the correct calculation at the moment the debts were made. This person is also identified as a debtor without malice and capacity to foresee. The last type of passive overindebted consumer is the one that for external reasons and unforeseen situations has suffered a brutal loss of resources due to unemployment, divorce, illness, all called "life accidents."[33]

We would like to acknowledge that the experiences of debt renegotiation in Brazil directed to the treatment of overindebtedness have occurred not judicially as the same line of work had been done at the Public Defender's Office of the state of Rio de Janeiro/Defensoria Pública do Rio de Janeiro[34] and of the Protection Service

[33]Leitao and Maria (2000), p. 237.

[34]Article 1°—The Public Defendor's Office is an essential institution of the State. Its function is to give whole and free legal assistance inside and outside of the courts to the needy as considered according the law. Complementary law # 80, of January 12, 1994.

of Consumers/PROCON[35] of São Paulo. These experiences present a common origin since they were inspired in a field research coordinated by Professor Dr. Cláudia Lima Marques of the Universidade Federal do Rio Grande do Sul, in partnership with the state's Public Defender's Office/Defensoria Pública.

27.3.2 Stricto Sensu *Proceeding*

The proceeding starts by the consumers voluntary wish, who cannot be a minor and has to be capable according to the requirements of article 5°[36] of the Brazilian Civil Code, with or without lawyer's assistance. The proceeding must observe the following requirements:

1. Filling out the standard forms with his/hers information and to whom will be explained about the bona fide status about the veracity of the facts. The form will be available at the court house and will be filling with guidance from a trained worker.
2. After filling out the standard form the consumer will receive the folder containing the "10 commandments to prevent the overindebtedness."

   The making of the folder entitled "Manual of the Overindebtedness Consumer" aimed to reinforce the pedagogical and preventive aspect of the project, especially because similar initiatives oriented toward the prevention (education and guidance) of consumer overindebtedness are new in Brazil, where education for consumers is not even part of the school curricula. Although the education and information to consumers about their rights and duties is one of the principles of the National Policy for Consumer Relations (article 44°, IV, CDC).[37] In a final analysis, the consumer education becomes real the fundament of the democratic state of Law, which has prevision on article 1°, II, of the Brazilian Federal Constitution by taking the citizenship to another level also having the legal support of article 5°, XXXII, and 170, V, of the aforementioned constitution:

---

[35]Created by the Law #9.192 of November 23, 1995 and the Law Decree # 41.170, of September 23 1996 the PROCON foundation is an institution connected to the Citizen Defense and Justice Department of the state of São Paulo, it has juridical personality of public law with technical, administrative and financial autonomy. The PROCON/SP is a pioneer institution to protect consumers in Brazil and is a synonym of protection to consumers' rights. The fruits of this work have been ripen aiming a balance in the consumer relations and a search to always improve it throughout the services rendered by the institution and to improve the life quality of the population as well as for a more conscious citizen.

[36]Article 5°: "The minority ends at the age of 18 years completed when the person is capable of all the acts of a civil life."

[37]The Public Defender's Office of the state of Rio de Janeiro and the PROCON of São Paulo were the first ones to create a Center to Help Consumers with Debt aiming the prevention of overindebtedness and its treatment throughout renegotiation with the creditors.

3. The proceedings are exempt of jurisdictional fees because the condition of 'overindebted' is equivalent to the legal provision of the articles 1°[38] e 2°[39] of the Law # 1.060/50 describing exemption of the fees based on the benefit of Free Legal Assistance.
4. The overindebted at the moment of filling the standard form is already subpoena to come to the renegotiation hearing with a set date.
5. The invitation standard letter will be send—preferably by electronic mail—setting the date to the renegotiation hearing with all the creditors indicated on the standard form.
6. RENEGOCIATION HEARING: it is a conjoint hearing with all the creditors and the consumer in the same opportunity to preserve the fast pace of the project and to guarantee a minimum amount to the living expenses of the overindebted consumer.

   This minimum amount for the living expenses called by the French as "rest a vivre" was a target of concern for the legislator that in 1998 with article 331-2[40] of the *Code de la Consommation*, some changes on the system of treatment of overindebtedness were created because of the belief that in solving the debts, one could not take all the means to maintain the debtor's existence. Moreover, after some experience dealing with the treatment of overindebtedness, we have come to realize that if a person or family cannot have the minimum to cover their living expenses, the possibility to honor their debts is unlikely.

   The demand for the minimum amount to cover the living expenses as a way to guarantee the debtor's resources for his/her maintenance cannot be less than the

[38] Article 1°: " The federal and state public power will guarantee the Free Legal Assistance will be given to the citizens independently of cooperation with the municipalities and the regional chapter of the Bar associations of Brazil (OAB)."

[39] Article 2°: "The benefit expressed by this Law – the right to file a lawsuit in its criminal, civil, military or on the labor areas - will be given to the nationals and foreigners that have residence in the country. The law considers 'needy' under its determinations those with an economical situation that cannot afford to pay for the legal fees and for a lawyer' service – without causing damage to its own maintenance and of his/her family.

[40] Article. L. 331-2: (Law # 95-125 of February 8 1995, article. 29, article 30 Diário Oficial of February 9, 1995, valid as 1 August 1st 1995) (Law # 98-657 of July 29, 1998, article 87 Diário Oficial of July 31,1998). The council has as its mission to treat the following conditions that are inserted in this chapter for the situation of the overindebtedness of consumers when they cannot fulfill their obligations with their creditors before the due date.

The amount or reimbursements that result from the application of the articles L.331-6 or L.331-7 is fixed according to the article L.145-2 of the Labor Code which determines to keep the portion of the income that cannot be taken away from the debtor. This is done to assure that the family will be safe with the minimum necessary resources to their existence. This is an amount of resources cannot be inferior to the 'minimum amount of insertion' (*revenu minimum d'insertion*) for the family, which is indicated on the plan structure according to article L. 331-6 or on the recommendations of articles L. 331-7 e L. 331-7-1.

minimum amount respected by law in accordance with article L.145- 2 of the Labor Code or less than the minimum amount of insertion (RMI).[41]

The project did not adopt a specific formula to calculate the minimum amount because it is a complex task and cannot be reduced to any easy mathematical formula—like some used on juridical decisions that consider that overindebtedness cannot go beyond one-third of the consumer's income.[42] We consider that it would only be reasonable for the consumer to honor the agreement when a sufficient amount is preserved to pay for home expenses such as water and electricity bills, food, education, health, rent expenses, house-related expenses, among other things necessary for the well-being of the family cell.[43]

As for the content, the renegotiation can consist of installments of the debt, of concession on extension with alteration on due dates for payment, of reduction of fees or even partial or total forgiveness of the debt.

The conciliation during the hearing can have the characteristic of a mediation or occur during an existing lawsuit:

7. SUCCESSFUL AGREEMENT AND CONCILIATING PROCEDURES: the judge coordinator of the project will sign the agreement conciliation terms giving it legal enforcement.

---

[41]The French juridical Law system has treated about the minimum amount in their Labor Code on article L145-2: *(Law # 73-4 January 2, 1973 Diário Oficial of January 3 1973), (Law # 91-650 of July 9 1991 article 48, article 49 Diário Oficial of July 14,1991 started on August 1°, 1992), (Law # 98-657 of July 29 1998 article 88 Diário Oficial of July 31, 1998), (law # 2002-73 of January 17, 2002 article 71 Diário Oficial of January18, 2002).* The amounts that can be taken from the person's income have to respect the limits of the living expenses according to the decree of the state Council. This decree will establish the conditions on which the parameters and the extenuate circumstances will be revised taking in consideration the evolution of the economical circumstances. To determine the amount that cannot be taken will be considered the accessories and even profits in *in natura,* after taxes. It will also be considered as an amount that cannot be taken if the consumer's income only have the amount of minimum insertion. Are exempted the amounts presented by the worker and the gifts received toward the family.

[42]Alain Gouriou finds surprising that the Appeals' Court qualifies the use of the 'good sense rule' based on that the 'good sense' leads to think that the important is not so much the percentage of the debt but the amount of income after the deduction of the installment to be paid. A debt fee of 50% will not have the same importance for a home that earns 12,000 F monthly and for another one earning 50,000 F. According to the author the statistical methods of analysis and selection of risks demonstrates this criterion having a lower detection risk power. As a result the lower risk of incident of payment do not correspond necessarily to the lowest rate of debt, in the same way the higher debt rates are not synonym of strong probability of insolvency when the other criteria are met. (GOURIOU, La responsabilité..., page 56).

[43]In the Swiss Law has an interesting point. It presents an indication of a basic regimen to verify the capacity of reimbursement that is articulated around three principles: (a) the amount received must allowed the consumer to get reimbursement for the credit ; (b) this reimbursement value has to leave a minimum vital amount to the consumer expenses; (c) aiming to reduce the risk of overindebtedness on a long run the capacity verification of the reimbursement should have been made under a fictitious base of installments of 36 months. The criteria were described by Stauder, Le prêt responsable..., page 1029–1047.

The minutes of the renegotiation hearing are written in the document, identifying each creditor, the amount of debt, the method of payment, and penalty fees in case of nonfulfillment of the obligation. If there is a pending lawsuit, the minutes should express the suspension or extinction of the lawsuit.

Related issues are about the competence to take the agreement document with legal enforcement to the court in case the parts do not obey the agreement. It is also determined in the document the place to start the lawsuit, which is the local residence of the consumer—according to the rules of public order and social interest in consumer relations specified in articles 1°[44] and 101, part I,[45] both of the Consumer Defense Code.

Moreover, also registered in the minutes are some specific effects that were inspired by the French legislation reinforcing the responsibility of the overindebted in following the terms of the agreement—receiving a warning about the solemn characteristics of it.

The effects are as follows:

The debts will be due before the deadline if:

(a) Intentionally you give false information or produce forged documents with the goal of making use of the benefits of the proceedings for overindebtedness;
(b) By hiding or feign the totality or even part of your assets aiming to fraud creditors or the collection process;
(c) You take other loans without the creditors' agreement and your debt situation is aggravated or if you practice acts of disposition with your patrimony while treating the overindebtedness situation.

8. UNSUCCESSFULL AGREEMENT WITHOUT A PENDING LAWSUIT: the overindebted is oriented to seek for his/her rights on the Judiciary at the Court House or even at the Civil Special Jurisdiction (Small Claims Court).[46]
9. UNSUCCESSFULL AGREEMENT WITHIN THE PENDING LAWSUIT: the pending lawsuit will be taken to its original jurisdiction to follow its regular proceedings.

---

[44]Article 1°: "The present article establishes rules of public and social interest on the terms of the article 5°, XXXII, article 170, V, of the Brazilian Federal Constitution and article 48 and its transitory dispositions".

[45]Article 101, I: "In the action of civil responsibility of the supplier of products and services without damaging the exposed on Chapters I e II of this title will be observed the following rules: I – the lawsuit can be proposed on the local court house of the consumer's residence".

[46]Law # 9.099/95, article 3: "The Small Claims Court/Juizado Especial Cível has jurisdiction for the conciliation, its processing and judgment over the civil cases of less complexity such as: I. suits where the amount of the case do not exceed 40 (forty) times the minimum wage; II. Those cases described in the article 275, II, of the Brazilian Civil Procedure Code/Código de Processo Civil; III. Eviction's action for owners' personal use; IV. Ownership actions over property which value do not exceed the amount limited on item I of this article."

27.4 Conclusion

Respecting political, economic, and cultural peculiarities; improving consumer rights; and regarding overindebtedness mean, first of all, marching forward to fighting social exclusion, present in developing countries, members of Mercosul. This goal was significantly consecrated by the Reform of 1998 in the French overindebtedness disciplinarian legislation, seen in article 1 of the Law of July 29, 1998: "La présente loi tend à garantir sur l'ensemble du territoire l'accès effectif de tous aux droits fondamentaux dans les domaines de l'emploi, du logement, de la proteccion de la santé, de la justice, de l'éducation, de la formation et de la culture, de la protection de la famille et de l 'enfance."

Furthermore, the overindebtedness study in the current credit approval conditions is reflected in the family microeconomy and social macroeconomy, reaffirming Bruno Oppetit[47] when he said that economy and law, turning to the juridical tutelage of social phenomena, walk together.

This social-economical dimension of the overindebtedness notices that the market maintenance through the ever-increasing production of goods, services, and information, will depend on the financial "health" of this consumer and his reinsertion in the production cycle, which is only possible through specific juridical tutelage destined to prevent and solve indebtedness situations.

In this analysis, we must take into consideration that the adoption of a prevention and treatment of the overindebtedness system will reflect in the internal economy of the countries as it makes possible the reinsertion of the consumers in the economical track, with consequent reflex in the external relations among the countries in the block.

10 COMMANDMENTS TO PREVENT OVERINDEBTEDNESS:

1) DO NOT SPEND more than you earn.
2) BE CAREFULL with easy access credit.
3) Do not make debt without REFLECTING upon it and SPEAKING to your family.
4) READ the contract and the prospectus.
5) DEMAND information about monthly and annual interest rates.
6) DEMAND the previous total amount of the debt and EVALUATE if it is compatible with your income.
7) COMPARE the competition interest rates.
8) DO NOT transfer over to you third party's debts.
9) DO NOT MAKE debts and GIVE OUT your information through the telephone or through the Internet.
10) SET ASIDE part of your income for your personal expenses.

---

[47] Oppetit (1998), p. 169.

TEST:
AM I UNDER OVERINDEBTEDNESS?
( ) Do my debts correspond to 50% or more of my income?
( ) Do I need extra work to pay my debts at the end of each month?
( ) Is the money from my salary all used up before the end of the month?
( ) Are my debts causing family problems?
( ) Can I pay on time the electric bill, the water bill, food, rent and/or home-expenses-related bills?
( ) Am I suffering from depression due to worries about my debts?
( ) Is my name under cadasters such as SPC, CERASA, CCF?
( ) Have I been always paying my debts after the due date?
( ) Have I already borrowed money from a family member or from a friend to pay my obligations?
( ) Is my family not aware of my difficulties?

WHAT CAN I DO?
If you are a person (this situation does not apply to a business or company) and the situations shown in this test do apply to you, look for the "Pilot Project" of the judiciary. This project has its focus on treating "consumer overindebtedness" situations in the jurisdictions of Charqueadas e Sapucaia do Sul (South of Brazil). This project aims to mediate the renegotiations of the debts with all the creditors, in an amicable way, according to the family budget, preserving the minimum amount for the family's basic needs. If there is no "pioneer project" in your town's courthouse, look for the Public Defenders or an attorney or the PROCON (Service to Protect the Consumer).

References

Andorno LO, Argentin R (1997) L'Endettement. L.G.D.J., Paris

Benjamin AHdeV (1993) A proteção do consumidor nos países menos desenvolvidos: a experiência da América Latina. http://www.bdjur.stj.gov.br

Castilla GO (2000) Deber de información en la Ley 17.189, de 20 de setiembre de 1999. Revista de Direito do Consumidor, São Paulo, 34:45–77

Fellous BE (2003) Proteção do consumidor no Mercosul e na União Européia.: Revista dos Tribunais, São Paulo

Kilborn JJ (2006) Comportamentos econômicos, superendividamento; estudo comparativo da insolvência do consumidor: buscando as causas e avaliando soluções. Direitos do consumidor endividado. Revista dos Tribunais, São Paulo

Lorenzetti RL, Marques CL (2005) Contratos de servicios a los consumidores. Rubinzal-Culzoni, Buenos Aires

Leitao M, Maria M et alii (2000) O endividamento dos consumidores. Almedina, Coimbra, pp 214–217

Marques CL (2006) Sugestões para uma lei sobre o tratamento do superendividamento de pessoas físicas em contratos de crédito ao consumo: proposições com base em pesquisa empírica de 100 casos no Rio Grande do Sul. Direitos do consumidor endividado. Revista dos Tribunais, São Paulo, pp 255–309
Mmarques CL (2002) Contratos no Código de Defesa do Consumidor, 4th edn. Revista dos Tribunais, São Paulo
Mosset IJ, Wajntraub JH (2008) Ley de defensa del consumidor, Santa Fé, p. 201
Oppetit B (1998) Droit et Modernité. Presses Universitaires de France, Paris
Sabsay DA, Onaindia JM (2000) La Constitución de los Argentinos. Errepar, Buenos Aires
Souza MA (1996) A política legislativa do consumidor no Direito comparado. Nova Alvorada Edições Limitada, Belo Horizonte

Chapter 28
"Withholding Credit" and Elderly Overindebtedness

Johannes Doll and Rosangela L. Cavallazzi

28.1 Introduction

Elderly people often have difficulty getting a credit from a bank. However, in Brazil, they not only have ease of getting credit, but also banks try to lure them with very aggressive marketing. How does that happen?

The specific reason for the interest of banks in the elderly began with Law 10.820/2003, which allowed retirees to consign up to 30% (actually 35%) of their retirement for the payment of credit.[1] The law provides for an irrevocable and irretrievable authorization and even collects dismissal fees.[2] To understand this law and other

We thank Prof. Saulo Neves de Oliveira for the competent translation from the Portuguese original to the English text.

[1]The current text of Law 10,820 is as follows: "Article 1. Employees governed by the Consolidation of Labor Laws, approved by Decree-Law No. 5,452, dated May 1, 1943, may authorize, irrevocably and irreversibly, the payroll discount or their available remuneration Of the amounts related to the payment of loans, financing, credit cards and leasing operations granted by financial institutions and leasing companies, when foreseen in the respective contracts."

[2]See the text of Art. 1 of the Law 10.820, in the redaction of the Law 13.172, 2015: ". § 1° The discount mentioned in this article may also relate to severance pay owed by the employer, if provided for in the respective loan agreement, financing, credit card or lease, up to a limit of 35% (thirty five percent), 5% (Five percent) exclusively for: I—the amortization of expenses incurred by means of a credit card; Or II—the use for the purpose of withdrawal by means of the credit card.

J. Doll (✉)
Faculty of Education, Federal University of Rio Grande do Sul, Porto Alegre, Brazil
e-mail: johannes.ufrgs@gmail.com

R.L. Cavallazzi
PROURB, Federal University of Rio de Janeiro, Rio de Janeiro, Brazil

Law Department, Pontifical Catholic University of Rio de Janeiro (PUCRJ), Rio de Janeiro, Brazil
e-mail: rosangela.cavallazzi@gmail.com

C. Lima Marques, D. Wei (eds.), *Consumer Law and Socioeconomic Development*,
DOI 10.1007/978-3-319-55624-6_28

rules[3] that followed—with further increase in vulnerable situations—it is necessary to understand the profound changes that occurred in Brazil in recent decades.

Pragmatically, easier access to credit for seniors has been quite ambiguous. What may seem positive and therefore guarantee rights has often complicated consequences. Thus, a series of questions arises: how do older people deal with this easy access to credit? What do the elderly use this money for? Do they have knowledge of the consequences of this assignment of their retirements? How do elderly (mainly) live in the contemporary world consumption with its aggressive and intrusive marketing practices? Are these credits, in fact, positive for the elderly? What are the risks that these credits can bring? Is this not, in essence, an economic exploitation of a highly vulnerable group of our society that calls for better legal protection?

This article aims to answer some of these questions. In a first step, it will be presented the development in Brazil in recent decades, which is focused on political, economic, and demographic issues. The second part is dedicated to presenting the specific situation of elderly people in our consumer world. The third part will address the "withholding credit" with its introduction and development. Although this type of credit has been implemented in the Brazilian market only in 2004, its standards have suffered profound changes during these last 12 years, an indication of the complexity of this type of credit. In this part, there will be a more detailed analysis of the legal foundations and how the Brazilian courts are dealing with the withholding credit. The last part will present data from a research of UFRGS-PROCON-SP on the profile of people who get the consigned credit and the reasons and the consequences of applying for this credit.[4]

Finally, conclusions point to challenges both in law as well as in education fields. For the authors, it seems necessary for a better kind of regulation and specific educational effort to fulfill the objective of the withholding credit, a secure and smooth way to a fair credit for a socially vulnerable group.

28.2 Last Decade Changes in Brazil

The Brazilian society has profoundly changed in recent decades. We highlight below some political, economic, and demographic elements to understand the situation of the elderly people in relation to the pitfalls of a consumerist society.

---

§ 2°. The regulation shall provide for the limits of the value of the loan, of the provision consignable for the purposes of the caput and of the commitment of the rescission funds for the purposes of paragraph 1 of this article."

[3]Law 10.820/2003, changed by the Law 13.172, from the 21st of October of 2015, conversation of the MP 681, from the 10th of July of 2015. In 2004, the Law 10.953 included the text of the Law 10.820 which established a limit of 30% for discounts and withholdings on payroll of amounts related to the payment of loans, financing and leasing operations. In 2015, the limit was amplified to 35% to allow the amortization of expenses incurred by credit card and drawings by such means (Law 13.172, of the 21th of October of 2015).

[4]The research data were first published in Doll (2009), p. 287ss.

Since 1889, when Emperor Dom Pedro II was removed by a military coup, Brazil has been a republican state. However, the existing oligarchic structures[5] up to this time have changed very little, being a republic, and also remained mainly during the different forms of government, being democratic or a dictatorship. In the Cold War tensions of the 1960s, a military coup took in 1964 President-elect João Goulart's power; his policy was branded by the military as "socialist" and turned Brazil into a military dictatorship. The strongly nationalist policy of the military to attempt progress through prestigious projects did not modify the unjust structure of society. During the 1980s[6] it became evident that the project of the military dictatorship could not solve the problems of the Brazilian society. The economic problems had gotten worse, and the political credibility of the military was lost. Strikes and protest movements definitively led to a process of redemocratization, which took place in stages. Important brands in this way were the new Federal Constitution of 1988 and the first free election of the republic president in 1989.

Even more than the political structure of the society, the Brazilian economy has changed a lot. In the early twentieth century, Brazil was almost exclusively an exporter of agricultural products and raw materials, with its economy based mainly on coffee, sugar, and rubber. Around the mid-twentieth century, many governments, especially of Getúlio Vargas and Juscelino Kubitschek, encouraged industrialization and modernization of the Brazilian economy, which led to the founding of large public companies and the concentration of economic development in the major regions of São Paulo and Rio de Janeiro. To protect domestic production, there were created high import taxes. This protected development led at the same time to a certain technological imbalance between Brazilian production compared to world production. During the 1970s, an "economic miracle" took place in Brazil, with growth rates around 10%, development supported by strong government investment, and favorable global economic conditions. But in the second half of the 1970s, this development declined, and the 1980s were marked by great economic problems to the point that these years were named as the "lost decade."

At this time, external debt increased greatly, mainly because of the economic policy of funding development through foreign credits, of the oil crisis, and of inflation in the United States, which led to a decrease in credit supply in the global market. Different economic plans (Cruzado I, Cruzado II, Collor Plan) tried to deal with the economic crisis and especially with the high inflation that reached more than 2000 (two thousand)% per year. Only in the mid-1990s, the "Real Plan" achieved the break of the vicious circle of inflation.[7] In addition to the gradual transition to the new currency "Real," several other economic measures were taken, such as flexibility to dollar exchange, high-interest policy, and strong liberalization

[5]See: Raymundo (1958). Raymundo (1974).

[6]See: Movimento *Diretas Já* started in the decade of 1980. http://www12.senado.gov.br/jornal/edicoes/2014/02/25/senadores-ressaltam-a-paz-do-movimento-diretas-ja. Accessed in 31/01/2016.

[7]See: Brum (1998).

of imports.[8] Over time, these changes have led to a stabilization of the economy and presented solid growth rates in the following decades.[9] A radical decrease of the foreign debt and a growing internal market has led to the strengthening of the Brazilian industry and entry of international investments since 2004. The growth of the economy, accompanied by a decrease in unemployment, together with social programs, such as the "Bolsa Família Programme," led to the formation of a new middle class, for some authors,[10] or a new working class, to others,[11] and a certain reduction of social injustice. However, dependence on the world market, both in relation to financial matters and in relation to production, remains high, exposing the Brazilian economy to changes and global crises.[12]

An important aspect to be considered is the very particular way the banking policies related to credit work in Brazil. For a long time, it has been extremely difficult to get a credit. High interest rates, designed to stop inflation, as well as very high demands on collateral by banks made it difficult to work with credits, both in the individual level and in the business environment. This changed profoundly. Credit interest rates remain very high, but in a context of economic stabilization in Brazil, these interest rates attracted foreign investment, also considering the global economic situation.[13] With the abundant presence of money in the financial market, lending money became interesting to banks and the extremely restrictive policy of granting credits gave way for a credit spraying strategy. This policy change of the banks, granting credits came, in general, without proper information and care that characterize the "responsible credit,"[14] committing the supplier to the overindebtedness prevention process and offering a conscious consumer choice.[15] On one hand, this change increased purchasing power, strengthened the internal market, and contributed thus to the development of the Brazilian economy. On the other hand, it increased the risk of indebtedness and overindebtedness. Data from the National Financial System[16] clearly demonstrate this process. While in January 2004 the credit volume was R$ 417.8 billion, this almost quadrupled in 6 years to R $ 1.71 trillion in January 2011. This means the bank credit/GDP ratio went from 24.3 to 46.5% in this period.

---

[8]On the occasion of the 20th anniversary of the currency "Real" there were a number of reports and analyzes of its success. See, e.g., Bourroul and Ferreira (2016).

[9]While economic growth in the 1980s was less than one percent per year, after the 1994 reform were registered solid growth rats: 1995–1998: 2.5%; 1999–2002: 2.1%; 2003–2006: 3.5%; 2007–2009: 3.6% (Fonte: IPEA, 2010, S. 60).

[10]See: Pochmann (2014). Neri (2011).

[11]See: Souza (2012).

[12]See: Doll et al. (2015), p. 9ss.

[13]See: Barbosa and Meurer (2016).

[14]The principle of responsible lending was developed in the doctoral thesis of Lima (2014). See also: Cavallazzi et al. (2010), p. 74ss.

[15]See: de Lima (2014).

[16]See: Flores (2016).

Table 28.1 Child mortality, fertility rate, and life expectation

	Child mortality	Fertility rate	Life expectation
1960	121 ‰	6.21	51.6
1980	69 ‰	4.06	61.8
2000	30 ‰	2.39	70.4
2010	22 ‰	1.86	73.4

Source: IBGE (Brazilian Institute of Geography and Statistics), 2012

It is also necessary to highlight the demographic changes of the Brazilian society. Brazil was long known as a young country, which was true, at least until 1960. The high fertility rate (6.2 children per woman of reproductive age), low life expectancy of 51.6 years, the high percentage of children (0–14 years, 43% of the population), and the relatively small number of elderly people (over 60 years, 4.7% of the population) have led to the classical population pyramid. However, the change of a young country to an aging country happened relatively fast in the case of Brazil, mainly caused by the sharp drop in the fertility rate (1960: 6.2 children, 2010: 1.86 children per woman of reproductive age) and a strong decrease in child mortality (1960: 121‰, 2010: 22‰). This, accompanied with progress in the area of health and hygiene, led to a rapid increase in life expectancy (2010: 73.4 years) and an increase in the elderly population (2010: over 60 years, 10.8% of population). While the Brazilian population in the last 50 years almost tripled (1960: 70 million, 2010: 190.7 million), there are actually six times more elder people in 1960 (1960: 3.3 million; 2010: 20.5 million). Note the following table, (See Table 28.1).

This evolution obviously represents a challenge for Brazilian policy in dealing with this rapid process of population aging.[17]

28.3 The Financial and Legal Situation of Elderly People in Brazil

In the 1960s, there were in Brazil very few people, especially physicians and social workers, who were concerned with the coming demographic changes.[18] In general, these issues were not perceived by the wider population. Also were not noted the first initiatives of the Ministry of Social welfare on an elderly people policy.[19] Similarly, the first practical work with groups for the retired and elderly by experts and social workers happened without public attention. Hence, the general population was taken by surprise when in 1992, suddenly, the elderly people took to the streets their fight for an appropriate adjustment of pensions, a fight that became

[17]See: de Freitas Elizabeth et al. (2011).

[18]See: Lopes (2000).

[19]See: Rodrigues (2001) pp. 149–158.

known as the struggle for adjustment of 147% of retirees and pensioners,[20] which by the way was victorious. In the 1990s, the issue of population aging gained more political attention, which can be observed with the approval of a specific law for the elderly, Law 8.842/94 of "The National Policy for the Elderly." The purpose of this law is to guarantee the social rights of the elderly, as well as their autonomy, integration, and effective participation in society.[21] Despite the importance of this law and the increasing number of elderly people, it became known only in the groups of experts and professionals. In the media (newspapers, television), it did not receive more attention. It took nearly a decade for the subject of aging to gain public attention. In fact, in 2003, Law 10.741/2003, "Statute of the Elderly" was published and received much attention from the media, and since then, almost every day there are news and articles about the elderly, senior meetings, the process of aging, and what to do to age well. The "Statute of the Elderly" follows, in general, the National Policy for the Elderly Law (Law 8.842/94) and adds a more protective sense, banning a number of discriminatory actions in relation to the elderly and establishing punishments. In addition to these two main laws regarding the elderly, there are a number of specific laws, particularly on health, at federal, state, and municipal levels. For the topic of this article, it matters more the aspects of consumer protection, which in fact, does not appear in these laws. On the other hand, the 1990 Consumer Defense Code (CDC) mentions the elderly in its Article 39, IV, and prohibits expressly the use of their limitations and vulnerability.[22]

Regarding the vulnerability presumed in the case of consumers (Article 4, I CDC), it now affects not only the consumers and their families but also the space of legal relations in the consumer society,[23] as the place of increasing weakness.[24] This is because of the hegemony of overindebted people who felt in that situation mostly by unexpected life events such as unemployment, illness, divorce, death in the family, etc., as has been demonstrated in numerous empirical studies, by reason of which we highlight the research of 2005 coordinated by Claudia Lima Marques.[25] The exacerbation of the vulnerability is in full harmony with contemporary society, high fragility conditions, and economic and social adversity. In this perspective, the vulnerability is explained by two conditions or relevant aspects: fragility and consumer subordination in relation to the credit provider.[26]

---

[20]See: Simões (1998).

[21]See: Rodrigues (2001), pp. 149–158.

[22]See: Marques et al. (2013).

[23]See: Silva and Cavalazzi (2013), pp. 13–45.

[24]"The situation of vulnerability in the process of granting credit to young people and the elderly becomes more serious. The fragility inherent in the relationship, due to age, comprehension capacity and health conditions, creates exceptional conditions so that the various types of vulnerability simultaneously permeate the whole process, as a rule without full compliance with the duty to inform (An obligation attached to the Principle of Good Faith Objective), preventing the possibility of reflection on the need for credit and the ability to assume the payment conditions, resulting in hypervulnerability." Cavallazzi et al. (2010), pp. 74–111.

[25]See: Marques and Cavalazzi (2006), pp. I–VI.

[26]See: Cavallazzi et al. (2010), pp. 74–111.

The contracts of the withholding credit, as well as other loan agreements, are adhesion contracts and standardized contracts. In other words, it was only in the past that contracts of this kind were negotiated on two parts, discussing the content and the conditions seeking the reciprocity of the obligations. Henri Acselrad, when analyzing processes and relationships in the field of environmental vulnerability, explains that "even when we consider that the vulnerability is socially produced and that political and institutional practices contribute to turn vulnerable certain social groups, the locus of observation tends to be the individual and not the process." In this perspective, the author concludes that, in line with the consumers' right:

> If the vulnerability is due to a historical relationship established between different social groups, to eliminate the vulnerability will require that the causes of deprivations suffered by the people or social groups are outdated and there is a change in the relationships that they have with the wider social space in which they live.

Precisely because of the numerous restrictions and consequent vulnerabilities of the consumer in relation to the provider, the counterpoint to the standardized adhesion contracts is the microsystems, for example, the "Statute of the Elderly" and the Consumer Defense Code, establishing new paradigms (the principle of the objective good faith), recognizing legal pluralism, and thus giving visibility to the relationship between unequals, in conditions of vulnerability and economic lack of sufficiency.

On the issue of this essay about consigned credit and overindebtedness of the elderly, the best lesson is from Claudia Lima Marques, who claims that the elderly consumer is a consumer "disputed" with his "enhanced vulnerability," whose special vulnerability "is on his 'age' and 'social condition', as outlined in the CDC, which makes some services (health services) or products (medicines) essential to the maintenance of life."[27]

Therefore, it is necessary to explain the financial situation of the elderly in Brazil. For a long time, the image of old age in Brazil was related to poverty, financial losses because of a decrease in retirement or pension benefits, and high costs of medicines.[28] This, combined with a general rejection of old age and aging,[29] is also the reason that advertising and marketing ignored this age group for a long time. In fact, the situation of the elderly in Brazil is very heterogeneous, and it does not differ from the general population. Since 1990, we can notice some improvements for the elderly, particularly by the expansion of social services, by some changes in retirement roles, and by a real increase in the minimum wage. In 1983, it was still almost a fifth of the elderly (19.1%) who did not receive any income, and in 2003 it was only 12%.[30] The data of 2007 show that the population

[27]See: Marques Claudia Lima.

[28]See: Grin (1999), p. 72 e seg.

[29]See: de Beauvoir (1990).

[30]See: Camarano (2006).

living below the poverty line covers much less elderly (7.7%) than this group represents in the general population (12.5%).[31]

In Brazil, there is a social assistance program for elderly people without own resources, the "assistance benefit for the elderly and the disabled person." Until 1993, this benefit was a quarter of a minimum wage for people over 70 and disabled person without own resources. From this date, the benefit has been increased to a minimum wage. The Statute of the Elderly from 2003 reduced the minimum age for this benefit from 70 to 65 years. This program has been very important, especially for the elderly, who have greater financial difficulties. In 2007, there were 2.68 million beneficiaries, the vast majority being the older people.[32]

Retirement is the main way to guarantee an income for the elderly people, but not everyone is included in the retirement system. Mainly, the rural population historically had difficulty accessing this benefit. Therefore, the expansion of the benefit to this group by the Constitution of 1988, supplemented by Laws 8.212 (Costing Plan) and 8.213 (Benefit Plans) in 1991, represents an important contribution to the economic basis of a considerable group of elderly people. Retiring requires a determined age (men 60, women 55) and proof of having worked in agriculture: "producer situation, partner, sharecropper and tenant farmers, prospectors and fishermen, as well as their spouses" (Article 195, § 8, of the Federal Constitution of 1988). Unlike other retirements, it is a noncontributory form, so it is guaranteed without the need of having contributed to the social welfare system. Zimmermann demonstrates how this retirement has gained importance since its implementation in 1991, almost doubling the number of beneficiaries within 4 years (1991: 4,080,400 benefits; 2003: 7,029,020).[33] Another important aspect is that the benefit is also given to spouses, even if the husband has also received retirement. Thus, this significantly strengthens the position of women in rural areas, for they do not depend on her husband's retirement because they have their own.[34] The rural retirement becomes also an important economic factor for rural families and communities in general. As Tavares revealed, 80% of elderly retirees in a rural community in Viçosa (MG) were responsible for half of the income of their families.[35]

Retirement is the main source of income for elderly people, but it is not the only one. Especially, men are still often working even if already retired, either in the same profession or in another, often migrating to the informal work.[36] Data from

[31]See: IBGE (2008).

[32]See: Guimarães (2008).

[33]Data from Dataprev, *apud* Zimmermann, Clóvis. A previdência rural brasileira no contexto das políticas públicas. Revista Espaço Acadêmico, n° 48, 2005. Acessível em: http://www.espacoacademico.com.br/048/48czimmermann.htm. Acesso em 31/01/2016.

[34]See: Kreter and Bacha (2006), pp. 467–502.

[35]See: Oliveira Tavares et al. (2011), pp. 94–108.

[36]See: Doll (2002), p. 8: "In 1991, casual work represented 41.3% of the total labor force, but rose to 51.3% in 2000. This high number of informal work is a problem, especially for Social Insurance benefits, because these workers do not pay contributions. Beside the high risks for such workers there is only a relatively small part of the population who support the Social Insurance System (only 43.5% of all formal and informal workers; IBGE/PNAD 1999)."

2006 reveal that 32% of men over 60 continue with a paid activity. An analysis of the sources of the income of elderly people shows that around half comes from retirement (49%), followed by the new work (39%) and other sources (13%).[37]

For an analysis of the financial situation of the elderly, it is important to consider the real minimum wage increase in the recent years. As its adjustment, in general terms, above the inflation rate, there was an increase of purchasing power of approximately 90% in the last 12 years. This has been an advantageous situation for the elderly people who receive a retirement, pension, or welfare benefit of one minimum wage—because the value cannot be less than a minimum wage, as determined by the Constitution. So while the value of the higher pensions tends to reduce its real value over time by smaller adjustment than inflation, a government policy to deal with the alleged deficit of social welfare, retirement of one minimum wage increases its purchase power.

Briefly it can be said that the financial situation of the elderly population in Brazil is, compared with the population in other age groups, not so bad.[38] A lot of the elderly could, during their life, buy a small house or an apartment. And even with the retirement reform in 1999, which introduced a ceiling for retiring and difficult early retirement, it represents a small but reliable source of income. Thus, retirement becomes an important economic factor, not only for the elderly but also for families who live with the elderly.[39] This safe and reliable income becomes especially important in the current economy, marked by insecurity, unemployment, informal work, and difficulties of the new generations entering the labor market.[40] The 2000 census indicated that 62.4% of the elderly are primarily responsible for the family income and in 20% of all Brazilian families, the elderly are family heads, thus a much higher percentage than what the elderly represent in the general population. A number of studies have demonstrated that this coexistence and financial transfers between generations usually happen in agreement and are generally advantageous for both older and younger people, linking to a better state of health of the older people and general advantages for the younger ones.[41]

28.4 Withholding Credit: Development and the "Credit Hangover"

The rapid growth of elderly people in Brazil in recent decades associated with the availability of regular and stable incomes became interesting to economics. In December 2015, the Ministry of Social Welfare paid more than 27 billion reais

[37] See: Neri (2007).

[38] See: Camarano and Kanso (2011).

[39] See: Camarano (2006).

[40] See: Beck (1999).

[41] See: Camarano et al. (2004).

(R$ 27,128,497,403) to more than 26 million (26,133,763) of retirees and pensioners (data: Statistical Bulletin of the Ministry of Social Welfare, 12/2015), a fact that results in an average of a little more than R$ 1000 (one thousand) for retirement or pension (Statistical Bulletin of Social Welfare, 2015).

In this context of the discovery of elderly people as consumers and the interest of banks to spray the credit system appears the consigned or withholding credit, in line with public policy, despite the validity of the Consumer Defense Code microsystem. The consigned or withholding credit was opened with a series of normative instructions, which started in December 2003 with Law 10.820[42] and was preceded on December 26, 2001, by the Direct Unconstitutionality Action (ADIn) proposed by banks, which aim to exclude bank-nature activities, finance, credit, and insurance from the application of the Consumer Protection Code (CDC).

The legal situation of the elderly in Brazil met its watershed moment in 2006 with the vote of Minister Eros Grau[43] in the Direct Unconstitutionality Act 2591-1 proposed in 2003, in terms of consumer protection with the recognition of the consumer relationship. It was the first step toward the implementation of the microsystem of the Consumer Defense Code on financial institutions:

> Also there is no doubt regarding the characterization of the financial institution client as a consumer for the purposes of Article 170 of the Constitution of Brazil. The relationship between bank and client is clearly a consumer relationship.[44]

Therefore, understanding the financial and legal situation of the elderly in Brazil demands to relate the size of this category of consumers to the market of banks and financial institutions with the possibilities and obstacles of legal protection.

---

[42] As previously registered, the Law 10.820/2003 was amended by Law 13,172, of October 21, 2015, in turn conversion of MP 681, of July 10, 2015.

[43] After recognition of a Motion for Clarification by the Attorney General, the Brazilian Institute of Consumer Policy and Law—BRASILCON and the Brazilian Institute of Consumer Defense—IDEC (as amici curiae), the menu of judgment of direct action of unconstitutionality n. 2591 is replaced by the following: Art. 3°, § 2°, DO CDC. Código De Defesa Do Consumidor. Art. 5 o, XXXII, DA CB/88. Art. *170, V, DA CB/88. Instituições financeiras. Sujeição delas ao código de defesa do consumidor. Ação direta de inconstitucionalidade julgada improcedente.*

1. As instituições financeiras estão, todas elas, alcançadas pela incidência das normas veiculadas pelo Código de Defesa do Consumidor.

2. "Consumidor", para os efeitos do Código de Defesa do Consumidor, é toda pessoa física ou jurídica que utiliza, como destinatário final, atividade bancária, financeira e de crédito.

3. Ação direta julgada improcedente.

Tribunal pleno embargos de declaração na ação direta de nconstitucionalidade 2.591-1 distrito federal Relator: min. Eros grau embargante(s): procuradoria-geral da república em 14 12/2006.

http://www.mpsp.mp.br/portal/pls/portal/docs/1/808763.PDF.

[44] Vote-view minister eros degree direct action of unconstitutionality 2,591-1 federal district reporter: min. Carlos velloso applicant: national confederation of the financial system - consif advocates: ives gandra s. Martins and others required: president of the republic required: national congress. In 07/06/2006 court full direct action of unconstitutionality 2,591-1 federal district reporter originating: min. Carlos villainous rapporteur for the accordion minister eros degree.

When the withholding credit was implemented, it was expected that banks fulfill the promise of lower interest rates and of course ensuring responsible lending, given that it was a form of credit with virtually no risk to the banks. In fact, the only risk was that the retiree or pensioner could come to die, a risk that was calculated by banks at 2% to 2.50% per month.[45] Still, banks have not taken the risk of death and currently charge the families in case that the borrower comes to die.

The consigned credit had a huge success, also stimulated by an aggressive advertising campaign by banks. In addition to regular advertising, well-known actors also at an advanced age were employed on television clips that advised this "friendly credit" to retirees. Various techniques have been used to sell the product in this campaign. One of the ways used was to take up the boundary between the private sphere and the economic interest. The "Friendly Credit" remembers much more a friend lending money than a professional economic contract. Another way to show the credit was related to specific fears of older people (loneliness, health) and finally using the authority of the speeches of famous people. The tendency to exaggerate positives and hide credit problems led to some legal processes.

In addition to the massive advertising campaign, there was an emphasis on direct contacts. Intermediaries, called "pastinhas," made contact with elderly people to obtain the credit. For a long time, it was almost impossible for elderly people to pass in front of a bank without being addressed to contract a withholding credit. While it was not banned, there were offers made by telemarketers.

With the situation of retirees and pensioners, the advantages (lower interest rates) of the new credit and the aggressive marketing showed results; the "withholding credit" was a huge success. In the first seven months, banks lent in this credit modality more than 11.5 billion reais at 6.8 million contracts in total. From 2004 to December 2007, 30.6 billion reais were contracted in 23.6 million contracts. In fact, the trend remains strong. Just in May 2012, 2.9 billion reais were lent in 876,326 contracts. From the data, it is evident that it is generally done in small amounts. On average, the amount that is borrowed is around R$ 1500 (one thousand, five hundred) to be paid in 33 installments. Most contractors have an income of up to a minimum wage.

The great success of the withholding credit, however, could not hide the problems from its beginning. Thus, the National Institute of Social Security ("Instituto Nacional do Seguro Social"—INSS) had to change the rules, especially in the initial phase, to protect retirees and pensioners, to regulate banks' practices, and to prevent crimes against the elderly. Between January 2005 and January 2008, the standards and rules have been amended eight times. Most of the changes refer to the practices

[45]In view of the high interest that at that time reached 141% a year for a credit on overdraft and 52.5–55.8% for a normal credit, payroll lending rates would have been a little lower. Even so, the National Council of Social Welfare found himself obliged, in June 2006, introducing a ceiling interest of 2.9% per month. Since then, interest rates fell slightly, and arrived at 2.14% per month, recently (D.O.U. 11/09/2015), interest rose again to 2.34% per month.

of banks, in an effort to protect consumers. Some of these reveal the tendency of banks to abuse the situation of consumers, for example, for not delivering copies of the contracts and printing them in small print and so on. To get a larger number of contracts, banks facilitated the hiring to the point of making room for many abuses against consumers. The practice of contracting a withholding credit by phone might serve as an example. Although the rules provided only hiring through written or electronic ways, it happened in many cases that the contracts were made via phone. It opened a huge space for fraud by people who have succeeded, usually easily, in getting the data of elderly people and making an contract on their behalf. So in September 2005, contracting by telephone was explicitly prohibited, but fraud still happens in some cases.

Something similar happened to the obligation of banks to provide information to its customers. For many elderly people, it is difficult to understand exactly their obligations and why they are in debt. In an intervention study with elderly women, it was evident that several of them were totally unaware of what "interest" meant.[46] To ensure greater transparency of fees and interest, banks have been required since July 2005 to disclose the interest per month and per year, including all fees and taxes. In May 2006, banks were prohibited from charging specific hiring rates and, in June 2006, introduced a ceiling for the interest that could be charged.

Particularly, two subjects have been changed several times and thus demonstrate the difficulties that the INSS had to address the issue. The first refers to the time extension in which the credit must be repaid. At the beginning, it was restricted to 36 months. In July 2005, it was fully opened; banks could choose the length freely. But in September 2005, the former limit of 36 months was reintroduced and continued until January 2008, when it was extended to 60 months. In 2014, the number of monthly installments was increased to 72 installments, being 6 years to repay the credit.

The second critical point was the use of credit cards. In July 2005, the possibility of using withholding credit for funding a special credit card was opened. At this time, it was possible to commit up to 10% of the income with a card. But in November of the same year, this possibility was removed by the argumentation that this would facilitate overindebtedness of elderly consumers. A working group was instituted to examine the issue, and in January 2008, the use of credit card was authorized again with specific rules regarding the interest and the issuance of the card. The ceiling of the card interest rates, which had fallen to a limit of 3.06% per month, rose again (D.O.U of 9/11/2015) to 3.36% per month.

The constant change of rules is obviously problematic. On one hand, it can be argued that the INSS showed a high sensitivity to the challenge of introducing a credit for retirees and pensioners unaccustomed to banking practices. This argument is sustained on the fact that the INSS in the first years kept updated information also with fraud and problem reports available on its website by a team

[46]See: Buaes (2011).

of journalists who gathered information from various sources.[47] On the other hand, these constant changes also create insecurity. Although it is possible to access the latest rules on the website of the Ministry of Social Welfare, this feature is not available to the great majority of elderly people who, due to low incomes and little education, are unlikely to be Internet users.[48] Thus, there remains the impression that an important instrument of social inclusion of elderly people through secure and regular access to credits was introduced hastily. This impression is reinforced by the fact that only in July 2005, more than a year after the official implementation of consigned credit, the population was informed through a national television campaign and radio about the existence and the rules of consigned credit.

Difficulties with the withholding credit demanded initiatives by older consumers themselves in the fight for their rights. One of the important partners in this fight is the PROCON, a public organization of consumer protection, which serves as an intermediary between the consumer and provider in almost all states and major cities. As PROCONS also have records of consumer complaints, they are an important reference to know the problems that affect consumers. Regarding consigned credit, the following complaints are the main ones: lack of clarity in the offer and information, lack of transparency in relation to marketing and advertising, not to deliver a copy of the agreement to the consumer, unfair terms, referral credit cards without request, contracts via phone, even after banned.

In the following, we will analyze in detail the rules that support and amend the withholding credit. So Law 10.820, which provided the authorization to discount in payroll, in an irrevocable and irreversible way, of the amounts corresponding to the payment of loans, financing, and leasing transactions granted by financial institutions and leasing companies, found itself in conflict with constitutional guarantees[49] for wage protection.

The chronology of rules on the withholding credit for the retired started when in May 2004 Law no. 10.953, amending Law no. 10.820 of December 17, 2003, extends the application of withholding credit for the retired by the INSS. That means that Article 6 of Law 10.820 stated that Social Security would collect the installments due from retirees or pensioners in contracts and then would transfer the money to financial institutions. With the amendment of the 2004 10.953 Law, Article 6, it started to allow banks to automatically retain the values of the installments in time to pay benefits to retirees without the intermediation of Social Security. This means, once assigned the withholding credit, the credit rate will be automatically debited from the pension without any possibility to stop that process, even in case of high vulnerability.

[47]Unfortunately this service stopped in 2011, claiming that there was an exchange of the journalists group.

[48]See: Doll (2007), pp. 109–124.

[49]"Unavailability, intangibility, irreconcilability and irreducibility are the structuring principles of the legal tradition of constitutionalism based on the defense of human labor and labor law" Cavallazzi et al. (2010), pp. 74–111.

By this way, the regulatory amendment puts the elderly pensioner and retired completely without coverage of state protection and establishes a legislation that ignores the consumer's vulnerability.

At the structural level of the possibilities of the legal field, the CDC microsystem remains strong, but the legislative situation presents a number of obstacles and possibilities intermittently.[50]

Law No. 10.953 includes the text of Law 10.820, the ceiling of 30% for discounts and withholdings on payroll of amounts related to the payment of loans, financing, and leasing operations.

In the normative chronology of obstacles to the protection of elderly consumers in consigned credit, the most harmful and sophisticated assault is undoubtedly Law 13.172 of 2015, which extends the discount from 30% to 35%, and 5% of these are intended for amortization of debts incurred by card and for use with the purpose of withdrawal by credit card.

The legislation related to the withholding credit invariably justifies its purpose with access to credit with the possible reduction of interest to retirees and pensioners, goals that could offer advantages to both sides. Let us look at a research on the reality of the facts.

28.5 Consigned Credit: Data from a Brazilian Study

The PROCON of São Paulo and the Research Group "Education and Aging" of the Federal University of Rio Grande do Sul (UFRGS), together with members of the School of Law and the School of Education from the same university, conducted an empirical study[51] between 2006 and 2007 in order to obtain a better understanding

[50]Between 2006 and 2011 we can record the following normative instructions: 03/14/2006—Banks should reformulate paycheck credit advertising for pensioners (Source: State Attorney of the State of Rio Grande do Sul). 03/03/2008—New rules of payroll loans come into force (Source: Agência Brasil). 9/02/2008—DECREE N° 6.386: Regulates the art. 45 of Law No. 8,122 of December 11, 1990, and provides for the processing of payroll deductions under the Integrated System of Human Resources Administration (SIAPE). 01/12/2010 (MJ)—The Department of Consumer Protection and Defense (DPDC) launches the Handbook Prevention and Treatment of the Superdependent. 5/10; 2010—Publication of Res. 382/2010 State Secretariat for Planning and Management (Seplag) implements a new payroll loan system in the State of Rio de Janeiro. 07/7/2011—Interest rates have third highest followed in the year in May, says Anefac. (Source: G1.) For the individual, rate was at 6.87%, the highest since June 2010. For legal entity, rate stood at 4.03%, the highest since July 2009. 14/01/2011 Central Bank prohibits exclusivity agreements for payroll-deductible loans. Circular 3,522, "financial institutions, in the provision of services and in the contracting of transactions, are prohibited from entering into agreements, contracts or agreements that prevent or restrict the access of clients to credit operations offered by other institutions.

[51]Research Project UFRGS "O idoso frente ao empréstimo consignado: implicações educacionais", PI: Johannes Doll.

of the consequences of a withholding credit to elderly people. The study aimed to answer the following questions:

1. What is the profile of retirees or pensioners who hire a consigned credit?
2. What are the reasons for a credit of this type?
3. What are the consequences of this credit to elderly people's lives?

The study was conducted in two major Brazilian cities, São Paulo and Porto Alegre. It was used as a questionnaire to register the data on the socioeconomic profile with social data, family structure, housing and financial situation, including a section on the withholding credit. Given the fact that in Brazil a large part of the elderly population has problems with written language, the questionnaire was completed by trained interviewers. The focused group sought to be elderly people of lower middle class, based on the assumption that this group should have particular problems with the withholding credit. Thus, in São Paulo, the interviews were conducted in a center for the elderly (2006/2007), and in Porto Alegre, these contacts were made with community groups (2007). The participation in the study totaled to 215 elderly, 125 in São Paulo and 90 in Porto Alegre. In 81 (37.7%) of the cases, people reported having at least one withholding credit. These data are consistent with the general data, according to which at least one-third of retirees and pensioners already had a withholding credit. An analysis of data from participants demonstrates that this consumer profile closely approximates the elderly people profile in Brazil in general. Still, this is not a representative group for all elderly in Brazil but a selection of people who usually attend social centers or community groups for the elderly.

28.5.1 *Participants' Profile*

In a first step, this study presents the sociodemographic data of the participants to then examine whether there was a difference between the group of those who hired a consigned credit and the group of elderly without consigned credit.

Participants were 69 years old on average. Regarding marital status, they were divided into two major groups, those who were married or living in stable relationships (39.1%) and those who had lost their partner (39.5%). Two smaller groups were constituted by the separated (11.6%) and single (9.8%). As Brazil had until 1960 high fertility rates, it was expected that the participants still had many children. This was confirmed by data indicating that 45.6% had between three and five children and 34% between five and six children. The group with few children (1–2) was relatively small (16.3%), while very large families with seven or more children were already very rare (2.3%). However, it should be noted that the research was performed in capitals where the trend for smaller families is greater. In rural areas, families should probably be bigger.

Almost all participants lived in houses and were often their owners (83.7%); few lived in rental houses (5.1%) or transferred houses (7.4%). The research data are consistent with data from the Brazilian Institute of Geography and Statistics (IBGE). The National Household Survey (PNAD) data of 2006 states that 91% of the population lives in households and 75% are owners.[52] In general, the elderly people live with other family members, but also 21.4% live alone. It can be observed that in Brazil, the number of elderly people living alone is lower than in many other countries, but it is growing. The family group of older people is generally small, more than half live together with up to three people, only 11.6% live with five or more people.

Also, the income of the group is expected. Less than a third (29.3%) has an income of a minimum wage (MW), 31.6% between one and two MW and a quarter (27.9%) between two and four MW. Only a very small group (1.9%) has more than 10 MW. Thus, the income of the studied group is a little lower than the general income in Brazil at that time, where 14.7% had less than one MW, 23.3% between two and four MW and 8.6% were over 10 SM (PNAD 2006 data). This confirms that the income of participants is within the overall Brazilian reality and that this group in fact belongs to the lower middle class.

The educational level among elderly people is generally lower than among young people, for the educational system in Brazil in school time of the current elderly was not as embracing as it is today. A considerable part of them had never been to school, and many of them evaded after a few years. The collected data confirm this expectation. Among the participants, 18.6% had no formal education and almost half of them (47.9%) had only between one and 4 years of schooling. These data are in accordance with the Brazilian reality in general.[53] Briefly, approximately two-thirds (66.5%) possess a very poor education suggesting that the ability to deal with language in written form is very limited. This is an important information regarding how the population of the elderly deals with banking contracts.[54]

The health situation is reasonable for a large proportion of participants (41.9%), according to their own statements. The trend is improving as 27.4% considered their health good and 8.4% very good. On the downside, 15.8% rated their health as problematic and 6.5% as very bad.

An interesting question is whether there are sociodemographic differences between people who hired a withholding credit and who did not. In other words, would there be a specific profile of someone who hires withholding credit? In fact, there are some differences but very small and in some specific features.

[52]In fact, the situation in Brazil has changed a bit in the last decade, but for reasons of comparability we will work here with 2006 data, the time of the survey research data. See: www.ibge.gov.br/home/estatistica/populacao/trabalhoerendimento/pnad2006.

[53]The representative survey "Elderly in Brazil," conducted by Perseus Abramo Foundation and SESC/SP reaches similar results, 70% of 2,136 respondents had a maximum schooling of 4 years. See: Santos et al. (2007).

[54]See data of the "Credit and Overindebtedness Observatory" of UFRGS-MJ, in Marques (2014b), pp. 99–145.

Table 28.2 Income, education, and health condition comparing people who hired the consigned credit (HC) and people who did not hire (DH) the consigned credit

Income			Education			Marital status		
	HC %	DH %		HC %	DH %		HC %	DH %
Ignored	0	0.7	No schooling	12.3	22.2	Single	13.8	7.4
Without income	0	0.7	1–3 years	30	27.4	Married	31.3	43.7
Up to 1 MW	26.3	31.1	4 years	17.5	20.7	Separated	11.3	11.9
1–2 MW	36.3	28.9	5–7 years	21.3	10.4	Widowed	43.8	37
2–4 MW	30.0	26.7	8–10 years	16.3	12.6		100	100
4–7 MW	3.8	8.2	11–14 years	2.5	4.4			
7–10 MW	2.5	0	15 years and plus	0	2.2			
Over 10 MW	1.3	2.2		100	100			
Missing data	0	1.5						
	100	100						

HC—Hired consigned credit
DH—Did not hire consigned credit
Source: UFRGS research data

Regarding education, there is a small but interesting difference that follows the function of a U. Thus, it is mainly the group in the middle, considering education and income, who hires withholding credits, while the poorest and the richest are more in the group of those who do not contract. Another difference is that there are fewer participants married or in stable unions among those who take credit than singles and widowers (see Table 28.2).

And finally, there is a very small difference in health.[55] People who have contracted a withholding credit tend to evaluate their health worse than people who did not. Obviously, it is not possible to determine the cause and the effect. This means that it is possible that people with a more fragile health need more money to treat and therefore need more often a credit. But it is also not to discard the possibility that concerns about credit worsen the health status of the elderly. Data are the following. (See Table 28.2).

Briefly, the data suggest that participants correspond in general terms to the profile of elderly people in Brazil. Most are integrated to their family and have a stable economic situation, indicated by their house and regular income, although not high. Education is weak, as in most of Brazilian elderly, where two-thirds have a problem with reading and nearly one-third can be considered functionally illiterate. These are important capabilities when it comes to signing a banking contract. During the interviews, it became clear that most of the elderly had a very

[55]In the questionnaire, participants rated their health status according to a Likert scale from very good (=1) to very bad (=5). Among those who had made a loan, the value in relation to health was slightly worse (2.93) compared to those without loan (2,80).

rudimentary and confused view about their credit and its characteristics, an impression that was confirmed dramatically in subsequent qualitative studies.[56]

28.5.2 *Reasons for Contracting a Withholding Credit*

The second research question was: what are the reasons that retirees indicate for getting a credit? What is the money of credit used for? As it is possible to observe in Table 28.3, there are different reasons for hiring a credit. (See Table 28.3).

The most frequent reason for contracting a withholding credit was to help a family member. Due to the high interest, it seems very reasonable to ask parents or grandparents to make a withholding credit with lower interest rates. When the relative for whom the retired did the credit returns the money, there is no problem. But the fact is that for the bank, only the elderly person who made the claim bears the responsibility to repay the debt. When the relative cannot return the money, either for reasons of unemployment or other reasons, the debt liability is exclusively for the elderly. Another problematic point is that it opens the door to financial violence against the elderly, a violence that has grown in recent times.[57] The Elderly Statute is very clear in considering it a crime in Article 102:

> Art. 102. Appropriating or divert assets, income, pension or any other income of the elderly, giving them different application of its purpose:
>
> Penalty - imprisonment of one (1) to four (4) years and a fine.

Still, this help from the elderly to the family occurs as research shows.

The second reason for contracting the credit pointed by elderly is renovating and fixing their own house. That is also a reasonable investment and a good way of expending money from credit—for improving of living and consequently of life quality. The third reason is contracting the credit to pay other debts. That reason

Table 28.3 Reasons for hiring a credit

For family members (relatives)	Housing renovation	Payment of debts	Health problems	Basic needs	Home appliance acquisition	Traveling	Funeral
24	23	15	13	13	3	2	1

In the answers, it was possible to mark more than one reason; because of that, the total number is higher than the 81 persons who contracted a credit
Source: UFRGS research data

[56]See: Buaes (2011).

[57]See, for example, the notice of 20/09/2015 "A violência financeira contra o idoso cresce com a crise", where the withholding credit is named as one of the instruments to explore the elderly. Available in: http://www.otempo.com.br/capa/economia/viol%C3%AAncia-financeira-contra-o-idoso-cresce-22-com-a-crise-1.1116196. Acsess in 31/01/2016.

could be considered problematic and not as reasonable as earlier reasons identified. In one way, it is certainly good to contract a credit with lower interests to pay debts with higher interests. However, as evidenced in this study, several elderly were situated in a kind of vicious circle being continuously in debt. Many times, interviewees related how they had been contacted to contract a new credit when they had reached half of their credit payments. As most of elderly people are unaware of the banking rules or have a very vague vision about them, they end up contracting another credit, sometimes not the withholding credit but a regular bank credit in disadvantageous conditions for the elderly. This vicious circle was evident in interviews with participants in Porto Alegre, where 16 participants only had a contract but 11 had two contracts at the same time and 13 had three contracts or more at the same time. The largest number of contracts was a participant with eight contracts. From these data, we suspect that the reason for paying a credit contract with another is a strong indicator of overindebtedness.

Income from retirement and pension is not very high and is generally insufficient to cover expenditures for extraordinary events such as an illness. Data from the research demonstrated that problems with health are also one of the main reasons to hire a withholding credit. But the most disturbing reason is the fact that credit becomes necessary to cover the costs of basic needs, a reason that 16.3% of participants indicated. When the regular income is not enough to pay the expenses of daily life, what is the situation when this income is further reduced by credit payments that could reach 35%?

Other surveys reach similar reasons, even with small differences. Newton Freitas quotes an IBOPE (the Brazilian Public Opinion and Statistics Institute) survey ordered by the Brazilian Association of Banks (ABBC), which provides the following results:

> The resources of the consigned credit according to the survey serve to: 1) pay down debt, 55%; 2) help the family, 12%; 3) Property reform, 19%; 4) health, 8%; 5) financing car, 2%; 6) purchase of household appliances, 2%; 7) Travel, 1%; 8) others 2%. The average of the operations is R $ 2,938.90, with an average term of 28.11 months and installments of R $ 166.35. The average compromised money is 20%. (Valor, São Paulo, 29 ago. 2006, p. C8) (*apud* http://www.newton.freitas.nom.br/artigos.asp?cod=139.)

The aspect that did not appear in our research was "financing a car"; however, the other reasons are quite similar. Another point that draws attention is the "pay down debt" that appeared as one of the main reasons that the IBOPE survey (55%) did not appear with the same strength in our research.

28.5.3 The Consequences of a Withholding Credit

One of the main features of the withholding credit is that the installments are deducted directly from retirement or pension. This means that the value of incomes in the years followed the credit decreases by up to 35% and may even exceed this percentage with current legislation.[58] If the income reduction is already planned and integrated on the family budget, there is no problem. However, it became clear in interviews that many elderly people were surprised by this reduction. Among the 81 participants with a consigned credit, 33% indicated that they had to reduce their spending. Most saved on basic needs (58%), buying less or cheaper food. Others cut in health spending (12%), saving on drugs or canceling health insurance. Still, others delayed bills to pay (5%) or, in one case, took another loan to pay the first.

It is normal to make some restrictions to pay a claim; however, when this economy reaches fundamental and basic needs such as food or health, it becomes problematic. And if there is a need to take a credit to pay a previous credit, the circular path to overindebtedness is already outlined.

How do older people evaluate their experiences with the withholding credit? At this point, the opinions are divided. For a third of the participants (35%), the situation has improved with the credit. For a quarter (24%), there was not much change. But for a large group of respondents (41%), the situation worsened with the withholding credit. And the group of São Paulo is even more pessimistic about it. Among respondents, 54% indicated that their situation has worsened with the credit.

It is therefore understandable that a considerable group (42.5%) would not want to repeat the experience with consigned credit. Just to illustrate, a lady, during the interviews, said that she made the credit for her daughter but she did not return the value. Thus, the mother had to be responsible for all payments. Still, more than half (57.5%) indicated that they would contract the withholding credit again. Even if the experience with this type of credit was not very positive, it is still the cheapest way to get money.

At this point, the evaluation of the participants in this study is quite different from other published data. Newton Freitas mentions a survey by Vox Populi ordered by the ABBC (Brazilian Association of Banks), according to which 91% of retirees and pensioners are satisfied with the withholding credit, 43% considered it great and 48% good.[59]

Probably it would need a more detailed analysis of the groups interviewed to explain these differences. Moreover, there is the assumption that the research having been made shortly after the credit release may have been influenced by the situation of "honeymoon" with the withholding credit.

An analysis of the answers of the research participants shows that consigned credit is, in a number of cases, a good opportunity to get a necessary resource. But for 41% of the participants, the credit contract has worsened their situation. The problem was not the credit itself in most cases but the low income and the problematic economic situation of the elderly and also of their families. Still it is

[58]Law 10,820/2003, amended by Law 13,172, of October 21, 2015, conversion of MP 681, of July 10, 2015.

[59]See: (Valor, São Paulo, 19 ago. 2005, p. C3 *apud* http://www.newton.freitas.nom.br/artigos.asp?cod=139).

necessary to consider that the withholding credit also opened a new possibility of exploitation of elderly people, either by family or by banks, whose aggressive advertising and questionable marketing practices sometimes take the elderly to contract a credit they may not need and that will cause serious consequences for their income in the coming years. One of such questionable practices is, for example, the not clear relationship between large franchise stores and banks, whose internal links are for the older consumers—and not just for them—almost incomprehensible. Thus, when the elderly think they are making an installment purchase, they discover upon receiving the next retirement or pension income that they had contracted a withholding credit!

Considering the education level among elderly people, the social vulnerability becomes even more evident—around two-thirds (66.5%) have very poor schooling; from this total, 18.6% had no schooling and nearly half, 47.9%, have only 1 to 4 years of schooling.

Another important issue for the condition of vulnerability from the elderly is the fact that older people generally live together with other relatives, and the most frequent reason to contract a withholding credit was to help other family members.

The result of the research reinforces the thesis of overindebtedness as a social phenomenon and vulnerability as a relational process that not only affects consumers but has also broad implications for the whole family.

Thus, it is assumed that the prevention of overindebtedness demands changes in relationships between consumer and provider, change in conditions experienced by social groups affected by vulnerability and, in the case of the elderly, by hypervulnerability.[60]

28.6 Conclusions

Brazil has changed a lot in the last 50 years, and one of the principle aspects is the aging of the Brazilian society. In the last years, the economy and the banks have discovered the elderly people with their low but regular income as an interesting consumer group. A special form of credit, the withholding credit for retirees and pensioners, gave the elderly access to credits. In fact, this form of credit has shown an explosive development by reaching in a few years around a third of all retirees and pensioners.

An analysis of the conditions of the elderly, the characteristics of this type of credit, and its impact on the lives of people bring a differentiated picture. It can be argued that this type of credit allows reasonable access to credit with more favorable conditions in relation to interest rates for a group with traditional difficulties of getting any credit. When this type of credit is used in a planned,

[60]See: Schmitt (2014).

thought-out, and rational way, this can be a good option. But it has to be considered that the elderly are a specific group of consumers with a high grade of vulnerability.

On the other hand, this credit is not only an inclusion of elderly people in the consumption world, but it is an excellent deal for the banks, for trade, and for the policy. Despite of being the interest a little lower than the normal market, the total security of banks to receive payments, transferred directly by the INSS to banks, makes the withholding credit a highly profitable business. For the trade, this credit is interesting because the elderly with cash in hand are great consumers. The withholding credit has become a very common form of payment for consumer goods because there is often a partnership between trade and banks. And for the government, the withholding credit represented a cash injection in the internal market and stimulated the economy. The use of withholding credit as a resource to solve market complaints became evident when tourism claims—almost immediately—were answered by a tourism plan that enables to fund domestic travel through withholding credit.[61]

At first glance, this credit seems to be very positive, but it is possible to perceive it as a double-edged sword, considering the high risk that after the "honeymoon" there comes a great "hangover," especially for elderly consumers. Our analysis has shown that older people are, in fact, a highly vulnerable group, and therefore it is necessary to think of protective measures, measures that help solve problems, such as an existing overindebtedness combined with educational measures.

The study confirmed that the risk of overindebtedness is worsened in the face of certain conditions set forth—usually linked to negligence in granting credit—on the relationship between the consumer and the credit provider.

Affirming that the elderly are a particularly vulnerable group does not mean that it refers to all people over 60 years. In fact, some elderly are still professionals, artists, and politicians and do not seem—at first—to need special protection. However, the technical vulnerability mode affects all consumers, including professionals and those with higher education. Looking at the vast majority of the elderly population, we find explicit four risk factors for vulnerability. The first aspect relates to illiteracy and low education, pointed in national surveys and the research presented here. The fact that two-thirds of older people have great difficulties in dealing with a written text makes the assumption highly problematic that older people can really understand the banking and credit contract signed by them.

The second aspect relates to the financial situation. Even if the financial situation of the elderly is not much worse than the general population, the relatively small income and the increase in certain expenses, mainly medicines, put much of the elderly population in a fragile economic situation. And when any negative event happens such as illness, death of family members, separation, unemployment (of the children), often credit is presented as the last exit. But once a person becomes indebted, it is usually very difficult to get rid of the debt, given the income already reduced from the necessary expenses.

[61]See: Notícia de (2007).

The third aspect that contributes to the vulnerability of the elderly is the health issue. Aging is not a disease, but the risk of contracting a disease increases significantly with aging, especially chronic degenerative diseases such as cancer, Parkinson's disease, dementias, all diseases for which the health system itself is barely adequate. Indeed, while the first phase of old age is often marked by new discoveries and new chances, advanced old age is a phase marked much more by loss, limitations, and fragility.[62]

The fourth factor relates to the fast changes that are taking place in the contemporary world. The elderly were socialized into a world of 50 or more years ago, and it was at this time that they developed their competencies and abilities. These competencies and abilities generally are not of great help in today's world, and even much less in the contemporary world marked by consumerism, precarious relations, and instability.[63] This makes the elderly an easy victim to abusive practices, aggressive marketing, and crimes.

In short, these aspects elucidate the affirmations of Claudia Lima Marques about the vulnerability of the elderly consumer:

> The elderly is a disputed consumers, especially in the countryside, but may be suffering from discriminatory practices and clauses without due attention be given (...) With regard to the consumer 'elderly' (so indistinctly considered one whose age is above 60 years), is, however, a consumer of potentiated vulnerability [. . .] it is true that the particular vulnerability of the elderly is linked to his 'age' and 'social status', as outlined in the CDC, which makes some services (health services) or products (medicines) essential to sustaining life. Health and age are united and in conflict, making contracting a search for dignity, social inclusion and equality.[64]

Given the vulnerability of the elderly consumer, especially in relation to consigned credit, we would like to highlight, as a conclusion, three measures that are needed to make consigned credit a quiet and safe way of access to credit for elderly people and not a trap.

The first measure would be of the required legal protection. It is important to ensure the access of retirees and pensioners to relevant information about credit in general, credit interest, the total amount to be paid and inhibit abusive practices and misleading advertising. Also, it is important to mention that the limitations imposed, for example, in relation to the commitment of income (first 30%, now 35%) and the number of installments (initially 36 months, now 72 months) serve as protection of elderly consumers, and the trend to extend these restrictions is a dangerous path that might lead to overindebtedness. It is also important that these rules are complied.[65]

---

[62]Baltes and Smith (2006), pp. 7–31.

[63]Bauman (2007).

[64]Marques (2014a), p. 381.

[65]Especially regarding the percentage of assignment to credit payment is known that there is no effective control. Seniors come to commit much more of their retirement than 30%/35% of their retirement or pension. See: http://www2.camara.leg.br/camaranoticias/noticias/ECONOMIA/414256-governo-alerta-para-endividamento-de-idosos-com-emprestimo-consignado.html.

The second important measure refers to older consumers who entered into a superindebtedness process. Given the ease that exists in going into overindebtedness, there is a need to promote means to assist them in getting out of this situation. An initiative in this direction is the "Processing of Consumer over-indebtedness Pilot Program," now existing in various courts of Brazil (Rio Grande do Sul, Paraná, São Paulo, Paraiba, Pernambuco and Brasilia) and aims the renegotiation of debts in front of a judge.[66]

Finally, the third measure is an adequate financial education to adult and elderly people. Perhaps that should be the first. This is because information campaigns and workshops on how to handle money, credit, and consumption are important, but to provoke a more profound change it is necessary to enter into an open dialogue with the community groups involved. As shown by the doctoral thesis of Caroline Stumpf Buaes,[67] simply teaching older people to fill tables to ensure control over the economic situation is not enough. The really relevant is an educational process, entering in the horizon of understanding of the specific population group in a way that collective constructions of meaning of the group itself can create new interpretations of the world (Paulo Freire). In this process, those involved begin to understand themselves as active actors in this "game" of consumption and finance, which leads to a reflexive stance that opens up new options of action. A financial education process in this perspective of Paulo Freire[68] leads to more profound and lasting changes and opens thereby possibilities for a more peaceful experience of elderly people with the contemporary world of consumption and credit.

References

Baltes PB Smith J (2006) Novas fronteiras para o future do envelhecimento. A Terceira Idade. SESC, São Paulo, 17(36):7–31

Barbosa LOS, Meurer R (2016) Determinantes do Investimento Estrangeiro em Carteira no Brasil de 1995 a 2009. Available on: http://www.anpec.org.br/encontro2010/inscricao/arquivos/379-3aea02569b5db847df4f0ff590d26381.docx. Accesso in 31/01/2016

Bauman Z (2007) Vida líquida. Zahar, Rio de Janeiro

de Beauvoir S (1990) A velhice. Nova Fronteira, Rio de Janeiro

Beck U (1999) Schöne neue Arbeitswelt. Campus Verlag, Frankfurt/Main

Bertoncello KRD (2015) Superendividamento do Consumidor - Mínimo existencial - Casos concretos. Revista dos Tribunais, São Paulo

Bourroul M, Ferreira M (2016) 20 anos do plano Real. Accessible at: http://20anosdoreal.epocanegocios.globo.com/. Access in 31/01/2016

[66]This pilot project, created by Judge Clarissa Costa Lima and Karen Berontcello, is part of a growing concern of investigators, judges and lawyers about the indebtedness effects. See, por exemplo, Marques et al. (2010), Lima, Clarissa Costa. O direito de recomeçar: Em busca de um modelo para o tratamento do superendividamento no Brasil. Tese de doutorado, Faculdade de Direito, UFRGS. Bertoncello (2015).

[67]Buaes (2011). See also: Buaes (2015), pp. 105–127.

[68]A pedagogy that can overcome the naive perception of reality. See: Freire (2008).

Brum A (1998) Desenvolvimento Econômico Brasileiro, 19ª edn. Vozes, Petrópolis

Buaes CS (2011) Sobre a construção de conhecimentos: uma experiência de educação financeira com mulheres idosas em um contexto popular. UFRGS/PPGEDU, Tese de Doutorado

Buaes CS (2015) Perspectivas de Educação Financeira com Idosos em um Contexto Popular. Educação e Realidade 40:105–127

Camarano AA (2006) Envelhecimento da população brasileira: uma contribuição demográfica. In: Freitas EV, Py L, Cançado FAX, Doll J, Gorzoni ML (eds) Tratado de Geriatria e Gerontologia. 2 edn. Guanabara Koogan, Rio de Janeiro

Camarano AA, Kanso S (2011) Aspectos socioeconômicos do Envelhecimento Populacional. In: Freitas EV, Py L, Cançado FAX, Doll J, Gorzoni ML (eds) Tratado de Geriatria e Gerontologia, 3 edn. Guanabara Koogan, Rio de Janeiro

Camarano AA, Kanso S, Mello JL (2004) Como vive o idoso brasileiro? In: Camarano AA (ed) Os novos idosos brasileiros: muito além dos 60? IPEA, Rio de Janeiro

Cavallazzi RL, Silva Sayonara GL, de Lima CC (2010) Tradições inventadas na sociedade de consumo: crédito consignado e a flexibilização da proteção ao salário. Revista de Direito do Consumidor. vol. 76, out

de Freitas Elizabeth V et al (2011) Tratado de geriatria e gerontologia. GEN-Koogan, Rio de Janeiro

de Lima CC (2014) O tratamento do superendividamento e o direito de recomeçar dos consumidores. Revista dos Tribunais, São Paulo

Doll J (2002) The situation of elderly workers in Brazil, in TALES, Third Age learning studies. Proceedings of the XII International Seminar, Saskatoon, Canada, vol. 12

Doll J (2007) Educação, cultura e lazer. In: Anita Liberalesso Neri (Org.) Idosos no Brasil. Vivências, desafios e expectativas na terceira idade. Editora fundação Persei Abramo - Edições SESC, SP, São Paulo, pp 109–124

Doll J (2009) Elderly Consumer Weakness in 'Withholding Credit'. In: Niemi J, Ramsay I, Whitford WC (eds) Consumer credit, debt and bankruptcy – Comparative and international perspective. Hart Publishing, Oxford

Doll J, Ramos AC, Buaes CS (2015) Apresentação -Educação e Envelhecimento, in Educação e Realidade, Porto Alegre, 40(1), jan./mar

Flores T (2016) Bolha de Crédito? O Aumento do crédito e do endividamento das famílias no Brasil. Acessível em: http://www.portaldeauditoria.com.br/artigos/Bolha-de-Cr%C3%A9dito.asp. Acesso em 20/01/2016

Freire P (2008) Educação e Mudança, 31ª edn. Paz e Terra, São Paulo

Grin DG (1999) A reinvenção da velhice, EDUSP, São Paulo

Guimarães D (2008) Benefício Continuado – o difícil direito à tranquilidade. IPEA, desafios, ano 5, edição 45, 2008. Acessível em: http://ipea.gov.br/desafios/index.php?option=com_content&id=1199:reportagens-materias&Itemid=39. Acesso em 20/01/2016

IBGE (2008) Síntese de Indicadores Sociais: uma análise das condições de vida da população brasileira. Instituto Brasileiro de Geografia e Estatística, Rio de Janeiro

Kreter AC, Bacha CJC (2006) Avaliação da eqüidade da Previdência no meio rural do Brasil. Revista de Economia e Sociologia Rural

Lopes A (2000) Os desafios da Gerontologia no Brasil. Alínea, Campinas, SP

Marques CL (2014a) Contratos no Código de Defesa do Consumidor, 7th edn. São Paulo, RT

Marques CL (2014b) Estudo sobre a vulnerabilidade dos analfabetos na sociedade de consumo: o caso do crédito consignado a consumidores analfabetos. Revista de Direito do Consumidor 95:99–145

Marques CL, Benjamin AHV, Miragem B (2013) Comentários ao Código de Defesa do Consumidor, 4th edn. São Paulo, Revista dos Tribunais

Marques CL, Cavalazzi R (2006) Lunardeli. Direitos do Consumidor endividado: Superendividamento e Crédito. RT, São Paulo

Marques CL. Solidariedade na doença e na morte: sobre a necessidade de ações afirmativas em contratos de planos de saúde e de planos funerários frente ao consumidor idoso. Revista Trimestral de Direito Civil 8/3-41

Marques CL, Lima CC, Bertoncello KRD (2010) Prevenção e tratamento do superendividamento. DPDC/SDE, Brasília

Movimento Diretas Já started in the decade of 1980. http://www12.senado.gov.br/jornal/edicoes/2014/02/25/senadores-ressaltam-a-paz-do-movimento-diretas-ja. Accessed in 31/01/2016

Neri MC (2007) Renda, consumo e aposentadoria: evidências, atitudes e percepções. In: Neri AL (ed) Idosos no Brasil: vivências, desafios e expectativas na terceira idade. Editora Fundação Perseu Abramo, Edições SESC SP, São Paulo

Neri M (2011) A nova classe média: o lado brilhante da base da pirâmide. Saraiva, São Paulo

Notícia de 2007 Plano Nacional de Turismo prevê crédito consignado para viagens. Available in: http://memoria.ebc.com.br/agenciabrasil/noticia/2007-05-16/plano-nacional-de-turismo-preve-credito-consignado-para-viagens. Access in 31/01/2016

Oliveira Tavares V, Damiano Teixeira KM, Wajnman S, Saraiva de Loreto M das D (2011) Interface entre a renda dos idosos aposentados rurais e o contexto familiar. Textos e Contextos, Porto Alegre, 10(1), jan./jul

Pochmann M (2014) O mito da grande classe média: capitalismo e estrutura social. Boitempo, São Paulo

Raymundo F (1958) Os Donos do Poder - formação do patronato político brasileiro. Editora Globo, Porto Alegre

Raymundo F (1974) Machado de Assisa - pirâmide e o trapézio. Companhia Editora Nacional, São Paulo

Rodrigues NC (2001) Política Nacional do Idoso – Retrospectiva Histórica. Estudos Interdisciplinares sobre o Envelhecimento, pp 149–158

Santos GA, Lopes A, Neri AL (2007) Escolaridade, raça e etnia: elementos de exclusão social de idosos. In: Neri AL (ed) Idosos no Brasil: vivências, desafios e expectativas na terceira idade. Editora Fundação Perseu Abramo, Edições SESC, São Paulo

Schmitt CH (2014) Consumidores hipervulneráveis – A proteção do idoso no mercado de consumo. Atlas, São Paulo

Silva SGCLd, Cavalazzi RL (2013) Vulnerabilidade e direitos: Lei e jurisprudência sobre consumo e trabalho na sociedade contemporânea. In: Revista de Direito do Consumidor, vol 86

Simões J (1998) A maior categoria do país: o aposentado como ator político. In: Barros ML (ed) Velhice ou terceira idade? Estudos antropológicos sobre identidade, memória e política. Fundação Getúlio Vargas, Rio de Janeiro

Souza J (2012) Os batalhadores brasileiros: nova classe média ou nova classe trabalhadora? 2th edn. Editora UFMG, Belo Horizonte

Chapter 29
Consuming, Consumption, and Overindebtedness in (Hyper) Contemporaneity

Diogenes Faria de Carvalho

29.1 Introduction

Companies are now known by the elements that characterize them; we hear talk of an information society, a network society, and an exclusionary society. Among other ideas, there is a logic that drives a society to offer, which then attracts the society that consumes, which in turn provides opportunities for a credit society and ultimately produces a society in debt.

There are a variety of paradigms that explain the construction of the world. Man, in his eternal contradiction, is a genius with his creation potential but is reduced to something different as he cannot dominate his relationship with his inventions. His findings lead him to exaggerate, whether with inventions, the accumulation of resources or with consumption.

Social position allows us to build a new identity, that of being able to buy. The notion of consumption in this sense moves in another direction. The value to be had in relation to work as something creative and as a creative source gave way to consumption and the facilities surrounding it. Consumerism allows consumers the ability to relate with pleasure and with a sense of social belonging to the object consumed.

The hypercontemporaneous world is marked by hyperconsumption and turbo-consumers who are all compulsive and uncontrolled individualists. They are in pursuit of the happiness announced in shop windows. Emotional consumption takes on the role of providing well-being, and when you do not consume all you want, you open up space for depression, stress, anxiety, restlessness. This is the disorientation of the hyperconsumer.

Contemporary society has created solutions for the pleasures of life such as those on show in the store windows, but individuals cannot attain them fully. Educated in

D.F. de Carvalho (✉)
Faculty of Law, Federal University of Rio Grande do Sul, Porto Alegre, Brazil
e-mail: Dfcarvalho01@hotmail.com

C. Lima Marques, D. Wei (eds.), *Consumer Law and Socioeconomic Development*,
DOI 10.1007/978-3-319-55624-6_29

that world of consumption, they survive the feelings of frustration and of being social failures with the joys that are provided by credit—buy now and pay later.

The formation of the consumer's consent at the time of purchase is his weak point and becomes the target of suppliers in order to stimulate the purchase of goods and services. Consumer law is primarily occupied with the study of this aspect — in order to avoid the emergence of new problems in a society that has been characterized by the connection between production-consumption-consumerism-credit-indebtedness.

According to this scenario, human relations are established insofar as one consumes. Why do we consume? To satisfy the needs for pleasure, affirmation, and recognition. New needs require new desires; consumption gives way to consumerism. So consumer culture has allowed the creation of extraordinary mechanisms to maintain the consumer active. Credit guarantees access to the object of desire with the promise of a future payment.

Credit consumption has made Brazil the home of credit funding. Hope of access to the world of consumption finds itself frustrated by exclusion driven by growing defaults. Overindebtedness has become the worst consequence for consumer culture and makes the consumer its victim.

In the absence of responsible credit, the consumer society requires instruments of prevention and treatment for overindebtedness. The prospect is to help reintegrate one's dignity through the updating of the Consumer Protection Code as a tool to establishing guidelines capable of guaranteeing the right to start over.

29.2 Consumption

Consumption is an elusive, ambiguous, complex social phenomenon. It is a furtive and vague concept because although it is a requirement for social reproduction within any human society, we only become aware of its existence when it is perceived within western standards as superfluous, ostentatious, or conspicuous.

According to Veblen (1899/1987), consumption removes the consumer from the world of need and uses the struggle for status as its argument. Consumption "is an activity that is done every day, sometimes in a festive way such as arranging a meeting with friends, celebrating an important event or to reward us for a particularly important achievement" (Bauman 2008c, p. 37, author's translation).

It was the *Theory of the Leisure Class: an Economic Study of Institutions*, by Veblen (1899/1987) that first opened up this perspective on the issue of consumption, marking its place in contemporary culture. In the book, the author notes an intellectual force, in the sense of removing consumption from its simple reflex-effect position in production and positing it as a phenomenon capable of assuming a more serious tone as a discourse about social relations. Veblen's (1899/1987) view goes beyond the consumption — utility model and allows the economic view to prevail. According to him, the cultural meaning contained in this phenomenon and its practices reach new proportions.

Durkheim (1987) also sees consumption as a social fact, and beginning with Veblen (1899/1987) you can see that consumption shares the intrinsic nature of a social fact, with it being coercive, extensive, and external to the individual. Consumption becomes a coercive power as it builds a system of representations, through products and services, which they collectively share, acting as a social force in relation to the individual.

In this sense, consumption practices are social, in both their symbolic and concrete use. It is always social, and in it nothing is created that does not have a layer of public significance. Consumption is governed by collective representations encoded emotions, mandatory feeling systems of thought and by the cultural order that invents, enables and supports it.

It is important to also highlight the ideas of Arendt (2010) in clarifying the relationship between labor and consumption because in her views, they are two stages of the same process, which is imposed on men by the necessities of life and highlights the idea that if you live in a society of workers, or people who work—all human activities are linked to work—but reduced to a common denominator, that of providing the necessities of life and, furthermore, producing them in abundance. She points out: "Whatever we do, we must do so in order to earn our own living; this is the verdict of society" (Arendt 2010, p. 139, author's translation). Thus, we live in a society of production and consequently of consumption.

But we see that consumption has a broader context.

> It has been observed that consumption is an eloquent discourse open to multiple readings; it is a message in code, allowing us to get close to and distinguish different groups; as operators of a system to classify people and spaces through things. Series of products, objects and services are organized, by consumption, groups of people, social groups, lifestyles, tastes, perspectives and desires, all of which involve us in a permanent communication system, of power and prestige in social life.

It is important to state that although each and every member of society is an active consumer of goods and services, not all have a role in the production chain. Barbosa and Campbell (2006) highlight that the unemployed, children, pensioners, the sick, and some others do not produce any wealth from an economic point of view but consume permanently.

Consumption is a vague and porous concept; it can be understood as manipulation or use, other times as purchase or exhaustion and fulfillment. Barbosa and Cambell (2006, p. 23, author's translation) state that consumption "derives from the Latin consumere, which means using everything to the point of exhaustion or destruction; and in English it means more and more." We note also that in Brazil, the term has been used closer to the first definition, which sounds negative, while in fact consummation has a more positive sense, that of accomplishment.

Societies that make use of consumer goods and services to meet the needs for satisfying hunger, quenching thirst, providing shelter from the cold, are farther from the hypeconsumerism of shopping facilities and the credit that neoliberalism and globalization provide. The physical and biological needs of the contemporary world lend to it a sense of exhaustion, preventing people from using them as mediators in social relations.

Rather, these needs are overvalued to justify the act of buying and continuously providing status to people. This new social situation of humanity allows us to build a new identity, to buy more and strengthen the subjective boundaries between social groups. Consumption has always been associated with the purchase of any product or service. The social sciences have started to treat social reproduction and the construction of subjectivity and identity as synonymous with consumption. As such,

> The use and enjoyment, the reclassifying of goods and services, which has always corresponded to cultural experiences being perceived as distinctly ontological, were grouped under the label of consumption and interpreted in this light. They add, by adopting a style of clothing, by adopting a specific type of diet, or listening to a particular type of music, we can either consume in the sense of an experience, or building a specific identity through the usage of some product, or better, self-discovery or even resisting the advance of consumerism in our lives, as suggested by the theory of cultural studies.

Consumption, according to Barbosa and Campbell (2006), is a topic that encompasses various activities, actors, and a diversity of products and services that are not restricted to those provided in the form of goods. In other words, consumption is at the same time a social process that relates to multiple forms of use of goods and services and the different forms of accessing them; a mechanism perceived by the social sciences as a producer of meaning and identity, regardless of the acquisition of property; a manner that completely different social groups use to define different situations in terms of lifestyle and identity from day to day.

29.2.1 Consumption and the Illness of (Hyper) Contemporaneity

The notion of consumption today has moved in another direction. The value it had in relation to work as a creating and creative source has given way to the alienation of consumption and the facilities surrounding it. The consumerist expression is aggregated to the acquisition of the superfluous without any connotation of guilt; instead, it now implies it provides lenders with a higher quality of being over those who do not necessarily have these items. Having has become identified with pleasure, importance, social belonging, the inverted criteria that are now accepted by society.

To get a broader sense of proportion concerning what consumptive actions have taken, it is necessary to highlight the importance of them and how they reflect on the individual and the social collective. Impulsive actions, even indirectly, can reach the social masses; behaviors can become fashion,[1] the habit of many.

The value of property may be the result of human judgment; more often than not, it can be determined by analyzing the environment, the meaning they acquire after having been purchased. Douglas and Isherwood (2009, p. 41) state that "[...] the theory of consumption has to be a culture of theory and a theory of social life. To separate the organization's culture is to float towards the sea of relativism." Drawing on methods and principles of anthropology and economics, the authors investigate consumption as an element in the social process and strive to demonstrate that it "must be recognized as part of the same social system that explains the willingness to work, itself part of the social need to relate to others, and to have material mediators for these relations" (Douglas and Isherwood 2009, p. 26, author's translation).

Throughout the work "The World of Goods: Towards an Anthropology of Consumption," criticisms of the theory of demand are developed as a pillar of economic science as it does not answer the famous question posed by the authors: why do people want goods? The idea of blatant consumption, as conceived in the thought of Veblen (1899/1987), who had questioned the purely utilitarian notion of consumption, attacks the argument that proposes an overly simplified proposal for the theory of emulation; in other words, according to this theory, individuals compete against each other, measuring their success by how much they have more than others.

Consumption exceeds the mere satisfaction of basic needs; it is a phenomenon and, above all, cultural. The very term "culture of consumption" means to emphasize that the world of commodities, and its principles of organization are central to the understanding of modern society. Thus, for Baudrillard (2010, p. 91, author's translation), "consumption appears as a system that ensures the organization of signs and of group integration: constituting simultaneously a moral (ideological value system) and a system of communication or exchange structure."

Consumer goods have become associated with beauty, luxury, exoticism, and status, becoming increasingly difficult to decipher their original or functional use. For Baudrillard (2010), the culture of consumption is effectively a no-depth culture in which all values have been cross-evaluated. Featherstone (1995) points to consumption practices, the purchase and display of these consumables, and says they cannot be understood simply by exchange value concepts or instrumental rational calculation.

Featherstone (1995) calls this phenomenon, aesthetical life, wherein the consumer culture confronts people with images and dreams, to design reality, in which

[1]As can be seen in Simmel's discussions (1995), from the perspective of Marques (2011), in the work *Contracts in the Consumer Protection Code*: "The first modern German sociologist, studying fashion, affirmed that the human being is dualistic in essence, which determines that their actions are directed by (Trieb) antagonistic and plural impulses, of social integration, called "sozialismus", and personal satisfaction, and the economy, or the social context, can objectify in an individual a distinct representation. Fashion, or consumption, can mean the coming together of these two instincts in contemporary man; as part of the consumer society and yet differentiated from it precisely because he can consume." (Marques 2011, p. 205).

> [...]the aestheticization of life refers to the fast flow of signs and images that saturate the fabric of everyday life in contemporary society. The theory of this process relied much on the fetishism of Marx's theory of commodity, developed in various forms by Lukacs, the Frankfurt School, Benjamin, Haug, Lefebvre, Baudrillard and Jameson. For Adorno, the increasing dominance of the exchange value not only suppressed the original use value of things and replaced it with an abstract exchange value, but also left merchandise free to acquire an ersatz or secondary use value, which Baudrillard subsequently appoints as sign-value, the centrality of the commercial manipulation of images through advertising, media exhibitions and performances and shows the urban fabric of daily life, which determines, therefore, a constant reactivation of desires through images. Thus, consumer society should not be seen only as disclosing a dominant materialism, as it also confronts people with dream- images that speak of desires and which estheticize and fantasize reality (Featherstone 1995, p. 100, author's translation).

The Marxist theory of fetishism[2] in has since been developed in various ways by various authors, Lukacs, Hug, and others. While the value of these forms quickly removed the original value of things, it also left them free to obtain an ersatz or secondary value. On the other hand, the constant reactivation of desires through images is brought about through manipulation. This world of symbols, meanings, and social imagination is focused on by Lipovetsky and Roux (2010), who elected to study, among other issues, advertising, fashion, luxury, and consumption.

The hypercontemporaneous world is organized around four structural poles: hypercapitalism, hyperindividualism, hypertechnocracy, and hyperconsumption, a hypertrophied and exponential form of commercial hedonism. The author is dedicated to the study of the culture of excess and immediacy, the classification of the society of hyperconsumption as the unfolding fruit of capitalism, formed by turboconsumers who are compulsive and uncontrolled individualists. They are in search of happiness to complete them, eager to try out the various forms of pleasure available in consumer culture.

[2]According to Marx (1977), "fetishism is a social relation between people mediated by things. The result is the appearance of a direct relationship between things and not between people. People act like things and things like people. In the case of the production of goods, the exchange of goods is the only way in which different isolated producers of goods relate to each other. Thus, the value of goods is determined independently by individual producers and each producer must produce his goods in terms of satisfaction of others' needs. The result is that the same commodity (or the market) seems to determine the will of the producer and not the opposite. Marx (1977) states that commodity fetishism is something intrinsic to the production of goods, as in capitalist society, the production process becomes autonomous with respect to the will of man. Such autonomy will disappear only when the human being consciously controls the production process, a free association of individuals, which can only be done by abolishing private ownership of the means of production and turning them into collective property, ending the commercial character of the goods and only preserving its value in use. This means a revolution between the relation of production and distribution in life. Marx also argues that classical political economy cannot remove itself from commodity fetishism, since it considers the production of goods as a natural given and not as an historical mode of production and therefore transitory. The result is that this fetishism that occurs in the production and exchange of goods, produces a theoretical underestimation of the exchange over the production process. Hence the cult of the market on the part of some economists who consider supply and demand as the fundamental determinants of the price of goods." Available at: http://pt.wikipedia.org/wiki/Fetichismo_da_mercadoria accessed: 14 March 2015 at 17h23.

Consumption becomes a way to satisfy small pleasures, often to make up for a lack of love, social ties, or recognition. According to Lipovetsky and Roux (2010, p. 249, author's translation), "the more fragile or frustrating the social and interpersonal relationships become, the more it exacerbates the malaise [. . .] destined to raise an emotional reaction. Homo psychologicus became the great multiplier of Homo consumericus."

Lipovetsky and Roux (2010) divide capitalism into three phases, the first from 1880 to the end of World War II—the stage of distribution, where wide demand absorbed the entire production of industries that cropped up every day. The second, between 1950 and 1980, is the stage of abundance, mass consumption, and the beginning of the fierce competition between firms to satisfy consumers. The third and current phase is one in which the link between the consumer and consumer goods is no longer linked to the object. Consumption is to be held on to, or sought after, because of the search for emotional satisfaction. Thus, it can be said that the second phase has inherited the pleasure of purchasing from the purchase itself, and in the third, what is sought is comfort and well-being. The ultimate goal is for autoconsumption to achieve pleasure, a satisfaction in itself.

Immediate pleasure is provided by the purchase of the product or service, not only the purchase itself but also the act of buying, either because of advertising or something seen in a window at a mall, just as with the effects of drug use. The relief that justifies all the effort for its realization is long working hours and privations of all sorts.[3]

The happiness experienced by the consumer leads consumers to buy to show their joy. It serves both to provide happiness and to prove it: the unfortunates purchase hope to achieve such happiness; the happy ones shop to demonstrate and reaffirm. It appears that these are the subjective definitions of consumption. While consumption makes visible the identity of persons, purchases reflect the cultural and unique identity of its actors.[4]

---

[3]A whole culture is developed that invites us to taste the pleasures of the moment, to achieve happiness here and now, to live for ourselves; a culture that no longer prescribes resignation, and which is the new Gospel, flashing in neon letters: buy and enjoy, this is the truth. Thus governs the consumer society, whose ambition is proclaimed to liberate the pleasure principle, taking man out of his needy past, one of inhibition and asceticism. The discipline and rigor of its imposition gives rise to the application of material desires, a celebration of leisure and consumption, perpetual enchantment with private happiness (Lipovetsky and Roux 2010, p. 87, author's translation).

[4]This area now is not so much to show an outward sign of wealth or success as to create a pleasant and aesthetic context of life 'that has to do with us', a friendly and personalized cocoon. No doubt that this cocoon results from the purchase of standard goods but at all times, these items are reinterpreted, arranged in new compositions that express an individual identity, and what matters is not so much the value of status, but the private value of each one's house, making it possible for a "creator consumer." At least partially, I reveal who I am, as a unique individual, through what I buy, the objects that populate my personal and family universe, through the signs which make up my life. "At a time when traditions, religion or politics are less likely to produce a core identity, consumption is responsible more and more for creating a new identity function. In the race for things and leisure, and in a more or less conscious way, homo consumericus strives to give a tangible response while also being superficial, to the eternal question: who am I?" (Lipovetsky and Roux 2010, p. 38/39, author's translation).

The concept of emotional consumption introduced by Lipovetsky and Roux (2010) is not the same idea propagated by marketing experts, i.e. one that gives consumers affective, imaginary, and sensory experiences, but a consumption that provides a subjective well-being.[5]

However, Lipovetsky and Roux (2012) identified the problems that are related to consumption such as depression, stress, anxiety, restlessness, and disorientation of the hyperconsumer. The authors reaffirm their understanding of

> Compulsive shopping, as the over-indebtedness of households, addiction to video games, cyber dependencies, addictions, vicious behavior, the anarchy of eating behaviors, bulimia and obesity. If hyper- capitalism is the contemporary advent of the professional consumer, who is also an expert, responsible, and conscious of his health, prices, quality of life, he is also an anomic consumer, less and less self-possessed. We observe so, a flood of phenomena that are synonymous with excesses and lack of self-control, of dysfunctional behavior, of pathological and compulsive consumption (Lipovetsky and Roux 2012, p. 59, author's translation).

There is, in contemporary society, a diverse range of solutions to the pleasures of life exposed in shop windows, but individuals cannot fully obtain these. Educated in that world of consumption, they live their feelings of frustration and social failures. According to Lipovetsky and Roux (2012, p. 60, author's translation), "under-consumption brings with it exclusion, shame to oneself, auto stigmatization."

Another point noted by Lipovetsky and Roux (2005a, b) is that of blatant consumption, highlighting the value of luxury, not the luxury of millionaires, unattainable by most people, but the luxury of purchasing goods with famous prestigious brand names, items that also provide pleasure, manifested as a right to superfluities.

Luxury reduces the cultural imagination of people more so than conspicuous consumption. For Lipovetsky and Roux (2005a, b), the world lives with brands and has brought about an epoch where creating a product is no longer enough; now it is necessary to create identity or its culture. Lipovetsky and Roux (2012, p. 95, author's translation) points out that "the hyper consumer first purchases a brand, and with it a supplement for the soul, of dreams and identity: for the global consumer in the extreme, what was once just a scent now has the intoxication of a Chanel bottle"

Consumption, in this context, should be noted for its central role in the social reproduction process in any society, that is, that every act of consumption is essentially cultural. But it should also be considered from another point of view as

[5]It is hard to deny that universal consumption brings a multitude of benefits, such as material well-being, better health, information and communication. "It helps to make possible a greater autonomy for individuals in their daily actions. At the same time, it sets in motion a process of disorientation by the enormous choices that we benefit from in terms of products, models, fashion, travel, styles, and brands. It generates in the hyper-contemporaneous buyer, new uncertainties linked to the opening of the range of choices, which are expressed even in cultural consumption" (Lipovetsky and Roux 2012, p. 58, author's translation).

addressing the consumer - subject in contemporary society in relation to the pursuit of pleasure and recognition that before consumption, emotional consumption takes place.

The illnesses of contemporary times, including mental illness, have common elements seen in traits of helplessness, lack of references, also known as the clinic of emptiness. To Macêdo (2012), the main diseases of this time are "panic; depression; food related disorders such as bulimia and anorexia; psychosomatics and its addictions and other elements" (Macêdo 2012, p. 100, author's translation).[6]

Consumerism becomes a kind of manic symptom, whose function is to express the denial of depression by the fundamental failure of the subject in their relations with each other in a contemporary context. Since helplessness is the first cause of not only neurotic suffering but also cultural invention, this in turn points to the paradoxical character of the notion of helplessness in psychoanalysis. In fact, he suffers from helplessness but is also subject to its inevitability as a driving force for the construction of culture.

Social exclusion becomes a reality for people who do not follow all its dictates. This separatist context exerts great influence on the overindebtedness of consumers, which in addition to three other aspects — the growing production of industrial goods, the extension of the credit system, and the formation of consumer culture — can be considered as a cause of the current situation facing citizens who often have their livelihood and families tied up with installments or unnecessary expenses.

Individuals are subjected to their desires, and suppliers present their products with a total promise of gratification. We see then, a culture developing around an image, an appearance, fitness, or youth, which finds support in its demand for this subject. Subjectivity becomes a key part to the success for these suppliers since the subject has its demand satisfied, deceptively, by the products offered.

From this reading of the subject, as observed by Freud (1986b), it is possible to reflect on consumer culture in modern society. According to the author, birth is the first experience of anxiety and helplessness through which the individual passes, for with the cutting of the umbilical cord an irreversible process of adaptation and struggle for survival is initiated. The child, when he leaves the uterine world, starts a development process towards concrete reality. Symbolically, this marks the journey from complete gratification to a permanent lack.

In the Project for Scientific Psychology (Freud 1986a), the concept of helplessness is developed, identifying it as a differential and constitutive feature of the

[6]The psychopathology of postmodernity is characterized by certain privileged forms of operational psychopathology, in which, what is always at stake is the individual's failure to attain self-glorification and the aesthetics of existence: clinical diagnoses always arise from the failure of the subject to participate in the culture of narcissism. When you are depressed and in a panic, the subject cannot come to terms with the allure of the aesthetics of his existence, and is considered a failure according to the axial values of this world view (Birman 2001, pp. 167–69, author's translation).

human being, which can never be overcome by the subject because it will always seek ways in which to, even if deceptively, suppress it. This helplessness or emptiness is not only constitutive of the subject but also a constituent. Human beings will always be engaged in a constant search for what can satisfy them.

Thus, consumer society thrives only when its participants perpetuate this sense of becoming unstuck. Dissatisfaction is compounded by frustration and unhappiness in a totally futile battle, noting that anything that is not authentic can generate happiness.

Overindebtedness is linked to the complex relationship between the individual and society or, that is, consumption as a form of social relationship between people and institutions or as a social reproduction mechanism. The phenomenon has produced impacts and consequences of various orders, in society, in family life, in interpersonal relationships, and in intrapsychic conflicts.

Bauman (1999a, b) in his work "Modernity and Ambivalence" says that the consumer market requires identikits, announcing that —

> Businesses require increased efforts to show their social context by trying to sell goods, that is, as part of a special lifestyle, so that the consumer perspective can consciously acquire self-identifying symbols that it would like to own. The market also offers tools to 'build identity' that can be used differentially, i.e., that produce results somewhat different from each other and are so 'custom' made, 'tailored', best to meet the requirements of individuality. Through the market, various elements of the 'identikit' can be put together making up the complete self [...] The attraction of identities promoted by the market lies in the self-torments and the subsequent search for social approval (Bauman 1999a, b, p. 216, author's translation).

In an environment highly incentivized to purchase, the consumer decision process is always formed by the putting together of a variety of variables. Thus, the formation of the consumer's consent at the time of purchase is his weak point; suppliers target this to stimulate the purchase of goods and services. Consumer law must also deal with the study of this aspect very effectively in order to avoid the emergence of new problems in this society characterized by mass production and hence mass consumption. This is the consumer society, of consumerism and of credit.

Access to credit stands out as an indispensable element in allowing the individual to participate in this consumer culture. After all, only those who have financial resources can participate in the consumer market. Credit allows essential conditions for the acquisition of goods and in bringing services to fruition. Receiving a line of credit is often presented as the only way to access consumption (Carpena and Cavallazzi 2006).

Loans to consumers not only meet but also create needs. Linked to the consumption pattern, the subject becomes identified as belonging to a particular class or group. Thus, debt has become an inherent fact in economic activity, serving also as a means to finance it (Costa 2002). Numerous consumers are borrowing money to consume goods and services, whether they are essential or not. During times of consumption we live either in a real economy or in a culture of debt., We make full use of the credit period, inevitably consuming more but with less need (Marques 2006).

These are times of consumption characterized by the consumption of our every day, a preponderance of wanting and much buying. This is the era of consumerism, the hypercontemporaneous, associated with the sale of happiness — buying yourself a funded illusion, with a fragmented life of credit. Overindebtedness becomes the cause and consequence of this scenario, giving rise to the modern malaise, the oppression of dignity, and so muting consumer hope. The time of consumption and consumerism is the disorder of our time, with its (un)human consequences.

29.3 Happiness on Credit in a Consumer Society

Consumer society is seen as the society of opulence, there is a kind of fantastic consumption evident and an abundance created by the multiplication of objects, services, and goods. According to Baudrillard (2010), it is a phenomenon characteristic of developed societies from the second half of the twentieth century, a society in which the logic of mass consumption has changed the world of moralizing prescriptions and eradicated coercive imperatives, a culture in which happiness overrides everything.

Happiness, as such is represented by a type of society that promotes, encourages, or strengthens the choice of a lifestyle and an existential consumer strategy. Bauman (2008a), looking at consumer society, describes it as a figure of liquefaction versus the strength of past ages, consumer society in opposition to the society of producers.

To Bauman (2008a), social changes taking place in modern society, in the field of human and labor relations, social institutions, public and private life, gives rise to the idea that the strength of social institutions succumbs irreversibly to liquefaction. The consequences are seen by contemporary-liquid individuals because the dynam ics of social change dissolve ties (both social and emotional) at great speed. The liquefaction of the structures reveals a sense of freedom, punctuated by emblems like temporariness and detachment. In this liquid society, the individualization of relations occurs, to the point where satisfaction is achieved immediately even without the need for interaction with others, reinforcing the notion of modern liquid, or freedom.

The fluidity or liquidity metaphors are employed to capture the nature of this phase in the history of contemporary times. Fluids move, drip, squirt, spill, leak, flood; they are filtered, distilled, sprayed, unlike the solids that are hardly changed. Thus, contemporary fluidity is associated with lightness, fragility, disposability, mobility, and the adaptation of the current society.

In the contemporary context, there is a detachment from the idea of conservation and durability. The individualization of the relationship ultimately gives rise to diseases typical of contemporary times, such as the fragility of affective ties, family abandonment, and loneliness, depression, bipolar and consuming disorders. Nothing is durable or permanent, for example, family legacy, savings, old loves; everything seems to have value only when in liquidity, i.e., when circulating.

In this scenario, Bauman (2008b) shows the rise of consumption as a major social force guiding the present and explains everyday consumer society by making clear the relationship between this liquefaction and consumption. He demonstrates that the individual establishes human relations only to the extent that it consumes. This Marxist fetishism is cited by Bauman (2008a) as one of the current social influences, affecting the sense of belonging of individuals in consumer society and the need to constantly update. He points out that the consumer himself becomes a commodity:

> We must remember, however, that in a consumer society, where human relationships tend to be led and mediated by consumer goods markets, a sense of belonging is not obtained by following given procedures or guided by these style trends to which it aspires, but rather by the aspirants own metonymic identification with the trend. The process of self-identification is pursued, and its results are presented with the help of visible brands usually to be found in stores. In postmodern tribes (as Mafiosi prefers to denominate the style trends of the consumer society), emblematic figures and their visible brands (indications that suggest dress codes and/or conduct) replace the totems of the original tribes. Having the emblems of these emblematic figures and their chosen styles on display, in fact, grants the recognition and the acceptance sought after, as being to the forefront is the only way to ensure such recognition at the desired time (Bauman 2008a, p. 108, author's translation).

Reinforcing the idea that individuals are goods, Bauman (2008a) explains that the incessant need for consumption goes beyond the purchase of material goods. It also consumes values, appearances, habits, and lifestyles when viewed as consumers in a modern-liquid society. Bauman (2009a, p. 105, author's translation) also posits that consumer society has as its premise, the satisfaction of human desires in a way that no past society has achieved, such that, "the promise of satisfaction, however, will remain only seductive while the desire to continue is unfulfilled; which is important, as there is a suspicion that desires have not been fully and completely satisfied."

Consumer society becomes one of permanent non-satisfaction in this sense. Bauman adds:

> The non-fulfillment of desires and the firm and eternal belief that every act aiming to satisfy them leaves much to be desired and can be improved are the ads in the economy that target the consumer [. . .] One way to cause this effect is to belittle and devalue consumer products soon after they have been put out into the universe of consumer desires. Another form even more effective, however, is to remove it from the limelight. This is a method to ensure that the satisfaction of every need/want/desire in a way that always creates new needs/wants/desires and inevitably ensures that what begins as a need will end as compulsion or addiction, does not in fact take place. And this is what happens, as the urge to look in stores, and only in these places, for solutions to problems, for relief from pain and anxiety, is only one aspect of behavior which can reduce a habit while still eagerly encouraging one to engage in it. (Bauman 2009a, pp. 105–106, author's translation).

The search for belonging by contemporary-liquid consumers is based on the need to secure one's social position, resonating as self-confidence, while everyone eagerly seeks approval. Thus, the basis for self-esteem can be presented as the approval and admiration of others, which may result in the individual's increasing fragility.

With this malaise in our civilization, Bauman (1998, p. 36, author's translation) states that "in this world, human bonds are hidden in successive meetings, identities are successfully protected behind masks, the story of life continues in a series of episodes, whose enduring consequence is the ephemeral equality of memory." It reinforces the fragility of human bonds seeking recognition and approval at all costs within a consumerist logic—"recognition is like the fake rabbit in a hunt; always chased by dogs, never caught in its jaws" (Bauman 1998, p. 59, author's translation). Consumer society or the consumer, becomes a society that seeks to answer the question, "why do we consume"? And for that matter, there is a series of widely accepted responses ranging from satisfaction of needs to the emulation of others, the narcissistic pursuit of pleasure, affirmation, recognition, identity, or the affirmation of a status.

29.3.1 From Consumers to Consumerists: The Era of Accumulation

There are some well known modern views on the historic process, the idea of a time of need has been replaced by a time of possibilities, random time, i.e., several unexpected opportunities appearing at any one moment and becoming unexpected obstacles. At this time, consumer society is a non-recurring or linear, a one-dimensional fact. It used to be so for people in other societies.

Others argue that time is pointillist or dotted,[7] marked by plenty of breaks and discontinuities, by gaps between successive points, and by the disruption of the links between them — an incongruous time with little cohesion, with many possibilities, fragmented, or even sprayed into a variety of perennial moments.

Consumer society has deepened social inequalities, given that the ability to or not to consume is one of the criteria for social inclusion or exclusion; consequently, there is also a strong capitalistic influence. We are part of a society of consumers, which judges and evaluates its members mainly by their capacity and conduct in relation to consumption.

Given the fact that contemporary consumerist society has been manipulated, it is observed that through consumerism, people come to offer you small joys as compensation for the lack of love, bonds, and recognition. In accordance with Lipovetsky and Roux (2012, p. 56, author's translation), "the more individual social bonds become fragile or frustrating, consumerism increasingly triumphs as a refuge." It is a different kind of consumption, which is basically characteristic of and an occupation for human beings as individuals; consumerism has become an attribute of society.

[7]It would be the equivalent of a line of ants, where they represent the points (the styling changes, new trends) while the actual line is our life.

Consumerism as a kind of social arrangement results from the recycling of wills and human desires, making them the main driving force in our operational society. According to Bauman (2008a, p. 41, author's translation), "consumerism coordinates systemic reproduction, integration and social stratification, besides forming individual humans, playing at the same time an important role in the group and in the individual self-identification process."[8]

New needs require new desires; today's consumerism is not concerned with the simple satisfaction of needs but the identification of needs and the seeking of approval by others—a need always based on comparison, vanity, envy, and the need for inclusion in the group.

Consumer goods are means or instruments used to obtain this standard admiration from each other, in a contemporary social context. The pace set by the consumer culture ultimately creates false needs that feed the desire of the subject engaged in the search for the object of consumption. No doubt alienated desires of consumption, once satisfied, are quickly replaced by others in an incessant rhythm of consumerism.

For Bauman (2008b), in the solid-modern era of producers, there is an incentive to accumulate durable goods, durable and immune to time, one whose satisfaction lies in the long-term promise of security. On the other hand, in a liquid-modern society, based on the existence of consumers, there is a transformation of the human desires of stability and satiety. Prosperity is disconnected from the idea of meeting needs and becomes linked to the volume and intensity of growing desires, which leads to the immediate use of and quick replacement of used objects, i.e., consumerism.

The idea of happiness can come untied from the satisfaction of needs, becoming linked to the continuously growing aspiration for ideas. New needs require new products, which in turn require new desires.

Consumer society promotes, encourages, or strengthens the choice of a lifestyle fully oriented to attaining immediacy. Businesses reject any alternative option, using training and increasingly early pressure, through a series of refined techniques that encourage rampant consumption from as early as childhood. Bauman (2008a) transcribes an example where it is clear that the purpose of business is to educate its potential customers from childhood into a life of consumption:

> Mattel, provides the example of a company that has flooded the toy market with Barbie dolls, reaching $ 1.7 billion in sales alone in 1996. It promised young consumers that they

[8]On the path leading to this (consumer society), the human desire for stability must be transformed, and indeed transform itself, from being the principle asset of the system and its greatest risk, perhaps even potentially fatal, possibly causing disruption or malfunction. It could hardly be any other way, as consumers, in sharp contrast to previous forms of life, associate happiness, not so much with satisfying needs (such as their "official versions" tend to imply), but the volume and intensity of ever-increasing desires, which in turn implies the immediate use and rapid replacement of desire intended to satisfy it. It combines, as Don Slater accurately identified, the insatiability of desire with the urgency and the need to "always look for goods to satisfy" (Bauman 2008a, p. 44, author's translation).

> would sell them the next Barbie at a discount if they brought the doll back to the store when she was "worn" (Bauman 2008a, p. 132, author's translation).

To be part of this society, we need to be consumers by vocation, through which consumption becomes a guide for deceptively free choices, impregnated with predetermined content. There is no difference of class, gender, or age; everyone needs to spend to keep up with socially acceptable positions.

When Barbosa and Campbell (2006) discusses the act of shopping, he says it is one of the ways in which individuals search for themselves and their place in the world. To buy is to expose the personality to various possibilities, while you decide what you need or want. To buy consciously, is to look internally into one's memory and desire. Shopping is an interactive process open to dialogue not only with people, places, and things but also with part of the self. A dynamic, reflective, and revelatory process, capable of moulding people.

One of the consumerist characteristics of the individual is to live permanently with the problem of unresolved identity, say Barbosa and Campbell (2006):

> We discovered that people are monitoring their reactions to various products and services, thus establishing their tastes and desires. But as postmodernists like to point out, in contemporary society, individuals change their tastes and preferences by, either following changing fashions, or by seeking a higher status, thereby going through a process of recreating. This seems to contradict the hypothesis that consumption allows people to discover who they really are; which had already found an answer to the question, "why should we exchange a specific identity for another"? [...] The first crucial point to be appreciated is that people actually change the level of their taste or preference; it does not represent a change in the way in which identity is recognized or designed. It is still the self being defined by desire, or our character being determined by our preferences. In this regard, the much emphasized variability and mutability of the perceived content of the identity is not as significant as the manifest continuity in the process involved in this discovery [...] This is because consumption, which, in the sense here treated by me, can be seen as an activity that involves the exploration of self, and can also be seen as an answer to ontological insecurity or existential angst (Barbosa and Campbell 2006, p. 56, author's translation).

In this way, confidence is acquired to overcome the existential angst and convince ourselves that we actually are alive. It is a psychological need that can be satisfied over and over again. However, it is impossible for the same stimulus to produce the same intensity of reaction as the first time. Consequently, one needs regular exposure to new stimuli to avoid boredom and to satisfy the continuous quest for ontological reaffirmation.

Birman (2001) states that we construct a kind of social bond in which the bond is loose, poor, light, superficial, with no room for the experiences of loss and grief, and as being rooted and fixed in the same liquid-modern idea as developed by Bauman (2009b). In this scenario, individualities are disposable, as well as their identities and all their erotic and emotional bonds. Otherness and difference will give rise to equality and massification. A social scene is portrayed which states that to have is to be; partnerships and groups disintegrate and become dependent on the market. The citizen gives way to the consumer; there is a clear otherness, and the trend is toward the reduction of humanity to the size of the image.

The culture of this image is an effect of the practice of the production of consumer subjectivity. Consumption becomes a dependent subject; advertising manipulates the power of individual purchasing decisions, transferring it to companies that end up making their own product. In this dependency network, the consumer is perpetually dissatisfied and bored, or in other words, willing to consume.

29.3.2 The (Lack of) Hopes of Consumption and Overindebtedness

Etymologically, the word credit comes from *credere*, meaning confidence. Credit is associated with two concepts, namely, trust and time. It is defined as a means of inspiring confidence (the loan) for a specified time (period). It is characterized as the result of a period between the loan to the creditor and that of the debtor, which is only possible because the lender believes the borrower will fulfill his obligation within the time limits agreed." The concept of credit should not be confused with the concept of promise, of security, or of faith in due performance because it is an exchange of a present (merchandise) for a future good (money). Credit for consumption implies constant movement, stimulating the economy, even driving this movement, with no turning back, always looking to do it in an ever-increasing manner.

Brazil has become the homeland of regular payments. In the modern economy, we cannot forget the context in which credit is included, as the driver of mass consumption and one of the most important policies of our public authorities in the fight against under-consumption and the threat of an economic slowdown. It is no longer conceived as a necessary evil but rather as a force that imposes social and economic development on the country. The author states:

> It is necessary to also consider that debt depends on the borrower having access to credit, being encouraged to consume more and more, through the promptings of advertising, aggressive selling techniques and the creation of new forms of credit which multiplies day by day. The emergence of a new culture of debt has made credit a normal feature, accepted as part of an individual's life, and even seen as a manifestation of freedom and autonomy in the home. This change in people's behavior in relation to credit can be noted through the constant complaints filed in the database of the Social Security Ombudsman, of those who do not accept the restrictions on lending, with the limitation of an assignable margin of 30% of the benefit.

Over-indebtedness is a theme in vogue in Brazil, and the new Brazilian reality calls for an adequate legal instrument to account for the new issues that arise in the consumer market, pertaining to credit agreements. To Carpena and Cavallazzi (2007), over-indebtedness is a problem of social content, as he points out:

> This statement is confirmed daily in the news: it cannot escape the reader's attention that today we have an economically stable Brazil, with a considerable expansion of credit on

> offer, which largely affects the lower classes, more numerous but less educated when it comes to the issues around consumption. In research published in late 2005, it was found that the granting of credit to individuals already accounts for 45.8% of bank loans and has increased 30% in the last 12 months, while real wages (the amount of people working and total wages adjusted for inflation) increased only 5% in the same period (Carpena and Cavallazzi 2007, p. 77, author's translation).

Brazil is now an economy of consumption, of spending in every way. Saving money does not seem to be a cherished value. Where does this behavior stem from? Why has Brazil become the home of regular monthly repayments? These are the hopes and frustrations of consumers from the point of view of consumer over-indebtedness—where do we go from here?

By multiplying the purchasing power of Brazilians, we see that this universal amplification of everything, including repayments, has become crucial to the increase of income in the country, or better, most of the new car buyers, new travelers, and new homeowners are credit borrowers with increasingly longer term funding.

Portuguese author Leitão Marques et al. (2000) recognizes that consumer debt is not a problem in itself because it contributes to increasing the well-being of families. However, she warns that debt becomes a problem when repayment default occurs, with the situation worsening when the household income does not include all their financial commitments, that is, when there is already a shortage in addition to the debt.

Excessive indebtedness or indebtedness is best defined by Marques (2006), as the overall inability of the individual physical debtor, a lay consumer, to in good faith pay all current and future debts. In this sense, Leitão Marques et al. (2000) state:

> Over-indebtedness, also known as bankruptcy or consumer insolvency, refers to situations where the debtor finds himself unable, in a durable or structured form, to pay all of his debts, or even when there is a serious threat that he may not be able to do so when they become due. Over-indebtedness can be active, if the borrower is actively contributing to putting himself in an impossible situation to make repayments, for example, not planning commitments and continuing to exaggeratedly accumulate creditors in relation to actual and expected revenues; or passively, when unforeseen circumstances occur (unemployment, precariousness of employment, divorce, illness or family death, accidents, etc.) seriously affecting the borrower's repayment capacity, putting him in an impossible situation to comply with his obligations (Leitão Marques et al. 2000, p. 2, author's translation).

There is, in fact, a distinction between passive and active over-indebtedness. In this case, the consumer abuses credit (Paisant 2002), by accumulating debts. The passively over-indebted, in turn, is a consumer who does not actively contribute to the emergence of the solvency and liquidity crisis, with its brutal reduction of resources linked to the twists and turns of life (Costa 2002).

In this sense, Marques (2006) contributes:

> Indeed, so many accidents of life (unemployment, wage cuts, divorces, illnesses, accidents, deaths, births of children, etc.) and credit abuse can create a solvency or liquidity crisis (unpredictably low-resources, high interest rates, high or low dollar exchange rates, additional need for loans etc.) for individuals and families, whether they be of the middle classes

> or of the poorer classes, leading to an inability to cope with the size of their current and future debts, making it impossible to pay in good faith, which the doctrine correctly termed indebtedness, or as I prefer, over-indebtedness [...] which readily results in their total exclusion from the consumer market (Marques 2006, pp. 258–260, author's translation).

The corresponding use of multiple forms of financing gives rise to intense consumption. Financial management has become more sophisticated because of the means of payment used, such as credit cards, debit cards, store cards, credit facilities, coexisting with other regular accounts, personal loans, mortgage loans, and car loans. Credit starts to be used as much for the purchase of a house as with the payment of health care, food, and leisure. Multi-indebtedness marks the cultural and financial life of these individuals who now are over-indebted.

Debt is an intrinsic phenomenon of modern society in which the citizen acquires a status in his community in proportion to the goods consumed: whoever has more is more! And the search for status is an integral part on the list of human needs (Scheweriner 2006).

As Bauman assures us (2010, p. 31, author's translation), "the credit agreement is the very success of the banks. It is the predictable result of transforming men, women, old and young, into debtors. They have reached their goal: producing a race of eternal debtors and perpetuating the indebted being, to the extent that accumulating more debt is seen as the only real instrument and salvation for existing debts." The next loan is the way to suspend the execution of the previous debt.

He notes that one of the most widely accepted arguments to explain the phenomenon of the global financial crisis is the absence of regulation, in particular in the financial and banking sector. And so we have the question, "where do we go from here?" The primary considerations of Professor Claudia Lima Marques (2006) are very much to the point, acknowledging that the challenge posed by the expansion of credit for consumption, in the absence of legislation to guide this mass of consumers, in addition to the Code of Consumer Protection and the general principle of good faith, has fomented a crisis of solvency and confidence. On one hand, there was an increase in bank profits and the inclusion in the banking system of millions of consumers, but from another point of view, there are an increasing number of individual actions being taken by people in debt, particularly through judicial revision.

According to Bauman's reasoning (2010, p. 29, author's translation), the relationship between work, salary, and shopping took on a new meaning with credit and in particular with credit cards. With the card you can reverse the order: first buy, then work, to pay. "Thanks be to God and the grace of banks [...] with the credit card you are free to administer your satisfaction, to get things when you want to, not when you earn enough to buy them."

All that notwithstanding, "in consolidated consumer societies, the over indebtedness of the subject is treated as a legal problem [...] special legislation has been prepared to avoid (prevention) and resolve this problem (treatment)" (Marques 2006, p. 265, author's translation). Likewise, Lima and Bertoncelo conclude that information and freedom of choice are essential to ensure consumer consent, integrity, and to prevent over-indebtedness.

The authors continue:

> To enhance the protection of consumers also means making progress in combating social exclusion [...] This socioeconomic dimension of over-indebtedness identifies that the maintenance of the market with its increasing production of goods, services and information will depend on the financial health of the consumer and their reintegration into the production cycle, which is only possible by means of specific legal protection to prevent and solve debt situations (Lima and Bertoncelo, pp. 207–208, author's translation).

What this article proposes is that the purchase of products and services has taken on unimaginable proportions, from consumption to consumerism, credit indebtedness, of dignity (and the lack of it) to hope. The hope of a fresh start according to Lima (2014) becomes a challenge to build a sustainable economy and protect consumers. She states:

> The factors that contribute to the over-indebtedness of individuals need to be considered by the legislature. The following are the main ones: deregulation of the credit market; reduction of the welfare state; credit democratization; impulsivity of consumers; consistent market failure in information streaming; lack of financial education of consumers; an incomplete consumer heuristic that leads them to badly assess the risk of over-indebtedness; granting of reckless credit by suppliers in fulfilling their obligation in assessing the consumer's repayment ability; creating new forms of credit (credit cards, payroll loans, online loans); advertising that encourages credit without alerting to the risks of super-indebtedness and the accidental events of life (unemployment, divorce, illness, and other unforeseen events that may prevent the payment of debts) (Lima 2014, p. 178, author's translation).

The hope for a solution is to update the Consumer Protection Code, which would furnish an opportunity for the treatment of and prevention of over-indebtedness. As Lima (2014) tells us, the creation of a differentiated protection against the state of over-indebtedness by consumers is consistent with the fundamental objective of the Federal Constitution — to eradicate poverty and marginalization and reduce inequalities, in addition to ensuring the right of access to justice, promoting the prevention of human dignity — all of which are cited respectively in Articles 1.3°, III, and Article 5°, XXXV, Federal Constitution of Brazil.

The author suggests a hybrid model for a Brazilian law that contemplates the phenomenon of over-indebtedness, to include elements of the French and American systems and the experience of reconciliation such as those at the Courts of Justice in the state of Rio Grande do Sul. Among some possible guidelines for the Brazilian legislature, she points out:

a) The regulation of bankruptcy should not only be directed to the repayment of creditors, but should consider the mitigation of the social effects of indebtedness on the debtor, his family and society;
b) The failure to provide for measures to mitigate the negative consequences of stigma, guilt, moral hazard, and other factors that may hinder the attainment of the objectives;
c) Bankruptcy should be included, welcoming both passive and active consciousness concerning over-indebtedness, the latter through the analysis of their good faith in each case;

d) The failure to provide for a conciliatory phase to design agreed payment plans, encouraging the repayment of debt and compliance with all contracts;
e) Payment plans should contain the necessary measures to enable the repayment of debts according to the budget of the consumer, while not compromising the minimum required and should be safeguarded as a guarantee for human dignity;
f) The duration of the plans can be set by the legislator, applying equally to all consumers, or by a judge according to the circumstances of each case. Short term plans are recommended because they increase the chances of compliance;
g) Consumers with no assets and no income, i.e. those in no financial position to meet a payment plan should not be discriminated against by the bankruptcy system, while recommending a particular scheme to avoid increasing social exclusion;
h) The cancellation of debts is recommended in the most serious situations of over-indebtedness, i.e. when the consumer in good faith has no assets and no income to repay creditors [...] but may be subject to the fulfillment of certain duties (Lima 2014, pp. 179–180, author's translation).

This is the spirit of PLS 283/2012 (a proposed law of the Brazilin Senate), rather than amend Law No. 8,078/90 of the Consumer Protection Code, to improve credit discipline and regulate the prevention and treatment of over-indebtedness. It is a legislative proposal that rescues the dignity of consumers who were living on the margins of society, in an indebted state. The disagreements that consumption and consumerism were able to create between having and being brought about the ills of the era of consumption, of hyper consumption. "What is the hope"? It is the right to start over.

Without intending to comment on the text completely, mention is made of some important aspects of this scenario yet to be constructed. In the above example, the text of Article 6, XI, XII, and XIII was proposed for inclusion among the basic rights of consumers, ensuring responsible lending practices, financial education, prevention and treatment of cases of over-indebtedness, and revision or debt renegotiation, among other measures.

Article 37, § 2, mentions as abusive, and discriminatory some issues such as: advertising: of whatever nature that incites violence, exploits fear or superstition, takes advantage of the lack of judgment and inexperience of a child, disrespects environmental values, or is capable of inducing the consumers to behave in a way that is harmful or dangerous to their health or safety, and advertising that, among other things, contains direct instructions to a child to consume and which is capable of promoting any form of discrimination or sense of inferiority generally among children and adolescents or uses children or adolescents as spokespersons on behalf of the instruction to consume.

Regarding the conciliatory plan, the project under discussion in Article 104-A gives the super-indebted consumer the possibility of establishing a debt renegotiation process in court. The process aims to achieve a conciliatory hearing in the presence of all creditors, who will receive a payment plan, with a maximum term of five years, respecting a minimum income necessary to survive and any guarantees already agreed. Section 2° of the article in question is important and motivational, in which it understands the legislator as someone often occupied with the attendance or non-attendance of the creditor, attributing to his absence the suspension of debt liability and all live charges.

As previously presented, Lima (2014) suggested minimum guidelines that should be adopted by the Brazilian legislature. PLS 283/2012 (proposed Senate law) will, when approved, with no detrimental changes, minimize the social effects of over-indebtedness, with special attention to the consumer-debtor aspect.

29.4 Conclusion

This article offers a reasoned commentary on some points (for and against) to contextualize these contemporary times of consumption; these, in turn, are the human consequences of the consumer being. It envisions a subject drunk on the desire to have, to buy goods, and to use products.

The point of view explored in the main body of the text starts with the idea of the need to recognize the existence of a multiplicity of paradigms to explain the world. The globalized world, and consequently consumption across borders, has made consumers believe in a false empowerment, believing it to be an omnipresent, omniscient, and omnipotent subject.

Society and its somewhat unreal relationship with its occupant, human kind, has reached a time when creator and creature must establish guidelines that provide harmony between humans, their inventions, and their desires. Consumer society, in this context, requires us to ask the questions: what is consumer society? Where is the society of consumption, and to where is this society of consumption headed?

Consumption is so indispensable, necessary, and opportune, and in the full sense of the Latin *consumere* has come to mean something that is about to run out or be destroyed. Social reproduction and the construction of subjectivity and identity are treated as synonyms of consumption. A new era allows us to speak of hyper-contemporaneity and consumption in which a world of goods is emphasized, to the extent that the consumer should be understood as a consumer of symbols and signs.

The hyper-contemporaneous world, as has been stated, is organized around four structural poles: hyper-capitalism, hyper-individualism, hyper-technocracy, and hyper-consumption, an exponential and hyper-trophied form of commercial hedonism, formed by turboconsumers who are compulsive, uncontrolled individuals, buying happiness and who have endless desires fuelled by consumer culture.

It must be concluded that consumption has taken on a central role in the process of social reproduction, i.e., the act of consumption is essentially cultural, but it should also be analyzed from a new perspective, addressing the contemporary subject-consumer, who seeks pleasure and recognition before consumption, and who acts upon emotional consumption.

The negative features of contemporaneity, including mental illness, have converged into traits of helplessness, with a lack of references. This is the clinic of emptiness, and from that context we see the useless, modern search for available identities in consumption and consumerism. It is the consumer society, thriving on the production of eternal feelings of helplessness, contradicting the sale of happiness, and feeding on the preprogramed unhappiness of consumers.

Access to credit has become essential for the individual to be able to participate in this consumer culture. The consumer society is also the credit society, immersed in accelerating social inequalities, which seeks to segmentize its members by their capacity for consumption.

In this scenario, overindebtedness confirms the gap between the consumer and their dignity. From the original term *credere*, which means trust, credit has come to signify hopelessness when referring to consumer over-indebtedness.

To finish with, we have two logical conclusions: (a) debt is an intrinsic phenomenon of modern society in which the citizen acquires status in his community in proportion to the goods they consume, and (b) it is possible to explain the phenomenon of the global financial crisis by the lack of regulation, in particular, in the financial and banking sector.

Where are we going? In consolidated consumer societies, the theme of over-indebtedness is part of the legal agenda. While it enhances consumer protection, it advances the fight against social exclusion. Certainly, maintaining the market requires good consumer financial health, which is only possible by means of legal protections specialized in preventing and treating conditions of debt distress.

We are waiting on the Consumer Protection Code to be updated. Rather than amending Law No. 8078/90, the proposed PLS 283/2012, (Public Senate Law), aims to improve credit discipline and regulate the prevention and treatment of over-indebtedness. It is a legislative proposal that rescues the dignity of consumers. As we stated previously, the disagreements that consumption and consumerism were able to create between having and being, determine the ills of the era of consumption and hyper-consumption. *The hope?* The right to start over, since it guarantees responsible lending practices and good consumer financial education, the prevention of and treatment of situations of over-indebtedness and debt renegotiation when necessary.

References

Arendt H (2010) A condição humana. Forense Universitária, Rio de Janeiro

Barbosa L, Campbell C (2006) Cultura, Consumo e Identidade. Editora FGV, Rio de Janeiro

Baudrillard J (2010) A sociedade de consumo Tradução de Artur Morão. Edições 70, Lisboa

Bauman Z (1998) O mal-estar da pós-modernidade. Tradução de Mauri Gama e Cláudia Martinelli Gama. Zahar, Rio de Janeiro

Bauman Z (1999a) Modernidade e ambivalência. Tradução de Marcus Penchel. Zahar, Rio de Janeiro

Bauman Z (1999b) Globalização: as conseqüências humanas. Marcus Penchel (Trad.). Jorge Zahar, Rio de Janeiro

Bauman Z (2008a) Vida para consumo: a transformação das pessoas em mercadorias. Tradução de Carlos Alberto Medeiros. Zahar, Rio de Janeiro

Bauman Z (2008b) A sociedade individualizada: vidas contadas e histórias vividas. Tradução de José Gradel. Zahar, Rio de Janeiro

Bauman Z (2008c) Vida a crédito: conversas com Citali Rovirosa-Madrazo. Tradução de Alexandre Werneck. Zahar, Rio de Janeiro

Bauman Z (2009a) A arte da vida. Tradução de Carlos Alberto Medeiros. Zahar, Rio de Janeiro

Bauman Z (2009b) Vida líquida. Tradução de Carlos Alberto Medeiros. Zahar, Rio de Janeiro

Bauman Z (2010) Mundo-consumo: ética del individuo em la aldea global. Traducido por Albino Santos Mosquera. Paidós, Buenos Aires

Birman J (2001) Subjetividades contemporâneas. In: Psychê – Revista de Psicanálise. São Paulo, ano V, n. 7, pp 151–169

Carpena Hde, Cavallazzi RL (2006) Superendividamento: proposta para um estudo empírico e perspectiva de regulação. In: Marques CL, Cavallazzi RL (coord) Direitos do Consumidor Endividado: superendividamento e crédito. RT, São Paulo

Carpena Hde, Cavallazzi RL (2007) Uma lei para os consumidores superendividados. Revista de Direito do Consumidor, n°61, pp 76–89, jan./mar.

Costa JP (2002) Sociedade de Controle. São Paulo

Douglas M, Isherwood B (2009) O mundo dos bens: para uma antropologia do consumo. Tradução Plínio Dentzien. Editora UFRJ, Rio de Janeiro

Durkheim É (1987) La Science sociale et l'action. Presses Universitaires de France, Paris

Featherstone M (1995) Cultura de consumo e pós modernidade. Studio Nobel, São Paulo

Freud S (1895/1986) Projeto para uma psicologia científica. In: Obras psicológicas completas de Sigmund Freud: edição standard brasileira; com comentários e notas de James Strachey e Alan Tyson; traduzido por Jayme Salomão. 2ª. Edição. Imago, Rio de Janeiro

Freud S (1900/1986) A interpretação dos sonhos. In: Obras psicológicas completas de Sigmund Freud: edição standard brasileira; com comentários e notas de James Strachey e Alan Tyson; traduzido por Jayme Salomão. 2ª. Edição. Imago, Rio de Janeiro

Leitão Marques MM et al (2000) O endividamento dos consumidores. Almedina, Lisboa

Lima CC (2014) O tratamento do superendividamento e o direito de recomeçar dos consumidores. Editora Revista dos Tribunais, São Paulo

Lipovetsky G, Roux E (2005a) O luxo Eterno: da idade do sagrado ao tempo das marcas. Tradução Maria Lúcia Machado. Companhia das Letras, São Paulo

Lipovetsky G, Roux E (2005b) A sociedade pós- moralista: o crepúsculo do dever e a ética indolor dos novos tempos democráticos. Tradução de Armando Braio Ara. Manole, Barueri

Lipovetsky G, Roux E (2010) Felicidade paradoxal: ensaio sobre a sociedade do hiperconsumo. Tradução de Patrícia Xávier. Edições 70, Lisboa

Lipovetsky G, Roux E (2012) A cultura-mundo: resposta a uma sociedade desorientada. Tradução de Maria Lúcia Machado. Companhia das Letras, São Paulo

Macêdo KB (2012) O desamparo do indivíduo na modernidade. In Ecos Revista, v. 2, p. 99–107

Marx K (1977) A critique of political economy. Vintage Books, New York

Marques CL (2006) Sugestões para uma lei sobre tratamento do superendividamento de pessoas físicas em contratos de crédito ao consumo: proposições com base em pesquisa empírica de 100 casos no Rio Grande do Suk. In: Marques CL, Cavallazzi RL (coord) Direitos do Consumidor Endividado: superendividamento e crédito. RT, São Paulo

Marques CL (2011) Contratos no código de defesa do consumidor: o novo regime das relações contratuais. RT, São Paulo

Paisant G (2002) El tratamiento del sobreendeudamiento de lós consumidores em derecho francês. Revista de Direito do Consumidor. RT, São Paulo, n. 42

Scheweriner MER (2006) Comportamento do consumidor: identificando necejos e supérffluos essenciais. Saraiva, São Paulo

Veblen T (1987) A teoria da classe ociosa: um estudo econômico das instituições. Tradução de Olívia Krahenbuhl. Nova Cultural, São Paulo

Printed by Printforce, the Netherlands